THE SOCIAL PSYCHOLOGY
OF GOOD AND EVIL

THE SOCIAL PSYCHOLOGY OF
GOOD
AND
EVIL

Edited by Arthur G. Miller

THE GUILFORD PRESS
New York   London

Library of Congress Cataloging-in-Publication Data

The social psychology of good and evil / edited by Arthur G. Miller.
    p. cm.
Includes bibliographical references and index.
    ISBN 1-57230-989-X (hard)   ISBN 1-59385-194-4 (paper)
    1. Aggressiveness. 2. Violence. 3. Helping behavior. 4. Good and evil.
5. Social psychology—Research. I. Miller, Arthur G., 1940–
    HM1116.S63 2004
    303.3'72—dc22

                                                           2003020008

About the Editor

Arthur G. Miller, PhD, is Professor of Psychology at Miami University in Oxford, Ohio. He received his doctorate in social psychology from Indiana University in 1967 and spent 1979–1980 at Princeton University on a National Institute of Mental Health fellowship, studying with Ned Jones. Dr. Miller's professional affiliations include the American Psychological Association, the American Psychological Society, the Society of Experimental Social Psychology, and the Society for Personality and Social Psychology. He has written *The Obedience Experiments: A Case Study of Controversy in Social Science* (1986, Praeger) and edited *In the Eye of the Beholder: Contemporary Issues in Stereotyping* (1982, Praeger). Dr. Miller's primary teaching and research interests include stereotyping and stigma, biases in attribution and social judgment, and judgmental reactions to diverse explanations of evil and violence.

CONTRIBUTORS

Nadia Ahmad, MA, Department of Psychology, University of Kansas, Lawrence, Kansas

Craig A. Anderson, PhD, Department of Psychology, Iowa State University, Ames, Iowa

Elliot Aronson, PhD, Distinguished Visiting Professor, Department of Psychology, Stanford University, Stanford, California

C. Daniel Batson, PhD, Department of Psychology, University of Kansas, Lawrence, Kansas

Roy F. Baumeister, PhD, Department of Psychology, Florida State University, Tallahassee, Florida

David M. Buss, PhD, Department of Psychology, University of Texas at Austin, Austin, Texas

Nicholas L. Carnagey, MS, Department of Psychology, Iowa State University, Ames, Iowa

Claire Champion, MA, Department of Psychology, Arizona State University, Tempe, Arizona

Jennifer Crocker, PhD, Department of Psychology, University of Michigan, Ann Arbor, Michigan

Bella M. DePaulo, PhD, Visiting Professor, Department of Psychology, University of California at Santa Barbara, Santa Barbara, California

John F. Dovidio, PhD, Department of Psychology, Colgate University, Hamilton, New York

Joshua D. Duntley, MA, Department of Psychology, University of Texas at Austin, Austin, Texas

Nancy Eisenberg, PhD, Department of Psychology, Arizona State University, Tempe, Arizona

Susan T. Fiske, PhD, Department of Psychology, Princeton University, Princeton, New Jersey

Samuel L. Gaertner, PhD, Department of Psychology, University of Delaware, Newark, Delaware

Gordon Hodson, PhD, Department of Psychology, University of Wales Swansea, Swansea, Wales, United Kingdom

Kerry Kawakami, PhD, Department of Psychology, York University, Toronto, Ontario, Canada

Shawna J. Lee, MSW, MPP, Department of Psychology, University of Michigan, Ann Arbor, Michigan

James J. Lindsay, PhD, Department of Psychology, University of Minnesota, Minneapolis, Minnesota

Arthur G. Miller, PhD, Department of Psychology, Miami University, Oxford, Ohio

Charlene L. Muehlenhard, PhD, Department of Women's Studies, University of Kansas, Lawrence, Kansas

Jason A. Nier, PhD, Department of Psychology, Connecticut College, New London, Connecticut

Allen M. Omoto, PhD, Department of Psychology, Claremont Graduate University, Claremont, California

Lora E. Park, MA, Department of Psychology, University of Michigan, Ann Arbor, Michigan

Zoë D. Peterson, MA, Department of Psychology, University of Kansas, Lawrence, Kansas

Jody A. Resko, MS, MPhil, Department of Epidemiology and
Population Health, Albert Einstein College of Medicine, Bronx,
New York

Mark Snyder, PhD, Department of Psychology, University
of Minnesota, Minneapolis, Minnesota

Ervin Staub, PhD, Department of Psychology, University
of Massachusetts, Amherst, Massachusetts

E. L. Stocks, MA, Department of Psychology, University of Kansas,
Lawrence, Kansas

Jeff Stuewig, PhD, Department of Psychology, George Mason
University, Fairfax, Virginia

June Price Tangney, PhD, Department of Psychology, George Mason
University, Fairfax, Virginia

Carlos Valiente, PhD, Department of Family and Human Development
Arizona State University, Tempe, Arizona

Kathleen D. Vohs, PhD, Sauder School of Business, University of British
Columbia, Vancouver, British Columbia, Canada

Thomas Ashby Wills, PhD, Department of Epidemiology and
Population Health, Albert Einstein College of Medicine, Bronx,
New York

Philip G. Zimbardo, PhD, Department of Psychology, Stanford
University, Stanford, California

PREFACE

Although the initial planning for this book occurred in the spring of 2001, the attacks on September 11, 2001, have lent a special urgency to its primary focus. Social psychologists have been preoccupied with aggressive or harmful as well as prosocial behaviors for many decades. The events of 9/11—the vivid depictions of death and suffering on a massive scale, and the displays of helping behaviors on the part of so many individuals—have made the issues of good and evil particularly salient to everyone, not just researchers. The attackers were immediately labeled by President Bush and countless media analysts as "evil," or "the evildoers," and the term "hero" was used with equal fervor to describe the many helpers who not only aided victims but, in some instances, were destined to join their ranks. The media coverage has been nonabating as well, with innumerable attempts on the part of journalists, historians, behavioral and political scientists, and others to discuss every conceivable facet of the attacks and their impact on our society.

These reactions are, of course, not unusual. Atrocities and tragedies—whether it be the Holocaust, the Oklahoma City bombing, inactive witnesses to the murder of Kitty Genovese, the enslavement of millions of African citizens in the United States, or countless acts of torture and terrorism throughout the world—have always prompted the asking of difficult questions: How could people do these things to other people? *Why* would they do them? Is it something about particular individuals, about culture or society, about unique circumstances, perhaps their complex interaction, that is responsible? Will these horrific events happen again? Can they be prevented? How can we reconcile these terrible acts with the demonstrable kindness and decency of so many people? Is there such a thing as human nature? Are people basically good, evil, both, or neither? This book will certainly not answer all of these questions, or perhaps any of them, in any truly satisfactory manner. They are fair questions to ask, however, and their answers should be sought.

The basic objective of this book is to examine conceptions of good and evil in contemporary social psychology, and to develop a compendium on what some of the most eloquent and informed spokespersons in social psychology have to say about some of the most fundamental and vexing issues in social life. I have asked a number of prominent social psychologists to present their current views as established theorists and researchers who have devoted a major portion of their illustrious careers to these issues.

ACKNOWLEDGMENTS

A number of individuals have played a vital role in the development of *The Social Psychology of Good and Evil*. First, of course, I wish to thank my colleagues who contributed chapters. Their expertise, enthusiasm, and responsiveness to my frequent memos helped sustain my own energy and perseverance for the project. I also take this opportunity to mention, with gratitude, a number of social psychologists who for many years have been particularly influential and inspirational to my thinking about social psychology generally, and about issues pertaining to this volume in particular. I refer here to the late Edward E.(Ned) Jones, the late Stanley Milgram, John M. Darley, and Herbert C. Kelman. The Department of Psychology at Miami University has always been a very congenial and supportive environment for me, and I will always be appreciative of the many students, both undergraduate and graduate, who have studied social psychology with me, to my considerable benefit.

Seymour Weingarten, Editor in Chief at The Guilford Press, has been a continuous source of sage advice at every phase of this book's development, and Laura Patchkofsky, Senior Production Editor, has been extraordinarily helpful and responsive to my continuous pledges of "just this one more addition."

Finally, I would like to dedicate this book to members of my family— to my wife, Sandy; my parents, Mollie and Irving; my daughters, Robi and Lani; to Scott; and (of course!) to grandson Jared. They have cared about this book and have been an invaluable source of gentle encouragement.

CONTENTS

III. The Self-Concept in Relation to Good and Evil Acts

IV. The Possibilities for Kindness

CHAPTER 1

INTRODUCTION AND OVERVIEW

ARTHUR G. MILLER

Rage and disgust can serve for a time to satisfy the transitory ego-defensive needs of tourists and dilettantes; such feelings are melted away from minds that are held in the fires of the Holocaust for prolonged periods. What remains is a central, deadening sense of despair over the human species. Where can one find an affirmative meaning in life if human beings can do such things? Along with this despair there may also come a desperate new feeling of vulnerability attached to the fact that one *is* human. If one keeps at the Holocaust long enough, then sooner or later the ultimate personal truth begins to reveal itself: one knows, finally, that one might either do it, or be done to. If it could happen on such a massive scale elsewhere, then it can happen anywhere; it is all within the range of human possibility, and like it or not, Auschwitz expands the universe of consciousness no less than landings on the moon. (Kren & Rappoport, 1980, p. 126)

Those who refused to obey the orders of authorities, and came to the aid of persecuted people, were neither saints nor heroes. Rather, their goodness was that of ordinary men and women who were responsive to the victims' manifest need for help. . . . Our observations confirm one of the most salient features of the accounts of rescuers' actions during the Nazi era in Europe: Helping happened progressively and was seldom premeditated. . . . Then, gradually, as the helpers became more involved in what they were doing, these initial modest steps evolved into more major, organized undertakings that made it possible to save large numbers of people from arrest, deportation, and murder. . . . Yes, the chances that evil will be perpetuated are increased when it is rendered banal, but goodness does not disappear in the process of making evil commonplace. . . . With respect to rescuers, we found that those who aided persecuted people acted in ways best conceptualized in terms of the *ordinariness of goodness*. (Rochat & Modigliani, 1995, pp. 197–198)

1

Among the vast array of interests investigated by social psychologists, two questions have always been of paramount importance:

1. Are people behaving in the best interests of others and of themselves?
2. Are they harming others and possibly themselves as well?

In searching for answers, social psychology has produced an extraordinarily rich and diverse body of theory and research on the general subjects of good and evil, the conditions under which people are kind and helpful to others, and under which they harm and perhaps even kill others. The major objective of this book is to present a significant, contemporary representation of the research literature on good and evil, as interpreted by social psychologists who have had a very influential role in contributing to our scientific understanding of these subjects.

The title—*The Social Psychology of Good and Evil*—merits elaboration. Most social psychologists would agree that the perspective of social psychology is one that emphasizes the influence of a person's context or social environment on his or her behaviors—what Ross and Nisbett (1991) refer to as the "power of situations" (p. 3). A related assumption is that a person's particular interpretation or construal of his or her context is a key factor, that is, their definition of the situation rather than someone else's physical or objective characterization of it. A variety of cognitive, attributional, and emotional processes are also characteristic of social-psychological conceptualizations of good and evil, as will be noted in the chapters to follow.

The causal role of individual differences or personality factors, however, is viewed more diversely. Many social psychologists consider individual differences to be crucial determinants of behavior, either alone or, more often, in their interaction with specific situations (e.g., Berkowitz, 1999; Funder & Ozer, 1983; Newman, 2002; Sabini, Siepman, & Stein, 2001). However, there is also an extremely strong belief on the part of many social psychologists, as well as considerable empirical evidence, that personal or dispositional factors are frequently very weak predictors of behavior, even though they are perceived, *erroneously*, to be the key determinant of individuals' behavior. Moreover, the lay observer frequently underestimates the impact of situational forces on behavior. This intuitive pattern of causal (mis)understanding is termed the "fundamental attribution error" or "correspondence bias" (Gilbert & Malone, 1995; Ross & Nisbett, 1991). Both of these views of the role of individual differences— that is, their substantive as well as their illusory role—are emphasized in this book. The issue of perception is particularly germane to the concerns of this volume, because many of the actions normally considered to be good as well as evil seem to evoke an instinctive tendency to endow the actor with moral traits that correspond to the acts themselves—that is, people who do good deeds *are*, themselves, good; those who do evil *are* evil. The sense in which these perceptions are accurate as well as inaccurate is an important issue considered here.

The terms *good* and *evil* also warrant some clarification. Clearly, these are value-laden, perhaps even grandiose, words with a long history of usage on the part of both laypersons and scholars in a host of intellectual disciplines. They certainly have religious overtones, among many others. The term *evil*, in particular, might seem particularly vague or controversial, hardly a scientifically precise construct. Yet we see an explicit emphasis on evil in the works of a growing number of social psychologists—for example, Baumeister (1997), Darley (1992), Miller (1999), Staub (1989), Waller (2002), and Zimbardo (1995). The term *evil* does not, in principle, seem less capable of ultimately achieving social-scientific status, at least comparable to that of its many terminological kin—for example, *aggression, violence, hostility, anger, harming, hate, coercion*—all of which have definitional problems of their own.

Berkowitz (1999) has noted, however, that the term *evil* is used inconsistently and far too loosely. For example, with respect to the behavior of subordinates in the Milgram obedience studies and the alleged linkage of the results to the Holocaust, Berkowitz is critical of the traditional social-psychological treatment of this issue. Focusing solely on subordinates who follow orders rather than the instigators who issue these orders reflects a serious failure to recognize degrees of evil. In some instances, *evil* refers to particularly onerous or egregious acts, such as genocide, torture, terrorism, rape, or child abuse. In these contexts, social scientists appear to use the term *evil* in a way similar to that of the layperson (Darley, 1992). In other cases, the term is used not solely with respect to the horrific nature of the acts but more specifically in relation to the proclivity of ordinary or "good" persons to engage in a wide variety of aggressive or criminal actions, particularly when they are part of organizational or hierarchically structured bureaucracies (Darley, 1992; Kelman & Hamilton, 1989).

Illustrating this usage of the term *evil* is its appearance in Hannah Arendt's famous phrase, "the banality of evil," in her account of Adolf Eichmann (1963). Reflecting the impact of Arendt's thesis, the term *ordinary* itself is used frequently in the context of explaining evil—for example, in Browning, *Ordinary Men* (1992); Waller, *How Ordinary People Commit Genocide and Mass Killing* (2002); and Katz, *Ordinary People and Extraordinary Evil* (1993). Goldhagen also uses the term in *Hitler's Willing Executioners: Ordinary Germans and the Holocaust* (1996), but his use of *ordinary* is essentially personal or characterological, explicitly *not* social-psychological in the sense of emphasizing external influences on the part of the perpetrators. This linkage of our ideas of *evil* and *ordinary* is highly consistent with the social-psychological perspective that focuses on normative behaviors characteristic of most people rather than specific types of persons.

Another perspective on the term *evil* reflects an assumption of escalation—that is, that actions of truly great evil frequently are the end result of processes in which the initial seeds may have appeared as relatively trivial or minor hurtful acts. Studying minor or mundane offenses may tell us about far more sinister ones. Baumeister (1997) has noted, for example, that "learning about why people break promises can tell us something about why people commit mass murder" (p. 9).

The contributors in this book are interested in diverse, harmful actions as displayed by large numbers of ordinary people—not necessarily by extremely maladjusted, sadistic, radically bigoted, or hateful people. This is not, of course, to deny the existence of such types of individuals nor their proclivity for engaging in evil acts; indeed, several authors emphasize the role of personality factors in specific domains. Many of the harmful behaviors considered in this volume likely fall short of intuitive conceptions of evil. Nevertheless, I think the term *evil* has a heuristic value in alerting us to the potential within most of us to engage in an extremely broad range of harmful actions. (Readers will note a variety of terminology across the chapters.)

The word *good* may initially seem less objectionable or controversial than *evil*, but it undoubtedly has its share of definitional vagueness. Behaviorally, the word refers to positive or prosocial acts—for example, acts involving helping, social inclusion, assistance, support, volunteerism, and empathy. As with *evil*, however, the term *good* refers to a "fuzzy" category. Not all positive or beneficial acts would be viewed as equally good, and we lack a precise set of terms to describe varying gradations of prosocial actions. Perhaps the most well-known social-psychological analyses of "good" behaviors are the bystander intervention studies of Latané and Darley (1970), prompted by the failure of witnesses to intervene on behalf of Kitty Genovese. Studies in the Latané and Darley tradition have dramatically shown the importance of situational factors in determining helping behaviors—behaviors which the layperson readily attributes to inner qualities of helping individuals (or the lack thereof). As is noted in this book, however, there are many forms of good acts or kindnesses, in addition to assisting in emergencies, that people provide for others.

It is useful to consider a number of issues involved in the study of good and evil. Some of these factors are addressed explicitly in the chapters to follow, others not. Nevertheless, the reader should find it of value to keep the following issues in mind.

GOOD AND EVIL: IN WHOSE EYES?

Social psychology has always emphasized the crucial role of social perception—that the reality or factual status of a social act depends often critically on "the eye of the beholder"—on specifically *who* is interpreting or imposing meaning on the event. There are many eyes or lenses to consider in this volume. Prototypical acts of harming involve a perpetrator and a victim. Considering the perspective of *both* of these participants is crucial, for each may present an extremely different version of what has happened (Baumeister, Stillwell, & Wotman, 1990). Similarly, acts of helping or kindness involve the benefactor or helper and the recipient of the aid. Their stories may also differ considerably in what has happened and why.

In addition to the parties most closely involved, there are other perspectives as well—those of bystanders (involved or uninvolved), authorities, friends, family members, and, crucially, the views of those who analyze these behaviors—social psychologists, other social scientists and academics, journalists, and the interested layperson. These many "viewers" of good and evil—and the reader of this book is yet another—may converge on a relatively common understanding of what has transpired, or, far more likely, form very different points of view or lines of reasoning. These diverse accounts or conceptual orientations are a mixed blessing, I think. They are undoubtedly a constant source of controversy and may be viewed as a powerful obstacle to achieving a consensually agreed-upon understanding. On the other hand, they are fascinating phenomena in themselves, part of the very essence of good and evil, not something apart. One major source of the diverse constructions of good and evil are the preexisting beliefs, theories, and biases held by the observer—be they perpetrator, victim, helper, recipient, scientist, or layperson (Lord, Ross, & Lepper, 1979). Readers are encouraged to note these perspective biases throughout this book, even those that may exist in themselves.

GOOD AND EVIL: TWO SIDES OF A COIN?

Categorizing social behaviors dichotomously as good or evil, kind or cruel, is a seemingly reasonable idea. When someone screams at us in traffic, the harmful intent requires little amplification, and when someone helps a blind person across a busy street, there is little doubt about what has transpired. Yet the distinction is hardly this simple. For one thing, motives matter considerably. A person might scream at us quite justifiably for something we have done, or even to warn us of an impending danger. A person may help someone in a genuinely empathic way, zealously, nobly, but also perhaps begrudgingly, inappropriately, or for purely self-presentational effects.

In addition, how shall we regard the *absence* of a particular, perhaps expected, behavior? Is the failure to help tantamount to an act of harming? Not always, but certainly on occasion. This was the context of the Kitty Genovese episode, and the Latané and Darley (1970) studies could have been considered, justifiably, as focusing on "bystander harming" rather than helping behaviors. Similarly, when acts of harming are prevalent or more likely, the failure to harm could, in a meaningful sense, be considered an act of helping. For example, Milgram (1974) noted an extreme decrease in destructive obedience when participants first observed two peers (accomplices of the experimenter) refusing to obey orders. Thus, role models for disobedience influenced research participants to also disobey authority, and, in so doing, to help the victim. Studies of Christians helping Jews during the Holocaust are also illustrative (e.g., Rochat & Modigliani, 1995). Rochat and Modigliani (1995), in their account of help provided to persecuted Jews by French villagers in LeChambon, title their article "The Ordinary Quality of Resistance," again reflecting social psychology's conceptual orientation toward behaviors within the potential repertoire of many people, not only uniquely heroic individuals. In considering the diverse emphases in this book, readers may wish to reconsider the nature of good and evil; their differences will, of course, often be glaring, but there are similarities as well. That one person's good may be another's evil—that "one person's terrorist may be another person's freedom fighter"—remind us of the intriguing overlap, ambiguity, and potential for heated controversy inherent in these seemingly disparate terminological domains.

UNDERSTANDING GOOD AND EVIL: IS TO EXPLAIN TO FORGIVE EVIL AND TO DEBUNK HEROISM?

When a social psychologist offers a theoretical explanation for a harmful or helpful act, the particular explanation is likely to include a causal analysis of the actor's behavior. This analysis may or may not imply that the actor is personally responsible for his or her behavior. For example, explanations that emphasize situational or external causes are likely to be interpreted as relatively exonerating toward perpetrators of harmful acts (Miller, Buddie, & Kretschmar, 2002; Miller, Gordon, & Buddie, 1999).

There is considerable evidence that writers on the subjects of evil and violence are concerned that their explanations will be misconstrued as indirect forms of forgiving or condoning the perpetrators whose actions they are explaining (Miller et al., 1999, 2002). Moreover, Miller and colleagues (1999) have reported evidence indicating that the very process of generating an explanation for an aggressive act may produce a more lenient or exonerating posture in the person generating the explanation, as well as the person reading such an account. Explanations may create resistance or controversy if they construe the responsibility of actors in a manner with which consumers (e.g., readers, other researchers) of their explanation disagree. The same principle applies to explanations of good acts. Explanations may be resisted if they seem to rob the helping individual of what, to many observers, seems to be well-deserved personal credit—that is, that he or she is a hero or a special and genuinely kind or caring individual.

In the chapters of this volume, the reader may find it of value to consider the manner in which good and evil behaviors are explained, specifically whether the explanations seem more or less acceptable or persuasive because of the manner in which they interpret the perpetrator's or helper's degree of personal responsibility and intentionality—or lack thereof—for his or her behaviors. Ideally, perhaps, explanations should not be evaluated in relation to their implied moral approval or disapproval of the persons whose actions are being addressed. I have little doubt, however, that this particular feature of explanations can be an influential factor affecting the manner in which particular explanations or theories of good and evil are received and evaluated (e.g., Mandel, 1998).

IMAGES OF HUMAN NATURE

In a book of this kind, I think it is appropriate to encourage readers to think about the images of human nature that are conveyed in the various chapters. It is likely that most people entertain an intuitive feeling regarding what people are like in general—good, evil, kind, selfish, trustworthy, etc. In considering the perspectives on good and evil presented here, it should be of interest to assess whether a coherent conception of human nature emerges. Darley (1992), in describing the effect of certain social organizations on the individual, has noted:

> The possibility of being evil is latent in all of us, and can be made actual and active, among other ways, by the conversion process. The person who goes a certain distance in the process has been fundamentally changed, and is now capable of doing harm in an autonomous way. He or she has "changed, changed utterly," has become evil. (p. 209)

We can immediately envision a corollary thesis that the possibility of being good is latent in all of us as well. After reading this book, the reader may wish to consider whether he or she agrees with these assumptions of latent evil and goodness—if so, why; if not, why not; and what other conceptualization of human nature might seem warranted? Are chapter authors, as well as readers, fundamentally optimistic or pessimistic regarding the possibilities for significant improvements in the human condition?

CHAPTER OVERVIEWS

The four chapters in Part I provide conceptual perspectives on good and evil. Evil behavior might seem to prevail in this section, perhaps reflecting the relatively greater attention that evil has received by social psychologists. However, I have also located some chapters that focus conceptually on helping behaviors in later sections of the book (for example, Chapter 14 by Batson and his colleagues). As noted earlier, in any conceptualization of evil, there are inevitably implications for *not* being evil as well. We can learn a great deal about the positive, noble aspects of behavior by focusing on the more destructive tendencies of human beings.

Zimbardo (Chapter 2) argues that good people may perform the most horrific acts. Classic studies on this theme in the history of social psychology are considered, as well as the social-psychological principles and processes responsible for these behaviors. The author explicitly contrasts the situationist perspective with a dispositional orientation, and strongly endorses the former. This conclusion is very unappealing to many people, who "rush to the dispositional" in their intuitive understanding of evil. Just as external accounts of evil have an exonerating implication regarding perpetrator culpability, Zimbardo notes that locating the causes of evil in *evil people* lets situational arrangements "off the hook" in terms of their powerful role in influencing behavior. It also, of course, lets off the hook all of those people who deem themselves *not* evil at all, and by some accounts, this might include virtually everyone! As Baumeister (1997) has noted, "Evil usually enters the world unrecognized by the people who open the door and let it in. Most people who perpetrate evil do not see what they are doing as evil" (p. 1). Zimbardo brings the "person" into focus by emphasizing psychological transformations that occur within individuals, once they are embedded in situationally defined roles. Contemporary issues of genocide, terrorism, torture, and war are also discussed. Of particular interest are Zimbardo's analysis of heroes, those who resist situational pressures, and his position on the apparently exonerating implications of situationist analyses.

Staub (Chapter 3) focuses on the role of basic human needs in the commission of constructive as well as destructive acts. These needs (e.g., security, positive identity, feelings of effectiveness and control, positive connection to other people, autonomy, comprehension of reality, and transcendence) are presumed to be universal, though shaped by culture and profoundly influenced by specific events. Staub describes a complex evolution of diverse processes, involving external conditions such as difficult life conditions, and internal processes such as stereotyping and scapegoating. Participating in genocidal murder or engaging in the most benevolent behaviors are, for Staub, crucially dependent upon the manner in which life circumstances promote the frustration or fulfillment of basic needs or motives. Socialization practices that contribute to aggression (e.g., neglect, punitiveness, and lack of guidance) frustrate basic needs, whereas those that contribute to altruism (e.g., warmth, affection, positive guidance) effectively fulfill basic needs. Staub concludes with an application of his conceptual perspective to the psychological climate of post-9/11 U.S. society.

In Chapter 4, Baumeister and Vohs construe evil and violence in terms of four basic root causes. Similar to Staub, these authors emphasize the role of fundamental needs or motives; for example, the need to obtain what one wants and the need to live up to one's ideals. What happens when a person's pride, self-esteem, or honor is threatened is of particular interest (also considered in Part III of this book). These authors address an issue of crucial significance to this volume, namely the importance of attending to the perspective of perpetrators as well as victims in attempting to understand the nature of evil. For a variety of reasons—which are, themselves, of considerable interest—the perpetrator's point of view is likely to be overlooked or trivialized, with unfortunate consequences. How can people behave more positively? Self-control is one answer, but to settle simply for the restraint of basic motives for evil seems less than a complete victory. The reader might ask whether these authors seem overly pessimistic in their depiction of human nature.

Duntley and Buss (Chapter 5) present an evolutionary perspective. Their approach, different in important ways from traditional social-psychological accounts, nevertheless emphasizes a number of processes that are very social-psychological, particularly those involving social perception, categorical thinking, and the designation of others as friendly or dangerous. The authors also note the importance of considering the diverse perspectives of all actors in episodes of harming or helping. Addressing what they regard as misconceptions regarding evolutionary views of social behavior—for example, the perceived inevitability of inherited behavioral tendencies and the failure to distinguish between what people ideally prefer in human nature and what appears to be the reality—these authors explain how humans have evolved adaptations to benefit as well as harm particular others. Human complexity, flexibility, and a sensitivity to contexts are intrinsic elements to the evolutionary perspective. Humans seem to have the capacity for evil as well as good.

Part II focuses on a number of specific domains of evil and violence. Although the five chapters in this section hardly exhaust the seemingly endless litany of harming behaviors that have been studied by social psychologists, they represent areas that have been unusually active in terms of research and scholarly discussion.

Fiske (Chapter 6) notes that people frequently categorize each other automatically and unintentionally on the basis of race, gender, age, and other protected group memberships. The consequences, in terms of stereotyping, prejudice, and discrimination, can be devastating. The author addresses the crucial issues of controllability and responsibility for personal biases. As noted earlier, the tendency for social-psychological explanations to be perceived, correctly or not, as exonerating perpetrators of evil is a very serious issue. Nowhere is this matter more succinctly raised than in a consideration of cognitive biases underlying stereotyping and prejudice. Although the lack of intent or awareness is, in itself, an intriguing and complex matter, Fiske suggests that people are, in fact, able, *if motivated*, to respond to others as unique individuals, not necessarily as members of social categories. She also discusses the legal and ethical implications for the unbiased treatment of others.

Dovidio, Gaertner, Nier, Kawakami, and Hodson (Chapter 7) consider the nature of contemporary racial bias, which, they contend (in line with Fiske's discussion), may be largely unconscious and unintentional. This aversive racism framework considers how well-intentioned whites, who are convinced that they are not prejudiced and in fact explicitly embrace egalitarian values, may simultaneously hold, without awareness, negative beliefs and feelings about blacks. Displaying a major theme in this volume—that good people can do evil—the authors indicate that these unconscious biases are typically rooted in normal, generally functional, cognitive, motivational, and sociocultural processes. The authors stress both the relatively subtle and situationally sensitive manifestations of aversive racism as well as the key role of rationalization processes that allow biased observers to remain unaware of their own racism. The authors also discuss the implications of holding people responsible for their racial biases, the possibilities for gaining control over, and changing, racial biases, and strategies for improving intergroup relations.

Anderson and Carnagey (Chapter 8) discuss research and theory relevant to the General Aggression Model (GAM). Their approach reflects an important tradition of research on aggression in social psychology, influenced by Leonard Berkowitz. Their model illustrates the complex, multivariate causes of aggression as well as the interaction between personality and situational factors. Individual differences in the personality of the potential aggressor play a major role in this chapter, with important aspects of hostility occurring automatically and without awareness. The authors note the effects of media violence, weapons, and violent video games on behavior. They also discuss the implications of GAM for personal versus societal responsibility, child-rearing practices, and public policy. Anderson and Carnagey review basic conceptual definitions of aggression and challenge the value of retaining the conventional distinction social psychologists have made between impulsive (i.e., hostile, reactive) and instrumental (i.e., premeditated, proactive) aggression.

In Chapter 9 I observe that social psychologists have, for several decades, interpreted the obedience studies as answering the central question of the Holocaust: How could so many apparently ordinary people, under the dictates of blatantly malevolent authority, participate directly, or even indirectly, in the extermination of millions of Jews and other groups? A perusal of current texts in social psychology, for example, reveals an extraordinary coverage of the Milgram experiments, invariably highlighting their relevance to genocide, in general, and the Holocaust, in particular. The obedience experiments, in documenting harmful obedience on the part of a large, representative sample of participants, are seen as empirical verification of Arendt's influential thesis on the banality of evil. In contrast to the prevailing view, a number of social psychologists have expressed grave reservations regarding generalizations from the obedience studies to the Holocaust. These criticisms draw sharp distinctions between the essential nature of the Holocaust and the laboratory context of the obedience research. Contributing to the intense controversies are the exonerating implications of social-psychological explanations of the destructive obedience. Explaining the Holocaust as a result of intentional, voluntary, evil behaviors on the part of extremely anti-Semitic Germans locates the attribution of personal responsibility in the perpetrators, themselves. This is a picture very different from the conclusions of the Milgram experiments, and for some at least, a far more preferable theoretical position to hold regarding the Holocaust. I advocate a reexamination of Milgram's research in the light of current criticisms and suggest that social psychologists consider relevant Holocaust scholarship in more detail when discussing the relevance of the obedience experiments to understanding the Holocaust.

Muehlenhard and Peterson (Chapter 10) highlight the many controversies involved in either studying or attempting to prevent sexual violence. The effects of personal biases or preexisting points of view are vividly documented, as decisions or conclusions in this area relate closely to one's values and theories about power, violence, sexuality, and gender. That many of these preconceptions are implicit and not consciously monitored is problematic. Definitions matter immensely. For example, should researchers limit their study of sexual violence to acts involving blatant coercion, or should they include a broader range of behaviors encompassing subtler forms of coercion? The perceived seriousness of sexual violence depends critically on how broadly inclusive or specific the victimizing acts are regarded. The causes and consequences of the trivialization as well as exaggeration of sexual violence are considered. The specific perspective emphasized in the analysis again looms large: Should we focus on victims, perpetrators, or society? The consequences of each of these emphases are discussed, particularly with respect to issues of victim blaming and attribution of responsibility. For example, conceptual treatments that focus on society (e.g., sexist norms, implicit beliefs and stereotypes) may perpetuate the idea that no single individual is responsible—that violence is "society's" fault. The complex aspects of the violence versus sex distinction in rape are also considered.

Part III includes three chapters that address, in a variety of contexts, the role of the self in acts of harm-doing and kindness. A core theme is that people are generally motivated to protect or affirm their self-concept in the face of diverse threats. A variety of aggressive, harmful actions may restore a person's sense of self-respect, honor, justice, or deservingness. The self may also be instrumental in acts of kindness and helping. (The more positive or prosocial dimensions of the self are also considered in Part IV.)

In Chapter 11, Crocker, Lee, and Park suggest that when people are preoccupied with protecting and enhancing their self-esteem, their behavior may impact very negatively on both the self and others. Defensiveness, anger, and aggression associated with fragile egotism are likely when people perceive threats in areas strongly connected with their self-worth. The authors review a variety of research programs demonstrating that anger and antisocial behaviors are greater in people who stake their self-worth on external, often uncontrollable, contingencies. Acts of generosity and kindness are more likely to be committed by individuals who base their self-esteem on internal sources such as virtue or fidelity, but the question remains as to whether the primary beneficiary is the "other" or the "self." Is the self-esteem construct overrated by social psychologists? Are people personally responsible for the behavioral effects of their needs for esteem? These and other issues are considered.

In perhaps no other specific area in this volume is the line between good and evil more blurred than in the case of lying and deceit. DePaulo (Chapter 12) notes that lying is widely condemned, yet even more widely practiced. Lies vary in their seriousness but invariably carry a poor moral image, at least in the abstract. In the arenas of actual life, people are adept at strategic lying to manage the challenges and dilemmas of their lives. DePaulo notes that, by definition, lying is intentional—a deliberate attempt to mislead—yet some lies appear to be essentially mindless and automatic. Although motivations for lying vary, the self-concept is frequently a primary beneficiary of successful lying. We may also, of course, lie to help others—for example, by not telling them bad news—as well as to harm them. The author includes a discussion of hypocrisy, "scrupulous honesty," and the morality of lying, giving readers an instructive portrait of social psychology "at work" on a problem of great complexity and social consequence.

Similar to lying, guilt and shame seem relevant to both the good and evil dimensions of human behavior, as people hesitate, or perhaps agonize, about the course of action ahead or just taken. Tangney and Stuewig (Chapter 13) note that shame and guilt are often cited as "moral emotions" because of the presumed role they play in deterring immoral and antisocial behavior. These authors question this assumption. With respect to actions with moral significance—for example, helping, telling difficult truths, lying, cheating—they ask if shame and guilt are helpful guides to effective behaviors. The authors review recent research on the nature and implications of shame and guilt. They note that these two so-called moral emotions are not equally "moral." Guilt and empathy generally influence people in positive directions, but shame appears more destructive in its effects on behavior. Tangney and Stuewig highlight the adaptive functions of guilt, in contrast to the hidden costs of shame, and differentiate the relationship of shame and guilt to a variety of behaviors central to the concerns of this book.

In an explicit sense, the five chapters in Part IV focus more on "the good" side of human nature in contrast to the explicit focus of Part II. Although the picture is actually more complex—and there is a considerable amount of hostility and harming considered in this section as well—the chapters are framed to highlight the possibilities for kindness and helping. The positive and negative social behaviors of children and adolescents are noted in several chapters in this section, illustrating the important interplay between social and developmental psychology.

Batson, Ahmad, and Stocks (Chapter 14) discuss the empathy–altruism hypothesis: the idea that empathic emotion evokes motivation with an ultimate goal of increasing another's welfare. They find considerable support for this hypothesis. Although the implications in terms of social behaviors might seem uniformly positive, the authors paint a more ambiguous picture. Empathy-induced altruism can indeed lead to more helping of those in need, to less harm, to increased cooperation, and to improved attitudes toward stigmatized groups. However, empathy-induced altruism may also have very negative effects. For example, aware of the burdensome aspects of empathy on obligatory helping, people may intentionally avoid feelings of empathy, turning away from those in need. Empathy-induced altruistic motivation can also lead to biased favoritism toward those for whom we especially care, even though fairness dictates impartiality. Empathy hardly seems evil, but the authors suggest that it is, by no means, always a good thing. It depends on the situation.

Eisenberg, Valiente, and Champion (Chapter 15) take a social–developmental perspective and review the relations of various modes of empathy-related responding to children's prosocial as well as more problematic behaviors. They consider both situational and dispositional causes of empathy-related responses. One particular focus concerns the manner in which parental expressions of emotion may contribute to the development of empathy and sympathy and the role of emotion-related regulation in this process. The authors deal with the relative contributions of personality and situational factors and the degree to which empathy-related behaviors are automatic or consciously controlled. They suggest that empathy is more often a relatively automatic response (though susceptible to purposeful enhancement, for example, by perspective-taking), whereas prosocial behaviors, per se, are more likely to be under voluntary control. Eisenberg and colleagues also note the implications of their research for social policies and interventions.

Wills and Resko (Chapter 16), focusing on adolescent behavior, emphasize the supportive context of a person's social relationships. Their approach emphasizes the classic social-psychological thesis regarding the crucial role of other people on a given person's good or evil actions. Altruistic behavior may be influenced by supportive relationships with parents, peers, teachers, etc.; conversely, aggressive, antisocial behaviors may be influenced by isolation, loneliness, or rejection. Drawing from theory and research on family support and substance use, Wills and Resko note that supportive relationships promote altruistic behavior through positive emotions, positive self-perceptions and optimism, and patterns of active, engaged coping. However, isolation or social rejection may increase destructive behaviors by eliciting anger, avoidant coping, and a greater tolerance for deviance. Paradoxically, however, peer support—perhaps the very prototype of a positive social influence—can also lead to undesirable outcomes under certain conditions. Wills and Resko discuss the processes by which supportive relationships influence deviance and how intermediate variables can lead to altruistic or aggressive outcomes. They conclude with a discussion of the implications of their model for interventions to reduce destructive behaviors and enhance prosocial actions.

If, on occasion, the spotlight in this book seems to shine more emphatically on evil and harm-doing than on the more benevolent capacities of people, a powerful counterweight is provided by Snyder, Omoto, and Lindsay in Chapter 17. These authors discuss the psychology of volunteerism. In contrast to social psychology's traditional emphasis on the more fleeting aspects of help or its absence in emergency situations, Snyder and colleagues are concerned with acts of sustained helping in which people intentionally help others, make continuing commitments to do so, and sustain these commitments without any prior obligations to the recipients of their services. Using a functional theoretical approach that emphasizes multiple processes of personality and motivation, the authors discuss research using diverse methodologies, samples of volunteers, and settings. They also describe theory-guided research examining the effects of volunteerism on those who volunteer, on the recipients of the services, and on the volunteers' social networks. Snyder and colleagues are interested in how the functional approach to the psychology of citizen participation can contribute to linkages between basic research and a variety of practical problems.

Aronson (Chapter 18) first examines situational factors that contribute to violence and intergroup hostility in schools. A primary focus concerns the ways of reducing violence and promoting harmonious, compassionate, social relationships. With respect to recent, highly publicized murders in school settings, Aronson proposes that intergroup separation and conflict—the exclusionary cliques so prevalent in middle and high schools—create an atmosphere of rejection and humiliation. Taunting, teasing, and bullying in these settings are commonplace. Consistent with issues considered in Part III, Aronson views the consequences of these extremely hurtful behaviors and the emotions they elicit to be the crux of the problem. Reactions on the part of the "losers" in this hierarchical status system vary: They may suffer quietly and privately, they may contemplate suicide, or they may attempt to harm or kill their fellow students. Using extensive research on the jigsaw classroom, Aronson argues for the power of situational arrangements to foster an atmosphere of interdependence, in which students benefit personally from helping others do well. Aronson views social-psychological principles as uniquely effective in showing us how to transform interpersonal and intergroup hostility into genuinely compassionate human relationships. This approach—an extremely optimistic one—reflects one of social psychology's most well-documented principles regarding the power of specific contextual arrangements to override the effects of negative, seemingly intransigent, personal attitudes or feelings, and to generate more effective and benevolent interpersonal dynamics.

REFERENCES

Arendt, H. (1963). *Eichmann in Jerusalem: A report on the banality of evil.* New York: Viking Press.

Baumeister, R. F. (1997). *Evil: Inside human violence and cruelty.* New York: Freeman.

Baumeister, R. F., Stillwell, A., & Wotman, S. R. (1990). Victim and perpetrator accounts of interpersonal conflict: Autobiographical narratives about anger. *Journal of Personality and Social Psychology, 59,* 994–1005.

Berkowitz, L. (1999). Evil is more than banal: Situationism and the concept of evil. *Personality and Social Psychology Review, 3,* 246–253.

Browning, C. R. (1992). *Ordinary men: Reserve police battalion 101 and the final solution in Poland.* New York: HarperCollins.

Darley, J. M. (1992). Social organization for the production of evil. *Psychological Inquiry, 3,* 199–218.

Funder, D. C., & Ozer, D. J. (1983). Behavior as a function of the situation. *Journal of Personality and Social Psychology, 44,* 107–112.

Gilbert, D. T., & Malone, P. S. (1995). The correspondence bias. *Psychological Bulletin, 117,* 21–38.

Goldhagen, D. J. (1996). *Hitler's willing executioners: Ordinary Germans and the Holocaust.* New York: Knopf.

Katz, F. E. (1993). *Ordinary people and extraordinary evil: A report on the beguilings of evil.* Albany: State University of New York Press.

Kelman, H. C., & Hamilton, V. L. (1989). *Crimes of obedience: Toward a social psychology of authority and responsibility.* New Haven, CT: Yale University Press.

Kren, G. M., & Rappoport, L. (1980). *The Holocaust and the crisis of human behavior.* New York: Holmes & Meier.

Latané, B., & Darley, J. M. (1970). *The unresponsive bystander: Why doesn't he help?* New York: Appleton-Century-Crofts.

Lord, C. G., Ross, L., & Lepper, M. R. (1979). Biased assimilation and attitude polarization: The effects of prior theories on subsequently considered evidence. *Journal of Personality and Social Psychology, 37,* 2098–2109.

Mandel, D. R. (1998). The obedience alibi: Milgram's account of the Holocaust reconsidered. *Analyse & Kritik, 20,* 74–94.

Milgram, S. (1974). *Obedience to authority: An experimental view.* New York: Harper & Row.

Miller, A. G. (1999). Harming other people: Perspectives on evil and violence. *Personality and Social Psychology Review, 3,* 176–178.

Miller, A. G., Buddie, A. M., & Kretschmar, J. (2002). Explaining the Holocaust: Does social psychology exonerate the perpetrators? In L. S. Newman & R. Erber (Eds.), *Understanding genocide: The social psychology of the Holocaust* (pp. 301–324). New York: Oxford University Press.

Miller, A. G., Gordon, A. K., & Buddie, A. M. (1999). Accounting for evil and cruelty: Is to explain to condone? *Personality and Social Psychology Review, 3,* 254–268.

Newman, L. S. (2002). What is a "social-psychological" account of perpetrator behavior? The person versus the situation in Goldhagen's *Hitler's willing executioners.* In L. S. Newman & R. Erber (Eds.), *Understanding genocide: The social psychology of the Holocaust* (pp. 43–67). New York: Oxford University Press.

Rochat, F., & Modigliani, A. (1995). The ordinary quality of resistance: From Milgram's laboratory to the village of LeChambon. *Journal of Social Issues, 51,* 195–210.

Ross, L. D. (1977). The intuitive psychologist and his shortcomings: Distortion in the attribution process. In L. Berkowitz (Ed.), *Advances in experimental social psychology* (Vol. 10, pp. 173–220). New York: Academic Press.

Ross, L. D., & Nisbett, R. E. (1991). *The person and the situation: Perspectives of social psychology.* New York: McGraw-Hill.

Sabini, J., Siepmann, M., & Stein, J. (2001). The really fundamental attribution error in social psychological research. *Psychological Inquiry, 12,* 1–15.

Staub, E. (1989). *The roots of evil: The origins of genocide and other group vio-lence.* New York: Cambridge University Press.

Waller, J. (2002). *Becoming evil: How ordinary people commit genocide and mass killings.* New York: Oxford University Press.

Zimbardo, P. G. (1995). The psychology of evil: A situationist perspective on re-cruiting good people to engage in anti-social acts. *Research in Social Psychol-ogy (Japan), 11,* 125–133.

PART I

CONCEPTUAL PERSPECTIVES ON GOOD AND EVIL

CHAPTER 2

A Situationist Perspective on the Psychology of Evil

Understanding How Good People Are Transformed into Perpetrators

PHILIP G. ZIMBARDO

I endorse the application of a situationist perspective to the ways in which the antisocial behavior of individuals and the violence sanctioned by nations can be best understood, treated, and prevented. This view, which has both influenced and been informed by a body of social-psychological research and theory, contrasts with the traditional perspective that explains evil behavior in dispositional terms: Internal determinants of antisocial behavior locate evil within individual predispositions—genetic "bad seeds," personality traits, psychopathological risk factors, and other organismic variables. The situationist approach is to the dispositional as public health models of disease are to medical models. Following basic principles of Lewinian theory, the situationist perspective propels external determinants of behavior to the foreground, well beyond the status as merely extenuating background circumstances. Unique to this situationist approach is the use of experimental laboratory and field research to demonstrate vital phenomena, that other approaches only analyze verbally or rely on archival or

The political views expressed in this chapter represent solely those of a private citizen/patriot, and in no way should be construed as being supported or endorsed by any of my professional or institutional affiliations.

correlational data for answers. The basic paradigm presented in this chapter illustrates the relative ease with which ordinary, "good" men and women can be induced into behaving in "evil" ways by turning on or off one or another social situational variable.

I begin the chapter with a series of "oldies but goodies"—my laboratory and field studies on deindividuation, aggression, vandalism, and the Stanford prison experiment, along with a process analysis of Milgram's obedience studies, and Bandura's analysis of "moral disengagement." My analysis is extended to the evil of inaction by considering bystander failures of helping those in distress. This body of research demonstrates the underrecognized power of social situations to alter the mental representations and behavior of individuals, groups, and nations. Finally, I explore extreme instances of "evil" behavior for their dispositional or situational foundations: torturers, death-squad violence workers, and terrorist suicide bombers.

Evil can be defined as intentionally behaving, or causing others to act, in ways that demean, dehumanize, harm, destroy, or kill innocent people. This behaviorally focused definition makes the individual or group responsible for purposeful, motivated actions that have a range of negative consequences for other people. The definition excludes accidental or unintended harmful outcomes, as well as the broader, generic forms of institutional evil, such as poverty, prejudice, or destruction of the environment by agents of corporate greed. However, it does include corporate forms of wrongdoing, such as the marketing and selling of products with known disease-causing, death-dealing properties (e.g., cigarette manufacturers or other substance/drug dealers). The definition also extends beyond the proximal agent of aggression, as studied in research on interpersonal violence, to encompass those in distal positions of authority whose orders or plans are carried out by functionaries. Such agents include military commanders and national leaders, such as Hilter, Stalin, Mao, Pol Pot, Idi Amin, and others whom history has identified as tyrants for their complicity in the deaths of untold millions of innocent people.

History will also have to decide on the evil status of President George W. Bush's role in declaring a pre-emptive, aggressive war against Iraq in March 2003, with dubious justification, that resulted in widespread death, injury, destruction, and enduring chaos. We might also consider a simpler definition of evil, proposed by my colleague, Irving Sarnoff: "Evil is knowing better but doing worse."

We live in a world cloaked in the evils of civil and international wars, of terrorism (home-grown and exported), homicides, rapes, domestic and child abuse, and countless other forms of devastation. The same human mind that creates the most beautiful works of art and extraordinary marvels of technology is equally responsible for the perversion of its own perfection. This most dynamic organ in the universe has served as a seemingly endless source of ever viler torture chambers and instruments of horror in earlier centuries, the "bestial machinery" unleashed on Chinese citizens by Japanese soldiers in their rape of Nanking (see Chang, 1997), and the recent demonstration of "creative evil" in the destruction of the World Trade Center by "weaponizing" commercial airlines. We continue to ask, *why?* Why and how is it possible for such deeds to continue to occur? How can the unimaginable become so readily imagined? These are the same questions that have been asked by generations before ours.

I wish I had answers to these profound questions about human existence and human nature. Here I can offer modest versions of possible answers. My concern centers around how good, ordinary people can be recruited, induced, seduced into behaving in ways that could be classified as evil. In contrast to the traditional approach of trying to identify "evil people" to account for the evil in our midst, I focus on trying to outline some of the central conditions that are involved in the transformation of good people into perpetrators of evil.

LOCATING EVIL WITHIN PARTICULAR PEOPLE: THE RUSH TO THE DISPOSITIONAL

"Who is responsible for evil in the world, given that there is an all-powerful, omniscient God who is also all-Good?" That conundrum began the intellectual scaffolding of the Inquisition in the 16th and 17th centuries in Europe. As revealed in *Malleus Maleficarum,* the handbook of the German Inquisitors from the Roman Catholic Church, the inquiry concluded that "the Devil" was the source of all evil. However, these theologians argued the Devil works his evil through intermediaries, lesser demons, and, of course, human witches. So the hunt for evil focused on those marginalized people who looked or acted differently from ordinary people, who might qualify, under rigorous examination of conscience and torture, as "witches," and then put them to death. The victims were mostly women who could be readily exploited without sources of defense, especially when they had resources that could be confiscated. An analysis of this legacy of institutionalized violence against women is detailed by historian Anne Barstow (1994) in *Witchcraze.* Paradoxically, this early effort of the Inquisition to understand the origins of evil and develop interventions to cope with it instead fomented new forms of evil that fulfill all facets of my definition. The phenomenon of the Inquisition exemplifies the notion of simplifying the complex problem of widespread evil by identifying *individuals* who might be the guilty parties and then making them "pay" for their evil deeds.

Most traditional psychiatry as well as psychodynamic theory also locate the source of individual violence and antisocial behavior within the psyches of disturbed people, often tracing it back to early roots in unresolved infantile conflicts. Like genetic views of pathology, such psychological approaches seek to link behaviors society judges as pathological to pathological origins—be they defective genes, "bad seeds," or premorbid personality structures. However, this view overlooks the fact that the same violent outcomes can be generated by very different types of people, all of whom give no hint of evil impulses. My colleagues and I (Lee, Zimbardo, & Berthoff, 1977) interviewed and tested 19 inmates in California prisons who had all recently been convicted of homicide. Ten of these killers had a long history of violence, showed lack of impulse control (on the Minnesota Multiphasic Personality Inventory), were decidedly masculine in sexual identity, and generally extraverted. The other murderers were totally different. They had never committed any criminal offense prior to the homicide—their murders were totally unexpected, given their mild manner and gentle disposition. Their problem was an *excessive* impulse control that inhibited their expression of any feelings. Their sexual identity was feminine or androgynous, and the majority were shy. These "shy sudden murderers" killed just as violently as did the habitual criminals, and their victims died just as surely, but it would have been impossible to predict this outcome from any prior knowledge of their personalities, which were so different from the more obvious habitual criminals.

The concept of an authoritarian personality syndrome was developed by a team of psychologists (Adorno, Frenkel-Brunswick, Levinson, & Sanford, 1950) after World War II who were trying to make sense of the Holocaust and the broad appeal of fascism and Hitler. Their dispositional bias led them to focus on identifying a set of personality factors that might underlie the fascist mentality. However, they overlooked the host of processes operating at political, economic, societal, and historical levels, all of which influenced and directed so many millions of individuals into a constrained behavioral channel of hating Jews and other minority groups, while endorsing and even applauding the views and policies of their dictator.

This tendency to explain observed behavior by reference to internal dispositional factors while ignoring or minimizing the impact of situational variables has been termed the fundamental attribution error (FAE) by my colleague Lee Ross (1977). We are all subject to this dual bias of overutilizing dispositional analyses and underutilizing situational explanations when faced with ambiguous causal scenarios we want to understand. We succumb to this effect because our educational institutions, social and professional training programs, and societal agencies are all geared toward a focus on individual, dispositional orientations. Dispositional analyses are a central operating feature of cultures that are based on individualistic rather than collectivist values (see Triandis, 1994). Thus, it is individuals who are lauded with praise and fame and wealth for achievement and are honored for their uniqueness, but it is also individuals who are blamed for the ills of society. Our legal, medical, educational, and religious systems all are founded on principles of individualism.

Dispositional analyses of antisocial, or non-normative, behaviors typically include strategies for behavior modification, whereby deviant individuals learn to conform better to social norms, or facilities for excluding them from society via imprisonment, exile, or execution. Locating evil within selected individuals or groups carries with it the "social virtue" of taking society "off the hook" as blameworthy; societal structures and political decision making are exonerated from bearing any burden of the more fundamental circumstances that create racism, sexism, elitism, poverty, and marginal existence for some citizens. Furthermore, this dispositional orientation to understanding evil implies a simplistic, binary world of good people, like us, and bad people, like them. That clear-cut dichotomy is divided by a manufactured line that separates good and evil. We then take comfort in the illusion that such a line constrains crossovers in either direction. We could never imagine being like *them*, of doing their unthinkable dirty deeds, and do not admit them into our company because they are so essentially different as to be unchangeable. This extreme position also means we forfeit the motivation to understand how they came to engage in what we view as evil behavior. I find it helpful to remind myself of the geopolitical analysis of the Russian novelist Alexander Solzhenitsyn, a victim of persecution by the Soviet KGB, that the line between good and evil lies in the center of every human heart.

THE TRANSFORMATION OF GOOD PEOPLE INTO AGENTS OF DESTRUCTION

My bias is admittedly more toward situational analyses of behavior and comes from my training as an experimental social psychologist as well as from having grown up in poverty, in a New York City ghetto of the South Bronx. I believe that dispositional orientations are more likely to correlate with affluence: The rich want to take full credit for their success, whereas the situationists hail more from the lower classes who want to explain the obvious dysfunctional lifestyles of those around them in terms of external circumstances rather than internal failures. I am primarily concerned with understanding the psychological and social dynamics involved when an ordinary, "good" person begins to act in antisocial ways and, in the extreme, behaves destructively toward the property or person of others. I saw, firsthand, my childhood friends go through such transformations, and I wondered how and why they changed so drastically and whether I could also change like that (e.g., they were bullied, failed in school, parents fought all the time, nothing to look forward to). I was similarly fascinated with the tale of the behavioral transformation of Robert Louis Stevenson's good Dr. Jekyll into the murderous Mr. Hyde. What was in his chemical formula that could have such an immediate and profound impact? Even as a child, I wondered if there were other ways to induce such changes, since my friends did not have access to his elixir of evil before they did such bad things to other people. I would later discover that social psychology had recipes for such transformations.

Our mission is to understand better how virtually anyone could be recruited to engage in evil deeds that deprive other human beings of their dignity, humanity, and life. The dispositional analysis has the comforting side effect of enabling those who have not yet done wrong to righteously assert, "Not *me*, I am different from those kinds of people who did that evil deed!" By positing a "me–us–them" distinction, we live with the illusion of moral superiority firmly entrenched in the pluralistic ignorance that comes from not recognizing the set of situational and structural circumstances that empowered others—like ourselves—to engage in deeds that they too once thought were alien to their nature. We take false pride in believing that "I am not that kind of person."

I argue that the human mind is so marvelous that it can adapt to virtually any known environmental circumstance in order to survive, to create, and to destroy, as necessary. We are not born with tendencies toward good or evil but with mental templates to do *either*. What I mean is that we have the potential to be better or worse than anyone who has existed in the past, to be more creative and more destructive, to make the world a better place or a worse place than before. It is only through the recognition that no one of us is an island, that we all share the human condition, that humility takes precedence over unfounded pride in acknowledging our vulnerability to situational forces. If we want to develop mechanisms for combating such malevolent transformations, then it seems essential to learn to appreciate the extent to which ordinary people can be seduced or initiated into the performance of evil deeds. We need to focus on discovering the mechanisms among the causal factors that influence so many to do so much bad, to commit so much evil throughout the globe. (See also the breadth of ideas presented by Baumeister, 1997; Darley, 1992; Staub, 1989; Waller, 2002.)

THE MILGRAM OBEDIENCE EXPERIMENTS

The most obvious power of the experimental demonstration by Stanley Milgram (1974) of blind obedience to authority lies in the unexpectedly high rates of such compliance, with the majority—two-thirds—of the subjects "going all the way" in shocking a victim with apparently lethal consequences. His finding was indeed shocking to most of those who read about it or saw his movie version of the study, because it revealed that a variety of ordinary American citizens could so readily be led to engage in "electrocuting a nice stranger." But the more significant importance of his research comes from what he did after that initial classic study with Yale College undergraduates. Milgram conducted 18 experimental variations on more than a *thousand* subjects from a variety of backgrounds, ages, both genders, and all educational levels. In each of these studies he varied one social-psychological variable and observed its impact on the extent of obedience to the unjust authority's pressure to continue to shock the "learner-victim." He was able to demonstrate that compliance rates of those who delivered the maximum 450 volts to the hapless victim could soar to 90% *or* could be reduced to less than 10% by introducing a single variable into the compliance recipe.

Milgram found that obedience was maximized when subjects first observed peers behaving obediently; it was dramatically reduced when peers rebelled or when the victim acted like a masochist asking to be shocked. What is especially interesting to me about this last result are the data Milgram provides on the predictions of his outcome by 40 psychiatrists who were given the basic description of the classic experiment. Their average estimate of the percentage of U.S. citizens who would give the full 450 volts was fewer than 1%. Only sadists would engage in such sadistic behavior, they believed. In a sense, this is the comparison level for appreciating the enormity of Milgram's finding. These experts on human behavior were *totally* wrong because they ignored the situational determinants of behavior in the procedural description of the experiment and overrelied on the dispositional perspective that comes from their professional training. Their error is a classic instance of the FAE at work. In fact, in this research, the average person does *not* behave like a sadist when an apparently masochistic victim encourages him or her to do so.

Milgram's intention was to provide a paradigm in which it was possible to quantify "evil" by the number of buttons a subject pushed on a shock generator, which allegedly delivered shocks to a mild-mannered confederate, playing the role of the pupil or learner, while the subject enacted the teacher role. Some of the procedures in this research paradigm that seduced many ordinary citizens to engage in evil offer parallels to compliance strategies used by "influence professionals" in real-world settings, such as salespeople, cult recruiters, and our national leaders (see Cialdini, 2001).

TEN INGREDIENTS IN THE SITUATIONIST'S RECIPE FOR BEHAVIORAL TRANSFORMATIONS

Among the influence principles in Milgram's paradigm for getting ordinary people to do things they originally believed they would not do are the following:

1. Presenting an acceptable justification, or rationale, for engaging in the undesirable action, such as wanting to help people improve their memory by judicious use of punishment strategies. In experiments this justification is known as the "cover story" because it is intended to cover up the procedures that follow, which might not make sense on their own. The real-world equivalent of the cover story is an ideology, such as "national security," that often provides the nice big lie for instituting a host of bad, illegal, and immoral policies.

2. Arranging some form of contractual obligation, verbal or written, to enact the behavior.

3. Giving participants meaningful roles to play (e.g., teacher, student) that carry with them previously learned positive values and response scripts.

4. Presenting basic rules to be followed, which seem to make sense prior to their actual use, but then can be arbitrarily used to justify mindless compliance. "Failure to respond must be treated as an error" was a Milgram rule for shock omissions as well as for false commissions. But then what happens when the learner complains of a heart condition, wants to quit, then screams, followed by a thud and silence? The learner's apparent inability to respond to the teacher's testing due to death or unconsciousness must be continually challenged by further shocks, since omission equals commission. The proceedings do not make sense at all: How could the teacher be helping to improve the memory of a learner who is incapacitated or dead? All too many participants stopped engaging in such basic, obvious critical thinking endeavors as their confusion and stress mounted.

5. Altering the semantics of the act and action: from hurting victims to helping learners by punishing them.

6. Creating opportunities for diffusion of responsibility for negative outcomes; others will be responsible, or it will not be evident that the actor will be held liable.

7. Starting the path toward the ultimate evil act with a small, insignificant first step (only 15 volts).

8. Increasing each level of aggression in gradual steps that do not seem like noticeable differences (only 30 volts).

9. Gradually changing the nature of the influence authority from "just" to "unjust," from reasonable and rational to unreasonable and irrational.

10. Making the "exit costs" high and the process of exiting difficult by not permitting usual forms of verbal dissent to qualify as behavioral disobedience.

Such procedures are utilized across varied influence situations, in which those in authority want others to do their bidding but know that few would engage in the "end game" final solution without first being properly prepared psychologically to do the "unthinkable." I would encourage readers to engage in the thought exercise of applying these compliance principles to the tactics used by the Bush administration to cajole Americans into endorsing the preemptive invasion of Iraq (discussed further later in the chapter).

LORD OF THE FLIES AND THE PSYCHOLOGY OF DEINDIVIDUATION

William Golding's (1954) Noble prize-winning novel of the transformation of good British choir boys into murderous beasts centers on the point of change in mental state and behavior that follows a change in physical appearance. Painting themselves, changing their outward appearance, made it possible for some of Golding's characters to disinhibit previously restrained impulses to kill a pig for food. Once that alien deed of killing another creature was accomplished, they could then continue on to kill, with pleasure, both animals and people alike. Was Golding describing a psychologically valid principle in his use of external appearance as catalyst to dramatic changes in internal and behavioral processes? That is the question I answered with a set of experiments and field studies on the psychology of deindividuation (Zimbardo, 1970).

The basic procedure involved having young women deliver a series of painful electric shocks to each of two other young women whom they could see and hear in a one-way mirror before them. Half were randomly assigned to a condition of anonymity, or deindividuation, half to one of uniqueness, or individuation. The appearance of the four college student subjects in each deindividuation group was concealed, and they were given identifying numbers in place of their names. The comparison individuation subjects in the four-woman groups were called by their names and made to feel unique. They were asked to make the same responses of shocking each of two female "victims"—all with a suitable cover story, the big lie that they never questioned.

The results were clear: Women in the deindividuation condition delivered twice as much shock to both victims as did the women in the individuated comparison condition. Moreover, the deindividuated subjects shocked both victims, the one previously rated as pleasant and the other as unpleasant, more over the course of the 20 trials, whereas the individuated subjects shocked the pleasant woman less over time than they did the unpleasant one. One important conclusion flows from this research and its various replications and extensions, some using military personnel: Anything that makes a person feel anonymous, as if no one knows who he or she is, creates the potential for that person to act in evil ways—if the situation gives permission for violence.

HALLOWEEN DISGUISES AND AGGRESSION IN CHILDREN

Outside the laboratory, *masks* may be used to create the anonymity needed to disinhibit typically restrained behavior. For example, people mask themselves at Carnival rituals in many Catholic countries. Children in the United States don masks and costumes for Mardi Gras and Halloween parties. Bringing the laboratory to the party, so to speak, Fraser (1974) arranged for elementary school children to go to a special, experimental Halloween party given by their teacher. There were many games to play and for each game won, tokens were earned that could be exchanged for gifts at the end of the party. Half the games were nonaggressive in nature, and half were matched in content but involved aggression: Physical confrontations between two children were necessary to reach the goal and win the contest. The experimental design was a within-subject (A-B-A) format: in the first phase the games were played without costumes; then the costumes arrived and were worn as the games continued; finally, the costumes were removed and the games went on for the third phase (each phase lasted about an hour). The data are striking testimony to the power of anonymity. Aggression increased significantly as soon as the costumes were worn, more than doubling from the initial base level average. When the costumes were removed, aggression dropped back well below the initial base rate. Equally interesting was the second result: that aggression had negative instrumental consequences on winning tokens—that is, it costs money to be aggressive—but that cost did not matter when the children were anonymous in their costumes. The least number of tokens won occurred during the costumed anonymity phase, when aggression was highest.

CULTURAL WISDOM OF CHANGING
WARRIORS' APPEARANCES

Let us leave the laboratory and the fun and games of children's parties to enter the real world, where these issues of anonymity and violence may take on life-and-death significance. Some societies go to war without having the young male warriors change their appearance, whereas others always include ritual transformations of appearance by painting or masking the warriors (as in *Lord of the Flies*). Does that change in external appearance make a difference in how warring enemies are treated? After reading my Nebraska Symposium chapter, Harvard anthropologist John Watson (1973) posed a research question, then went to the human area files to find the answer, then published the data: (1) the societies that did or did not change appearance of warriors prior to going to war, and (2) the extent to which they killed, tortured, or mutilated their victims. The results are striking confirmation of the prediction that anonymity promotes destructive behavior, when permission is also given to behave in aggressive ways that are ordinarily prohibited. Of the 23 societies for which these two data sets were present, the majority (12 of 15, 80%) of societies in which warriors changed their appearance were those noted as most destructive, whereas only one of the eight societies in which the warriors did *not* change appearance before going to battle was noted as destructive. Cultural wisdom dictates that when old men want usually peaceful young men to harm and kill other young men like themselves in a war, it is easier to do so if they first change their appearance by putting on uniforms or masks or painting their faces. With that anonymity in place, out goes their usual internal focus of compassion and concern for others.

THE THEORETICAL MODEL OF DEINDIVIDUATION AND BANDURA'S MODEL OF MORAL DISENGAGEMENT

The psychological mechanisms involved in getting good people to do evil are embodied in two theoretical models, the first elaborated by me (Zimbardo, 1970) and modified by input from subsequent variants on my deindividuation conceptions, notably by Diener (1980). The second is Bandura's model of moral disengagement (1998, 2003), which specifies the conditions under which anyone can be led to act immorally, even those who usually ascribe to high levels of morality.

Bandura's model outlines how it is possible to morally disengage from destructive conduct by using a set of cognitive mechanisms that alter (1) one's perception of the reprehensible conduct (e.g., by engaging in moral justifications, making palliative comparisons, using euphemistic labeling for one's conduct); (2) one's sense of the detrimental effects of that conduct (e.g., by minimizing, ignoring, or misconstruing the consequences); (3) one's sense of responsibility for the link between reprehensible conduct and the detrimental effects (e.g., by displacing or diffusing responsibility); and (4) one's view of the victim (e.g., by dehumanizing him or her, attributing the blame for the outcome to the victim).

Dehumanization in Action: "Animals" by Any Other Name Are College Students

A remarkable experiment by Bandura, Underwood, and Fromson (1975) reveals how easy it is to induce intelligent college students to accept a dehumanizing label of other people and then to act aggressively based on that stereotyped term. Four participants were led to believe they were overhearing the research assistant tell the experimenter that the students from another college were present to start the study in which they were to deliver electric shocks of varying intensity to the participants (according to the dictates of a reasonable cover story). In one of the three randomly assigned conditions, the subjects overheard the assistant say to the experimenter that the other students seemed "nice"; in a second condition, they heard the other students described as "animals"; in the third group, the assistant did not label the students in the alleged other group.

The dependent variable of shock intensity clearly reflected this situational manipulation. The subjects gave the highest levels of shock to those labeled in the dehumanizing way as "animals," and their shock level increased linearly over the 10 trials. Those labeled "nice" were given the least shock, whereas the unlabelled group fell in the middle of these two extremes. Thus, a single word—*animals*—was sufficient to incite intelligent college students to treat those so labeled as if they deserved to be harmed. On the plus side, the labeling effect resulted in others being treated with greater respect if someone in authority labeled them positively. The graphed data is also of interest: On the first trial there is no difference across the three experimental treatments in the level of shock administered, but with each successive opportunity, the shock levels diverge. Those shocking the so-called "animals" shock them more and more over time, a result comparable to the escalating shock level of the deindividuated female students in my earlier study. That rise in aggressive responding over time, with practice, or with experience belies a self-reinforcing effect of aggressive or violent responding: It is experienced as increasingly pleasurable.

What my model adds to the mix of what is needed to get good people to engage in evil deeds is a focus on the role of cognitive controls that usually guide behavior in socially desirable and personally acceptable ways. The shift from good to evil behavior can be accomplished by knocking out these control processes, blocking them, minimizing them, or reorienting them. Doing so suspends conscience, self-awareness, sense of personal responsibility, obligation, commitment, liability, morality, and analyses in terms of costs–benefits of given actions. The two general strategies for accomplishing this objective are (1) reducing cues of social accountability of the actor (i.e., "No one knows who I am, nor cares to know"), and (2) reducing concerns for self-evaluation by the actor. The first eliminates concerns for social evaluation and social approval by conveying a sense of anonymity to the actor and diffusing personal responsibility across others in the situation. The second strategy stops self-monitoring and consistency monitoring by relying on tactics that alter states of consciousness (e.g., via drugs, arousing strong emotions or hyperintense actions, creating a highly focused present-time orientation wherein there is no concern for past or future), and by projecting responsibility outside the self and onto others.

My research and that of other social psychologists (see Prentice-Dunn & Rogers, 1983) on deindividuation differs from the paradigm in

Milgram's studies in that there is no authority figure present, urging the subject to obey. Rather, the situation is created in such a way that subjects act in accordance to paths made available to them, without thinking through the meaning or consequences of those actions. Their actions are not cognitively guided, as they are typically, but directed by the actions of others in proximity to them or by their strongly aroused emotional states and situationally available cues, such as the presence of weapons.

Environmental Anonymity Breeds Vandalism

It is possible for certain environments to convey a sense of anonymity on those who live in, or pass through, their midst. The people living in such environments do not have a sense of community. Vandalism and graffiti may be interpreted as an individual's attempt for public notoriety in a society that deindividuates him or her.

I conducted a simple field study to demonstrate the ecological differences between places ruled by anonymity versus those conveying a sense of community. I abandoned used but good-condition cars in the Bronx, New York City, and in Palo Alto, California, one block away from New York University and Stanford University, respectively. License plates were removed and hoods raised slightly to serve as ethological "releaser cues" for the potential vandals' attack behavior. It worked swiftly in the Bronx, as we watched and filmed from a vantage point across the street. Within 10 minutes of officially beginning this study, the first vandals surfaced. This parade of vandals continued for 2 days, by which time there was nothing of value left to strip; then they simply began destroying the remains. In 48 hours we recorded 23 separate destructive contacts by individual or groups, who either took something from the abandoned vehicle or did something to wreck it. Curiously, only one of these episodes involved adolescents; the rest of the vandals were adults, many well dressed and many driving cars, so that they might qualify as, at least, lower middle class. Anonymity can make brazen vandals of us all. But what about the fate of the abandoned car in Palo Alto? Our time-lapse film revealed that no one vandalized any part of the car over a 5-day period. When we removed the car, three local residents called the police to say that an abandoned car was being stolen (the local police had been notified of our field study). That is one definition of "community," where people care about what happens on their turf, even to the person or property of strangers, with the reciprocal assumption that they would also care about them.

I now feel that any environmental or societal conditions that contribute to making some members of society feel that they are anonymous—that no one knows or cares who they are, that no one recognizes their individuality and thus their humanity—makes them potential assassins and vandals, a danger to my person and my property—and yours (Zimbardo, 1976).

THE FACES OF THE "ENEMY": PROPAGANDA IMAGES
CONDITION US TO KILL ABSTRACTIONS

We need to add a few more operational principles to our arsenal of variables that trigger the commission of evil acts by men and women who are ordinarily good people. We can learn about some of these principles by considering how nations prepare their young men (admittedly, women are now members of the armed forces in many countries, but it is primarily the men who are sent into combat zones) to engage in deadly wars, and how they prepare citizens to support the risks of going to war, especially a war of aggression. This difficult transformation is accomplished by a special form of cognitive conditioning. Images of "The Enemy" are created by national propaganda to prepare the minds of soldiers and citizens alike to hate those who fit the new category of "your enemy." This mental conditioning is a soldier's most potent weapon, for without it, he could probably never fire his weapon to kill another young man in the cross-hairs of his gun sight. A fascinating account of how this "hostile imagination" is created in the minds of soldiers and their families is presented in *Faces of the Enemy* by Sam Keen (1986; see also his companion video). Archetypal images of the enemy are created by propaganda fashioned by the governments of most nations against those judged to be the dangerous "them"— the outsiders who are also "our" enemies. These visual images create a consensual societal paranoia that is focused on the enemy who would do harm to the women, children, homes, and god of the soldier's nation, way of life, and so forth. Keen's analysis of this propaganda on a worldwide scale reveals that there are a select number of attributes utilized by "homo hostilis" to invent an evil enemy in the minds of good members of righteous tribes. The enemy is aggressive, faceless, a rapist, godless, barbarian, greedy, criminal, a torturer, harbinger of death, a dehumanized animal, or just an abstraction. Finally, there is the enemy as worthy, heroic opponent to be crushed in mortal combat—as in the video game of the same name.

Ordinary Men Murder Ordinary Men, Women, and Children: Jewish Enemies

One of the clearest illustrations of my fundamental theme of how ordinary people can be transformed into engaging in evil deeds that are alien to their past history and to their moral development comes from the analysis of British historian Christopher Browning. In *Ordinary Men: Reserve Police Battalion 101 and the Final Solution in Poland* (1992) he recounts that in March 1942 about 80% of all victims of the Holocaust were still alive, but a mere 11 months later about 80% were dead. In this short period of time, the *Endlösung* (Hitler's "Final Solution") was galvanized by means of an intense wave of mass mobile murder squads in Poland. This genocide required mobilization of a large-scale killing machine at the same time as able-bodied soldiers were needed on the Russian front. Since most Polish Jews lived in small towns and not the large cities, the question that Browning raised about the German High Command was "where had they found the manpower during this pivotal year of the war for such an astounding logistical achievement in mass murder?" (p. xvi).

His answer came from archives of Nazi war crimes, in the form of the activities of Reserve Battalion 101, a unit of about 500 men from Hamburg, Germany. They were elderly family men, too old to be drafted into the army, from working-class and lower middle-class backgrounds, with no military or police experience, just raw recruits sent to Poland without warning of, or any training in, their secret mission: the total extermination of all Jews living in the remote villages of Poland. In just 4 months they had shot to death at point blank range at least 38,000 Jews and had deported another 45,000 to the concentration camp at Treblinka. Initially, their commander told them that this was a difficult mission which must be obeyed by the battalion, but any individual could refuse to execute these men, women, and children. Records indicate that at first about half the men refused, letting the others commit the mass murder. But over time, social modeling processes took their toll, as did any guilt-induced persuasion by buddies who did the killing, until by the end, up to 90% of the men in Battalion 101 had participated in the shootings, even proudly taking photographs of their up-close and personal slaughter of Jews.

Browning makes clear that there was no special selection of these men, only that they were as "ordinary" as could be imagined—until they were put into a situation in which they had "official" permission, even encouragement, to act sadistically and brutally against those arbitrarily labeled as "the enemy."

Let us go from the abstract to the personal for a moment: Imagine you witnessed your own father shooting to death a helpless mother and her infant child, and then imagine his answer to your question, "Why did you do it, Daddy?"

The War on Iraq: A Spurious Creation of Evil Terrorists and Infusion of National Fears

Fast forward to our time, our nation, our citizenry, and the fears of terrorism instilled by the destruction of the World Trade Center towers since that unforgettable day of September 11, 2001. The initial press and official reaction was to label the perpetrators of this horrific deed as "hijackers," "murderers," "criminals." Soon the label changed to "terrorists" and their deeds described as "evil." *Evil* became the coin of the realm, used repeatedly by the media as fed by the administration, and with an ever-widening net of inclusiveness. Osama bin Laden, the mastermind of 9/11, was the first culprit designated as evil. But when he proved elusive, escaping from the war zone in Afghanistan, it became necessary for the administration's war on terrorism campaign to put a new face and a new place on terrorism. Of course, terrorism works its generation of fear and anxiety by its very facelessness and nonlocal ubiquity. Several countries were labeled by our president as the "axis of evil," with the leader of one of those countries, Iraq, designated as so evil that he, Saddam Hussein, had to be removed from power by all means necessary.

A propaganda campaign was created to justify a preemptive war against Saddam Hussein's regime by identifying the clear and imminent threat to the national security of the United States posed by the alleged weapons of mass destruction (WMD) this evil leader had at his disposal. Then a link was erected between him and the terrorist networks to whom, allegedly, he would sell or gift these WMD. Over time, many Americans began to believe the falsehoods that Saddam Hussein was involved in the 9/11 terrorist attacks, was in complicity with Osama bin Laden, and had ready and operational an arsenal of deadly weapons that threatened U.S. security and well-being. Magazine images, newspaper accounts, and vivid TV stories contributed to the "evilization" of Saddam Hussein over the course of a year.

The vulnerability to terrorism that Americans continued to experience on deep, personal levels—in part, sustained and magnified by the administration's issuance of repeated (false) alarms of imminent terrorist attacks on the homeland—was relieved by the action of officially going to war. The public and Congress strongly supported a symmetrical war of "shock and awe"—to rid Iraq of the feared WMD and destroy Hussein's evil menace. Thus, for the first time in its history, the United States endorsed what the majority believed to be a justified aggressive war that has already cost billions of dollars, untold thousands of deaths (soldiers *and* civilians), totally destroyed a nation, weakened the United Nations, and will enmesh the United States in a prolonged, Vietnam-like, "no exit" scenario for years to come.

When no WMD were uncovered, despite the alleged best intelligence reports and aerial photos of them presented by the Secretary of State to the United Nations, collective cognitive dissonance reduction seeped in to maintain the belief that was still a "necessary" and "good" war against evil (Festinger, 1957). After many months of an all-out, desperately intense search of every part of Iraq, American troops and intelligence forces have not unearthed a single WMD! So the original reason for going to war is being played down and is being replaced by the mantra that Iraq is the new front in our worldwide fight against terrorism, thus it is good we are in control of the destiny of Iraq. But who cares what the truth really is regarding the deceptive reasons for going to war, if the United States is now safer and the president is a commander-in-chief of decisive action—as his image crafters have carefully depicted him in the media. This national mind control experiment deserves careful documenting by unbiased social historians for the current and future generations to appreciate the power of images, words, and framing that can lead a democratic nation to support *and even relish* the unthinkable evil of an aggressive war.

The Socialization of Evil: How the "Nazi Hate Primers" Prepared and Conditioned the Minds of German Youth to Hate Jews

The second broad class of operational principles by which otherwise good people can be recruited into evil is through education/socialization processes that are sanctioned by the government in power, enacted within school programs, and supported by parents and teachers. A prime example is the way in which German children in the 1930s and 1940s were systematically indoctrinated to hate Jews, to view them as the all-purpose enemy of the new (post–World War I) German nation. Space limitations do not allow full documentation of this process, but I touch on several examples of one way in which governments are responsible for sanctioning evil.

In Germany, as the Nazi party rose to power in 1933, no target of Nazification took higher priority than the reeducation of Germany's youth. Hitler wrote: "I will have no intellectual training. Knowledge is ruin to my young men. A violently active, dominating, brutal youth—that is what I am after" (*The New Order,* 1989, pp. 101–102). To teach the youth about geography and race, special primers were created and ordered to be read starting in the first grade of elementary school (see *The New Order,* 1989). These "hate primers" were brightly colored comic books that contrasted the beautiful blond Aryans with the despicably ugly caricatured Jew. They sold in the hundreds of thousands. One was titled *Trust No Fox in the Green Meadows and No Jew on His Oath.* What is most insidious about this kind of hate conditioning is that the misinformation was presented as facts to be learned and tested upon, or from which to practice penmanship. In the copy of the *Trust No Fox* text that I reviewed, a series of cartoons illustrates all the ways in which Jews supposedly deceive Aryans, get rich and fat from dominating them, and are lascivious, mean, and without compassion for the plight of the poor and the elderly Aryans.

The final scenarios depict the retribution of Aryan children when they expel Jewish teachers and children from their school, so that "proper discipline and order" could then be taught. Initially, Jews were prohibited from community areas, like public parks, then expelled altogether from Germany. The sign in the cartoon reads, ominously, "One-way street." Indeed, it was a unidirectional street that led eventually to the death camps and crematoria that were the centerpiece of Hitler's Final Solution: the genocide of the Jews. Thus, this institutionalized evil was spread pervasively and insidiously through a perverted educational system that turned away from the types of critical thinking exercises that open students' minds to new ideas and toward thinking uncritically and close-mindedly about those targeted as the enemy of the people. By controlling education and the propaganda media, any national leader could produce the fantastic scenarios depicted in George Orwell's (1981) frightening novel *1984.*

The institutionalized evil that Orwell vividly portrays in his fictional account of state dominance over individuals goes beyond the novelist's imagination when its prophetic vision is carried into operational validity by powerful cult leaders or by agencies and departments within the current national administration of the United States. Previously I have outlined the direct parallels between the mind control strategies and tactics Orwell attributes to "The Party" and those that Reverend Jim Jones used in dominating the members of his religious/political cult, Peoples Temple (Zimbardo, 2003a). Jones orchestrated the suicide/murders of more than 900 U.S. citizens in the jungles of Guyana 25 years ago, perhaps as the grand finale of his experiment in institutionalized mind control. I learned from former members of this group that not only did Jones read *1984,* he talked about it often and even had a song commissioned by the church's singer, entitled "1984 Is Coming," that everyone had to sing at some services. I will leave it to the reader to explore the similarities between the mind control practices in *1984* and those being practiced on U.S. citizens in the past few years (see Zimbardo, 2003b).

THE STANFORD PRISON EXPERIMENT: A CRUCIBLE OF HUMAN NATURE WHERE GOOD BOYS ENCOUNTERED AN EVIL PLACE

Framing the issues we have been considering as, in essence, who wins when good boys are put in an evil place casts it as a neo-Greek tragedy scenario, wherein "the situation" stands in for the externally imposed forces of "the gods and destiny." As such, we can anticipate an outcome unfavorable to humanity. In more mundane psychological terms, this research on the Stanford prison experiment synthesized many of the processes and variables outlined earlier: those of place and person anonymity that contribute to the deindividuation of the people involved, the dehumanization of victims, giving some actors (guards) permission to control others (prisoners), and placing it all within a unique setting (the prison) that most societies throughout the world acknowledge provides some form of institutionally approved sanctions for evil through the extreme differentials in control and power fostered in prison environments.

In 1971, I designed a dramatic experiment that would extend over a 2-week period to provide our research participants with sufficient time for them to become fully engaged in their experimentally assigned roles of either guards or prisoners. Having participants live in a simulated prison setting day and night, if prisoners, or work there for long 8-hour shifts, if guards, would also allow sufficient time for situational norms to develop and patterns of social interaction to emerge, change, and crystallize. The second feature of this study was to ensure that all research participants would be as normal as possible initially, healthy both physically and mentally, and without any history of involvement in drugs or crime or violence. This baseline was essential to establish if we were to untangle the situational versus dispositional knot: What the situation elicited from this collection of similar, interchangeable young men versus what was emitted by the research participants based on the unique dispositions they brought into the experiment. The third feature of the study was the novelty of the prisoner and guard roles: Participants had no prior training in how to play the randomly assigned roles. Each subject's prior societal learning of the meaning of prisons and the behavioral scripts associated with the oppositional roles of prisoner and guard was the sole source of guidance. The fourth feature was to create an experimental setting that came as close to a *functional simulation* of the psychology of imprisonment as possible. The details of how we went about creating a mindset comparable to that of real prisoners and guards are given in several of the articles I wrote about the study (see Zimbardo, 1975; Zimbardo, Haney, Banks, & Jaffe, 1973).

Central to this mind set were the oppositional issues of power and powerlessness, dominance and submission, freedom and servitude, control and rebellion, identity and anonymity, coercive rules and restrictive roles. In general, these social-psychological constructs were operationalized by putting all subjects in appropriate uniforms, using assorted props (e.g., handcuffs, police clubs, whistles, signs on doors and halls), replacing corridor hall doors with prison bars to create prison cells, using windowless and clock-less cells that afforded no clues as to time of day, applying institutional rules that removed/substituted individual names with numbers (prisoners) or titles for staff (Mr. Correctional Officer, Warden, Superintendent), and that gave guards control power over prisoners.

Subjects were recruited from among nearly 100 men between the ages of 18 and 30 who answered our advertisements in the local city newspaper. They were given a background evaluation that consisted of a battery of five psychological tests, personal history, and in-depth interviews. The 24 who were evaluated as most normal and healthiest in every respect were randomly assigned, half to the role of prisoner and half to that of guard. The student-prisoners underwent a realistic surprise arrest by officers from the Palo Alto Police Department, who cooperated with our plan. The arresting officer proceeded with a formal arrest, taking the "felons" to the police station for booking, after which each prisoner was brought to our prison in the reconstructed basement of our psychology department.

The prisoner's uniform was a smock/dress with a prison ID number.

The guards wore military-style uniforms and silver-reflecting sunglasses to enhance anonymity. At any one time there were nine prisoners on "the yard," three to a cell, and three guards working 8-hour shifts. Data were collected via systematic video recordings, secret audio recordings of conversations of prisoners in their cells, interviews and tests at various times during the study, postexperiment reports, and direct, concealed observations.

For a detailed chronology and fuller account of the behavioral reactions that followed, readers are referred to the above references, to Zimbardo, Maslach, and Haney (1999), and to our new website: *www.prisonexp.org*. For current purposes, let me simply summarize that the negative situational forces overwhelmed the positive dispositional tendencies. The Evil Situation triumphed over the Good People. Our projected 2-week experiment had to be terminated after only 6 days because of the pathology we were witnessing. Pacifistic young men were behaving sadistically in their role as guards, inflicting humiliation and pain and suffering on other young men who had the inferior status of prisoner. Some "guards" even reported enjoying doing so. Many of the intelligent, healthy college students who were occupying the role of prisoner showed signs of "emotional breakdown" (i.e., stress disorders) so extreme that five of them had to be removed from the experiment within that first week. The prisoners who adapted better to the situation were those who mindlessly followed orders and who allowed the guards to dehumanize and degrade them ever more with each passing day and night. The only personality variable that had any significant predictive value was that of F-scale authoritarianism: The higher the score, the more days the prisoner survived in this totally authoritarian environment.

I terminated the experiment not only because of the escalating level of violence and degradation by the guards against the prisoners that was apparent when viewing the videotapes of their interactions, but also because I was made aware of the transformation that I was undergoing personally (see the analysis by Christina Maslach of how she intervened to help bring light to that dark place and end the study; in Zimbardo et al., 1999). I had become a Prison Superintendent in addition to my role as Principal Investigator. I began to talk, walk, and act like a rigid institutional authority figure more concerned about the security of "my prison" than the needs of the young men entrusted to my care as a psychological researcher. In a sense, I consider the extent to which I was transformed to be the most profound measure of the power of this situation. We held extended debriefing sessions of guards and prisoners at the end of the study and conducted periodic checkups over many years. Fortunately, there were no lasting negative consequences of this powerful experience.

Before moving on, I would like to share parts of a letter sent to me recently (e-mail communication, October 18, 2002) by a young psychology student, recently discharged from military service. It outlines some of the direct parallels between the aversive aspects of our simulated prison many years ago and current despicable practices still taking place in some military boot-camp training. It also points up the positive effects that research and education can have:

> I am a 19-year-old student of psychology [who watched] the slide show of your prison experiment. Not too far into it, I was almost in tears. . . . I joined the United States Marine Corps, pursuing a childhood dream. To make a long story short, I had become the victim of repeated illegal physical and mental abuse. An investigation showed I suffered more than 40 unprovoked beatings. Eventually, as much as I fought it, I became suicidal, thus received a discharge from boot camp. . . .
>
> The point I am trying to make is that the manner in which your guards carried about their duties and the way that military drill instructors do is unbelievable. I was amazed at all the parallels of your guards and one particular D. I. who comes to mind. I was treated much the same way, and even worse, in some cases.
>
> One incident that stands out was the time, in an effort to break platoon solidarity, I was forced to sit in the middle of my squad bay (living quarters) and shout to the other recruits "If you guys would have moved faster, we wouldn't be doing this for hours," referencing every single recruit who was holding over his head a very heavy foot locker. The event was very similar to the prisoners saying #819 was a bad prisoner. After my incident, and after I was home safe some months later, all I could think about was how much I wanted to go back to show the other recruits that as much as the D. I.s told the platoon that I was a bad recruit, I wasn't.
>
> Other behaviors come to mind, like the push-ups we did for punishment, the shaved heads, not having any identity other than being addressed as, and referring to other people as, "Recruit So-and-So"—which replicates your study. The point of it all is that even though your experiment was conducted 31 years ago, my reading the study has helped me gain an understanding I was previously unable to gain before, even after therapy and counseling. What you have demonstrated really gave me insight into something I've been dealing with for almost a year now. Although, it is certainly not an excuse for their behavior, I now can understand the rationale behind the D. I.'s actions as far as being sadistic and power hungry.

THE FAILURE OF THE SOCIAL EXPERIMENT
OF THE U.S. CORRECTIONAL SYSTEM

As much joy that such personal reactions bring to someone whose vision has always been for psychological research to make a difference in people's lives, I have been saddened by the lack of impact the Stanford prison experiment has had on the correctional system in the United States. When

Craig Haney and I recently did a retrospective analysis of our study, with contrasting views of U.S. and California correctional policies over the past 30 years, our conclusions were disheartening (Haney & Zimbardo, 1998). Prisons continue to be failed social experiments that rely on a dispositional model of punishment and isolation of offenders. Gone is any sense of the modifiable situational determinants of crime or of basic rehabilitation practices that might reduce persistently high rates of recidivism. The United States is now the prison center of the universe, with more than 2 million citizens incarcerated, *greater than any other nation,* and growing. Our analysis revealed that prison conditions had significantly worsened in the decades since our study, as a consequence of the politicization of prisons, with politicians, prosecutors, DAs, and other officials taking a hard line on crime as a means of currying favor of an electorate made fearful of crime by media exaggerations. Misguided policies about sentencing for crack cocaine use and sale and the "Three Strikes" rulings have put a disproportionately large number of African American and Hispanic men behind bars for long sentences. There are now more African American men wasting away in the nation's prison system than fulfilling their potentials in our higher educational system.

THE EVIL OF INACTION

Our usual take on evil focuses on violent, destructive actions, but *nonac*tion can also become a form of evil, when assistance, dissent, and disobedience are needed. Social psychologists heeded the alarm when the infamous Kitty Genovese case made national headlines. As she was being stalked, stabbed, and eventually murdered, 39 people in a housing complex heard her screams and did nothing to help. It seemed obvious that this was a prime example of the callousness of New Yorkers, as many media accounts reported. A counter to this dispositional analysis came in the form of a series of classic studies by Latané and Darley (1970) on bystander intervention. One key finding was that people are less likely to help when they are in a group, when they perceive that others are available who could help, than when those people are alone. The presence of others diffuses the sense of personal responsibility of any individual.

A powerful demonstration of the failure to help strangers in distress was staged by Darley and Batson (1973). Imagine you are a theology student on your way to deliver the sermon of the Good Samaritan in order to have it videotaped for a psychology study on effective communication. Further imagine that as you are heading from the psychology department to the video taping center, you pass a stranger huddled up in an alley in dire distress. Are there any conditions that you could conceive that would *not* make you stop to be that Good Samaritan? What about "time press"?

Would it make a difference to you if you were late for your date to give that sermon? I bet you would like to believe it would not make a difference, that you would stop and help no matter what the circumstances. Right? Remember, you are a theology student, thinking about helping a stranger in distress, which is amply rewarded in the Biblical tale.

The researchers randomly assigned students of the Princeton Theological Seminary to three conditions that varied in how much time they thought they had between receiving their assignment from the researchers and getting to the communication department to tape their Good Samaritan speeches. The conclusion: Do not be a victim in distress when people are late and in a hurry, because 90% of them are likely to pass you by, giving you no help at all! The more time the seminarians believed they had, the more likely they were to stop and help. So the situational variable of *time press* accounted for the major variance in extending or withholding help, without any need to resort to dispositional explanations about theology students being callous or cynical or indifferent, as Kitty Genovese's nonhelpers were assumed to be—another instance of the FAE, one that needs to be reversed.

THE WORST OF THE APPLES IN THE EVIL BARREL: TORTURERS AND EXECUTIONERS?

There is little debate but that the systematic torture by men and women of their fellow men and women represents one of the darkest sides of human nature. Surely, my colleagues and I reasoned, here was a place where dispositional evil would be manifest: among torturers who did their dirty deeds daily, for years, in Brazil as policemen sanctioned by the government to extract confessions through torturing so-called enemies of the state. We began by focusing solely on the torturers, trying to understand both their psyches and the ways they were shaped by their circumstances, but we had to expand our analytical net to capture their comrades-in-arms who chose, or were assigned to, another branch of violence work—death-squad executioners. They shared a "common enemy": men, women, and children who, though citizens of their state, even neighbors, were declared by "the authorities" to be threats to the country's national security. Some had to be eliminated efficiently, wheras those who might hold secret information had to be made to yield it up and confess to their treason.

In carrying out this mission, these torturers could rely, in part, on the "creative evil" embodied in the torture devices and techniques that had been refined over centuries since the Inquisition by officials of The Church and, later, of the National State. But our current-day torturers added a measure of improvisation to accommodate the particular resistances and resiliencies of the enemy standing before them, claiming innocence, refusing to acknowledge their culpability, or not succumbing to intimidation. It took time and emerging insights into exploitable human weaknesses for these torturers to become adept at their craft, in contrast to the task of the death-squad executioners, who, wearing hoods for anonymity and sporting good guns and group support, could dispatch their duty to country swiftly and impersonally. For the torturer, it could never be "just business." Torture always involves a personal relationship, essential for understanding what kind of torture to employ, what intensity of torture to use on this person at this time: wrong kind or too little; no confession, too much, and the victim dies before confessing. In either case, the torturer fails to deliver the goods. Learning to select the right kind and degree of torture that yields up the desired information makes rewards abound and praise flow from the superiors.

What kind of men could do such deeds? Did they need to rely on sadistic impulses and a history of sociopathic life experiences to rip and tear flesh of fellow beings day in and day out for years on end? Were these violence workers a breed apart from the rest of humanity—bad seeds, bad tree trunks, bad flowers? Or, is it conceivable that they were programmed to carry out their deplorable deeds by means of some identifiable and replicable training processes? Could a set of external conditions—that is, situational variables—that contributed to the making of these torturers and killers be identified? If their evil deeds were not traceable to inner defects but attributable to outer forces acting upon them—the political, economic, social, historical, and experiential components of their police training—then we might be able to generalize, across cultures and settings, those principles responsible for this remarkable transformation. Martha Huggins, Mika Haritos-Fatouros, and I interviewed several dozen of these violence workers in depth and recently published a summary of our methods and findings (Huggins, Haritos-Fatouros, & Zimbardo, 2002). Mika had done a similar, earlier study of torturers trained by the Greek military junta, and our results were largely congruent with hers (Haritos-Fatouros, 2003).

We learned that sadists are *selected out* of the training process by trainers because they are not controllable, get off on the pleasure of inflicting pain, and thus do not sustain the focus on the goal of confession extraction. From all the evidence we could muster, these violence workers were not unusual or deviant in any way prior to practicing this new role, nor were there any persisting deviant tendencies or pathologies among any of them in the years following their work as torturers and executioners. Their transformation was entirely understandable as a consequence of (1) the training they were given to play this new role, (2) group camaraderie, (3) acceptance of the national security ideology, and (4) the belief in socialist-communists as enemies of their state. They were also influenced by being made to feel special—above and better than peers in public service—by the secrecy of their duties and by the constant pressure to produce desired results regardless of fatigue or personal problems. We report many detailed case studies that document the ordinariness of these men engaged in the most heinous of deeds, sanctioned by their government at that time in history, but reproducible at this time in any nation whose obsession with national security and fears of terrorism permit suspension of basic individual freedoms.

SUICIDE BOMBERS:
SENSELESS FANATICS OR MARTYRS FOR A CAUSE?

Not surprisingly, what holds true for the Brazilian violence workers is comparable to the nature of the transformation of young Palestinians from students to suicide bombers killing Israelis. Recent media accounts converge on the findings from more systematic analyses of the process of becoming a suicidal killer (see Atran, 2003; Bennet, 2003; Hoffman, 2003; Merari, 1990, 2002; Myer, 2003). There have been more than 95 suicide bombings by Palestinians against Israelis since September, 2000. Originally, and most frequently, the bombers were young men, but recently a half dozen women have joined the ranks of suicidal bombers. What has been declared as senseless, mindless murder by those attacked and by outside observers is anything but to those intimately involved. It was mistakenly believed that it was poor, desperate, socially isolated, illiterate young people with no career and no future who adopted this fatalistic role. That stereotype has been shattered by the actual portraits of these young men and women, many of whom were students with hopes for a better future, intelligent and attractive youth, connected with their family and community.

Ariel Merari, an Israeli psychologist who has studied this phenomenon for many years, outlines the common steps on the path to these explosive deaths. Senior members of an extremist group first identify particular young people who appear to have an intense patriotic fervor, based on their declarations at public rallies against Israel or their support of some Islamic cause or Palestinian action. These individuals are invited to discuss how serious they are in their love of their country and their hatred of Israel. They are then asked to commit to being trained in how to put their hatred into action. Those who make the commitment are put into a small group of three to five similar youth who are at varying stages of "progress" toward becoming agents of death. They learn the tricks of the trade from elders: bomb making, disguise, selecting and timing targets. Then they publicize their private commitment by making a videotape on which they declare themselves to be "living martyrs" for Islam and for the love of Allah. In one hand they hold the Koran, a rifle in the other, their headband declaring their new status. This video binds them to the final deed, since it is sent home to the family of the recruit before they execute the final plan. The recruits also realize that not only will they earn a place beside Allah, but their relatives will also be entitled to a high place in heaven because of their martyrdom. A sizable financial incentive is bestowed on their family as a gift for their sacrifice.

Their photo is emblazoned on posters that will be put on walls everywhere in the community the moment they succeed in their mission. They will be immortalized as inspirational models. To stifle concerns about the pain from wounds inflicted by exploding nails and other bomb parts, they are told that before the first drop of their blood touches the ground, they will already be seated at the side of Allah, feeling no pain, only pleasure. An ultimate incentive for the young males is the promise of heavenly bliss with scores of virgins in the next life. They become heroes and heroines, modeling self-sacrifice to the next cadre of young suicide bombers.

We can see that this program utilizes a variety of social-psychological and motivational principles in turning collective hatred and general frenzy into a dedicated, seriously calculated program of indoctrination and training for individuals to become youthful "living martyrs." It is neither mindless nor senseless, only a very different mind set and with different sensibilities than we have been used to witnessing among young adults in our country. A recent television program on female suicide bombers went so far as to describe them in terms more akin to the girl next door then to alien fanatics. Indeed, that very normalcy is what is so frightening about the emergence of this new social phenomena—that so many intelligent young people could be persuaded to envision and welcome their lives ending in a suicidal explosive blast.

To counteract the powerful tactics of these recruiting agents requires the provision of meaningful, life-affirming alternatives to this next generation. It requires new national leadership that is willing and able to explore every negotiating strategy that could lead to peace instead of death. It requires these young people across national boundaries to openly share their values, their education, and their resources and to explore their commonalities, not highlight their differences. The suicide, the murder, of any young person is a gash in the fabric of the human connection that we elders from every nation must unite to prevent. To encourage the sacrifice of youth for the sake of advancing ideologies of the old might be considered a form of evil from a more cosmic perspective that transcends local politics and expedient strategies.

CONCLUSIONS

It is a truism in psychology that personality and situations interact to generate behavior, as do cultural and societal influences. However, I have tried to show in my research over the past 30 years that situations exert more power over human actions than has been generally acknowledged by most psychologists or recognized by the general public. Along with a hardy band of experimental social psychologists, I have conducted research demonstrations designed, in part, to provide a corrective balance to the pervasive fundamental attribution error. Nevertheless, the traditional dispositional perspective continues to dominate Anglo-American psychology fueled by reliance on the individualist orientation central in our institutions of medicine, education, psychiatry, law, and religion. Acknowledging the power of situational forces does not excuse the behaviors evoked in response to their operation. Rather, it provides a knowledge base that shifts attention away from simplistic "blaming the victim" mentality and ineffective individualistic treatments designed to change the evil doer, toward more profound attempts to discover causal networks that should be modified. Sensitivity to situational determinants of behavior also affords "risk alerts" that allow us to avoid or modify prospective situations of vulnerability.

Please consider this Zimbardo homily that captures the essence of the difference between dispositional and situational orientations: "While a few bad apples might spoil the barrel (filled with good fruit/people), a barrel filled with vinegar will *always* transform sweet cucumbers into sour pickles—regardless of the best intentions, resilience, and genetic nature of those cucumbers." So, does it make more sense to spend our resources on attempts to identify, isolate, and destroy the few bad apples or to learn how vinegar works so that we can teach cucumbers how to avoid undesirable vinegar barrels?

My situational sermon has several related dimensions. First, we should be aware that a range of apparently simple situational factors can impact our behavior more compellingly than we would expect or predict. The research outlined here, along with that of my colleagues presented in this volume, points to the influential force of numerous variables: role playing, rules, presence of others, emergent group norms, group identity, uniforms, anonymity, social modeling, authority presence, symbols of power, time pressures, semantic framing, stereotypical images and labels, among others.

Second, the situationist approach redefines heroism. When the majority of ordinary people can be overcome by such pressures toward compliance and conformity, the minority who resist should be considered *heroic*. Acknowledging the special nature of this resistance means that we should learn from their example by studying *how* they have been able to rise above such compelling pressures. That suggestion is coupled with another that encourages the development of an essential but ignored domain of psychology—heroes and heroism.

Third, the situationist approach should, in my view, encourage us all to share a profound sense of personal humility when trying to understand those "unthinkable," "unimaginable," "senseless" acts of evil. Instead of immediately embracing the high moral ground that distances us good folks from those bad ones and gives short shrift to analyses of causal factors in the situations that form the context of the evil acts, the situational approach gives all others the benefit of "attributional charity." This means that any deed, for good or evil, that any human being has ever performed or committed, you and I could also perform or commit—given the same situational forces. If so, it becomes imperative to constrain our immediate moral outrage that seeks vengeance against wrongdoers and turn our efforts toward uncovering the causal factors that could have led them in that aberrant direction.

The obvious current instantiation of these principles is the rush to characterize terrorists and suicide bombers as "evil" people, instead of working to understand the nature of the psychological, social, economic, and political conditions that have fostered such generalized hatred of an enemy nation, including our own, that young people are willing to sacrifice their lives and murder other human beings. The "war on terrorism" can never be won solely by the current administration's plans to find and destroy terrorists—since any individual, anywhere, at any time, can become an active terrorist. It is only by understanding the *situational determinants of terrorism* that programs can be developed to win the hearts and minds of potential terrorists away from destruction and toward creation— not a simple task, but an essential one that requires implementation of social-psychological perspectives and methods in a comprehensive, long-term plan of attitude, value, and behavior change.

REFERENCES

Adorno, T. W., Frenkel-Brunswick, E., Levenson, D. J., & Sanford, R. N. (1950). *The authoritarian personality.* New York: Harper & Row.

Atran, S. (2003, May 5). Who wants to be a martyr? *The New York Times,* p. A23.

Bandura, A. (1998). Mechanisms of moral disengagement. In W. Reich (Ed.), *Origins of terrorism: Psychologies, ideologies, theologies, states of mind* (pp. 161–191). New York: Cambridge University Press.

Bandura, A. (2003). The role of selective moral disengagement in terrorism and counterterrorism. In F. M. Mogahaddam & A. J. Marsella (Eds.), *Understanding terrorism* (pp. 121–150). Washington, DC: American Psychological Association.

Bandura, A., Underwood, B., & Fromson, M. E. (1975). Disinhibition of aggression through diffusion of responsibility and dehumanization of victims. *Journal of Personality and Social Psychology, 9,* 253–269.

Barstow, A. L. (1994). *Witchcraze: A new history of the European witch hunts.* New York: HarperCollins.

Baumeister, R. F. (1997). *Evil: Inside human cruelty and violence.* New York: Freeman.

Bennett, J. (2003, May 30). A scholar of English who clung to the veil. *The New York Times,* pp. A1, A14.

Browning, C. R. (1992). *Ordinary men: Reserve police battalion 101 and the final solution in Poland.* New York: HarperPerennial.

Chang, I. (1997). *The rape of Nanking: The forgotten holocaust of World War II.* New York: Basic Books.

Cialdini, R. B. (2001). *Influence: Science and practice* (4th ed.). Boston: Allyn & Bacon.

Darley, J. M. (1992). Social organization for the production of evil. *Psychological Inquiry 3,* 199–218.

Darley, J. M., & Batson, D. (1973). From Jerusalem to Jericho: A study of situational and dispositional variables in helping behavior. *Journal of Personality and Social Psychology, 27,* 100–108.

Diener, E. (1980). Deindividuation: The absence of self-awareness and self-regulation in group members. In P. B. Paulus (Ed.), *The psychology of group influence* (pp. 209–243). Hillsdale, NJ: Erlbaum.

Festinger, L. (1957). *A theory of cognitive dissonance.* Palo Alto, CA: Stanford University Press.

Fraser, S. C. (1974). *Deindividuation: Effects of anonymity on aggression in children.* Unpublished manuscript, University of Southern California, Los Angeles.

Golding, W. (1954). *Lord of the flies.* New York: Capricorn Books.

Haney, C., & Zimbardo, P. G. (1998). The past and future of U.S. prison policy: Twenty-five years after the Stanford Prison Experiment. *American Psychologist, 53,* 709–727.

Haritos-Fatouros, M. (2002). *The psychological origins of institutionalized torture.* London: Routledge.

Hoffman, B. (2003, June). The logic of suicide terrorism. *The Atlantic Monthly,* 40–47.

Huggins, M., Haritos-Fatouros, M., & Zimbardo, P. G. (2002). *Violence workers: Police torturers and murderers reconstruct Brazilian atrocities.* Berkeley: University of California Press.

Keen, S. (1986). *Faces of the enemy: Reflections of the hostile imagination.* New York: HarperCollins.

Kramer, H., & Sprenger, J. (1971). *The malleus maleficarum.* New York: Dover. (Original work published 1486)

Latané, B., & Darley, J. M. (1970). *The unresponsive bystander: Why doesn't he help?* New York: Appleton-Century-Crofts.

Lee, M., Zimbardo, P. G., & Berthof, M. (1977). Shy murderers. *Psychology Today, 11,* 69–70, 76, 148.

Merari, A. (1990). The readiness to kill and die: Suicidal terrorism in the Middle East. In W. Reich (Ed.), *Origins of terrorism: Psychologies, theologies, states of mind* (pp. 192–200). New York: Cambridge University Press.

Merari, A. (2002, October). *Suicide terrorism.* Paper presented at the First Conference of the National Center for Disaster Psychology and Terrorism, Palo Alto, CA.

Milgram, S. (1974). *Obedience to authority.* New York: Harper & Row.

Myer, G. (2003, May 30). A young man radicalized by his months in jail. *The York Times,* pp. A1, A14.

The new order (The Third Reich). (1989). Alexandria, VA: Time Life Books.

Orwell, G. (1981). *1984.* New York: Signet.

Prentice-Dunn, S., & Rogers, R. W. (1983). Deindividuation and aggression. In R. G. Geen & E. I. Donnerstein (Eds.), *Aggression: Theoretical and empirical reviews—issues in research* (Vol. 2, pp. 155–171). New York: Academic Press.

Ross, L. (1977). The intuitive psychologist and his shortcomings. In L. Berkowitz (Ed.), *Advances in experimental social psychology* (Vol. 10, pp. 173–220). New York: Academic Press.

Staub, E. (1989). *The roots of evil: The origins of genocide and other group violence.* New York: Cambridge University Press.

Waller, J. (2002). *Becoming evil: How ordinary people commit genocide and mass killing.* New York: Oxford University Press.

Watson, R. I., Jr. (1973). Investigation into deindividuation using a cross-cultural survey technique. *Journal of Personality and Social Psychology, 25,* 342–345.

Zimbardo, P. G. (1970). The human choice: Individuation, reason, and order versus deindividuation, impulse, and chaos. In W. J. Arnold & D. Levine (Eds.), *1969 Nebraska Symposium on Motivation* (pp. 237–307). Lincoln: University of Nebraska Press.

Zimbardo, P. G. (1975). On transforming experimental research into advocacy for social change. In M. Deutsch & H. Hornstein (Eds.), *Applying social psychology: Implications for research, practice, and training* (pp. 33–66). Hillsdale, NJ: Erlbaum.

Zimbardo, P. G. (1976). Making sense of senseless vandalism. In E. P. Hollander & R. G. Hunt (Eds.), *Current perspectives in social psychology* (4th ed., pp. 129–134). Oxford, UK: Oxford University Press.

Zimbardo, P. G. (2003a). Mind control in Orwell's *1984*: Fictional concepts become operational realities in Jim Jones' jungle experiment. In M. Nussbaum, J. Goldsmith, & A. Gleason (Eds.), *1984: Orwell and our future.* Princeton: Princeton University Press.

Zimbardo, P. G. (2003b). Phantom menace: Is Washington terrorizing us more than Al Qaeda? *Psychology Today, 36,* pp.34–36.

Zimbardo, P. G., Haney, C., Banks, C., & Jaffe, D. (1973, April 8). The mind is a formidable jailer: A Pirandellian prison. *The New York Times Magazine,* pp. 38 ff.

Zimbardo, P. G., Maslach, C., & Haney, C. (1999). Reflections on the Stanford Prison Experiment: Genesis, transformation, consequences. In T. Blass (Ed.), *Obedience to authority: Current perspectives on the Milgram Paradigm* (pp. 193–237). Mahwah, NJ: Erlbaum.

CHAPTER 3

BASIC HUMAN NEEDS, ALTRUISM, AND AGGRESSION

ERVIN STAUB

In this chapter I describe a conception of universal psychological needs—needs shared by all human beings—and how the fulfillment of these needs creates a strong potential for people to become caring and helpful, whereas their frustration creates a strong potential for hostility and aggression. This view is different from the belief or assumption that human beings are either helpful or aggressive, kind or cruel, good or evil *by nature*. Although I make the assumption that basic human needs are part of our nature, I also contend that it is through experiences that either fulfill or frustrate these needs that inclinations and motives to help or harm others develop. Still, in a sense, it could be said that the fulfillment or frustration of basic psychological needs provide "natural" bases (bases rooted in our nature and common human experiences) for goodness and evil.

This chapter explores the origins of helping and harming others. *Evil* is an extreme and sometimes repeated form of people harming others. Evil might be defined as "intensely harmful actions, which are not commensurate with instigating conditions, and the persistence or repetition of such acts. A series of actions also can be evil when any one act causes limited harm, but with repetition, these cause great harm" (Staub, 1999b, p. 180). A parent persistently diminishing and derogating a child might be an example of the latter form of evil. Evil actions can be conscious and intended—as in the case of plans formulated to destroy a group—or performed without the conscious intention to destroy. Although from a social-psychological perspective, it is best to consider *actions* as evil, a "group's or person's habitual, spontaneous reactions to certain kinds of events can [also] become highly destructive" (Staub, 1999b, p. 179), so that, in a sense, the person or group has become evil.

Goodness refers to actions that benefit others; it is an extreme form of helping others.

> The greater the benefit and the more effort and/or sacrifice it requires, the greater the goodness. Goodness, like evil, can come in an obvious form, like a single heroic act that saves someone's life. Or it can take the form of persistent efforts to save people, as in the case of people in the U.S. who through the underground railroad helped slaves escape, or Hutus in Rwanda who endangered themselves to save Tutsis. Heroic acts and such persistent acts of goodness require great effort, courage, and at times even the willingness to endanger one's life. But goodness can also take the form of persistent engagement in helping people or creating positive social change which does not involve great danger. It can consist of small, repeated acts that bring benefit to others, like kindness by a neighbor or relative toward a child who is neglected or badly treated at home, kindness that can help the child develop normally. . . . (Staub, 2003, p. 6)

Individuals and groups helping and harming others, including their extreme forms, goodness and evil, are the outcomes of normal psychological processes and the development or psychological and social evolution of individuals and groups, under the influence of these processes.

BASIC HUMAN NEEDS: AN INTRODUCTION

In a number of publications I have proposed that there are universal, or basic, human needs, and that their degree and, to some extent, mode of fulfillment or frustration develop the potentials that exist in every person for kindness or cruelty (Staub, 1989, 1996b, 1999b, 2003, in preparation-a, in preparation-b). Their fulfillment or frustration can lead to psychological and social processes that develop inclinations in individuals and groups to turn toward people in positive ways, or to turn away from or against people in avoidant, defensive, or hostile ways. Other experiences, added to histories of need fulfillment or frustration, can lead individuals and groups to develop persistent motives for helping or aggression. The fulfilment of basic needs also fosters effective functioning, well-being, and continued growth or optimal human functioning.

A number of psychological theorists have proposed the existence of central needs, motives, and beliefs ranging from Freud (sex and aggression, pleasure) and Adler (overcoming inferiority, maintaining self-esteem, etc.) to Rogers (1961), Epstein (1993), Janoff-Bulman (1992), and many more.

A few psychologists and other social and behavioral scientists have proposed what are usually referred to as human needs theories (Christie, 1997; Deci & Ryan, 1985; Maslow, 1968, 1987; McCann & Pearlman, 1990; Murray, 1938; Pearlman & Saakvitne, 1995). They describe somewhat varied but overlapping needs as central to human functioning, and their fulfillment as central to well-being. The best known among these theorists is Abraham Maslow (1968), who proposed a hierarchy of needs ranging from physiological needs, to safety needs, belongingness and love needs, esteem needs, and growth or being needs, with "self-actualization" the most advanced need.

Maslow believed that lower needs must be fulfilled before the next higher need in the hierarchy could be fulfilled. To some degree guided by his theory, Maslow (1987) tried to understand what a self-actualized person is like. In an informal research project, he studied a small group of people whom he had identified as self-actualized, either through interviews or by using their own and others' writings about them. He found, among other things, that these individuals tended to be less focused on themselves than other people. I use the term *transcendence* to describe both the motive and the ways of behaving that characterize people who go beyond a focus on the self.

Kelman (1990) and Burton (1990) have used needs theory as a way of understanding why intractable conflict—persistent, seemingly unresolvable, violent conflict (Staub & Bar-Tal, 2003)—develops and why the groups involved in such conflict cannot resolve it. In Kelman's view, a threat or failure to fulfill needs for identity, security, dignity, and justice causes and/or maintains intractable conflict.

Empirical and/or theoretical considerations that support the claim that the needs discussed below are present in human beings have been described elsewhere (Staub, 2003, in preparation-b). Here I give a small sample of theorizing that supports the notion of basic needs. Baumeister and Leary (1995) have gathered extensive empirical support for the existence of a need to belong, "to form and maintain strong, stable, interpersonal relationships" (p. 497). Buss (2000) has drawn on evolutionary psychology to describe some roots of unhappiness in contemporary life. He suggests that human beings have evolved in small, close-knit communities—conditions absent in many modern settings, especially in big cities where people often do not even know their neighbors and there is no deep connection to others. Buss clearly suggests that a need for connection is frustrated in today's world (although he does not use the term *frustrated*), and further suggests that people can increase their happiness by creating deep connections to friends, family, and community.

Stevens and Fiske (1995) have noted that many theories suggest the existence of one or more basic motives—to belong, to understand, to be effective, to find the world benevolent, and to maintain self-esteem—and proposed evolutionary roots and reasons for the existence of these motives. Erikson's (1959) theory of developmental stages identifies a variety of needs, which in the terminology I use may be described as needs for security (trust), positive identity, positive connection to others, and autonomy. Terror management theory focuses on a particular form of insecurity and its consequences: the insecurity arising from an awareness of our mortality (McGregor et al., 1998; Pyszcznski, Greenberg, & Solomon, 1997).

Needs are theoretical constructs. One kind of support for a theory of needs is to identify relationships between antecedent conditions and consequences that seemingly result from them (see also Lederer, 1980), with the connection best explained by the presence, activation, and either satisfaction or frustration of basic needs. This is the strategy I use in demonstrating the role of basic needs in the helping versus harming of others, particularly in accounting for genocide and mass killing, and for the development of helpful versus aggressive behavior in children (and adults). Another strategy for future research is to identify individual differences in the early experience of need fulfillment and frustration and ascertain its relationship to the intensity and current form or construction of basic needs. To what extent are both of these related to habitual constructive or destructive modes of need fulfillment (see below) and to behavior under specific conditions of need arousal?

A CONCEPTION OF BASIC NEEDS: DEFINITIONS AND ASSUMPTIONS

Although the theory presented here assumes that basic needs are universal, it also assumes that the properties of needs and their modes of fulfillment are shaped by culture and personal experience. I consider the needs for (1) security, (2) effectiveness and control, (3) a positive identity, (4) connection, and (5) comprehension of reality to be basic, and the needs for long-term satisfaction and transcendence to be advanced basic needs. First I define these needs and discuss some assumptions about their properties and functioning (see also Staub, 2003, in preparation-b).

Security

The need for security encompasses the need to know or believe that we (as well as people who are important to us—family, group) are, and will continue to be, free of physical and psychological harm (i.e., of attack, injury, threat to our body or self-concept and dignity) and that we are, and will be, able to satisfy our essential biological needs (for food, water, etc.) and our need for shelter. That security is a basic need seems evident simply from observation; and also has a great deal of empirical support (Staub, 2003, in preparation-b).

That a particular need is basic does not mean that people cannot act contrary to it. In part, because we have varied needs, they may be in conflict under particular circumstances or, at times, expressed in ways that they may seem to be in conflict to outside observers. Suicide bombers certainly act contrary to a need for physical security. The may act, instead, to fulfill other needs. Palestinian suicide bombers, for example, may act to fulfill a need for effectiveness and control in the midst of the helplessness experienced under Israeli occupation. A need for connection also seems involved. Among Palestinians in 2003, much of the community, and especially the groups to which potential suicide bombers are reported to develop a connection, strongly support suicide bombing. Perhaps, paradoxically, a need for psychological security may also be involved, since distancing oneself from the fight against Israel could lead to a feeling of aloneness or ostracism in difficult times. Another need involved in this phenomena is a comprehension of reality. Those who become suicide bombers may develop a world view or understanding of reality in which their actions make sense, bring meaning, fulfill a cause, glorify their names, benefit their families, and even promise special fulfillment in an afterlife (Post, 2001). Given their worldview, connection to community, and the presumed glory that will surround their names, a need for positive identity may also be fulfilled in planning the suicide mission.

The example of suicide bombers points to something highly important about human beings, especially when we are attempting to understand great goodness involving extreme sacrifice and great evil involving extreme destruction: that we are capable of constructing ways of looking at events in which extraordinary and normally inconceivable acts become possible, even ideal. This kind of construction manifested in the shocking acts of killing, in which some Hutus killed their own children in the course of the genocide in Rwanda, because their father or mother was Tutsi, the group that was to be eliminated in the genocide (des Forges, 1999).

Basic needs are present in an undifferentiated form for very young children; over time, these undifferentiated needs develop into cognitive–emotional constructions that can be activated under particular circumstances. Being Hutu can become paramount in maintaining a positive identity, the other as Tutsi can be seen as a profound threat to identity and existence. This threat may combine with the very real danger of harboring a Tutsi, even one's own child, in the face of killers. These were the circumstances in Rwanda under which some parents killed their own children (Mamdani, 2001).

People also act contrary to the need for security to save lives. Rescuers of Jews in Nazi Europe and of Tutsis in Rwanda (as well as of designated victims in other genocides) endangered not only themselves in saving lives but often also their families (Oliner & Oliner, 1988). Later I address the important question of how such extreme commitment to others' welfare evolves, and how can we understand the role of basic needs in it.

Effectiveness and Control

The need for effectiveness and control is the need to know or believe that we have the capacity to (1) protect ourselves (as well as people important to us) from harm (danger, attack, etc.), (2) accomplish the things we set out to do (such as fulfilling important goals), and (3) lead purposeful lives that have the potential to impact our society or the world. Although most elements of this need (and of other needs) come into play very early in life, some become relevant later in life.

The need for security and that of effectiveness and control are inherently linked. By effective action we can protect ourselves from harm and bring about outcomes that enhance our security. For example, actually having control or believing that one has control over noise or electric shocks received in an experiment can have profound impact on physiological, cognitive, and psychological functioning (Glass & Singer, 1972; Lefcourt, 1973; Seligman, 1975; Staub et al., 1971). People attempt to exercise control even under extremely malevolent conditions when they attempt to save themselves in a genocide. Successful control in the face of such extreme danger results not only in survival but in significant psychological benefits.

Positive Identity

The need for a positive identity is the need to have a well-developed self and a positive conception of who we are and who we want to be (self-esteem)—which requires self-awareness and self-acceptance, including acceptance of our limitations. With increasing age, higher-level fulfillment of this need requires integration of different parts of ourselves. Coherence and inner harmony enable us, in turn, to lead increasingly purposeful lives.[1] Receiving esteem from others has been regarded by Maslow and other theorists as a basic need. Here it is seen as essential to fulfill certain basic needs, especially positive identity and positive connection.

Positive Connection

The need for positive connection is the need to have relationships in which we feel positively connected to other individuals or groups, such as close family ties, intimate friendships, love relationships, and relationships to

---

[1]This description points to a family of needs, where "members" of the "family" may, at times, conflict. For example, who we are and who we want to be can conflict with each other. A positive view is not the same as an integrated view. However, as a mature positive identity evolves, integration may enhance a positive view of the self, and who we want to be may become a part of who we are. The definition of positive identity also includes processes required for continued growth, such as self-awareness.

communities. The need for connection in the development of attachment in infants and for continued positive development in children is very well established. It is also clear that this is a lifelong need (Baumeister & Leary, 1995).

Comprehension of Reality

The need to comprehend reality is the need to have an understanding of people and the world (what they are like, how they operate) and of our own place in the world; to have views or conceptions that make sense of the world. This is a basic need, so any degree of comprehension is better than none. However, certain kinds of comprehension of reality—for example, seeing the world and people as hostile and dangerous due to an earlier history of need frustration—make the fulfillment of other basic needs more difficult.

Independence or Autonomy

The need for independence or autonomy is the need to make choices and decisions, to be one's own person, to be able to function as a spearate individual. As noted, some needs may stand in opposition to each other, especially under particular conditions. This is evidently the case with the need for autonomy, which can conflict with the need for connection. Cultures can intensify or lessen this inherent conflict. In well-functioning cultures all basic needs can be fulfilled to a reasonable extent; nevertheless, different cultures emphasize different needs. Western cultures emphasize individualism and autonomy, Eastern cultures connection and community (Triandis, 1994).

Culture is likely to affect the ease or difficulty with which needs are fulfilled; autonomy is a more difficult need to fulfill in collectivist cultures, connection in individualist cultures. Cultures also shape the manner in which needs are fulfilled. In collectivist cultures the need for effectiveness and control may be fulfilled more by "secondary control": Individuals align themselves with the group and important people in it, or exercise cognitive control by reorganizing their understanding of events. In individualist societies, members tend to take action to influence events—what has been referred to as primary control (Weiss, Rothbaum, & Blackburn, 1984). Affolter (2002), applying the basic needs conception described here, specifies different socialization practices related to particular needs in Western and Japanese cultures. With regard to the need for effectiveness and control, he suggests that in the West, "caretakers encourage exploration, autonomy, efficacy and individual initiative," whereas in Japan "caretakers encourage adaptation and integration into the group, capacity to contribute to preservation of harmony, emotional constraint and indi-

rect expression of feelings." The differences in socialization and in the use
of forms of control are likely to be a matter of degree, variations on
a continuum. However, with experience, individuals develop different
cognitive–emotional constructions of needs and pursue different modes of
gratification.

I view basic needs as equally basic, all needing to be fulfilled, with security possibly an exception; it may need to be fulfilled before other needs
can be addressed. The early fulfillment of these basic needs makes them
more resistant to frustration and easier to fulfill later in life. Early experiences, even in infancy, have relevance to the fulfillment of all needs, including positive identity. However, certain needs are especially important
during particular developmental phases or life periods. Likewise, important agents of need fulfillment can change, with parents especially important early in life and peers becoming more important in preadolescence in
relation to the needs for connection, identity, and perhaps comprehension
of reality.

I note two other needs here, which I consider advanced basic needs,
because both are significantly related to the prior fulfillment of the other
needs.

Long-Term Satisfaction

The need for long-term satisfaction is the need to feel and believe that
things are good in one's life and that life is progressing in a desirable way
(not necessarily in the moment, but overall) in the long run. I use the term
long-term satisfaction rather than *happiness* to convey stability even in the
midst of temporary distress, sorrow, or pain, which are inevitable in human life. The fulfillment of this need is primarily a byproduct of the fulfillment of other needs. A sense of goodness about one's life is already evident
in well-cared-for infants' increasing capacity to soothe themselves when
hungry or distressed (Shaffer, 1995). Mood, particularly a sense of well-
being, affects the frequency and extent of helping (and probably harming)
behaviors (for a review, see Staub, 1978). The fulfillment of this need for
long-term satisfaction has direct relevance to the emergence of helping and
probably harm-doing.

Transcendence of the Self

The need to experience a transcendence of the self is the need to go beyond
a focus on, and concern with, the self. Forms of transcendence include experiencing connection to nature, the universe, or spiritual entities, devot-
ing oneself to the welfare of others, or working for significant social
change.

This need increasingly emerges, in its positive, genuine form, as people fulfill the other basic needs. It may also be that, given the nature of their life experiences, people develop different capacities for transcendence. Certain socializing experiences, in addition to fulfilling basic needs, may promote connections to a greater extent to what is beyond oneself—nature, the spiritual realm, other people and their well-being, and so on. When basic needs are not fulfilled, those needs continue to press for satisfaction, so the need for transcendence does not emerge. When it is strongly present, but people do not act to fulfill it, some form of malaise or dissatisfaction with life develops (Coan, 1977).

Transcendence may be constituted by or expressed in psychological states, acts, and a whole way of being. A young child's complete engagement with an activity, a state of flow (Csikszentmihaly, 1990), is a transcendent state. A genuinely altruistic act, directed purely by the motivation to help, is transcendent, in that it goes beyond a focus on the self. Similarly to need fulfillment, such states and acts have shaping/socializing effects. Rescuers and heroic helpers are usually (although not always) experiencing a transcendence of the self. Maslow's (1987) description of self-actualized people in his pilot study may point to a group of people who experience transcendence as a way of being.

In addition to genuine transcendence, there is also "pseudo-transcendence," wherein the frustration of basic needs leads people to give themselves over to causes, extreme beliefs, and destructive movements. The underlying motivations is to relinquish a burdensome self, gain a new comprehension of reality, and experience connection. Depending on the nature of the movement a person joins and subsequent experiences in it, basic needs may get fulfilled and pseudo-transcendence may grow into genuine transcendence. This may happen in some religious movements. Even in some gangs, giving oneself over to the group—not necessarily a full pseudo-transcendence—can help fulfill basic needs. This may be the reason that, in earlier decades, before gangs turned violent and criminal, young people often moved on from youth gangs to live normal lives (Staub, 1996b). In contrast, in a destructive and violent ideological movement, the participants' basic needs may be fulfilled in the short run, but their engagement in destructive actions creates psychological wounds, often brings later dishonor and shame, and ultimately frustrates the basic needs they sought to fulfill.

Other Basic Needs

This list of needs is not meant to be exhaustive. For example, the need for bodily satisfaction or pleasure may be basic. It is also possible that having or creating justice is a basic need. People may live under unjust conditions for a long period of time without protest, but once they perceive their conditions as unjust, they tend to go to great length to correct them. However, rather than functioning as an independent need, justice and its flip side of injustice may play significant roles in fulfilling or frustrating other needs. The need for a positive identity, for one, is frustrated by the perception that one is not as well treated as others.

Other Central Assumptions

In other publications I have described a number of central assumptions (see Staub, 2003, in preparation-b), such as the essentially nonhierarchical nature of basic needs, the possibility of conflict between them, and that conditions and experiences that satisfy or frustrate one basic need often satisfy or frustrate others as well. For example, experiences of deep connection also tend to fulfill the need for a positive identity and shape comprehension of reality. Under conditions of security, in a benevolent environment, people are more likely to seek novelty (e.g., infants and toddlers use a good attachment figure as a secure base), which in turn helps fulfill the need for effectiveness, develops the self, and shapes comprehension of reality. The infant's need for security is satisfied by caretakers who respond to the infant's signals by providing food or relief from pain and discomfort. In addition, the caretaker's responsiveness satisfies the infant's need for effectiveness and control. The total experience—the valuing of the child inherent in good caregiving—helps develop positive attachment (Bretherton, 1992), contributes to a positive identity, and builds positive connection.

Constructive satisfaction of needs leads to continued growth. *Constructive* satisfaction means, first, that a need is satisfied in a way that does not frustrate (and might even satisfy) other needs. The environment and actions taken are both involved. For example, in a family that encourages both autonomy and connection in the children, reasonable autonomous behavior does not disrupt relationships, and connection does not close off or inhibit independence and autonomy. A person who satisfies the need for effectiveness and positive identity by aggressive means is likely to have difficulty satisfying either the need for connection or the need for security (since people tend to retaliate). Second, the constructive satisfaction of one person's needs does not frustrate others' basic needs or inhibit their ability to satisfy needs.

Destructive satisfaction refers to modes of satisfying a basic need that frustrate the fulfillment of another need or the needs of another person. Typically, the element of destructiveness emerges when attempts to satisfy needs occur under conditions that frustrate them or when a person attempting to satisfy a need has a past history of need frustration. An important assumption is that needs are powerful motives that press for satisfaction. When they cannot be constructively fulfilled, people learn to fulfill them in destructive ways—which, however, interferes with long-term need satisfaction and personal growth. For example, being overprotective might temporarily fulfill a parent's basic needs for connection, control, security (by making the child secure; Pearlman & Saakvitne, 1995), and even the child's need for connection. However, such parental protectiveness frustrates the child's need for autonomy, effectiveness and control, and the development of identity. In the long run, the relationship that develops between parent and child is likely to frustrate the fulfillment of the parent's needs as well. Another common cause of destructive attempts to satisfy needs is the occurrence of traumatic, overwhelming, or life-threatening events over which a person has no control; such events frustrate all basic needs, especially when the events involve victimization by other people. In response, a person may develop an intense need to exercise control over situations and people—a behavior that, in turn, interferes with the ability to develop positive relationships.

Internal psychological processes may also provide destructive means of need fulfillment. For example, blaming the self for bad treatment by others may lead a child or adult to believe that he or she can effectively protect him- or herself in the future by behaving in ways expected to bring good treatment (Janoff-Bulman, 1992), thereby gaining some sense of security and effectiveness. However, such behavior frustrates the need for a positive identity and is likely to inhibit people from initiating and developing relationships. It may also give a person a false sense of security. As I note in the discussion of genocide, below, a number of psychological processes that serve psychological needs, such as scapegoating others for life problems, contribute to the adoption of violent "solutions."

THE ROLE OF BASIC NEEDS IN THE ORIGINS OF GENOCIDE AND MASS KILLING

I apply this conception of basic needs first to an analysis of the origins of extreme violence by one group against another (Staub, 1989, 1996a, 2003). A frequent starting point for intense group violence is "difficult life conditions." These include intense economic problems, intense political disorganization, rapid social change, or some combination of these factors, together with the social chaos and disorganization that ensues from them. Conceptualizing these conditions as agents of basic need frustration makes the initial responses they almost always generate understandable as attempts at need satisfaction. These are psychological—emotional and cognitive—reactions that are generated in a whole group and expressed in observable, social ways that include (1) a shift from individual identities to greater identification with some group (e.g., an ethnic, ideological, or national entity); (2) elevating the group's status, which is often accomplished by diminishing other groups; (3) scapegoating (i.e., blaming) some group for the elevated group's life problems; and (4) adopting or creating destructive ideologies, which are visions of desirable social arrangements that are destructive because they include the identification of some group as an enemy that stands in the way of the ideology's fulfillment. Although these reactions partially satisfy some basic needs, they do not solve life problems. At the same time, they are the starting points for the discrimination, persecution, and violence that may end in attempted or actual genocide.

Increased identification with a particular group is evident in many ethnic conflicts and genocides. Focusing on one's membership in a group lessens insecurity, strengthens identity, and creates connection. Scapegoating is nearly universal when life problems are intense and persistent. Diminishing personal and group responsibility for life problems, including the inability to care for oneself and one's family, strengthens identity. By offering an understanding of the reasons for life problems, the scapegoating serves the need for comprehension of reality. It also serves the need for effectiveness and control, by suggesting that the problems can be solved by taking action against those who have caused them. Scapegoating also creates connection, as members of the group gain a sense of community through the shared belief—and later, through the action taken against the designated scapegoat.

Ideologies are related but perhaps even more universal elements than scapegoating on the road to genocide and mass killing. Adopting ideologies involving visions of a better society (such as nationalism) or a better world (such as communism and aspects of Nazism) offers a new comprehension of the world and provides connection to like-minded others, a positive identity (since one envisions and strives to create a "better world"), and effectiveness in place of helplessness (since one is part of a movement that engages in action to change the world).

Groups can perpetrate genocide even when there is no conflict of vital interests, which is the case when difficult life conditions are the central instigating factors. The psychological and social roots of genocide are always crucial, but in those instances, even more dominant. However, another important starting point for genocide and mass killing is intense, intractable conflict—long-lasting conflict that has been resistant to resolution and led to mutual violence (Staub & Bar-Tal, 2003). Whereas the conflict of real, concrete interests has important effects, the reasons for the difficulty in resolving the conflict are often psychological. Consistent with the theorizing of Kelman (1990) and Burton (1990), the conditions of life, the existing circumstances, as well as the actions of the other party and interactions between the parties all combine to frustrate the basic needs of each. Furthermore, in intractable conflicts, the group psychological and social processes I describe above that help fulfill basic needs also arise (Staub & Bar-Tal, 2003). Often difficult life conditions and group conflict combine to give rise to the preconditions for genocide. A prime example of this dynamic is the genocide that occurred in Rwanda (des Forges, 1999; Staub, 1999a).

Although these group psychological and social processes may satisfy basic psychological needs, at least temporarily, they also lead the groups to turn against one another. When certain societal/cultural characteristics are also present, and when "bystanders" are passive, an "evolution" is likely to follow. The scapegoat, or ideological enemy, becomes the object of discrimination and then of progressively increasing violence.

Individuals and groups change as a result of their actions. Discrimination and limited violence are justified by increased devaluation of the victim group as well as by the ideals of the ideology. Violence progressively increases, supported by changes in norms and standards of conduct in relation to the victim group, at times by changes in laws, and by the creation of paramilitary groups and other institutions that serve violence. Without countervailing forces, such as opposition within the society (i.e., active internal bystanders) or by outside groups and nations (i.e., active external bystanders), the progression of increasingly violent actions is likely to end in mass killing or genocide (Staub, 1989, 2003).

In the case of intractable conflict, the increasing violence tends to be mutual, although it may be especially escalated by one party or the other. Here also, people identify more with their group over time, thereby fulfilling their needs for identity, connection, and security. They strengthen their individual and group identity by blaming the other for the conflict and by developing group beliefs that make their own cause just (Bar-Tal, 1998, 2000; Staub & Bar-Tal, 2003). Mutual retaliation contributes to the escalation of violence.

Certain cultural characteristics make these processes more probable (Staub, 1989, 1999a). A central one is a history of "cultural devaluation"—a well-established devaluation of one or more subgroups of society—which "preselects" the devalued group as a potential scapegoat or ideological enemy (Staub, 1989). Another is very strong respect for authority. This leads people to rely more on guidance by and support from leaders than on their own perceptions and values. As a result, severe life problems and social chaos give rise to especially strong feelings of insecurity, threat to identity, and loss of comprehension of reality—whereupon people look for new leaders.

Past victimization of a group is another predisposing characteristic. Persecution and intense violence against one's group frustrates all basic needs and creates a feeling of vulnerability (i.e., a weakened identity) and a perception of the world as dangerous (i.e., a comprehension of reality that creates persistent insecurity). When there is new threat, the group may strike out to defend itself, even when defense is not necessary, thereby becoming perpetrators (Staub, 1998; Staub & Pearlman, 2001; Staub, Pearlman, & Miller, 2003). The likelihood of this response is enhanced when the group's collective memory emphasizes past victimization (Volkan, 1997).

The Serb violence during the 1990s may have been partly due to past Serb victimization as well as its centrality in collective memory. The persistence of conflict and violence between Palestinians and Israelis may also be partly due to past victimization. The Jews were victimized for many centuries before the Holocaust and to a horrific extent in the Holocaust, as well as by attacks on them early during the Israeli–Arab conflict, and by terrorist attacks and suicide bombers in subsequent years. The Palestinians have been victimized in the past 50-plus years, since the establishment of Israel, both by Israel—as many of them fled and became refugees, and for those who remained, through the occupation of territories in which they lived and the repressive practices used against them—and by Arab states, which (by failing to accept them) maintain their refugee status.

A culture and social arrangement that frustrates rather than fulfills the basic needs of members, or of a substantial subgroup, so that they become highly sensitive to new frustration, may be another predisposing cultural characteristic. A subordinate group in society may respond especially strongly to difficult life conditions; these difficult conditions further intensify the differences between the groups and enhance the experience of injustice in the subordinate group (Leatherman, DeMars, Gaffney, & Vayrynen, 1999). Strong legitimizing ideologies (Sidanius & Pratto, 1999) that justify the privilege of a dominant group may also contribute. When this privilege is challenged, the group's identity and comprehension of reality are also challenged. Given the ideology, and depending on members' image of the less privileged group as dangerous, so is their security. A cycle of escalation may ensue, leading to mass killing or genocide by one party or the other.

This conception of the influences leading to mass violence and of the role of basic needs in it seems applicable to many instances: the Holocaust, the genocide against the Armenians, the "autogenocide" in Cambodia, the disappearances (mass killing) in Argentina (Staub, 1989), the mass killing in Bosnia (Staub, 1996a), and the genocide in Rwanda (Staub, 1999a; see also Staub, 2003).

BASIC NEEDS AND THE PREVENTION OF VIOLENCE

A basic needs perspective can contribute to the development of strategies aimed at preventing intense group violence. For example, in place of a destructive ideology that focuses on enemies, an inclusive, connecting vision can fulfill needs while enabling members of all groups to join together in responding to life problems. The policies of the Roosevelt administration during the Depression seem to be an example of this inclusive worldview. Healing from past wounds can strengthen identity, increase the possibility of feeling a sense of control over events, and provide a more benevolent comprehension of reality. In general, in difficult times or at times of conflict, the more basic needs can be fulfilled by constructive means, without creating or intensifying enmity, the less likely that violence will develop.

Basic needs exert their influence in an automatic fashion. Individuals are usually not aware that they are shifting from seeing themselves as individuals to seeing themselves as group members, or that they are scapegoating, rather than correctly identifying, groups that have caused the often very complex life problems. They are also not aware that the psychological/social processes described here have the function of fulfilling basic needs. However, that does not mean that they cannot make choices and are not responsible. The actions groups take against other groups, and even the processes that precede them, can all be contemplated and examined for their meaning and consequences. The justification of violent actions by increased devaluation/blaming of the victim or the opponent can also be the object of self-reflection, and reflection about one's group. The resulting awareness can reveal (1) the problematic nature of the group's beliefs and actions, (2) their incorrectness (the scapegoated group is usually not responsible for life problems; the cause touted by one's group is not clearly just while that of the other unjust), and (3) their immorality (the discrimination and violence against the other are contrary to essential human values, often even the values of one's own group, at least when the process starts and before those values change).

In preventing violence between groups, especially renewed violence, education about the origins of violence may be of great value. In our work in Rwanda, my associates and I have used an exploration of the origins of genocide and group violence as part of an intervention with varied groups, serving varied purposes. This exploration consists of brief lectures in which we presented the origins of group violence (along the lines briefly described above), with many examples of specific cases (see Staub, 1989, 1996b, 1999a). This is usually followed by extensive discussion, in the course of which participants themselves apply the conception to Rwanda (Staub & Pearlman, 2003; Staub, Pearlman, & Miller, 2003).

The intervention included similar explorations of the impact of trauma, avenues to healing, as well as engagement by participants, in small groups, with their own painful experiences during the genocide. The participants worked with local nongovernmental organizations (NGOs) that worked with groups of people in the community on issues of healing, reconciliation, and community building. We evaluated the effects of the intervention not on the participants, but on the members of the community groups with whom our participants later worked. Both over time and in comparison to control groups, the intervention reduced trauma symptoms. It also led to a mutually more positive orientation between Tutsis and Hutus, as expressed in a greater awareness of the complex sources of genocide, seeing the other group in a more differentiated way (e.g., not all Hutus are bad; some tried to help during the genocide), and seeing the possibility of a better joint future. The intervention also led to "conditional forgiveness"—conditional on the other group's acknowledgment of its harmful actions and expressions of regret (Staub & Pearlman, 2001, 2003; Staub, Pearlman, Hagengimana, & Gubin, 2003).

The effects of exploring the origins of genocide were not separately evaluated for the groups but seemed powerful. In the course of the discussions, participants made comments that suggested that they felt humanized by understanding the actions taken against them as not simply pure evil, but as the horrible outcome of understandable human processes. They also felt more hopeful, saying, "If we understand how violence happens, we can take action to prevent it." The intervention we used is likely to have affected participants' comprehension of reality (how the incomprehensible—genocide—could happen), their identity ("We were not uniquely selected by God for such bad treatment"), and the potential to influence the future effectively (Staub & Pearlman, 2003; Staub et al., 2003).

The origins of group violence are rooted in situations, structures, and individuals. Difficult life conditions and group conflict can arise in any society, but their likelihood—and to a much greater extent, how they are dealt with—are affected by the societal characteristics I describe here. Culture and social institutions shape individual personality, rendering more or less likely the psychological and social processes in individuals that contribute to violence. Certain cultures and social and political institutions can develop in ways that make it likely that the group will easily engage in violence—in a sense, that it becomes evil. In contrast, cultures that help members develop constructive ways to fulfill basic needs, do not devalue others, and foster reasonable (rather than excessive) respect for authority render genocide and mass killing far less likely (Staub, 1989, 2003). Providing education about the origins of violence, including the role of basic needs and important psychological and social processes, and experiential education that develops constructive modes of need fulfillment may enhance individual self-awareness and reduce violence-generating processes. The inclusion of such education in schools and in other settings seems of great importance (Staub, 2002a).

SOCIALIZATION OF ALTRUISM AND AGGRESSION AND THE FULFILLMENT OR FRUSTRATION OF BASIC NEEDS

Here I briefly review socialization practices and experiences that promote altruism and aggression and show how these frustrate or fulfill basic needs.

Motivations for Helping and Harming People

If socializing processes that promote altruism fulfill basic needs, it is not surprising that those that promote aggression frustrate needs, since in terms of both outcomes—enhancing or diminishing people's well-being—

and mediating processes, altruism and aggression are opposites (Staub, 2003, in preparation-b). However, even children who develop caring or altruistic orientations may be taught to devalue certain groups and feel hostile and aggressive toward their members. In fact, socialization practices that fulfill basic needs and thereby provide a strong basis for caring about other people also enhance the power of the socializers to teach hostility toward outgroups. Thus, to render violence by groups against other groups less likely, it is important to develop in children the orientation of *inclusive caring* (Staub, 2002b) that extends to people beyond the group—ideally, to all human beings.

Researchers and theorists have differentiated several motivational sources of helping:

- *Selfish,* motivated by real or hoped for rewards, including the reciprocation of benefits, and the desire to avoid discomfort due to punishment or withdrawal of reinforcement.
- *Moral,* guided by adherence to internalized rules or principles such as justice, the sanctity of human life, or a norm of social responsibility.
- *Altruistic,* motivated by the desire to benefit others, to reduce their distress or enhance their well-being.

Similarly, motivations for harming others can be differentiated. The most prominent distinction has been between *hostile* aggression, motivated by the desire to harm, and *instrumental* aggression, which uses aggression as a tool by which to gain benefits for oneself (Berkowitz, 1993). *Defensive aggression,* which aims to protect the self (from real or imagined harm), is a common form of aggression (Toch, 1969) and can be differentiated from other forms of instrumental aggression. In this as well as in other kinds of aggression, hostile and instrumental motives frequently combine (Staub, 1996b).

Personal characteristics and circumstances join together to make it more or less likely that the motives that lead to helping versus aggressing arise and are expressed in action. People inclined to respond with altruistic motivation to others' needs are likely to be helpful under the widest range of conditions.

Altruistic motivation is likely to have at least two related roots. One is *empathy,* specifically the kind of empathy that generates *sympathy,* which includes both *feeling with* and *concern about* persons in distress or needing help (Batson, 1990; Eisenberg, 2002; Eisenberg & Fabes, 1998; Hoffman, 1975a, 1975b), in contrast to feeling "personal distress" in response to others' distress (Batson, 1990; Eisenberg, 2002; Eisenberg et. al, 1989). I call another root *prosocial value orientation;* the positive evaluation of human beings, together with a concern for, and a feeling of personal responsibility for, others' welfare. This orientation was found to be related to helping people in either physical or psychological distress (Feinberg, 1978; Grodman, 1979; Staub, 1978), to self-reports of varied forms of helping (Staub, 1995), and to constructive patriotism (Schatz & Staub, 1997), which combines love of country with the willingness to oppose policies that are contrary to humane values (see Staub, 2003). Beyond the motivation to help others, a feeling of efficacy is also required for, and contributes to (Midlarsky, 1971; Staub, 1995), people helping each other.

Affection and Nurturance versus Neglect and Harsh Treatment

Temperamental characteristics of children enter into the development of altruism and aggression (Coie & Dodge, 1998; Eisenberg & Fabes, 1998). For example, impulsiveness and related early temperamental characteristics have been linked to boys' aggression (Staub, in preparation-b). However, these characteristics are most likely to exert their influence in interaction with social experience. The expression of these characteristics is shaped by harsh treatment or lack of support and appropriate guidance by parents and other people. Similarly, temperamental dispositions appear to play a role in the emergence of empathy, but so do early socializing experiences (Zahn-Waxler & Radke-Yarrow, 1990). Social conditions such as poverty also play an important role, but they appear to exert influence primarily by affecting how parents relate to and guide their children (McLoyd, 1990).

Here, I focus on child-rearing practices. Becoming a caring, helpful, altruistic person or a hostile and aggressive one is the result of combinations or patterns of child-rearing practices (Staub, 1979, 1996a, 2003, in preparation-b). Early responsiveness by parents to their infants' needs and the provision of continuing nurturance, warmth, and affection are the core socializing practices and experiences for the development of helpful tendencies in children (Eisenberg, 1992; Eisenberg & Fabes, 1998; Hoffman, 1970a, 1970b, 1975a; Shaffer, 1995; Staub, 1971, 1979, 1996a, 1996b, 2003, in preparation-b; Yarrow & Scott, 1972). Neglect and harsh treatment—that is, rejection, hostility, the extensive use of physical punishment, and physical or verbal abuse—are the core socializing practices and experiences that contribute to the development of aggression (Coie & Dodge, 1998; Eron, Gentry, & Schlegel, 1994; Eron, Walder, Lefkowitz, 1971; Heussman, Eron, Lefkowitz, & Walder, 1984; Huesman, Lagerspetz, & Eron, 1984; Lykken, 2001; Staub, 1979, 1996a, 1996b, 2003, in preparation-b; Weiss et al., 1992; Widom, 1989a, 1989b).

Providing warmth, affection, and nurturance indicates that caretakers are responsive to the needs of the young child. Responsiveness to the infant's physical and social needs provides (fulfills the basic needs for) security and connection. Sensitive responding to the infant's signals also satisfies the need for efficacy and control. Responding to signals and satisfying needs also affirms the child and begins to develop the rudiments of a positive identity. Such sensitive parental responding is associated with the development of secure attachment (Ainsworth, Bell, & Stayton, 1974; Bretherton, 1992; Shaffer, 1995; Waters, Wippman, & Sroufe, 1979). In turn, secure attachment is associated with the development of sympathy (i.e., the feeling of sorrow or concern for the distressed or needy other; Eisenberg, 2002, p. 135), with helping peers by the time children are 3½ years old (Waters et al., 1979), and with the emergence of prosocial behavior in preschool (Kestenbaum, Farber, & Sroufe, 1989).

As children get older, love, affection, and caring about a child's welfare can take varied forms. For example, an in-depth, important study found that an essential characteristic of the parents of boys who have high self-esteem was caring about the child's welfare, expressed in many ways, and not necessarily by physical affection (Coopersmith, 1967). Sensitivity in caring about and responding to the child's feelings and needs—to who the child is—fulfills all basic needs. The child in such care develops connection to important adults and forms a positive orientation toward people in general. That this is the case is suggested by research findings that show that securely attached children are also capable of *creating* positive connections. Such children have positive relationships with peers in the early school years (Waters et al., 1979). Further in the developmental continuum, college students who rate their parents as affectionate and caring also have a positive view of their fellow humans and express concern about, and feelings of responsibility for, others' welfare (Staub & Operario, unpublished data). As noted earlier, such a prosocial value orientation is related to varied forms of helping.

In contrast, experiencing neglect and the ineffectiveness of one's signals, such as crying, to bring about the satisfaction of essential biological (and social) needs has severe negative effects. Research on institutionalized infants has shown that in institutions with poor caretaking, infants become depressed and die in significant numbers. Children who had lived in such institutions later show deficiencies in their capacity for human connection and in other domains (Shaffer, 1995; Thompson & Grusec, 1970). The conditions in such institutions frustrate infants' basic needs for security, connection, and effectiveness/control. Given inadequate staffing, infants are fed and cared for on schedule, and in sequence, when it is their turn, not when they are hungry or distressed. Their crying brings no response. They have no significant connection to anyone. Neglect beyond infancy also has extreme negative consequences. Emotional neglect—that is, inattention to the child as a person and to his or her efforts to feel connection and affirmation—has even more severe consequences than harsh treatment (Erikson & Egeland, 1996).

Harsh treatment also frustrates basic needs, increasingly so as it become more severe and abusive. Especially when it is unpredictable, it creates insecurity. When it is unavoidable, in that the child cannot prevent it, it creates a feeling of ineffectiveness. The child feels diminished; his or her connection with the caretaker is broken, and the child forms a view of people and the world as hostile and dangerous. This view, formed so early in life, interferes with the child's ability to develop connections to people in general.

Aggressive boys, as well as adults, may come to use aggression as a destructive mode of fulfilling needs for security, efficacy, positive identity, and even connection. They learn to interpret others' behavior toward themselves as hostile (Dodge, 1980, 1993) and consider aggression to be normal, appropriate, and even inevitable (Huesmann & Eron, 1984). When children are victimized by caretakers and also have models who coach them in aggressive responses (referred to as "violentization"), they may become intensely aggressive (Rhodes, 1999).

Guidance and Discipline

The experience of warmth and affection fulfills basic needs and provides the basis for caring about others' welfare. However, *guidance* is necessary. Parental permissiveness, which is the absence of guidance, has been associated with aggression in adolescents, independent of the warmth–hostility continuum (DiLalla, Mitchell, Arthur, & Pagliococca, 1988). In short, warmth and affection are not associated with prosocial behavior, especially generosity, when parents are overly permissive (Eisenberg, 1992; Eisenberg & Fabes, 1998; Staub, 1979).

Positive guidance itself fulfills basic needs. Structure and order that guidance provides in children's lives makes it easier for them to gain understanding of the world and develop self-guidance. By teaching children how to act in order to be successful in their efforts, guidance contributes to the development of a sense of efficacy and positive identity. Parents of high self-esteem children set high but achievable standards for them (Coopersmith, 1967). Guidance can help children set standards for themselves that make self-reinforcement possible. In addition, positive guidance uses the potentials/inclinations developed by the fulfillment of basic needs constructively. In contrast, inherent in harsh treatment is negative guidance—that is, the tendency to use force rather than verbal communication, and the modeling of aggression. In such parenting, guidance and a harsh, rather than moderate, form of discipline are one and the same. Parents' frequent use of their power via the denial or withdrawal of privileges makes the development of caring and helping less likely and the emergence of aggression more likely (Eisenberg & Fabes, 1998; Hoffman, 1970b; Staub, 1996a).

Positive guidance consists of rules set in a democratic manner for children. While parents or teachers exercise firm control, so that children will act in accordance with important rules, they also are responsive to children's explanations of or reasons for what they think and want (Baumrind, 1971, 1975). Adults also explain reasons for rules. Induction—that is, pointing out to children the consequences of their behavior for others—has been advocated and found useful in some research for promoting empathy and prosocial behavior (Eisenberg & Fabes, 1998; Hoffman, 2000). Such explanations use the positive orientation to other people provided by the fulfillment of basic needs to help children understand others' internal worlds, to develop empathy, and to cultivate feelings of responsibility to help, not harm, others (Staub, 1979). Providing examples of positive behavior toward other people is another important form of guidance, accomplishing similar goals. Through such guidance children learn *values* of caring, empathy, and sympathy as well as *actions* that benefit others.

When explicit guidance is limited—when rules and explanations that structure and help children understand reality are lacking—personal interactive experiences with people that both fulfill or frustrate basic needs and serve as models become even more powerful. However, explanations that are contrary to powerful personal experiences such as abuse will have little influence. Children who are not cared about cannot be instructed effectively to care about others. Guidance that promotes caring values but is combined with significant levels of harsh treatment will have limited effect.

Learning by Doing

Giving children opportunities to help others increases their later helping behavior (Staub, 1975, 1979, 2003). Children and adults learn by doing. Parents can engage in "natural socialization" (Staub, 1979) by giving children significant responsibilities for helping at home (Grusec, Kuczynski, Rushton, & Simutis, 1978; Whiting & Whiting, 1975) and by guiding them to engage in helpful actions in relation to peers, adults, or the community outside the home. There is also evidence that adults harming others increases their later harmful and aggressive actions (Buss, 1966; Goldstein, Davis, & Herman, 1975; Staub, 1989). I have discussed this phenomenon at the group level as well. Parents who allow violent behavior by children, or encourage aggression against peers, are likely to promote the development of aggressive tendencies (see also Staub, 2003).

Children learn "by doing" to be helpful for two reasons: First, their actions fulfill basic needs, and second, they develop values, beliefs, and skills that extend inclinations already developed through the fulfillment of basic needs. If the experience of engaging in helpful action has positive cultural meaning (which it often does, although there are subcultures in which it does not), and if it leads to others' improved welfare, basic needs for effectiveness, positive identity, and positive connection are fulfilled—both for the people helped and for the larger community whose values the person fulfills. Effective, helpful actions express and affirm the value of helping, thereby leading children to value others' welfare and to see themselves as helpful persons (Eisenberg & Cialdini, 1984; Grusec et al., 1978; Staub, 1979, 2003).

When they are not halted by negative consequences, aggressive actions also lead to more aggression by fulfilling basic needs and by affirming values that promote strength and power. However, aggression fulfills basic needs destructively (see the criteria on pp. 60–61). Behaving aggressively may create a feeling of effectiveness and control and affirm identity, but it also creates disconnection from the people harmed and also from the community, except in violent subcultures. Many aggressive youths, for example, are unpopular among their peers; however, they are unaware of their unpopularity. As a result they do not change and, indeed, become increasingly aggressive over time (Zakriski, Jacobs, & Coie, 1999).

BASIC NEEDS, THE LEARNING OF VALUES, AND EVOLUTION: AN OVERVIEW

The fulfillment of basic human needs and guidance (via induction, modeling, learning by doing, etc.) that promotes caring values and effectiveness/competence combine to foster helpful, altruistic tendencies. The fulfillment of basic needs is a base, to which other elements have to be added, in a manner that continues to fulfill rather than frustrate basic needs.

"Evolution" in the actions, beliefs, and psychological condition of individuals, and of whole groups, also plays a central role and constitutes another core process in the development of altruism and aggression, goodness and evil. This evolution relies on the processes already noted, such as prior fulfillment or frustration of basic needs and environmental influences that promote values and actions that encourage helping or aggression. The psychological changes in the course of the evolution lead to increasing devaluation of those harmed (and its extension to more people) or increasing concern about those helped (and its extension to people beyond one's group), and to a view of oneself as willing to use aggression or as helpful.

Another important aspect of this evolution may be how we construct our basic needs. With experience, needs are likely to be shaped and formed in cognitive–emotional constructions, which then shape, limit, or extend the way needs can be fulfilled. Since aggressive men (Toch, 1969) view toughness and strength as masculine ideals, they have to be tough and strong to fulfill their need for a positive identity. Feeling empathy and concern for people, except perhaps some intimates, will not fulfill their need for a positive identity. Increasing their empathy would not constitute a desirable "expansion of the self" for these individuals.

When people devalue a particular group, they cannot fulfill their need for connection by friendship with members of that group. Perpetrators learn to deal with consequences of their actions by closing off to the feelings of their victims—by learning to become less empathic (Staub & Pearlman, 2001, 2003). Over time, perpetrators' capacity to form connections to people in general may diminish. In the course of the evolution of helping or aggressive perspectives and behaviors, the cognitive–emotional construction of basic needs is likely to further develop in the same direction.

RESCUERS

Can we understand the behavior of heroic helpers or rescuers in terms of the conception advanced here? The term *rescuers* was first applied to the Christians in Nazi Europe who endangered themselves, and usually their families as well, by attempting to save the lives of Jews. There have been rescuers in other genocides as well, and perhaps in all of them. In Rwanda, I interviewed people who were rescued and, in one case, the rescuer as well.

Research on rescuers in the Holocaust suggests that their socialization was highly consistent with the socialization I described, based on research with children, as important in developing altruism. Rescuers received more love and affection and positive guidance in their early childhoods than others who were in similar situations to help but did not help. In cultures where physical punishment was common, the parents of these rescuers used explanation instead of physical punishment. They also were exposed to helpful models, often a parent who embodied moral values in his or her actions, and parents who were more inclusive, who engaged with people outside their own group in positive ways, including Jews (Oliner & Oliner, 1988). Thus, inclinations created by the fulfillment of basic needs were elaborated by further experience in ways that were likely to develop inclusive caring.

HEALING, NEED FULFILLMENT, RESILIENCE, AND ALTRUISM BORN OF SUFFERING

Victimization tends to lead to aggression. The reasons for this, mentioned in the discussion of the cultural characteristics that make violence probable, also apply to individuals who have been victimized. People who were abused as children are more likely to abuse their own children. Among violent criminals, the great majority report experiences of victimization at home or in their community (Gilligan, 1996; Rhodes, 1999). According to newspaper reports, at least, many of the school shooters who wreaked such carnage in recent years were victimized by peers.

However, not everyone who is victimized becomes aggressive. Many children who come from difficult backgrounds show resilience—that is, effective functioning despite their background (Masten, 2001; Rutter, 1987; Staub, in preparation-b). Can people who have been victimized, their basic needs deeply frustrated, still become kind and helpful? Some people, depending on their past experience with suffering and frustrated needs, may develop an intensely defensive or hostile stance against a perceived hostile world that they are unlikely to have, or at least to perceive, experiences in ways that would ameliorate such orientations to the world. However, other people who have been victimized become caring individuals who devote themselves to helping others or to protecting others from suffering the way they themselves have suffered. This is true, for example, of child survivors of the Holocaust (people who were children at the time), many of whom are in service professions (Valent, 1998) or work for positive social change, as well as many people who have been abused by parents in their childhood (O'Connell Higgins, 1994).

Victimization (and other trauma) deeply frustrate basic needs. I assume that for victimized children to become caring, altruistic people, they must experience the fulfillment of their basic needs, to some degree at least, and they must heal, to some degree, from the psychological wounds created by their victimization. Prior need fulfillment may protect them somewhat from the effects of victimization, and subsequent need fulfillment may enable them to envision the possibility of experiencing security, dignity, and positive connection.

In the case of genocide survivors, many experienced basic need fulfillment in their close, loving connections with their families and their group before the genocide, and to other survivors afterwards. In addition, many survivors were helped by other people, and some took courageous action on their own behalf. This was true of survivors of the Holocaust, for example, including young children who often engaged in amazing acts of initiative to help themselves or their families (Staub, in preparation-a). In the midst of horrific circumstances, such experiences fulfill needs for connection, effectiveness and identity, and a comprehension of reality—which, in turn, provide hope and makes caring for others possible.

Healing from past trauma requires the development of renewed trust in people. Resilience in children is usually facilitated by interest and support from, and positive connection to, one or more persons—teachers, counselors, relatives, neighbors. Temperamental characteristics of children also contribute to resilience (Rutter, 1987). This may be the case, at least in part, for children who are more outgoing and who more easily initiate active efforts to connect with potentially supportive others. Here again, basic needs are fulfilled—for effectiveness and control, connection and identity.

Healing and the fulfillment of basic needs enable people who have suffered to become open to the pain of others. Once that happens, they are able to understand and empathize with others' pain well, given their own experience. Identification with those who suffer may lead to increasing engagement and, over time, to a strong motivation to help. Research on the development of caring, helping, and altruism in children has focused on positive roots, as described in the earlier section of this chapter. Given the widespread observation that people who have suffered often devote themselves to helping others (e.g., O'Connell Higgins, 1994; Valent, 1998), the extent to which this occurs and the conditions required for such "altruism born of suffering" ought to be a focus for study.

OPTIMAL HUMAN FUNCTIONING, TRANSCENDENCE, AND THE GOOD SOCIETY

The fulfillment of basic needs is normally a matter of degree. Each person, inevitably, also experiences frustration and pain. Children and adults learn the limits of their effectiveness and struggle with inherent conflicts between needs, such as autonomy and connection, that may be enhanced by cultural or familial values and practices. They experience losses, as friends move away or people die, as well as rejection and other "life injuries" (Staub, in preparation-a). But if basic needs are fulfilled to a substantial degree, and children learn to regulate their feelings (Eisenberg, 2002), including feelings generated by need frustration, they will become people whose understanding of the meaning of frustration becomes integrated with their predominant experience of need satisfaction. This integration enables them to pursue need fulfillment in constructive ways.

As basic needs are fulfilled, they undergo transformation, become less pressing, and evolve into personal goals (Staub, 1980)—that is, the desire to bring about particular, valued outcomes. The outcomes that people value obviously differ, depending on their life experience. Varying realms of effectiveness, sources of positive identity, and connections to individuals or to a larger community become especially important.

The fulfillment of basic needs should bring about the capacity for continued personal growth. I see this attribute as the central defining characteristic of optimal human functioning. It is this continued growth that leads to the emergence and perhaps dominance of the need for transcendence, and to the ability to fulfill this need, in part, by altruistic endeavors. Here again, other influences that build on the base provided by need fulfillment are important in shaping the particular focus beyond the self and determining whether that focus includes the welfare of other people.

An interesting question is whether true transcendence (in contrast to pseudo-transcendence) ever leads people to devote themselves to an ideology, a movement with "higher" ideals, that advocates and leads to engagement in the destruction of others. Since humans are capable of tremendous cognitive transformations, such as dehumanizing other people and representing them as a threat to oneself, one's group, or all humanity, it is possible that promoting "altruistic transcendence" and ensuring that no "destructive transcendence" occurs may require an explicit development of inclusive caring.

The fulfillment of basic needs is not simply an individual matter or even a matter of what kind of parents, teachers, or peers a child happens to have. Families, peers, and schools are located in a society. Characteristics of a society affect the fulfillment of basic needs (see Staub, 2003). The devaluation of, and discrimination against, a group is likely to affect the security, identity, and perhaps other needs of its members. Poverty creates stress and negatively affects parenting (McLoyd, 1990), which, in turn, frustrates children's needs. Teenage single mothers are likely to have their own needs frustrated by their circumstances and to have difficulty fulfilling the needs of their children, especially if they are poor. Unless they receive ample support from others, they are much more likely to abuse their children than other mothers (Garcia-Coll, Hoffman, & Oh, 1987). Both the frequency of young single mothers and the support they receive can greatly vary across groups. In a society that helps its members fulfill basic needs constructively, there will be trust and positive reciprocity among members, so that basic needs are naturally fulfilled in everyday life. Such a society helps develop the effectiveness of its members, building social capital and enhancing the strength of the society as a whole (Affolter, 2002).

It would make tremendous sense to evaluate the "goodness" of societies in terms of the ease or difficulty of fulfilling basic human needs, and to identify desirable social changes in terms of their probable contribution to the fulfillment of basic needs. An essential task in promoting goodness and preventing evil is to shape cultural and societal institutions in a manner that helps adults and children fulfill their needs in constructive ways and uses the resulting potential and inclinations to further develop the values and orientations that promote goodness.

A POSTSCRIPT: BASIC HUMAN NEEDS, AGGRESSION, AND CARING IN A POST-9/11 UNITED STATES

The attack on the United States on September 11, 2001, seems to have been deeply wounding for Americans. It has obviously affected citizens' feelings of security. It certainly has affected the need for a positive identity.

Who are we, really, presumably the most powerful nation on earth, if such things can be done to us? Furthermore, who are we, if we generate such hostility in some people? This latter question did not lead, as it should have, to self-exploration on a policy level. Our leaders, instead, pointed to an evil other—which could have accompanied an exploration of the reasons for such a virulent hostility toward the United States, whether justified or not. The events of 9/11 also created a feeling of powerlessness and helplessness, at least until the war against Afghanistan, and then Iraq.

One possible reaction to 9/11 would have been increased empathy with others who have suffered from genocide, mass killing, or other violence against them. Not surprisingly, this empathic response has not happened. This empathy would be an element, a psychological underpinning, for what I have called altruism born of suffering. As I have suggested, this form of altruism requires prior healing. Instead, people in the United States turned to their leader to help fulfill their basic needs—to reestablish security, a positive identity, and so on.

"Authority orientation"—the extent of, respect for, and uncritical acceptance of the authority of leaders—is both a cultural characteristic and a tendency that is affected by current events and social conditions. Following 9/11 there was an increase in such authority orientation; people looked for, and accepted the guidance, words, and actions of the president. The use of questioning and critical judgment lessened—a lessening that was greatly reinforced by the uncritical attitude of the media and Congress.

This excess authority orientation may have led to some tragic judgments and actions on the part of our leaders and the American people and clearly leaves several tasks in its wake. One is to recreate what is the essence of American democracy: vigorous public debate. Genuine debate requires honesty. It requires showing dead Iraqis on television and not acting as if nobody, other than American soldiers and some really bad people in Iraq, had died or suffered as a result of the war. Without honesty and without true pluralism, much is lost.

Another task is to fulfill the basic needs of the people in the United States by constructive rather than destructive means. Self-defense is legitimate and necessary, but striking out in revenge, even it the target is unclear, is destructive both for others and the self. (In a survey reported by the *New York Times* before the war in Afghanistan began, over 60% of respondents wanted to attack that country, even if we didn't know exactly who was responsible for the 9/11 attacks.) Even if destructive need fulfillment temporarily strengthens feelings of security, identity, and so on, it creates problems not only for others but for the actor as well in the long run. Healing, attending to psychological wounds, grieving, and commemorating—*without* the distraction of revenge and violence—are important ways to fulfill basic needs in the wake of trauma.

Experiencing an increased empathy for others, which healing makes more likely, and taking constructive actions to improve U.S. actions and U.S. image in the world are other ways of fulfilling basic needs. Coming to see the world as a truly interconnected community, within which the United States is an extremely powerful country with a responsibility to help the people of other countries fulfill their material as well as basic psychological needs will, in turn, change the United States and its relationship to others. Such actions would help others, but they would also help the people of this country.

REFERENCES

Affolter, F. W. (2002). *Development policies for socio-emotional well-being.* Unpublished doctoral dissertation, School of Education, University of Massachusetts, Amherst.

Ainsworth, M. D. S., Bell, S. M., & Stayton, D. J. (1974). Infant–mother attachment and social development: Socialization as a product of reciprocal responsiveness to signals. In M. P. M. Richards (Ed.), *The integration of the child into a social world.* London: Cambridge University Press.

Bar-Tal, D. (1998). Societal beliefs in times of intractable conflict: The Israeli case. *International Journal of Conflict Management, 9,* 22–50.

Bar-Tal, D. (2000). *Shared beliefs in a society: Social psychological analysis.* Thousand Oaks, CA: Sage.

Batson, C. D. (1990). How social an animal? The human capacity for caring. *American Psychologist, 45,* 336–347.

Baumeister, R. F., & Leary, M. R. (1995). The need to belong: Desire for interpersonal attachments as a fundamental human motivation. *Psychological Bulletin, 117*(3), 497–529.

Baumrind, D. (1971). Current patterns of parental authority. *Developmental Psychology, 4,* 1–101.

Baumrind, D. (1975). *Early socialization and the discipline controversy.* Morristown, NJ: General Learning Press.

Berkowitz, L. (1993). *Aggression: Its causes, consequences, and control.* New York: McGraw-Hill.

Bretherton, I. (1992). The origins of attachment theory: John Bowlby and Mary Ainsworth. *Developmental Psychology, 28,* 759–775.

Burton, J. W. (1990). *Conflict: Human needs theory.* New York: St. Martin's Press.

Buss, A. H. (1966). The effect of harm on subsequent aggression. *Journal of Experimental Research in Personality, 1,* 249–255.

Buss, D. M. (2000). The evolution of happiness. *American Psychologist, 55,* 15–24.

Christie, D. J. (1997). Reducing direct and structural violence: The human needs theory. *Peace and Conflict: Journal of Peace Psychology, 3,* 315–332.

Coan, R. W. (1977). *Hero, artist, sage, or saint? A survey of views on what is variously called mental health, normality, maturity, self-actualization, and human fullfillment.* New York: Columbia University Press.

Coie, J. D., & Dodge, K. A. (1998). Aggression and antisocial behavior. In W. Damon (Series Ed.) & N. Eisenberg (Vol. Ed.), *Handbook of child psychology: Vol. 3. Social, emotional, and personality development* (5th ed). New York: Wiley.

Coopersmith, S. (1967). *The antecedents of self-esteem.* San Francisco: W. H. Freeman.

Csikszentmihaly, M. (1990). *Flow: The psychology of optimal experience.* New York: Harper & Row.

Deci, E. L., & Ryan, R. M. (1985). The dynamics of self-determination in personality and development. In R. Schwarzer (Ed.), *Self-related cognition in anxiety and motivation.* Hillsdale, NJ: Erlbaum.

des Forges, A. (1999). *Leave none to tell the story: Genocide in Rwanda.* New York: Human Rights Watch.

DiLalla, L. F., Mitchell, C. M., Arthur, M. W., & Pagliococca, P. M. (1988). Aggression and delinquency: Family and environmental factors. *Journal of Youth and Adolescence, 73,* 233–246.

Dodge, K. A. (1980). Social cognition and children's aggressive behavior. *Child Development, 51,* 162–170.

Dodge, K. A. (1993). Social cognitive mechanisms in the development of conduct disorder and depression. *Annual Review of Psychology, 44,* 559–584.

Eisenberg, N. (1992). *The caring child.* Cambridge, MA: Harvard University Press.

Eisenberg, N. (2002). Empathy-related emotional responses, altruism, and their socialization. In R. J. Davidson & A. Harrington (Eds.), *Visions of compassion: Western scientists and Tibetan Buddhists examine human nature.* New York: Oxford University Press.

Eisenberg, N., & Cialdini, R. B. (1984). The role of consistency pressures in behavior: A developmental perspective. *Academic Psychology Bulletin, 6,* 115–126.

Eisenberg, N., & Fabes, R. A. (1998). Prosocial development. In W. Damon (Series Ed.) & N. Eisenberg (Vol. Ed.), *Handbook of child psychology: Vol. 3. Social, emotional, and personality development* (5th ed). New York: Wiley.

Eisenberg, N., Fabes, R. A., Miller, P. A., Fultz, J., Mathy, R. M., Shell, R., & Reno, R. R. (1989). The relations of sympathy and personal distress to prosocial behavior: A multimethod study. *Journal of Personality and Social Psychology, 57,* 55–66.

Epstein, S. (1993). Emotion and self-theory. In M. Lewis & J. M. Haviland (Eds.), *Handbook of emotions.* New York: Guilford Press.

Erikson, E. H. (1959). Identity and the life cycle: Selected papers. *Psychological Issues, Vol. 1, Monograph 1.* New York: International Universities Press.

Erikson, M., & Egeland, B. (1996). The quiet assault: A portrait of child neglect. In J. Briere, L. Berliner, S. Bulkley, C. Jenny, & T. Reid (Eds.), *The handbook of child maltreatment* (pp. 4–20). Newbury Park, CA: Sage.

Eron, L. D., Gentry, J. H., & Schlegel, P. (Eds.). (1994). *Reason to hope: A psychosocial perspective on violence and youth.* Washington, DC: American Psychological Association.

Eron, L. D., Walder, L. O., & Lefkowitz, M. N. (1971). *Learning of aggression in children.* Boston: Little, Brown.

Feinberg, J. K. (1978). *Anatomy of a helping situation: Some personality and situational determinants of helping in a conflict situation involving another's psychological distress.* Unpublished doctoral dissertation, University of Massachusetts, Amherst.

Garcia-Coll, C. T., Hoffman, J., & Oh, W. (1987). The social ecology and early parenting of Caucasian adolescent mothers. *Child Development, 58,* 955–963.

Gilligan, J. (1996). *Violence: Our deadly epidemic and its causes.* New York: Putnam.

Glass, D. C., & Singer, J. E. (1972). *Urban stress: Experiments on noise and social stressors.* New York: Academic Press.

Goldstein, J. H., Davis, R. W., & Herman, D. (1975). Escalation of aggression: Experimental studies. *Journal of Personality and Social Psychology, 31,* 162–170.

Grodman, S. M. (1979). *The role of personality and situational variables in responding to and helping an individual in psychological distress.* Unpublished doctoral dissertation, University of Massachusetts, Amherst.

Grusec, J. E., Kuczynski, L., Rushton, J. P., & Simutis, Z. M. (1978). Modeling, direct instruction, and attributions: Effects on altruism. *Developmental Psychology, 14,* 51–57.

Hoffman, M. L. (1970a). Conscience, personality, and socialization technique. *Human Development, 13,* 90–126.

Hoffman, M. L. (1970b). Moral development. In P. H. Mussen (Ed.), *Carmichael's manual of child development.* New York: Wiley.

Hoffman, M. L. (1975a). Altruistic behavior and the parent–child relationship. *Journal of Personality and Social Psychology, 31,* 937–943.

Hoffman, M. L. (1975b). Developmental synthesis of affect and cognition and its implications for altruistic motivation. *Developmental Psychology, 11,* 607–622.

Hoffman, M. L. (2000). *Empathy and moral development: Implications for caring and justice.* New York: Cambridge University Press.

Huesmann, L. R., & Eron, L. D. (1984). Cognitive processes and the persistence of aggressive behavior. *Aggressive Behavior, 10,* 243–251.

Huesmann, L. R., Eron, L. D., Lefkowitz, M. M., & Walder, L. O. (1984). Stability of aggression over time and generations. *Developmental Psychology, 20*(6), 1120–1134.

Huesmann, L. R., Lagerspetz, K., & Eron, L. D. (1984). Intervening variables in the television violence–aggression relation: Evidence from two countries. *Developmental Psychology, 20,* 746–775.

Janoff-Bulman, R. (1992). *Shattered assumptions: Towards a new psychology of trauma.* New York: Free Press.

Kelman, H. C. (1990). Applying a human needs perspective to the practice of conflict resolution: The Israeli–Palestinian case. From J. Burton (Ed.), *Conflict: Human needs theory.* New York: St. Martin's Press.

Kestenbaum, R., Farber, E. A., & Sroufe, L. A. (1989). Individual differences in empathy among preschoolers: Relation to attachment history. *New Directions in Child Development, 44,* 51–64.

Leatherman, J., DeMars, P., Gaffney, X., & Vayrynen, R.(1999). *Breaking cycles of violence: Conflict prevention in intrastate crises.* West Hartford, CT: Kumarian Press.

Lederer, K. (1980). Introduction. In K. Lederer, J. Galtung, & D. Antal (Eds.), *Human needs: A contribution to the current debate.* Cambridge, MA: Oelgeschlager, Gunn & Hain.

Lefcourt, H. M. (1973). The function of the illusions of control and freedom. *American Psychologist, 28,* 417–425.

Lykken, D. T. (2001). Parental licensure. *American Psychologist, 56,* 885–894.

Mamdani, M. (2001). *When victims become killers: Colonialism, nativism, and the genocide in Rwanda.* Princeton, NJ: Princeton University Press.

Maslow, A. H. (1968). *Toward a psychology of being* (2nd ed.). Princeton, NJ: Van Nostrand.

Maslow, A. H. (1987). *Motivation and personality* (3rd ed.). New York: Harper & Row. (Original work published 1954)

Masten, A. S. (2001). Ordinary magic: Resilience processes in development. *American Psychologist, 59,* 227–238.

McCann, I. L., & Pearlman, L. A. (1990). *Psychological trauma and the adult survivor: Theory, therapy, and transformation.* New York: Brunner/Mazel.

McLoyd, V. C. (1990). The impact of economic hardship on Black families and children: Psychological distress, parenting, and socioemotional development. *Child Development, 61,* 311–346.

McGregor, H. A., Lieberman, J. D., Greenberg, J., Solomon, S., Arndt, J., Simon, L., & Pyszczynski, T. (1998). Terror management and aggression: Evidence that morality salience motivates aggression against worldview-threatening others. *Journal of Personality and Social Psychology, 74*(3), 590–605.

Midlarsky, E. (1971). Aiding under stress: The effects of competence, dependence, visibility, and fatalism. *Journal of Personality, 39,* 132–149.

Murray, H. A. (1938). *Explorations in personality.* New York: Oxford University Press.

O'Connell Higgins, C. (1994). *Resilient adults overcoming a cruel past.* San Francisco: Jossey-Bass.

Oliner, S. B., & Oliner, P. (1988). *The altruistic personality: Rescuers of Jews in Nazi Europe.* New York: Free Press.

Pearlman, L. A., & Saakvitne, K. W. (1995). *Trauma and the therapist: Countertransference and vicarious traumatization in psychotherpy with incest survivors.* New York: Norton.

Post, J. M. (2001). *The mind of the terrorist: Individual and group psychology of terrorist behavior.* Testimony prepared for Sub-Committee on Emerging Threats and Capabilities, Senate Armed Services Committee, November 15.

Pyszcznski, T., Greenberg, J., & Solomon, S. (1997). Why do we need what we need? A terror management perspective on the roots of human social motivation. *Psychological Inquiry, 8,* 1–20.

Rhodes, R. (1999). *Why they kill: The discoveries of a maverick criminologist.* New York: Knopf.

Rogers, C. R. (1961). *On becoming a person; A therapist's view of psychotherapy.* Boston: Houghton Mifflin.

Rutter, M. (1987). Psychosocial resilience and protective mechanisms. *American Journal of Orthopsychiatry, 57*(3), 316–331.

Schatz, R., & Staub, E. (1997). Manifestations of blind and constructive patriotism. In D. Bar-Tal & E. Staub (Eds.), *Patriotism in the lives of individuals and groups.* Chicago: Nelson-Hall.

Seligman, M. E. P. (1975). *Helplessness: On depression, development and death.* San Francisco: W. H. Freeman.

Shaffer, D. R. (1995). *Social and personality development.* Monterey, CA: Brooks–Cole.

Sidanius, J., & Pratto, F. (1999). *Social dominance: An intergroup theory of social hierarchy and opression.* Cambridge, UK: Cambridge University Press.

Staub, E. (1971). A child in distress: The influence of modeling and nurturance on children's attempts to help. *Developmental Psychology, 5,* 124–133.

Staub, E. (1975). To rear a prosocial child: Reasoning, learning by doing, and learning by teaching others. In D. DePalma & J. Folley (Eds.), *Moral development: Current theory and research.* Hillsdale, NJ: Erlbaum.

Staub, E. (1978). *Positive social behavior and morality. Vol. 1. Social and personal influences.* New York: Academic Press.

Staub, E. (1979). *Positive social behavior and morality. Vol. 2. Socialization and development.* New York: Academic Press.

Staub, E. (1989). *The roots of evil: The origins of genocide and other group violence.* New York: Cambridge University Press.

Staub, E. (1995). How people learn to care. In P. G. Schervish, V. A. Hodgkinson, M. Gates, & Associates (Eds.), *Care and community in modern society: Passing on the tradition of service to future generations.* San Francisco: Jossey-Bass.

Staub, E. (1996a). Altruism and aggression in children and youth: Origins and cures. In R. S. Feldman (Ed.), *The psychology of adversity.* Amherst: University of Massachusetts Press.

Staub, E. (1996b). The cultural–societal roots of violence: The examples of genocidal violence and of contemporary youth violence in the United States. *American Psychologist, 51,* 17–132.

Staub, E. (1998). Breaking the cycle of genocidal violence: Healing and reconciliation. In J. H. Harvey (Ed.), *Perspectives on loss and trauma: Assaults on the self.* Washington, DC: Taylor & Francis.

Staub, E. (1999a). The origins and prevention of genocide, mass killing and other collective violence. *Peace and Conflict: Journal of Peace Psychology, 5,* 303–337.

Staub, E. (1999b). The roots of evil: Personality, social conditions, culture and basic human needs. *Personality and Social Psychology Review, 3,* 179–192.

Staub, E. (2002a). From healing past wounds to the development of inclusive caring: Contents and processes of peace education. In G. Solomon & B. Nevo (Eds.), *Peace education: The concepts, principles, and practices around the world.* Mahwah, NJ: Erlbaum.

Staub, E. (2002b). Preventing terrorism: Raising "inclusively" caring children in the complex world of the 21st century. In C. E. Stout (Ed.), *The psychology of terrorism.* Westport, CT: Praeger.

Staub, E. (2003). *The psychology of good and evil: Children, adults and groups helping and harming others.* New York: Cambridge University Press.

Staub, E. (in preparation-a). Another form of heroism: Survivors saving themselves and its impact on their lives. In O. Feldman & P. Tetlock (Eds.), *Personality and politics: Essays in honor of Peter Suedfeld.*

Staub, E . (in preparation-b). *A brighter furture: Raising caring, nonviolent, morally courageous children.* New York: Oxford University Press.

Staub, E., & Bar-Tal, D. (2003). Genocide, mass killing and intractable conflict: Roots, evolution, prevention and reconciliation. In D. Sears, L. Huddy, & R. Jarvis (Eds.), *Handbook of political psychology.* New York: Oxford University Press.

Staub, E., & Pearlman, L. A. (2001). Healing, reconciliation and forgiving after genocide and other collective violence. In S. J. Helmick & R. L. Petersen (Eds.), *Forgiveness and reconciliation: Religion, public policy and conflict transformation.* Radnor, PA: Templeton Foundation Press.

Staub, E., & Pearlman, L. A. (2003). *Advancing healing and reconciliation in Rwanda and elsewhere.* Unpublished manuscript, University of Massachusetts at Amherst.

Staub, E., Pearlman, L. A., Hagengimana, A., & Gubin, A. (2003). *Healing, forgiving and reconciliation: An intervention and its experimental evaluation in Rwanda.* Unpublished manuscript, University of Massachusetts, Amherst.

Staub, E., Pearlman, L. A., & Miller, V. (2003). Healing the roots of genocide in Rwanda. *Peace Review, 15*(3), 287–294.

Stevens, L. E., & Fiske, S. T. (1995). Motivation and cognition in social life: A social survival perspective. *Social Cognition, 13,* 189–214.

Thompson, W. R., & Grusec, J. (1970). Studies of early experience. In P. H. Mussen (Ed.), *Carmichael's manual of child psychology* (Vol. 2, 3rd ed.). New York: Wiley.

Toch, H. (1969). *Violent men.* Chicago: Aldine.

Triandis, H. C. (1994). *Culture and social behavior.* New York: McGraw-Hill.

Valent, P. (1998). Child survivors: A review. In J. S. Kestenberg & C. Kahn (Eds.), *Children surviving persecution: An international study of trauma and healing.* Westport, CT: Praeger.

Volkan, V. (1997). *Blood lines: From ethnic pride to ethnic terrorism.* New York: Farrar, Straus & Giroux.

Waters, E., Wippman, J., & Sroufe, L. A. (1979). Attachment, positive affect, and competence in the peer group: Two studies in construct validation. *Child Development, 50,* 821–829.

Weiss, B., Dodge, K. A., Bates, S. E., & Pettit, G. S. (1992). Some consequences of early harsh discipline: Child aggression and a maladaptive social information processing style. *Child Development, 63,* 1325–1333.

Weiss, J., Rothbaum, F., & Blackburn, T. (1984). Standing out and standing in: The psychology of control in American and Japan. *American Psychologist,* pp. 955–975.

Whiting, B. B., & Whiting, J. W. M. (1975). *Children of six cultures: A psychocultural analysis.* Cambridge, MA: Harvard University Press.

Widom, C. S. (1989a). The cycle of violence. *Science, 224,* 160–166.

Widom, C. S. (1989b). Does violence beget violence? A critical examination of the literature. *Psychological Bulletin, 106*(1), 3–28.

Yarrow, M. R., & Scott, P. M. (1972). Limitations of nurturant and nonnurturant models. *Journal of Personality and Social Psychology, 8,* 240–261.

Zahn-Waxler, C., & Radke-Yarrow, M. (1990). The origins of empathic concern. *Motivation and Emotion, 14,* 107–130.

Zakriski, A., Jacobs, M., & Coie, J. (1999). Coping with childhood peer rejection. In S. A. Wolchik & I. N. Sandler (Eds.), *Handbook of children's coping: Linking theory and intervention.* New York: Plenum Press.

CHAPTER 4

FOUR ROOTS OF EVIL

ROY F. BAUMEISTER
KATHLEEN D. VOHS

The study of evil soon confronts any thoughtful person with a seeming paradox. On the one hand, there is evil aplenty: People perform violent, harmful, cruel, and oppressive acts all over the world, and they have done so throughout history. On the other hand, hardly anyone recognizes him- or herself as evil. Ironically, many who have perpetrated what history has come to condemn as some of the worst excesses regarded themselves as trying their best to do something good and noble.

How can there be so many evil acts without evil perpetrators? Has everything been just a series of huge misunderstandings? It would be absurd to dismiss the tortures, genocides, and other monumental crimes as simply a matter of misunderstanding. People have really made other people suffer and die, often in large numbers.

This chapter has two parts. In an effort to understand how so few evildoers can produce so much evil—or, rather, why the perpetrators do not see themselves as evil, even as their victims condemn them, the first recognizes the deep gulf that divides the thinking of victims and perpetrators. To achieve any kind of understanding requires us to reformulate the question of why people do evil acts. It becomes: Why do some people do things that others will regard as evil? The second part of the chapter explores five answers to that question: four root causes and one proximal cause.

VICTIMS AND PERPETRATORS

One of the great challenges in attempting to understand evil is to detach oneself from sympathetic identification with the victim's perspective. Most of us become interested in studying evil because we feel sympathy for those who have suffered, or even because we want to alleviate the suffering of (past or future) victims. We condemn the cruel and harmful acts of perpetrators, and the more we care about the victims, the more outrage we feel at the violent and oppressive treatment they describe having received at the hands of the perpetrators.

Outrage is an important moral stance, but it is not the best attitude for a scientist to take, especially if the goal is to arrive at an objective understanding of the facts. Indeed, outrage may make it all the more difficult to see the facts. Hence the scientist studying evil must take the morally dangerous step of moving away from the victim's perspective and trying to understand the perpetrator's motives, thoughts, feelings, and actions.

Some differences between perpetrator and victim thinking emerged from a study one of us conducted in the late 1980s (Baumeister, Stillwell, & Wotman, 1990). The study was not initially designed to investigate the nature of evil. Rather, the purpose was simply to learn about anger, which was (and still is) a problematic emotion whose full understanding has proven elusive to research psychologists. When experimenters want to study anger, they typically hire a confederate and instruct him or her to deliver a gratuitous, nasty, unprovoked insult to the research participant. This tactic succeeds: People often do get angry when they are insulted for no reason. But does this scenario correspond to real life? How often have you gone out of your way to deliver an unnecessary insult to someone you have just met?

In order to learn about how anger emerges and plays out in everyday life, this research project asked people to describe two important incidents from their own personal experience. The instruction for one was to relate an episode in which someone had made the participant angry. In the other, the instruction was to relate an episode in which the participant had made someone else angry. The order of writing the stories was counterbalanced. It was hoped that obtaining these pairs of stories would shed light, from both perspectives involved, on how anger arose—in effect, in one person as both victim and perpetrator.

One aspect of this research design bears repeating: Every participant wrote both kinds of story. This point is quite important. Most treatments of evil and violence have looked at perpetrators as wicked, malicious beings who are seemingly unlike normal, decent people (including their victims). The tendency to demonize perpetrators is deeply rooted and widespread. But this study got around it: everyone was both a victim and a perpetrator. Or, to put it another way, none of the findings of this study can be taken as showing that victims and perpetrators are different kinds of people, because they were exactly the same people. Thus, any differences we found must be attributed to the *roles* of victim and perpetrator and not to any personality differences between victims and perpetrators. Indeed, we probably biased the study against finding any differences by having everyone write both kinds of story at the same sitting. Everyone had to adopt both perspectives within the same laboratory session of less than an hour, so what they said in one kind of story would probably tend to resemble what they said in the other.

Despite this pressure toward similarity, the two sets of stories—those by victims and those by perpetrators—showed a series of important, systematic differences that shed light on how the psychological perspectives of victims and perpetrators differ, even when the same person switches from one to the other within a matter of minutes.

The time spans differed. Victim stories often began by providing background events leading up to the episode they meant to describe. Then they described the event itself, and typically they also included some discussion of what came after it. In many cases the consequences of the transgression were portrayed as continuing for years afterward, extending even to the present time and likely continuing into the future.

In contrast, perpetrator stories had much shorter time spans. Many of them simply described the event itself—as in, what happened on that particular day—without any reference to what came before or after it. When perpetrators did allude to the present, it was often to deny that there were any lasting consequences of their misdeed. Thus, whereas the victim would say something like "After that episode, I could never trust my roommate again, and our friendship is mostly over," the perpetrator stories would tend to end with "After the episode, we made up and now we are even better friends than we were back then." Indeed, when we coded for a category called "happy endings," in which the story about anger and transgression concluded on a positive, pleasant note, we found a large and significant difference: These were relatively common in the perpetrator stories but essentially absent from the victims' accounts.

To be sure, our research sample consisted of many everyday conflicts and misdeeds, few of which were sufficiently important to qualify for the grandiose term *evil*. Our assumption, however, is that similar processes operate in everyday transgressions as in large-scale misdeeds, and that if anything, the gap between victim and perpetrator would probably be even larger in horrendously evil events than in petty, everyday conflicts. With regard to time perspective, there is some evidence that this parallel is true. With regard to many of the great crimes of history, perpetrators are much quicker than victims to consign a misdeed to ancient history. Anyone who has lived in both Northern and Southern states of the United States knows that the South, which sees itself as victim, still bears the memory of the

Civil War much more keenly than the North. Undoubtedly, similar gaps can be recognized between European and African Americans on the issue of slavery, between European and Native Americans on the issue of internment and genocide, between Jewish and German attitudes toward the death camps, and many other historical events.

While researching a book on evil, one of us (Baumeister, 1997) came across a history of the Crusades as seen from the Arab perspective (Maalouf, 1987), and it makes a shocking contrast to most treatments of the Crusades by European and American historians (e.g., Runciman, 1951–1954). The Crusades really do seem like very ancient history, being mostly completed before the Middle Ages came to an end, but the Arab treatment was full of a still-fresh sense of grievance over the unprovoked (as they saw it) invasions and atrocities by Europeans which did lasting damage to the Arab cultures of the Middle East. The book ended with an assertion that if one wants to understand Arabs today, including the politics of oil and terrorism, it is necessary to appreciate that many Arabs still regard the Crusades as a defining moment in their relationship to Europe.

Another difference between victims and perpetrators was found in how each understood the perpetrators' reasons for their misbehavior. Victims, in particular, seemed to emphasize that there was no valid reason to explain the person's actions. The perpetrators in the victims' stories came across as performing nasty or unkind acts for no reason or perhaps out of sheer malice. Perpetrators rarely portrayed themselves that way, however. A few did say something like, "I don't know why I did it," but these were exceptions. Most of them—even when admitting that what they had done was wrong—described their intent usually in terms that depicted it as somewhat justifiable or at least understandable.

This discrepancy points to an important gap in understanding. The perpetrator's motives are often opaque to the victim. Perpetrators usually have an understanding of what they are trying to do and why, but victims cannot or will not see this perspective.

Another difference is in the degree of harm. Nor surprisingly, the victims depicted the harm as much greater than the perpetrators. To some extent, this finding can be interpreted as indicating that perpetrators downplay the bad consequences of their actions, but it could also signify that victims are prone to play up or even exaggerate the bad consequences.

Although our sympathy must remain with the victims, recognizing the lesser consequences seen by perpetrators may be important to any psychological effort to understand them. Often they may see their actions as "no big deal." Their repentance may seem inadequate not because they are inhuman monsters but because, in their own minds, the harm they have done is not on the same scale as what the victim perceives.

In attempting to deny the reality or extent of their misdeeds, perpetrators are sometimes captured by external events. That is, some lasting consequences are harder to deny than others. Undoubtedly the victim's perception of bad consequences is intensified by the fact that he or she is still suffering from them, whereas the perpetrator is less exposed to those consequences, and so it is easier to downplay them. Korbin (1989) studied a sample of women who had abused their children to the point of death. In her account, the child's death generally came as a severe shock to the mother, even though previous incidents of abuse had produced seemingly ample warnings. But bruises and broken bones heal, and so most of the mothers had regarded themselves as good mothers up until the moment they killed their children. They might have taken their child to an emergency room on several occasions, but still they managed to avoid facing up to their own abusiveness. For example, they would go to a different hospital each time, which prevented any of the medical staff from recognizing a pattern of abuse, and so each injury would be treated as a one-time event. The abusive woman might tell herself that all these different physicians had seen the child and not a single one had said anything to criticize or accuse her, so her own behavior must be within the normal, acceptable range. In any case, the event was soon put into the past, as the child healed and life went on. Only when the child died was there unmistakable proof that the woman was doing something bad.

Causation by victims was another important theme characterized by systematic discrepancies between victim and perpetrator accounts. Many of the perpetrator stories (again, even while admitting wrongdoing) noted that the victim had done something to precipitate or cause the conflict. "OK, I shouldn't have hit her, but she shouldn't have called me an idiot," they might say. In contrast, victim accounts almost never assigned any responsibility to the self. The victim stories thus resembled a script that anyone could recognize from violent movies, fairy tales, or horror flicks: The victim is entirely good and innocent, whereas the perpetrator attacks the victim for no apparent reason.

On this matter, the weight of evidence tends to be closer to the perpetrators' accounts. People rarely attack for no reason. Many studies have shown that perpetrators perceive themselves as under attack or as having been provoked (see Toch, 1993). In many cases a violent crime follows on the heels of an escalating exchange, in which both parties are initially rude or insulting to the other, and it is almost meaningless to ask "Who started it?".

We have tried to suggest that both victim and perpetrator roles contain some sources of bias and distortion. Our purpose in this is not to apologize for perpetrators—far from it—but simply to recognize that the truth is often elusive in such matters. Therefore, it is not scientifically appropriate to treat victim accounts as the clear truth while dismissing perpetrator accounts as self-serving lies (although, to be sure, sometimes that may be a fair description).

The study of narrative accounts we have described thus far had no way of discerning whether victims/perpetrators were telling the truth about the event, because there was no objective criterion of accuracy. Stillwell and Baumeister (1997) made one effort to ascertain whether the victim or the perpetrator role is more likely to produce biases. In their study, research participants were randomly assigned to take the role of either victim or perpetrator (those words were not used) while reading a story about a transgression and then retelling it in their own words, as if it had really happened to them. By comparing the participants' retellings with the original version of the story, line by line, it was possible to check for accuracy.

The results were startling. Both victims and perpetrators distorted their stories—and to almost identical degrees. The number of discrepancies between the victim stories and the original story was almost identical to the discrepancies in the perpetrator stories, and both tallies were significantly higher than what was found in a control group, who read the story without identifying with either character and then retold it in the third person. (In some ways, even that difference is surprising, because most researchers assume that memory is improved by identification with a character in the story and recalling it as if it were one's own experience.)

To be sure, the laboratory studies by Stillwell and Baumeister (1997) were simply pretend exercises, and they lacked one crucial factor that exists outside the laboratory: the risk of punishment and other consequences. Genuine criminals and other perpetrators have a reason to lie that did not exist in that laboratory simulation: They do not want to be punished. Hence, in everyday life, there is some reason to suspect that perpetrators may distort their accounts more than victims. Still, both victims and perpetrators significantly distorted their accounts in the lab studies, and they did so even when the experimenter offered them a cash inducement to furnish a thorough and accurate account. Perhaps pragmatic concerns could produce even more distortions, but apparently pragmatic concerns (in the form of a cash reward) are not sufficient to eliminate them.

In short, victims and perpetrators understand and interpret transgressions in systematically different ways, even when the same people occupy the victim and perpetrator roles. Moreover, both roles contain sufficient motivations for some degree of distortion. The truth may lie somewhere in between what the victim says and what the perpetrator says.

ROOT CAUSES OF EVIL

We turn now to consider the root causes of evil. The discrepancies between victims and perpetrators require us to change the basic question of "Why are some people evil?" or even "Why do some people do bad things?" into "Why do some people do things that others will regard as evil?" As outlined by Baumeister (1997), there are four main root causes: Violence is employed as (1) a means to an end, (2) in response to threatened egotism, (3) in a misguided effort to do good, and (4) a means of gaining sadistic pleasure.

Instrumentality: A Means to an End

The first and probably least surprising answer is that some people resort to violence as a means to get what they want. Some degree of conflict is probably inevitable in human social life. Two people may want the same thing, or they may want things that are incompatible with each other's preferences. There are many ways to resolve conflict, and violence is certainly one of them.

The goals toward which people employ violence are often quite ordinary. People use violence to get money, resources, power, and sex. They use it to win an argument or to get someone to stop doing something they dislike. These ends are not generally objectionable in themselves. After all, most people have some desire for money, land, power, sex, and the rest. The evil lies in the means, not the end. The resort to violence is what makes the activity evil.

In the long run, perhaps, violence is not an effective way to get what one wants. Many scholars have noted that evil or violent means fail to produce the desired result (see Baumeister, 1997). Assassination and terrorism fail to bring about the government one desires. Domestic violence fails to create the loving relationship one seeks. Wars harm both sides. Robbers and drug pushers do not retire as rich, happy individuals. Rape does not bring sexual satisfaction. Most murders are soon regretted as pointless and counterproductive.

Nonetheless, the long-term futility of the violence is not generally recognized by perpetrators. If anything, perpetrators are often focused in the here and now, and violence may be seen as the most promising way to get what they want as quickly as possible. Again, not surprisingly, violence is somewhat effective in the short run.

These views led Tedeschi and Felson (1994) to argue that the psychology of aggression should be merged with the psychology of influence. In their view, most aggression is essentially an attempt to influence someone else. People harm others to get them to do, or think, what the perpetrator wants.

Threatened Egotism

A second root cause of violence is threatened egotism (Baumeister, Smart, & Boden, 1996). People attack others who have wounded their pride or besmirched their honor. The image of self, rather than material gain, is thus the core issue in this category of violence.

The theory of threatened egotism flies in the face of some traditional psychological wisdom, which has long asserted that low self-esteem is an important cause of violence. The low self-esteem theory was widely repeated, but it never had any clear theoretical or empirical basis. Moreover, the view that low self-esteem causes violence gradually emerged as seriously at odds with the character of people with low self-esteem, as it was demonstrated in decades of study (see Baumeister, 1993, for an overview of multiple research programs on self-esteem). People with low self-esteem are generally shy, reluctant to take risks, slow to call attention to themselves, uncertain about which action to take, and prone to give in to what others say. None of these qualities seems conducive to violent action.

Studies of perpetrators gradually painted a very different picture (see Baumeister et al., 1996). Many of them seemed to have very favorable, even inflated, views of themselves. This inflation was observed in violent criminals, such as murderers and rapists, as well as other violent types, such as tyrants. It even fits violent groups, such as the Nazis (the "master race" is hardly a slogan of low self-esteem) and the Ku Klux Klan (whose theme of racial supremacy is, again, indicative of a highly favorable image of self).

After reviewing the evidence, however, Baumeister and colleagues (1996) concluded that it would be inaccurate to leap from low to high self-esteem as the assigned cause of violence. True, some people with favorable views of self are violent, but others are nonviolent. An important early study by Kernis, Grannemann, and Barclay (1989) showed both sides of high self-esteem. On a questionnaire measure of hostility, people with high self-esteem were found at both extremes. The important contribution of Kernis and colleagues was to sort people based on the *stability* of their self-esteem. Some people's self-esteem fluctuates from day to day in response to their successes and failures and how others treat them, whereas others experienced relatively stable self-esteem, regardless of circumstances. Kernis and colleagues found that people with high and stable self-esteem scored the lowest on hostility in their entire sample, whereas the people with high and unstable self-esteem scored the highest on hostility.

The finding that high self-esteem can push toward either more or less aggression has prompted researchers to begin looking beyond simple measures of self-esteem in their efforts to understand violence. Laboratory research by Bushman and Baumeister (1998) measured not only self-esteem but also narcissism, a trait defined as having an inflated, highly positive view of self, a deep sense of being better than others and of deserving special, preferential treatment, and an overarching concern with securing the admiration of others (e.g., Morf & Rhodewalt, 2001). Bushman and Baumeister measured these traits and then measured how aggressively people behaved in a laboratory task that ostensibly involved competing with someone else on a reaction time task. The winner of each trial could supposedly blast the other with aversive, stressful noise. Prior to the game, some participants were ostensibly insulted by their future opponent, whereas others were praised.

The results of these experiments supported the threatened egotism theory. The highest levels of aggression were found among people who scored high in narcissism and who had been insulted by their opponent in the game. Thus, people who were highly invested in a favorable image of themselves and who then encountered someone who disputed that flattering view were most prone to lash out and attack that person. Meanwhile, traditional, standard measures of self-esteem failed to predict aggression. Moreover, narcissists were not more aggressive toward everyone. They were no more or less aggressive than other people toward someone who had praised them, or toward a neutral third person (even if they had been insulted by someone else). Their aggression was limited to attacking the person who had criticized them.

Idealism: Doing Good by Doing Bad

The third root of evil is, in many ways, the most tragic. It consists of people who are motivated by high-minded ideals. They regard violence as a necessary means, often a distasteful and regrettable one, to accomplish something good and positive. In some cases, they regard it as their moral duty to perpetrate their violent acts.

Our sympathy for victims has obscured this aspect of the psychology of many perpetrators. It may be startling to realize that many of the perpetrators of the most horrific acts of violence in the 20th century were actually motivated by positive ideals. Unfortunately, idealism has produced the highest body counts of all the roots of evil. The highest tallies of deaths apart from war—and, in fact, surpassing all but the World Wars—were found in the Stalinist purges in the Soviet Union and in the Cultural Revolution in Maoist China. Both are now estimated to have killed about 20 million people. But both were guided by the hope of creating a communist or socialist utopia, in which all would be equal, people would care for each other and share all possessions in common, and no one would exploit innocent victims. And even if one doubts that Stalin or Mao sincerely embraced these ideals, it seems indisputable that most of the party cadres who carried out the arrests and executions did sincerely believe that they were doing the right thing, for the sake of their beloved country and the creation of the socialist paradise.

Nazi Germany has become perhaps the most enduring emblem of evil. Most historians agree on the estimate that the Nazi death camps killed about 6 million Jews; there were many other victims as well, including

Roma (Gypsies), homosexuals, and Communists, with the total number of victims approaching 12 million. Regardless of the exact number, the carnage was appalling, and the toll in human suffering incalculable. But the Nazis too were guided by high and ostensibly noble ideals. They also wanted to create an ideal society, where people (at least those of the approved ethnicity and nationality) would live together in respect and prosperity, cultivating an era of moral virtue. In fact, the SS officers who have come to stand as symbols of Nazi brutality were rigorously selected for their high moral character and supposedly comprised a moral elite.

If we turn away from the sheer number of bodies and instead focus on the proportion of deaths, the Khmer Rouge were the most successful murderers of the 20th century. Estimates of their death toll continue to rise, but now some experts are beginning to say that 2 million Cambodians died during their brief reign, out of a population of only about 7 million. Yet the Khmer Rouge were idealists too. They wanted to usher in the workers' (and peasants') paradise, ending inequality and oppression, and they also wanted to restore Cambodia to its mythologized former glory.

Outside the 20th century, similar conclusions emerge. The number of deaths in the Reign of Terror following the French Revolution cannot compete with the 20th-century mass murder campaigns, but at the time it was a profound shock to the civilized world. It was, in fact, so shocking that it had the effect of discrediting the idea of a democratic republic, at least in Europe, and revulsion against the months of bloodletting were a factor leading to the restoration of the French monarchy. Yet the Reign of Terror was supposed to usher in a more or less permanent era of public virtue. The men who ordered the deaths of specific people spoke incessantly, and seemingly sincerely, of their love for "the People" (at least, in the abstract). Killing a few bad people was seen as necessary to the greater good of the People. Nowadays the ideals of democracy and freedom are recognized as very positive, good things, but the first Europeans to try to institute them used killing as a way to promote them.

Closer to home, the tragedy of September 11, 2001, again reminds us that great violence is often employed in attempts to achieve high-minded ideologies. The violent means used by the Taliban and *jihadis* (Islamist radicals and disciples of their holy struggle) were aimed at achieving the goal of creating an Islamic superstate that would take control of the world and place it under Islamic rule. They focused their terrorism on the United States, as opposed to the rest of the world, because they saw the United States' involvement in the Israeli–Palestinian conflict and the bombing in Afghanistan as the cause of the Arab world's sufferings. Moreover, the war on the United States has created a newfound group of Islamic martyrs, some of whom were promised marriage to 72 virgins *after* their deaths. (In this case, the "means to an end" aspect of the Taliban's actions was secondary to their desire to establish a worldwide Islamic movement.) Once again, these ideals were not propagated by powerless people with few other means of influence; the terrorists who died when bombing the World Trade Center in New York City were born and raised in Saudi Arabia, which is the richest Arab state, and had been educated in the West. Not coincidentally, Saudi Arabia is the only Arab state created with the idea of mutual cooperation between religious leaders ("men of the pen") and military leaders ("men of the sword") ("The Difficult Future of Holy Struggle," 2002).

To remedy what they saw as the unnecessary suffering of their peoples and to disseminate their Islamic message, the *jihad* extremists advocated the use of terrorism in the United States—indeed, they prayed for it. As part of their daily prayer sessions, many Arab Muslims added a new genuflection, which ends with the plea, "May God destroy America" ("The Difficult Future of Holy Struggle," 2002). Osama bin Laden believed that the Taliban's barbarities and the consequent U.S. military reactions would breathe life into a mass movement in the Islamic world. However, this objective has been far from realized: Fighters in Pakistan, Saudi Arabia, Egypt, Palestine, Indonesia, or even in Afghanistan have never amounted to more than a few thousand. Once again, violence aimed at achieving idealistic intentions failed to produce desired effects.

In the United States today, and especially since the events of September 11, 2001, we like to think that we have finally recognized the fallacy of the argument that the ends justify the means. Yet that view lives on, even in our land. It is at least a relentless theme of movies and television shows. Countless police dramas and some medical ones feature a conflict between one person who insists on following proper procedures and rules, and another whose keen sense of the higher good makes him (or occasionally her) willing to bend the rules. One classic version of this theme was the movie character "Dirty Harry," played by Clint Eastwood in a long series of successful films. Dirty Harry was a cop who had endless conflicts with his superiors. They wanted him to follow standard procedures and respect the rights of suspects, but he knew that the only way to stop wicked murderers from claiming the lives of more innocent victims was to take all necessary actions. Waiting for a search warrant could spell the difference between life and death for another potential victim, and Harry would sooner act than wait.

For Dirty Harry and countless other characters (another very successful one was the *Beverly Hills Cop,* played by Eddie Murphy), the end justified the means. How many times has the theme depicted the clash between the one who insists on obeying the rules and the other who is anxious to catch the bad guys, even if it means bending or breaking them? And of all of those stories, how many times was the rule-follower depicted as the more sympathetic character? In Hollywood—generally accepted as one of the most powerful and ubiquitous sources of influence in our culture—the end nearly *always* justifies the means.

Sadism: The Joy of Hurting

The fourth root of evil is probably the most common in victims' accounts and fictional depictions but the least common in everyday life: sadism. When evildoers are regarded from outside as villains or bad guys, they are often perceived as enjoying the harm they inflict.

Sadism is the technical term for deriving enjoyment from inflicting harm or pain on others. The term is derived from the name of the Marquis de Sade, a French aristocrat, philosopher, and novelist, who sought to record all known sexual perversions in literature (often accompanied by flowery philosophical justifications for their practice). His grand ambition is remembered, somewhat inadequately, by naming one sexual practice after him: that of obtaining sexual pleasure from inflicting pain. The term *sadism,* as used here, however, does not refer specifically to sexual pleasure or indeed any sexual practice at all, but simply the pattern of enjoying hurting someone.

Abundant references to sadism are found in victim accounts, but its mention is far rarer in perpetrator accounts, and one could question whether it exists at all. Baumeister (1997) noted that the "myth of pure evil" denies that perpetrators can have any valid motives for their misdeeds, and so it is common to depict them as harming people simply for the fun of it. However, even though relatively few perpetrators admit to enjoying the infliction of harm (see McCall, 1994, and especially Bourke, 2000, for reports of those who do), a greater number of perpetrators allude to others who seem to enjoy it. These perpetrator accounts were sufficiently common to lead Baumeister to conclude that sadism is a genuine cause of violence, albeit a relatively uncommon one. Sadism may be the least frequently occurring of the four main roots of evil, although it can lead to extremes of cruelty far beyond what the others produce.

The very notion of sadism seemingly flies in the face of many observations about people, such as their tendency to empathize with each other, their reluctance to inflict harm, and the typically very negative reactions to first experiences with hurting. Soldiers in battle often find themselves unable or unwilling to kill enemy soldiers, even though that is their duty and the enemy is presumably trying to kill them. By the same token, when police officers kill someone in the line of duty, their reaction is often extremely negative. A vivid illustration of the impact of killing was furnished in Browning's (1992) account of a corps of middle-aged German reserve police officers who, to their surprise, found themselves ordered to execute all the Jews in a Polish village near where they were stationed. The men carried out their grisly task in a reluctant and inefficient way, sometimes even missing the targets at point-blank range because of their own inhibitions. That night, many had anxiety attacks, nightmares, and gastrointestinal problems. It is worth noting that these negative reactions were not the result of moral or philosophical objections—rather, they indicated a visceral disgust and alarm.

A theory of how sadism might occur despite the seemingly natural aversion to hurting was proposed speculatively by Baumeister (1997; see also Baumeister & Campbell, 1999), who applied the opponent process theory previously proposed by Solomon and Corbit (1974). That theory is based on the homeostatic mechanisms of the body: Any new demand is met with a change in the bodily processes (the A process), and afterward an opposing process (the B process) gradually returns the body to its normal, resting state. Solomon and Corbit observed that initially the A process dominates and the B process is slow and inefficient, but over time the B process can rise to dominance as it becomes faster and more efficient.

Hence, over time, opponent processes can induce people to seek out and enjoy activities/people/events that might be highly aversive at first. Falling is offered as one clear example. Falling is among the most deeply rooted, presumably innate fears in the human constitution, and falling into space generally induces an immediate sensation of panic. It may seem paradoxical, therefore, that many people seem to enjoy falling and base their leisure pastimes on it: bungee jumping, parachuting, diving off the high board, and the like. According to opponent process theory, the initial and natural panic reaction to falling calls forth an opposing reaction that resembles euphoria in order to restore the body to its homeostatic state. Over time, as one continues to jump, the panic dwindles and the euphoria becomes more pronounced, and so what once brought terror now brings pleasure.

This model can account for the emergence of sadism even if people are naturally averse to inflicting harm. The first time one hurts or kills someone, one has a strong negative reaction, but as one continues to perform such acts, the opponent process gradually yields more and more pleasure. Certainly the scattered observations on sadism seem to fit such a pattern. Enjoyment of sadistic acts is mainly reported or admitted by people who have been at it for a relatively long time.

Why does not everyone become a sadist? After all, every human body operates on the basis of homeostasis, and so everyone has opponent processes. In principle, therefore, anyone could become a sadist. But, clearly, most perpetrators do not become sadists, even when they engage in multiple acts of violence.

One possible answer is that a sense of guilt prevents most people from acknowledging that they might enjoy inflicting harm on others. Most people have some degree of conscience that would condemn them for taking pleasure in causing another to suffer. Hence, even if they started to experience the visceral pleasure of the opponent process in the course of harming someone, they would not allow themselves to enjoy it, let alone to pursue it.

There are some indications that more people could become sadists if they were not restrained by their own feelings of guilt. When guilt is not operating, however, people do seem better able to enjoy the suffering of others. In the United States, for example, it is considered acceptable to enjoy watching violent movies or shows, and, in fact, such films are often enormously profitable. Likewise, many people learn to enjoy hunting, even if they experience some distress the first time they kill an animal. This is not to say that hunters or fans of violent movies are sadists. But the idea of enjoying oneself while watching injury or death is not as far-fetched as it might at first seem, especially when guilt is eliminated.

Again, these are merely speculations designed post hoc to fit a sketchy lot of observations. They are reasonable in light of what we know now, but the data are far from convincing.

SELF-CONTROL: THE PROXIMAL CAUSE

Instrumentality, threatened egotism, idealism, and sadism are the four root causes of evil. The causal chain leads from them through a variety of possible mediators and moderators, to end in the violent act. In some ways, however, the most important cause is not any of those roots but what can be found at the other end of the causal chain, just before the violent act. In many cases, that final link in the chain involves a breakdown in self-control.

Most people have a set of inner restraints, scruples, and inhibitions that prevent them from acting on every impulse they might feel. And it is a good thing, too: Civilized life in human society would be chaotic, if not completely impossible, without these restraints. The capacity for self-regulation is more highly developed in human beings than in most (indeed, probably in any) other species. One of the central uses of these self-regulation processes is to override initial responses and impulses and allow the person to act in a more appropriate manner (Baumeister, Heatherton, & Tice, 1994).

Nowhere is this self-control mechanism more useful than in restraining aggression. The inevitability of conflict in human coexistence entails that people are often frustrated, angry, irritated, or dismayed with each other. Many of these interpersonal conflicts give rise to aggressive or violent impulses, but only a few of them lead to violence. Baumeister (1997) noted that he began his investigations by asking "Why is there evil?", but after reviewing all the many factors that contribute to aggression, he discovered a need to address the equally pressing question, "Why isn't there more evil than there is?" The answer is *self-control.* Simply put, most aggressive impulses are stifled.

It is fair to think of human aggressive tendencies in this way: Many events give rise to aggressive impulses, but self-control prevents people from acting on them. In a sense, self-control is the last defense against aggression; therefore, self-control failure may be an important cause of aggression. When the restraints cease to function, the aggressive *impulses* lead to aggressive *action*.

Consistent with this view, aggression increases in many situations that have been shown to undermine self-control. One of the best documented causes of violence is alcohol intoxication. Bushman and Cooper (1990) confirmed that intoxication leads to higher rates of aggression in many studies, and data from outside the laboratory confirm its role. Yet alcohol, by itself, does not lead to aggression. Alcohol merely increases the degree of aggression that a person displays in response to a provocation. When others are nice to you, a few drinks will not make you turn violent. But if someone insults you, a few drinks may be the difference between holding back and lashing out.

Data from criminology have confirmed the central importance of self-control. In their important work *A General Theory of Crime*, Gottfredson and Hirschi (1990) concluded that low self-control was the defining trait of many criminals. They offered a wealth of data to substantiate this view, and subsequent studies using trait measures have confirmed their conclusion. The point is that low self-control makes people more willing to act on a broad variety of antisocial and even illegal impulses.

Self-control failure is not always a factor, however. Sometimes people use self-control to enable them to act *more* violently. This dynamic is probably most common when idealism is the root of the evil enacted. Idealists may actively seek to live up to high moral standards, and some of them at least recognize that killing or harming others is contrary to such ideals. Lifton's (1986) accounts of Nazi physicians who struggled to reconcile their killing activities with their moral principles show that they often had to force themselves—that is, use self-control—to carry out their grisly tasks. Similarly, some of the Communist cadres who carried out the brutal and lethal repressions during the Ukrainian terror/famine also suffered qualms and had to exert self-control to confiscate the last scraps of food from starving peasant families.

Still, by and large, self-control operates to restrain aggression. When self-control fails, violence becomes more likely.

CONCLUSION

There is no single answer to the question of why people perform evil acts. Indeed, stated baldly, the question is almost unanswerable, because very few people perform what they themselves regard as evil actions.

An understanding of evil and violence begins with an appreciation of the different perspectives of victim and perpetrator. The two parties involved in an act of violence may often have strikingly different perceptions of what transpired. As compared with victim accounts, perpetrators' views of transgressions typically involve less severe harm and fewer lasting consequences, a shorter time span that is less connected to the present and future, more appreciation of mitigating factors, a much more substantial causal role for the victim, and a much more nuanced and comprehensible understanding of what they (the perpetrators) actually intended to do.

Four main roots of evil were identified. The first is instrumentality: Violence is one means to obtain what one wants, especially when that acquisition requires influencing others to comply. The second is threatened egotism: People turn violent when their cherished, flattering images of themselves are impugned by others. The third is idealism: Tragically, sometimes people seek to make the world a better place by harming or killing those who they think stand in the way of their utopian dream. Last, sadism is sometimes a cause of violence: Some people do seem to learn to derive pleasure from harming others. Opponent process theory offers one explanation of how these individuals might acquire that taste.

In many cases, however, people feel violent impulses but manage to refrain from acting on them. Self-regulation, also known as self-control, is a powerful internal antidote to violence. Violence erupts when self-control stops or breaks down, such as may occur under the influence of alcohol or emotional distress.

The root causes of evil are deeply entrenched in the fabric of human social relations. It does not appear that they can be eliminated easily. Hence, the best prospect for restraining violence may lie with the proximal cause. By encouraging and teaching people to develop and practice self-control, society may achieve some success at reducing evil and violence.

REFERENCES

Baumeister, R. F. (1993). (Ed.). *Self-esteem: The puzzle of low self-regard.* New York: Plenum Press.

Baumeister, R. F. (1997). *Evil: Inside human violence and cruelty.* New York: Freeman.

Baumeister, R. F., & Campbell, W. K. (1999). The intrinsic appeal of evil: Sadism, sensational thrills, and threatened egotism. *Personality and Social Psychology Review, 3,* 210–221.

Baumeister, R. F., Heatherton, T. F., & Tice, D. M. (1994). *Losing control: How and why people fail at self-regulation.* San Diego, CA: Academic Press.

Baumeister, R. F., Smart, L., & Boden, J. M. (1996). Relation of threatened egotism to violence and aggression: The dark side of high self-esteem. *Psychological Review, 103,* 5–33.

Baumeister, R. F., Stillwell, A., & Wotman, S. R. (1990). Victim and perpetrator accounts of interpersonal conflict: Autobiographical narratives about anger. *Journal of Personality and Social Psychology, 59,* 994–1005.

Browning, C. R. (1992). *The path to genocide: Essays on launching the final solution.* Cambridge, UK: Cambridge University Press.

Bushman, B. J., & Baumeister, R. F. (1998). Threatened egotism, narcissism, self-esteem, and direct and displaced aggression: Does self-love or self-hate lead to violence? *Journal of Personality and Social Psychology, 75,* 219–229.

Bushman, B. J., & Cooper, H. M. (1990). Effects of alcohol on human aggression: An intergrative research review. *Psychological Bulletin, 107,* 341–354.

The difficult future of holy struggle. (2002, January 5). *The Economist* [Online]. Available at *http://www.economist.com/displaystory.cfm?story_id=966016*

Gottfredson, M. R., & Hirschi, T. (1990). *A general theory of crime.* Palo Alto, CA: Standard University Press.

Kernis, M. H., Grannemann, B. D., & Barclay, L. C. (1989). Stability and level of self-esteem as predictors of anger arousal and hostility. *Journal of Personality and Social Psychology, 56,* 1013–1022.

Korbin, J. E. (1989). Fatal maltreatment by mothers: A proposed framework. *Child Abuse and Neglect, 13,* 481–489.

Lifton, R. J. (1986). *The Nazi doctors.* New York: Basic Books.

Maalouf, A. (1987). *The Crusades through Arab eyes.* New York: Schocken.

Morf, C. C., & Rhodewalt, F. (2001). Unraveling the paradoxes of narcissism: A dynamic self-regulatory processing model. *Psychological Inquiry, 12,* 177–196.

Runciman, S. (1951–1954). *A history of the Crusades.* New York: Cambridge University Press.

Solomon, R. L., & Corbit, J. D. (1974). An opponent-process theory of motivation: I. Temporal dynamics of affect. *Psychological Review, 81,* 119–145.

Stillwell, A. M., & Baumeister, R. F. (1997). The construction of victim and perpetrator memories: Accuracy and distortion in role-based accounts. *Personality and Social Psychology Bulletin, 23,* 1157–1172.

Tedeschi, J. T., & Felson, R. B. (1994). *Violence, aggression, and coercive actions.* Washington, DC: American Psychological Association.

Toch, H. (1993). *Violent men: An inquiry into the psychology of violence.* Washington, DC: American Psychological Association.

CHAPTER 5

THE EVOLUTION OF EVIL

JOSHUA D. DUNTLEY
DAVID M. BUSS

On the evening of July 24, 2002, in the thriving city of Houston, Texas, Clara Harris got into her Mercedes Benz and killed her husband, David Harris, in the parking lot of a hotel. Using her car as the device of murder, she ran into him once. Her anger still not allayed, she circled the lot and ran over him again. Witnesses differ in precisely how many times she backed up and crushed her husband with the 4,000-pound vehicle. One said five times, another four, and a third witness indicated only twice. Videotape from the hotel security cameras revealed that the correct number was three. Some think that Clara Harris is evil and deserves to rot in jail for the remainder of her life. But some view the homicide as justifiable, or at least understandable.

The circumstance that elicited the homicide was David Harris's affair with Gail Bridges, his former office coworker. Clara Harris discovered the affair through a private detective, whom she had hired when her suspicions were initially aroused. The morning of his death, David Harris swore to Clara that he would end the affair. Later that night, Clara, along with her stepdaughter Lindsey, began to search for David Harris. When they finally tracked him down at a hotel, according to Lindsey, "She said she could kill him and get away with it for what she's been through." Indeed, Clara had gone to great efforts to win her husband back after she discovered his affair. She made herself "real pretty so Dad would want her and not Gail," Lindsey said. During the week before the murder, Clara Harris spent time at a tanning salon, a beauty shop, and a gym. She also consulted a plastic surgeon, inquiring about breast implants.

It might also have aggravated Clara that the hotel was precisely the one where Clara and David had gotten married a decade earlier—on Valentine's Day. When she saw her husband emerge from the hotel elevator with his mistress, the two hand-in-hand, Clara Harris went "ballistic." She ripped the blouse off her rival's body and wrestled her to the ground. Although she clearly intended to do more damage, her husband separated the two women, and Clara was firmly escorted out of the hotel by the clerk on duty. As she left the lobby, David shouted, "It's over! It's over! It's over!"

It was then that Clara Harris became strangely calm, according to her stepdaughter, Lindsey, who accompanied her out of the hotel. Clara silently got into her Mercedes, and her tears stopped flowing. Clara was cool and composed as she suddenly stomped on the accelerator and rammed the car into her husband. She then ran over him again and again. Her stepdaughter tried to exit the vehicle, but had to wait until Clara stopped the car and the damage had finally come to an end. "You killed my Dad," Lindsey said, when the car finally stopped. In light of the circumstances, many in Texas do not judge Clara's horrific deed as evil. Some think that David Harris got exactly what he deserved.

Can good and evil be evaluated from an evolutionary perspective? In this chapter, we consider several related issues:

Have humans evolved adaptations to commit deeds that most would consider "evil"?

Have humans evolved defenses against the perpetration of evil on them?

Do the apparently universal cognitive categories of "good" and "evil" have special functional uses, aiding humans in solving critical, adaptive problems?

EVIL AS THE INFLICTION OF FITNESS COSTS

Evil has no direct analogue in the formal structure of evolutionary theory. Evolution by natural selection operates by the simple process of differential gene reproduction as a consequence of differences in heritable design. Heritable variants that lead to greater reproduction, compared with competing variants present in the population at the time, become represented in greater numbers in the next generation. Iterated over multiple generations, the process of selection leads to the evolution of adaptations that exist solely because they contributed, either directly or indirectly, to the reproductive success of their bearers. Thus, the process of natural selection is value-free. Whatever qualities lead to increased replicative success are those that evolve.

The evolutionary process of selection produces many products, and humans have little hesitation in labeling some of those products "good" and others "evil." At a first approximation, those we label as "evil" are behaviors or behavioral dispositions that result in a massive imposition of fitness costs on another individual or group. Indeed, as we argue later in the chapter, humans have evolved a specialized psychological categorization system for making these judgments.

The imposition of fitness costs on another individual can vary in magnitude from trivial to catastrophic. At the low end, someone bumping into you in the hall or stepping on your toe might be considered annoying, but probably not evil, unless these acts were repeated to the point of torture. At the high end are events such as robbing, maiming, rape, torture, and murder, with combinations of these usually viewed as embodying evil more fully than any considered alone. Intentional premeditated murder occupies the extreme end of the continuum, but within that broad class, some murders are considered to be more evil than others—murder with malice, murder without provocation, murder of young, defenseless children, murder of adolescent girls, serial murder, mass murder, and genocide. Some homicides, on the other hand, are considered excusable, justifiable, or even altruistic—for example, killing in self-defense, killing to protect a family member from harm, or killing to prevent a helpless stranger from being raped. Of course, as Baumeister (1997) points out, the judgment of the perpetrators and victims will surely differ in how evil these deeds are evaluated to be (a point that we will take up later). The key point here is that the acts we consider evil invariably involve the imposition of massive costs on victims, even though not all massive costs are considered to be evil.

By what metric do we judge acts to be costly? One contention of this chapter is that the deeds we view as evil occupy the extreme end of a continuum of reproductively relevant costs—that is, those that impose a massive fitness cost on the victim will be viewed to be the most evil. Humans, of course, do not think in these terms. We do not think to ourselves: "Gee, the damage done to Sally inflicts a large cost on her fitness, which impairs her relative gene replication . . . hence, it's evil." Rather, we propose that humans have evolved evaluative psychological mechanisms that function to gauge the magnitude of fitness costs inflicted on themselves, their allies, their children, and their extended families—roughly, the degree of evil. We have also evolved evaluative mechanisms to assess the magnitude of fitness benefits that others bestow on us and our vehicular allies—roughly, the degree of good. According to our evolutionary theory of good and evil, the degree of evil and of good judged by a person is partially a function of the person's degree of genetic relatedness to the person upon whom costs are inflicted or benefits are bestowed. Costs inflicted or benefits bestowed upon closer relatives would be more evil or good, respectively, than the same amounts of costs or benefits accruing to more distant genetic relatives. Degree of evil or good is also a function of "strategic confluence," that is, the degree to which other individuals are allied with us in achieving some goal (Buss, 1996). Thus, extreme fitness costs inflicted on a close friend would be judged as more evil than comparable costs inflicted on a stranger or an enemy. Indeed, massive fitness costs inflicted on an enemy are often judged to be good. In sum, the degree of strategic confluence, including individuals who are either genetic kin or non-kin allies, is predicted to mediate the degree to which an intentionally inflicted fitness cost is judged to be evil.

In order for these evaluative mechanisms to have evolved, however, there must have been evolutionarily recurrent deeds that humans performed that correspond to these psychological categorizations. Thus, before exploring the evolution of human judgments of good and evil and the functions of these psychological mechanisms, we must first explore why people inflict extreme levels of egregious harm on other people.

HUMAN PSYCHOLOGY AS THE END PRODUCT OF A COMPETITIVE EVOLUTIONARY PROCESS

From an evolutionary perspective, modern humans are the end products of a long line of successful reproducers. Indeed, all humans are evolutionary success stories. Each one of us owes his or her existence to an unbroken chain of ancestors, each of whom did what was necessary to survive and reproduce. If any one of our ancestors or their ancestors had failed at these tasks—for example, by dying before reaching reproductive age, failing to find a mate, failing to best competitors in attracting a mate, or failing to keep their own offspring alive so that they could mate—we would not be here to ponder the momentous issues of good and evil. As end products of this vast chain of events operating over deep evolutionary time, modern humans carry with them the adaptations that led to their ancestors' success and the genes that contribute to the reliable development of these adaptations. These adaptations comprise our universal human nature.

Aside from genetically identical twins and lifelong monogamous mates, the fitness interests of all individuals are, to some degree, unique and diverge from each other. Stated differently, humans are, to some extent, reproductive competitors with other humans to become ancestors. Competition need not be direct and need not involve overt contests. Indeed, competitors need never meet for competition to ensue. Scramble competition, for example, involves striving for the acquisition of limited or better resources in the external environment. Intrasexual competitors can compete with each other in individual courtship displays to attract a particular mate. Parents can compete with other parents merely by investing in their children's success. Although some of these forms of individual competition, such as investing in children, do not correspond to human intuitions about competition, they do embody competition at the formal level of natural selection, as much as two stags locking horns in direct combat or two humans clawing each other psychologically to get ahead in the status hierarchy.

Since all modern humans are the descendants of ancestors who succeeded countless times in direct and indirect competition, modern humans carry with them the competitive adaptations that led to their ancestors' success, and pass on the genes that contribute to the development of these adaptations to their children. Some of these adaptations function to inflict costs on other humans.

WHY HUMANS INFLICT HARM ON OTHER HUMANS

At an abstract level, there are two fundamental strategies for besting a competitor in a fitness contest. One strategy involves the acquisition of benefits that aid fitness—for example, scrambling for superior access to resources, displaying more alluring attractant signals to a mate, bestowing on children resources that aid their reproductive success, or aiding one's kin in a manner that increases inclusive fitness (Hamilton, 1964). The other strategy involves inflicting costs on competitors—for example, impairing their access to resources, interfering with their mate attractant signals, or harming a competitor's kin.

In the world of nonhuman animals, both strategies are seen in great abundance. Baby birds compete for their parents' food resources by "begging" with beaks wide open, but they also sometimes push a sibling out of the nest and hence commit siblicide. Male scorpionflies compete for females by securing insects to feed them as part of the nuptial gift, but they also jostle competing males away from the female, inflicting physical costs on their rivals. Among humans, intrasexual strategies of mate competition involve both sending attraction signals (Buss, 1988) and verbally derogating rivals (Buss & Dedden, 1990; Schmitt & Buss, 1996). Although damaging a rival's reputation may not be considered "evil" in the grand scheme of things, from the victim's perspective, the lost social status and consequent failure in mate competition may seem evil. Indeed, these status losses sometimes drive people to kill those they perceive as having harmed them. The emotion of vengeance may have evolved as a defense designed to staunch such costs or deter others from inflicting similar costs in the future.

In summary, we can expect selection to have favored the evolution of some adaptations that function to inflict costs on intrasexual rivals specifically and conspecific competitors generally. These costs vary from small to large in the currency of fitness damage to the recipient. As the fitness costs grow in magnitude, we become more and more inclined to label the actions as evil. According to our theory of the evolution of evil, humans have adaptations to inflict these costs—adaptations to steal rivals' resources, adaptations to damage rivals' reputations, adaptations to physically injure rivals, and adaptations to steal their mates. Humans also are likely to have evolved adaptations to kill (Buss & Duntley, 2003).

KILLING AS PROTOTYPICALLY EVIL

Probably no other class of human action is judged to be more evil than premeditated murder, and there may be no other class of actions that inflicts a greater fitness cost on the victim (Buss & Duntley, 2003; Duntley & Buss, 2003). Although no formal theory is needed to tell us that it is bad to be dead, killing is worse for a victim's fitness than is currently recognized by any existing psychological theory, except the homicide adaptation theory (Buss & Duntley, 2003). First, by being killed, the victim forfeits all future reproduction. He loses sexual access to his current partner as well as all future mating opportunities he may have acquired if he remained alive. With his death, he is no longer around to invest in his children. His children's survival and reproduction become imperiled as a result of his untimely death. It is known that the death of a parent can impair the survival of children, in some cultures by as much as 10% (Hill & Hurtado, 1996). If the children live and his mate remarries, the victim's children become stepchildren—the single largest risk factor for physical abuse and child homicide (Daly & Wilson, 1988). Furthermore, the victim's extended kin—his brothers and sisters, aunts and uncles, nephews and nieces, grandparents and grandchildren—all become more vulnerable as a consequence of his death through the loss of his protection and the perception of his family as exploitable. And if all of these fitness costs are not bad enough, his rivals benefit from his death. His mate becomes a potential sexual partner for his rivals. His resources become available for their taking. And his rivals' children now have a competitive edge over the victim's own children. His death, in short, can become his rivals' gain. In summary, killing may inflict more momentous fitness costs on a victim than any other single act—such a consequence constitutes prototypical evil from the perspective of the victim and the victim's friends and kin.

Reversing the perspective from victim to perpetrator yields interesting insights. As a thought experiment, consider that your assignment, should you decide to accept it, is to outreproduce your rivals. You can achieve this goal by various means—for example, besting them in the quest for high-quality food, developing more hygienic practices to better combat parasites and diseases, cultivating strategies that succeed in better attracting desirable mates, or investing more heavily or more skillfully in your children. But one remarkably effective strategy remains by which you could accomplish your mission in dramatic fashion—killing your rivals.

From the perspective of the inclusive fitness of the killer, killing a rival, in principle, can offer a bounty of benefits. By killing a rival, you may gain access to the rival's resources, since the rival is not around to protect them—resources such as land, food, tools, weapons, or shelter. Since rivals are often in competition for the same pool of potential mates, killing a rival can eliminate mating competition. The rival's existing mates become potential new mates for the killer. The killer's current and future children may have less competition in the next generation, thereby enhancing their fitness. The victim's losses, in short, can become a killer's gains.

This brief description of the potential benefits of killing a rival, of course, ignores the costs of killing, and indeed, killing can be a dangerous and costly strategy to carry out. Killers risk being injured or killed while attempting to carry out a murder. Even if "successful," the kin of the victim may extract revenge in the future. In some cultures, killers suffer retribution from the larger group. Furthermore, killing may harm the reputation of the perpetrator, hindering future access to social resources, including mates. The key point is *not* that killing is always, or even often, beneficial to the fitness of the killer. Rather, *killing historically has been potentially beneficial in the currency of reproductive fitness under some delimited circumstances* (i.e., when the risks are low, when costs are unlikely to be incurred, when the potential yield is large in magnitude, or when killing is the least costly strategy available amid an array of costly options). As a result of these benefits to the killer, combined with the costs to victims, as soon as homicide enters a population as a strategy, evolution will immediately select for coevolved defenses, resulting in an "arms race" of antagonistic coevolution.

DEFENDING AGAINST EVIL: ANTAGONISTIC COEVOLUTION

There can be little doubt that, from the victim's perspective, their killers or would-be killers would be considered evil. Before we consider the possible evolution of a universal cognitive category of evil, however, it is critical to consider the evolutionary events that would be set into motion once killing entered the human strategic repertoire. Because of the dramatic fitness costs of being killed, selection would act strongly to create defenses against killing—what we have called anti-homicide mechanisms (Duntley & Buss, 1998).

The intensity of selection is generally a function of two critical factors: (1) the fitness consequences, and (2) the frequency of the fitness-relevant events. There is no doubt that being killed inflicts enormous fitness damage on victims, fulfilling the first criterion. Given the magnitude of damage, the frequency of killing need not be high at all for selection to act consistently and strongly in fashioning anti-homicide defenses. The lifetime odds of being killed in the United States are roughly 1 in 200; they are 1 in 26 for certain groups such as inner-city males (Ghiglieri, 1999). Among more traditional societies, such as the Ghibusi tribe of Africa or the Yanomamo of Venezuela, as many as 30% of all males die at the hand of their fellow humans (Chagnon, 1988; Ghiglieri, 1999). Even among the so-called "peaceful" !Kung San of Botswana, murder rates are higher than in Los Angeles or Detroit. Paleontological evidence, which reveals arrowheads lodged in rib cages and crushing blows to ancient skulls, points to a long human history of killing (Buss & Duntley, 2003).

Although it is impossible to determine with precision the exact frequency of homicide over the long course of human evolutionary history, available evidence suggests that it was likely to be far from uncommon. And given the large fitness impact of being killed, even small rates of killing, such as the 0.5% rate that exists currently in the United States, would easily have met the required criteria for selection to have operated to fashion anti-homicide defenses.

Indeed, humans likely have evolved many different types of antihomicide defenses (Duntley & Buss, 2003). Stranger anxiety, for example, is an excellent candidate for an evolved anti-homicide strategy. It emerges predictably at 7–8 months of life, is specific to male strangers (who historically have been more dangerous to infants), and appears to be universal across cultures (Heerwagen & Orions, 2002; Marks, 1987; Marks & Nesse, 1994). Other potential anti-homicide defenses include ethnocentrism, fleeing mechanisms, mind-reading abilities specialized for detecting homicidal intent, and many others (Duntley & Buss, 2003).

Because humans risk getting killed in many different circumstances, a single anti-homicide adaptation would have been insufficient to combat all of the dangers. Being killed in infancy is different from being killed by an intrasexual rival in a status dispute as an adult. Being killed in a status dispute is different from being killed by a jealous mate who has suddenly discovered a sexual infidelity. Being killed by an enraged mate is different from being killed in tribal warfare. Given the many, varied, and evolutionarily recurrent circumstances in which the lives of humans have been endangered, selection will have forged a complex armament of defensive, anti-homicide devices.

Once anti-homicide defenses begin to evolve, however, killing becomes a more costly strategy to pursue. First, the success rate of the strategy becomes lower as a consequence of anti-homicide defenses, rendering fewer fitness benefits to the killer. Second, attempting to kill can be downright costly to the killer. Killers risk injury from intended victims, and they risk death, since "killing to prevent being killed," or killing in self-defense, is undoubtedly one of the anti-homicide defenses. Indeed, sometimes entire coalitions of individuals join forces to kill a killer. The upshot is that pursuing a homicidal strategy becomes less evolutionarily profitable as anti-homicide defenses evolve.

These anti-homicide defenses, by making killing less profitable, set in motion another evolutionary process: The coevolution of killer adaptations designed to circumvent the anti-homicide defenses. Selection will favor design features in killers that choose circumstances in which the costs of killing will not be incurred—for example, when the intended victim is particularly vulnerable or weak, when the intended victim lacks kin or coalitional support, or when the victim is caught by surprise. Selection will favor deceptive strategies in killers that include concealing homicidal intent from the victim in order to circumvent the activation of the victim's anti-homicide defenses.

As these more refined killer adaptations begin to evolve, selection will then favor the further evolution of increasingly sophisticated defenses. The consequence is a perpetual antagonistic coevolutionary arms race, as depicted in Figure 5.1.

From the victim's perspective, of course, being the target of a homicide renders the would-be killer evil. From the killer's perspective, how-

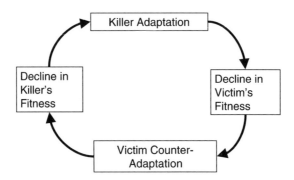

FIGURE 5.1. Antagonistic coevolution. This figure depicts the hypothesized process of the coevolution of homicide adaptations and anti-homicide defenses. Once an adaptation to kill conspecifics evolves within a population, it produces a decrease in the fitness of the killer's victims. This sets into motion countervailing selection that favors the evolution of defenses that function to prevent falling victim to murder. These defenses, in turn, create selection pressure for the evolution of more refined killer adaptations, such as those that circumvent the defenses of the victim (e.g., by using surprise or deception). To the extent that context-specific killing continues to provide fitness benefits to killers (on average), the coevolutionary arms race between homicidal adaptations and anti-homicide defenses will be perpetual in a way analogous to the coevolution of predators and prey.

ever, eliminating a victim may represent a "good," and the victim's anti-homicide strategies would thereby be viewed as evil.

THE FUNCTIONS OF COGNITIVE EVALUATIVE
MECHANISMS OF "EVIL" AND "GOOD"

It is not implausible that selection has fashioned privileged and universal cognitive categories of "evil" and "good" reserved precisely for monumental fitness-impairing motivations and fitness-bestowing motivations, respectively. The categorization of specific others as evil serves an important function: It targets a key threat to an individual's fitness, serves to encode an array of relevant fitness-damaging events in memory for subsequent strategic retrieval, and motivates action designed to circumvent the fitness threat (see Buss, 1989, for a more general argument about emotions as adaptations designed to deal with strategic interference).

Consider the case of the stepdaughter who is consistently beaten and sexually abused by her stepfather—events known to occur in nontrivial frequencies (Daly & Wilson, 1998). The stepdaughter's categorization of her stepfather as evil serves several important functions: (1) It tags fitness-damaging events for storage, (2) causes emotional arousal in response to fitness-damaging events (such as sexual abuse), and (3) motivates action designed to escape the fitness-damaging events. The fact that stepchildren leave home earlier, on average, than children who reside with both genetic parents may reflect this motivated action (Mitchell, Wister, & Burch, 1989). Historically, evaluative categories such as "evil" would have facilitated avoidance of cost-inflicting individuals.

The evolved category of evil, however, is likely to be a great deal more complex than this. Our ancestors faced many recurrently costly entities. It is likely that the category of evil only applies to some of those entities, and then to different degrees. We propose that an entity is more likely to be perceived as evil when it (1) engages in behaviors that inflict asymmetrically high levels of cost on a person relative to the benefits it receives, and (2) appears to desire to inflict harm.

An entity that inflicts great costs for small gains is more likely to be put into the special category of evil than when there is no asymmetry between costs inflicted and benefits received. Other factors equal, a person who kills for 10 million dollars is viewed as less evil than a person who kills for 10 dollars. And a person who kills someone in self-defense, in order to avoid being killed him- or herself, may not be viewed as evil at all. We propose that psychological mechanisms evolved to recognize other individuals who inflict great costs for relatively little gain. Categorization of such individuals as evil would serve the important adaptive function of helping to avoid becoming a victim of heavy costs.

The *intent* to do harm is an integral part of the definition of evil (Weiner & Simpson, 1989). It is not enough that some entity is costly to one's fitness. The entity must desire, or be perceived to desire, to inflict those costs. Over our evolutionary history, some entities would have been more recurrently associated with cost-inflicting events than others. Based on recurrent evolutionary experiences with cost-inflicting entities, the perception of desire to inflict costs likely evolved to be greater for some entities than others. It makes evolutionary sense that those entities that recurrently exhibited a closer causal relationship between their behavior and the infliction of costs would be perceived as more desirous of inflicting those costs and hence more evil. Snakes, for example, should be considered to be more evil than flowers (Mineka, 1992). And other humans (Buss & Duntley, 2003) can be considered the most evil entities of all. In the United States, homicide is among the top four leading causes of death for people between the ages of 1 and 44 (National Center for Health Statistics, 2002). The other causes of death include disease, accidents, and suicide. Of all causes of death, homicide is the only one with a directly and recurrently identifiable causal agent: another human. Over evolutionary time, this trend would have contributed to the evolution of a perception of other humans as potentially evil. However, the recurrent association of other humans with cost-inflicting behaviors, such as homicide, was not the only factor that must have contributed to the evolution of our perceptions of evil. Uncertainty about the intentions of others also would have played an important role.

There is a degree of uncertainty associated with all of our interactions with other humans. What does the other person hope to gain from this interaction? How much does he or she stand to lose as a result of this interaction? Over the history of our species, our ancestors would have had imperfect knowledge of the important factors associated with determining the likely costs and benefits of an interaction. They would have chosen specifically to engage in interactions that were likely to yield the greatest benefit at the lowest cost. Prior experience with an individual would have been among the most accurate ways of determining whether an interaction would be beneficial or costly, whether the intentions of another individual were good or evil. In the absence of prior experience, how would our ancestors have determined the intentions of others?

Error management theory (Haselton & Buss, 2000) proposes that humans evolved strategic cognitive biases that lead them to avoid high costs and not overlook significant benefits when making decisions under conditions of uncertainty. For example, men, but not women, have been shown to overperceive the sexual interest of a member of the opposite sex who acts friendly toward them (Haselton, 2002). This bias functions to decrease the likelihood that a man will overlook a situation where a significant boost to his fitness may be achieved.

A lifelong apprehensiveness or anxiety about the intentions of strangers, particularly men who are unknown, may be a cognitive bias that evolved to protect us from individuals who may want to inflict costs upon us for their own gain. The ancestral costs of assuming that an unknown male had beneficent intentions when, in fact, he intended to inflict harm would have been great. These costs would have provided selection pressure for the evolution of cognitive biases to assume that unknown individuals, particularly men who are more likely to inflict costs, had hostile intentions. In tribal societies, it is not uncommon that an approaching unknown adult male is intent on inflicting costs (Chagnon, 1983).

Some researchers have argued that our psychology of stereotyping may be an adaptive, energy-saving device (Macrae, Milne, & Bodenhausen, 1994). We propose that stereotyping may be adaptive by helping to make judgments under conditions of uncertainty. In the absence of other sources of information, a stereotype of another individual, though not completely accurate, would be better than no information at all in making decisions about how to interact with that person. Selection would have favored the evolution of stereotyping as a buffer against uncertainty if it provided individuals with an advantage in avoiding hostile conspecifics. Stereotyping would have evolved to help avoid heavy costs even at the price of missing out on some potentially beneficial interactions. The fact that most stereotypes are negative suggests that they are patterned in our psychology by evolved mechanisms designed to avoid some of the potentially heavy costs of interacting with unknown individuals.

PRINCIPLED PERSPECTIVE SHIFTS IN EVIL BASED ON FITNESS CONFLICTS

It should be clear from the preceding discussion that categorizations of good and evil hinge heavily on the perspective of the victim versus the perpetrator—a point that has been made by others (e.g., Baumeister, 1997). An evolutionary account, however, renders this intuitively obvious point a great deal more precise. In order to understand why, it is necessary to highlight the different levels of evolutionary analysis, and the precise ways in which perspectives on evil may shift predictably.

Consider a woman who is pregnant. She is young and has many potential reproductive years ahead of her. However, she is unmarried, lacks extended kin in close proximity, and lives in a nutritionally impoverished environment. In these and other circumstances, women often "spontaneously" abort the growing fetus. From the fetus's perspective, however, this is its only shot at life, which sets the stage for mother–fetus conflict (Haig, 1993). What is in the best fitness interests of the fetus (being born) differs fundamentally from what is in the best fitness interests of the incipient mother (aborting the fetus). A large body of evidence points to the co-evolution of adaptations in both mother and fetus to deal with this conflict. The perpetual arms race produces adaptations that may damage the mother (e.g., by producing hypertension). The key point is that what we often view as a harmonious relationship of self-evident unity of interests—mother and growing child—is actually fraught with evolutionary conflict. In this example, of course, neither the growing fetus nor the mother typically categorize the other as evil. But the disharmony between mother and fetus demonstrates that conflicts permeate all relationships from the moment of conception.

Although selection is generally regarded as operating in the strongest manner at the genic level, it can play out at many levels of analysis. What is good for a particular gene in the currency of fitness may be bad for the other genes in an individual's genotype, resulting in the phenomenon known as *intragenomic conflict* (e.g., Cosmides & Tooby, 1981). Furthermore, what is good for the genes of an individual can be bad for the genes of other individuals, leading to conflict between conspecifics. What is good for one intrasexual competitor (e.g., ascending in status) might be bad for another (e.g., being supplanted in the status hierarchy). What is good for one woman, such as mating with a highly desirable man, inevitably entails inflicting costs on intrasexual competitors who lose out and fail to obtain this particular mate. What is good for a man (e.g., obtaining sexual access to a woman through deception) might be bad for the woman (e.g., suffering damage to her reputation or other consequences of being deceived). What is good for one kinship group might be bad for another. What is good for one coalition of individuals might be bad for another. And, what is good for one species (e.g., surviving through predation) might be bad for another species (e.g., those preyed upon).

In sum, evolutionary psychology adds theoretical precision to the intuitively grasped perspective differences that characterize victims and perpetrators of horrendous deeds by yielding a precise analysis of the specific forms that conflict takes.

THE EXPLOITATION OF EVIL

Once psychological mechanisms have evolved to place other individuals into the cognitive category of "evil," these mechanisms can be exploited by others for their own purposes. People often exploit these mechanisms in order to forge alliances designed to inflict costs on competing individuals or groups. Just as President George W. Bush used the label "axis of evil" in an effort to forge alliances with other groups, Osama bin Laden labeled the United States "evil" in order to forge Arab alliances with other groups and to motivate and justify the infliction of massive fitness costs on Americans.

Stated differently, once the cognitive category of evil exists, it can be exploited by individuals or groups to justify the perpetration of massive fitness costs on their enemies. The exploitation of labeling others as evil operates in several ways: (1) it motivates others to join in, amplifying the fitness damage inflicted on enemies; (2) it decreases the overall costs of pursuing a strategy of inflicting such damage because the larger coalition renders success more likely and defeat less likely; and (3) it justifies to nonparticipants the validity of inflicting costs, thus lowering the odds that nonparticipants will ally with the victims.

The universal category of evil can be exploited in another way. Some individuals actively cultivate a reputation as evil to exploit and avoid being exploited by others. In the Iraqi regime of Saddam Hussein, dissenters were often killed, decreasing the likelihood of challenges to Hussein's power. These actions may be regarded as attempting to exploit the evolved psychological mechanisms in others that perceive evil in order to achieve particular ends.

Richard Dawkins notes that religion can be used as a vehicle to promote evil: "My point is not that religion itself is the motivation of wars, murders, and terrorist attacks, but that religion is the principal label, and the most dangerous one, by which 'they' as opposed to 'we' can be identified at all" (Dawkins, 2003, p. 158). Whether one subscribes to a particular belief system or not, religion is a pervasive feature of human experience. Some have pointed out that it appears as though our minds were prepared for religion by evolution (Boyer, 2001). This may be the case, but it is more likely to have occurred in a different sequence: The ideas that comprise the most popular religions exist in the form that they do because they appeal to different psychological adaptations—adaptations that evolved to solve particular ancestral problems. One problem religion helps to solve is the identification of social allies and social enemies (Dawkins, 2003). Another is establishing and maintaining group solidarity. When there is competition between groups for some tangible resource, combined with powerfully reinforced religious beliefs that life has no end, psychological adaptations that embrace religious belief systems may contribute to misguided, cost-inflicting acts toward other groups who are perceived to be evil.

THE EVOLUTION OF GOOD

Although this chapter focuses primarily on the evolution of evil, a few words can be said about the evolution of good. At one level of analysis, many of the arguments made for the evolution of evil can simply be reversed for the evolution of good. That is, people evaluate "good" when fitness benefits are delivered or received. The magnitude of the fitness benefits is predicted to be highly correlated with judgments of good—an altruistic gift of a house or car would be judged to be more "good" than an altruistic gift of a candy bar. As in the evolution of evil, perspective matters greatly in evaluating good. People who deliver fitness-relevant benefits to oneself, one's children, other genetic relatives, friends, and coalitional allies are "good." People who deliver fitness benefits to one's enemies are "evil."

Just as humans have evolved adaptations to inflict costs on other humans, we have also evolved adaptations to bestow benefits. Evolutionary psychologists have explored three classes of benefit-bestowing mechanisms: (1) altruism delivered to genetic relatives (e.g., Burnstein, Crandall, & Kitayama, 1994); (2) reciprocal altruism delivered among friends or allies (e.g., Bleske & Buss, 2001); and (3) benefit-delivering mechanisms that do not involve kin altruism or reciprocal altruism and in which the giver does not incur a cost to deliver a benefit (e.g., Tooby & Cosmides, 1996). Parents sometimes sacrifice their own lives so that their children may live, an example of kin altruism. Friends bestow resources on each other, an example of reciprocal altruism. If I give you a ride to school when I am already going there anyway, I deliver a benefit to you without incurring a cost to myself. Evolution by selection has undoubtedly fashioned many benefit-bestowing adaptations in humans.

At another level, the things we tend to single out as especially deserving of the label "good" involve bestowing benefits at a great cost to oneself, *without any apparent return benefit*. Thus, the soldier who throws himself on a grenade to save his buddies, Mother Teresa's devotion to helping others, the bystander who risks his life to save a stranger from drowning—these are all categorized as good and noble deeds. Indeed, it is precisely when there appear to be *no* return benefits to self, kin, or friends that we are especially prone to label a deed as admirable. The parent who donates $100,000 to her child's college education is not deemed as good as the person who makes the same donation to an impoverished stranger's child. When a beneficent deed benefits self, kin, or allies, we tend to "discount" the amount of good we attribute to the person performing it. Thus, the evolutionary analysis of "good" is not strictly the mirror image of the evolutionary analysis of evil.

People undoubtedly exploit and manipulate perceptions of "good," just as they exploit and manipulate perceptions of "evil." Thus, we expect that people will sometimes put "spin" on their delivery of benefits to others, presenting their actions as more altruistic and less self-serving than they actually may be. Conversely, others may attempt to publicly discount apparent acts of good by pointing to some hidden benefit the giver is receiving. Indeed, many acts of apparent self-sacrifice turn out to have hidden benefits to the bestower, complicating the analysis even further. Soldiers wounded in war fighting for "freedom" or "their country" often receive large boosts in prestige and social reputation through metals of valor. Women find these highly "altruistic" men to be especially attractive, and so the wounded soldier benefits in mating currency. Even the suicide bombers who commit acts regarded by their group as highly "good" receive benefits through "martyr" status and resources bestowed on their families.

In sum, an evolutionary analysis of "good" can be expected to shed much light on how people deliver benefits to others and manipulate the perceptions of others around the delivery of those benefits. Although these brief comments cannot do this complex topic justice, they suggest a few lines along which inquiry might proceed.

A COMPARISON OF THEORETICAL PERSPECTIVES ON EVIL

The use of violence against another person or group, particularly if it is perceived as unjustified, is undoubtedly the category of actions most likely to be viewed as evil (Anderson & Carnagey, Chapter 8; Baumeister & Vohs, Chapter 4, this volume). Violence is typically viewed as "not an effective way to get what one wants" (Baumeister & Vohs, Chapter 4, this volume). In response to the question "Why is there evil?", Baumeister proposes that evil stems fundamentally from a failure of self-control, an inability to stifle aggressive impulses. Our theory of the evolution of evil suggests that these formulations of evil are fundamentally incorrect.

First, let's consider the contention that violence is not an effective way to get what one wants (Baumeister & Vohs, Chapter 4, this volume). Citing the possibility that violent or aggressive strategies can result in prison sentences or other costs is beside the point from an evolutionary perspective. The key issue is whether selection has favored the contingent use of violence in some circumstances—whether the benefits of violence outweighed the costs, *on average,* relative to other strategic solutions over the sample space of relevant instances in the evolutionary past. Most social scientists, innocent of the logic of the evolutionary process, have intuitions that are wide off the mark when it comes to evaluating whether a particular strategy is "beneficial" or not. Selection, for example, can favor a strategy such as homicide, even if that strategy sometimes results in the strategist getting killed or imprisoned. The logic of this seemingly counterintuitive argument becomes clear when one realizes that selection operates *not* on whether a particular strategy is effective *in every instance,* but rather on whether the benefits of the strategy outweigh the costs, on average, across the entire sample space of instances in which it is deployed (relative to competing designs present in the population at the time). Thus, selection can produce adaptations that result in many instances of failure—bullies who sometimes get beaten up, thieves who sometimes get caught, cheaters who sometimes get ostracized, and killers who sometimes get killed. However, if the net fitness benefits outweighed the net fitness costs of these adaptations for evil, relative to competing designs, then selection will favor their evolution, eventually making them fundamental components of human nature.

Second, consider the argument that evil stems from an inability to control one's impulses (Baumeister & Vohs, Chapter 4, this volume). Our theory of the evolution of evil suggests an alternative explanation: that humans have evolved adaptations "designed" to solve certain adaptive problems in certain circumstances with behavior that appears "impulsive." Effective strategies sometimes require immediate action. Ponderous time delays and real-time extended reflection would result in failure. Stated differently, we propose that "impulsivity" is actually a design feature of certain adaptations that promotes their tactical effectiveness. The fact that they appear to external observers to be products of the lack of judicious reflection may speak to the profound inability of human intuitions to grasp the logic of evolved design, or to our moral judgments that classify certain strategies as good or bad. Speedy, immediate, real-time responses can be the product of adaptive design rather than "mechanism failure."

PRACTICAL IMPLICATIONS: FLEXIBILITY, TRACTABILITY, RESPONSIBILITY, AND MORALITY

Evolutionary psychology is a scientific discipline devoted to understanding the human mind and behavior, guided by a variety of evolutionarily based theories, hypotheses, and predictions. As a scientific discipline, it is concerned with description, explanation, and understanding, *not* with prescription, recommendation, or policymaking. Nonetheless, because evolutionary psychology is so often mischaracterized and misunderstood (e.g., Rose & Rose, 2000), it is worthwhile dispelling what we anticipate might be some common misconceptions based on our analysis.

At a broad level of analysis, evolutionary psychology envisions the human mind as consisting of a large collection of complex and interrelated mechanisms whose activation (or nonactivation) is highly contingent on specific forms of environmental and endogenous input. Just as callus-producing adaptations are activated only upon the receipt of environmental friction to the skin, psychological adaptations are activated only upon the receipt of certain forms of input. Male sexual jealousy, for example, is not an invariant "biological instinct" that wells up regardless of circumstances. Instead, jealousy is activated only by highly circumscribed input, such as the perception of cues to a mate's infidelity, the threat of mate poachers, or the opening of a discrepancy in the relative "mate values" of the members of a couple (Buss, 2000). Similarly, all of the actions judged to be "good" or "evil" are hypothesized to be the output resulting from the activation of evolved psychological mechanisms by specific forms of environmental, social, or endogenous input.

Human behavioral flexibility results from the functioning of a large number of psychological mechanisms, and their complexity, their interrelatedness, and their dependence on activation from various forms of input. Humans are not lumbering robots insensitive to context. Rather, adaptations arise precisely to deal with varying contexts, or in the language of evolutionary psychology, the different adaptive problems and contingencies an individual confronts over time. In short, an evolutionary analysis does not, and should not, lead to the erroneous view that human behavior is inevitable or intractable. Indeed, the greater the knowledge we have about our evolved psychological mechanisms and the contexts that trigger their activation, the greater will be our power to effect change in the domains where change is deemed desirable.

This point becomes especially important because when evolutionary analysis is seen as dooming us to inevitable courses of action and a pessimistic fate: "If evil has its foundation in evolved psychological mechanisms," this concern is sometimes expressed, "then we cannot hold people responsible for their actions; we are doomed to a pessimistic view of human nature; we cannot judge their actions to be morally wrong" (Rose & Rose, 2000).

This concern reflects several related misunderstandings. First, people can be held responsible for their actions; in fact, holding people responsible is one of the critical forms of environmental input that can be used to deter people from committing deeds we consider to be "evil." Nothing in an evolutionary analysis implies that people cannot be held responsible for their actions. Second, standards of morality themselves have a foundation in evolved psychological mechanisms—for example, the evolved moral emotions of *disgust, moralistic anger,* and *contempt* (Haidt, 2000; see Buss, 2004, for a review). Expressed moral emotions become part of the social input that can deter the adoption of certain actions people judge to be evil or wrong. Third, an evolutionary psychological analysis does not condone any actions—to do so would be to confuse what "is" with what "ought" to be, or the naturalistic fallacy, as it is commonly known. Many phenomena exist "in nature" that we do not condone and, in fact, try to eradicate—diseases and infant mortality, for example. In the same way, we may wish to eradicate the activation of certain evolved psychological mechanisms, such as those involved in motivating homicide and genocide.

Finally, it is important to avoid what has been called "the anti-naturalistic fallacy" or "the romantic fallacy"—the confusion of what one wants to be true with what is true. Many people cherish a view of human nature that is fundamentally kind and good, with acts of evil attributed to the ills of modern society, capitalism, or "the partriarchy." In the words of one anthropologist, "We have never quite outgrown the idea that some-where, there are people living in perfect harmony with nature and one an-other, and that we might do the same were it not for the corrupting influ-ences of Western culture" (Konner, 1990, p. 155). We may want human nature to be fundamentally good and free of evil, but that utopian view should not lead us to commit the romantic fallacy and confuse what ought to be with what really is.

According to our evolutionary analysis, human nature includes adap-tations to bestow benefits and adaptations to inflict costs on others, some-times massive costs such as killing. We have the capacity for good and evil. Only through deeper knowledge of our evolved psychology can we acquire the tools to deter the expression of the more pernicious components of human nature.

CONCLUSIONS

Our theoretical framework for the evolution of evil contains several key premises that make it unique among theories of evil. First, humans have evolved adaptations designed to harm other individuals in ways both small and large. In addition to whatever adaptations humans have evolved to de-liver benefits to particular others (and these are many in number—see Buss, 2004, for a recent summary), humans have also evolved adaptations to lie, cheat, steal, maim, and murder. The harm-inflicting adaptations are fundamental and universal components of human nature and cannot be at-tributed to the particulars of media, parents, teachers, capitalism, or cul-ture. Whether these harm-inflicting adaptations are expressed in manifest behavior is highly contingent on particulars of the social and physical envi-ronment—contingencies that are themselves essential components of the design of the adaptations.

Second, those harm-inflicting phenomena that are especially costly in fitness currencies, when inflicted intentionally, are those that humans tend to label as "evil." Certain types of killing are prototypical examples of evil—killings that are intentional, unprovoked, and inflict massive fitness costs on the victim.

Third, because humans have been victims of harm-producing adapta-tions in others, they have evolved defenses to prevent incurring these costs. Stranger anxiety, specific kinds of fears, stereotyping, xenophobia, cheater-detection, ostracism, and other anti-homicide mechanisms are but a few examples of these evolved defenses. We propose that many co-evolutionary arms races have been set into motion, as illustrated in Figure 5.1: Adaptations to inflict harm evolve to become more sophisticated and context-contingent to counter adaptations designed to defend against harm. Many of these coevolutionary arms races are perpetual, with no stable equilibrium.

Fourth, humans have evolved special cognitive mechanisms designed to categorize some phenomena as "good" and other phenomena as "evil." These cognitive mechanisms function to identify specific humans who intend, or are likely, to inflict massive costs on an individual. Intentionality is central. An entity that accidentally delivers massive harm is not considered "evil," nor is one that unintentionally delivers benefits considered "good."

Fifth, evolutionary psychology provides a principled, theoretical framework for adding precision to the intuition that "evil" depends critically on perspective. Precise perspective shifts are predicted to occur according to who is delivering the costs and who is the unfortunate victim of the costs. We predict that degree of genetic relatedness between the perpetrator and victim, for example, will strongly affect judgments of good and evil—a prediction not rendered by any other theory of good and evil.

All organisms that perceive can be deceived (Dawkins & Krebs, 1978). The psychological machinery of an organism potentially can be exploited for purposes that are contrary to the organism's fitness interests. Just as fishermen can use lures to exploit the sense organs of fish, psychopaths can exploit the cooperative mechanisms of their victims. Once a psychology of evil evolved, it became possible for other humans to exploit it in the service of their own ends. Invoking "evil" in other individuals or groups is often a psychological manipulation designed to enlist coalitional support for inflicting massive costs on the individual or group so labeled.

The theoretical framework for understanding "evil" proposed in this chapter contains many premises and predictions that are highly testable—predictions not generated by any other theory of evil. Understanding *why* people inflict massive costs on others requires understanding the underlying psychological mechanisms involved in the perpetration of these acts. Evolutionary psychology generally, and the coevolutionary arms races proposed here specifically, provide a cogent conceptual framework for understanding why these psychological mechanisms evolved, why humans have evolved defenses against them, and why the potential for evil resides within all of us today.

REFERENCES

Baumeister, R. F. (1997). *Evil: Inside human violence and cruelty*. New York: Freeman.

Bleske, A. L., & Buss, D. M. (2001). Opposite sex friendship: Sex differences and similarities in initiation, selection, and dissolution. *Personality and Social Psychology Bulletin, 27*, 1310–1323.

Boyer, P. (2001). *Religion explained*. New York: Basic Books.

Burnstein, E., Crandall, C., & Kitayama, S. (1994). Some neo-Darwinian decision rules for altruism: Weighing cures for inclusive fitness as a function of the biological importance of the decision. *Journal of Personality and Social Psychology, 67,* 773–789.

Buss, D. M. (1988). The evolution of human intrasexual competition: Tactics of mate attraction. *Journal of Personality and Social Psychology, 54,* 616–628.

Buss, D. M. (1989). Conflict between the sexes: Strategic interference and the evocation of anger and upset. *Journal of Personality and Social Psychology, 56,* 735–747.

Buss, D. M. (1996). The evolutionary psychology of human social strategies. In E. T. Higgins & A. W. Kruglanski (Eds.), *Social psychology: Handbook of basic principles* (pp. 3–38). New York: Guilford Press.

Buss, D. M. (2000). *The dangerous passion: Why jealousy is as necessary as love and sex.* New York: Free Press.

Buss, D. M. (2004). *Evolutionary psychology: The new science of the mind* (2nd ed.). Boston: Allyn & Bacon.

Buss, D. M., & Dedden, L. A. (1990). Derogation of competitors. *Journal of Social and Personal Relationships, 7,* 395–422.

Buss, D. M., & Duntley, J. D. (1998, July 10). *Evolved homicide modules.* Paper presented at the annual meeting of the Human Behavior and Evolution Society, Davis, CA.

Buss, D. M., & Duntley, J. D. (2003). Adaptations for murder: The evolution of homicide. *Behavioral and Brain Sciences.* Manuscript under review.

Chagnon, N. A. (1988). Life histories, blood revenge, and warfare in tribal population. *Science, 239,* 985–992.

Cosmides, L., & Tooby, J. (1981). Cytoplasmic inheritance and intragenomic conflict. *Journal of Theoretical Biology, 89,* 83–129.

Daly, M., & Wilson, M. (1998). *The truth about Cinderella: A Darwinian view of parental love.* London: Weidenfeld & Nicolson.

Dawkins, R. (2003). *A devil's chaplain: Reflections on hope, lies, science, and love.* New York: Houghton Mifflin.

Dawkins, R., & Krebs, J. R. (1978). Animal signals: Information or manipulation. In J. R. Krebs & N. B. Davies (Eds.), *Behavioural ecology: An evolutionary approach* (pp. 282–309). Oxford, UK: Blackwell Scientific.

Duntley, J. D., & Buss, D. M. (1998, July 10). *Evolved anti-homicide modules.* Paper presented at the annual meeting of the Human Behavior and Evolution Society, Davis, CA.

Duntley, J. D., & Buss, D. M. (2003). *The evolutionary psychology of anti-homicide: Adaptations to prevent being killed.* Manuscript under review.

Ghiglieri, M. P. (1999). *The dark side of man.* Reading, MA: Perseus Books.

Haidt, J. (2001). The emotional dog and its rational tail: A social intuitionist approach to moral judgment. *Psychological Review, 108,* 814–834.

Haig, D. (1993). Genetic conflicts in human pregnancy. *Quarterly Review of Biology, 68,* 495–532.

Hamilton, W. D. (1964). The genetical evolution of social behavior: I and II. *Journal of Theoretical Biology, 7,* 1–52.

Haselton, M. G. (2002). The sexual overperception bias: Evidence of a systematic bias in men from a survey of naturally occurring events. *Journal of Research in Personality, 37,* 34–47.

Haselton, M. G., & Buss, D. M. (2000). Error management theory: A new perspective on biases in cross-sex mind reading. *Journal of Personality and Social Psychology, 78,* 81–91.

Heerwagen, J. H., & Orians, G. H. (2002). The ecological world of children. In P. H. Kahn, Jr., & S. R. Kellert (Eds.), *Children and nature: Psychological, sociocultural, and evolutionary investigations* (pp. 29–64). Cambridge, MA: MIT Press.

Konner, M. (1990). *Why the reckless survive.* New York: Viking.

Marks, I. M. (1987). *Fears, phobias, and rituals: Panic, anxiety, and their disorders.* New York: Oxford University Press.

Marks, I. M., & Nesse, R. M. (1994). Fear and fitness: An evolutionary analysis of anxiety disorders. *Ethology and Sociobiology, 15,* 247–261.

Macrae, C. N., Milne, A. B., & Bodenhausen, G. V. (1994). Stereotypes as energy-saving devices: A peek inside the cognitive toolbox. *Journal of Personality and Social Psychology, 66,* 37–47.

Mineka, S. (1992). Evolutionary memories, emotional processing, and the emotional disorders. *Psychology of Learning and Motivation, 28,* 161–206.

Mitchell, B. A., Wister, A. V., & Burch, T. K. (1989). The family environment and leaving the parental home. *Journal of Marriage and the Family, 51,* 605–613.

National Center for Health Statistics (NCHS). (2002). *Atlas of United States mortality* [Online]. Available at: *http://www.cdc.gov/nchs/products/pubs/pubd/other/atlas/atlas.htm*

Rose, H., & Rose, S. (2000). *Alas poor Darwin: Arguments against evolutionary psychology.* New York: Harmony Books.

Schmitt, D. P., & Buss, D. M. (1996). Strategic self-promotion and competitor derogation: Sex and context effects on perceived effectiveness of mate attraction tactics. *Journal of Personality and Social Psychology, 70,* 1185–1204.

Tooby, J., & Cosmides, L. (1996). Friendship and the banker's paradox: Other pathways to the evolution of adaptations for altruism. *Proceedings of the British Academy, 88,* 119–143.

Weiner, E. S., & Simpson, J. A. (Eds.). (1989). *Oxford English dictionary.* Oxford, UK: Oxford University Press.

PART II

HARMING OTHERS: CONTEXTS, CAUSES, AND IMPLICATIONS

CHAPTER 6

WHAT'S IN A CATEGORY?

Responsibility, Intent, and the Avoidability of Bias against Outgroups

SUSAN T. FISKE

When I teach the psychology of racism—a course I have now taught over half-a-dozen times at two universities—a predictable low point occurs every semester. About halfway through the course, after we have covered the latest research on the social cognitive origins of bias, everyone in the course becomes profoundly discouraged and even depressed. If they could, they would give up and go home. But this is a university course, so they continue, partly to avoid the *W* on their transcript, partly out of curiosity to see how much worse it can get, and partly because I urge them to stay tuned because the news eventually gets better. What is so unpleasant about discovering the psychology of bias? It is not the focus on a few really bad apples—the ones who make the national news for unspeakable outgroup murders. It is not learning about the 10% of the population that harbors extreme, bigoted views, consistent with the views of people who go on to commit hate crimes. We all know about them from newspaper and television reports. But what is the news from academia, and why does it depress my students?

THE LATEST NEWS FROM BIAS RESEARCH

By some counts, 80% of the populations of Western democracies harbor benign intentions about intergroup relations but display subtle forms of bias. Subtle forms of bias are automatic, unconscious, and unintentional;

cool, indirect, and ambiguous; and often ambivalent. The implication of these subtle forms of bias is that people—observers and actors alike—cannot so easily detect, name, and control them. They escape notice, even the notice of those enacting the biases. Does that detection difficulty remove responsibility from the individual? But we are getting ahead of ourselves. First, the news.

Automatic, Unconscious, and Unintentional Bias

By far the biggest news in the last decade of research on bias is how underground it can be (Dovidio & Gaertner, 1986). Automaticity characterizes stereotypes, prejudice, and associated behavior. Sparked by findings that racial category labels can prime stereotypes, as indicated by more rapid accessibility and by studies suggesting that even relatively unprejudiced people have automatic stereotypic associations, scores of studies now support the essentially automatic aspect of stereotyping (Fiske, 1998, 2000; Macrae & Bodenhausen, 2000). For example, lexical decision tasks show that even subliminally presented outgroup category labels can activate stereotypically associated terms. That is, when people have to decide rapidly whether a series of letter strings (*apple, prebam, white, carnup*) are words or nonwords, they respond more rapidly to stereotypic words (*athlete*) when primed with a category label (*black*), even below awareness. In a more affective vein, outgroup category exemplars (such as outgroup faces or stereotypically ethnic names) easily activate negative evaluative terms.

Recent related work on brain imaging shows amygdala activation in response to pictures of unfamiliar outgroup faces, indicating what may be primitive emotional prejudices (Hart et al., 2000; Phelps et al., 2000). Furthermore, automatic activation of outgroup categories leads to behavior stereotypically associated with that group. The apparent automaticity of such biases corroborates Gordon Allport's (1954) provocative early insights about the inevitability of categorization. It also shocks well-intentioned people who prefer to consider prejudices as conscious and controllable (and therefore a tendency they could suppress).

Cool, Indirect, and Ambiguous Bias

The biases of the moderate, well-intentioned majority not only live underground, they also wear camouflage. It turns out that people's biases reflect ingroup comfort at least as much as outgroup discomfort, so derogation is less an issue than is simple neglect. For example, bias often consists in refusing positive emotions toward outgroups (Pettigrew, 1998a). Moderates rarely express open hostility toward outgroups, but they may withhold basic liking and respect; hence, their responses represent cool neglect. People more rapidly assign positive attributes to the ingroup than the outgroup (negative attributes often show a weaker, or even no, difference; Fiske, 1998). People withhold rewards from the outgroup, relative to the ingroup, reflecting ingroup favoritism (Brewer & Brown, 1998). They do not punish or derogate the outgroup but simply fail to share positive outcomes. The damage, thus, is relative and indirect.

Biases are indirect in other ways associated with norms for appropriate responses. If the situational norms do allow biases, they flourish. Biases appear most often when people have unprejudiced excuses for their apparent biases. If some people exercise neglect, then everyone else also avoids contact with the outgroup. If an outgroup member behaves poorly, providing an excuse for prejudice, the resulting exclusion is swifter and surer than it would be for a comparable ingroup member. Biases also appear in shared political policy preferences, whereby one might have principled reasons (excuses) for one's opinion, but one also just happens to have a whole series of policy preferences that all disadvantage the outgroup relative to the ingroup. Excuses for bias fulfill the social norm requiring rational, fair judgments, but controlled comparisons reveal greater bias toward outgroup than toward comparable ingroup members (Fiske, 1998).

People also engage in attributional "tricks" that discourage sympathy by blaming outgroups for their own unfortunate outcomes: Outgroups should try harder, but at the same time, they should not push themselves where they are not wanted (a Catch-22). For example, modern prejudice scales include items reflecting both perceived laziness and perceived intrusiveness (Pettigrew, 1998b).

The blame goes further than perceived lack of effort. Whereas ingroup members might be excused for their failures (due to extenuating circumstances), the outgroup members brought it on themselves (due to their unfortunate dispositions). People often attribute outgroups' perceived failings to their essence: some innate, inherent, enduring attribute, perhaps biological, that makes up the core of the category's distinctiveness.

In trying to make sense of outgroup category members, people exaggerate cultural differences (e.g., in ability, language, religious beliefs, sexual practices). The mere fact of categorizing people into "us" and "them," ingroup and outgroup, tends to exaggerate intercategory differences and diminish intracategory differences. In a nutshell: "They are all alike and different from us, besides." In all these ways, the bias of moderates is cool, indirect, and ambiguous.

Ambivalent and Mixed Bias

Besides being underground and camouflaged, people's biases are often complex. For example, moderate whites' ambivalent racism entails a mix of sympathy ("pro-black") and anti-black sentiment, which can tip over to a predominantly positive or negative response, depending on circumstances. In this view, blacks are both deviant (for allegedly not trying hard enough) and disadvantaged (given the reality of discrimination). As another example, ambivalent sexism demonstrates two correlated dimensions that differentiate hostile sexism (directed primarily toward nontraditional women) and subjectively benevolent sexism (directed primarily toward traditional women). In both cases, ambivalence indicates mixed forms of prejudice more subtle than unmitigated hostility (Fiske, 1998).

Mixed forms of bias turn out to be the rule, rather than the exception. We find that, although various outgroups all are classified as "them," the outgroups fall into different clusters (see Figure 6.1). Some elicit relatively less respect, and some elicit relatively less liking. That is, not only is the bias of well-intentioned moderates of the cool variety (withholding the positive, rather than assigning the negative), it is not even uniformly lacking in positive views. Specifically, some outgroups (e.g., Asians, Jews, career women, black professionals, rich people) are envied and respected for their perceived competence and high status, but they are resented and disliked as lacking in warmth because they compete with the ingroup. Other outgroups (e.g., older people, disabled people, housewives) are pitied and disrespected for their perceived incompetence and low status, but they are nurtured and liked as being warm because they do not threaten the

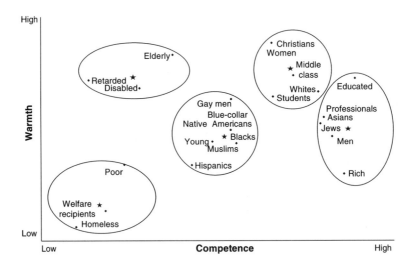

FIGURE 6.1. A map of group stereotypes along dimensions of competence and warmth, showing groups in areas high on one dimension but low on the other. From Fiske, Cuddy, Glick, and Xu (2003). Copyright 2003 by the American Psychological Association. Reprinted by permission.

ingroup. Only a few outgroups (primarily poor people of any race) receive contempt, both dislike and disrespect, because they are simultaneously seen as low status and exploiting the ingroup.

The implication of the ambivalent and mixed form of bias is system justification. The subordinated, pitied groups have an incentive to cooperate because they receive care in return for not challenging the hierarchy. The dominant group maintains its relative advantage in status due to the position of the subordinated group. On the other hand, the envied, competitive groups have an incentive to support the system because they are perceived to be succeeding in it, even if they are socially excluded by the culturally dominant group. For the dominant group, respecting the envied group members acknowledges the ground rules for competition (which favor them also), but disliking them justifies their social exclusion.

Moderate Biases Predict Exclusion

Subtle forms of bias predict personal interactions that are pervaded by discomfort and anxiety (e.g., Heatherton, Kleck, Hebl, & Hull, 2000). Nonverbal indicators (e.g., distance, posture, tone of voice) and self-reports reveal interactions that are anything but smooth, mostly due to inexperience with the outgroup.

Moreover, people treat each other in ways that tend to confirm their biased expectations, leading both parties to maintain their distance. The self-fulfilling prophecy, expectancy effects, and behavioral confirmation all name related phenomena, whereby biased perceivers bring about the very behavior they anticipate, which is usually negative. All these interpersonal processes result in subsequent avoidance whenever people have any choice about the company they keep. Discretionary contact is minimized.

Furthermore, exclusion and avoidance extend to decisions about employment, housing, education, and justice, which tend to favor the ingroup and disadvantage the outgroup. Ample evidence indicates that relatively automatic, cool, indirect, ambiguous, and ambivalent biases permit allocation of resources to maintain ingroup advantage.

How Do Moderate Biases Originate?

Subtle prejudice emerges in response to people's internal conflict between ideals and biases, both acquired from the culture at large. People experience constant exposure to examples of bias in the media. At the same time, their direct, personal experience with outgroup members may be limited. Given substantial de facto residential and occupational segregation, most people lack experience in constructive intergroup interactions. The general media, then, supply their main sources of information about outgroups, so people easily develop unconscious associations and feelings that reinforce bias.

Nevertheless, the ideals of Western cultures tend to encourage tolerance of most outgroups. Complying with antiprejudice ideals requires a conscious endorsement of egalitarian norms against prejudice. Moderates also generally share personal values against prejudice.

The upshot is a conflict between relatively implicit, unconscious biases and explicit, conscious ideals to be unprejudiced. The internal conflict between biases and ideals tends to push awareness of the biases underground. The result is a "modern" form of prejudice that is subtle and aversive to the people that hold it.

Summary: The Dilemma

We have seen that people categorize each other automatically and unintentionally on the basis of race, gender, age, and other protected group memberships and, further, that stereotypes, prejudice, and discrimination tend to follow. Does a glimmer of hope suggest that, if properly motivated, people could move beyond their initial categorical reactions and respond to others as unique individuals? In other words, where does this analysis leave us in the quest to understand the moral implications of the newly discovered subtle biases?

NIGHTMARE ON OUR STREET: RESPONSIBILITY FOR BIASES

Until recently, these analyses would suggest that people are not responsible for their initial category-based reactions but are responsible only for what they do in response to their initial reactions. That is, if people cannot alter their impression formation processes that are launched along a trajectory guided by outgroup categories, then how can they possibly prevent themselves from responding in a biased manner? Precisely this issue was raised by Jones and colleagues (1984, p. 300): "Contemporary cognitive approaches to stereotyping . . . project a rather weary fatalism . . . [about] ingrained human proclivities." Hamilton (1979, p. 80) called the same problem "a rather depressing dilemma." This kind of concern was also described by Bargh (1999) in "The Cognitive Monster" this way:

> If it were indeed the case . . . that stereotyping occurs without an individual's awareness or intention, then the implications for society . . . were tremendously depressing. Most ominously, how could anyone be held responsible, legally or otherwise, for discriminatory or prejudicial behavior when psychological science had shown such effects to occur unintentionally? The legal profession has a term for such a dilemma: "the parade of horribles." (p. 363)

Legal Attributions of Responsibility

The responsibility dilemma is made explicit in legal settings, where discrimination is, by definition, intentional. The perpetrator must be demonstrated to have intended to disadvantage the protected group member(s). Unlawful discrimination has no category equivalent to involuntary manslaughter in the legal arena of murder.

The two legal standards for establishing discrimination both rely on intent. "Disparate treatment" discriminates against one group precisely because of race, gender, age, etc. (e.g., saying that one refuses to hire certain people because they are black would be the baldest example of this category). One might consider this behavior direct discrimination.

In contrast, "disparate impact" discrimination is indirect; it operates by way of a practice that appears neutral but has differential impact on a protected category (e.g., requiring all firefighters to be over 200 pounds would differentially impact women). In such a case the plaintiffs complain that the supposedly neutral practice is actually a pretext for excluding their category of people. If the defendants cannot demonstrate that the practice is, in fact, a business necessity, then the inference is made that it was indeed a pretext and that the defendant intended to discriminate.

The point here is that both types of discrimination assume intent. If one could show that all people universally operate on the basis of protected categories, and that they do so without intent or control (i.e., automatically), then perhaps one could argue that discrimination is an inevitable and blameless fact of social life.

This scenario gave me pause, more than once, when I served as an expert witness in discrimination cases. As I was educating the fact-finder (judge or jury) about the automaticity of ingroup–outgroup categorization and subsequent bias, I waited for the opposing attorney to demand how anyone could possibly be held responsible for intentional discrimination, according to the cognitive social account. At the time, I developed one psychological answer to this dilemma, the plaintiff's lawyers developed another, and the research community eventually generated a third.

Psychological Analysis of Intent

My original response to this dilemma was to examine closely the meaning of intent, according to lay, psychological, and legal definitions (Fiske, 1989). I found some agreement on three criteria for inferring intent, then applied those to the situation of perceiver bias. First, observers must agree that the perceiver had a *choice* between two modes of response. For example, most people would agree that one can hardly avoid flinching from touching an unexpectedly hot surface, even though one might choose, in an emergency, to grab a burning object in order to extinguish it. In social life, the equivalent perspective would argue that although people may feel uncomfortable around unfamiliar outgroup members, it is not a burning surface; they do have a choice about how they respond.

Corroborating this lay analysis, various psychological models argue for two modes of social cognition, one a more automatic form of response, and the other a more deliberate, thoughtful form of response (Chaiken & Trope, 1999). In impression formation specifically, I have argued that people's impression formation processes form a continuum, from relatively automatic, category-based processes to relatively thoughtful, individuated processes (Fiske, Lin, & Neuberg, 1999; Fiske & Neuberg, 1990). People have alternative modes available, so they have a choice.

The law makes a similar distinction between, for example, murder in self-defense (automatic) and premeditated murder (deliberate). Individuals are responsible for the latter but not for the former. Partly, this differentiation hinges on the idea that people have a choice in the latter case but not in the former one.

But the inference of intent in premeditated murder brings us to the second lay, psychological, and legal criterion for intent. People are more clearly acting with intention when they make the *hard choice*. The person who refuses to commit a murder, despite extreme provocation and strong impulse (e.g., in the moment of discovering one's spouse in flagrente delicto) is more obviously making a choice than the person who follows what is seen as a natural homicidal impulse. The person who grabs the burning object to extinguish it is attributed more intent than the person who flinches. In impression formation, the person who refuses to categorize but instead "individuates" another person, by gathering additional information and treating the person as unique, is acting with intent. The person who automatically categorizes another person, and acts accordingly, is less clearly acting with intent. Observers less often view impulse as fueled by intent; controlling the impulse is more clearly intentional.

The third criterion for inferring intent is *attention*. People are responsible for premeditated murder precisely because it involves deliberate thought and attention. Likewise, people are seen as deliberately controlling their individuation process because it requires attention and motivation. People have to gather information, consider it, synthesize it, and weigh it in the final impression; all that requires attention.

In summary, a psychological analysis of intent provides a basis in lay, legal, and social cognitive terms for inferring an individual's intent. Intent is clearest when the individual has a choice, makes the hard choice, and pays attention.

But what about meeting subsets of these criteria? What if a person has a choice and apparently makes the hard choice, but without thinking about it? A person who rushes into a burning building to save a child is widely acclaimed a hero—clearly having had a choice and having made the hard choice—though often the person reports doing it "without thinking." Nevertheless, we laud the person as responsible. What about a person who has a choice but makes the easy choice, although by thinking about it? An individual who follows an impulse to murder an unfaithful spouse, but does so after an interval of planning, is held more responsible than someone who does so in the passion of the moment. Similarly, what about an individual who (a) has an impulse to exclude an outgroup member (but demonstrably has a choice to either include or exclude), (b) thinks about it and justifies the exclusion (attention), and (c) acts accordingly (makes the easy choice)? That person would seem to be responsible for intentional action. What about the hardest case: An individual has an impulse to exclude the outgroup member (we know the person has a choice to follow or resist the impulse) but does not bother to think (no attention) and acts accordingly (makes the easy choice)? Perhaps we should have a category of involuntary but unlawful discrimination, slightly less egregious than premeditated discrimination. Drawing on the legal distinctions among types of murder, we could go from involuntary discrimination (like manslaughter, acting on impulse that greater control might have prevented) or negligent discrimination (like accidental homicide, acting in a thoughtless manner that attention might have prevented), up the levels to deliberate bigotry (like premeditated murder). The legal world has yet to adopt this theory, but they have devised another answer to the dilemma of individual responsibility in a world of relatively automatic bias.

Legal Analysis of Intent

Because people are motivated by social situations, organizations may be viewed as responsible for the actions of their individual members. The U.S. Supreme Court held, in a case in which I had served as an expert witness at the lower court level, that an organization acts as a body that cannot hold its employees to gender stereotypes (*Price Waterhouse v. Hopkins*, 1989): "We are beyond the day when an employer could evaluate employees by assuming or insisting that they matched the stereotype associated with their group" (p. 1790).

In another case in which I served as an expert witness (*Robinson v. Jacksonville Shipyards*, 1989), a Florida appeals court held that an organization knows—or should know—that its male employees are likely to act on sexually explicit materials (e.g., pin-up calendars in the workplace) in ways that sexually harass the female employees:

> Corporate defendant liability may be proved under one of two theories. Direct liability is incurred when an agent of the corporate employer is responsible for the behavior that comprises the hostile work environment, and the agent's actions were taken within the scope of the agency. . . . Indirect liabil-

ity attaches where the hostile environment is created by one who is not the plaintiff's employer, such as a coworker, or by an agent of the employer who is acting outside the scope of the agency, and the plaintiff can establish that the employer knew or should have known of the harassment and failed to take prompt, effective remedial action. (par. 25)

In addition to the attribution of intent to an organization, legal analyses complement psychological analyses in another manner. The Price Waterhouse decision is known in legal circles not for its relevance to organizational responsibility but for its relevance to the problem of mixed-motive discrimination. Suppose a decision is admittedly tainted by protected class membership (i.e., it took gender into account), but regardless, other factors (e.g., a difficult personality) would have denied the benefit (e.g., hiring, promotion) anyway. In a recent mixed-motive decision, the Supreme Court ruled that the burden of proof shifts to the defendant (i.e., employer). In other words, when the decision is tainted by a protected category (i.e., outgroup) membership, the decision maker is responsible for showing that prejudice was not the cause of the decision.

What is more, the Court recently ruled that indirect evidence (i.e., circumstantial evidence) of discriminatory animus is sufficient in a mixed-motive case wherein protected class membership is just one motivating factor in the decision. That is, an outgroup member does not necessarily need overt evidence of discriminatory intent but could use more subtle indicators, such as those described earlier as indicating modern forms of bias. In this case, Caesar's Palace employed the plaintiff as its only female warehouse worker. The company treated her less favorably than comparable men and also failed to protect her from a supervisor who stalked her. Notice that these actions are actually *failures* to act, consistent with subtle forms of discrimination in which people withhold benefits from outgroup members and neglect them, while benefiting the ingroup.

These legal analyses therefore address the intent issue in two ways that complement psychological analyses. First, they accept the concept of organizational responsibility, which would be outside the purview of a psychological analysis (because intent is attributed to a group and because moral responsibility is allocated; see Hamilton & Sanders, 1999). Second, the legal analyses complement psychological perspectives on intent by analyzing mixed-motives settings, in which both the category and individual attributes are in play. The results suggest suspicious motives whenever a group makes a decision tainted by category membership.

Recent Research on Intent

Earlier this section listed three possible answers to the automaticity dilemma: my initial analysis of intent, legal analyses of responsibility, and the recent research on automaticity and control. This third response to the question of automaticity—which so dismays well-intentioned people—comes from the same researchers whose work provoked the dilemma in the first place.

All is not lost for the well-intentioned. Recent evidence suggests that people's initial gut-level responses may be influenced by their frame of mind—that is, by their motivation. People do not inevitably activate and use their ingroup–outgroup categories. It depends on how overloaded and motivated they are, and it depends on their values and goals, as well as the nature of the information they confront.

In other words, category activation apparently is not *unconditionally* automatic. Although people can instantly identify another person's category membership (especially gender, race, and age), they may not always activate the associated stereotypic content, for example, under mental overload. People's long-term attitudes also can moderate access to biased associations: Lower levels of chronic prejudice can attenuate activation of stereotypes. And temporary processing goals matter as well: Category activation can depend on various short-term motivations, including relevance for self-enhancement and accurate understanding (Fiske, 2004).

Promising as they are, these findings remain controversial. For example, they may depend on the nature of the stimuli: Ease of category activation probably differs, depending on whether perceivers encounter verbal labels (easy), photographs (harder), or a real person (hardest). Some researchers believe that social categories inevitably activate associated biases, whereas others believe the activation depends entirely on short-term situational goals and long-term individual differences (Devine, 2001).

Whether bias is conditionally or unconditionally automatic, either way, people's long- and short-term motives *do* matter. If category activation is unconditionally automatic, less prejudiced perceivers still can override their automatic associations with subsequent controlled processes. If category activation is conditionally automatic, then people may be able to inhibit the biased associations in the first place.

Moreover, even if people do *activate* biases associated with a category, they may not *apply* (or use) those biases. For example, once the category is activated, other information may be consistent or inconsistent with it, and perceivers must decide what to do about the conflicting information. Inconsistency resolution and subsequent individuation of the other person require resources that are allocated according to the perceiver's motivation and capacity. Overriding category activation to avoid using the category depends on metacognitive decisions (i.e., reflecting on one's thinking patterns) and higher-level executive functions (i.e., deliberate control), not just on sheer brute attentional capacity. Other qualifications to the use of activated categories go beyond the perceiver's motivation and capacity: For example, category use depends on the nature of the stimuli (e.g., category abstractions are more likely to encourage assimilation, whereas exemplars encourage contrast) and the perceiver's theory about whether people's dispositions are fixed entities or flexible states (Fiske, 2004, chap. 4).

Inhibition of category activation and its application both turn out to challenge even the most determined moderate. Direct suppression sometimes causes only a rebound of the forbidden biases. Depending on cognitive capacity, practice, age, and motivation, people can suppress or inhibit many effects of social categories.

Indeed, we have recently found that even amygdala activation to cross-race faces vanishes when people adopt individuating goals (e.g., Would this person like broccoli?) or nonsocial goals (Is there a dot on this photograph?) (Wheeler & Fiske, 2001). The take-home message to lay people is: Bias is more automatic than you think but less automatic than we psychologists thought.

WHERE DOES THIS LEAVE THE RESPONSIBILITY FOR GOOD AND EVIL IN INTERGROUP PERCEPTIONS?

These analyses create a new set of criteria for attributing intent (and therefore responsibility) for biased responses. The recent research findings, in particular, take responsibility and situational pressures one step further back in the psychological processes of biased impression formation. Assume that right-thinking people want to avoid biases against people from other groups. People with the right values (e.g., egalitarianism), the right organizational incentives (e.g., cross-category teamwork), the right motivation (e.g., motivation to avoid prejudice), can, in fact, get beyond (sometimes even prevent) their automatic use of category-driven impression formation and decision making. People demonstrably have a choice and can choose the hard choice, if they pay sufficient attention.

This conclusion suggests legal and ethical implications for the unbiased treatment of others. Organizations can be educated to understand that people's initial impulse is to categorize others and to favor the ingroup. In response to this knowledge, organizations can structure their incentives so that people from different categories learn to work well together. Individuals can be accountable for their treatment of others. Interdependent teams can learn to work together. In each case, overriding the default response is key, and knowing that it is indeed the default response can help individuals and organizations take responsibility for treatment of underrepresented groups—for good or ill.

REFERENCES

Allport, G. (1954). *The nature of prejudice*. Reading MA: Addison-Wesley.
Bargh, J. A. (1999). The cognitive monster: The case against the controllability

of automatic stereotype effects. In S. Chaiken & Y. Trope (Eds.), *Dual-process theories in social psychology* (pp. 361–382). New York: Guilford Press.

Brewer, M. B., & Brown, R. J. (1998). Intergroup relations. In D. T. Gilbert, S. T. Fiske, & G. Lindzey (Eds.), *Handbook of social psychology* (4th ed., Vol. 2, pp. 554–594). New York: McGraw-Hill.

Chaiken, S., & Trope, Y. (Eds.). (1999). *Dual-process theories in social psychology.* New York: Guilford Press.

Devine, P. G. (2001). Implicit prejudice and stereotyping: How automatic are they? Introduction to the special section. *Journal of Personality and Social Psychology, 81,* 757–759.

Dovidio, J. F., & Gaertner, S. L. (Eds.) (1986). *Prejudice, discrimination, and racism.* San Diego, CA: Academic Press.

Fiske, S. T. (1989). Examining the role of intent: Toward understanding its role in stereotyping and prejudice. In J. S. Uleman & J. A. Bargh (Eds.), *Unintended thought* (pp. 253–283). New York: Guilford Press.

Fiske, S. T. (1998). Stereotyping, prejudice, and discrimination. In D. T. Gilbert, S. T. Fiske, & G. Lindzey (Eds.), *Handbook of social psychology* (4th ed., Vol. 2, pp. 357–411). New York: McGraw-Hill.

Fiske, S. T. (2000). Stereotyping, prejudice, and discrimination at the seam between the centuries: Evolution, culture, mind and brain. *European Journal of Social Psychology, 30,* 299–322.

Fiske, S. T. (2004). *Social beings: A core motives approach to social psychology.* New York: Wiley.

Fiske, S. T., Cuddy, A. J., Glick, P., & Xu, J. (2003). A model of (often mixed) stereotype content: Competence and warmth respectively follow from perceived status and competition. *Journal of Personality and Social Psychology, 82,* 878–902.

Fiske, S. T., Lin, M. H., & Neuberg, S. L. (1999). The Continuum Model: Ten years later. In S. Chaiken & Y. Trope (Eds.), *Dual-process theories in social psychology* (pp. 231–254). New York: Guilford Press.

Fiske, S. T., & Neuberg, S. L. (1990). A continuum of impression formation, from category-based to individuating processes: Influences of information and motivation on attention and interpretation. In M. P. Zanna (Ed.), *Advances in experimental social psychology* (Vol. 23, pp. 1–74). New York: Academic Press.

Hamilton, D. L. (Ed.). (1979). *Cognitive processes in stereotyping and intergroup behavior.* Mahwah, NJ: Erlbaum.

Hamilton, V. L., & Sanders, J. (1999). The second face of evil: Wrongdoing in and by the corporation. *Personality and Social Psychology Review, 2,* 222–233.

Hart, A. J., Whalen, P. J., Shin, L. M., McInerney, S. C., Fischer, H., & Rauch, S. L. (2000). Differential response in the human amygdala to racial outgroup versus ingroup face stimuli. *Neuroreport, 11,* 2351–2355.

Heatherton, T. F., Kleck, R. E., Hebl, M. R., & Hull, J. G. (2000). *The social psychology of stigma.* New York: Guilford Press.

Jones, E. E., Farina, A., Hastorf, A. H., Markus, H., Miller, D. T., & Scott, R. A. (1984). *Social stigma: The psychology of marked relationships.* New York: Freeman.

Macrae, C. N., & Bodenhausen, G. V. (2000). Thinking categorically about others. In S. T. Fiske, D. L. Schacter, & C. Zahn-Waxler (Eds.), *Annual review of psychology* (Vol. 51, pp. 93–120). Palo Alto, CA: Annual Reviews.

Pettigrew, T. F. (1998a). Intergroup contact theory. In J. T. Spence, J. M. Darley, & D. J. Foss (Eds.), *Annual review of psychology* (Vol. 49, pp. 65–85). Palo Alto, CA: Annual Reviews.

Pettigrew, T. F. (1998b). Reactions toward the new minorities of Western Europe. In J. Hagan & K. S. Cook (Eds.), *Annual review of sociology* (Vol. 24, pp. 77–103). Palo Alto, CA: Annual Reviews.

Phelps, E. A., O'Connor, K. J., Cunningham, W. A., Funayama, E. S., Gatenby, J. C., Gore, J. C., & Banaji, M. R. (2000). Performance on indirect measures of race evaluation predicts amygdala activation. *Journal of Cognitive Neuroscience, 12,* 729–738.

Price Waterhouse v. Hopkins, 109 U.S. 1775 (1989).

Robinson v. Jacksonville Shipyards, Inc. (Fla. 1989; Case No. 86–927).

Wheeler, M. E., & Fiske, S. T. (2001, November). *fMRI study of three cognitive tasks that differentially modulate stereotype accessibility and human amygdala response to racial outgroup faces.* Poster presented at the meeting of the Society for Neuroscience, San Diego, CA.

CHAPTER 7

Contemporary Racial Bias
When Good People Do Bad Things

JOHN F. DOVIDIO
SAMUEL L. GAERTNER
JASON A. NIER
KERRY KAWAKAMI
GORDON HODSON

That good and evil exist in the world is clear. Of that, there is little debate. We know that some people are capable of great selflessness, and that most people maintain high moral standards for themselves and others, give the welfare of others high priority, and place equality among their most central values (Kluegel & Smith, 1986). We also know that some people are capable of doing great harm, intentionally and unintentionally, to others. Racism reflects an essential kind of selfishness and evil that has pervaded human existence across cultures and across time (Jones, 1997). Racism provides both psychological benefits (e.g., enhanced self-esteem; Fein & Spencer, 1997) and material advantages (e.g., access to economic resources; Dovidio & Gaertner, 1998; see also Blank, 2001) to the perpetrator. The problem is that the same people—average people, "good" people—can be responsible for both good and bad deeds. Good people are often racist, and they are often racist without being aware of it.

Racism is easy to recognize in its most blatant forms. The traditional form of racism in the United States has involved open and direct expression ranging from derogatory comments to public lynching and murder. In contemporary times, racism has produced racial segregation in neighborhoods and schools and open discrimination in employment and educational opportunity (Jones, 1997). Due, in part, to the civil rights legislation of the 1960s, however, the nature of racism has changed. This legislation defined racism not only as morally bad but also as legally wrong. It became clear that good people should not discriminate.

We naively began our research on racism with a simple assumption: Based on differences in their expressed racial attitudes (see Adorno, Frenkel-Brunswik, Levinson, & Sanford, 1950), conservative whites would behave in a more racially discriminatory way than would liberal whites. Perhaps embedded in this assumption was our own value judgment that liberals (like us) were somehow "better" than conservatives, at least, when it came to race relations (see also Dovidio, 2001). However, we discovered, somewhat serendipitously, that racial discrimination was complex and occurs in subtle as well as overt ways.

In this initial study of contemporary racism (Gaertner, 1973), white participants residing in Brooklyn, New York, were selected for a field experiment on helping on the basis of their liberal or conservative orientations, as indicated by their political party affiliations, which were a matter of public record. Both the liberal and the conservative households received wrong-number telephone calls that quickly developed into requests for assistance. The callers, who were clearly identifiable from their dialects as being black or white, explained that their car was disabled and that they were attempting to reach a service garage from a public phone along the parkway. The callers further claimed that they had no more change to make another call and asked the participant to help by calling the garage. If the participant agreed to help and called the number, ostensibly of the garage, a "helping" response was scored. If the participant refused to help or hung up after the caller explained that he or she had no more change, a "not helping" response was recorded. If the participant hung up before learning that the motorist had no more change, the response was considered to be a "premature hang-up."

The first finding from this study was direct and predicted. Conservatives showed a higher "helping" response to whites than to blacks (92% vs. 65%), whereas liberals helped whites somewhat, but not significantly, more than blacks (85% vs. 75%). By this measure, conservatives were more biased against blacks than were liberals. However, what is good and bad behavior is not always obvious or straightforward. Additional inspection of the data revealed an unanticipated finding. Liberals "hung up prematurely" much more often on blacks than they did on whites (19% vs. 3%), and especially often on a black male motorist (28%). Conservatives did not discriminate in this way (8% vs. 5%). From the perspective of black callers, the consequence of a direct "not helping" response and of a "premature hang-up" was the same: They would be left without assistance. From the perspective of the participants, however, the consequences were different. Whereas a "not helping" response was a direct form of discrimination because it should have been clear to participants that their help was needed, a "premature hang-up" was a more indirect form because participants disengaged from the situation before they learned of the other person's dependence on them, and thus participants never overtly refused assistance. Consequently, both conservative and liberal whites discriminated against blacks but in different ways.

These findings and the conceptual work of Kovel (1970) challenged our views of good and bad and prompted us to reevaluate our assumptions about the nature of liberals' racial attitudes and good intentions. They also stimulated a line of research on contemporary racism that we have conducted over the past 30 years. Specifically, this work has focused on a particular type of contemporary racism, "aversive racism." Aversive racism is hypothesized to be qualitatively different from the old-fashioned, blatant kind, and it is presumed to characterize the racial attitudes of most well-educated and liberal whites in the United States. It is more indirect and subtle than the traditional form of prejudice, but its consequences are no less evil. In this chapter, we first consider the nature of aversive racism. Second, we offer experimental evidence of its existence and operation in the behavior of whites toward blacks. Third, we examine how aversive racism can contribute to interracial miscommunication and distrust. Fourth, we explore approaches for combating aversive racism. And finally, we discuss the social implications of aversive racism.

THE NATURE OF AVERSIVE RACISM

Whereas overt expressions of prejudice have declined significantly over the past 35 years (Dovidio & Gaertner, 1998, 2000; Schuman, Steeh, Bobo, & Krysan, 1997), contemporary forms of prejudice continue to exist and affect the lives of people in subtle but significant ways (Dovidio & Gaertner, 1998; Gaertner & Dovidio, 1986). In these subtler, contemporary forms of prejudice, bias is expressed in indirect, often unintentional, ways. Nevertheless, the consequences of these prejudices (e.g., the restriction of economic opportunity) may be as significant for people of color and as pernicious as those of the traditional, overt form of discrimination (Dovidio & Gaertner, 1998; Gaertner & Dovidio, 1986; Sears, 1988).

Aversive Racism, Duality, and Ambivalence

A critical aspect of the aversive racism framework is the conflict between the denial of personal prejudice and the underlying unconscious negative feelings and beliefs. Because of current cultural values, most whites hold strong convictions concerning fairness, justice, and racial equality. However, because of a range of normal cognitive, motivational, and socio-cultural processes that promote intergroup biases, most whites also de-velop some negative feelings toward, or beliefs about, blacks. The exis-tence of these nearly unavoidable racial biases along with the simultaneous desire to be nonprejudiced comprise a basic duality of attitudes and beliefs in aversive racists that can produce racial ambivalence (see also Katz & Hass, 1988; Katz, Wackenhut, & Hass, 1986). We recognize that all rac-ists are not aversive or subtle, that old-fashioned racism still exists, that there are individual differences in aversive racism, and that some whites may not be racist at all. Nevertheless, we propose that aversive racism gen-erally characterizes the racial attitudes of a large proportion of whites who express apparently nonprejudiced views—that is, good people who are not as good as they think they are.

Negative Feelings and Beliefs

In contrast to traditional approaches that emphasize the *psychopathology* of prejudice (e.g., Adorno et al., 1950; see also Duckitt, 1992), the nega-tive feelings and beliefs that underlie aversive racism are hypothesized to be rooted in *normal,* often adaptive, psychological processes (see Dovidio & Gaertner, 1998; Gaertner & Dovidio, 1986). These processes involve both individual factors (such as cognitive and motivational biases and so-cialization) and intergroup elements (such as realistic group conflict or bi-ases associated with the mere categorization of people into ingroups and outgroups). These biases are also functional: Racism offers advantages. Discriminating against others can boost self-esteem and promote feelings of control and superiority (Fein & Spencer, 1997; Tajfel & Turner, 1979). Discrimination also offers tangible economic advantages to members of the majority group and serves to maintain that group's political, social, and corporate power (Blumer, 1958; Bobo, 1999). These negative biases may occur spontaneously, automatically, and without full awareness (Dovidio & Gaertner, 1998). In addition, in contrast to the feelings of open hostility and clear dislike of blacks, the negative feelings that aversive racists experience are typically more diffuse, such as feelings of anxiety and uneasiness.

Subtle Bias

The aversive racism framework also helps to predict when discrimination against blacks and other minority groups will or will not occur. Whereas old-fashioned racists exhibit a direct and overt pattern of discrimination, aversive racists' actions may appear more variable and inconsistent because of the duality of their attitudes and the resulting, potential ambivalence. Sometimes they discriminate (manifesting their negative feelings), and sometimes they do not (reflecting their egalitarian beliefs). Our research has provided a framework for understanding this pattern of discrimination.

Because aversive racists consciously recognize and endorse egalitarian values and because they truly aspire to be good and just people, they will *not* discriminate in situations in which discrimination would be obvious to others and to themselves. Specifically, we propose that when people are presented with a situation in which the appropriate response is clear, in which right and wrong are clearly defined, aversive racists will not discriminate against blacks. In these contexts, aversive racists will be especially motivated to avoid feelings, beliefs, and behaviors that could be associated with racist intent. Wrongdoing, which would directly threaten their nonprejudiced self-image, would be too obvious. However, because aversive racists still possess negative feelings, these negative feelings eventually will be expressed, but they will be expressed in subtle, indirect, and rationalizable ways. For instance, discrimination will occur when appropriate (and thus inappropriate) behavior is not obvious or when the aversive racist can justify or rationalize a negative response on the basis of some factor other than race. Under these circumstances, aversive racists may engage in behaviors that ultimately harm blacks but do so in ways that allow them (the aversive racists) to maintain their self-image as good people and that insulate them from ever having to recognize that their behavior was racially motivated.

Generally, then, aversive racists may be identified by a constellation of characteristic responses to racial issues and interracial situations. First, aversive racists, in contrast to old-fashioned racists, endorse fair and just treatment of all groups. Second, despite their conscious good intentions, aversive racists unconsciously harbor negative feelings toward blacks and therefore try to avoid interracial interaction. Third, when interracial interaction is unavoidable, aversive racists experience anxiety and discomfort, and consequently they try to disengage from the interaction as quickly as possible. Fourth, because part of the discomfort that aversive racists experience is due to a concern about acting inappropriately and appearing prejudiced, aversive racists strictly adhere to established rules and codes of behavior in interracial situations that they cannot avoid. Fifth, their negative feelings get expressed in subtle, rationalizable ways that disadvantage minorities or unfairly benefit the majority group.

The term *aversive*, as a descriptor for this form of racism, thus refers to two aspects of this bias. It reflects the nature of the emotions associated with blacks, such as anxiety, that lead to avoidance and social awkwardness rather than to open antagonism. It also reflects the fact that, because of their conscious adherence to egalitarian principles, these whites find any indication that they might be prejudiced to be aversive.

In general, then, the aversive racism framework considers this form of prejudice as a critical factor influencing the expression of racial bias by whites toward blacks. Although social influences can directly influence the level of bias that is expressed (Pettigrew, 1959, 1998), we emphasize the *moderating* role of situational factors on whether the unconscious negative aspects of aversive racists' attitudes are manifested in terms of racial discrimination. That is, whether the situation is one in which a negative act toward a black person would be attributed to racial intent, by others or by the aversive racist him- or herself, determines whether bias will or will not be expressed.

Consistent with the aversive racism perspective, other theories of contemporary racism also hypothesize that bias is currently expressed more subtly than in the past. One such approach is the symbolic racism theory (Sears, 1988; Sears, Henry, & Kosterman, 2000) and a closely related derivation, the modern racism theory (McConahay, 1986). According to the symbolic racism theory, negative feelings toward blacks that whites acquire early in life persist into adulthood but are expressed indirectly and symbolically, in terms of opposition to busing or resistance to Affirmative Action policies, rather than directly or overtly, as in voicing support for segregation. McConahay (1986) further proposes that because modern racism involves the rejection of traditional racist beliefs and the displacement of anti-black feelings onto more abstract social and political issues, modern racists, such as aversive racists, are relatively unaware of their racist feelings. However, whereas symbolic and modern racism are subtle forms of contemporary racism that seem to exist among political conservatives, aversive racism seems to be more strongly associated with liberals.

We have found consistent support for the aversive racism framework across a broad range of situations (see Dovidio & Gaertner, 1998; Gaertner & Dovidio, 1986). Our work mainly considers the influence of contemporary racial biases of whites toward blacks because of the central role that racial politics has played in the history of the United States. In addition, much of the research reported in this chapter focuses on the responses of white college students—well-educated and typically liberal people—who are presumed to represent a prime population for aversive racism. Nevertheless, we note that many of the findings and principles we discuss extend to biases exhibited by liberal noncollege populations (e.g., Gaertner, 1973) and to biases toward other groups (e.g., Hispanic; Dovidio, Gaertner, Anastasio, & Sanitioso, 1992). In the next sections, we describe examples of a series of different studies to illustrate the operation of aversive racism.

AVERSIVE RACISM AND CONTEMPORARY BIAS

The evidence we present in this section comes from paradigms involving emergency intervention and employment or admission selection decisions.

Emergency Intervention

One of our earliest experiments (Gaertner & Dovidio, 1977) demonstrates how aversive racism can operate in fairly dramatic ways. The scenario for the experiment was inspired by an incident in the mid-1960s in which 38 people witnessed the stabbing of a woman, Kitty Genovese, without a single bystander intervening to help. What accounted for this behavior? Feelings of responsibility play a key role (see Darley & Latané, 1968). If a person witnesses an emergency knowing that he or she is the only bystander, that person bears all of the responsibility for helping. Consequently, the likelihood of helping is high. In contrast, if a person witnesses an emergency but believes that there are several other witnesses who might help, then the responsibility for helping is shared. Moreover, if the person believes that someone else will help or has already helped, the likelihood of that bystander taking action is significantly reduced.

We created a situation in the laboratory in which white participants witnessed a staged emergency involving either a black or white victim. We led some of our participants to believe that they would be the only other person in the study besides the victim. We led others to believe that there would be other white people also participating in the session. While participants were performing a task over an intercom system with a black or white confederate in an adjacent room, the session was interrupted by a crash of falling chairs, which apparently injured the confederate. We predicted that, because aversive racists do not act in overtly bigoted ways, whites would not discriminate when they were the only witness and the responsibility for helping was clearly focused on them. However, we anticipated that whites would be much less helpful to black than to white victims when they had a justifiable excuse not to get involved, such as the belief that one of the *other* witnesses would take responsibility for helping.

The results nicely reflected these predictions. When white participants believed that they were the only witness, they helped both white and black victims very frequently (over 85% of the time) and equivalently. There was no evidence of blatant racism. In contrast, when they thought there were other witnesses and they could rationalize a decision not to help on the basis of some factor other than race, they helped black victims only half as often as white victims (37.5% vs. 75%). These results illustrate the operation of subtle biases in relatively dramatic, spontaneous, and apparently life-threatening circumstances involving a failure to help, rather than an action intentionally aimed at doing harm. This research, therefore, shows that although the bias may be subtle and the people involved may be well-intentioned, its consequences may be severe.

Selection Decisions

Labor statistics continue to demonstrate fundamental disparities in the economic status of blacks relative to whites—a gap that has not only persisted but also, in some important aspects (e.g., family income), has widened in recent years (see Blank, 2001). Aversive racism may be one factor that contributes to disparities in the workplace. Subtle biases can influence both the access of blacks to the workplace and their performance in it.

At the time of hiring, aversive racism can affect how qualifications are perceived and weighed in a manner that systematically disadvantages black relative to white applicants. In particular, the aversive racism framework suggests that bias will not be expressed when a person is clearly qualified or unqualified for a position, because the appropriate decision is obvious. However, bias is expected when the appropriate decision is unclear, for example, because of ambiguous evidence about whether the candidate's qualifications meet the criteria for selection or when the candidate's file has conflicting information (e.g., some strong and some weak aspects).

In one study of hiring decisions (Dovidio & Gaertner, 2000), we presented college students with excerpts from an interview and asked them to evaluate candidates for a position in an ostensibly new program for peer counseling at their university. Specifically, white participants evaluated a black or white candidate who had credentials that were systematically manipulated to represent very strong, moderate, or very weak qualifications for the position. The findings were supportive of the aversive racism framework. When the candidates' credentials clearly qualified them for the position (strong qualifications) or the credentials clearly were not appropriate (weak qualifications), there was no discrimination against the black candidate. However, when candidates' qualifications for the position were less obvious and the appropriate decision was more ambiguous (moderate qualifications), white participants recommended the black candidate significantly less often than the white candidate with exactly the same credentials. Moreover, when we compared the responses of participants in 1989 and 1999, we found that the pattern of subtle discrimination in selection decisions remained essentially unchanged, although overt expressions of prejudice (measured by items on a self-report prejudice scale) had declined over this 10-year period.

In subsequent research (Hodson, Dovidio, & Gaertner, 2002), participants were asked to help make admissions decisions for the university. Again we found no racial bias when applicants had uniformly strong or uniformly weak college board scores and records of high school achievement. When applicants were strong on one dimension (e.g., on college board scores) and weak on the other (e.g., high school grades), however, black applicants generally tended to be recommended less strongly than white applicants. Moreover, participants changed how they weighed the criteria to justify their decisions as a function of race. For black applicants, they gave the weaker dimension (college board scores or grades) greater weight in their decisions, whereas for white applicants they assigned the stronger of the qualifications more weight. Taken together, these findings suggest that when given latitude for interpretation, whites give white candidates the "benefit of the doubt"—a benefit they do not extend to blacks.

The behavior of aversive racists is thus characterized by two types of inconsistencies. First, aversive racists exhibit an apparent contradiction between their expressed egalitarian attitudes and their biased (albeit subtle) behaviors. Second, sometimes (in clear situations) they act in an unbiased fashion, whereas at other times (in ambiguous situations) they are biased against blacks. For blacks who may not understand the dynamics but who suffer the consequences, these inconsistencies can create a climate of suspicion and distrust. In the next section, we explore how the contradictions and inconsistencies of aversive racism can produce awkward and inefficient interactions that, often inadvertently, have disparate and negative consequences for blacks.

INTERRACIAL INTERACTION AND PERFORMANCE

Once on the job, aversive racism can exert subtle influences on the behavior of whites in interracial work groups and, thereby, on the outcomes for blacks. Effective teamwork on the job requires social coordination as well as task-relevant skills. The duality of aversive racists' conscious egalitarian ideals and their unconscious negative feelings may produce mixed, potentially contradictory, signals that interfere with effective interracial interaction and further contribute to interracial distrust.

Dissociated Attitudes

Beginning with our earliest work on the aversive racism framework, we hypothesized that there is commonly a dissociation between whites' conscious and unconscious racial attitudes and beliefs. Recent research in social cognition has yielded new techniques for assessing unconscious, as well as conscious, attitudes and stereotypes. These techniques thus provide direct evidence about the influence of factors previously only assumed to be involved in aversive racism.

Borrowing from work in cognition more generally, researchers have made a fundamental distinction between explicit and implicit processes (Devine, 1989; Greenwald & Banaji, 1995). Explicit attitudes and stereotyping operate in a conscious mode and are exemplified by traditional self-report measures of these constructs. Implicit attitudes and stereotypes, in contrast, are evaluations and beliefs that are automatically activated by the mere presence (actual or symbolic) of the attitude object. They commonly function in an unconscious and unintentional fashion. Implicit attitudes and stereotypes are typically assessed using response latency procedures, memory tasks, physiological measures (e.g., galvanic skin response), and indirect self-report measures (see Blair, 2001; Dovidio, Kawakami, & Beach, 2001).

Along with other researchers using response-time measures based on the assumption that racial attitudes operate like other stimuli to facilitate responses and decision making about related concepts (e.g., doctor–nurse), we have found consistent evidence of whites' generally negative implicit (unconscious) attitudes toward blacks (e.g., Dovidio, Evans, & Tyler, 1986; Fazio, Jackson, Dunton, & Williams, 1995; Gaertner & McLaughlin, 1983; Greenwald, McGhee, & Schwartz, 1998; Wittenbrink, Judd, & Park, 1997). Moreover, supportive of the aversive racism framework, whites' unconscious attitudes are largely dissociated from their conscious, self-reported attitudes. The correlation between these different types of attitudes is, on average, .24 (Dovidio et al., 2001). The development of these new techniques thus allows us to examine the independent influence of conscious and unconscious attitudes on whites' behaviors toward blacks, as well as the joint influence of these different types of attitudes.

We hypothesize that this disassociation between the conscious (explicit) and unconscious (implicit) attitudes of aversive racists can subtly shape the ways that whites and blacks interact and further contribute to the different perceptions that whites and blacks develop about their situations. If whites are unaware of their negative implicit attitudes, they may also be unaware of how their behaviors in interracial interactions may be influenced by these racial biases. In contrast, blacks, observing the negative behaviors of whites with whom they are interacting, may form very different impressions about whether racial bias is operating and the degree to which it is intentionally determined. Blacks (and other minority groups) may be vigilant to signs of bias and readily attribute these actions to intentional racism (Shelton, 2000; Vorauer & Kumhyr, 2001). We examine the implications of this aspect of our framework in the next section.

Conflicting Attitudes, Mixed Messages

We propose that the dissociation between the positive conscious attitudes and the negative unconscious attitudes of aversive racists fundamentally affects the ways these racists interact with blacks. In particular, conscious and unconscious attitudes influence behavior in different ways and under different conditions (Dovidio, Kawakami, & Gaertner, 2002; Dovidio, Kawakami, Johnson, Johnson & Howard, 1997; Fazio et al., 1995; Wilson, Lindsey, & Schooler, 2000). Conscious attitudes shape deliberative, well-considered responses, for which people have the motivation and opportunity to weigh the costs and benefits of various courses of action. Unconscious attitudes influence responses that are more difficult to monitor and control (e.g., some nonverbal behaviors; see Chen & Bargh, 1997; McConnell & Leibold, 2001) or responses that people do not view as an indication of their attitude and thus do not try to control.

For instance, we have found that whites' unconscious negative attitudes predict nonverbal cues of discomfort (increased rate of blinking) and aversion (decreased eye-contact) toward blacks, whereas whites' self-reported conscious attitudes predict overt evaluations and indications of liking toward blacks (Dovidio, Kawakami, et al., 1997). Thus, aversive racists who have positive conscious attitudes and who want to be good and supportive of blacks but who also harbor unconscious negative attitudes are likely to convey mixed messages in interracial interactions. Given these conflicting signals, it is not surprising that blacks are likely to approach interracial interactions with anxiety, guardedness, and underlying mistrust (Hyers & Swim, 1998; Shelton, 2000).

These communication obstacles and interaction problems are exacerbated by the fact that whites and blacks have fundamentally different perspectives on the attitudes implied and the actions demonstrated by whites during these interactions. Whites have full access to their conscious attitudes and are able to monitor and control their more overt and deliberative behaviors. They do not have access to their unconscious attitudes or to their less obvious behaviors. As a consequence, whites' beliefs about how they are behaving or how blacks perceive them would be expected to be based primarily on their conscious attitudes and their more overt behaviors, such as the verbal content of their interaction with blacks, and not on their unconscious attitudes or less deliberative (i.e., nonverbal) behaviors. In contrast to the perspective of whites, the perspective of black partners in these interracial interactions allows them to attend to both the spontaneous (e.g., nonverbal) and the deliberative (e.g., verbal) behaviors of whites. To the extent that the black partners attend to whites' nonverbal behaviors, which may signal more negativity than their verbal behaviors, blacks are likely to form more negative impressions of the encounter and be less satisfied with the interaction than are whites (Shelton, 2000).

To investigate this possibility, we conducted another experiment (Dovidio et al., 2002) in which we assessed perceptions of interracial interactions by whites and blacks, and we related those perceptions to white participants' conscious attitudes, measured on a self-report prejudice scale, and unconscious attitudes, assessed with a response-latency technique. Then we arranged dyadic conversations between a black and a white participant on a race-neutral topic. We videotaped the interactions and subsequently asked one set of coders to rate the nonverbal and verbal behaviors of white participants and another set of observers to rate their global impressions of participants from a videotape recorded from their partners' perspective.

As we hypothesized, white participants' self-reported racial attitudes predicted their deliberative behaviors, such as their verbal friendliness toward black relative to white partners, which in turn predicted whites' impressions of how friendly they behaved in interactions with the black relative to the white partner. Thus, whites' conscious attitudes, controllable behaviors, and self-impressions were all consonant. Unconscious racial attitudes, measured via response latencies, did not predict these verbal behaviors or whites' impressions of how they behaved. However, as we also anticipated, we found that white participants' unconscious racial attitudes predicted biases in their *nonverbal* behaviors, which then predicted how they were perceived by their partners.

Because white participants and their partners based their impressions on different aspects of the participants' attitudes, the conscious and unconscious attitudes were dissociated and their impressions of the interaction were generally uncorrelated ($r = .11$). white participants typically reported that they found the interaction satisfying, and they expressed contentment with their contributions. Their black partners, however, reported being relatively dissatisfied with the exchange and were uneasy about their partners' behaviors. Despite white participants' good intentions, the impressions they made were not as good as they thought. Moreover, both members assumed that their partner shared their impression of the interaction.

Taken together, our findings on the effects of conscious and unconscious attitudes in interracial interaction suggest that the nature of contemporary biases can shape the everyday perceptions of white and black Americans in ways that interfere with the development of communication and trust that are critical to long-term positive intergroup relations. These different perspectives and experiences of whites and blacks in interracial interaction, which happen inadvertently and occur daily, can have summative effects over time (Feagin & Sikes, 1994) that contribute to the climate of misperception and distrust that characterizes contemporary race relations in the United States. The majority of U.S. blacks today have a profound distrust of the police and legal systems, and about a third are overtly distrustful of whites, in general (Anderson, 1996). In addition, blacks commonly believe that conspiracies inhibit their progress as a group (Crocker, Luhtanen, Broadnax, & Blaine, 1999; DeParle, 1990, 1991).

The mixed messages that aversive racists often convey can create fundamental miscommunication in interracial interactions and produce divergent impressions among interactants that can undermine their ability to interact efficiently in task-oriented situations as well as effectively in social situations.

Interracial Performance

The different and potentially divergent impressions that blacks and whites may form during interracial interactions can have significant impact on these individuals' effectiveness in task-oriented situations. Cannon-Bowers and Salas (1999) have argued that effective teamwork requires two types of skills: those associated with the technical aspects of the job and those associated with being a member of the team. Regarding the latter factor, team competencies include the knowledge, skills, and attitudes required to work effectively with others. In addition to manifesting itself in terms of different impressions and perceptions, contemporary bias can influence personal relations and group processes in ways that unintentionally but adversely affect outcomes for blacks.

We (Dovidio, Gaertner, Kawakami, & Hodson, 2002) examined these processes in interracial dyads in which a black participant was paired with a white student who was identified as (1) a traditionally high-prejudiced person (expressed biases openly), (2) an aversive racist (expressed egalitarian views but showed evidence of unconscious bias), or (3) a low-prejudiced white (held egalitarian views and showed little evidence of unconscious bias). These participants engaged in a problem-solving task about challenges to college students. For example, in one task they were asked to identify the five most important items that incoming students need to bring to campus. Because there were no objective measures of the quality of their team solution, we focused on the quality of their interaction (as reflected in their perceptions of friendliness and trustworthiness and feelings of satisfaction) and in their efficiency (as indexed by their time to complete the task).

In general, whites' impressions of their own behavior were related primarily to their publicly expressed attitudes, whereas blacks' impressions of whites were related mainly to whites' unconscious attitudes. Specifically, whites who expressed egalitarian ideals (i.e., low-prejudiced whites and aversive racists) reported that they behaved in friendlier ways than did those who expressed their biases openly (i.e., high-prejudiced whites). black partners perceived whites who showed no evidence of unconscious bias (i.e., low-prejudiced whites) to be friendlier than those who had unconscious biases (aversive racists and high-prejudiced whites). Of all three groups, blacks were least trustful of aversive racists.

Our results further revealed that whites' racial attitudes could be systematically related to the efficiency of the interracial teams. Teams with low-prejudiced whites solved the problem most quickly. Interracial teams involving high-prejudiced whites were next most efficient. Teams with aversive racists were the least efficient. Presumably, the conflicting messages displayed by aversive racists and the divergent impressions of the team members' interaction interfered with the team's effectiveness. To the extent that blacks are in the minority in an organization and are dependent on high-prejudiced whites or aversive racists, their performance is likely to be poorer objectively than the performance of whites who predominantly interact with other whites. Thus, even when whites harbor unconscious and unintentional biases toward blacks, their actions can have effects on interracial processes and outcomes that are sometimes even more detrimental than those of old-fashioned racists.

Overall, we have offered a range of evidence across time, populations, and paradigms that illustrates how aversive racism—racism among people who are good and well-intentioned—can influence the nature of interracial interactions and directly or indirectly produce disparate outcomes between blacks and whites. As we noted earlier, although the bias of aversive racists may be subtle and unintentional, its ultimate consequences may be just as evil as old-fashioned racism. In the next section we examine strategies for combating this insidious type of bias.

COMBATING AVERSIVE RACISM

Traditional prejudice-reduction techniques have been focused on changing conscious attitudes—old-fashioned racism—and obvious expressions of bias. Attempts to reduce this direct, traditional form of racial prejudice have typically involved educational strategies to (1) enhance knowledge and appreciation of other groups (e.g., multicultural education programs), (2) emphasize norms that prejudice is wrong, and (3) utilize direct (e.g., mass media appeals) or indirect (e.g., dissonance reduction) attitude change techniques (Stephan & Stephan, 2001). However, because aversive racists are not aware of their unconscious negative attitudes and only discriminate against blacks when they can justify their behavior on the basis of some factor other than race, they will not see the relevance of these approaches to themselves. Aversive racists recognize that prejudice is bad, but they do not recognize that *they* are prejudiced. Thus, like a virus that has mutated, racism has evolved into different forms that are not only more difficult to recognize but also to combat.

We believe, however, that aversive racism can be addressed with techniques aimed at its roots at both individual and collective levels. At the individual level, strategies to combat aversive racism need to be directed at unconscious attitudes. Aversive racists' conscious attitudes are already favorable and may, in fact, be instrumental in motivating change. At the intergroup level, interventions can be targeted at processes that support aversive racism, such as ingroup favoritism (Gaertner & Dovidio, 2000).

Addressing Unconscious Attitudes and Beliefs

As we note earlier, aversive racism is characterized by conscious (explicit) egalitarian attitudes and negative, unconscious (implicit) attitudes and beliefs. In their model of dual attitudes, Wilson and colleagues (2000) argue that systems of dual attitudes, such as those involved in aversive racism, typically arise developmentally. The person's original attitudes become unconscious and automatically activated through repeated occurrence, practice, and ultimately overlearning (Wyer & Hamilton, 1998). Given the historic socialization of whites and the repeated exposure to negative images of blacks in the mass media, most whites develop negative attitudes and stereotypic beliefs about blacks that become internalized and habitualized relatively early in life (Devine, 1989). Aversive racists, however, also subsequently develop a strong conscious commitment to equality and to nonprejudiced attitudes and behaviors. Nevertheless, according to Wilson and colleagues' model, the original attitude is not expunged. It remains stored in memory on implicit, unconscious levels, whereas the newer attitude is explicit and conscious. In general, explicit attitudes can change and evolve relatively easily, whereas implicit attitudes are much more difficult to alter because they are based in overlearning and habitual reactions.

Just because they are unconscious and automatically activated does not mean that aversive racists' unconscious, negative attitudes are immutable and inevitable. If unconscious attitudes and stereotypes can be learned, we propose that they can also be unlearned or inhibited by equally well-learned countervailing influences. Devine and Monteith (1993) observed, "Although it is not easy and clearly requires effort, time, and practice, prejudice appears to be a habit that can be broken" (p. 336). We have found that with extensive practice, either imposed externally or self-motivated, it is possible to change implicit beliefs.

Imposed Practice

Individuals can develop "auto-motive" control of their actions through frequent and persistent pursuit of a goal, such as to not be biased or not to stereotype (Bargh, 1990). As Monteith, Sherman, and Devine (1998) note, "Practice makes perfect. Like any other mental process, thought suppression processes may be proceduralized and become relatively automatic" (p. 71).

Consistent with this line of reasoning, in a series of studies (Kawakami, Dovidio, Moll, Hermsen, & Russin, 2000) we found that automatic stereotype activation can be reduced and eliminated with training to not stereotype members of a group. In particular, participants in this research practiced extensively to respond in ways either consistent with prevailing racial stereotypes (by indicating "yes" to stereotype-consistent pairings of black and white photographs and traits and responding "no" to stereotype-inconsistent pairings) or to negate racial stereotypes (by responding "no" to stereotype-consistent pairings and "yes" to stereotype-inconsistent pairings). At the end of the session, participants performed a response latency task to assess their unconscious, automatically activated racial stereotypes. Whereas those participants who were in the condition in which they responded affirmatively to conventional stereotypic associations showed equivalent evidence of unconscious racial stereotypes before and after the training exercise, those who practiced negating stereotypes demonstrated a significant decrease in unconscious stereotyping after training. These effects of practice in negating stereotypes were still evident up to 24 hours following the training.

Although such direct strategies appear to be promising, these kinds of intensive and time-consuming approaches may be limited in their general applicability. Alternative promising strategies, however, take advantage of aversive racists' genuine interest in nonprejudicial states to motivate significant and enduring change.

Motivation and Self-Regulation

Because aversive racists consciously endorse egalitarian values and truly want to be nonprejudiced, it may be possible to capitalize on their good intentions and induce self-motivated efforts to reduce unconscious biases upon becoming aware of them. Work by Devine, Monteith, and their colleagues (e.g., Devine & Monteith, 1993; Monteith & Voils, 1998) has revealed that when low-prejudiced people recognize discrepancies between their potential behavior toward minorities (i.e., what they *would* do) and their personal standards (i.e., what they *should* do) they feel guilt and compunction, which produces motivation to respond without prejudice in the future. In their process model of prejudice reduction, Devine and Monteith (1993) further suggest that individuals who are committed to maintaining egalitarian standards learn to reject old, biased ways of responding and to adopt new, nonprejudiced ways. Over time and with practice, these people learn to reduce prejudicial responses and to respond in ways that are consistent with their nonprejudiced personal standards. Thus, this process of self-regulation, which is initiated by making people aware of their potential for racial bias, may produce changes in even unconscious negative responses when extended over time.

We directly investigated this possibility. In our study (see Dovidio, Kawakami, & Gaertner, 2000), white participants who were categorized as low or high in prejudice (on the basis of their self-reported prejudice) completed a task, modeled after the procedures of Devine and Monteith (1993), making them aware of discrepancies between what they would do and what they should do (i.e., their personal standards) in interracial situations. We assessed emotional reactions and, using a response-latency task, initial unconscious racial stereotyping. Three weeks later, participants returned to the laboratory and completed the unconscious stereotyping tasks and another measure of the "would–should" discrepancy.

We hypothesized that initial discrepancies between one's actions (what one would do) and one's personal standards (what one should do) would generate stronger feelings of guilt and compunction and produce more self-initiated efforts at change in low-prejudiced than in high-prejudiced participants. The effects of this self-regulatory process were expected to be reflected in decreased discrepancies and unconscious stereotyping.

As anticipated, in the first session greater discrepancies between what they would do and should do produced higher levels of guilt primarily in low-prejudiced participants, not in high-prejudiced participants. These findings indicate the potential initiation of self-regulatory processes for low- but not high-prejudiced participants. When participants returned 3 weeks later, we found an overall greater alignment (i.e., smaller discrepancy) between what they would and should do—an indication that both high- and low-prejudiced participants showed a decrease in overt expressions of bias. However, as hypothesized, low- and high-prejudiced whites differed in terms of the extent to which they internalized these changes. Low-prejudiced whites who had larger initial discrepancies showed greater reductions in unconscious stereotyping ($r = -.56$); in contrast, the relationship was weaker ($-.07$) and nonsignificant for high-prejudiced whites. These findings demonstrate that the good intentions of aversive racists can be harnessed to produce self-initiated change in even unconscious biases with appropriate awareness, effort, and practice over time.

Strategies that emphasize intergroup processes, such as intergroup contact and social categorization and identity, offer alternative, complementary approaches to these individual-level approaches. We examine one such approach in the next section.

Redirecting Ingroup Bias

Social categorization, particularly in terms of ingroups ("we's") and outgroups ("they's") is a fundamental process that contributes to aversive racism (Gaertner et al., 1997). In general, the mere categorization of people into ingroups and outgroups has a profound influence on social perception, affect, cognition, and behavior. When others are distinguished by their ingroup or outgroup membership, people exaggerate differences between members of the groups (Abrams, 1985; Turner, 1985), spontaneously experience more positive feelings toward ingroup members (Otten &

Moskowitz, 2000), remember more positive information about ingroup members (Howard & Rothbart, 1980), and behave more helpfully to ingroup members (Dovidio, Gaertner, et al., 1997). Because race is a fundamental type of social categorization in the United States, race is associated with strong ingroup biases.

The process of social categorization, however, is not completely unalterable. Categories are hierarchically organized, with higher-level categories (e.g., nations) more inclusive of lower level ones (e.g., cities or towns). By modifying a perceiver's goals, motives, perceptions of past experiences, expectations, as well as factors within the perceptual field and the situational context, there is opportunity to alter the level of category inclusiveness that will be most influential in a given situation. This malleability of the level at which impressions are formed is important because of its implications for altering the way people think about members of ingroups and outgroups, and consequently about the ways whites, in general, and aversive racists, in particular, respond to blacks.

Because categorization is a basic process that is fundamental to intergroup bias, we have targeted it as a way of addressing the effects of aversive racism. In the next section we explore how the forces of categorization can be harnessed and redirected toward the reduction, if not the elimination, of racial biases. This approach is represented by the common ingroup identity model (Gaertner & Dovidio, 2000; Gaertner, Dovidio, Anastasio, Bachman, & Rust, 1993).

The Common Ingroup Identity Model

The common ingroup identity model is rooted in the social categorization perspective of intergroup behavior and recognizes the central role of social categorization in reducing as well as in creating intergroup bias (Tajfel & Turner, 1979). Specifically, if members of different groups are induced to conceive of themselves more as a single, superordinate group rather than as two separate groups, attitudes toward former outgroup members will become more positive through processes involving pro-ingroup bias. Thus, changing the basis of categorization from race to an alternative dimension can alter who is "we" and who is "they," undermining a contributing force to contemporary forms of racism, such as aversive racism. Substantial evidence in support of the common ingroup identity model has been found (Gaertner & Dovidio, 2000).

For example, two studies reported by Nier, Gaertner, Dovidio, Banker, and Ward (2001) illustrate the effectiveness of this approach for addressing racial biases. Study 1 was a laboratory experiment in which white college students, in a session with a black or white confederate, were induced to perceive themselves as separate individuals participating at the same time or as members of the same laboratory team. The participants evaluated their black partners significantly more favorably when they were teammates than when they were just individuals without common group connections. In contrast, the evaluations of the white partner were virtually equivalent in the team and individual conditions. Thus, inducing a common ingroup identity was particularly effective in producing positive responses toward blacks.

Study 2 was a field experiment conducted at the University of Delaware football stadium prior to a game between the University of Delaware and Westchester State University. Black and white students approached fans from both universities just before the fans entered the stadium. These fans were asked if they would be willing to be interviewed about their food preferences. Our student interviewers wore either a University of Delaware or Westchester State University hat. By selecting white fans wearing clothing that identified their university affiliation, we systematically varied whether fans and our interviewers had a common or different university identities in a context in which we expected university identities to be particularly salient. We predicted that making a common identity salient would increase compliance with the interviewer's request, particularly when the interviewer was black.

Supportive of predictions from the common ingroup identity model, white fans were significantly more cooperative with a black interviewer when they shared a superordinate university identity than when they did not (60% vs. 38%). For white interviewers, with whom they already shared racial group membership, the effect was much less pronounced (43% vs. 40%). Thus, in field and laboratory settings, racial outgroup members were accorded especially positive reactions when they shared common ingroup identity with white participants, compared to when the context did not emphasize their common group membership. These studies suggest the value of combating aversive racism at its roots, by strategically controlling the forces of ingroup favoritism that can produce subtle racial biases associated with aversive racism (see Gaertner et al., 1997).

SUMMARY AND CONCLUSIONS

In this chapter, we have described the concept of aversive racism, considered the factors that contribute to aversive racism, demonstrated empirically how it affects outcomes for blacks and interracial interactions, and explored how it can be combated. Despite apparent consistent improvements in expressed racial attitudes over time, aversive racism continues to exert a subtle but pervasive influence on the lives of black Americans. This bias is expressed in indirect and rationalizable ways that restrict opportunities for blacks while insulating aversive racists from ever having to confront their prejudices. It is an elusive phenomenon that plays a critical, moderating role. When an interracial situation is one in which an action could be readily attributed to racial bias, aversive racists carefully monitor their interracial behaviors and do not discriminate. In fact, they may respond even more favorably to blacks than to whites as a way of affirming their nonprejudiced self-images. When the situation is ambiguous, when norms for appropriate behavior are not clear, when the circumstances permit a justification for negative behavior on the basis of some factor other than race, or when aversive racists are not conscious of their actions, however, their bias is expressed, often subtlety.

The inconsistency of aversive racists' behavior may appear to be self-serving, systematically providing advantages to whites while avoiding attributions of blame, which suggests a kind of deceptiveness based on evil intentions. Nevertheless, we caution that the biases of aversive racists are genuinely unconscious and unintentional. They are truly well-intentioned people. Thus, just as our initial assumptions about discrimination among conservatives and liberals proved to be too simple, we note that characterizations of aversive racists as bad or good people are also oversimplifications that obscure and distort the complicated dynamics of contemporary racism.

Are, then, aversive racists evil people? Baumeister's (1996) social-psychological analysis of evil suggests that the answer to this question is complex. Baumeister argues that the folk conception of evil is based on several factors. The most prominent factor that determines whether evil has occurred, in the eyes of the layperson, is whether harm has been *intentionally* inflicted on another person. When one individual intentionally harms another, the behavior is much more likely to be considered evil. However, Baumeister observes that very little human behavior actually fits this conception of evil, and that most harmful or violent acts that people commit are *not* performed out of a wanton desire to harm another person deliberately.

Contemporary racism, in general, and aversive racism, in particular, can be viewed through this same lens. Whereas discriminatory behavior is common in the United States, intentional malicious acts of discrimination seem to be somewhat rare. (Hate crimes are a notable exception; see Boeckmann & Turpin-Petrosino, 2002.) The motivations and causes of prejudice do not usually reflect a malicious desire to harm those from other racial or ethnic groups. As we have discussed, the conscious motivations of most whites is to treat blacks fairly; discrimination arises largely out of unconscious psychological processes. Thus, from this perspective, aversive racism clearly does not fit the popular notion of evil as a malicious and deliberate act designed intentionally to harm another individual.

However, when the consequences of these discriminatory acts are considered, this behavior can hardly be described as morally neutral. This kind of discrimination reflects a new form of evil that should not be judged by conventional legal and moral standards. Perhaps the morality of racism in the United States should be assessed by its profoundly damaging effects rather than its subtle causes or the degree of intentionality that characterizes it. Judged by this yardstick, contemporary racism is an evil act committed by people who are not evil and who, by most normal standards, are good people. Nevertheless, the fact that the motivation for aversive racists' biases may be unconscious and their discrimination may be unintentional and subtle should not ultimately exonerate them from responsibility for their bad actions.

The challenge of addressing aversive racism resides in its elusiveness. Because aversive racists are unaware of their unconscious negative attitudes and truly embrace their egalitarian self-image, they are motivated to deny the existence of these feelings and not to recognize or take responsibility for the adverse impact of their behavior on blacks. In addition, the subtle processes underlying discrimination motivated by aversive racism can be identified and isolated under the controlled conditions of the laboratory. However, at the societal and organizational levels, at which the controlled conditions of an experiment are rarely possible and multiple factors may simultaneously shape decision making, this process presents a substantial challenge to the equitable treatment of members of disadvantaged groups. For example, Krieger (1995), in the *Stanford Law Review*, observed: "Herein lies the practical problem. . . . Validating subjective decisionmaking systems is neither empirically nor economically feasible, especially for jobs where intangible qualities, such as interpersonal skills, creativity, and ability to make sound judgments under conditions of uncertainty are critical" (p. 1232). Thus the operation of aversive racism may go largely unnoticed and unaddressed in naturalistic settings.

In addition, to the extent that discrimination reflects ingroup favoritism (see also Gaertner et al., 1997), it is particularly difficult to address legally. Krieger (1998) adds:

> Title VII is poorly equipped to control prejudice resulting from ingroup favoritism. . . . Ingroup favoritism manifests itself gradually in subtle ways. It is unlikely to trigger mobilization of civil rights remedies because instances of this form of discrimination tend to go unnoticed. If they are noticed, they will frequently seem genuinely trivial or be economically unfeasible to pursue. . . . For this reason as for others, we cannot expect existing equal opportunity tools adequately to prevent, identify, or redress this more modern form of discrimination. (pp. 1325–1326)

As we have proposed, new techniques are needed to address this, and other, contemporary forms of racism.

Developing interventions at the individual, intergroup, and societal levels that not only control the expressions of aversive racism but also address its negative components has critical social implications. Aversive racism represents a latent form of bias whose expression is strongly moderated by social circumstances and norms. A change in conditions or norms can allow this bias to operate more directly and openly. For instance, research on interracial aggression has demonstrated that under normal circumstances, whites are not more aggressive and harmful toward blacks than toward whites. Overt and unprovoked aggression toward blacks would readily be perceived as racist. However, when whites are first antagonized by another person's aggressiveness, when they feel freed from prevailing norms through conditions that make them feel anonymous and deindividuated, or when norms change from censuring to supporting aggression, whites exhibit more aggressiveness toward blacks than toward other whites (Donnerstein & Donnerstein, 1973; Donnerstein, Donnerstein, Simon, & Ditrichs, 1972; Kawakami, Spears, & Dovidio, 2002; Rogers & Prentice-Dunn, 1981). Thus, if left unaddressed, aversive racism provides the seed for bias to emerge when conditions allow or encourage a more open expression of discrimination.

Although we have focused our chapter on the attitudes of whites toward blacks, we note that many of the principles of aversive racism apply to the responses of the majority group to minority groups in contexts in which egalitarian ideals are valued and discrimination is censured (Dovidio et al., 1992). For instance, Pettigrew and Meertens (1995) have found that whereas blatant prejudice in Europe is related to the unconditional exclusion or severe limitation of immigrants, subtle prejudice is associated with constraints in immigration, such as prerequisite educational levels, that can be justified on the basis of factors ostensibly unrelated to race or ethnicity. However, paralleling the scenario that we described for race relations, when conditions change and people feel threatened—such as after the terrorist attacks of September 11, 2001, in the United States—subtle biases may become more open and result not only in incidents of overt violence but also directly in attitudes and political actions against immigrants and immigration (Esses, Dovidio, & Hodson, 2002).

In conclusion, good and evil are difficult to disentangle in regard to aversive racism because they are tightly intertwined within the same individual. On the one hand, biases associated with normal human functioning and socialization in a society with racist traditions form the basis for the development of aversive racists' unconscious negative attitudes. On the other hand, aversive racists truly aspire to be good people, and they see themselves as nonprejudiced. They sincerely embrace principles of fairness, justice, and racial equality. The good and evil behaviors of aversive racists are contextually determined: These individuals do not discriminate when wrongdoing would be obvious to others and to themselves, but they will exhibit bias, unintentionally, when right and wrong is not clearly defined or when the action can be justified on the basis of some factor other than race. Nevertheless, the good intentions of aversive racists can be harnessed to bring their unconscious attitudes and beliefs in line with their egalitarian values. We believe that addressing aversive racism at its roots is essential for moving toward a truly egalitarian society. Simply controlling the negative expressions of aversive racism today cannot, by itself, guarantee racial harmony or equality tomorrow.

REFERENCES

Abrams, D. (1985). Focus of attention in minimal intergroup discrimination. *British Journal of Social Psychology, 24,* 65–74.

Adorno, T. W., Frenkel-Brunswik, E., Levinson, D. J., & Sanford, R. N. (1950). *The authoritarian personality.* New York: Harper.

Anderson, J. (1996, April 29, May 6). Black and blue. *The New Yorker,* 62–64.

Bargh, J. A. (1990). Auto-motives: Preconscious determinants of social interaction. In E. T. Higgins & R. M. Sorrentino (Eds.), *Handbook of motivation and cognition. Vol. 2: Foundations of social behavior* (pp. 93–130). New York: Guilford Press.

Baumeister, R. F. (1996). *Evil: Inside human cruelty and violence.* New York: Freeman.

Blair, I. V. (2001). Implicit stereotypes and prejudice. In G. B. Moskowitz (Ed.), *Cognitive social psychology: The Princeton symposium on the legacy and future of social cognition* (pp. 359–374). Mahwah, NJ: Erlbaum.

Blank, R. M. (2001). An overview of trends in social and economic well-being, by race. In N. J. Smelser, W. J. Wilson, & F. Mitchell (Eds.), *Racial trends and their consequences* (Vol. 1, pp. 21–39). Washington, DC: National Academy Press.

Blumer, H. (1958). Race prejudice as a sense of group position. *Pacific Sociological Review, 1,* 3–7.

Bobo, L. (1999). Prejudice as group position: Micro-foundations of a sociological approach to racism and race relations. *Journal of Social Issues, 55*(3), 445–472.

Boeckmann, R. J., & Turpin-Petrosino, C. (2002). Understanding the harm of hate crimes. *Journal of Social Issues, 58,* 207–225.

Cannon-Bowers, J. A., & Salas, E. (1999). Team performance and training in complex environments: Recent findings from applied research. *Current Directions in Psychological Science, 7,* 83–87.

Chen, M., & Bargh, J. (1997). Nonconscious behavioral confirmation processes: The self-fulfilling consequences of automatic stereotype activation. *Journal of Experimental Social Psychology, 33,* 541–560.

Crocker, J., Luhtanen, R., Broadnax, S., & Blaine, B. E. (1999). Belief in U.S. government conspiracies against blacks among black and white college students: Powerlessness or system blame? *Personality and Social Psychology Bulletin, 25,* 941–953.

Darley, J. M., & Latané, B. (1968). Bystander intervention in emergencies: Diffusion of responsibility. *Journal of Personality and Social Psychology, 8,* 377–383.

DeParle, J. (1990, October 29). Talk of government being out to get blacks falls on more attentive ears. *The New York Times,* p. B7.

DeParle, J. (1991, August 11). For some blacks, social ills seem to follow white plans. *The New York Times,* p. E5.

Devine, P. G. (1989). Stereotypes and prejudice: The automatic and controlled components. *Journal of Personality and Social Psychology, 56,* 5–18.

Devine, P. G., & Monteith, M. J. (1993). The role of discrepancy-associated affect in prejudice reduction. In D. M. Mackie & D. L. Hamilton (Eds.), *Affect, cognition, and stereotyping: Interactive processes in intergroup perception* (pp. 317–344). Orlando, FL: Academic Press.

Donnerstein, E., & Donnerstein, M. (1973). Variables in interracial aggression: Potential ingroup censure. *Journal of Personality and Social Psychology, 27,* 143–150.

Donnerstein, E., Donnerstein, M., Simon, S., & Ditrichs, R. (1972). Variables in interracial aggression: Anonymity, expected retaliation, and a riot. *Journal of Personality and Social Psychology, 22,* 236–245.

Dovidio, J. F. (2001). On the nature of contemporary prejudice: The third wave. *Journal of Social Issues, 57,* 829–849.

Dovidio, J. F., Evans, N., & Tyler, R. B. (1986). Racial stereotypes: The contents of their cognitive representations. *Journal of Experimental Social Psychology, 22,* 22–37.

Dovidio, J. F., & Gaertner, S. L. (1998). On the nature of contemporary prejudice: The causes, consequences, and challenges of aversive racism. In J. Eberhardt & S. T. Fiske (Eds.), *Confronting racism: The problem and the response* (pp. 3–32). Newbury Park, CA: Sage.

Dovidio, J. F., & Gaertner, S. L. (2000). Aversive racism and selection decisions: 1989 and 1999. *Psychological Science, 11,* 319–323.

Dovidio, J. F., Gaertner, S. L., Anastasio, P. A., & Sanitioso, R. (1992). Cognitive and motivational bases of bias: The implications of aversive racism for attitudes toward Hispanics. In S. Knouse, P. Rosenfeld, & A. Culbertson (Eds.), *Hispanics in the workplace* (pp. 75–106). Newbury Park, CA: Sage.

Dovidio, J. F., Gaertner, S. L., Kawakami, K., & Hodson, G. (2002). Why can't we just get along? Interpersonal biases and interracial distrust. *Cultural Diversity and Ethnic Minority Psychology, 8,* 88–102.

Dovidio, J. F., Gaertner, S. L., Validzic, A., Matoka, K., Johnson, B., & Frazier, S. (1997). Extending the benefits of re-categorization: Evaluations, self-disclosure and helping. *Journal of Experimental Social Psychology, 33,* 401–420.

Dovidio, J., Kawakami, K., & Beach, K. (2001). Implicit and explicit attitudes: Examination of the relationship between measures of intergroup bias. In R. Brown & S. L. Gaertner (Eds.), *Blackwell handbook of social psychology. Vol. 4: Intergroup relations (pp. 175–197). Oxford, UK: Blackwell.*

Dovidio, J. F., Kawakami, K., & Gaertner, S. L. (2000). Reducing contemporary prejudice: Combating explicit and implicit bias at the individual and intergroup level. In S. Oskamp (Ed.), *Reducing prejudice and discrimination* (pp. 137–163). Hillsdale, NJ: Erlbaum.

Dovidio, J. F., Kawakami, K., & Gaertner, S. L. (2002). Implicit and explicit prejudice and interracial interaction. *Journal of Personality and Social Psychology, 82,* 62–68.

Dovidio, J., Kawakami, K., Johnson, C., Johnson, B., & Howard, A. (1997). The nature of prejudice: Automatic and controlled processes. *Journal of Experimental Social Psychology, 33,* 510–540.

Duckitt, J. (1992). *The social psychology of prejudice.* Westport, CT: Praeger.

Esses, V. M., Dovidio, J. F., & Hodson, G. (2002). Public attitudes toward immigration in the United States and Canada in response to the September 2001 "Attack on America." *Analysis of Social Issues and Public Policy, 2,* 69–85.

Fazio, R. H., Jackson, J. R., Dunton, B. C., & Williams, C. J. (1995). Variability in automatic activation as an unobtrusive measure of racial attitudes: A *bona fide* pipeline? *Journal of Personality and Social Psychology, 69,* 1013–1027.

Feagin, J. R., & Sikes, M. P. (1994). *Living with racism: The black middle-class experience.* Boston: Beacon Press.

Fein, S., & Spencer, S. J. (1997). Prejudice as self-image maintenance: Affirming the self through derogating others. *Journal of Personality and Social Psychology, 73,* 31–44.

Gaertner, S. L. (1973). Helping behavior and racial discrimination among liberals and conservatives. *Journal of Personality and Social Psychology, 25,* 335–341.

Gaertner, S. L., & Dovidio, J. F. (1977). The subtlety of white racism, arousal, and helping behavior. *Journal of Personality and Social Psychology, 35,* 691–707.

Gaertner, S. L., & Dovidio, J. F. (1986). The aversive form of racism. In J. F. Dovidio & S. L. Gaertner (Eds.), *Prejudice, discrimination, and racism* (pp. 61–89). Orlando, FL: Academic Press.

Gaertner, S. L., & Dovidio, J. F. (2000). *Reducing intergroup bias: The common ingroup identity model.* Philadelphia: Psychology Press.

Gaertner, S. L., Dovidio, J. F., Anastasio, P. A., Bachman, B. A., & Rust, M. C. (1993). The common ingroup identity model: Recategorization and the reduction of intergroup bias. In W. Stroebe & M. Hewstone (Eds.), *European review of social psychology* (Vol. 4, pp. 1–26). New York: Wiley.

Gaertner, S. L., Dovidio, J. F., Banker, B., Rust, M., Nier, J., Mottola, G., & Ward, C. (1997). Does racism necessarily mean anti-blackness? Aversive racism and pro-whiteness. In M. Fine, L. Powell, L. Weis, & M. Wong (Eds.), *Off white* (pp. 167–178). London: Routledge.

Gaertner, S. L., & McLaughlin, J. P. (1983). Racial stereotypes: Associations and ascriptions of positive and negative characteristics. *Social Psychology Quarterly, 46,* 23–30.

Greenwald, A., & Banaji, M. (1995). Implicit social cognition: Attitudes, self-esteem, and stereotypes. *Psychological Review, 102,* 4–27.

Greenwald, A., McGhee, D., & Schwartz, J. (1998). Measuring individual differences in implicit cognition: The implicit association test. *Journal of Personality and Social Psychology, 74,* 1464–1480.

Hodson, G., Dovidio, J. F., & Gaertner, S. L. (2002). Processes in racial discrimination: Differential weighting of conflicting information. *Personality and Social Psychology Bulletin, 28,* 460–471.

Howard, J. M., & Rothbart, M. (1980). Social categorization for in-group and out-group behavior. *Journal of Personality and Social Psychology, 38,* 301–310.

Hyers, L. L., & Swim, J. K. (1998). A comparison of the experiences of dominant and minority group members during an intergroup encounter. *Group Processes and Intergroup Relations, 1,* 143–163.

Jones, J. M. (1997). *Prejudice and racism* (2nd ed.). New York: McGraw-Hill.

Katz, I., & Hass, R. G. (1988). Racial ambivalence and value conflict: Correlational and priming studies of dual cognitive structures. *Journal of Personality and Social Psychology, 55,* 893–905.

Katz, I., Wackenhut, J., & Hass, R. G. (1986). Racial ambivalence, value duality, and behavior. In J. F. Dovidio & S. L. Gaertner (Eds.), *Prejudice, discrimination, and racism* (pp. 35–59). Orlando, FL: Academic Press.

Kawakami, K., Dovidio, J. F., Moll, J., Hermsen, S., & Russin, A. (2000). Just say no (to stereotyping): Effects of training in trait negation on stereotype activation. *Journal of Personality and Social Psychology, 78,* 871–888.

Kawakami, K., Spears, R., & Dovidio, J. F. (2002). Disinhibition of stereotyping: Context, prejudice and target characteristics. *European Journal of Social Psychology, 32,* 517–530.

Kluegel, J. R., & Smith, E. R. (1986). *Beliefs about inequality: Americans' views of what is and what ought to be.* New York: Aldine de Gruyter.

Kovel, J. (1970). *White racism: A psychohistory.* New York: Pantheon.

Krieger, L. H. (1995). The content of our categories: A cognitive bias approach to discrimination and equal employment opportunity. *Stanford Law Review, 47,* 1161–1248.

Krieger, L. H. (1998). Civil rights *perestroika*: Intergroup relations after affirmative action. *California Law Review, 86,* 1251–1333.

McConahay, J. B. (1986). Modern racism, ambivalence, and the modern racism scale. In J. F. Dovidio & S. L. Gaertner (Eds.), *Prejudice, discrimination, and racism* (pp. 91–125). Orlando, FL: Academic Press.

McConnell, A. R., & Leibold, J. M. (2001). Relations among the Implicit Association Test, discriminatory behavior, and explicit measures of racial attitudes. *Journal of Experimental Social Psychology, 37,* 435–442.

Monteith, M. J., Sherman, J., & Devine, P. G. (1998). Suppression as a stereotype control strategy. *Personality and Social Psychology Review, 1,* 63–82.

Monteith, M. J., & Voils, C. (1998). Proneness to prejudiced responses: Toward understanding the authenticity of self-reported discrepancies. *Journal of Personality and Social Psychology, 75,* 901–916.

Nier, J. A., Gaertner, S. L., Dovidio, J. F., Banker, B. S., & Ward, C. M. (2001). Changing interracial evaluations and behavior: The effects of a common group identity. *Group Processes and Intergroup Relations, 4,* 299–316.

Otten, S., & Moskowitz, G. B. (2000). Evidence for implicit evaluative in-group bias: Affect-based spontaneous trait inference in a minimal group paradigm. *Journal of Experimental Social Psychology, 36,* 77–89.

Pettigrew, T. F. (1959). Regional differences in anti-Negro prejudice. *Journal of Abnormal and Social Psychology, 59,* 28–36.

Pettigrew, T. F. (1998). Intergroup contact theory. *Annual Review of Psychology, 49,* 65–85.

Pettigrew, T. F., & Meertens, R. W. (1995). Subtle and blatant prejudice in Western Europe. *European Journal of Social Psychology, 25,* 57–76.

Rogers, R. W., & Prentice-Dunn, S. (1981). Deindividuation and anger-mediated interracial aggression: Unmasking regressive racism. *Journal of Personality and Social Psychology, 41,* 63–73.

Schuman, H., Steeh, C., Bobo, L., & Krysan, M. (1997). *Racial attitudes in America: Trends and interpretations.* Cambridge, MA: Harvard University Press.

Sears, D. O. (1988). Symbolic racism. In P. A. Katz & D. A. Taylor (Eds.), *Eliminating racism: Profiles in controversy* (pp. 53–84). New York: Plenum Press.

Sears, D. O., Henry, P. J., & Kosterman, R. (2000). Egalitarian values and contemporary racial politics. In D. O. Sears, J. Sidanius, & L. Bobo (Eds.), *Racialized politics: The debate about racism in America* (pp. 75–117). Chicago: University of Chicago Press.

Shelton, J. N. (2000). A reconceptualization of how we study issues of racial prejudice. *Personality and Social Psychology Review, 4,* 374–390.

Stephan, W. G., & Stephan, C. W. (2001). *Improving intergroup relations.* Thousand Oaks, CA: Sage.

Tajfel, H., & Turner, J. C. (1979). An integrative theory of intergroup conflict. In W. G. Austin & S. Worchel (Eds.), *The social psychology of intergroup relations* (pp. 33–48). Monterey, CA: Brooks–Cole.

Turner, J. C. (1985). Social categorization and the self-concept: A social cognitive theory of group behavior. In E. J. Lawler (Ed.), *Advances in group processes* (Vol. 2, pp. 77–122). Greenwich, CT: JAI Press.

Vorauer, J. D., & Kumhyr, S. M. (2001). Is this about you or me? Self- versus other-directed judgments and feelings in response to intergroup interaction. *Personality and Social Psychology Bulletin, 27,* 706–719.

Wilson, T. D., Lindsey, S., & Schooler, T. Y. (2000). A model of dual attitudes. *Psychological Review, 107,* 101–126.

Wittenbrink, B., Judd, C., & Park, B. (1997). Evidence for racial prejudice at the implicit level and its relationship with questionnaire measures. *Journal of Personality and Social Psychology, 72,* 262–274.

Wyer, N., & Hamilton, D. (1998). The balance between excitation and inhibition in stereotype use. In R. Wyer (Ed.), *Advances in social cognition: Vol. 11. Stereotype activation and inhibition* (pp. 227–242). Mahwah, NJ: Erlbaum.

CHAPTER 8

VIOLENT EVIL AND THE GENERAL AGGRESSION MODEL

CRAIG A. ANDERSON
NICHOLAS L. CARNAGEY

CONTEXT

On April 20, 1999, the 110th anniversary of Adolf Hitler's birthday, Eric Harris and Dylan Klebold murdered 13 people and wounded another 23 in their high school in Littleton, Colorado. On September 11, 2001, in a coordinated attack, terrorists hijacked four commercial jets and succeeded in flying two of them into the World Trade Center Towers in New York City, and one into the Pentagon. The fourth, apparently targeted for the U.S. Capitol in Washington, DC, crashed in a Pennsylvania field when passengers attacked the hijackers. The final death toll was over 2,800 (The National Obituary Archive, 2002).

We label the most extreme forms of aggression as "violent evil" in this chapter. Hopes that the horrors of World War II and the Holocaust would produce a worldwide rejection of such inhuman actions and a resulting end of genocidal practices, a cessation of wars among nations, and a reduction in homicide rates have been dashed by the realities of war, homicide, and genocide in the last half of the 20th century. The litany of recent genocidal events is both long and depressing, including major massacres in Uganda, Cambodia, Rwanda, Burundi, Zaire, Bosnia, Serbia, Croatia, Hercegovina, among others. The beginning of the 21st century has not provided much relief either, as clearly illustrated by the September

11, 2001 terrorist attacks, the subsequent "war on terrorism" in Afganistan, the escalating conflict between the Israelis and Palestinians, the ethnic/religious massacres in India, and the recent (and continuing) war in Iraq.

Of course, human violence is not new. Archeological and historical evidence makes it clear that violence was prevalent among our hunter/gatherer ancestors 25,000 years ago, among the Greek, Egyptian, and Roman societies 2,000–3,000 years ago, among most societies in the last two centuries, and in almost every society today. Although technological advances have made mass violence easier to accomplish, "people" today are not more violence-prone than they were thousands of years ago. Nonetheless, the prevalence of violence in contemporary society, the efficiency of modern weapons, and differences in violence rates between societies have collectively inspired a resurgence of interest in understanding such behavior at individual, group, and societal levels. The hope, of course, is that such understanding will lead to significant reductions in future rates of violence at each level of analysis.

As is apparent throughout the chapters in this book on good and evil, the predominant "evil" is violence, usually defined as an intentional action directed at one or more fellow humans and designed to inflict great harm on those target individuals. There are, of course, many variants and degrees of evil. In this chapter we focus on aggression and violence and demonstrate how the General Aggression Model (GAM) can be used to integrate the many factors that contribute to the evil of violence (Anderson & Bushman, 2002b; Anderson & Huesmann, in press; Lindsay & Anderson, 2000). Also apparent from many chapters in this book is the fact that good and evil are two sides of the same coin. Identifying and understanding factors that lead to violent evil also yield valuable insights into factors that lead to good. Furthermore, many shining examples of the best of human actions are essentially actions taken to thwart or resist violent evil. We focus on violent evil in this chapter for the sake of brevity, but we invite readers to consider how our model can also be used to further understand heroic actions, such as that displayed by passengers who thwarted the terrorists attempting to crash their hijacked jet into the U.S. Capitol, by Gandhi and followers who conducted a successful nonviolent revolution in India, and by Martin Luther King, Jr., and followers who used similar nonviolent means to reduce institutionalized racial injustices.

LEVELS OF ANALYSIS

Violence may be analyzed at several different levels, ranging from the individual human to *homo sapiens* as a species. In our view, the most interesting levels are the individual, the small group, the subculture, and the society. This does not mean that evolutionary analyses are unimportant. Indeed, such analyses and cross-species comparisons have contributed much to the scientific study of violence (e.g., Geary, 1998; Malamuth & Heilmann, 1998). However, it is clear that humans have a *built-in* capacity for violence and that the likelihood of that capacity being realized in actual behavior varies widely and systematically. We believe that the study of this variablility is fascinating, has already led to a very good understanding of violence and to societal changes that effectively reduce violence, and will ultimately lead to more successful attempts to reduce unwarranted violence at all levels of analysis.

Many chapters in this book identify key factors at the group, subculture, and societal levels. We find these developments exciting. Our focus on the individual in society is based on the fact that only individuals "behave" in either good or evil ways. To be sure, historical, economic, and social forces greatly influence the individual's behavior, but they must do so by influencing some aspect of the individual. In our explication of GAM, we note how and where such higher-level factors operate on the individual.

THE GENERAL AGGRESSION MODEL

Definitions and Scope

Aggression is usually defined by social psychologists as *behavior directed toward another individual and carried out with the intent to cause harm.* Furthermore, the perpetrator must believe that the behavior will harm the target, and that the target is motivated to avoid the behavior (Baron & Richardson, 1994; Berkowitz, 1993; Geen, 2001). Violence is usually defined as physical aggression at the extremely high end of the aggression continuum, such as murder and aggravated assault. All violence is aggression, but much that is aggression is not violence. For example, one child pushing another off a tricycle is aggression but not violence. A school shooting involves both aggression and violence. Some criminologists and public health officials use quite different definitions of violence and seem largely uninterested in aggression or the aggression–violence continuum (Surgeon General, 2001). For some, *violence* requires actual serious physical harm to another person through the performance of an act that must be illegal. Such a restricted definition may be useful in some contexts, but the social-psychological definitions are much more valuable for understanding violent evil. For instance, some Holocaust participants maintained that because they were following legitimate orders, they should not be held responsible for their actions, even though they knew that the victims would be killed. That is, they proposed that because their actions were technically legal, they therefore were neither aggressive nor evil. The social-psychological definition does not include an "illegal" component and so does not falter in this context. Similar arguments can be made for focusing on the *attempt* to cause harm rather than on whether or not that attempt succeeded.

Several additional changes in the conceptualization of aggression are necessary to create a truly general model of human aggression. All involve discarding traditional dichotomous categorization schemes. Three such categorization schemes have been discarded in previous work: affective (hostile) versus instrumental aggression, impulsive versus premeditated aggression, and proactive versus reactive aggression (Anderson & Bushman, 2002b; Anderson & Huesmann, 2003; Bushman & Anderson, 2001). Historically, *affective* aggression has been conceived as an impulsive and thoughtless (i.e., unplanned) form of behavior, driven by anger, having the ultimate motive of harming the target, and occurring as a reaction to some perceived provocation. It is sometimes called hostile, impulsive, or reactive aggression. *Instrumental* aggression is conceived as a premeditated, proactive rather than reactive means of obtaining some goal other than harming the victim. *Impulsive* aggression is usually conceived as thoughtless (i.e., automatic, fast, without consideration of consequences), reactive, and affect laden. *Premeditated* aggression, in contrast, is usually conceived as thoughtful (i.e., deliberative, slow, instrumental), proactive, and affectless. Proactive and reactive aggression are frequently used interchangeably with instrumental and affective, respectively, but they have slightly different emphases. *Proactive* aggression is usually conceived as occurring without provocation, is thoughtful, and has little or no affect. *Reactive* aggression is a response to a prior provocation and usually is accompanied by anger (Dodge & Coie, 1987; Pulkkinen, 1996).

The three main problems with these either/or dichotomies are that (1) many common aggressive behaviors contain elements that do not fit the dichotomous schemes; (2) the dichotomous schemes do not fit what is known about the interplay of automatic and controlled cognitive perception and decision processes; and (3) the dichotomous distinctions are themselves confounded with each other in contradictory ways. Apparently instrumental aggression can contain much hostile affect; some angry outbursts appear to be coldly calculated; some proactive aggression has a distinctly emotional aspect; and apparently instrumental considerations of potential consequences can be made both automatically and without awareness. For example, frequent use of aggression to obtain valued goals can become so automated or habitual that it becomes impulsive (Bargh & Pietromonaco, 1982; Schneider & Shiffrin, 1977; Shiffrin & Schneider, 1977).

To deal with the affective/instrumental dichotomy, we introduced and illustrated the distinction between proximate and ultimate goals (Anderson & Bushman, 2002b; Bushman & Anderson, 2001). A proximate goal is one that most immediately guides behavior, whereas the ultimate goal is the broader reason for doing that behavior. In this new conceptual scheme, intention to harm still is a necessary definitional feature of all aggression, but it is necessary only as a *proximate* goal. The *ultimate* goal, however, may be solely to inflict harm (pure affective aggression), solely to gain some other goods or resource (pure instrumental aggression), or a mixture of hostile and instrumental goals. In essence, we can separately evaluate the degree to which an ultimate goal has hostile and instrumental components.

Similarly, a dimensional approach resolves other dichotomous anomalies. Any aggressive act can be characterized along each of the following dimensions:

- Degree of hostile or agitated affect present
- Automaticity
- Degree to which the primary or ultimate goal is to harm the victim versus benefit the perpetrator
- Degree to which consequences were considered

This dimensional framework yields a clearer understanding of mixed-motive aggression, quick but consequence-sensitive aggressive acts, and other forms of aggression that have been problematic for traditional dichotomous approaches (Anderson & Bushman, 2002b; Anderson & Huesmann, 2003; Bushman & Anderson, 2001).

The need to address the dichotomy of direct versus indirect aggression emerged while preparing this chapter. Indirect aggression is usually defined as aggressive behavior committed outside the presence of the victim, such as telling stories and lies behind someone's back to get him or her in trouble or taking a person's things when he or she is not present. Direct aggression is committed in the presence of the target. This distinction has been highlighted by several research groups who have found substantial gender differences, with males using relatively more direct and females relatively more indirect forms of aggression (Bjorkqvist, Lagerspetz, & Kaukiainen, 1992; Crick & Grotpeter, 1995; Lagerspetz, Bjorkqvist, & Peltonen, 1988; Lagerspetz & Bjorkqvist, 1992). The problem with this dichotomy is that it confounds two dimensions: visibility of the act and actor to the victim, and propinquity to the act that actually produces the harm. Consider the case of a Nazi guard who forces Jewish prisoners to board a train for a death camp. The act takes place in the presence of the victims and so would seem to be a case of direct aggression. However, the execution of those prisoners might take place hundreds of miles away, some weeks or months later, and may not occur for all of the prisoners. This makes the act seem more like indirect aggression. We propose that the direct/indirect dichotomy be discarded in favor of the two dimensions of *visibility* and *propinquity*.

The Basic Model

Background

The General Aggression Model is a dynamic, social–cognitive, developmental model that includes situational, individual (personological), and biological variables and provides an integrative framework for domain-specific theories of aggression. GAM is largely based on social learning and social–cognitive theories developed over the past three decades by a large number of scholars from social, developmental, and personality psychology (e.g., Bandura, 1973, 1977, 1983, 1986; Berkowitz, 1989, 1993; Dodge, 1980, 1986; Crick & Dodge, 1994; Huesmann, 1982, 1988, 1998; Mischel, 1973; Mischel & Shoda, 1995). These scholars prepared the stage for GAM's integrative view by delineating how social behavior moves under the control of internal self-regulating processes, and by illustrating the underlying learning and developmental processes. Social behavior depends upon the individual's construal of events in the present environment, including the person's interpretation of these events, beliefs about typical ways of responding to such events, perceived competencies for responding in different ways, and expectations regarding likely outcomes. These cognitions provide a basis for some stability of behavior across a variety of situations (because each individual tends to resolve situational ambiguities in characteristic ways), but also allow considerable situational specificity (because of reality constraints upon possible construals).

GAM also draws heavily on research that elucidates the development and use of knowledge structures for perception, interpretation, decision making, and action (e.g., Bargh, 1996; Collins & Loftus, 1975; Fiske & Taylor, 1991; Higgins, 1996; Wegner & Bargh, 1998). Knowledge structures develop from experience; influence all types of perception, from basic visual patterns to complex behavioral sequences; can become automatized with use; are linked to affective states, behavioral programs, and beliefs; and guide interpretations and behavioral responses to the social and physical environments. One particularly important breakthrough was the discovery that even very complex decision and judgment processes can become automatized with practice. That is, decisions that initially require considerable conscious thought can, in fact, become effortless and occur with little or no awareness. For example, a person who repeatedly "learns" through experience or through cultural teachings that a particular type of person (e.g., Palestinian, Israeli) is a "threat" can automatically perceive almost any action by a member of that group as dangerous and remain unaware of the multiple inferences he or she made in coming to that perception. This dynamic can easily lead to a "shoot first, ask questions later" mentality. Indeed, this automaticity of hatred, suspicion, and preemptive aggression aptly characterizes the conditions leading to many of the most heinous massacres and acts of genocide throughout history.

Three particularly important types of knowledge structures are (1) *perceptual schemata,* which are used to identify phenomena as simple as everyday physical objects (e.g., chair, person) or as complex as social events (e.g., personal insult); (2) *person schemata,* which include beliefs about a particular person (e.g., George W. Bush) or groups of people (e.g., Hutus, Tutsis); and (3) *behavioral scripts,* which contain information about how people behave under varying circumstances (e.g., a restaurant script).

Knowledge structures include affect in three different way. First, knowledge structures contain links to experiential affect "nodes" or concepts. When a knowledge structure containing anger is activated, anger is experienced. Second, they include knowledge about affect, such as when a particular emotion should be experienced, how emotions influence people's judgments and behavior, and so on. Third, a script may include affect as an action rule (Abelson, 1981). For example, a "personal insult" script may prescribe aggressive retaliation but only if anger is at a high level or fear is at a low level. Figure 8.1 displays two types of knowledge structures: a general schema about guns and a behavioral script for retaliation. Concepts with similar meanings (e.g., hurt, harm) and concepts that are frequently activated simultaneously (e.g., gun, shoot) become strongly linked. In Figure 8.1, line thickness represents association strength, and distance represents dissimilarity of meaning. The figure also illustrates how network associations can activate specific behavioral scripts. If the nodes *gun, kill, hurt,* and *harm* are activated, the retaliation script will be strongly primed; once primed, the script becomes a more likely tool for

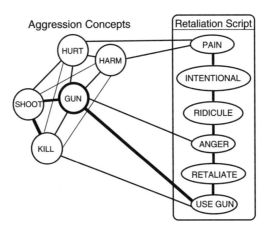

FIGURE 8.1. Simplified associative network of aggression concepts and a retaliation script. From Anderson, Benjamin, and Bartholow (1998). Copyright 1998 by the American Psychological Society. Reprinted by permission.

interpreting an ambiguous situation involving ridicule, thereby increasing the likelihood of retaliation.

Single Episode Cycle

GAM focuses on the "person in the situation," called an *episode,* consisting of one cycle of an ongoing social interaction. Figure 8.2 presents a simplified version of the main foci of the model. The three main foci concern (1) person and situation inputs; (2) present internal state, consisting of the cognitive, affective, and arousal routes though which input variables have their impact; and (3) outcomes of the underlying appraisal and decision processes.

Inputs. The input level consists of two types of *proximate* causes. Situational causes are features of the present situation that increase (or inhibit) aggression—for example, factors such as an insult, an uncomfortable temperature, presence of a weapon, presence of one's religious leader. Personological causes include whatever the person brings to the current situation—for example, factors such as attitudes, beliefs, and behavioral tendencies. Biological effects (e.g., hormones, genetics) operate via biosocial interaction effects (e.g., the interaction of a biological vulnerability with an abusive environment) on personological causes (e.g., Anderson & Huesmann, 2003; Raine, Brennen, Farrington, & Mednick, 1997).

Present Internal State. Input variables influence behavior through the *present internal state* that they create. The internal states of most interest concern cognition, affect, and arousal. A given input variable may influ-

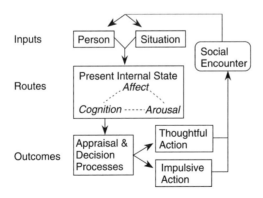

FIGURE 8.2. The general aggression model: Episodic processes. From Anderson and Bushman (2002b). Copyright 2002 by Annual Reviews. Reprinted by permission.

ence aggression by influencing one, two, or all three aspects of the present internal state. Furthermore, the dashed line connecting the three aspects in Figure 8.2 illustrate that each may influence the others. This means that a given input variable may have direct or indirect effects on each aspect of the present internal state. For example, research on temperature effects has found that hot temperatures appear to directly increase hostile affect and physiological arousal and to indirectly increase hostile cognition (e.g., Anderson, Anderson, & Deuser, 1996; Anderson, Anderson, Dorr, DeNeve, & Flanagan, 2000).

Sometimes person and situation variables combine interactively in their effects on present internal state, as in Anderson, Anderson, Dill, and Deuser's (1998) finding that pain and trait hostility interactively affect aggressive cognitions. At other times they combine additively, as in Anderson's (1997) finding that exposure to media violence and trait hostility both increased feelings of state hostility but that the two variables did not interact.

Outcomes. The third stage includes several complex appraisal and decision processes, ranging from the relatively automatic to the heavily controlled (cf. Robinson, 1998; Smith & Lazarus, 1993). Results from the inputs enter into the appraisal and decision processes through their effects on present internal state. In Figure 8.3 relatively automatic processes are labeled "immediate appraisal," whereas more controlled processes are labeled "reappraisal." The outcomes of these decision processes determine the final action of the episode. The final action then cycles through the social encounter to become part of the input for the next episode, as depicted in Figure 8.2.

The appraisal and decision processes depicted in Figure 8.3 derive

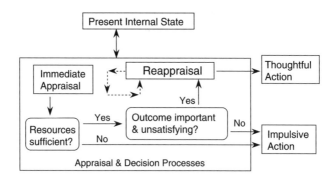

FIGURE 8.3. Appraisal and decision processes: Expanded view. From Anderson and Bushman (2002b). Copyright 2002 by Annual Reviews. Reprinted by permission.

from research in many areas but most specifically from work on spontaneous inference processes (Krull, 1993; Krull & Dill, 1996; Uleman, 1987) and explanation/attribution processes (Anderson, Krull, & Weiner, 1996). Immediate appraisal is automatic: It is relatively effortless, spontaneous, and occurs without awareness. Present internal state determines the content of the immediate appraisal. And as noted earlier, both person and situation factors determine the present internal state.

Immediate appraisals include affective, goal, and intention information. A threat appraisal may include fear and anger-related affect, an aggression goal, and a specific intention to carry out that goal. Responses to the same objective situation differ considerably from person to person, depending on each person's social learning history (i.e., personality) and present state of mind (i.e., which knowledge structures are currently most accessible).

Whether reappraisal occurs depends on two factors: availability of resources (e.g., time, cognitive capacity) and whether the immediate appraisal is judged as both important and unsatisfactory. If resources are insufficient or if the outcome is deemed unimportant or satisfactory, impulsive action occurs—action that may be aggressive or nonaggressive, depending on the content of the immediate appraisal.

If reappraisal occurs, a search is activated for an alternative view of the situation. Different knowledge structures may be recruited and tested, including different scripts and memories of similar events. Numerous reappraisal cycles may occur, but at some point the process ceases and a thoughtful course of action occurs. That action may be nonaggressive, but an important aspect of this model is that thoughtful action may well be highly aggressive—whether of a cold, calculating type or a hot, affective type. Indeed, the reappraisal process can increase the level of anger, as past "wrongs" by the target person are dredged up from memory or as the damage to one's social image becomes more apparent. Also note that present internal state is affected by both types of appraisal, indicated by the double-headed arrow in Figure 8.3.

In sum, all social behavior, including aggression, is the result of the proximate convergence of situational factors (i.e., instigators or inhibitors of aggression) and personological factors (i.e., propensity or preparedness to aggress or to avoid aggression). These input variables influence social behavior by determining the present internal state and subsequent appraisal and decision processes. The emitted social behavior, in turn, moves the social encounter along to its next episodic cycle.

Developmental Cycle

From this social–cognitive perspective, *personality* is the sum of a person's knowledge structures (Anderson & Huesmann, 2003; Mischel & Shoda,

1995; Sedikides & Skowronski, 1990), constructed from countless experiences throughout the life span, influenced by biological factors as well as situational ones. At any given point in time, how a person construes and responds to the social world depends on the situational factors in his or her world and on the knowledge structures he or she has acquired and uses habitually.

The process by which hostile schemas, aggressive scripts, and other types of knowledge structure are activated is a cognitive one that can, with practice, become completely automatic and operate without awareness (Schneider & Shiffrin, 1977; Todorov & Bargh, 2002). By viewing each episodic cycle depicted in Figure 8.2 as a learning trial, we can understand the development of an aggressive personality as the result of a series of learning episodes that prepare the individual to behave aggressively or violently in a number of differing situations. Many of the perceptual, appraisal, and decision processes underlying such behavior can take place with little thought, effort, or awareness. This social–cognitive learning aspect of GAM and similar models, in conjunction with the judgment and decision-making aspects of the model, (1) clarifies how situational and personological variables produce more (vs. less) aggressive individuals in general, (2) accounts for the specificity and generality of a given individual's pattern of aggressive (or nonaggressive) behaviors across time and situation, and (3) provides a sound basis for constructing interventions designed to prevent the development of inappropriately aggressive tendencies or to change such tendencies after they have developed.

Biosocial Interactions. Inherited biological factors clearly influence risk for aggression but do not entirely determine level of aggression expressed (Raine et al., 1997). Biological predispositions manifest themselves through "interactions" with the social context in which the organism develops. Such interactions allow biological factors to influence social behavior by affecting the developing knowledge structures (such as scripts, beliefs, and schemas) and through their influence on affective components of these knowledge structures. Recent evolutionary theorizing about aggression, specifically the recognition of the importance of "calibration" through learning experiences in the emergence of inherited behavior patterns (e.g., Buss & Shackelford, 1997a, 1997b; Daly & Wilson, 1994; Malamuth & Heilmann, 1998), fits this biosocial interaction perspective quite well. Similar conclusions have been reached by social–developmental researchers (e.g., Huesmann, 1997; Tremblay, 2000). It is also interesting to note the relevance of the old learning concept of "preparedness" (Seligman, 1970), the idea from the animal learning literature that it is easier to link some stimulus–response pairs than others. Preparedness relates to human aggression in at least two ways. First, certain emotional states and behavioral syndromes appear to be easily linked, such as frustration, pain, anger, and aggression (e.g., Berkowitz, 1993). Second, biological (i.e., genetic, hormonal) effects on aggression may operate by preparing some individuals to more easily learn frustration–anger–aggression linkages, and by preparing others (i.e., those who become nonaggressive people) to more easily learn the negative consequences of aggression (e.g., Soubrie, 1986).

Aggression-Related Variables. Figure 8.4 presents a schematic summary of these developmental and personality processes in relation to five broad categories of aggression-related variables that have been identified by various researchers as key elements in what we call aggressive personality. Although each of the five categories focuses on "aggressive" elements, it is important to remember the flip sides of these five coins. For example, anti-aggression beliefs and attitudes are also relevant, even though there is not a separate "box" for them.[1]

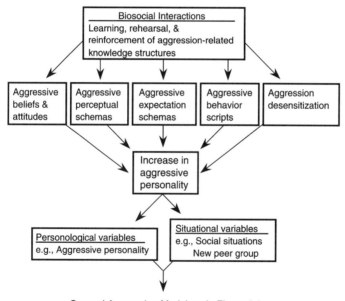

FIGURE 8.4. The General Aggression Model: Developmental/personality processes in relation to five categories of aggressive-related variables.

---

[1]Note that *aggressive personality* is not conceived as a unitary construct. There are many types of aggressive people, differing in which kinds of aggression they display in response to different types of situations.

The bottom half of Figure 8.4 links this developmental–personality portion of GAM back to the social episode portion, illustrating how both the past and the future influence social behavior in the present situation. Past biosocial interactions of certain types lead to increases in aggressive personality. Expectations about the future are a part of this social—cognitive view of personality. Personality (i.e., personological variables) influences the construal of, and reaction to, new social encounters, thus bringing both the past and the future into the present social episode. In addition, changes in personality can bring about systematic changes in types of situations that the person will encounter most frequently in the future. For example, a child who becomes more aggressive over time will experience a shift in friendship patterns and relationships with teachers and family members. Such a child tends to become a social outcast, associating with other aggressive children and being shunned by more socially adept peers. Interactions with teachers and parents deteriorate as well. In essence, the child's social environment becomes more aggressive and confrontational in many ways.

Violence Escalation Cycle

Figure 8.5 illustrates the violence escalation cycle, which has been described by many aggression scholars, is discussed in several chapters in the present volume, and fits GAM quite well. "A" and "B" can represent two people, two groups, two religions, two nations—basically any dyadic units in which members of the dyad are in conflict with each other. Some initial triggering event sets the cycle in motion. One person's "appropriate and justified" retaliation is the other's next provocation. Very often, the initial events are lost in the distant past, but once started, the cycle tends to persist. There are three key points. First, as most grandparents, most religions, and most aggression scholars have noted, violence begets violence. The cyclical nature of violent acts is so apparent in day-to-day interactions among children as well as nations that further elucidation seems unnecesary. Unfortunately, people and nations involved in such cycles often cannot "see" what seems apparent to others. For example, many U.S. citizens consider the U.S. "War on Terrorism" in Afghanistan and the "preemptive" war on Iraq as appropriate and justified responses to the events of 9/11 and to other threats, but fail to understand how it is that others around the world, including Arab groups in the Gulf region, might perceive one or both wars as unjustified overreactions, outright religious wars, or an imperialistic grab for oil. Many of the U.S. political leaders seem to be truly puzzled by the fact that many recent U.S. military actions can be perceived by others as "evil" works demanding a forceful response. Our point is not that the United States is wrong and that Osama bin Laden and Saddam Hussein are right, but merely to illustrate how difficult it can

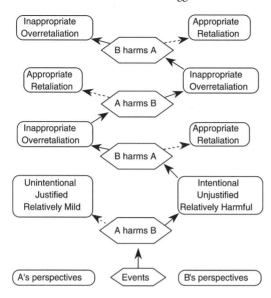

FIGURE 8.5. The violence escalation cycle.

be to perceive our own involvement in an ongoing cycle of violence. If we truly understand the cycle and our place in this particular one, then we cannot be surprised that "terrorist" groups are reappearing in Afghanistan or that guerilla warfare against U.S. troops in Iraq has emerged and is escalating.

Second, retaliation typically occurs at a higher or more extreme level than the most recent provocation. This is the "escalation" aspect of the cycle. When the cycle invovles two individuals, the escalation is often absolute. That is, if person A makes cutting remarks to person B, B may escalate to a punch or slap; A may then escalate to a knife, B to a gun. At the level of nations, the escalation is often relative, in the sense that each side may increase the harm it does relative to what it did in an earlier cycle, but the nations may differ dramatically in their ability to inflict harm on the other. The Isreali–Palestinian conflict is of this nature. The Palestinians cannot begin to inflict the number of deaths on Isrealis that the Isrealis can inflict on the Palestinians. The same imbalance exists in the U.S. wars on terrorism. Again, we do not wish to promote one political or religious position over another but are merely trying to illustrate key points about cycles of violence.

Third, the upward pressure toward ever-increasing levels of violence stems largely from perspective biases, in which the most recent perpetrators view the harmful act they just committed as appropriate and justified, whereas the most recent victims view the harmful act committed against them as an inappropriate overreaction. These differential perspective biases are fueled by many of the knowledge structures discussed in the previous section.

Successful intervention requires that (1) the parties in conflict are separated (at least, temporarily) so that the escalation cycle can be stopped; (2) key underlying knowledge structures are changed (e.g., extremely hostile stereotypes or beliefs about the other side, beliefs about the moral superiority of one's own position, expectations about the eventual effectiveness of one's violent course of action); and (3) knowledge structures that facilitate peaceful coexistence be created or made more salient (e.g., establishing common goals and plans to achieve those goals, as well as expectations that they can be achieved). Of course, the specific knowledge structures that need to be changed vary from case to case as well as from level to level (i.e., two individuals vs. two gangs vs. two nations). However, as GAM makes clear, the same basic processes are at work regardless of the level at which the escalation cycle has been engaged.

Risk Factors

Multiple Causes

Research from several perspectives reveals that a wide variety of risk and protective factors influence the incidence of individual and collective violent evil between and within various societies. Examples of these factors include accessibility of guns (O'Donnell, 1995), global warming (Anderson, Bushman, & Groom, 1997), different cultural norms about violence (Nisbett & Cohen, 1996), and the widespread exposure to violent entertainment media (Anderson et al., in press; Anderson & Bushman, 2001, 2002b). However, no one causal factor, by itself, explains more than a small portion of differences in violence. For example, it is now well established that exposure to media violence is a risk factor for development of aggressive and violent individuals. Four broad types of converging evidence provide consistent results on this point: Cross-sectional correlation studies, longitudinal studies, laboratory experiments, and field experiments all point to the same simple conclusion (Anderson & Bushman, 2002c). Compared to the effect sizes of other more well-known medical effects, such as secondhand smoking effects on lung cancer (Bushman & Anderson, 2002a), the media violence effects are sizeable but still account for only 3–4% of the variance in aggression. The effect size on the most extreme forms of violent evil is likely smaller. But the same is true for other violence risk factors. Violent evil is most likely to emerge in environments with multiple risk factors, environments that provide aggressive models, frustrate and victimize people, reinforce aggression, and teach people that aggression is acceptable and successful.

Types of Causes

It is convenient to divide risk factors for violent evil into proximate and distal causes (Anderson & Huesmann, 2003). As discussed earlier, *proximate* causes are those *person* and *situation* variables that are present and active in the current social episode. *Distal* causes are *environmental* and *biological* modifiers that exert their influence over a long period of time. As illustrated in Figure 8.6, distal factors operate by increasing proximate factors that facilitate aggression or by decreasing proximate factors that inhibit aggression. For the most part, distal factors are seen as influencing the individual's personal preparedness to aggress (i.e., aggressive personality). For example, repeated exposure to media violence can create highly accessible retaliation scripts that are easily activated on future occasions. As noted earlier, however, systematic changes in aggressiveness also produce systematic changes in the person's social environment. Thus, distal factors can also systematically change the situational contexts in which a person habitually resides. Finally, it is useful to remember that some biological and some environmental modifiers operate as both proximate and distall causal factors. Exposure to a violent movie both primes aggression-related knowledge structures in the immediate situation and constitutes an additional learning trial that teaches the viewer beliefs that will have longer-lasting effects.

Table 8.1 lists a variety of causes of aggression and violence, including causal factors described in greater detail by a number of authors in this volume. Though not exhaustive, the list is intended to illustrate how vari-

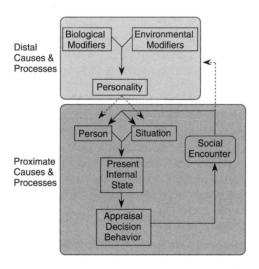

FIGURE 8.6. The General Aggression Model: Overall view.

TABLE 8.1. Proximate and Distal Causal Factors in Violent Evil

Proximate causal factors	Distal causal factors
Person	Environmental modifiers
Unstable high self-esteem	Maladaptive families and parenting
Narcissism	Violent neighborhood
Self-image	Cultural norms that support violence
Long-term goals	Victimization experiences
Self-efficacy beliefs for violent	Deprivation
and nonviolent behavior	Difficult life conditions
Normative beliefs about aggression,	Group conflict
retaliation, etc.	Fear-inducing events
Attitudes toward violence	Lack of bystander intervention
Hostile attribution, expectation,	in violent encounters
and perception biases	Diffusion of responsibility
Aggression scripts	Exposure to violent media
Dehumanization of others	Association antisocial peers
Cultural stereotypes	
Moral justification for violence	Biological modifiers
Displacement of responsibility	Low arousal
	Low serotonin
Situation	ADHD
Social stress	Hormone imbalances
Provocation	Executive functioning deficits
Frustration	
Pain/discomfort	
Bad moods	
Weapons	
Violent scenes	
Violent media	
Noise	
Temperature	
Threatening or fearful stimuli	
Exercise	
Alcohol and other drugs	

ous types of factors are well organized by GAM, and how even societal-level factors eventually operate through their influence on the individual in a specific social encounter.[2]

For example, consider a Palestinian youth growing up on the West Bank during the last 15 years. The social, economic, and cultural environment has been filled with deprivation, fear, hate, and violence. The cultural norms and everyday experiences have provided ample opportunity for the youngster to learn to hate and dehumanize his or her Israeli "ene-

---

[2]For citations of relevant empirical articles on these factors, see Anderson and Huesmann (2003); Berkowitz (1993); Geen (2001); Miller (1999); and various chapters in this volume.

mies," to develop violent behavioral scripts, and to become quite prepared to engage in "heroic" (i.e., terrorist) attacks on Israeli citizens. Indeed, it is difficult to imagine an environment better suited to create a generation of people prepared to behave violently toward their neighbors. Though the conditions are considerably different in many ways, Isrealis growing up during this time period also have been exposed to conditions conducive to creating people who are psychologically prepared to behave violently toward their neighbors. Indeed, the recent series of suicide bombings by Palestinians and military attacks by Israelis illustrates the violence escalation cycle all too well, despite truly heroic efforts by many individuals on both sides of the conflict to end the conflict.

In addition to the heuristic value provided by organizing research findings from several voluminous literatures, GAM also bolsters research on how to intervene in group conflicts at several levels. For instance, key factors outlined by Staub (e.g., 1989, 1998) in numerous writings all fit well with GAM: the initial need to stop the violence, provide economic development, work toward reducing (and eventually eliminating) mutual distrust and fear, promote healing and reconciliation, and promote cultural change in ways that give people on both sides a stake in the success of peace (e.g., promoting democratic reforms). Similarly, the work by Kelman (1998, 2001) fits GAM well. Not only do these approaches to the reduction of the broad types of violent evil fit GAM, but GAM provides a meaningful theoretical context within which we can understand how these approaches work at the level of the individual engaging in social encounters.

CONCLUDING ISSUES AND COMMENTS

An Interactionist Perspective

Like any good theory, the General Aggression Model is a work in progress. Most of our early studies on this model came from the heat/aggression domain, whereas most of our recent empirical work has been focused on media violence. Throughout all of this work, though, the intent has been to create and test hypotheses about human aggression, in general. As it turns out (not entirely by chance), a focus on these two domains naturally led us to create a model that takes a very strong interactionist perspective. It is an interactive model in several ways. First, GAM is largely predicated on the ubiquity of social encounters or interactions of the person with his or her social environment (broadly conceived to include thinking about fictitious characters as well as truly social interactions with real people). Second, GAM illustrates the dynamics underlying interactions between situational and personological variables. Third, GAM explicitly incorporates biological factors (admittedly, with less precision) as they interact with enviromental factors to influence the preparedness of the individual to aggress within specific contexts. Finally, and perhaps most importantly in the context of this chapter, GAM includes a structure that explicates how multiple levels of violence-related factors operate on the individual, from very general societal factors through subcultures, neighborhoods, schools, peers, family, and so on.

Causality and Personal Responsibility

Though it has become fashionable in some scientific quarters to eschew causal language in favor of eviscerated terms such as *linkages* or *associations,* GAM is explicitly a causal model. This does not mean that correlational evidence is ignored or that the difficulties in establishing clear, causal connections from correlational data are overlooked. The causal focus reflects an underlying belief that good theory is intended to be useful for social action, and that we do not take social action on the basis of linkages unless we believe them to be causal. Thus, GAM specifies that violent evil is indeed *caused by* the conjunction of numerous converging risk factors.

This causal language is sometimes misinterpreted as suggesting that the perpetrators of violence are not seen as carrying responsibility for their violence, or that society should not hold them responsible. From a social action perspective, however, perpetrators must be held responsible for their actions. Several key aggression-inhibiting factors rely on the individual's belief that he or she is responsible for his or her own behavior (i.e., self-regulation processes) and will be held responsible by others (i.e., social regulation). GAM (and other social–cognitive models) brings the future into the present by noting the effects of expected future outcomes on present behavioral decisions. When individuals or groups of individuals come to believe either that they are not responsible or that they will not be held accountable by others, the stage is set for the occurrence of violent evil. Indeed, as several writers in this volume have noted, a key ingredient of genocidal attacks is the blurring of personal responsibility. In sum, modern society cannot afford to allow abdication of personal responsibility, even if it sometimes seems unfair to hold individuals (or nations) responsible for violent acts that were "caused," at least partially, by extraneous factors over which they had no control. For example, there are several recent homicide cases in which the defense used a violent video game defense. Although we agree that violent video games (like other violent media) are a cause of increased aggressiveness, we disagree with a position that totally removes responsibility from the person who actually committed the homicide.

Social, Political, and Cultural Implications

Research on human aggression, as organized by the General Aggression Model, has numerous public policy implications at several levels. It tells us how to raise children who will not be prone to using violence to resolve conflicts. It suggests how to construct successful prevention programs and intervention methods and helps us understand why prevention is easier than intervention, why intervention is easier at earlier ages than later ones, and why some programs "work" and others do not (e.g., Anderson, 2000; Anderson & Bushman, 2002b; Anderson & Huesmann, 2003).

GAM and the research it summarizes can also provide a guide for international political action in the face of conflict between nations and between disparate groups within nations. It suggests what sorts of short-term interventions are most likely to provide a useful interruption in some ongoing cycles of violence as well as what types of programs are most likely to yield desirable long-term results. At the most global level, this work suggests that citizens of this planet must not sit quietly on the sidelines when major genocidal events are taking place.

Finally, the model suggests that modern society must beware of creeping cultural shifts toward greater acceptance of violence in everyday life. It makes clear that each generation learns an array of aggression-related knowledge structures both from direct sources, such as family, school, churches, and peers, and from indirect sources, such as the mass media. When a society allows (or creates) a shift toward greater acceptance of violence in everyday life, it is a shift that comes with an immediate price and a long-term risk. The immediate price is obvious. There will be more assaults, murders, rapes, and the quality of life will decline. The long-term risk may be less obvious. The next generation will internalize the new, more aggression-tolerant norms and hence be prepared to allow even further shifts toward greater acceptance of everyday violence. Furthermore, such tolerance of violence may well increase a nation's willingness to go to war to further its aims. Although still in very early stages of data analysis, we have some evidence indicating that changes in the framing of news reports about 9/11 events and the "war on terrorism" may have led to systematic changes in attitudes toward violence—changes that facilitated acceptance among the U.S. population of the use of war in Afghanistan and Iraq as a legitimate, appropriate, and even desirable foreign policy (Anderson & Carnagey, 2003). Recent discussions throughout the United States about the lack of civility and about the pervasiveness of media violence are touching on this same issue of creeping shifts in violence acceptability. GAM and the knowledge structure approach on which it is based provides insight into how such cultural shifts take place and into potential ways to slow or reverse them.

ACKNOWLEDGMENTS

This chapter borrows heavily from Anderson and Bushman (2002b) and Anderson and Huesmann (2003).

REFERENCES

Abelson, R. P. (1981). Psychological status of the script concept. *American Psychologist, 36,* 715–729.

Anderson, C. A. (1997). Effects of violent movies and trait irritability on hostile feelings and aggressive thoughts. *Aggressive Behavior, 23,* 161–178.

Anderson, C. A. (2000). Violence and aggression. In A. E. Kazdin (Ed.), *Encyclopedia of psychology* (Vol. 8, pp. 162–169). New York & Washington, DC: Oxford University Press and the American Psychological Association.

Anderson, C. A., Anderson, K. B., & Deuser, W. E. (1996). Examining an affective aggression framework: Weapon and temperature effects on aggressive thoughts, affect, and attitudes. *Personality and Social Psychology Bulletin, 22,* 366–376.

Anderson, C. A., Anderson, K. B., Dorr, N., DeNeve, K. M., & Flanagan, M. (2000). Temperature and aggression. In M. Zanna (Ed.), *Advances in experimental social psychology* (Vol. 32, pp. 63–133). New York: Academic Press.

Anderson, C. A., Benjamin, A. J., & Bartholow, B. D. (1998). Does the gun pull the trigger? Automatic priming effects of weapon pictures and weapon names. *Psychological Science, 9,* 308–314.

Anderson, C. A., Berkowitz, L., Donnerstein, E., Huesmann, L. R., Johnson, J., Linz, D., Malamuth, N., & Wartella, E. (in press). The influence of media violence on youth. *Psychological Science in the Public Interest.*

Anderson, C. A., & Bushman, B. J. (2001). Effects of violent video games on aggressive behavior, aggressive cognition, aggressive affect, physiological arousal, and prosocial behavior: A meta-analytic review of the scientific literature. *Psychological Science, 12,* 353–359.

Anderson, C. A., & Bushman, B. J. (2002a). The effects of media violence on society. *Science, 295,* 2377–2378.

Anderson, C. A., & Bushman, B. J. (2002b). Human aggression. *Annual Review of Psychology, 53,* 27–51.

Anderson, C. A., & Bushman, B. J. (2002c). Media violence and the American public revisited. *American Psychologist, 57,* 448–450.

Anderson, C. A., Bushman, B. J., & Groom, R. W. (1997). Hot years and serious and deadly assault: Empirical tests of the heat hypothesis. *Journal of Personality and Social Psychology,16,* 1213–1223.

Anderson, C. A., & Carnagey, N. L. (2003, May 29–June 1). *9/11-induced changes in attitudes towards violence.* Invited address presented at the American Psychological Association Convention, Atlanta, GA.

Anderson, C. A., & Huesmann, L. R. (2003). Human aggression: A social—cognitive view. In M. Hogg & J. Cooper (Eds.), *Handbook of social psychology* (pp. 296–323). London: Sage.

Anderson, C. A., Krull, D. S., & Weiner, B. (1996). Explanations: Processes and consequences. In E. Higgins & A. Kruglanski (Eds.), *Social psychology: Handbook of basic principles* (pp. 271–296). New York: Guilford Press.

Anderson, K. B., Anderson, C. A., Dill, K. E., & Deuser, W. E. (1998). The interactive relations between trait hostility, pain, and aggressive thoughts. *Aggressive Behavior, 24,* 161–171.

Bandura, A. (1973). *Aggression: A social learning theory analysis.* Englewood Cliffs, NJ: Prentice-Hall.

Bandura, A. (1977). *Social learning theory. New York: Prentice Hall.*

Bandura, A. (1983). Psychological mechanism of aggression. In R. G. Geen & E. I. Donnerstein (Eds.), *Aggression: Theoretical and empirical reviews* (Vol. 1, pp. 1–40). New York: Academic Press.

Bandura, A. (1986). *Social foundations of thought and action: A social–cognitive theory.* Englewood Cliffs, NJ: Prentice-Hall.

Bargh, J. A. (1996). Automaticity in social psychology. In E. T. Higgins & A. W. Kruglanski (Eds.), *Social psychology: Handbook of basic principles* (pp. 169–183). New York: Guilford Press.

Bargh, J. A., & Pietromonaco, P. (1982). Automatic information processing and social perception: The influence of trait information presented outside of conscious awareness on impression formation. *Journal of Personality and Social Psychology, 43,* 437–449.

Baron, R. A., & Richardson, D. R. (1994). *Human aggression* (2nd ed.). New York: Plenum Press.

Berkowitz, L. (1989). Frustration–aggression hypothesis: Examination and reformulation. *Psychological Bulletin, 106,* 59–73.

Berkowitz, L. (1993). *Aggression: Its causes, consequences, and control.* New York: McGraw-Hill.

Bjorkqvist, K., Lagerspetz, K., & Kaukiainen, A. (1992). Do girls manipulate and boys fight? Developmental trends in regard to direct and indirect aggression. *Aggressive Behavior, 18,* 117–127.

Bushman, B. J. (1998). Priming effects of violent media on the accessibility of aggressive constructs in memory. *Personality and Social Psychology Bulletin, 24,* 537–545.

Bushman, B. J., & Anderson, C. A. (2001a). Is it time to pull the plug on the hostile versus instrumental aggression dichotomy? *Psychological Review, 108,* 273–279.

Bushman, B. J., & Anderson, C. A. (2001b). Media violence and the American public: Scientific facts versus media misinformation. *American Psychologist, 56,* 477–489.

Buss, D. M., & Shackelford, T. K. (1997a). From vigilance to violence: Mate retention tactics in married couples. *Journal of Personality and Social Psychology, 72,* 346–361.

Buss, D. M., & Shackelford, T. K. (1997b). Human aggression in evolutionary psychological perspective. *Clinical Psychology Review, 17,* 605–619.

Collins, A. M., & Loftus, E. F. (1975). A spreading activation theory of semantic processing. *Psychological Review, 82,* 407–428.

Crick, N. R., & Dodge, K. A. (1994). A review and reformulation of social information processing mechanisms in children's adjustment. *Psychological Bulletin, 115,* 74–101.

Crick, N. R., & Grotpeter, J. K. (1995). Relational aggression, gender, and social-psychological adjustment. *Child Development, 66,* 710–722.

Daly, M., & Wilson, M. (1994). Evolutionary psychology of male violence. In J. Archer (Ed.), *Male violence* (pp. 253–288). London: Routledge.

Dodge, K. A. (1980). Social cognition and children's aggressive behavior. *Child Development, 51,* 620–635.

Dodge, K. A. (1986). A social information processing model of social competence in children. In M. Perlmutter (Ed.), *The Minnesota Symposium on Child Psychology* (Vol. 18, pp. 77–125). Hillsdale, NJ: Erlbaum.

Dodge, K. A., & Coie, J. D. (1987). Social information-processing factors in reactive and proactive aggression in children's peer groups. *Journal of Personality and Social Psychology, 53,* 1146–1158.

Fiske, S. T., & Taylor, S. E. (1991). *Social cognition.* New York: McGraw-Hill.

Geary, D. C. (1998). *Male, female: The evolution of human sex differences.* Washington, DC: American Psychological Association.

Geen, R. G. (2001). *Human aggression.* Philadelphia: Open University Press.

Higgins, E. T. (1996). Knowledge activation: Accessibility, applicability, and salience. In E. T. Higgins & A. W. Kruglanski (Eds.), *Social psychology: Handbook of basic principles* (pp. 133–168). New York: Guilford Press.

Huesmann, L. R. (1982). Information processing models of behavior. In N. Hirschberg & L. Humphreys (Eds.), *Multivariate applications in the social sciences* (pp. 261–288). Hillsdale, NJ: Erlbaum.

Huesmann, L. R. (1988). An information processing model for the development of aggression. *Aggressive Behavior, 14,* 13–24.

Huesmann, L. R. (1997). Observational learning of violent behavior: Social and biosocial processes. In A. Raine, D. P. Farrington, P. O. Brennen, & S. A. Mednick (Eds.), *The biosocial basis of violence* (pp. 69–88). New York: Plenum Press.

Huesmann, L. R. (1998). The role of social information processing and cognitive schemas in the acquisition and maintenance of habitual aggressive behavior. In R. G. Geen & E. Donnerstein (Eds.), *Human aggression: Theories, research, and implications for policy* (pp. 73–109). New York: Academic Press.

Kelman, H. C. (1998). Social-psychological contributions to peacemaking and peacebuilding in the Middle East. *Applied Psychology: An International Review, 47,* 5–28.

Kelman, H. C. (2001). The role of national identity in conflict resolution: Experiences from Israeli-Palestinian problem-solving workshops. In R. D. Ashmore & L. Jussim (Eds.), *Rutgers Series on Self and Identity: Vol. 3. Social identity, intergroup conflict, and conflict resolution* (pp. 187–212). London: Oxford University Press.

Krull, D. S. (1993). Does the grist change the mill?: The effect of perceiver's goal on the process of social inference. *Personality and Social Psychology Bulletin, 19,* 340–348.

Krull, D. S., & Dill, J. C. (1996). On thinking first and responding fast: Flexibility in social inference processes. *Personality and Social Psychology Bulletin, 22,* 949–959.

Lagerspetz, K. M., & Bjorkqvist, K. (1992). Indirect aggression in girls and boys.

In L. R. Huesmann (Ed.), *Aggressive behavior: Current perspectives* (pp. 131–150). New York: Plenum Press.

Lagerspetz, K. M., Bjorkqvist, K., & Peltonen, T. (1988). Is indirect aggression typical of females? Gender differences in aggressiveness in 11- to 12-year-old children. *Aggressive Behavior, 14,* 403–414.

Lindsay, J. J., & Anderson, C. A. (2000). From antecedent conditions to violent actions: A general affective aggression model. *Personality and Social Psychology Bulletin, 26,* 533–547.

Malamuth, N. M., & Heilmann, M. F. (1998). Evolutionary psychology and sexual aggression. In C. H. Crawford & D. L. Krebs (Eds.), *Handbook of evolutionary psychology* (pp. 515–542). Mahwah, NJ: Erlbaum.

Miller, A. G. (Ed.). (1999). Special issue: Perspectives on evil and violence. *Personality and Social Psychology Review, 3*(3), 176–275.

Mischel, W. (1973). Toward a cognitive social learning reconceptualization of personality. *Psychological Review, 80,* 252–283.

Mischel, W., & Shoda, Y. (1995). A cognitive–affective system theory of personality: Reconceptualizing situations, dispositions, dynamics, and invariance in personality structure. *Psychological Review, 102,* 246–268.

The National Obituary Archive. (2002). Retrieved November 27, 2002, from *http://www.arrangeonline.com/notablePersons/honorroll.asp*

Nisbett, R. E., & Cohen, D. (1996). *Culture of honor: The psychology of violence in the South.* Boulder, CO: Westview Press.

O'Donnell, C. R. (1995). Firearm deaths among children and youth. *American Psychologist, 50,* 771–776.

Pulkkinen, L. (1996). Proactive and reactive aggression in early adolescence as precursors to anti- and prosocial behavior in young adults. *Aggressive Behavior, 22,* 241–257.

Raine, A., Brennen, P. A., Farrington, D. P., & Mednick S. A. (Eds.). (1997). *Biosocial bases of violence.* London: Plenum Press.

Robinson, J. (1998). Theoretical issues in the role of appraisal in emotion: Cognitive content versus physiological change. In R. Hoffman & M. Sherrick (Eds.), *Viewing psychology as a whole: The integrative science of William N. Dember* (pp. 449–469). Washington, DC: American Psychological Association.

Schneider, W., & Shiffrin, R. M. (1977). Controlled and automatic human information processing: I. Detection, search, and attention. *Psychological Review, 84,* 1–66.

Sedikides, C., & Skowronski, J. J. (1990). Towards reconciling personality and social psychology: A construct accessibility approach. *Journal of Social Behavior and Personality, 5,* 531–546.

Seligman, M. E. P. (1970). On the generality of the law of learning. *Psychological Review, 77,* 406–418.

Shiffrin, R. M., & Schneider, W. (1977). Controlled and automatic human information processing: II. Perceptual learning, automatic attending, and general theory. *Psychological Review, 84,* 127–190.

Smith, C. A., & Lazarus, R. S. (1993). Appraisal components, core relational themes, and the emotions. *Cognition and Emotion, 7,* 233–269.

Soubrie, P. (1986). Reconciling the role of central serotonin neurons in humans and animal behavior. *Behavioral and Brain Sciences, 9,* 319–364.

Staub, E. (1989). *The roots of evil: The origins of genocide and other group violence.* New York: Cambridge University Press.

Staub, E. (1998). Breaking the cycle of genocidal violence: Healing and reconciliation. In J. Harvey (Ed.), *Perspectives on loss: A sourcebook* (pp. 231–238). Philadelphia: Taylor & Francis.

Surgeon General. (2001). *Youth violence: A report of the Surgeon General.* Rockville, MD: U.S. Department of Health and Human Services.

Todorov, A., & Bargh, J. A. (2002). Automatic sources of aggression. *Aggression and Violent Behavior, 7,* 53–68.

Tremblay, R. E. (2000). The development of aggressive behavior during childhood: What have we learned in the past century? *International Journal of Behavioral Development, 24,* 129–141.

Uleman, J. S. (1987). Consciousness and control: The case of spontaneous trait inferences. *Personality and Social Psychology Bulletin, 13,* 337–354.

Wegner, D. M., & Bargh, J. A. (1998). Control and automaticity in social life. In D. T. Gilbert, S. T. Fiske, & G. Lindzey (Eds.), *The handbook of social psychology* (4th ed., Vol. 1, pp. 446–496). New York: McGraw-Hill.

CHAPTER 9

WHAT CAN THE MILGRAM OBEDIENCE EXPERIMENTS TELL US ABOUT THE HOLOCAUST?

Generalizing from the Social Psychology Laboratory

ARTHUR G. MILLER

If in this study an anonymous experimenter could successfully command adults to subdue a fifty-year old man, and force on him painful electric shocks against his protests, one can only wonder what government, with its vastly greater authority and prestige, can command of its subjects.

—MILGRAM (1965, p. 75)

Indeed, the inspiration for Milgram's study was the Holocaust, in which seemingly normal individuals (e.g., guards at prison camps) followed the orders of authority figures to the point of committing horrific acts. . . . The fact that these processes appear to be similar to those that occurred at some of humankind's darkest moments, such as the Holocaust, is what makes his results so compelling.

—ARONSON, WILSON, AND BREWER (1998, p. 133)

His [Milgram's] obedience explanation of the Holocaust is oversimplified, misleading, and of potential social danger.

—MANDEL (1998, p. 78)

If we compare the Holocaust with Milgram's research . . . the differences are brutally clear. Although we may be upset, saddened, even disappointed by the behavior of Milgram's subjects, the terms that are routinely used to describe the horrors of the Holocaust—

e.g., atrocity, inhumanity, hatefulness, wickedness—are simply preposterous in the context of Milgram's studies. Those terms suggest a psychological state that is almost the antithesis of that observed in the lab studies.

—FENIGSTEIN (1998, p. 71)

Stanley Milgram's research on obedience to authority, conducted over 40 years ago, is the most well-known research in social psychology and, perhaps, in all of social science. A major reason for the unabating visibility of the obedience experiments is their association with the Nazi Holocaust. This linkage was noted by Milgram, himself, in his first published account of his research in 1963. In the intervening decades, countless enthusiasts have endorsed the view that these studies contain vital insights into the Holocaust, in particular, the propensity of ordinary human beings, under the dictates of malevolent authority, to fail significant tests of moral judgment. As Brown (1985) commented in his influential social psychology text:

> Perhaps Hannah Arendt and all those who have agreed with her about Eichmann were too credulous; the man was, after all, on trial for his life. Yet she made the startling claim that "in certain circumstances the most ordinary decent person can become a criminal." That should not be so if monstrous deeds presuppose a monstrous character. However, the most famous series of experiments in social psychology, Stanley Milgram's (1974) experiments on obedience to malevolent authority, confirm Arendt's prophetic claim. (pp. 2–3)

However, there have also been critics who find the associations of the Milgram research to the Holocaust (termed *M–H* in this chapter) completely unwarranted (Miller, 1986). Recently, a number of particularly vehement criticisms have been directed at the M–H linkage. These critics— social psychologists, themselves—present perspectives on the Holocaust that contrast sharply with the implications of the obedience research.

This chapter examines the associations between the obedience experiments and the Holocaust, charts the evidence and diverse commentary regarding these associations, and draws some conclusions regarding the contribution that the obedience research makes—and does not make—in terms of understanding the Holocaust. First, I briefly review Milgram's major empirical findings and interpretation (Milgram, 1963, 1974). Second, the associations made to the Holocaust are considered. I also summarize recent empirical findings regarding reactions to explanations of the Holocaust that focus on obedience to authority, as well as on other causal factors. The chapter concludes with an appraisal of the M–H thesis and suggestions for further consideration.

THE OBEDIENCE EXPERIMENTS: A SYNOPSIS
OF THE EMPIRICAL FINDINGS

The Experimental Paradigm

Milgram (1963) created a laboratory scenario described to research participants as one concerned with punishment and learning. Participants, who
were volunteers of diverse ages and backgrounds (primarily male), arrived
at the Yale University laboratory and encountered a white-coated experimenter of stern demeanor and another apparent volunteer (an accomplice). An elaborate staging then occurred in which the other participant,
in the role of "learner," was to receive electric shocks for mistakes that he
would make on a word-association task. The device which the "teacher"
(the real participant) would use to administer the shocks was a realistic
"shock generator," labeled as delivering shocks from 15 to 450 volts. Participants were instructed to administer increasingly severe shocks for each
error made on a series of memory trials. No actual shocks were delivered,
although the learner acted as if he were receiving the punishment. Although he was located in an adjoining room (in the basic paradigm), he
emitted audible sounds of pain, in clear hearing of the participant. Pound-
ing on the wall, the learner also mentioned a recently diagnosed "heart
problem" and, ultimately, demanded repeatedly to be released. Milgram's
intent was to produce an intense moral conflict for the participant—
whether to obey the experimenter but at the cost of continuing to harm a
protesting victim, or to side with the learner but, in so doing, disobey the
experimenter and ruin the experiment.

The learner was programmed to make "errors" on the memory task.
If the participant resisted administering the appropriate shock, the experimenter responded with a sequence of four increasingly strident prods, concluding with the exhortation, "You have no other choice, you must go on"
(Milgram, 1963, p. 374). Refusals to continue punishing the learner beyond this prod terminated the experiment. The prods thus operationalized
the experimenter's authority, conveying the expectation that the participant was obliged to obey all instructions to punish the learner.

The Major Findings

Milgram reported (1963) two startling findings in his initial paper on the
experiment. First, 65% of the participants obeyed orders to the end of the
shock series. Various groups (e.g., psychiatrists, undergraduate students)
were given a description of the laboratory situation and asked to predict
the obedience rate of 100 hypothetical persons; the respondents invariably
underestimated the obtained results by extremely wide margins. Milgram's
initial report thus constituted evidence of the most dramatic kind, given
that *nobody* expected what, in fact, had occurred (Milgram, 1974, Ch. 3).

In their stunning contradiction to commonsense reasoning, Milgram's results could be likened to the Holocaust itself. Both scenarios revealed ordinary people willing to treat other people with unimaginable cruelty, and in both instances, the coercive influence of authority figures seemed to be of critical importance.

A second major finding was the intense stress observed in many participants. Regarding these emotional experiences as one of the key findings of the research itself, Milgram (1963) was extremely graphic in his description:

> In a large number of cases, the degree of tension reached extremes that are rarely seen in sociopsychological laboratory studies. Subjects were observed to sweat, tremble, stutter, bite their lips, groan, and dig their fingernails into their flesh. These were characteristic rather than exceptional responses to the experiment. . . . At one point he [one of the participants] pushed his fist into his forehead and muttered: "Oh God, let's stop it." And yet he continued to respond to every word of the experimenter, and obeyed to the end. . . . I observed a mature and initially poised businessman enter the laboratory smiling and confident. Within 20 minutes, he was reduced to a twitching, stuttering wreck, who was rapidly approaching a point of nervous collapse. (pp. 375–377)

Evidence regarding the tension experienced by Milgram's participants is based largely on his reports (1963, 1974), and a vivid documentation of stress in Milgram's film (1965) of the obedience project. A variety of situational factors that weakened the authority were invariably associated with less obedience. A control condition that allowed participants to select their own shock level, under no authority pressures, produced only the most minimal level of punishment. Thus it could be safely concluded that most participants, whether maximally obedient or not, found the task decidedly onerous. This conjunction of *high rates of obedience on the part of persons who appear to detest what they are doing to the victim* is crucially important and discussed later in this chapter.

Confirmation of Milgram's Findings

A number of studies have confirmed Milgram's major findings (Miller, 1986, Ch. 4). Research in the Netherlands has provided evidence of destructive obedience, using a procedure in which participants are ordered to harass another person taking a test as part of a job interview (Meeus & Raaijmakers, 1995). Again, the specific situational arrangements are critically relevant to the observed obedience. The key finding, however, is an extraordinarily high level of destructive obedience (90%) in the baseline condition, exceeding Milgram's initial finding. Although there have been methodological criticisms of the Milgram paradigm (Milgram, 1972;

Miller, 1986, Ch. 6), the current view on the part of most social psychologists is that the Milgram findings are a reliable phenomenon in the laboratory.

Initial Conclusions: The Power of the Situation

Milgram's interpretation emphasized the extraordinary influence of diverse contextual features faced by his participants. Paramount was the perceived legitimacy of the experiment, inherent in the larger context of a scientific study. Also key were the participants' voluntary commitment to the experiment and the rapidity with which events occurred in the course of the study. Participants thus became involved in a graduated escalation of harming, the endpoint of which was very unlikely to be foreseen at the start. Because participants were randomly assigned to the different situational arrangements, and because obedience was shown to vary correspondingly, Milgram repeatedly emphasized the power of the situation to override personal feelings: "One might suppose that a subject would simply break off or continue as his conscience dictated. Yet, this is very far from what happened" (1963, p. 377). In the baseline experiment, therefore, a large percentage of seemingly good people engaged in extremely destructive actions under an experimenter's orders. Because the "learner" eventually stopped responding to the experimental task, it was conceivable that in the eyes of at least some participants, the learner had either become unconscious or had died.

The Role of Individual Differences

Milgram found that within any specific experimental variation, there were typically variations among individuals in their degree of obedience. In the baseline (1963) study, 35% defied the experimenter at some point prior to the end (450 v. shock level). Precisely why some individuals obeyed fully while others did not, although of considerable interest, has not been clarified, unfortunately (Blass, 1991; Miller, 1986; Miller, Collins, & Brief, 1995). Possibly due, in part, to the ethical problems in conducting this type of research, there have been relatively few replications. To examine the personality factors operative in acts of destructive obedience would also require relatively large samples. Berkowitz (1999) has suggested that the failure to examine individual differences limits the generalizations that can be made from this research to the Holocaust. At least some of Milgram's participants were more heroic in being able to disengage themselves from the experiment, suggesting that those who were totally obedient may have lacked some aspect of personal character or values, thus leaving them in their role as an obedient participant (e.g., Kelman & Hamilton, 1989).

SOURCES OF CONTROVERSY

The controversial impact of Milgram's experiments, perhaps as well
known as the experimental findings themselves, is based on three factors:
the ethical and methodological status of the research, and the linkage of
Milgram's studies to the Nazi Holocaust (Miller, 1986). The ethical issue
deserves at least a brief consideration, because it is related to the Holocaust linkage as well.

The Ethical Controversy

The Milgram experiments have always been regarded, even by their most
zealous supporters, as at least approaching the limits of ethical propriety
in terms of the amount of stress and anxiety that was experienced by many
participants. Although there is no documented evidence that any person
was harmed, either in Milgram's studies or any subsequent research on
obedience, there is no question that Milgram approached the limits of ethical propriety, specifically in terms of respecting current provisions regarding the participants' right to withdraw from the experiment (American
Psychological Association, 2002; Miller, 1986, Ch. 5). One resolution,
commonly noted in discussions of this issue, is to conclude that the benefits of the obedience research outweighed the costs in terms of subjects'
stress levels. Milgram's postexperiment debriefing procedure was also very
extensive and included follow-up correspondence with each participant.

There is, however, a meaningful connection between the ethical aspects of the obedience research and the generalizations that can be made
from the experiments, themselves. The extreme stress and emotional conflict described by Milgram, which were the basis for the ethical controversy (e.g., Baumrind, 1964), also define the operative generalizations that
may be inferred convincingly, for example, to the Holocaust. As will be
seen, the participants' personal motivation *not* to harm the victim is
extremely relevant to the M–H thesis.

What Are the Participants' Personal Feelings and Objectives
in the Milgram Paradigm?

Although the most common interpretation of Milgram's findings is that
participants did not personally wish to harm the learner, the motives generated in this paradigm may well have been more mixed or ambivalent in
many participants. Unfortunately, the manner in which people actually regard the act of *punishing others when they make mistakes*—that is, the key
behavior in the Milgram paradigm—has been virtually ignored in discussions of the obedience research. However, an examination of recent re-

search on *corporal punishment* suggests that this form of harming is a widely accepted form of child discipline (Gershoff, 2002; Strauss, 1994). Most people are hardly unequivocally opposed to the use of physical punishment under absolutely any circumstances. That a majority approve the use of capital punishment in this country might serve as another illustration. It is also likely that in the late 1950s, the rationale of administering physical pain (i.e., shocks) to induce better learning may have seemed at least somewhat less surprising than it would today.

Key aspects of the arguments linking the obedience studies to the Holocaust rest not simply upon what actions people perform in these studies *but why they perform them, and what they are experiencing while doing so.* Many participants may have had a complex mixture of feelings about what they were being ordered to do; that is, they may not have been *totally* opposed personally to shocking the learner, even though they did have reservations and were not willing to inflict significant punishment when left to their own accord. Precisely how people regard punishment, both physical and nonphysical, is thus one of the many unanswered questions with important relevance to the M–H argument.

The Issue of Generalizing Research Findings

Research findings rarely "speak for themselves." Generalizing the results of research to specific nonresearch contexts frequently produces disagreement because the applicability of a study is often a matter of *interpretation* rather than empirical or statistical fact, and people obviously may differ in their interpretations (e.g., Banaji & Crowder, 1989; Miller, 1995). Often, it is not the superficial similarities between a research project and an analogous "real world" setting that are crucial to the generalization process (Henshel, 1980). Rather, as Mook (1983) has noted: "Ultimately, what makes research findings of interest is that they help us understand everyday life. That understanding, however, comes from theory or the analysis of mechanism; it is not a matter of 'generalizing' the findings themselves" (p. 386). At times, the linkage between research and nonresearch settings is relatively straightforward. For example, a number of generalizations from Milgram's studies have been made to the kinds of obedience pressures that exist in hierarchical social organizations, corporations, and other bureaucracies (e.g., Brief, Buttram, Elliott, Reizenstein, & McCline, 1995; Darley, Messick, & Tyler, 2001; Hamilton & Sanders, 1999; Kelman & Hamilton, 1989). These analyses have provoked no noticeable controversy. Hamilton and Sanders (1995), for example, see great value in the Milgram experiments in terms of explaining how contemporary bureaucratic organizations may create conditions for subordinate deference to authorities:

Most of the organized ways in which people do wrong happen when they go to work. It is part of Milgram's (1974) legacy that psychologists realize no question is more important for the next millennium than that of how human social organization can be made more humane. We need to learn, literally, who in the world really expects organizational actors to be autonomous moral beings. Perhaps then we may better understand when and why they are not. (p. 85)

As will be noted, however, generalizing the obedience research to the Holocaust has been anything but noncontroversial.

The First Challenge to the Obedience Interpretation of the Holocaust

In her influential ethical criticism of Milgram's studies, Baumrind (1964) was extremely skeptical of linking the obedience research to the Holocaust. She noted that the SS officers were not under the impression that the ultimate authority, Hitler, was kindly disposed toward the victims. The victims also were not social peers of the SS but rather were dehumanized to an extreme degree. Baumrind contended that the conflict expressed by many subjects was evidence of their concern for the learner—another major weakness in the Nazi analogy.

In Milgram's (1964) rebuttal, he agreed partially with Baumrind— that is, he noted that he was not attempting to study the Holocaust per se. Arguing that his paradigm was only an analogy to the Holocaust, he clarified that his primary intent was not to explain the Holocaust:

Baumrind mistakes the background metaphor for the precise subject matter of investigation. The German event was cited to point up a serious problem in the human situation: the potentially destructive effect of obedience. But the best way to tackle the problem of obedience, from a scientific standpoint, is in no way restricted by "what happened exactly" in Germany. What happened exactly can *never* be duplicated in the laboratory or anywhere else. The real task is to learn more about the general problem of destructive obedience using a workable approach. (p. 851)

If Milgram and others had subsequently continued studying the processes of destructive obedience without a continuous preoccupation with its linkage to the Holocaust, the course of scholarship relating to the obedience research would likely have been very different. However, connections to the Holocaust *were* to become the most salient reaction to the obedience studies. Indeed, the obedience studies were soon to become world renowned, and Milgram often extrapolated his laboratory findings to a variety of global instances of destructive obedience—in addition to the Holocaust, he opined on the mass suicides under Jim Jones at Jonestown, the My Lai massacre, and other horrific events (e.g., Milgram, 1974, pp. 179–189).

Why Is the Generalizability Issue Controversial?

Preexisting points of view or theoretical orientations held by the observer of a study (i.e., critics, students, readers) are a major source of controversy. One's initial position or perspective may induce powerful biases in terms of how a research finding is interpreted or appraised (e.g., Greenwald, Pratkanis, Leippe, & Baumgardner, 1986; Kunda, 1990; Lord, Ross, & Lepper, 1979). Information that contradicts one's prevailing attitude or theory is likely to be devalued and subjected to intense scrutiny. Information that is consistent with one's theoretical view or leads to a preferred conclusion is more likely to be readily endorsed. Contributing to the importance and often insidious effects of these biases is the fact that people are likely to be unaware of these effects, claiming, instead, that their reactions to a particular study are objective and factually based.

The sources of these confirmatory biases are diverse—it could be a formal theoretical orientation, a political position, a religious or ethical conviction, a highly personal, emotional feeling, etc. Social psychologists who adopt a strongly situationist view of behavior invariably endorse the obedience experiments, whereas social psychologists taking a more dispositional or personality-oriented view of behavior are more critical (e.g., Berkowitz, 1999), particularly in terms of their generalization to the Holocaust. In dramatizing the power of situations, social psychologists frequently note that the lay observer is not similarly attuned to situational pressures but rather biased toward dispositional explanations—what is often termed the fundamental attribution error or correspondence bias (Gilbert & Malone, 1995)—that is, if you do not agree with the situational view, you are simply committing a serious attributional error.

Generalizations from a social-psychological explanatory perspective are convincing only to the degree that the conceptualization of the domain to which the research is generalized (e.g., Holocaust) is also plausibly construed in compatible terms. Thus, for a social-psychological analysis of the Holocaust to be convincing—that is, to be persuasive to those who might not initially think about the Holocaust in social-psychological terms—it must describe the Holocaust as caused, in key respects, by processes of social influence and external pressure in addition to (or perhaps rather than) personality factors or traits of moral character in individual actors. In essence, there must be a conceptual fit or match between both elements of the generalization: the research and the target domain of the generalization. If this match is not present, disagreement will automatically ensue.

THE HOLOCAUST: A DEFINITION

In this chapter, the term *Holocaust* refers to the systematic and planned killing of millions of Jews, largely during the latter parts of the war. The Holocaust is generally considered to have been the result of a highly efficient bureaucracy or social organization (Darley, 1992; Hilberg, 1985). It is virtually uncontested that the policy of genocide was instigated by Adolf Hitler and other high-ranking Nazi officials (Mandel, 2002). It is further assumed here that the murder of Jews on the scale of genocide would not have occurred without this key factor of authorization from the upper echelons of the Nazi hierarchy. In describing the motives of the instigators, there is a general consensus that an ideological world view of Jews was of central importance. Bauer (2001) has noted that the Nazi regime extended anti-Semitism to a radically new form, essentially coupling it with a more elaborate ideology of racial purification: "Nazi ideology saw in the Jews a universal devilish element, so the pursuit of Jews was to have been a global, quasi-religious affair, the translation into practice of a murderous ideology" (p. 27). Sabini and Silver (1980) describe the diverse actions, performed by those who were given orders, that comprised the Holocaust:

> It is not the angry rioter we must understand but Eichmann, the colorless bureaucrat, replicated two million times in those who assembled the trains, dispatched the supplies, manufactured the poison gas, filed the paper work, sent out the death notices, guarded the prisoners, pointed left and right, supervised the loading–unloading of the vans, disposed of the ashes, and performed the countless other tasks that also constituted the Holocaust. (p. 330)

A central question in this chapter concerns the perpetrators' primary motives in the killing operations. In terms of the M–H thesis, the issue of motives is of critical importance and a source of great controversy.

GENERALIZING FROM THE MILGRAM EXPERIMENTS TO THE HOLOCAUST (M–H): ARGUMENTS IN SUPPORT OF THE M–H THESIS

What can the obedience experiments tell us about the Holocaust? Positions on this issue can generally be divided into those that endorse the generalizations and those opposing them. I begin with an examination of the pro-generalization arguments.

Milgram's Position

In the opening paragraph of his first publication on the obedience research, Milgram (1963) made an explicit association between the experiments and the Holocaust:

> Obedience, as a determinant of behavior, is of particular relevance to our time. It has been reliably established that from 1933–45 millions of innocent persons were systematically slaughtered on command. Gas chambers were built, death camps were guarded, daily quotas of corpses were produced with the same efficiency as the manufacture of appliances. These inhumane policies may have originated in the mind of a single person, but they could only be carried out on a massive scale if a very large number of persons obeyed orders. (p. 371)

Given that the Holocaust, itself, has been the focus of intense controversies within a host of academic disciplines—for example, reactions to Goldhagen's *Hitler's Willing Executioners* (1996)—it is understandable that any scientific experiment claiming a meaningful connection to the Holocaust would prompt similar reactions. Certainly this controversy accompanied the obedience studies. My impression is that it was Milgram's reference to the Holocaust in conjunction with the startling results of his 1963 report that set into motion the unparalleled impact of this study. Baumrind's ethical criticisms (1964) in *The American Psychologist*, appearing only a few months after the original obedience publication, also had the unintended effect of introducing the obedience studies to a large readership.

People, Milgram stated, are often obsessed with carrying out their jobs; they become dominated by "an administrative, rather than a moral, outlook" (1974, p. 186). He emphasized the role of the mission itself, its noble purpose: "In the experiment, science is served by the act of shocking the victim against his will; in Germany, the destruction of the Jews was represented as a 'hygienic' process against 'jewish vermin' (Hilberg, 1961)" (p. 187). He addressed the role of silence in the process of destructive obedience: "In Nazi Germany, even among those most closely identified with the 'final solution,' it was considered an act of discourtesy to talk about the killings. . . . Subjects in the experiment most frequently experience their objections as embarrassing" (p. 187). Milgram was careful to note that obedience was not, in its essence, a bad or dangerous activity, and that it could have life-enhancing consequences.

Milgram's Recognition of Distinctions between His Research and the Holocaust

By the appearance of Milgram's 1974 book, the linkage of the obedience research to the Holocaust had already become extremely well known and cited in diverse texts. Here Milgram explicitly recognized important *differences* between his experimental paradigm and the Nazi Holocaust:

> The experiment is presented to our subjects in a way that stresses its positive human values: increase of knowledge about learning and memory processes. . . . By contrast, the objectives that Nazi Germany pursued were themselves morally reprehensible, and were recognized as such by many Germans. [Milgram does footnote the idea that the regime itself viewed killing Jews as a virtuous activity to cleanse the Reich of subhuman vermin.]
>
> The maintenance of obedience in our subjects is highly dependent upon the face-to-face nature of the social occasion and its attendant surveillance. . . . The forms of obedience that occurred in Germany were in far greater degree dependent upon the internalization of authority . . . to resist Nazism was itself an act of heroism, not an inconsequential decision, and death was a possible penalty. Penalties and threats were forever around the corner, and the victims themselves had been thoroughly vilified and portrayed as being unworthy of life or human kindness. Finally our subjects were told by authority that what they were doing to their victim might be temporarily painful but would cause no permanent damage, while those Germans directly involved in the annihilations knew that they were not only inflicting pain but were destroying human life. So, in the final analysis, what happened in Germany from 1933 to 1945 can only be fully understood as the expression of a unique historical development that will never again be precisely replicated. (pp. 176–177)

Thus, Milgram explicitly articulated key distinctions between his studies and the Holocaust—precisely what many critics have accused him (and legions of his advocates) of completely ignoring in his analysis. Nevertheless, Milgram's position on the M–H issue varied. At times, he was a strong proponent of the linkage. He felt that he had identified a fundamental psychological process that was common to both the laboratory and the real-world context:

> Yet the essence of obedience, as a psychological process, can be captured by studying the simple situation in which a man is told by a legitimate authority to act against a third individual. This situation confronted both our experimental subject and the German subject and evoked in each a set of parallel psychological adjustments. (1974, p. 177)

Milgram's views could thus be termed complex and diverse by his supporters or inconsistent and ambiguous by his detractors. Clearly, however, the linkage between Milgram's studies and the Holocaust was to become the prevailing thesis in the eyes of most social psychologists. Numerous scholars, other than social psychologists, have both championed and refuted the M–H thesis (Miller, 1986).

Social Psychology Textbooks: Positions on the M–H Linkage

Where can we find discussions of the obedience experiments? I am tempted to answer, "Not quite everywhere, but close to it!" I wish to focus, however, on social psychology textbooks, which have been the primary source for generations of students and social scientists. To assess the current treatment of the M–H thesis, I examined seven recent editions of popular textbooks. The Milgram obedience research continues to receive extraordinary attention. The number of pages allotted to the obedience research varied between five and 15, most accounts featuring detailed analyses of the many experimental variations in Milgram's paradigm and photographs from his laboratory. Contemporary authors emphasize a point that Milgram himself regarded as highly underappreciated, namely the extraordinary degree to which harmful obedience to authority is responsive to variations in the specific experimental context:

> The degree of obedience varied sharply depending upon the exact manner in which the variables of the experiment are arranged in an experimental condition. Yet, in the popular press, these variations are virtually ignored, or assumed to be of only minor importance. (1979, pp. 7–8)

In this context, there is a tendency for many people to misunderstand the obedience experiments even after hearing a discussion of the research and watching Milgram's filmed account of the study (Safer, 1980). Instead of recognizing (correctly) the situationally specific nature of obedience, that is, that (the same) people may be highly obedient in some circumstances but very defiant in others, many observers conclude, erroneously, that most people are simply obedient to destructive orders *regardless of the situation.* For example, one frequently observes the assertion that Milgram's primary finding is that people are "blindly obedient" to authority, a finding virtually completely at odds with Milgram's actual observations. As I have noted, this tendency to infer personal or internal causes of behavior, even when it occurs under highly constraining circumstances, is viewed by many social psychologists as a major judgmental error or attributional bias (Ross & Nisbett, 1991).

From the perspective of this chapter, however, the most salient element in all of these textbook accounts of Milgram's research is the assertion that the obedience research provides crucial insights into the causes of the Holocaust. Consider the following excerpts:

> Would you be cruel if ordered? How did Nazi Germany conceive and implement the inconceivable slaughter of 6 million Jews? These evil acts occurred because thousands of people followed orders. They put the prisoners on trains, herded them into crowded showers, and poisoned them with gas. How could people engage in such horrific actions? Were these folks normal human

beings? Stanley Milgram (1974) wondered. So he set up a situation where people were ordered to administer increasing levels of electric shock to someone who was having difficulty learning a series of words . . . the experimental results were quite disturbing: nearly two-thirds of the participants fully complied. . . . Milgram's conclusion also makes it hard to attribute the Holocaust to unique character traits in the German people: "The most fundamental lesson of our study," he noted, is that "ordinary people, simply doing their jobs, and without any particular hostility on their part, can become agents in a terrible destructive process." (Myers, 2002, pp. 4, 222)

The virtual annihilation of the European Jewish community could not have happened without the cooperation of thousands of ordinary citizens—bureaucrats, soldiers, janitors, doctors, railroad workers, carpenters. Why did so many people comply with the Nazi regime? Did their compliance emerge from pathological characteristics of the German people? Or, more frighteningly, did following orders arise out of the normal operation of everyday social processes, such as simple obedience to authority? Social psychologists have used scientific methods to seek answers to these questions. (Taylor, Peplau, & Sears, 2000, p. 224)

Milgram argued that his study of obedience gave us insights into the horrible events in Nazi Germany. . . . If, as Milgram's research indicates, a majority of people will deliver painful shocks to a heart patient on the orders of a research scientist who has no real authority over them, it becomes less surprising that solders will kill innocent civilians and that cult members will kill themselves at the direction of more personally relevant authority figures. (Kenrick, Neuberg, & Cialdini, 2002, pp. 28, 201)

Perhaps the most vivid example of people's willingness to follow those with authority is seen in the atrocities committed against the Jews by the Nazis during World War II. . . . Although the most common examples of blind faith in following orders occur in emergency or wartime situations, there is nowhere a more striking and, we think, more terrifying example of how blindly people follow orders than in the demonstrations of Stanley Milgram (1963, 1965). (Worchel, Cooper, Goethals, & Olson, 2000, p. 355)

According to social psychologists, most of the German guards and citizens who participated in the Holocaust were not madmen but ordinary people exposed to extraordinary social influences (p. 288). [This is a figure caption to a death camp scene, with mounds of victims at Nordhausen, Germany.] Thus the Milgram studies do not show that people have an evil streak that shines through when the surface is scratched. Instead, these studies demonstrate that social pressures can combine in insidious ways to make humane people act in an inhumane manner. (Aronson, Wilson, & Akert, 2002, p. 295)

During World War II, troops in the German army frequently obeyed commands to torture and murder unarmed civilians—millions of them. In fact, the Nazis established horrible but highly efficient death camps designed to eradicate Jews, Gypsies, and other groups they felt were inferior or a threat to their own

racial purity. These events are described in vivid detail in the National Holocaust Museum in Washington, D.C., and we strongly recommend that you visit
this museum if you ever get the chance to do so (see Figure 9.14). In an effort to
gain insights into the nature of such events, Milgram designed an ingenious, if
unsettling, laboratory simulation. (Baron & Byrne, 2003, p. 383)

Ross and Nisbett (1991), in their influential book, also addressed the M–
H issue:

> That there were many Germans who were not fiends yet knowingly played a
> role in sending the victims of Naziism to their horrible fates, we do not
> doubt. It is certainly the case that many Nazi concentration camp guards led
> blameless lives, both before and after their horrible service (Steiner, 1980).
> To explain such complicity, therefore, we must assume the existence of a spe-
> cific social and situational context that could induce ordinary people to com-
> mit extraordinarily evil deeds. As it happens, at roughly the same time Arendt
> was developing her thesis about the banality of evil, Stanley Milgram was
> demonstrating it in his laboratory. (p. 53)

Similar quotations have been commonplace in most social psychology
textbooks for decades, as shown in previous analyses of textbook constructions of the obedience research (Miller, 1986, 1995; Saltzman, 2000).
Generations of college students (and many others) have been exposed to
these explicit associations between the obedience experiments and the
Holocaust. What are the underlying reasons for these consistent M–H
associations?

Major Elements in the M–H Thesis

The Central Role of Obedience to Authority

It is virtually uncontested in text accounts that obedience to authority was
a major feature of the Nazi Holocaust. A policy of genocide, instigated by
a relatively small group of the Nazis, was obeyed and enacted by countless
subordinates, who were in varying degrees of proximity to the actual killing operations. Milgram created a laboratory procedure that produced
harmful behaviors under the directives of an authority—behaviors *that
would not have occurred without such directives*—and thus captured a key
feature of the Holocaust in the psychological laboratory. It is this general
position that characterizes social-psychological accounts of the obedience
experiments.

Good People Are Capable of Harming Others Under Orders

Milgram's participants were not screened for any personal traits regarding
hostility, aggression, anger, prejudice, etc. Randomly assigned to varying

conditions of the experimental situation, most participants were capable of either obeying or defying the experimenter's orders to inflict punishment. Thus, as with many phenomena studied by social psychologists, destructive obedience to authority appears well within the repertoire of most people (Miller, Buddie, & Kretschmar, 2002). It does not require a significant degree of mental illness or psychological disturbance to harm others under orders. This reality, of course, does not deny the existence of special types of persons who would be even more likely to engage in extreme acts of harm toward others.

The implication that might be drawn from the "normality" thesis noted above is that many, if not most, of the Germans who were involved in the Holocaust were, like Milgram's subjects, basically good, adjusted people—or *at least would have been thus considered in the context of the society within which they lived*. Thus, while those instigating the genocidal policy of the Holocaust might well have been extremist in their ideological zeal, which included virulent anti-Semitism (Mandel, 2002), there is no need to ascribe similar traits to the countless subordinates who obeyed their orders. In *Ordinary Men: Reserve Police Battalion 101 and the Final Solution in Poland*, Browning (1992) makes a similar point. Units of over-age, rear-echelon reservists brought to Poland from Hamburg—neither committed Nazis nor racial fanatics—participated in the direct shooting deaths of at least 38,000 Jews and the deportation of even more. Acknowledging that "this story of ordinary men is not the story of all men" and that, similar to Milgram's findings, there were individual differences in the degrees of killing behavior, Browning nevertheless concludes with a highly situational perspective on the Holocaust:

> The collective behavior of Reserve Police Battalion 101 has deeply disturbing implications. There are many societies afflicted by traditions of racism and caught in the siege mentality of war or threat of war. Everywhere society conditions people to respect and defer to authority, and indeed could scarcely function otherwise. Everywhere people seek career advancement. In every modern society, the complexity of life and the resulting bureaucratization and specialization attenuate the sense of personal responsibility of those implementing official policy. Within virtually every social collective, the peer group exerts tremendous pressures on behavior and sets moral norms. If the men of Reserve Police Battalion 101 could become killers under such circumstances, what group of men cannot? (pp. 188–189)

The thesis that ordinary people are fully capable of being influenced to inflict severe pain on others is counterintuitive and provocative—it defies what people predict to occur, and it defines a larger moral image of human nature. It is saying that evil is not committed only by evil people— what Baumeister (1997) and Darley (1992) have termed the "myth" of evil—but is within the repertoire of most people. College students, given a description of the Milgram experiment, tend to regard those who obey the experimenter's orders as hostile or aggressive, and they cannot imagine themselves behaving as, in fact, the majority did in Milgram's baseline experiment (Miller, Gillen, Schenker, & Radlove, 1974).

Arendt's Thesis on the Banality of Evil

In terms of historical documentation, the most significant association that social psychologists make to the obedience research is to "the banality of evil," used by the philosopher Hannah Arendt (1963) in her book *Eichmann in Jerusalem: A Report on the Banality of Evil* (Miller, 1995). Arendt, a court reporter for *The New Yorker* at the trial of Adolf Eichmann in Israel, challenged the prevailing view of Eichmann as a "scourge, a hangman, and a monster" (Segev, 1993, p. 332):

> The trouble with Eichmann was precisely that so many were like him, and that the many were neither perverted nor sadistic, that they were, and still are, terribly and terrifyingly normal. From the viewpoint of our legal institutions, and of our moral standards of judgment, this normality was much more terrifying than all the atrocities put together. (Arendt, 1963, p. 276)

Stanley Milgram was among the first to note the correspondence between Arendt's thesis and his findings:

> After witnessing hundreds of ordinary people submit to the authority in our own experiments, I must conclude that Arendt's conception of the *banality of evil* comes closer to the truth than one might dare imagine. The ordinary person who shocked his victim did so out of a sense of obligation . . . and not from any peculiarly aggressive tendencies. (1974, p. 6)

Milgram's reference to the banality of evil was itself important in terms of investing his research with both political and moral significance. The obedience research seemed to provide empirical verification of Arendt's extraordinarily counterintuitive description of Eichmann.

Arendt's judgment of Eichmann was instantly controversial. She was accused of "going against the way of thinking that grounds evil deeds in evil natures, that claims men *do* evil because they *are* evil" (Young-Bruehl, 1982, p. 342). The Milgram studies were also immediately controversial, and for precisely the same reason. Both Milgram and Arendt had converged, almost simultaneously, on the astonishing idea that rather ordinary people, in the dutiful conduct of their occupation, could perform unconscionable evil (Brown, 1985; Miller, 1995). Generations of social psychologists have endorsed the obedience studies as a reflection of the banality of evil. This linkage has not been uncontested, however, as will be seen.

Attributing Responsibility and Self-Serving Justifications

One of Milgram's (1974) central arguments was that obedience to authority was powerfully driven by subordinates' ability to absolve themselves of personal responsibility for the actions they were performing—what Milgram termed the "agentic shift." Although there is very little empirical support for this particular theoretical process, the idea is intuitively compelling. People often do what authorities tell them to do, even if it goes against their personal desires or preferences. Sabini and Silver (1980) suggest a clear linkage between the obedience studies and the Holocaust on this issue, but argue that obedience to authority does not provide a moral justification for reallocating personal responsibility for immoral actions committed under that authority:

> Eichmann and Milgram's subjects lost the right to be unconcerned with the moral implications of their actions just when the German state and the experimenter's demands became immoral. Milgram's obedient subjects and Hitler's murderers ought to have seen that these institutions were no longer legitimate, could no longer claim their loyalty, and could no longer settle for them the question of moral responsibility. (p. 336)

Sabini and Silver's judgment on the moral illegitimacy of the behavior inside Milgram's laboratory does not, however, detract from the idea that from the participants' point of view, they may well have felt personally absolved, at least to a degree.

Once in the process of obeying increasingly disturbing commands, what allows the participant to continue obeying? Contemporary social psychology has provided considerable empirical evidence suggesting the powerful role of self-justification and self-affirming rationalizations for one's behavior (Aronson, 1992; Bandura, 1999; Kelman & Hamilton, 1989; Kunda, 1990). People typically are motivated to preserve a strong sense of personal self-esteem and therefore interpret their own actions so as to maintain this sense of virtue (e.g., Bandura, Underwood, & Fromson, 1975; Bersoff, 1999). In terms of the contemporary emphases upon processes of construal and self-serving biases, the behavior of Milgram's participants is even more understandable than it was at the time of Milgram's (1974) own effort to provide a theoretical account.

The Extreme Level of "Pain" Administered in Milgram's Laboratory

I am unaware of any other research program in social science that has involved a comparable level of physical pain being inflicted by research participants (only, of course, in the eyes of these perpetrators). As noted, this aspect of the experiment led to the extreme stress and tension experienced by many participants, thus contributing to the ethical controversy. However, it was also the apparent infliction of pain in the obedience research that added to the validity of the Holocaust analogy, in terms of the pain (and, of course, far worse fates) experienced by Holocaust victims.

Why Social Psychologists Have Not Emphasized Anti-Semitism as an Explanation of the Holocaust

In an earlier period, social psychologists emphasized personality as a key factor in the anti-Semitism that was believed to culminate in the Holocaust—for example, the classic studies on the authoritarian personality (Adorno, Frenkel-Brunswik, Levinson, & Sanford, 1950). For a variety of reasons, this approach was largely abandoned. In discussing the obedience experiments, social psychology text authors rarely expand upon the thesis that German culture was rampant with widespread or uniquely extremist anti-Semitism. Instead, a variety of examples of genocide and massacres are noted in addition to the Holocaust (e.g., Armenia, My Lai, Jonestown, Rwanda, ethnic cleansing in Serbia, etc.). Destructive obedience to malevolent authority is seen as a generic problem in social life. The "particulars," in terms of the specific identities of the victims or perpetrators, are largely a matter of historical rather than psychological significance. As interesting as the Holocaust is to all who ponder human nature, for social psychologists, the My Lai massacre, the mass suicides at Jonestown, and other genocides are also, in principle, very relevant. For example, Kelman and Hamilton (1989) have examined numerous real-world scenarios of organizational corruption and harm-doing. Although none is of the same destructive magnitude as the Holocaust, it is still possible, from a scientific perspective, to seek the common themes and dynamics underlying a wide array of scenarios and events that are highly unique on the surface. The uniquely Jewish aspect of the Holocaust is generally given minimal consideration by social psychologists. If prejudice is included, it is generalized to the idea that the potential for destructive obedience would, understandably, be even heightened when the victims are a despised outgroup (e.g., Mook, 1983).

CRITICISMS OF THE M–H LINKAGE

If one were to examine only social psychology textbooks (and other texts in social sciences more generally), one would emerge with a clear conviction that the linkage of the obedience research to the Holocaust is one of social psychology's most dramatic and compelling messages. One would not surmise that there is a completely opposing point of view, a set of vehement criticisms authored not by skeptics from other academic quarters but from social psychologists themselves. As noted earlier, one criterion for a convincing argument of the generalizability of a research finding is that the research context and target domain share a sufficient number of critically important features—in particular, underlying psychological processes. One may conclude that the research does *not* generalize to a given target either because of particular features of the research itself or because one construes the target as not involving features or processes that are central to the research. Both of these types of criticism have been made regarding the linkage of the obedience experiments to the Holocaust.

Obedience to Authority: Inconsistent with the Sadism and Egregious Cruelty of the Holocaust

If the obedience paradigm is to relate meaningfully to the Holocaust, we would need evidence that subordinates in the Holocaust obeyed authority with great reluctance and personal distaste for what they were ordered to do (i.e., similar to what was observed in Milgram's studies). However, a number of writers have argued that there is no compelling evidence for this type of conflicted obedience in the Holocaust. Fenigstein (1998) points to three features of killers' actions in the Holocaust—an absence of a guilty conscience, the lack of mechanistic killing, and the presence of a clear choice not to participate—that, in his view, were *not* characteristic of the participants in the obedience experiments:

> In general, the historical evidence on the spontaneity, initiative, enthusiasm, and pride with which the Nazis degraded, tortured, and killed their victims, is utterly incompatible with the concept of obedience, and simply has no counterpart in the behavior that Milgram observed in his laboratory studies. . . . The terms that are routinely used to describe the horrors of the Holocaust— e.g., atrocity, inhumanity, hatefulness, wickedness—are simply preposterous in the context of Milgram's studies. (pp. 68, 71)

Berkowitz (1999) has noted that "social psychology's general belief in the overriding power of the immediate situation has contributed greatly to the widespread contention that Milgram's observations capture the 'central dynamic' of the Holocaust" (p. 250). Berkowitz suggests that an emphasis on the type of obedience observed in Milgram's studies fails to recognize the sadism involved in many of the killings and the crucial importance of distinguishing between "truly egregious injustices, such as the Nazis' Final Solution . . . and somewhat lesser misdeeds" (p. 250).

Obedience and Authority: Conceptual Ambiguities

Lutsky (1995) is critical of the imprecise use of the term *obedience* in relating the obedience studies to the Holocaust (and other contexts). His major objection is that the term *obedience* is used both as a *description* of behavior (i.e., subjects "obeying" an experimenter's orders to inflict punishment) and as an *explanation* of that behavior. There is also ambiguity inherent in the concept of *authority,* which may refer to expertise, to the power to reward and punish a subordinate, or to a role of legitimized power that induces a sense of moral obligation to obey. Finally, Lutsky notes that whereas Milgram emphasized the *reluctance* expressed on the part of his obedient subjects, this reluctance, in itself, hardly requires the explanatory concept of obedience. For many decades, social psychologists have shown that people often engage in behaviors that are not correspondent with their beliefs or feelings. Lutsky acknowledges the role of authority in Nazi Germany but argues that social psychology has vastly overemphasized the importance of obedience as understood in terms of the Milgram paradigm:

> What I want to suggest below is that when our references rely on the model of obligatory obedience in the Milgram experiment, they do not adequately represent the behavior of perpetrators in the Holocaust nor do they prompt new social psychological understandings of that behavior. . . . What an emphasis on obedience slights, however, are voluntary individual and group contributions to Nazi ideology, policy, bureaucracy, technology, and ultimately, inhumanity. . . . Perhaps if we recognize that obligatory obedience addresses only a part of the tragedy of the Holocaust, we will consider anew why people were attracted to authority . . . how they perceived their circumstances and why they were unwilling or unable to alter them, how individuals responded to peer behavior and the social dilemmas they faced . . . and why so many people used the opportunity provided by the Nazis to further their own interests, even if that meant tolerating or contributing to genocide. (pp. 62–63)

Obedience: Too Limited in Its Explanatory Power

Similarly, Staub (1989) has provided an instructive emphasis upon a diverse set of processes responsible for genocide—not only the Holocaust, but a number of other genocidal events as well. As does Lutsky, Staub has a more complex view of the Holocaust, in which obedience is viewed as a relevant but hardly dominant feature:

> While obedience is an important force, it is not the true motive for mass killing or genocide. The motivation to obey often comes from a *desire* to follow a leader, to be a good member of a group, to show respect for authority. Those who willingly accept the authority of leaders are likely to have also accepted their views and ideology. Guided by shared cultural dispositions, the shared experience of difficult life conditions, shared motivations that result from them, and shared inclinations for ways to satisfy motives, people *join* rather than simply obey out of fear or respect. We must consider not only

how those in authority gain obedience but how the motivations of the whole group evolve. . . . A society's strong respect for authority is *one* source of genocidal violence. A tendency to like and obey is *one* characteristic of perpetrators. (pp. 29–30)

For Staub, the power of the situation—that is, the prototypic social-psychological explanation—can mask the vital importance of individuals' personal choices and goals, even if they are also in a subordinate position in relation to authorities. Bandura (1999) has voiced a similar argument:

The sanctioning of harmful conduct in everyday life differs in two important ways from the direct authorizing system examined by Milgram (1974). Responsibility is rarely assumed that openly. . . . Obedient functionaries do not cast off all responsibility for their behavior as if they were mindless extensions of others. If they disowned all responsibility, they would perform their duties only when told to do so. It requires a strong sense of responsibility, rooted in ideology, to be a good functionary. (p. 197)

Darley (1995) takes a similar perspective:

Obviously I violently object to those who would equate the behavior of the subjects in the Milgram situation with the behaviors of Nazi doctors, concentration camp executioners, or Serbian snipers who assassinate children . . . the actions of the subjects in the Milgram obedience studies are different in important ways from the actions of concentration camp executioners, or soldiers perpetrating massacres, but the psychological community's presentation of these results no longer recognizes these differences. (p. 133)

Darley acknowledges that the behavior of Milgram's participants is "condemnable" because they inflict pain on an individual who has withdrawn his consent to participate. But, nevertheless, the operative dynamic in the Milgram paradigm is a very literal form of obedience to authority—intrinsically different from what Darley sees, in the Holocaust, as the voluntary perpetration of atrocities.

Changes in Perpetrators over Time: Not Addressed in the Obedience Experiments

A key feature of harm-doing, particularly as it occurs in group and organizational contexts, is the escalation of harm over time (Baumeister, 1997; Darley, 1992, 1995; Darley et al., 2001; Zimbardo, 1995). People first commit themselves to a course of action, then find themselves behaving badly toward others in a manner they did not envision at the outset, then engage in a variety of justification or rationalization processes to reassure themselves of the moral legitimacy of their harming actions (Bandura, 1999). The momentum is decidedly in the direction of maintaining, if not escalating, the destructive acts. For a variety of reasons, dropping out, quitting, whistle blowing, and other acts of defiance are unlikely to occur, at least on the part of most people, particularly if they do not have group support. The Milgram experiments do not, in themselves, capture this temporal dynamic of harm-doing in real contexts, but Darley suggests that Milgram at least has shown how the temporal drift toward evil may look in its earliest phase—the initial stage of a harm-doing process—which, if "continued by organizational forces, will bring people to do independently, calmly, and willingly what they first did only reluctantly, stressfully, and under protest" (1995, p. 134). Furthermore:

> The person who is induced into participation, and who goes far enough in the conversion process so that he or she autonomously and intelligently initiates evil actions, is an individual who has become evil. . . . The possibility of being evil is latent in all of us, and can be made actual and active, among other ways, by the conversion process. The person who goes a certain distance in the process has been fundamentally changed, and is now capable of doing harm in an autonomous way. He or she has "changed, changed utterly," has become evil. (Darley, 1992, p. 209)

The Dehumanized Status of Holocaust Victims: Neglected in Discussions of Obedience

For a number of commentators, the Milgram experiments fail to capture the most important feature of the Holocaust—namely, the dehumanized status of Jews (and others, including homosexual individuals and those with mental illness). The extreme symptoms of stress involved in obedience, emphasized as a key finding in Milgram's report, would likely not occur if the victims were viewed in dehumanized terms. Fenigstein (1998) has noted:

> If the Nazi perpetrators were "ideologically prepared" to see their Jewish victims as vermin, as less than human, and as hated enemies that threatened their way of life, their destruction could hardly be seen as morally repugnant. (p. 65)

Fenigstein argues that if this moral resistance is lacking, "obedience is unnecessary as an explanation" (p. 66). Browning repeatedly noted that on occasion, the soldiers who quit shooting did so because of physical revulsion, but "did not express any ethical . . . principles behind this revulsion" (1992, p. 74). Guilt and remorse, apparently central to the conflict in Milgram's laboratory, are not to be found in the Holocaust killers, according to Fenigstein. Browning (and others) report very graphic indicators of purely physical revulsion: "The shooters were gruesomely besmirched with blood, brains, and bone splinters. It hung on their clothing" (p. 65). Thus, a key distinction must be made between *distress*—which apparently was experienced by Nazi murderers—and *personally held moral values contradictory to the orders*—which were not experienced. Guilt and remorse were not experienced because the objects of their brutality were not, in their eyes, human beings. Fenigstein points out that after the war, the accused Nazi killers would have been expected to engage in a variety of self-absolving apologies and expressions of guilt and regret to mitigate their crimes and minimize their punishment. However, "in the absence of any such expression, it is difficult to escape the conclusion that these men simply did not feel that they had performed any morally repugnant actions" (1998, p. 67).

A widespread view of the Holocaust is that the Nazis had no choice but to obey their orders—but this view appears to be based almost entirely on statements made by these perpetrators at the postwar trials (e.g., Nuremburg), such as, "I had no choice, I was following orders." On this point, Fenigstein (1998) cites Browning, Goldhagen, and others: "There is not a single instance on record of harsh punishment ever being used, or even being possible, for disobeying a killing order" (p. 69).

Berkowitz (1999) also has expressed misgivings, specifically regarding Arendt's banality of evil thesis that was endorsed by Milgram and so many others. Berkowitz emphasizes that Arendt herself was struck by the sadistic nature of the murders of Jews:

> No one had issued orders that infants should be thrown into the air as shooting targets, or hurled into the fire alive, or have their heads smashed against walls. . . . Innumerable individual crimes, one more horrible than the next, surrounded and created the atmosphere of the gigantic crime of extermination. (Blass, 1993, p. 36, cited in Berkowitz, 1999, p. 250)

The dissimilarity between such actions and the obedience shown in Milgram's laboratory is, for the critics, an overwhelming reality that certainly rules out any obvious linkage or generalizability.

Is to Explain to Condone?—to Understand to Forgive?

A major concern of critics is that an explanation of the Holocaust from the perspective of the obedience experiments exonerates the perpetrators. Before examining the specific arguments, I should note that there is a general concern often expressed by those studying violence and evil that their explanation will be construed as forgiving harm-doers:

Some would argue that rather than studying Nazi evil, it should simply be recognized for what it is and condemned. Any efforts at understanding the causes of the Third Reich only serve to explain such actions, thus making them seemingly understandable and perhaps even excusable or justifiable. (Zillmer, Harrower, Ritzler, & Archer, 1995, p. 13)

Some went on to make a compelling case for leaving the whole subject alone. Their argument was that Nazi evil should merely be recognized and isolated: rather than make it an object of study, one should simply condemn it. Psychological study in particular, it was feared, ran the risk of replacing condemnation with "insights." (Lifton, 1986, p. xi)

I also fear that some readers may see me as exculpating killers; I have no such intention. . . . Although outrage is easier to feel in the face of uncomprehended evil, to understand is not necessarily to forgive. (Staub, 1989, pp. xiii–xiv)

The policemen in the battalion who carried out the massacres and deportations, like the much smaller number who refused or evaded, were human beings. I must recognize that in the same situation, I could have been either a killer or an evader—both were human—if I want to understand and explain the behavior of both as best I can. This recognition does indeed mean an attempt to empathize. What I do not accept, however, are the old cliches that to explain is to excuse, to understand is to forgive. Explaining is not excusing; understanding is not forgiving. (Browning, 1992, p. xx).

Despite the disavowing assertions of these writers, Miller and colleagues (Miller, Gordon, & Buddie, 1999; Miller et al., 2002) have suggested that their concerns about appearing too condoning are well founded in terms of the cognitive and emotional effects of explanations. In contrast to the intuitive, first-impression reactions of the lay person to the Holocaust—in whom reactions of anger, horror, shock, disgust, disbelief, and revulsion are virtually automatic—explicit theoretical accounts by social scientists are likely to be more complex, less exclusively reliant upon denigrating the personal moral character of perpetrators, and devoid of personal invective and anger on the part of the theorist. Baumeister (1997) has noted that formal (e.g., social science) explanations are also more likely, relative to the accounts of laypersons, to take into account the perspective of perpetrators, a perspective with exonerating implications: "There is ample reason to fear that understanding can promote forgiving. Seeing deeds from the perpetrator's point of view does change things in many ways" (p. 386). Sabini and Silver (1980), who have provided the strongest endorsement of the M–H thesis, acknowledge this possibility but are resolved not to exonerate perpetrators:

The thrust of [this] chapter has been to bring the phenomena of the camps closer to home, to see how this horror, this inhumanity could have been the product not only of deranged individuals but of normal people placed in deranged and degrading circumstances. We have attempted to draw links between what we know the artisans of the Holocaust did and what ordinary, American people have done in laboratory settings. . . . There is, however, a danger in this. The task of making something understandable is to make us see how it could have happened by showing how it is akin to something we can already grasp. There is a common tendency to slide from understanding to excusing. We are accustomed to thinking that once we have understood how someone came to do something, we are then compelled to forgive. In this case we cannot allow understanding to lead to excuse or forgiveness." (pp. 356–357)

Does Milgram's Interpretation Exonerate Those Who Obey Malevolent Authority?

In my view, the answer to this question is a qualified "yes." Consider the following from Milgram (1974):

> It is the old story of "just doing one's duty" that was heard time and time again in the defense statements of those accused at Nuremberg. But it would be wrong to think of it as a thin alibi concocted for the occasion. Rather, it is a fundamental mode of thinking for a great many people once they are locked into a subordinate position in a structure of authority. The disappearance of a sense of responsibility is the most far-reaching consequence of submission to authority (p. 8). . . . For the social psychology of this century reveals a major lesson: Often, it is not so much the kind of person a man is as the kind of situation in which he finds himself that determines how he will act. (p. 205)

Milgram's explicit refutation of the "alibi" argument is of particular significance in terms of contemporary criticisms. It is the position one might expect to hear from a defense attorney in a criminal trial, that is, in refuting claims that his or her client was lying and making excuses to escape conviction or punishment (e.g., Colman, 1991).

There is, however, a statement, located somewhat obscurely, that contradicts the above conclusion. This occurs in Milgram's (1964) rebuttal to Baumrind's (1964) widely known ethical criticism of the obedience research. Responding to Baumrind's contention that, methodologically, obedience to authority could not, in principle, be analyzed in a laboratory situation because the baseline for expected obedience was so extraordinarily high in that setting, Milgram countered as follows:

> Baumrind feels that the experimenter *made* the subject shock the victim. This conception is alien to my view. The experimenter tells the subject to do some-

thing. But between the command and the outcome there is a paramount force, the acting person who may obey or disobey. I started with the belief that every person who came to the laboratory was free to accept or to reject the dictates of authority. This view sustains a conception of human dignity insofar as it sees in each man [sic] a capacity for *choosing* his own behavior. (p. 851)

It is difficult, of course, to reconcile the idea of "freedom of choice" expressed here with Milgram's earlier-cited (and far more widely noted) views regarding the power of the situation. Perhaps because Milgram was challenging Baumrind's very personal ethical criticisms of his research, he disclaimed the accusation that he forced his participants to obey. In fact, many of Milgram's participants did disobey the experimenter, which strongly supports his position. Yet in my view, Milgram's more basic theoretical view is one that is likely to be perceived as exonerating harmful obedience.

In a recent analysis of the diverse interpretive constructions of the Holocaust in American culture, historian Peter Novick (1999) has commented on the impact of the obedience studies. In the context of Arendt's thesis on the banality of evil, he notes the different meaning that "following orders" acquired as a result of Milgram's experiments.

In the mid-sixties Milgram's work began to reach an audience wider than the readership of the *Journal of Abnormal [and Social] Psychology*. By then, Arendt's version of Eichmann had also entered common discourse. . . . A kind of synergy developed between the symbol of Arendt's Eichmann and the symbol of Milgram's subjects, invoked in discussing everything from the Vietnam war to the tobacco industry, and, of course, reflecting back on discussions of the Holocaust. It was in large part as a result of the acceptance of Arendt's portrait of Eichmann (with an assist from Milgram) that "just following orders" changed, in the American lexicon, from a plea in extenuation to a damning indictment. (p. 137)

Novick thus endorses Milgram's view that the concept of following orders has powerful explanatory value—an unpleasant reality of the human predicament—despite its more superficial image as an exonerating rationalization for destructive acts.[1]

---

[1]In his address to the nation on March 17, 2003, prior to ordering the invasion of Iraq, President George W. Bush recognized but explicitly disavowed the exonerating implications of obedience to authority: "And all Iraqi military and civilian personnel should listen carefully to this warning. . . . Do not obey any command to use weapons of mass destruction against anyone. War crimes will be prosecuted. War criminals will be punished. And it will be no defense to say, 'I was just following orders.' "

Critics of the Exonerating Implications of the Obedience Experiments

In a scathing critique of the relevance of the M–H thesis, Mandel (1998) describes two "social dangers" inherent in the "just following orders" claim, which he construes as the essential meaning of the experiments conveyed by social psychologists: "The first is that it is offensive to survivors (and to our memories of victims) who know all too well that there was much more behind the way they were viciously brutalized, mocked, and tormented than a mere obligation to follow orders" (p. 91).

Mandel is the first scholar, to my knowledge, to voice the position that one should consider the impact of certain types of explanations of the Holocaust on those for whom the issue is of particular emotional significance. However, he then suggests that social scientists should not try to construct theories "that comfort any particular group" (p. 90), that they "should, of course, seek the truth even if it is a terrible truth and they should reveal what they find. Nevertheless care should be taken in how explanations are communicated, especially when they have a clear potential to cause harm" (p. 91). Obedience, for example, should be given a qualified causal significance in the Holocaust, and its role should be placed in the context of the crucial importance of many other factors.

The second "social danger" of the obedience explanation relates specifically to the exoneration problem:

> The second, negative social ramification of the oversimplified obedience account is that it insidiously serves the function of exonerating Nazi war criminals (and an untold number of other evildoers) by reaffirming exactly what many of them—even the highest-ranking Nazi officials on trial at Nuremberg ... claimed in their defense: that they too were "just following orders." (p. 91)

Mandel accuses Milgram (and all who have championed his studies in connection with the Holocaust) of providing an obedience alibi, of "siding with the enemy":

> Holocaust perpetrators have asserted the obedience alibi as an assurance of their innocence. Social scientists have asserted the obedience alibi as an ostensibly situationist explanation of the Holocaust. Though the intent of one group has differed from the other, the message conveyed has been strikingly similar. (p. 91)

Mandel concludes with an unusually vitriolic summarization of Milgram's position on the Holocaust, calling him "uninformed by fact and displaying a bizarre illogic," revealing a "dangerous form of pseudoscientific overconfidence" (p. 92).

In a strong critique of a central thesis of traditional social psychology—that is, that behavior is under the powerful causal control of situational factors—Sabini, Siepmann, and Stein (2001a, 2001b) have recently advocated a pronounced reemphasis on the role of "the person" and of dispositions in social-psychological theory and research. They noted:

> And, indeed, the overly broad message that situations, not dispositions, cause behavior seems to erode responsibility for behavior. This message lets people off the hook for what is their fault (as well as for what is not their fault) and denies them praise for what they should be praised for. If claiming that situations are more important than dispositions lets the innocent off the hook, it does so by a blanket denial of human responsibility, and that is dehumanizing, not humanizing. (2001a, p. 46)

Berkowitz (1999) also implies that there is a condoning aspect to the radical situationist view of obedience, common to social-psychological discussions of the Holocaust. In his view, situationist accounts of evil—and, in particular, the behavior of Milgram's obedient participants—have virtually no meaningful relationship to the heinous acts of the Holocaust perpetrators. Implying that all harmful acts, be they in a laboratory or extermination camps, are a reflection of situationally imposed evil is unacceptable:

> Social psychology's relative inattention to the great atrocities committed during the extermination program reflects the field's failure to establish a conception of evil that differentiates among categories of wrongdoing. In so doing, there is a danger of trivializing terrible actions. In not distinguishing conceptually between truly egregious injustices such as the Nazis' Final Solution and somewhat lesser misdeeds, . . . we basically place all of these behaviors in the same psychological category and thus run the risk of regarding all of them as equally bad. (p. 250)

Fenigstein (1998) also sees an alibi in the Milgram studies:

> The concept of the agentic state is frighteningly evocative, for example, of the litany of "I was just following orders" heard repeatedly at the Nuremberg trials. Although Milgram argued that these defense claims actually represent serious and significant psychological truths, the possibility that these men were simply trying to avoid or mitigate punishment for the crimes must obviously be considered (as the Nuremberg jurists, in fact, often did). Thus, it is difficult to find convincing evidence for the agentic state by examining the testimony (or psychiatric protocols, e.g. Lifton 1986) of war criminals. (p. 62)

Instigators of the Holocaust: A Neglected Factor

Recent commentators have suggested that social psychologists, in their devotion to the obedience experiments, have essentially ignored a major element in Milgram's paradigm: the authority issuing the harmful orders. Who are the authorities? How do they achieve this status? What factors induce them to develop the harmful orders that others appear so inclined to obey? These questions have received virtually no attention in contemporary social psychology. Berkowitz's views are representative:

> Milgram's (1974) obedience research does not represent significant features of the Holocaust, especially the sadism that occurred not infrequently, and disregards the vital difference between those who initiated the murderous policy and the others who followed their orders. . . . The evil of Adolph Eichmann's actions surely did not match those of Adolph Hitler or even those of Reinhardt Heydrich, described by Arendt (1963) as "the real engineer of the Final Solution (p. 36)." (1999, pp. 246, 250).

In a recent analysis of the instigator issue, Mandel (2002) makes a sharp distinction between instigators—those who originate acts of collective violence—and perpetrators—those who execute such acts. Focusing on Hitler, Mandel applies a number of social-psychological principles (regarding cognition, emotion, motivation, behavior) that help explain Hitler's role. Mandel notes, however:

> My attempt to "normalize Hitler" by examining his behavior from a subjectivist and situationist perspective does not imply, as some might wrongly assume, that there is a Hitler in all of us. However, I hope that this chapter may convince the reader that social-psychological accounts of evil do not necessitate a view of people as fundamentally good either. Lay dispositionist accounts of evil may erroneously portray evildoers as monsters, but situationist accounts may also erroneously portray evildoers as good-intentioned souls who are swept along by the power of bad situations. (p. 279)

THE M–H THESIS IN RECENT ANALYSES OF OBEDIENCE AND GENOCIDE

Given the uniformly positive endorsement of the M–H thesis in social-psychology texts, it is of interest to note how the Milgram experiments are discussed in texts devoted more exclusively to analyses of obedience and genocide. A number of social psychologists have written or edited books on these topics (Baumeister, 1997; Blass, 2000; Katz, 1993; Kelman & Hamilton, 1989; Newman & Erber, 2002; Staub, 1989; Waller, 2002). All of these sources refer to the obedience experiments in the context of the Holocaust, genocide, and other crimes. These books generally present highly detailed, multifaceted analyses, involving numerous processes interacting in complex patterns (e.g., social-psychological, personality, organizational, historical, legal, cultural, political). Understandably, the concept of destructive obedience to authority emerges as only one causal dynamic among many others. Clearly, the inhumane treatment of other people raises complex questions about human nature, and requires extensive conceptual frameworks to cover the vast domains involved in this subject.

Among the works noted above, Staub is the most critical of the M–H thesis. As noted earlier, his primary contention is that most people who participate in genocidal behaviors do so voluntarily. Recognizing the impact of the obedience research, Staub nevertheless has serious reservations:

> Milgram's dramatic demonstration of the power of authority, although of great importance, may have slowed the development of a psychology of genocide, as others came to view obedience as the main source of human destructiveness. (p. 29)

The other authors are generally more positive in endorsing the M–H thesis but all recognize the crucial role of other processes as well, in particular the dehumanization of the Jews and other victims as well as the cruelty and sadism that were routinely inflicted by many perpetrators. Waller (2002), for example, takes a complex view of the M–H thesis. He first outlines several important features of the Milgram experiments that do not generalize convincingly to the Holocaust—for example, the transient nature of the laboratory experience, the anguish displayed by Milgram's participants, and the presumably benevolent attitude of the authority to the welfare of the victims. Yet he also sees a crucial validity to the M–H linkage:

> It would be inaccurate to characterize the subjects' motivations and behavior in Milgram's Yale laboratory as exactly equivalent, either morally or psychologically, to that of those who commit atrocities in mass killing and genocide. However, it is just as inaccurate to say that Milgram's research is without relevance to our study of extraordinary evil. He correctly focuses our attention on the social and situational pressures that can lead ordinary people to commit extraordinary evil. (p. 108)

Thus, in these more extensive discussions of evil and genocide, one observes elements of the M–H thesis that are highly congruent with those characterizing social psychology texts, as well as consistent with some of the pointed criticisms I have described in this chapter. Readers who are interested in pursuing the M–H thesis would benefit considerably in examining the broad contexts that these analyses provide. It should also be possible for authors of social psychology texts to incorporate, in their discussion of the M–H thesis, at least a synopsis of the more detailed and contextually rich analyses contained in these more extended treatments of genocide and evil.

ARE SOCIAL-PSYCHOLOGICAL EXPLANATIONS
OF HARM-DOING PERCEIVED
AS EXONERATING PERPETRATORS?: EMPIRICAL EVIDENCE

Miller and colleagues (1999) tested the hypothesis that a social-psychological explanation of a harmful act would be perceived as more condoning toward the perpetrator than would an explanation focused on dispositions of the perpetrator. The essential underlying rationale for their study derived from Weiner's (1995) model of the attribution of responsibility. Social-psychological explanations of harm-doing that emphasize the influence of external forces tend to describe perpetrators as relatively low in personal responsibility and thus should elicit a relatively condoning impression, in comparison to a more dispositionally framed explanation of the same behavior.

Participants were first given a synopsis of an experiment on cheating modeled after Diener and Wallbom (1976), who found evidence that people would cheat less if they were in a situation that accentuated self-awareness (e.g., having a mirror in front of them as they worked alone on a test). Participants were assigned to one of two conditions. In the *social-psychological explanation* condition, results were provided (to participants in Miller et al.) that indicated a powerful situational effect: 5% cheating in the mirror condition, 90% cheating in the no-mirror condition (similar to the actual results of Diener & Wallbom). The discussion emphasized the power of the situation to influence cheating behavior and the implications of random assignment to conditions. In the *personality explanation* condition, the results indicated the total absence of any situational effect. In order to clarify the failure to obtain the expected effect, the researcher had administered a follow-up study, in which the same participants returned to complete an "honesty test" (e.g., "It is important never to lie," "Cheating is probably more common than most people realize," etc). A new set of results was then presented, showing that only 5% of those scoring high on the honesty test had cheated in the earlier session, whereas 90% of those scoring low on the honesty test had cheated. The discussion section emphasized the failure of the situational manipulation and the power of the individual participant's level of honesty to predict cheating behavior.

After participants read either the social-psychological or personality results and explanation, they were given two sets of measures. On the *researcher's impressions* form, they were asked to estimate the researcher's views concerning various aspects of the study. As predicted, participants who had read a social-psychological explanation of cheating viewed the researcher as significantly more condoning toward the perpetrators than did subjects who had read a dispositional explanation—that is, less responsible, less intentional, and less blameworthy. However, when giving *their personal impressions,* participants held cheaters accountable for their behavior, regardless of the type of explanation they had read. Thus, subjects essentially ignored the situational implications of the social-psychological explanations when giving their personal judgments about the cheater.

To extend this analysis to the primary focus of this chapter, a follow-up study was recently conducted.[2] Two very distinct explanations of the Holocaust were written. An *obedience* explanation was based closely on the Milgram research and emphasized key elements of the social-psychological perspective. Included in this explanation were two quotations from Milgram: "These inhumane policies may have originated in the mind of a single person, but they could only have been carried out on a massive scale if a very large number of persons obeyed orders" (1963, p. 371) and "it is not so much the kind of person one is, but the kind of situation one is in, that determines our actions" (1974, p. 205).[3] The second explanation, termed the *anti-Semitism* explanation, emphasized that the Holocaust was essentially caused by the virulent anti-Semitism that characterized the German people. For this explanation, a number of quotations from Goldhagen's (1996) *Hitler's Willing Executioners* were used. Representative of this explanation is the following:

> This explanation is that "antisemitism moved many thousands of 'ordinary' Germans . . . to slaughter Jews. Not economic hardship, not the coercive means of a totalitarian state, not social psychological pressure . . . but ideas about Jews that were pervasive in Germany, and had been for decades, induced ordinary Germans to kill unarmed, defenseless Jewish men, women, and children by the thousands, systematically and without pity." (p. 9)

Participants read both explanations, being assigned randomly to read either the obedience or anti-Semitism explanation first in order. After reading each explanation, participants rated it on a number of judgmental items. As expected, participants reading the obedience explanation in comparison to the anti-Semitism explanation rated the perpetrators as substantially lower in responsibility, intentionality, and blameworthiness. They also evaluated the obedience explanation as providing a relatively greater justification and excuse on the part of the perpetrators, and as portraying the perpetrators as significantly less evil and violent. Interestingly, participants were, on average, very similar in their personal endorsements of both types of explanations.[4]

---

[2] Olga Levina provided invaluable assistance in the conceptualization and analysis of this research. Further information about this study may be obtained from the author.

[3] This is a slight modification of the original quotation in Milgram (1974), which is as follows: "It is not so much the kind of person a man is as the kind of situation in which he finds himself that determines how he will act" (p. 205).

CONCLUSIONS

In previous commentary, I strongly supported the M–H thesis (e.g., Miller, 1986):

> The experiments cast a shadow. They warn against relegating the potential for Holocaust-like events to the past, to a time of unenlightenment, to an era of primitive passions. They have an unsettling, futuristic relevance. They signify that destructive obedience, in a variety of contexts, may be a disaster "waiting to happen." (p. 258)

The world has surely witnessed numerous Holocaust-like events in recent years—so-called ethnic cleansing in Serbia, genocide in Africa, pervasive sexual abuse of children and its concealment in religious institutions, worldwide terrorism, shockingly destructive corruption in leading financial institutions, and fatal disasters in the space program traced to organizational malfeasance, to name only a few. I have no doubt that obedience to authority has been a significant element in all of them.

However, my own views regarding the M–H thesis have become more complex or perhaps ambivalent. My objectives in this final section are to identify what I view to be some important issues underlying the controversies, to suggest a resolution of at least some of them, and to make suggestions for further inquiry.

Good People Doing Evil: Confronting the Counterintuitive and Controversial

The obedience research is often portrayed by its supporters as *the* prototype of a counterintuitive finding. They highlight the naiveté of the lay perceivers' presumption that only evil people do evil deeds. As Novick (1999) observed, Daniel Goldhagen's book has, in fact, been extremely popular, despite some resistance among scholars. The reason is that Goldhagen's explanation, in its extremely dispositional orientation, distances the perpetrators from the average reader. Goldhagen thus indicts rather than exonerates perpetrators. In essence, he is telling readers what they want to hear:

---

[4]For further discussion on the condoning implications of social-psychological explanations of the Holocaust, see Miller et al. (2002). Miller et al. (1999) have also observed that simply generating an explanation of more mundane examples of harm-doing—in contrast to not explaining but simply reading about such acts—may produce a condoning bias in the person generating the explanation. Folkes and Whang (2003) have recently confirmed these findings, noting that explanations tend to produce a cognitive elaboration of the harming behavior, including an increased awareness of situational causes.

It is a comforting argument: if such deep and long-standing hatred is a necessary precondition for mass murder, we're a lot safer than many of us think. But the desire to frame the perpetrators in the traditional way remains powerful—which is why Goldhagen's book was a runaway bestseller" (Novick, 1999, p. 137).[5]

The obedience research captures these issues in a startling way, and is particularly instructive in provoking students to engage in critical thinking regarding their own susceptibility to destructive influences from authorities.

The Prestige of Contributing to an Understanding of the Holocaust

The Holocaust is obviously a very daunting and intriguing domain of inquiry. To be able to claim—in classes and in writing—that one's academic discipline has important things to say about the Holocaust is extremely gratifying. There is, I think, an undeniable degree of prestige or intellectual status inherent in contributing significantly to an understanding of the Holocaust. It is not surprising, therefore, that many social psychologists take pride in claiming the Milgram experiments as *their* unique contribution to Holocaust scholarship. Certainly the extensive coverage given to the obedience studies in contemporary texts is consistent with this line of reasoning.

The powerful meaning of the obedience research for many social psychologists may, however, have also imposed, unwittingly, a subtle judgmental bias or "blind spot." In a provocative experiment relevant to this discussion, Wilson, DePaulo, Mook, and Klaaren (1993) have shown that the perceived importance of a research topic can influence people to overlook methodological flaws in the research. Research participants (research psychologists and medical faculty) were shown brief descriptions of fictitious research studies, either on an important or unimportant topic (e.g., on cardiovascular disease vs. on heartburn, on hypertension vs. on dandruff). Except for the stated topic of study, the versions of the studies were identical and included a variety of obvious flaws and methodological errors (e.g., lack of control groups, lack of random assignment). The results indicated that participants were significantly more likely to recommend the "important topic" study for publication and to regard it as methodologically more rigorous in comparison to the "unimportant topic" study. Wilson and colleagues concluded:

---

[5]Goldhagen's book, *Hitler's Willing Executioners* (1996), although extremely popular, has also been extraordinarily controversial. A useful reference is Shandley (1998).

People are often blind to a loved one's faults. It is a disturbing comment on the nature of scientific assessment that a similar process can occur when trained scientists evaluate research: Our infatuation with the importance of the topic of a study can make us overlook its imperfections. (p. 325)

I would suggest that a similar effect may have occurred with respect to the M–H thesis. That is, the uniquely provocative and stimulating aspects of the obedience research may have induced some commentators (myself included) to be, at least on occasion, too zealous and unreflective in making strong inferences regarding causes of the Holocaust. Such inferences may, of course, be perfectly reasonable to make, but only if forged in a careful weighing of the many relevant arguments, specifically including those dissenting from the prevailing pro-M–H thesis.

Single-Cause Explanations: Costs and Benefits

Critics of the M–H linkage argue that a reliance on the Milgram studies to explain the Holocaust provides too simplistic an account of the horrific event. Thus, when social psychologists suggest or imply that obedience on the part of normal, adjusted persons to malevolent authority was *a major cause*—perhaps *the* major cause—of the Holocaust, they are going to provoke criticism. There is no statistical or empirical means of verifying such a conclusion, and virtually anyone, upon reflection, would agree with the countering view that a historical epoch such as the Nazi Holocaust would undoubtedly be attributable to a large number of major causal factors. Of course, one could also apply the "too simplistic" objection to those who argue that extreme anti-Semitism and the resulting dehumanization of the Jews were *the major causes* of the Holocaust.

Complex answers may sound more convincing than simpler ones. However, influential forces in the academic world reinforce the tendency to identify the key causal factor of a phenomenon. To conclude simply that a complex phenomenon such as the Holocaust has a multiplicity of determinants operating in some combination might be seen as obvious or lacking in discernment—perhaps vague, ambiguous, or (worse) even boring. Those who advance a more concise and sharply defined analysis are likely to be regarded as more persuasive and perhaps more brilliant or creative (Amabile, 1983). It is my impression that social psychologists tend to emphasize the *distinctive* role of destructive obedience, not merely the plausibility of its playing *some part* in the Holocaust.

Because the Holocaust rarely receives substantial consideration in social psychology texts other than that associated with the obedience experiments, the critics are persuasive in suggesting that students emerge with, at best, a very narrow view. If the "missing components"—for example, the horrific cruelty and sadism, the dehumanization, the psychology of the instigators—were to receive their deserved consideration *in conjunction with a discussion of destructive obedience,* at least some of the controversy would undoubtedly recede. There would still, however, be dissenting voices regarding the M–H thesis because, as we have seen, a number of scholars and commentators remain convinced that obedience to authority, specifically on the part of large numbers of subordinates who were ideologically and emotionally opposed to the orders they were given, was an extremely minor (if that) causal factor in the Holocaust—regardless of how surprising or provocative this assertion may seem.

The M–H linkage has seemingly become part of social psychology's received wisdom. Lee Ross (1988) has observed:

> Milgram's demonstrations have become much more than a topic for internecine debate among psychologists. Perhaps more than any other empirical contributions in the history of social science, they have become part of our society's shared intellectual legacy—that small body of historical incidents, biblical parables, and classic literature that serious thinkers feel free to draw on when they debate about human nature or contemplate human history. (p. 101)

Shared legacy or not, the M–H linkage clearly deserves a thorough reexamination, even by its most ardent supporters, on the basis of the evidence reviewed in this chapter.

Is Authorization for Murder Superfluous, Given Extremist Anti-Semitic Beliefs?

Fenigstein (1998) has suggested that "the vast majority of those who did the killing believed it was just and necessary and would have been willing to kill Jews, even in the absence of orders to do so" (p. 65). To argue that masses of individuals, steeped in vitriolic hatred of Jews, would spontaneously engage in murderous activities on anything approaching the magnitude of the Holocaust seems unwarranted. Social psychologists have known for many years that attitudes or feelings do not necessarily predict behavior. One can personally agree with the orders one receives—recall Oliver North, during the Iran/Contra hearings, proudly asserting that he would "march up the hill and salute," upon receiving any orders from an authority. However, this agreement hardly implies that orders are superfluous. Fenigstein's comment illustrates, in my view, an extremist and indefensible position, likely caused by what he perceives to be the equally implausible thesis linking the obedience experiments to the Holocaust. A more convincing position would be that the *simultaneous occurrence* of genocidal orders in the presence of intense hatred and dehumanization of Jewish victims was of critical importance to the creation of the Holocaust.

The Milgram experiments only document one part of this position, but it could be a critically important dynamic without in any way minimizing the crucial role of the second component.

The Obedience Alibi: Does Social Psychology Condone Destructive Obedience?

Do the obedience experiments provide an excuse or justification for the perpetrators of the Holocaust? Critics of the M–H linkage contend that they do, and I have noted that there is now empirical evidence that social-psychological explanations of harming behaviors are, in fact, perceived as condoning in comparison to more dispositional accounts. "I was only obeying orders" was the standard defense at the Nuremburg trials, and this plea stands on rather firm social-psychological ground—indeed, consider Milgram's observation that this claim was "not a thin alibi, concocted for the occasion." Writers on violence and evil alert their readers that they personally do not condone or excuse the harmful behaviors they are seeking to explain. Yet critics of the M–H thesis see precisely this kind of "forgiveness" in Milgram's situational analysis and, more generally, in the writings of contemporary social psychologists (Miller et al., 2002).

It is understandable that many people might react very negatively to a theoretical analysis of the Holocaust that appears to be incongruent with their intensely negative emotional reactions to the perpetrators and their terrible deeds. Theories that locate the causes of such acts inside the perpetrators—that is, in their *evil* nature—are, for many, far more appealing (Miller et al., 1999). Goldhagen states the "bottom line" to this general point of view: "Simply put, the perpetrators, having consulted their own convictions and morality and having judged the mass annihilation of Jews to be right, did not *want* to say no" (1996, p. 14).

Some critics may thus be motivated to see defects in the M–H linkage because this thesis contradicts their preferred conclusion that perpetrators are responsible for their actions and deserve severe punishment. In contrast, the M–H thesis appears to normalize and condone their behavior. As noted earlier, there is an extensive research literature documenting the powerful biasing effects of personal beliefs and theoretical allegiances on the processing of new information. The same line of reasoning would apply, of course, to those with a different conceptual orientation. Adherents to the M–H linkage would be expected to be far less enthusiastic about theories emphasizing personal or characterological determinants of perpetrator behavior (e.g., Goldhagen, 1996). Of course, as we have noted, critics may object to the M–H thesis for reasons quite distinct from the alibi or condoning issue, yet there is the possibility that the strong reaction against the condoning implication itself motivates the critics to find *additional* defects in the M–H association.

Might the converse of the above also be true? That is, might those who champion a strongly situational view of harm-doing and endorse the M–H thesis prefer that theoretical explanation because it condones the actions of perpetrators? It is difficult to argue that scholars or researchers would have, underlying their theoretical work, a strong personal motive to forgive perpetrators of atrocities, thereby endorsing situational views of evil because they have a condoning premise. A number of commentators (Miller et al., 2002) have suggested that social-psychological explanations of the Holocaust are actually very skeptical and accusatory toward the proclivity of most of *us* to commit harmful, even evil, deeds. That is, situational analyses are only superficially exonerating—at a deeper level, they implicate all of us. Zimbardo, Maslach, and Haney (2000) have noted:

> Thus, any deed that any human being has ever done, however horrible, is possible for any of us to do—under the right or wrong situational pressures. That knowledge does not excuse evil; rather it democratizes it, shares its blame among ordinary participants, rather than demonizes it. (p. 206)

However, this kind of reasoning would undoubtedly be rejected by critics of the M–H thesis, who, as we have seen, find it ludicrous to "indict everyone" as potential genociders, when, in their view, the perpetrators of the Holocaust were so distinctively different from most people.

One of the difficult issues surrounding the relationship between explanation and exoneration concerns the role of values and moral judgment. The sentiment appears widely shared that the effort to understand the causes of evil or violence should not—indeed, must not—drift into an apologetic or accepting posture. Yet as I have discussed, there may be a number of cognitive and affective processes, related to social-psychological explanations, which in fact lead to a degree of exoneration, either in fact or as perceived (Miller et al., 1999). Is this necessarily an untenable position for a scholar or researcher? Perhaps not. Baumeister (1997) has offered a particularly eloquent thought on this complicated matter. He suggests that to understand may require a *temporary* moratorium on condemnation, but that this need not be the end of the story: "It is a mistake to let moral condemnation interfere with trying to understand—but it would be a bigger mistake to let that understanding, once it has been attained, interfere with moral condemnation" (p. 387).

Taking the Perspective of Victims as well as Perpetrators

Critics of the M–H thesis may find the obedience experiments unacceptable because they appear to take the perpetrator's perspective. In Milgram's research (and other studies of obedience) the entire focus is on those who obey—why they obey, when they obey, why they stop obeying, their anguish in obeying, etc. In addition, the conceptual framework is comprised entirely of external causal factors. The victim is not even a real victim but an accomplice of the researcher. One can appreciate how some commentators would find this scenario completely at odds with their construal of the Holocaust, in which the suffering of genuine victims is the essence of the matter.

Social-Psychological Accounts of the Holocaust: Reasonable or Deficient?

One can take either of two positions on the association between the Milgram experiments and the Holocaust as typically portrayed in social psychology texts. From one perspective, the discussion in current social psychology can be seen as reasonable. It could be argued that introductory courses in social psychology (and other social sciences) are not the appropriate context for getting into complex historical details on such matters as the Holocaust. Thus, the mention of a "possible" linkage between the Milgram studies and historical episodes of genocide is not only reasonable but professionally responsible. After all, the connection has, in fact, been a major concern from the initial appearance of Milgram's studies in 1963.

The other perspective is less generous. Social psychologists should become more familiar with contemporary historical analyses of the Holocaust (e.g., Bauer, 2001; Gellately, 2001; Johnson, 1999; Newman & Erber, 2002), and weave more specific documentation of obedience (or its absence) in these sources into their discussions of the obedience research. Although sources with this kind of detail are available (e.g., Kelman, 1973; Sabini & Silver, 1980), they are rare and not represented in more standard texts. Newman (2001) has made a similar point with respect to Arendt's thesis on the banality of evil. However, Newman's argument is not simply that social psychologists fail to deal *sufficiently* with Holocaust scholarship but that they deal with it *erroneously*. He argues that social psychologists have failed to read Arendt's (1963) book *Eichmann in Jerusalem* carefully (if at all), and present an essentially erroneous concept of Arendt's own interpretation of the banality of evil. Read more thoroughly, Arendt's portrait of Eichmann is hardly that of the simple bureaucrat with his reputedly cold, emotionless demeanor. Newman quotes Arendt's view of Eichmann's stance: "I will jump into my grave laughing, because the fact that I have the death of five million Jews on my conscience gives me extraordinary satisfaction" (p. 11). Thus, the portrait of Eichmann (and by casual inference, all Nazis) as a stolid, dutiful employee without emotional enthusiasm is simply incorrect. What this all leads to, ultimately, is that Eichmann's banality of evil (in Arendt's actual report) is *not* reflective of the behavior of Milgram's subjects. Milgram's subjects were portrayed as greatly distressed and conflicted, features that were not characteristic of Eichmann, and, in fact, were contradictory to Arendt's portrait.

Newman (2001) suggests that many social psychologists are biased. They have engaged in a "rush to judgment," taking Arendt's one statement that Eichmann was not a sadistic monster and concluding (erroneously) that his personality did not matter at all:

> And if that was so, then what was left? Situational pressures. So Arendt's book was framed in terms of a set of issues that did not really map onto her ideas so well, and in the process, they got distorted. Needless to say, there was also a motivational element at work, too. Social psychologists interpreted her work in a way that was consistent with their preferred conclusions. (p. 16)

Weaknesses in Social-Psychological Coverage of the Obedience Research

There is no question that one weakness of the obedience research resides in the lack of a substantiated *theory*. Milgram's (1974) account of the agentic shift has received minimal support (Darley, 1992, 1995; Mantell & Panzarella, 1976), and other than post-hoc explanations of the demonstrable finding that obedience to authority varies sharply with specific situational arrangements (Milgram, 1974; Ross & Nisbett, 1991), there is really no conclusive theory to account for destructive obedience—or defiance, either. The matter of disobedience to authority has also received insufficient attention. Some individuals disobeyed Milgram's experimenter; crucially important, if relatively rare, help was provided to Jews during the Holocaust (Rochat & Modigliani, 1995). If one agrees with Mook (1983) and others that what generalizes in the truest sense from laboratory findings is "theoretical understanding," the M–H thesis rests on a somewhat shaky foundation. This lack of solid grounding, of course, has hardly stopped social psychologists (and scholars from other disciplines) from pursuing the M–H argument, but making the argument is obviously not tantamount to making it convincingly or persuasively. One approach would be to consider how the concepts of obedience and authority have been pursued in other contexts. A particularly useful example is the analysis of ethical problems in organizations (e.g., Darley et al., 2001; Kelman & Hamilton, 1989; Strudler & Warren, 2001). Social psychologists would be advised to examine these and related works to sharpen their conceptual understanding of obedience to authority in a variety of organizational settings.

What Can the Obedience Experiments Tell Us about the Holocaust?

On the basis of the evidence considered in this chapter, the answer is a complex one. There is no question, in my opinion, that the experiments document obedience to malevolent authority on the part of a representative sample of persons. That many ordinary persons will, upon receiving instructions from a researcher, inflict what they perceive as unbearable pain upon a protesting peer is still, to me, a stunning discovery, with powerful implications for real-life settings, including those involving torture and genocide. Because the Holocaust also involved malevolent authority, obedience on the part of an extremely large number of persons, and the infliction of pain of every imaginable kind, the M–H thesis is thus convincing—*to this point*. The experiments certainly generalize to those persons in Nazi Germany who obeyed orders, despite having personal reservations about what was happening to the Jews, and who did *not* harbor what Goldhagen terms eliminationist, anti-Semitic beliefs. I do not think we would be able to understand the behavior of these individuals—and the countless bystanders, who may be said to have obeyed by omission (Staub, 1989)—as well as we do had the obedience research not been conducted.

On the other hand, the critics pose some very compelling arguments to those who would assert the presence of a strong inference regarding the M–H thesis. I would suggest that any serious discussion of the M–H thesis that did not include a simultaneous consideration of the importance of dehumanization would constitute an inadequate coverage of the issues. To my knowledge, an obedience experiment that includes, as a major independent variable, the dehumanization of the victim, has not been performed. Dehumanization has been well documented (e.g., Bandura, 1999; Bandura et al., 1975), but the joint effects of *obedience pressures* and *victim dehumanization* have not received attention. (Milgram envisioned this study in his NSF research proposal, but he never actually performed it.) Until this type of research is performed, it is impossible to make strong inferences regarding the M–H thesis on the basis of the Milgram studies alone. Anti-Semitism in Nazi Germany is simply too compelling a reality to dismiss as crucial simply because Milgram demonstrated that prejudice on the part of obedient persons was not necessary to obtain extreme harmdoing. Milgram's participants may have harmed the learner for one set of reasons, and Holocaust perpetrators may have harmed their victims for other reasons. All acts of harming—even if done under orders to harm—are not necessarily comparable in their underlying causes. The critics are on solid ground here.

It should also not be surprising, at least at this point, that the exoneration of harm-doers is viewed very negatively by many people, including at least some social psychologists. One might think that this problem could be resolved simply by saying, "Well, that's only how social-psychological explanations are *perceived*—they actually do not provide moral approval for harm-doing." Sabini and Silver (1980) take this position. I do not think this approach is effective, at least for students who are just being introduced to these matters, because this kind of answer simply begs another question; that is, if the social-psychological perspective seems to be excusing the perpetrators, why do you then say that it really does *not* excuse the perpetrators?[6] I have no solution at this point, but the critics are pointing to a serious gap in our understanding not only of obedience or the Holocaust, but crucially, of the impact of our explanations on others. This, among other issues considered in this chapter, is an important area for further inquiry.

REFERENCES

Adorno, T., Frenkel-Brunswik, E., Levinson, D., & Sanford, R. N. (1950). *The authoritarian personality.* New York: Harper.

Amabile, T. M. (1983). Brilliant but cruel: Perceptions of negative evaluators. *Journal of Experimental Social Psychology, 19,* 146–156.

American Psychological Association. (2002). Ethical principles of psychologists and code of conduct. *American Psychologist, 57,* 1060–1073.

Arendt, H. (1963). *Eichmann in Jerusalem: A report on the banality of evil.* New York: Viking Press.

Aronson, E. (1992). The return of the repressed: Dissonance theory makes a comeback. *Psychological Inquiry, 3,* 303–311.

Aronson, E., Wilson, T. D., & Akert, R. M. (2002). *Social psychology* (4th ed.). Upper Saddle River, NJ: Prentice-Hall.

Aronson, E., Wilson, T. D., & Brewer, M. B. (1998). Experimentation in social psychology. In D. Gilbert, S. Fiske, & G. Lindzey (Eds.), *The handbook of social psychology* (4th ed., pp. 99–142). Hillsdale, NJ: Erlbaum.

Banaji, M. R., & Crowder, R. G. (1989). The bankruptcy of everyday memory. *American Psychologist, 44,* 1185–1193.

Bandura, A. (1999). Moral disengagement in the perpetration of inhumanities. *Personality and Social Psychology Review, 3,* 193–209.

Bandura, A., Underwood, B., & Fromson, M. E. (1975). Disinhibition of aggression through diffusion of responsibility and dehumanization of victims. *Journal of Research in Personality, 9,* 253–269.

Baron, R. A., & Byrne, D. (2003). *Social psychology* (10th ed.). Boston: Allyn & Bacon.

Bauer, H. (2001). *Rethinking the Holocaust.* New Haven, CT: Yale University Press.

Baumcister, R. F. (1997). *Evil: Inside human violence and cruelty.* New York: Freeman.

Baumrind, D. (1964). Some thoughts on the ethics of research: After reading Milgram's "behavioral study of obedience." *American Psychologist, 19,* 421–433.

Berkowitz, L. (1999). Evil is more than banal: Situationism and the concept of evil. *Personality and Social Psychology Review, 3,* 246–253.

Bersoff, D. M. (1999). When good people sometimes do bad things: Motivated

---

[6]Kelman and Hamilton (1989) provide an informative discussion on this issue (see Chapter 3, pp. 53–76). They note: "Our goal is to clarify how responsibility may be 'lost' where it is most essential to retain it: in the military bureaucratic hierarchies of the modern world" (p. 76).

reasoning and unethical behavior. *Personality and Social Psychology Bulletin, 25,* 28–39.

Blass, T. (1991). Understanding behavior in the Milgram obedience experiment: The role of personality, situations, and their interactions. *Journal of Personality and Social Psychology, 60,* 398–413.

Blass, T. (1993). Psychological perspectives on the perpetrators of the Holocaust: The role of situational pressures, personal dispositions, and their interaction. *Holocaust and Genocide Studies, 7,* 30–50.

Blass, T. (Ed.). (2000). *Obedience to authority: Current perspectives on the Milgram paradigm.* Mahwah, NJ: Erlbaum.

Brief, A. P., Buttram, R. T., Elliott, J. D., Reizenstein, R. M., & McCline, R. L. (1995). Releasing the beast: A study of compliance with orders to use race as a selection criterion. *Journal of Social Issues, 51,* 177–193.

Brown, R. (1985). *Social psychology* (2nd ed.). New York: Free Press.

Browning, C. R. (1992). *Ordinary men: Reserve Police Battalion 101 and the final solution in Poland.* New York: HarperCollins.

Colman, A. M. (1991). Crowd psychology of South African murder trials. *American Psychologist, 46,* 1071–1079.

Darley, J. M. (1992). Social organization for the production of evil. *Psychological Inquiry, 3,* 199–218.

Darley, J. M. (1995) Constructive and destructive obedience: A taxonomy of principal-agent relationships. *Journal of Social Issues, 51,* 125–154.

Darley, J. M. (1999). Methods for the study of evil-doing actions. *Personality and Social Psychology Review, 3,* 269–275.

Darley, J. M., Messick, D. M., & Tyler, T. R. (Eds.). (2001). *Social influences on ethical behavior in organizations.* Mahwah, NJ: Erlbaum.

Diener, E., & Wallbom, M. (1976). Effects of self-awareness on antinormative behavior. *Journal of Research in Personality, 10,* 107–111.

Fenigstein, A. (1998). Were obedience pressures a factor in the Holocaust? *Analyse & Kritik, 20,* 1–20.

Folkes, V. S., & Whang, Y. (2003). Account-giving for a corporate transgression influences moral judgment: When those who "spin" condone harm-doing. *Journal of Applied Psychology, 88,* 79–86.

Gellately, R. (2001). *Backing Hitler: Consent and coercion in Nazi Germany.* New York: Oxford University Press.

Gershoff, E. T. (2002). Corporal punishment by parents and associated child behaviors and experiences: A meta-analytic and theoretical review. *Psychological Bulletin, 128,* 539–579.

Gilbert, D. T., & Malone, P. S. (1995). The correspondence bias. *Psychological Bulletin, 117,* 21–38.

Goldhagen, D. J. (1996). *Hitler's willing executioners: Ordinary Germans and the Holocaust.* New York: Knopf.

Greenwald, A. G., Pratkanis, A. R., Leippe, M. R., & Baumgardner, M. H. (1986). Under what conditions does theory obstruct research progress? *Psychological Review, 93,* 216–229.

Hamilton, V. L., & Sanders, J. (1995). Crimes of obedience and conformity in the workplace: Surveys of Americans, Russians, and Japanese. *Journal of Social Issues, 51,* 67–88.

Hamilton, V. L., & Sanders, J. (1999). The second face of evil: Wrongdoing in and by the corporation. *Personality and Social Psychology Review, 3,* 222–233.

Henshel, R. L. (1980). The purposes of laboratory experimentation and the virtues of deliberate artificiality. *Journal of Experimental Social Psychology, 16,* 466–478.

Hilberg, R. (1985). *The destruction of the European Jews* (rev. and definitive ed.). New York: Holmes & Meier.

Johnson, E. A. (1999). *Nazi terror: The Gestapo, Jews, and ordinary Germans.* New York: Basic Books.

Katz, F. E. (1993). *Ordinary people and extraordinary evil: A report on the beguilings of evil.* Albany: State University of New York Press.

Kelman, H. C. (1973). Violence without moral restraint: Reflections on the dehumanization of victims and victimizers. *Journal of Social Issues, 29,* 25–61.

Kelman, H. C., & Hamilton, V. L. (1989). *Crimes of obedience: Toward a social psychology of authority and responsibility.* New Haven, CT: Yale University Press.

Kenrick, D. T., Neuberg, S. L., & Cialdini, R. B. (2002). *Social psychology: Unraveling the mystery* (2nd ed.). Boston: Allyn & Bacon.

Kunda, Z. (1990). The case for motivated reasoning. *Psychological Bulletin, 108,* 480–514.

Lifton, R. J. (1986). *The Nazi doctors: Medical killing and the psychology of genocide.* New York: Basic Books.

Lord, C. G., Ross, L., & Lepper, M. R. (1979). Biased assimilation and attitude polarization: The effects of prior theories on subsequently considered evidence. *Journal of Personality and Social Psychology, 37,* 2098–2109.

Lutsky, N. (1995). When is "obedience" obedience? Conceptual and historical commentary. *Journal of Social Issues, 51,* 55–65.

Mandel, D. R. (1998). The obedience alibi: Milgram's account of the Holocaust reconsidered. *Analyse & Kritik, 20,* 74–94.

Mandel, D. R. (2002). Instigators of genocide. In L. Newman & R. Erber (Eds.), *Understanding genocide: The social psychology of the Holocaust* (pp. 259–284). New York: Oxford University Press.

Mantell, D. M., & Panzarella, R. (1976). Obedience and responsibility. *British Journal of Social and Clinical Psychology, 15,* 239–245.

Meeus, W. H. J., & Raaijmakers, Q. A. W. (1995). Obedience in modern society: The Utrecht studies. *Journal of Social Issues, 51,* 155–175.

Milgram, S. (1963). Behavioral study of obedience. *Journal of Abnormal and Social Psychology, 67,* 371–378.

Milgram, S. (1964). Issues in the study of obedience: A reply to Baumrind. *American Psychologist, 19,* 848–852.

Milgram, S. (1965). Some conditions of obedience and disobedience to authority. *Human Relations, 18,* 57–76.

Milgram, S. (1972). Interpreting obedience: Error and evidence—a reply to Orne and Holland. In A. G. Miller (Ed.), *The social psychology of psychological research* (pp. 138–154). New York: Free Press.

Milgram, S. (1974). *Obedience to authority: An experimental view.* New York: Harper & Row.

Milgram, S. (1979). Preface to the second French edition. In *Obedience to authority: An experimental view* (p. 9). Paris: Calmann-Levy.

Miller, A. G. (1986). *The obedience experiments: A case study of controversy in social science.* New York: Praeger.

Miller, A. G. (1995). Constructions of the obedience experiments: A focus upon domains of relevance. *Journal of Social Issues, 51,* 33–53.

Miller, A. G., Buddie, A. M., & Kretschmar, J. (2002). Explaining the Holocaust: Does social psychology exonerate the perpetrators? In L. Newman & R. Erber (Eds.), *Understanding genocide: The social psychology of the Holocaust* (pp. 301–324). New York: Oxford University Press.

Miller, A. G., Collins, B. E., & Brief, D. E. (1995). Perspectives on obedience to authority: The legacy of the Milgram experiments. *Journal of Social Issues, 51*(3), 1–19.

Miller, A. G., Gillen, B., Schenker, C., & Radlove, S. (1974). The prediction and perception of obedience to authority. *Journal of Personality, 42,* 23–42.

Miller, A. G., Gordon, A. K., & Buddie, A. M. (1999). Accounting for evil and cruelty: Is to explain to condone? *Personality and Social Psychology Review, 3,* 254–268.

Mook, D. G. (1983). In defense of external invalidity. *American Psychologist, 38,* 379–387.

Myers, D. G. (2002). *Social psychology* (7th ed.). New York: McGraw-Hill.

Newman, L. S. (2001). *The banality of secondary sources: Why social psychologists have misinterpreted Arendt's thesis.* Unpublished manuscript, University of Illinois at Chicago, Department of Psychology.

Newman, L. S., & Erber, R. (Eds.). (2002). *Understanding genocide: The social psychology of the Holocaust.* New York: Oxford University Press.

Novick, P. (1999). *The Holocaust in American life.* New York: Houghton Mifflin.

Rochat, F., & Modigliani, A. (1995). The ordinary quality of resistance: From Milgram's laboratory to the village of Le Chambon. *Journal of Social Issues, 51,* 195–210.

Ross, L. D. (1977). The intuitive psychologist and his shortcomings: Distortion in the attribution process. In L. Berkowitz (Ed.), *Advances in experimental social psychology* (Vol. 10, pp. 173–220). New York: Academic Press.

Ross, L. D. (1988). Situationist perspectives on the obedience experiments. *Contemporary Psychology, 33,* 101–104.

Ross, L. D., & Nisbett, R. E. (1991). *The person and the situation: Perspectives of social psychology.* New York: McGraw-Hill.

Sabini, J. P., Siepmann, M., & Stein, J. (2001a). Authors' response to commentaries. *Psychological Inquiry, 12,* 41–48.

Sabini, J. P., Siepmann, M., & Stein, J. (2001b). The really fundamental attribution error in social psychological research. *Psychological Inquiry, 12,* 1–15.

Sabini, J. P., & Silver, M. (1980). Destroying the innocent with a clear conscience: A sociopsychology of the Holocaust. In J. E. Dimsdale (Ed.), *Survivors, victims, and perpetrators: Essays on the Nazi Holocaust* (pp. 329–358). New York: Hemisphere.

Safer, M. A. (1980). Attributing evil to the subject, not the situation: Student reactions to Milgram's film on obedience. *Personality and Social Psychology Bulletin, 6,* 205–209.

Saltzman, A. L. (2000). The role of the obedience experiments in Holocaust studies: The case for renewed visibility. In T. Blass (Ed.), *Obedience to authority: Current perspectives on the Milgram paradigm* (pp. 125–143). Mahwah, NJ: Erlbaum.

Segev, T. (1993). *The seventh million: The Israelis and the Holocaust.* New York: Hill & Wang.

Shandley, R. R. (1998). *Unwilling Germans? The Goldhagen debate.* Minneapolis: University of Minnesota Press.

Staub, E. (1989). *The roots of evil: The origins of genocide and other group violence.* New York: Cambridge University Press.

Staub, E. (1999). The roots of evil: Social conditions, culture, personality, and basic human needs. *Personality and Social Psychology Review, 3,* 179–192.

Strauss, M. A. (1994). *Beating the devil out of them: Corporal punishment in American families.* New York: Lexington.

Strudler, A., & Warren, D. E. (2001). Authority, heuristics, and the structure of excuses. In J. M. Darley, D. M. Messick, & T. R. Tyler (Eds.), *Social influences on ethical behavior in organizations* (pp. 155–173). Mahwah, NJ: Erlbaum.

Taylor, S. E., Peplau, L. A., & Sears, D. O. (2000). *Social psychology* (10th ed.). Upper Saddle River, NJ: Prentice-Hall.

Waller, J. (2002). *Becoming evil: How ordinary people commit genocide and mass killing.* New York: Oxford University Press.

Weiner, B. (1995). *Judgments of responsibility: A foundation for a theory of social conduct.* New York: Guilford Press.

Wilson, T. D., DePaulo, B. M., Mook, D. G., & Klaaren, K. J. (1993). Scientists' evaluations of research: The biasing effects of the importance of the topic. *Psychological Science, 4,* 322–325.

Worchel, S., Cooper, J., Goethals, G. R., & Olson, J. M. (2000). *Social psychology.* Belmont, CA: Wadsworth.

Young-Bruehl, E. (1982). *Hannah Arendt: For the love of the world.* New Haven, CT: Yale University Press.

Zillmer, E. A., Harrower, M., Ritzler, B. A., & Archer, R. P. (1995). *The quest for the Nazi personality: A psychological investigation of Nazi war criminals.* Hillsdale, NJ: Erlbaum.

Zimbardo, P. G. (1995). The psychology of evil: A situationist perspective on recruiting good people to engage in anti-social acts. *Research in Social Psychology, 11,* 125–133.

Zimbardo, P. G., Maslach, C., & Haney, C. (2000). Reflections on the Stanford Prison Experiment: Genesis, transformations, consequences. In T. Blass (Ed.), *Obedience to authority: Current perspectives on the Milgram paradigm* (pp. 193–237). Mahwah, NJ: Erlbaum.

CHAPTER 10

CONCEPTUALIZING SEXUAL VIOLENCE

Socially Acceptable Coercion and Other Controversies

CHARLENE L. MUEHLENHARD
ZOË D. PETERSON

It is not controversial to say that sexual violence is a serious problem that merits efforts to prevent it. Dig deeper into the meanings of this statement, however, and controversy abounds. Anyone involved in studying or preventing sexual violence needs to make decisions that are likely to be controversial—decisions that reflect values and implicit or explicit theories about power, violence, sexuality, and gender. In this chapter we discuss controversies about defining sexual violence, dilemmas surrounding whether to focus research and prevention efforts on victims, perpetrators, or society, and the issues involved in acknowledging that sexual violence does not have uniformly severe consequences. We primarily address rape, but we also draw examples from the literature on child sexual abuse and domestic violence.

DEFINING SEXUAL VIOLENCE: WHAT COUNTS?

> [Rape is the] culturally disvalued use of coercion by a male
> to achieve the submission of a female to sexual intercourse.
> —LEVINE (1959, p. 965)

Definitions are important for practical reasons: To do research on the prevalence or consequences of sexual violence, it is necessary to decide what will count as sexual violence. Definitions are also political, however: Drawing the line between which behaviors are and are not considered sexual violence requires making value judgments about what forms of influence are coercive, what sexual behaviors are important enough to count, and how gender should be construed.

We illustrate this point by discussing definitions of rape. Rape can generally be defined as one person's use of coercion to obtain sex from another person (Estrich, 1987; Muehlenhard, Powch, Phelps, & Giusti, 1992). We organize our discussion around the elements of this general definition. First, we address what counts as *coercion;* that is, what forms of influence are considered coercive and thus unacceptable, and what forms of influence are considered noncoercive and thus acceptable? Second, what counts as *sex?* What sexual behaviors, if coerced, are considered to constitute rape? Finally, which *persons* count? Here, we focus on how gender is constructed in various definitions of rape.

What Counts as Coercion?

If rape is defined as using coercion to obtain sex from another person, it is necessary to distinguish between coercive and noncoercive forms of influence. In some cases, this distinction is fairly noncontroversial; in other cases, it is extremely controversial. There is a general consensus that it is coercive and thus unacceptable to obtain sex using force—although, as we illustrate below, deciding what counts as force can itself be controversial. The acceptability of using psychological pressure to obtain sex is even more controversial. Psychologists acknowledge that people exert power over each other not only by using obvious, direct forms of influence but also by using subtler, indirect forms of influence (Falbo & Peplau, 1980; see also French & Raven, 1959; Ng, 2001; Raven, 1999). Indirect forms of influence can be extremely powerful, but because they are subtle, there is controversy about whether to consider them coercive.

We begin our discussion by considering definitions of rape that conceptualize coercion in terms of *force.* We then move to definitions of rape that conceptualize coercion in terms of lack of *consent.* Both conceptualizations are problematic.

Definitions Involving Force

Some definitions of rape are formulated around the notion of "force" (Estrich, 1987). What constitutes force? In some cases, consensus about whether force has been used would be high. For example, consensus is likely if the perpetrator struck the victim into unconsciousness or physically overpowered the victim such that the victim was unable to move. The victim would have had no choice.

Cases involving *threats* of force yield less consensus, however. In such cases, the victim could be construed as having had a choice—even if it is a choice with only bad options—about whether to engage in sex or to risk the threatened force. In some cases, such as if the perpetrator had held a gun or a knife, most people would see the alternative to giving in to sex— that is, facing the risk of being shot or stabbed—as sufficiently negative that they would say that there was no real choice (this would be what Lamb, 1996, p. 37, called "choiceless choices").

When the alternative to having sex is less extreme—such as when the threat is less lethal or less clearly communicated—consensus is even less likely. Consider the Maryland case, *State v. Rusk* (cited in Estrich, 1987; Schulhofer, 1998). A woman, Pat, met a man, Rusk, at a bar. He persuaded her to drive him home at about 1:00 A.M. After she twice refused his invitation to come inside, he took her keys; being unfamiliar with the neighborhood and scared, she followed him inside. She did not leave when he went to the bathroom. He then pulled her onto the bed, removed her blouse, and asked her to remove her slacks and his clothing, which she did. She begged him to let her leave and asked him, "If I do what you want, will you let me go without killing me?" When she cried, he began to lightly choke her (her version) / heavily caress her (his version). She asked again if he would let her go if she had sex with him, and he said that he would. She complied, performing fellatio and vaginal intercourse. In court she testified that she complied because she was "really scared" because of the "look in his eyes" (quoted in Estrich, 1987, pp. 63–64).

Rusk was convicted of rape, defined in Maryland law as intercourse by force or threat of force (Schulhofer, 1998). The case was appealed, and ultimately the conviction was upheld. As the case went through the appeals process, however, 11 of the 21 judges involved concluded that the conviction should be reversed. For example, three Court of Appeals judges wrote, "She may not simply say, 'I was really scared,' and thereby transform consent or mere unwillingness into submission by force. These words do not transform a seducer into a rapist. She must follow the natural instinct of every proud female to resist, by more than mere words" (cited by Estrich, 1987, pp. 64–65). In response, Estrich wrote,

> In a very real sense, the "reasonable" woman under the view of the eleven judges who voted to reverse Mr. Rusk's conviction is not a woman at all. Their version of a reasonable person is one who does not scare easily, one who does not feel vulnerable, one who is not passive, one who fights back, not cries. The reasonable woman, it seems, is not a schoolboy "sissy"; she is a real man. (p. 65)

Estrich (1987) argued that there are many problems with definitions predicated on force. Force is necessary to subdue victims only if they resist, but it is often unreasonable for victims to resist. As Estrich pointed out, the law does not require victims of robbery to resist. The victim's claims of being afraid to resist raise the issue of the reasonableness of the basis for this fear. Whose standards should apply here? Generally men are larger than women, have greater upper body strength, and are likely to have more experience with fighting; thus, Estrich argued, men and women are likely to have different perspectives on the reasonableness of fear and the advisability of resisting.

The situation gets even murkier when the threat is something other than physical harm. In everyday language, people often use the word *force* when referring to decisions based on contingencies other than physical harm. Consider the headline in *The New York Times,* "Car Rental Industry Is Forced to Shift Ways" (Maynard, 2002, p. C1). The article went on to say that because of changing rental patterns, "companies are being forced both to streamline their businesses aggressively and to venture into new areas" (p. C1). In this example, the alternative to changing their business practices would not have been injury or death. Rental companies were "forced" to change their practices to avoid financial difficulties. If a wife has sex with her husband because the alternative would be divorce, leading to financial difficulties, has she been forced to have sex?

Definitions Involving Consent

Estrich (1987) described a North Carolina case (*State v. Alston*) in which a woman left her physically abusive boyfriend. A month later, he came to her school, grabbed her arm, and told her that she was coming with him. She agreed to walk with him if her released her arm. He threatened to "fix" her face to show that he was not "playing." She told him the relationship was over. He said he had a right to have sex with her again. They went to his friend's house, and she told him that she did not want to have sex with him. He "pulled her up from the chair, undressed her, pushed her legs apart, and penetrated her. She cried" (p. 61). Alston was convicted of rape, but the North Carolina Supreme Court reversed the conviction. They agreed that the sex was nonconsensual, but the law was written in terms of force. Because she did not physically resist, Alston did not need to use force.

Based on this example, it might seem that rather than defining rape as *forced* sex, it would be less problematic to define rape as *nonconsensual* sex. Unfortunately, this approach is also fraught with problems.

One problem involves the focus of the analysis. Whereas focusing on force requires examining the *perpetrator's* behavior and intentions, focusing on consent requires examining the *victim's* behavior and intentions (Estrich, 1987). This focus can lead to blaming the victim (we return to this topic later).

Another problem involves how to conceptualize consent (Muehlenhard et al., 1992). Should we think of consensual sex as sex accompanied by a *feeling* of willingness or as sex accompanied by an *overt expression* of willingness?

Defining consensual sex as requiring a *feeling* of willingness—and, conversely, defining rape as sex that occurs without a feeling of willingness—is problematic. Because no one can ever truly know another person's feelings, such a definition would mean that we could never really know if rape had occurred.

Defining consensual sex as requiring an *overt expression* of willingness—and, conversely, defining rape as sex that occurs without such an expression—is also problematic. If rape is defined as sex that occurs without an explicit *verbal* statement of consent, then a lot of sex in which the participants are willing and eager would fit the definition of rape. People often do not communicate their sexual consent verbally (Hall, 1998; Hickman & Muehlenhard, 1999). In one study of college students, both women and men reported that they most often showed their consent to sexual intercourse by doing nothing—that is, by not saying no, not resisting, not stopping the other person (Hickman & Muehlenhard, 1999).

Clearly, it is problematic to define rape as sex without verbally communicated consent. What about defining rape as sex without verbally *or nonverbally* communicated consent? This approach is also problematic. Nonverbal communication is easily misinterpreted. There is evidence that people consider a wide array of nonverbal behaviors as signaling sexual desire or consent, even when the signaler does not intend to send such a signal. Examples include a woman inviting a man on a date, going to his home, letting him pay the dating expenses, having a reputation for having sex with other people, wearing tight or revealing clothing, or attending a party where alcohol or drugs are present (Bostwick & DeLucia, 1992; Goodchilds & Zellman, 1984; Muehlenhard, 1988; Muehlenhard, Friedman, & Thomas, 1985). Furthermore, on average, men interpret such behaviors as signaling sexual desire or consent more than do women (Abbey, 1982; Bostwick & DeLucia, 1992; Goodchilds & Zellman, 1984; Hickman & Muehlenhard, 1999; Muehlenhard, 1988). Although gender differences in inferences about consent are small and are unlikely when communication is direct (Hickman & Muehlenhard, 1999), defining rape in terms of nonverbal communication of consent opens the door for actual—or professed—misunderstandings.

Conditions Complicating Consent

Numerous types of circumstances can complicate the relationship between what someone expresses and what she or he actually feels. For example, under conditions of duress, as discussed above, overt expressions of consent might not correspond with internal feelings of consent. A person could comply with a demand only because complying is the least bad of a set of bad options.

Bart and O'Brien (1985) suggested a continuum ranging from consensual sex to altruistic sex to compliant sex (i.e., sex in which "there is no overt threat of force, but the woman knows that if she does not comply, there will be unpleasant consequences," p. 56) to rape. They concluded that "few women have only engaged in consensual sex" (p. 56). Russell (2000) also suggested that sexual experiences could be conceptualized along a continuum: "If one were to see sexual behavior as a continuum with rape at one end and sex liberated from sex-role stereotyping at the other, much of what passes for normal heterosexual intercourse would be seen as close to rape" (p. 246).

It is informative to think about circumstances that could constrain a person's decision about whether to engage in sex and the conditions that might be required to constitute freely given consent. A person's decision about whether to engage in sex could be constrained by numerous factors: by the desire to maintain a relationship, to avoid a partner's anger, to avoid hurting a partner's feelings, to gain more sexual experience, to prove one's heterosexuality, to conform to one's image of normality, to fulfill self-perceived obligation, to avoid physical harm, to get something that one needs, and so forth (Impett & Peplau, 2003; Muehlenhard & Cook, 1988; O'Sullivan & Allgeier, 1998). A student in our research group, Timothy Dupree, provided insight into such constraints when he described women in his neighborhood who had sex with men in exchange for rides to the grocery store. The women had no cars, and there were no grocery stores in their impoverished neighborhood, so they "chose" to have sex with men in exchange for rides.

In contrast, freely given sexual consent might require that none of these constraints be present—that whether or not one decides to engage in sex, one will feel secure in one's relationship, will be free from physical harm, will be free from the partner's anger, will have what one needs, and so forth.

At its most extreme, this argument can be used to suggest that members of oppressed groups can never freely consent to sex. MacKinnon (1989) argued that women's sexuality is a socially constructed response to women's powerlessness in relation to men (e.g., constructed as a form of self-protection) and not an expression of women's own agency or autonomy. She implied that women cannot freely refuse or consent to sexual interactions because sexuality is defined and constructed by men. Thus, if one broadens the definition of coercion far enough, all sexual interactions in which women participate could be viewed as sexual violence against women. In response to MacKinnon's argument, Atmore (1999) stated that "it does not make sense to call something rape when it also appears to be sex-as-usual and when it involves normative ideas about gendered behavior" (p. 198).

To further complicate matters, power may be one of the things that makes a potential sexual partner appealing, and conversely, being viewed as sexually attractive by a potential sexual partner may give an individual power over that potential partner (Felson, 2002). If a power differential can directly relate to sexual interest and desire, do power differences between sexual partners automatically constitute coercion? Felson (2002) argued that they do not. He contended that "a sexual encounter based on mutual attraction is not coercive, even if there is an apparent power differential" (p. 124)—even, for example, if it occurs between an older male professor and his younger female student.

It is unrealistic to expect to create a society in which sexual decisions are never constrained by contingencies, power differences, and so forth. Indeed, in commenting on an article that one of us had coauthored (Muehlenhard & Schrag, 1991) outlining various sources of nonviolent coercion, Schulhofer (1998) noted that "truly voluntary consent, as Muehlenhard and Schrag conceive it, exists for none of us in this lifetime" (p. 53). Nevertheless, in evaluating the coerciveness involved in an act, it is useful to think about the range of options available to the person and the contingencies she or he faces when deciding whether to have sex.

Distinguishing between Consensual Sex and Wanted Sex

Sometimes rape is defined in terms of unwanted sex. For example, the Sexual Experiences Survey, a widely used scale in research on rape, classifies women as rape victims if they report having had sexual intercourse when they "didn't want to" because a man used physical force or gave them alcohol or drugs (Koss, Gidycz, & Wisniewski, 1987, p. 167).

Substantial research indicates that people often feel ambivalent about sex and that a dichotomous model, which conceptualizes sex *either* as wanted and consensual *or* as unwanted and nonconsensual, is overly simplistic. Muehlenhard (2002) proposed a more complex model of wanting and not wanting sex. This model allows for more than two levels of wantedness, recognizes that there are numerous dimensions on which sex can be wanted or unwanted and that sex can be wanted on some dimensions and simultaneously unwanted on others, distinguishes between wanting or not wanting the sexual act itself and wanting or not wanting the consequences of the act, and—of particular relevance here—distinguishes between *wanting or not wanting* the act and *consenting or not consenting* to the act.

Several studies illustrate the usefulness of this more complex model. When we asked students about their first experiences with sexual intercourse, we found that the majority (63%) reported wanting the act but not wanting the consequences of the act (Muehlenhard, Peterson, Mac-Pherson, & Blair, 2002). One woman in the sample reported an experience with nonconsensual sexual intercourse that would qualify as rape under state law. She described it as "sex w/aggression. I said no, he said yes—to the point that it happened." Nevertheless, she reported that there were reasons for wanting to have sexual intercourse: She was sexually interested in him, she was in love with him, and she wanted a relationship with him. Thus, she described an incident that was *wanted* (at least, in some ways) but that was *nonconsensual*.

The converse—*unwanted consensual* sex—also occurs. O'Sullivan and Allgeier (1998) asked students in committed dating relationships to keep diaries of their sexual interactions for 2 weeks. They found that 38%—50% of the women and 26% of the men—reported engaging in unwanted consensual sex during the 2-week period. The most commonly reported reasons for consenting to unwanted sex were satisfying the partner's needs/promoting relationship intimacy and avoiding relationship tension. In a literature review, Impett and Peplau (2003) suggested several perspectives for thinking about the factors that contribute to unwanted consensual sex, including gender perspectives (generally, more women than men report having consented to unwanted sex), motivational perspectives (e.g., an insecure attachment style; Impett & Peplau, 2002), and relationship maintenance perspectives (e.g., relationship commitment). Impett and Peplau (2003) also noted that "it is sometimes difficult to determine whether an individual has freely consented to engage in sex" (p. 88). These researchers placed consenting to unwanted sex on a continuum ranging from unwilling compliance because of physical force or threat of harm, to psychological pressure, to situations in which "an individual does not want sex but responds positively to a partner's sexual initiation under no duress or coercion" (p. 88), which they regarded as prototypical incidents of "clearly consensual" but unwanted sex. It is not clear how Impett and Peplau would evaluate the reasons cited most frequently by O'Sullivan and Allgeier's respondents. Is a decision to have sex in order to avoid relationship tension made freely or under duress? Is a decision to have sex in order to promote relationship intimacy or to satisfy the partner's needs a freely made decision? Does it depend on the contingencies—on what would happen if intimacy were not promoted or if the partner's needs were not satisfied?

In summary, there are no uniformly accepted standards that deem certain conditions sexually coercive. The type of influence used to obtain sex and the circumstances of the individuals involved are all likely to affect people's judgments. Often, when people think about rape, they think of the more physically forceful, direct uses of power (e.g., people asked to write about the "typical" rape tend to describe high levels of aggression; Ryan, 1988), but limiting the definition to such blatant incidents leaves more subtle uses of indirect power unchallenged.

What Counts as Sex?

Many sexually related behaviors lie in the murky area somewhere between "sex" and "not sex." For example, Sanders and Reinisch (1999) found that 99.5% of college students reported that they would say that they had "had sex" if they had engaged in penile–vaginal intercourse; this percentage was 81% for anal sex, 41% for oral sex, and 14% for touching another person's genitals. Other researchers have found similar percentages (Bogart, Cecil, Wagstaff, Pinkerton, & Abramson, 2000; Pitts & Rahman, 2001).

Which behaviors are counted as sex influence which behaviors are counted as rape (Bart & O'Brien, 1985; Peterson & Muehlenhard, 2003). Bart and O'Brien (1985) studied women who self-identified as having been raped or as having thwarted a rape attempt. They found that most women who had experienced forced phallic sex (e.g., penile–vaginal intercourse, fellatio, penile–anal sex, interfemoral penile penetration) labeled themselves as having been raped. In contrast, most women who had experienced forced nonphallic sex (e.g., vaginal penetration by fingers or objects, cunnilingus, fondling, or lack of penile penetration because of loss of erection or other reason) but not phallic sex labeled themselves as having avoided rape. Bart and O'Brien speculated that this phenomenon occurred partly because phallic sex increases the likelihood of pregnancy and sexually transmitted diseases and partly because phallic sex is more likely than nonphallic sex to result in the man's orgasm. "It may be that if the man can have an orgasm at the woman's expense, she feels raped" (p. 20). This phenomenon may also reflect the more general phallocentric nature of sex in this culture (Rotkin, 1986).

Similarly, in a study of women who reported experiences that met the legal definition of rape, Peterson and Muehlenhard (2003) found that whether women labeled their experience as rape was significantly predicted by whether they considered the experience to be sex. Although nonconsensual digital penetration of a woman's vagina counts as rape, based on the state's legal definition, most women who experienced this form of penetration did not consider their experience to be sex or rape. Interestingly, this phenomenon also occurred for a few women who reported vaginal penetration by the man's penis. For example, one woman wrote, "He didn't force me to totally have sex. He inserted his penis into me once or twice but nothing else" (p. 20). These women did not consider the experience to be rape because they did not consider it to be sex.

Which Persons Count?: The Role of Gender

Defining sexual violence requires making decisions about which persons to include in the definition—which, in turn, requires decisions about how to construe gender. Some researchers choose to emphasize gender differences by defining rape as something that men do to women or by studying only female victims and male perpetrators. Others choose to minimize gender differences by defining rape in a gender-neutral way or by studying both women and men, asking them identical questions, and interpreting their answers without considering how their differing roles or circumstances might influence their responses. Numerous arguments have been made in support of each approach (see Muehlenhard, 1998; Muehlenhard & Kimes, 1999, for reviews).

Advantages and Disadvantages of a Gender-Differences Approach

A gender-differences approach acknowledges the role of gender in sexual violence. Sexual violence is not gender neutral: More women than men experience sexual violence, and more men than women perpetrate sexual violence (Struckman-Johnson, Struckman-Johnson, & Anderson, 2003; Tjaden & Thoennes, 2000). Women fear sexual violence more than men (Poirier, 1996) and restrict their behavior more than men (Gordon & Riger, 1989). Paradoxically, however, we would not have this information if researchers had taken a strict gender-differences approach, studying only women when asking questions about being victimized and only men when asking questions about victimizing others. This point highlights an important disadvantage of the gender-differences approach.

A gender-differences approach has other disadvantages as well: It ignores female perpetrators. It neglects and invalidates the experiences of victims other than female victims of male perpetrators. Furthermore, a gender-differences approach perpetuates gender dualism and essentialism (Atmore, 1999; Renzetti, 1999). Essentializing gender differences might suggest that men cannot be held accountable for perpetrating sexual violence because violence is simply a part of their nature or their upbringing. It may perpetuate the stereotype that women are naturally passive and helpless (White & Kowalski, 1994). Renzetti (1999) summarized the problem well: "Since we construct sex and gender in oppositional terms—what men are, women are not, and vice versa—it is women's 'nature' to be passive; the respectable woman, the feminine woman, is socially constructed as a natural victim" (p. 49).

Helliwell (2000) argued from an anthropological standpoint that emphasizing gender differences in sexual violence leads Western feminists to wrongly universalize the experience of rape. From this perspective, men are viewed as naturally equipped to rape, so it is assumed that rape must be a universal phenomenon, despite anthropological evidence that rape does not occur in all cultures. Helliwell further suggested that by emphasizing biological gender differences, some feminists may fail to observe the ways in which rape actually creates social inequality between the genders.

Advantages and Disadvantages of a Gender-Similarities Approach

In contrast, taking a gender-similarities approach to studying sexual violence avoids research bias—that is, it is not predicated on the assumption that some research questions are relevant only to one gender. It challenges gender stereotypes, such as stereotypes of women's passivity, women's helplessness, and men's sexual insatiability. It acknowledges the experiences of male victims and victims of female perpetrators. It forces researchers to go beyond gender in theorizing about the nature of sexual violence, considering variables such as personality, psychopathology, and so forth (Muehlenhard, 1998).

On the other hand, a gender-similarities approach can gloss over important gender differences. In this culture, there are gender differences in the likelihood of experiencing sexual violence, in the extent to which fear of rape limits individuals' freedom, and in the meanings and consequences of sexual violence (Estrich, 1987; Muehlenhard, 1998; Tjaden & Thoennes, 2000).

Radical feminists have argued that a gender-similarities approach perpetuates gender inequality. For example, MacKinnon (1990) argued that "gender neutrality means that you cannot take gender into account . . . neutrality enforces a non-neutral status quo" (p. 12).

Furthermore, a gender-similarities approach could result in a backlash against feminist activism aimed at addressing violence against women. For example, reports of women's violence toward men have been used by opponents of the women's movement to argue against funding shelters for battered women (Gelles & Strauss, 1988). (Note, however, that gender-differences approaches have also resulted in backlash. Researchers taking gender-differences approaches have been a target of critics such as Gilbert [1991] and Roiphe [1993], who argued that feminists have exaggerated the prevalence and seriousness of violence against women.)

"Double Visions"

It is possible to use both approaches. For example, Kimball (1995) argued that both the differences tradition and the similarities tradition contribute to our understanding of gender. She recommended practicing "double visions" by approaching social issues using both perspectives.

Conclusion: The Advantages and Disadvantage of Narrow versus Broad Definitions

In conclusion, definitions of rape and other forms of sexual violence vary along many dimensions. Some definitions are narrow; others are broad.

Narrow definitions tend to label only the most extreme acts as "sexual violence." Thus, they can be regarded as perpetuating the status quo, however coercive, by labeling only the "*culturally disvalued* use of coercion" as sexual violence (Levine, 1959, p. 965, emphasis added). Culturally acceptable forms of coercion are not considered to be sexual violence. Such narrow definitions tend to perpetuate existing power relations by ignoring the more indirect ways in which powerful people exert their influence over others.

On the other hand, as definitions of sexual violence are broadened to include more socially acceptable forms of coercion, it becomes increasingly difficult to distinguish between sex that is entirely consensual (if there is such a thing) and sex that is coerced. The harm caused by sexual violence can be obscured (e.g., Gold, Hughes, & Swingle, 1996, found links between child sexual abuse and subsequent adolescent and adult sexual victimization when they used narrow definitions but not when they used broad definitions). The power that can come from labeling an act as "sexual violence" can be diminished as this category covers more and more acts.

WHERE SHOULD WE FOCUS OUR RESEARCH ON RAPE PREVENTION: ON VICTIMS, PERPETRATORS, OR SOCIETY?

> The Israeli parliament suggested a curfew on women when the rape rate increased. However, Prime Minister Golda Meir suggested a curfew on men because they were the ones doing the raping.
>
> —BART AND O'BRIEN (1985, p. 2)

Rape researchers and activists face political and ethical dilemmas when choosing the focus of their efforts. Researchers can choose to focus on victims by exploring attitudes, behaviors, and personality characteristics that increase or decrease the risk of being raped. Alternatively, researchers can focus on the attitudes, behaviors, and personality characteristics of perpetrators. Finally, researchers can focus on society, identifying stereotypes, social norms, and institutions that support and perpetuate rape. Similarly, activists can focus their rape-prevention efforts on potential victims, on potential perpetrators, or on society. Each of these approaches could help address the problem of rape, but each is also controversial in its political and ethical implications.

Research Focusing on Victims

Rape research focused on victims has provided valuable information about risk factors for victimization. For example, research suggests that women are at greater risk of rape if they frequently get intoxicated (Muehlenhard & Linton, 1987; Testa & Dermen, 1999), engage in casual sex (Testa & Dermen, 1999), or attend fraternity parties (Ullman, 1997), or if they have a history of child sexual abuse (Muehlenhard, Highby, Lee, Bryan, & Dodrill, 1998).

Such findings can help reduce the risk of rape. Identifying risky situations and behaviors can help individuals make informed choices about their behaviors. Identifying background factors or personality characteristics that lead to patterns of repeated victimization can suggest appropriate therapeutic interventions to help alter these patterns.

However, different rape prevention strategies implicitly suggest different views of responsibility for rape (Krulewitz & Kahn, 1983). Rape prevention based on findings about victims' traits and behaviors may implicitly suggest that those who are most at risk for rape—that is, women—should alter and restrict their behavior to avoid being raped. For example, information suggesting that attending parties is risky might be interpreted to mean that women should avoid parties in order to avoid being raped. This approach puts the burden of preventing rape on potential victims rather than potential perpetrators and limits women's freedom.

Furthermore, focusing rape prevention on victims may be viewed as blaming the victim. Individuals who engage in risky behaviors and are raped might be blamed—by others and by themselves—for contributing to their own victimization. Such victim blaming is often evident in the legal system; when crime victims are seen as behaving in ways that contribute to their own victimization, legal cases against perpetrators are sometimes dismissed or the charges are reduced (Miethe, 1985).

An alternative to focusing on risk factors for victimization is to focus on resistance strategies women have used to thwart rape attempts. For example, research shows that active resistance strategies (e.g., physically fighting, screaming, and running away) are more strongly associated with thwarting attempted rape, whereas passive resistance strategies (e.g., pleading, crying, reasoning, or doing nothing) are associated more strongly with experiencing completed rape (Bart & O'Brien, 1985; Ullman 1997; Ullman & Knight, 1993; Zoucha-Jensen & Coyne, 1993).

Focusing on resistance strategies has advantages over focusing on risk factors. Focusing on resistance rather than on risk factors is less likely to lead to the suggestion that women limit their behavior to avoid rape. Educating women about active resistance strategies, rather than suggesting that they rely on men to protect them, challenges gender stereotypes and can serve as a method of empowerment. Rozee and Koss (2001) argued that women benefit from the message that they can resist rape, even in cases where attempts at resistance fail, because women who resist are less likely to experience self-blame following rape experiences.

However, research that focuses on helping women protect themselves from rape may inherently suggest that some rape victims could have avoided being raped if only they had behaved differently. Rape victims are sometimes judged as deserving greater blame if they do not resist forcefully enough (Deitz, Littman, & Bentley, 1984; Ong & Ward, 1999), and historically, rape victims in legal cases have been required to prove that they resisted adequately in order to ensure successful prosecution of their rapists (Estrich, 1987). There is a danger that research suggesting that women can resist rape may be used to suggest that women who do not resist successfully were "asking for it."

Some researchers who have studied rape avoidance have explicitly addressed this danger: Levine-MacCombie and Koss (1986) pointed out that research suggesting that women can and do successfully avoid rape should not be interpreted to mean that all rape is avoidable if the victim responds "correctly"; in some cases, rapists are so determined and aggressive that any attempt at resistance is futile. Bart and O'Brien (1985) emphasized that "since some women are raped on one occasion and avoid rape on another . . . , we want to stress that the women's 'personality' does not cause rape. They are not 'victimization prone.' Women do not cause rape!!!" (p. 55). Although Bart and O'Brien discussed how naiveté and concern about seeming "paranoid" or hurting people's feelings can make it difficult for women to resist rape, they clarified that they do not blame women when these traits result in rape: "Blaming a woman growing up in this culture for being raped is like blaming her for speaking English" (p. 56).

In contrast, Lamb (1996) suggested that there are benefits to acknowledging victims' responsibility for their victimization—at least, for some victims some of the time. She offered several reasons for this suggestion. First, she argued that victims blame themselves and that telling them that they are wrong to do so does them a disservice:

> Victims blame themselves. . . . [I]f we truly listen to victims and honor their perspectives, we see that by advocating a cognitive view of their experience that is so at odds with what they themselves are feeling, by telling them that we know more about their agency in the world than they do, and by informing them that they are sadly mistaken in their perception of choice and free will we do them an injustice. (p. 22)

Second, Lamb (1996) argued that self-blame can serve many purposes: It can be a way to master anxiety, maintain an illusion of control, and maintain a view of the world as meaningful and benevolent (see also Herman, 1992; Langer, 1975; Presson & Benassi, 1996).

Third, Lamb suggested that powerlessness is the most demeaning aspect of victimization and that telling victims that there was nothing that they could have done to prevent their victimization only increases their sense of powerlessness: "Doesn't it seem strange to advocate a totally deterministic view to women who themselves do not hold that view and to women we hope to empower?" (1996, p. 22). She argued that regarding victimization solely as a result of external social forces undermines the possibility of change.

Crocker (2003) made a similar point regarding possibilities for change. She stated that people are seldom either 0% or 100% responsible for bad things that happen to them. It is helpful to be connected to the reality of how things happen because the only aspects of their experiences that people can control are those for which they themselves are responsible.

Many rape victims have previously been victims of child sexual abuse (Muehlenhard et al., 1998). If we refuse to hold victims responsible for their subsequent behavior (e.g., if we refuse to hold a woman responsible for engaging in high-risk behaviors because she was sexually abused as a child), then we find ourselves in a problematic situation with respect to holding perpetrators responsible for their behavior (Lamb, 1996). Many perpetrators also have been victims of child sexual abuse (Fergusson & Mullen, 1999). If we refuse to hold victims responsible for their subsequent behavior, then it would be inconsistent to hold former victims responsible for perpetrating sexual abuse (Lamb, 1996, p. 9).

Related to these points, Felson (2002) summarized the problems with regarding female victims of male violence as necessarily blameless. He questioned the scientific merit of such a construction. Furthermore, citing work by Loseke on victims of domestic violence, he wrote that if shelter workers think of victims as nonviolent, passive, and blameless, they tend to be skeptical of clients who do not fit this theme. Women who describe their own provocative behavior are deemed to be "in denial" or are excluded from the shelter.

Similarly, Renzetti (1999) pointed out that often victims are judged as "true" or "worthy" (p. 48) victims only if they are perfectly innocent of any wrongdoing. Lamb (1999) made a similar point. Does a rape victim qualify as a true victim only if she avoided any behavior that might be viewed as contributing to her rape? This idea is suggested by some rape myths, which imply that women who behave in certain ways (e.g., "leading a man on," drinking alcohol, dressing "suggestively") deserve to have sex forced on them (Burt, 1980; Payne, Lonsway, & Fitzgerald, 1999). Should researchers acknowledge only "worthy" victims whose victim status is undeniable and whose lack of responsibility for their own victimization is unquestionable? Insisting that victims must be blameless might result in constructing the category "victim" so narrowly that it excludes many people who have been victimized.

Research Focusing on Perpetrators

One solution to the problems inherent in focusing on rape victims might be to conduct research that focuses on rape perpetrators. This approach has the advantage of implicitly placing responsibility for change where it justly belongs: on perpetrators. Research on perpetrators has identified numerous attitudes related to sexual aggression. For example, compared with other men, men who rape are more accepting of violence against women, feel more hostility toward women, believe myths about rape more strongly, and have a more authoritarian approach to relationships (Drieschner & Lange, 1999; Murnen, Wright, & Kaluzny, 2002).

It is helpful to identify attitudes related to rape perpetration because such attitudes can be addressed in rape prevention programs. Numerous rape prevention programs have demonstrated success in changing men's rape-supportive attitudes (e.g., Gilbert, Heesacker, & Gannon, 1991; Jones & Muehlenhard, 1990; Lee, 1987). Such programs place the responsibility for change on men rather than relying on women to avoid situations that pose a threat or suggesting that women learn to respond "correctly" if confronted with a rape attempt (Berkowitz, 2002).

Unfortunately, it is unclear whether rape prevention programs that change men's attitudes about rape also decrease men's likelihood of raping. Although rape prevention aimed at men is desirable, rapists and potential rapists may be unmotivated to change their behaviors (Lonsway, 1996). Krulewitz and Kahn (1983) reported that students perceived rape reduction strategies that required men to take action as less effective than rape reduction strategies that placed the responsibility for change on women. As the primary victims of rape, women are generally more motivated to prevent rape than are men, particularly men who are likely to rape.

An additional problem with focusing research on perpetrators is that holding men exclusively responsible for rape prevention can imply that women are powerless to protect themselves from rape. Such an implicit message can undermine women's sense of agency and lead to feelings of vulnerability. Hollander (2001) reported that in discussions about violence, both women and men perceived women as highly vulnerable to violence, and both perceived men as relatively invulnerable. Many women and men thought that women required the protection of men to avoid violence (Hollander, 2001). Women's fear of violence leads them to restrict their activities and to be hypervigilant to signs of potential violence (Hickman & Muehlenhard, 1997; Hollander, 2001; Poirier, 1996). Stereotypes of women as passive and helpless make them reliant on men and limit their freedom.

Lamb (1996) questioned the effectiveness of blaming perpetrators for their behavior. She pointed out that often blame leads to shame, and shame leads to anger, blaming others, and refusing to acknowledge the problem. Drawing parallels to alcoholism, she argued that blaming an alcoholic is likely to lead to shame and self-disgust, which in turn lead to more drinking to escape these feelings. In contrast, telling alcoholics that they have a disease and that it is not their fault can free them from shame and allow them to seek help. Although blame and responsibility can be distinguished conceptually (e.g., Shaver & Drown, 1986), this distinction can easily be lost.

Research Focusing on Society

A third possible approach to rape research is to focus on society. This focus allows rape researchers to illuminate the laws, stereotypes, power relations, and gender roles within our culture that contribute to the perpetuation of rape. Many feminists have argued that, ultimately, social change is the only way to eliminate the problem of rape (e.g., Brownmiller, 1975; Griffin, 1971).

For example, Burt (1980) provided evidence for the existence of widely held rape-supportive attitudes that she labeled "rape myths." Rape myths can function to justify rape and create a hostile environment for rape victims (Burt, 1980; Lonsway & Fitzgerald, 1994). Rape myths also influence rape laws and institutional responses to rapists and rape victims (Estrich, 1987). If rape myths go unnoticed and unchallenged, they may serve to excuse rape and discourage social change. For example, one commonly held myth about rape is that only deviant or mentally ill men rape (Burt, 1980; Lonsway & Fitzgerald, 1994). This myth gives support to the belief that rape is caused by just a few "bad apples" rather than by a more systemic problem—meaning that no change is needed at the societal level (Peterson & Muehlenhard, 2003). Similarly, the rape myth "Men don't usually intend to force sex on a woman, but sometimes they get too sexually carried away" (Lonsway & Fitzgerald, 1994) excuses rape as a mere accident rather than a malicious crime. By focusing research on societal beliefs regarding rape, researchers can identify and take steps to challenge rape-supportive attitudes that excuse rape and obscure the need for change.

However, such a research approach also has some major disadvantages. By focusing on how society perpetuates rape, researchers implicitly exonerate individual perpetrators. The suggestion that men who rape are simply the product of a patriarchal society relieves them of individual responsibility for their behavior. Focusing on society may perpetuate the idea that no one is responsible, that sexual violence is "society's" fault. Lamb (1996) noted, "Moral condemnation of violence and cruelty seems rather empty if there is no agent" (p. 13).

Additionally, a societal approach to rape prevention fails to account for the fact that most men are not rapists. If our patriarchal culture turns men into rapists, why do most men escape these influences?

Finally, research that focuses on society is unlikely to have an immediate or observable impact on rape prevention. Research findings on societal norms leave individual women without information about the relative risk of various situations or about how to defend themselves. This approach tells women, in effect, that all they can do to protect themselves is to try to effect social change, hoping that they are not raped in the meantime.

Conclusion: Choosing a Research Focus

Each of these three foci of rape research has the potential to contribute to the understanding and eventual reduction of rape. Each, however, has its risks, including the risk that it will lead to misinterpretations about responsibility and blame. We suggest that rape researchers not allow the fear of misinterpretation to obstruct their quest for scientific understanding. Nevertheless, it is important for researchers to consider the implications and interpretations of their approaches—both to forestall misinterpretation by others and to challenge their own assumptions about sexual violence.

ACKNOWLEDGING THAT SEXUAL VIOLENCE DOES NOT HAVE UNIFORMLY SEVERE CONSEQUENCES

The politics of research have caused many studies to have been undertaken in a less than complete way. For example, we know very little about what kinds of circumstances mediate positive and negative outcomes after sexual abuse. There has been little acknowledgement of the fact that although rape, child sexual abuse, and wife battering are terrible experiences to have gone through, many people have "survived" and moved beyond them, feeling as if their victimization is not something that has defined them or continues to affect them.
—LAMB (1996, p. 46)

On July 12th the U.S. House of Representatives voted 355–0 to condemn certain conclusions of our article; the Senate quickly followed suit.
—RIND, TROMOVITCH, AND BAUSERMAN (1999, p. 11)

Does sexual violence *always* have severe consequences? This question involves issues of politics, definitions, and meaning.

An article published in *Psychological Bulletin* illustrates the politics of this issue. Rind, Tromovitch, and Bauserman (1998) conducted a meta-analysis of 59 studies comparing the adjustment of college students who reported having experienced child sexual abuse (CSA) with those who did not report CSA. Their meta-analysis revealed small differences between the two groups, with CSA accounting for less than 1% of the variance in adjustment (r_u = .09, with a 95% confidence interval from .08 to .11). It also revealed that the outcomes reported by men were less negative than those reported by women.

These results could have been interpreted as a message of hope for victims of CSA and their families, contradicting the idea that individuals experiencing CSA are doomed to a life of depression and despair. Instead, through a complicated series of events, the authors—and the American Psychological Association, which publishes *Psychological Bulletin*—found themselves under attack (Rind et al., 1999).

The attack was initiated by the National Association for Research and Therapy of Homosexuality, a psychoanalytically oriented group that still regards homosexuality as a mental disorder. Conservative talk show host "Dr. Laura" Schlessinger and the conservative lobbying group, The Family Research Council, joined the attack (Rind et al., 1999). Finally, on July 12, 1999, the U.S. Congress voted to condemn the study and "any suggestion that sexual relations between children and adults . . . are anything but abusive [and] destructive" (Rind et al., 1999, p. 11).

The question of whether sexual violence has uniformly severe consequences—and, if not, what conditions affect the consequences—deserves careful thought. There are many aspects to consider. Here we discuss two such issues: other experiences that reproduce the dynamics of sexual violence, and individual differences in the meaning of sexual violence.

Other Experiences Reproducing the Dynamics of Sexual Violence

Experiences other than sexual violence—some obviously abusive, others not obviously abusive—can cause problems similar to those caused by sexual violence. These experiences make it difficult to assess the effects of sexual violence.

First, consider examples of obviously abusive experiences. In many studies of the consequences of rape, for example, researchers do not ask whether the research participants have experienced other forms of abuse, such as CSA, physical abuse, emotional abuse, or neglect; adolescent and adult physical and emotional abuse; or other crimes. Thus, these experiences are present in the target and control groups in unknown ways. Some researchers have suggested deleting such individuals from the control group. Such a procedure, however, would result in confounding the effects of rape with the effects of other experiences; there could be numerous explanations of the differences between the two groups (the target group, but not the control group, might have experienced physical abuse, emotional abuse, etc.). Excluding individuals who have had these experiences from both groups would also be problematic, given that individuals who have been raped often have also experienced CSA or other forms of abuse (Muehlenhard et al., 1998). Thus, a group of rape victims that excluded victims of other forms of violence would be an atypical, unrepresentative group of rape victims. Statistically controlling for relevant experiences could be a solution, but it would require large samples, and it would require researchers to decide which experiences to control for. These principles also apply to research on the consequences of CSA (Fergusson & Mullen, 1999).

Next, consider experiences that are not obviously abusive but that might be relevant. We illustrate this point using Finkelhor and Browne's (1986) model for conceptualizing the consequences of CSA. These researchers sought to understand and explain the symptoms experienced by victims of CSA by organizing them around four "traumagenic dynamics" or trauma-causing factors associated with CSA: traumatic sexualization (e.g., pairing sexuality with negative emotions or memories; fetishizing the child's sexual parts); stigmatization (e.g., making the child feel ashamed, blamed, or denigrated; pressuring the child to keep the experience secret); betrayal (e.g., betraying the child's trust; making the child feel unsupported by her or his parents); and powerlessness (e.g., using force against the child; making the child feel afraid; invading the child's "body territory"). Finkelhor and Browne theorized about how these dynamics can cause the emotions and behaviors that are sometimes seen in children or adults with CSA histories.

These traumagenic dynamics are not limited to CSA, however. Many experiences other than sexual abuse involve similar dynamics. Parents and religious authorities make many children feel guilty about their sexuality, thus pairing sexuality with negative emotions. Advertisements fetishize parts of children's and adolescents' bodies. Many children feel pressured to keep family or personal secrets. Many children are blamed for family problems. Many children feel stigmatized by medical problems, physical imperfections, or being different from other children. Many children feel unsupported by their parents. Many children feel powerless. Because of such experiences, many children who never experienced CSA still experience dynamics similar to those of CSA. Interestingly, however, these experiences are generally not thought of as abusive and destructive.

Related to this point, Rind and colleagues (1998) identified several family environment variables that accounted for more variance in adjustment than did CSA. For example, for nonsexual abuse and neglect, $r_u =$ .19; for conflict or pathology, $r_u = .14$; for traditionalism, $r_u = .16$. Furthermore, these variables were confounded with CSA; that is, CSA was more likely to occur in families where nonsexual abuse and neglect, conflict and pathology, and traditionalism were present. Thus, in some cases, problems that might appear to be consequences of CSA—problems more prevalent in the CSA group than in the no-CSA group—may actually be the consequences of nonsexual abuse or neglect, conflict or pathology, traditionalism, or other such factors.

Tavris (1992) made a similar point. She argued that some people, especially women who have been victims of CSA, assume that a history of CSA is the source of their problems, such as depression, interpersonal conflicts, unhappiness with their appearance, alcohol abuse, and bad relationships. She concluded, "Indeed, these problems are often the results of childhood sexual abuse, but many of them are also the sadly familiar laments of women who were not abused as children" (p. 316).

Individual Differences in the Meaning of Sexual Violence

Different individuals react differently to similar experiences. For example, in a study that has been cited as showing "the most clear cut" (Browne & Finkelhor, 1986, p. 169) relationship between the type of sexual act and the consequences, Russell (1986) examined the self-reported consequences of three levels of sexual abuse: "very severe" (attempted or completed vaginal, oral, or anal penetration); "severe" (attempted or completed contact with unclothed breasts or genitals or simulated intercourse); and "least severe" (sexual kissing or touching of the buttocks, thighs, legs, or clothed breasts or genitals). Russell found that the percentages of women in these three groups who described their experience as "very traumatic" were 54%, 35%, and 19%, respectively. The percentages who reported experiencing no trauma were 2%, 19%, and 27%, respectively. This means that some (2%) of the women who reported "very severe" abuse reported having experienced no trauma, whereas some (19%) of the women who reported the "least severe" abuse reported that it had been very traumatic.

Some of these individual differences can be accounted for by characteristics of the abuse. For example, in general, the effects of CSA seem to be more serious if the abuse is of longer duration, involves physical restraint or violence, or involves a father or stepfather (Fergusson & Mullen, 1999). Similarly, in general, the effects of rape seem to be more serious if the rape was especially brutal or if the victim perceived the rape to be life threatening (Resick & Nishith, 1997). Gender also seems to moderate the consequences. In general, the consequences of CSA seem to be more severe for girls than for boys (Fergusson & Mullen, 1999; Rind et al., 1998). The consequences of sexual violence and coercion seem to be more severe for women than for men (Satterfield & Muehlenhard, 1996; Struckman-Johnson et al., 2003; Tjaden & Thoennes, 2000).

Beyond situational characteristics and demographic variables, other variables seem to affect the consequences of sexual violence. For example, the consequences of rape are often more severe if the victim had experienced psychological problems or chronic stress prior to the rape (Resick & Nishith, 1997). Victims who were raped in a situation they had considered safe show more subsequent fear and depression than those who had perceived themselves to be in danger (Resick & Nishith, 1997).

Similar acts can *mean* different things to different people. For example, in order to identify factors that might provide insights into resisting rape, Bart and O'Brien (1985) studied women who had been sexually attacked. As discussed previously, they asked women to self-identify as having been raped or as having thwarted a rape attempt. Although most women who had experienced forced phallic sex labeled themselves as having been raped, two women who had experienced vaginal penetration by the perpetrator's penis considered themselves to have avoided rape because they had reacted quickly and made the perpetrator stop, and the penetration did not last long. Another woman self-identified as having avoided rape even though she had experienced forced fellatio and digital penetration and even though she had been robbed, beaten, and injured. The attackers had fled when a train arrived, but she had chased them, and they had been caught and arrested. During the interview, she said, "I believe he's done it before and . . . he would do it to my grandmother and my cousin, my little seven year old cousin. It made me really mad" (p. 88). As Bart and O'Brien commented, "What was one woman's rape seemed to be another woman's avoidance" (p. 9).

What an incident means to individuals can affect how they feel about it. For example, Gavey (1999) described experiencing an attempted rape. At age 16, she was "tricked into stopping at an older male co-worker's place. . . . I was thrown onto a bed . . . and he proceeded to jump on top of me and attempt to remove my pants. . . . I remember having to struggle as hard as I could" (p. 71). Later, she recalled that "being able to successfully prevent a forceful attempt at unwanted sex left me feeling strong, determined, and invulnerable" (p. 71). "I did not feel like a victim. I despised his actions, but I did not feel I had been harmed" (p. 72).

CONCLUSION

Although it is not controversial to say that sexual violence is a serious problem that merits efforts to prevent it, the topic is clearly fraught with controversy. Research and prevention efforts in this area require making decisions that involve value judgments about power, violence, sexuality, and gender. It can be rewarding to try to effect social change by conceptualizing sexual violence in ways that challenge the status quo and by gaining insights into sexual violence through scientific inquiry. Neither endeavor is without controversy, however.

Traditional conceptualizations of sexual violence are restricted to "culturally disvalued" (Levine, 1959, p. 965) forms of sexual coercion. One way to effect social change is to expand what counts as sexual coercion. For example, some forms of indirect influence are so widely accepted that they are almost invisible. Labeling these more subtle forms of influence as sexually coercive challenges social norms about what forms of influence are acceptable and unacceptable in the matter of obtaining sex.

Not surprisingly, suggesting conceptualizations that challenge the status quo is not always popular. For example, Roiphe (1993) ridiculed researchers and activists who suggested broader definitions of sexual coercion as "rape-crisis feminists" who treat women like children (pp. 61–62) and portray women as cowering, as "knocked on [their backs] by the barest feather of peer pressure . . . [and as] weak-willed, alabaster bodies, whose virtue must be protected from the cunning encroachments of the outside world" (p. 67).

Scientific inquiry can contribute to our understanding of the causes and effects of sexual violence. However, researchers risk censure if their results do not fall within a narrow window of allowable outcomes. In some cases, researchers have been condemned for *exaggerating* the problem (e.g., Gilbert, 1991, accused researcher Mary Koss of promoting a "phantom epidemic of sexual assault," p. 54; see Muehlenhard, Sympson, Phelps, & Highby, 1994, for more information). In other cases, researchers have been condemned for *minimizing* the problem (e.g., as discussed, the U.S. Congress voted to condemn Rind and colleagues' [1998] conclusions). Such an atmosphere constrains the questions researchers are likely to ask, the results they are likely to report, and the interpretations they are likely to make. Ultimately, this atmosphere limits our knowledge about sexual violence.

There are also constraints on the reactions expected from those who experience sexual coercion. Individuals who experience "culturally disvalued," unacceptable forms of sexual coercion are expected to experience severe consequences; those who do not may be labeled as defensive or in denial" (e.g., Bass & Davis, 1988, p. 42; see Gavey, 1999, and Lamb, 1999, for discussions). In contrast, individuals who experience culturally acceptable forms of sexual coercion are expected to experience no consequences (or, if they do, are expected not to complain about it); those who do may be mocked or ridiculed (e.g., Farrell, 1993; Roiphe, 1993). It would be helpful to those who experience sexual coercion if our culture took a more flexible approach instead of expecting a rigid correspondence between forms of sexual coercion and allowable outcomes.

As is clear from this chapter, there is no one "correct" way to conceptualize sexual violence. All approaches have advantages and disadvantages. The controversies that arise as a result of researchers' and activists' choices about these issues can serve an important heuristic value. Differing conceptualizations can result in new theoretical and empirical approaches to the study of sexual violence, which in turn can result in a fuller understanding and in new ways of addressing the problem.

REFERENCES

Abbey, A. (1982). Sex differences in attributions for friendly behavior: Do males misperceive females' friendliness? *Journal of Personality and Social Psychology, 42,* 830–838.

Atmore, C. (1999). Victims, backlash, and radical feminist theory (or, the morning after they stole feminism's fire). In S. Lamb (Ed.), *New versions of victims: Feminists struggle with the concept* (pp. 183–211). New York: New York University Press.

Bart, P. B., & O'Brien, P. H. (1985). *Stopping rape.* New York: Pergamon.

Bass, E., & Davis, L. (1988). *The courage to heal.* New York: Harper & Row.

Berkowitz, A. D. (2002). Fostering men's responsibility for preventing sexual assault. In P. A. Schewe (Ed.), *Preventing violence in relationships: Interventions across the life span* (pp. 163–196). Washington, DC: American Psychological Association.

Bogart, L. M., Cecil, H., Wagstaff, D. A., Pinkerton, S. D., & Abramson, P. R. (2000). "Is it sex?" College students' interpretations of sexual behavior terminology. *Journal of Sex Research, 37,* 108–116.

Bostwick, T. D., & DeLucia, J. L. (1992). Effects of gender and specific dating behaviors on perceptions of sex willingness and date rape. *Journal of Social and Clinical Psychology, 11,* 14–25.

Browne, A., & Finkelhor, D. (1986). Initial and long-term effects: A review of the research. In D. Finkelhor (Ed.), *A sourcebook on child sexual abuse* (pp. 143–179). Thousand Oaks, CA: Sage.

Brownmiller, S. (1975). *Against our will: Men, women, and rape.* Toronto: Bantam.

Burt, M. R. (1980). Cultural myths and supports for rape. *Journal of Personality and Social Psychology, 38,* 217–230.

Crocker, J. (2003, June). *The worthy self: New findings in self-esteem research.* Workshop sponsored by Cortext Continuing Education, Kansas City, MO.

Deitz, S. R., Littman, M., & Bentley, B. J. (1984). Attribution of responsibility for rape: The influence of observer empathy, victim resistance, and victim attractiveness. *Sex Roles, 10,* 261–280.

Drieschner, K., & Lange, A. (1999). A review of cognitive factors in the etiology of rape: Theories, empirical studies, and implications. *Clinical Psychology Review, 19,* 57–77.

Estrich, S. (1987). *Real rape.* Cambridge, MA: Harvard University Press.

Falbo, T., & Peplau, L. A. (1980). Power strategies in intimate relationships. *Journal of Personality and Social Psychology, 38,* 618–628.

Farrell, W. (1993). *The myth of male power: Why men are the disposable sex.* New York: Simon & Schuster.

Felson, R. B. (2002). *Violence and gender reexamined.* Washington, DC: American Psychological Association.

Fergusson, D. M., & Mullen, P. E. (1999). *Child sexual abuse: An evidence based perspective.* Thousand Oaks, CA: Sage.

Finkelhor, D., & Browne, A. (1986). Initial and long-term effects: A conceptual framework. In D. Finkelhor (Ed.), *A sourcebook on child sexual abuse* (pp. 180–198). Thousand Oaks, CA: Sage.

French, J. R. P., Jr., & Raven, B. H. (1959). The bases of social power. In D. Cartwright (Ed.), *Studies in social power* (pp. 150–167). Ann Arbor, MI: Institute for Social Research.

Gavey, N. (1999). "I wasn't raped, but . . .": Revisiting definitional problems in sexual victimization. In S. Lamb (Ed.), *New versions of victims: Feminists struggle with the concept* (pp. 57–81). New York: New York University Press.

Gelles, R. J., & Strauss, M. A. (1988). *Intimate violence.* New York: Simon & Schuster.

Gilbert, B. J., Heesacker, M., & Gannon, L. J. (1991). Changing men's sexual aggression–supportive attitudes: A psychoeducational intervention. *Journal of Counseling Psychology, 38,* 197–203.

Gilbert, N. (1991). The phantom epidemic of sexual assault. *The Public Interest, 103,* 54–65.

Gold, S. N., Hughes, D. M., & Swingle, J. M. (1996). Characteristics of childhood sexual abuse among female survivors in therapy. *Child Abuse and Neglect, 20,* 323–335.

Goodchilds, J. D., & Zellman, G. L. (1984). Sexual signaling and sexual aggression in adolescent relationships. In N. M. Malamuth & E. Donnerstein (Eds.), *Pornography and sexual aggression* (pp. 233–243). Orlando, FL: Academic Press.

Gordon, M. T., & Riger, S. (1989). *The female fear.* New York: Free Press.

Griffin, S. (1971). Rape: The all-American crime. *Ramparts, 10,* 26–35.

Hall, D. S. (1998). Consent for sexual behavior in a college student population. *Electronic Journal of Human Sexuality, 1.* Retrieved on September 15, 2003, from *http://www.ejhs.org/volume1/consent1.htm*

Helliwell, C. (2000). "It's only a penis": Rape, feminism, and difference. *Signs, 25,* 789–816.

Herman, J. L. (1992). *Trauma and recovery.* New York: Basic Books.

Hickman, S. E., & Muehlenhard, C. L. (1997). College women's fears and precautionary behaviors relating to acquaintance rape and stranger rape. *Psychology of Women Quarterly, 21,* 527–547.

Hickman, S. E., & Muehlenhard, C. L. (1999). "By the semi-mystical appearance of a condom": How young women and men communicate sexual consent in heterosexual situations. *Journal of Sex Research, 36,* 258–272.

Hollander, J. A. (2001). Vulnerability and dangerousness: The construction of gender through conversations about violence. *Gender and Society, 15,* 83–109.

Impett, E. A., & Peplau, L. A. (2002). Why some women consent to unwanted sex with a dating partner: Insights from attachment theory. *Psychology of Women Quarterly, 26,* 359–369.

Impett, E. A., & Peplau, L. A. (2003). Sexual compliance: Gender, motivational, and relationship perspectives. *Journal of Sex Research, 40,* 87–100.

Jones, J. M., & Muehlenhard, C. L. (1990, November). *Using education to prevent rape on college campuses.* Paper presented at the annual meeting of the Society for the Scientific Study of Sex, Minneapolis, MN.

Kimball, M. M. (1995). *Feminist visions of gender similarities and differences.* New York: Harrington Park Press.

Koss, M. P., Gidycz, C. A., & Wisniewski, N. (1987). The scope of rape: Incidence and prevalence of sexual aggression and victimization in a national sample of higher education students. *Journal of Consulting and Clinical Psychology, 55,* 162–170.

Krulewitz, J. E., & Kahn, A. S. (1983). Preferences for rape reduction strategies. *Psychology of Women Quarterly, 7,* 301–312.

Lamb, S. (1996). *The trouble with blame: Victims, perpetrators, and responsibility.* Cambridge, MA: Harvard University Press.

Lamb, S. (1999). Constructing the victim: Popular images and lasting labels. In S. Lamb (Ed.), *New versions of victims: Feminists struggle with the concept* (pp. 108–138). New York: New York University Press.

Langer, E. (1975). The illusion of control. *Journal of Personality and Social Psychology, 32,* 311–328.

Lee, L. A. (1987). Rape prevention: Experiential training for men. *Journal of Counseling and Development, 6,* 100–101.

Levine, R. (1959). Gusii sex offenses: A study in social control. *American Anthropologist, 61,* 965–990.

Levine-MacCombie, J., & Koss, M. P. (1986). Acquaintance rape: Effective avoidance strategies. *Psychology of Women Quarterly, 10,* 311–320.

Lonsway, K. A. (1996). Preventing acquaintance rape through education: What do we know? *Psychology of Women Quarterly, 20,* 229–265.

Lonsway, K. A., & Fitzgerald, L. F. (1994). Rape myths: In review. *Psychology of Women Quarterly, 18,* 133–164.

MacKinnon, C. A. (1989). *Towards a feminist theory of the state.* Cambridge, MA: Harvard University Press.

MacKinnon, C. A. (1990). Liberalism and the death of feminism. In D. Leidholdt & J. G. Raymond (Eds.), *The sexual liberals and the attack on feminism* (pp. 3–13). New York: Pergamon.

Maynard, M. (2002, November 27). Car rental industry is forced to shift ways. *The New York Times,* p. C1.

Miethe, T. D. (1985). The myth or reality of victim involvement in crime: A review and comment on victim-precipitation research. *Sociological Focus, 18,* 209–220.

Muehlenhard, C. L. (1988). Misinterpreted dating behaviors and the risk of date rape. *Journal of Social and Clinical Psychology, 6,* 20–37.

Muehlenhard, C. L. (1998). The importance and danger of studying sexually aggressive women. In P. B. Anderson & C. Struckman-Johnson (Eds.), *Sexually aggressive women: Current perspectives and controversies* (pp. 19–48). New York: Guilford Press.

Muehlenhard, C. L. (2002, April). *"Was the sex [ ] wanted [ ] unwanted (check one)?" Re-examining the concept of consent.* Invited plenary address presented at the Western Region Conference of the Society for the Scientific Study of Sexuality, Manhattan Beach, CA.

Muehlenhard, C. L., & Cook, S. W. (1988). Men's self-reports of unwanted sexual activity. *Journal of Sex Research, 24,* 58–72.

Muehlenhard, C. L., Friedman, D. E., & Thomas, C. M. (1985). Is date rape justifiable? The effects of dating activity, who initiated, who paid, and men's attitudes toward women. *Psychology of Women Quarterly, 9,* 297–310.

Muehlenhard, C. L., Highby, B. J., Lee, R. S., Bryan, T. S., & Dodrill, W. A. (1998). The sexual revictimization of women and men sexually abused as children: A review of the literature. *Annual Review of Sex Research, 9,* 1–47.

Muehlenhard, C. L., & Kimes, L. A. (1999). The social construction of violence: The case of sexual and domestic violence. *Personality and Social Psychology Review, 3,* 234–245.

Muehlenhard, C. L., & Linton, M. A. (1987). Date rape and sexual aggression in dating situations: Incidence and risk factors. *Journal of Counseling Psychology, 34,* 186–196.

Muehlenhard, C. L., Peterson, Z. D., MacPherson, L. A., & Blair, R. L. (2002, June). *First experiences with sexual intercourse: Wanted, unwanted, or both? Application of a multidimensional model.* Paper presented at the Midcontinent Regional Conference of the Society for the Scientific Study of Sexuality, Big Rapids, MI.

Muehlenhard, C. L., Powch, I. G., Phelps, J. L., & Giusti, L. M. (1992). Definitions of rape: Scientific and political implications. *Journal of Social Issues, 48*(1), 23–44.

Muehlenhard, C. L., & Schrag, J. L. (1991). Nonviolent sexual coercion. In A. Parrot & L. Bechhofer (Eds.), *Acquaintance rape: The hidden crime* (pp. 115–128). New York: Wiley.

Muehlenhard, C. L., Sympson, S. C., Phelps, J. L., & Highby, B. J. (1994). Are rape statistics exaggerated? A response to criticism of contemporary rape research. *Journal of Sex Research, 31,* 144–146.

Murnen, S. K., Wright, C., & Kaluzny, G. (2002). If "boys will be boys," then girls will be victims? A meta-analytic review of the research that relates masculine ideology to sexual aggression. *Sex Roles, 46,* 359–375.

Ng, S. H. (2001). Influencing through the power of language. In J. P. Forgas & K. D. Williams (Eds.), *Social influence: Direct and indirect processes* (pp. 185–197). Philadelphia: Psychology Press.

Ong, A. S. J., & Ward, C. A. (1999). The effects of sex and power schemas, attitudes toward women, and victim resistance on rape attributions. *Journal of Applied Social Psychology, 29,* 362–376.

O'Sullivan, L. F., & Allgeier, E. R. (1998). Feigning sexual desire: Consenting to unwanted sexual activity in heterosexual dating relationships. *Journal of Sex Research, 35,* 234–243.

Payne, D. L., Lonsway, K. A., & Fitzgerald, L. F. (1999). Rape myth acceptance: Exploration of its structure and its measurement using the Illinois Rape Myth Acceptance Scale. *Journal of Research in Personality, 33,* 27–68.

Peterson, Z. D., & Muehlenhard, C. L. (2003). *Was it rape? The function of women's rape myth acceptance and definitions of sex in predicting rape acknowledgment.* Manuscript submitted for publication.

Pitts, M., & Rahman, Q. (2001). Which behaviors constitute "having sex" among university students in the UK? *Archives of Sexual Behavior, 30,* 169–176.

Poirier, J. L. (1996). *The fear of rape: A comparison with other common fears of female and male college students.* Unpublished master's thesis, University of Kansas, Lawrence.

Poirier, J., & Muehlenhard, C. L. (2000, November). *Feeling more vulnerable to stranger rape while knowing that acquaintance rape is more common: Exploring the paradox.* Paper presented at the annual meeting of the Society for the Scientific Study of Sexuality, Orlando, FL.

Presson, P. K., & Benassi, V. A. (1996). Illusion of control: A meta-analytic review. *Journal of Social Behavior and Personality, 11,* 493–510.

Raven, B. H. (1999). Reflections on interpersonal influence and social power in experimental social psychology. In A. Rodrigues & R. V. Levine (Eds.), *Reflections on 100 years of experimental social psychology* (pp. 114–134). New York: Basic Books.

Renzetti, C. (1999). The challenge to feminism posed by women's use of violence in intimate relationships. In S. Lamb (Ed.), *New versions of victims: Feminists struggle with the concept* (pp. 42–56). New York: New York University Press.

Resick, P. A., & Nishith, P. (1997). Sexual assault. In R. C. Davis, A. J. Lurigio, & W. G. Skogan (Eds.), *Victims of crime* (2nd ed., pp. 27–52). Thousand Oaks, CA: Sage.

Rind, B., Tromovitch, P., & Bauserman, R. (1998). A meta-analytic examination of assumed properties of child sexual abuse using college samples. *Psychological Bulletin, 124,* 22–53.

Rind, B., Tromovitch, P., & Bauserman, R. (1999, November). *The clash of media, politics, and sexual science: An examination of the controversy surrounding the* Psychological Bulletin *meta-analysis on the assumed properties of child sexual abuse.* Paper presented at the joint annual meeting of the Society for the Scientific Study of Sexuality and the American Association of Sex Educators, Counselors, and Therapists, St. Louis, MO.

Roiphe, K. (1993). *The morning after: Sex, fear, and feminism on campus.* Boston: Little, Brown.

Rotkin, K. (1986). The phallacy of our sexual norms. In S. Bem (Ed.), *Psychology of sex roles* (pp. 384–391). Acton, MA: Copley.

Rozee, P. D., & Koss, M. P. (2001). Rape: A century of resistance. *Psychology of Women Quarterly, 25,* 295–311.

Russell, D. E. H. (1986). *The secret trauma: Incest in the lives of girls and women.* New York: Basic Books.

Russell, D. E. H. (2000). The backlash: Feminists blamed for creating a phantom epidemic of rape and child sexual abuse. In D. E. H. Russell & R. M. Bolen, *The epidemic of rape and child sexual abuse in the United States* (pp. 239–254). Thousand Oaks, CA: Sage.

Ryan, K. M. (1988). Rape and seduction scripts. *Psychology of Women Quarterly, 12,* 237–245.

Sanders, S. A., & Reinisch, J. M. (1999). Would you say you "had sex" if . . .? *Journal of the American Medical Association, 281,* 275–277.

Satterfield, A. T., & Muehlenhard, C. L. (1996, November). *The role of gender in the meaning of sexual coercion: Women's and men's reactions to their own experiences.* Paper presented at the annual meeting of the Society for the Scientific Study of Sexuality, Houston, TX.

Schulhofer, S. J. (1998). *Unwanted sex: The culture of intimidation and the failure of the law.* Cambridge, MA: Harvard University Press.

Seligman, M. E. P. (1991). *Learned optimism.* New York: Knopf.

Shaver, K. G., & Drown, D. (1986). On causality, responsibility, and self-blame: A theoretical note. *Journal of Personality and Social Psychology, 50,* 697–702.

Struckman-Johnson, C., Struckman-Johnson, D., & Anderson, P. B. (2003). Tactics of sexual coercion: When men and women won't take no for an answer. *Journal of Sex Research, 40,* 76–86.

Tavris, C. (1992). *The mismeasure of woman.* New York: Simon & Schuster.

Testa, M., & Dermen, K. H. (1999). The differential correlates of sexual coercion and rape. *Journal of Interpersonal Violence, 14,* 548–561.

Tjaden, P., & Thoennes, N. (2000). *Full report of the prevalence, incidence, and consequences of violence against women* (No. NCJ 183781). Washington, DC: U.S. Department of Justice.

Ullman, S. E. (1997). Review and critique of empirical studies of rape avoidance. *Criminal Justice and Behavior, 24,* 177–204.

Ullman, S. E., & Knight, R. A. (1993). The efficacy of women's resistance strategies in rape situations. *Psychology of Women Quarterly, 17,* 23–38.

White, J. W., & Kowalski, R. M. (1994). Deconstructing the myth of the nonaggressive woman: A feminist analysis. *Psychology of Women Quarterly, 18,* 487–508.

Zoucha-Jensen, J. M., & Coyne, A. (1993). The effects of resistance strategies on rape. *American Journal of Public Health, 83,* 1633–1634.

PART III

SELF-CONCEPT IN RELATION TO GOOD AND EVIL ACTS

CHAPTER 11

THE PURSUIT OF SELF-ESTEEM

Implications for Good and Evil

JENNIFER CROCKER
SHAWNA J. LEE
LORA E. PARK

North Americans generally view self-esteem as an unmitigated good, integral to a meaningful, satisfying, and fulfilling life. From a young age, parents, teachers, and popular culture teach us that feeling good about ourselves is a high priority (Miller, 2001). Thousands of self-help books, child-rearing guides, and television shows hail the benefits of increasing self-esteem. The self-esteem movement, based on the assumption that high self-esteem leads to positive outcomes (Benson, Galbraith, & Espeland, 1998; Glennon, 1999; Miller, 2001), aimed to raise children's self-esteem to combat social problems, such as academic underachievement, high dropout rates, crime, teenage pregnancy, eating disorders, drug and alcohol abuse, and interpersonal aggression (Branden, 1994; Dawes, 1994; McElherner & Lisovskis, 1998; Mecca, Smelser, & Vasconcellos, 1989; Seligman, 1998).

Underlying this cultural concern with self-esteem is the belief that feelings of worthlessness and low self-esteem lead people to do things that are harmful and destructive to themselves and to others; in other words, low self-esteem is one source of evil. The belief in the costs/disadvantages of low self-esteem and the benefits of high self-esteem seem so pervasive that many psychologists have assumed that self-esteem is a universal and fundamental human need (Allport, 1955; Epstein, 1985; Greenberg, Pyszczynski, & Solomon, 1986; James, 1890; Maslow, 1968; Rogers, 1961; Rosenberg, 1979; Solomon, Greenberg, & Pyszczynski, 1991; Steele, 1988; Taylor & Brown, 1988; Tesser, 1988), even arguing that humans evolved as a species to pursue self-esteem (Leary & Baumeister, 2000; Leary & Downs, 1995).

In recent years, however, researchers have questioned the idea that self-esteem is an unmitigated, universal good (Baumeister, 1998; Baumeister, Campbell, Krueger, & Vohs, 2003; Dawes, 1994; Heatherton & Ambady, 1993; Heatherton & Vohs, 2000). A review of the literature yields little support for the notion that increasing self-esteem reduces social problems (Baumeister, 1998); in fact, researchers have found that even among those with high self-esteem, *threats* to self-esteem lead people to respond in ways that may exacerbate, rather than ameliorate, social problems (Baumeister, 1998; Crocker & Park, in press; Heatherton & Vohs, 2000). These findings have led scientists to criticize the self-esteem movement (Baumeister, 1999; Seligman, 1998), criticism echoed in the popular media (Goode, 2002; Slater, 2002). Recent research on self-esteem and its description in the popular media have created confusion about self-esteem. Is low self-esteem a root of evil, or is high self-esteem a root of evil?

In our view, neither high nor low self-esteem is a cause of good or evil. Instead, much of what is considered evil stems from the *pursuit* of self-esteem: from the desire to prove to oneself and others that one is wonderful and worthy, not worthless. Concern with feelings of self-worth and self-esteem—feeling competent, superior, having the regard of others—can lead people to lose sight of the consequences of their behavior for others, and focus instead on how their behavior *feels* to themselves and *looks* to others. Consequently, pursuing self-esteem is sometimes incompatible with doing good or behaving in ways that ultimately satisfy our fundamental human needs for relatedness, learning, and autonomy. In fact, doing good sometimes requires abandoning ego concerns and risking failure, disapproval, or rejection—all of which can take a toll on self-esteem.

The *American Heritage Dictionary* includes several meanings for the word *evil*. We use the word here to refer to the consequences of action, to "something that causes harm, misfortune, or destruction," rather than the moral intent behind the action, as suggested by the definition, "morally bad or wrong; wicked." In our view, much that causes harm, misfortune, and destruction—from petty slights, looking down on others, and ignoring another's need for social support, to prejudice, aggression, violence, and even war—stems from the struggle to prove one's worth and value. The pursuit of self-esteem is not morally wrong or wicked, it need not have evil intent, but, as we will see, it can cause harm, misfortune, and destruction to the self and to others.

THE PURSUIT OF SELF-ESTEEM

People pursue self-esteem when they become concerned with the question, "Am I wonderful and worthy, or am I worthless?" We assume, like most other researchers, that people want to feel good about themselves and believe that they have worth and value as a person. How do people arrive at the belief that they are worthy and wonderful, and have value? In some cultural and religious meaning systems, this is not a relevant question; every person has worth and value by virtue of being human, a living creature. In these meaning systems, one's worth or value does not need to be proved, earned, or deserved; it is a given. In North American culture, however, people commonly assume that some people have more worth or value than others, and that their worth or value as a person depends on what they are or do. Self-worth or self-esteem is *contingent* on satisfying standards of worth or value. Some people stake their self-worth on being beautiful or thin, others on being morally virtuous, others on accumulating wealth or professional success, and so on. Consequently, feelings of self-worth and self-esteem depend on perceived success or failure in those domains on which self-worth is contingent (Crocker & Wolfe, 2001).

For most North Americans, then, self-worth is not a given; it must be earned or deserved. People therefore strive to achieve success and avoid failure in those domains on which their self-worth is staked. Because success or failure in these domains can either prove one's worth and value or demonstrate one's worthlessness, people pursue self-esteem in these domains. Failure, or the threat of failure, in the areas on which self-worth is staked is particularly distressing and may trigger efforts to maintain, enhance, and protect self-esteem from the threat. Because it feels good to conclude that one is worthy and wonderful, and it feels bad to conclude that one is not, acceptable performance in these domains of contingency often feels compelling—the pursuit of self-esteem captures attention, provides motivation, and impacts emotions (Crocker & Wolfe, 2001). Because this pursuit is, first and foremost, about the self, people lose sight of other goals and the impact of their behavior on others when they are caught in the question of whether they are wonderful or worthless. The pursuit of self-esteem leads to heightened self-evaluation and preoccupation with the self, interferes with emotional and behavioral self-regulation, hinders the ability to maintain mutually caring, supportive relationships with others, and may ultimately contribute to interpersonal violence, aggression, and intergroup conflict. Hence, the pursuit of self-esteem can ultimately cause harm, misfortune, and destruction.

Cognitive Reactions to Ego Threat

Threats in domains of contingency trigger self-evaluation and self-preoccupation. For example, in an experiment, college students who scored high or low in basing their self-worth on academic competence completed either an easy or difficult version of the Remote Associates Test or were assigned to a control condition in which they rated their preference for words. Afterward, participants completed a thought-listing task. Students whose self-worth was staked on academic competence and took the difficult RAT test (failure condition) reported more negative self-evaluative thoughts than students whose self-worth was less contingent in the academic domain or students in the control condition (Park & Crocker, 2003).

Indeed, when self-worth is on the line, attention is focused on the self, often at the expense of others' needs and feelings. A recent study investigated the effects of a threat to contingent self-worth on subsequent interpersonal interactions (Park & Crocker, 2002). The results showed that among high self-esteem targets, those who were highly contingent on academic competence and in the ego-threat condition rated themselves as more preoccupied, less supportive, and less empathic toward another's personal problem and liked their partners less, compared to targets who were less contingent on academic competence. Partners, in turn, also perceived high self-esteem, highly contingent targets who were ego-threatened as being more preoccupied, less supportive, and less likable. These findings suggest that when people receive a threat to a domain of contingency (especially if they have high self-esteem), they become preoccupied with the self, which detracts from their ability to experience compassion toward another person's problem and, therefore, may hinder them from forming and maintaining mutually caring, supportive relationships with others.

Emotional Consequences

Affective reactions to events are more intense when they pertain to contingent domains than when they do not (Crocker & Wolfe, 2001). For example, a daily report study examined college seniors' responses to graduate school acceptances and rejections as a function of how much they based their self-worth on academic competence (Crocker, Sommers, & Luhtanen, 2002). Compared to students who based their self-esteem less on academic competence, those who highly based their self-worth in this domain experienced more dramatic decreases in state self-esteem and increases in negative affect on days they received rejection letters from graduate schools, and more dramatic increases in state self-esteem and positive affect on days they were accepted to graduate schools. Similarly, a study of college students majoring in either psychology or engineering found that those who were highly contingent on academic competence showed greater drops in self-esteem on days they received worse-than-expected grades, compared to students who were less contingent on academic competence (Crocker, Karpinski, Quinn, & Chase, in press). Taken together, these findings suggest that when people are threatened in contingent domains, they are likely to experience decreases in self-esteem and increases in negative affect and depressive symptoms.

Failure in contingent domains may also evoke negative self-relevant emotions, such as humiliation and shame. Shame leads to a painful scrutiny of the entire self and to feelings of global inadequacy and worthlessness (Tangney, Wagner, Hill-Barlow, Marschall, & Gramzow, 1996). These negative self-evaluations, in turn, can lead to anger. Consequently, the intense negative affect and loss of self-esteem that people experience in the face of failure in domains of contingency can result in emotional dysregulation: that is, the failure to control and modulate the intensity of emotional reactions to arousal-producing experiences (Muraven, Tice, & Baumeister, 1998; Walden & Smith, 1997). As part of emotional regulation processes, negative emotions initiate efforts to improve one's emotional state, which can involve switching from a long-term focus on inhibiting negative reactions to distress to a shorter-term focus on immediately improving one's emotional state (Tice, Bratslavsky, & Baumeister, 2001). When self-esteem is at stake, failure implies that one is worthless, so attempts to improve one's emotional state are focused frequently on identifying an explanation or excuse for the failure that protects self-esteem (Blaine & Crocker, 1993). When threatened in a domain of contingency, people may move quickly from feeling ashamed, humiliated, and worthless to blaming others for the failure. Feelings of shame are frequently accompanied by a sense of humiliated rage (Tangney et al., 1996). When pursuing self-esteem, people focus on and exaggerate feelings of anger and hostility, which are associated with blaming others for failure (Weiner, 1985). Rather than modulate negative affect, this reaction replaces shame and humiliation (feelings associated with worthlessness), with anger and hostility (feelings associated with the belief that the failure was unfair or someone else's fault) (Smith & Ellsworth, 1985)—feelings that are often expressed in maladaptive, destructive ways. Shame-prone individuals respond to anger-inducing events by expressing malevolent intentions, externalizing blame onto others, and engaging in indirect, direct, and displaced forms of aggression and hostility (Tangney et al., 1996). When pursuing self-esteem, people can become trapped in intensely negative emotional states (e.g., anger and even rage), as they struggle to replace feelings of worthlessness, shame, and humiliation with self-worth.

Behavioral Consequences

Emotional dysregulation, triggered by threats in domains on which self-worth is staked, can also have important implications for behavior. Paralleling emotional regulation, behavioral self-regulation is the process of inhibiting impulsive or immediate behavioral reactions to life events (Tice et al., 2001). People's efforts to regulate their emotions and to feel better about themselves in the short-term may come at the expense of longer-term goals (Tice & Bratslavsky, 2000; Tice et al., 2001). People who experience anger, frustration, or embarrassment often make risky decisions, ignoring relevant information on the costs and benefits of behavioral alternatives (Leith & Baumeister, 1996) and compromising behavioral self-regulation.

Poor behavioral self-control interferes with the ability to delay gratification in obtaining rewards, leads to a lack of persistence on important tasks, inability to control eating behavior, and increased vulnerability to depressive symptoms (Baumeister, Heatherton, & Tice, 1993; Muraven et al., 1998; Pyszczynski & Greenberg, 1987; Pyszczynski, Holt, & Greenberg, 1987). Breakdowns in emotional and behavioral regulation may also contribute to school underachievement, unsafe sexual behavior, crime, and violence (Baumeister, 1997, 1998; Baumeister et al., 1993; Muraven et al., 1998).

Additionally, emotional and behavioral dysregulation are linked to self-destructive behaviors such as alcohol and drug use and risky sexual behaviors (Cooper, Agocha, & Sheldon, 2000; Cooper, Frone, Russell, & Mudar, 1995; Cooper, Shapiro, & Powers, 1998). Lack of self-regulation and high arousal in the face of a negative mood increase the frequency of risk-taking behaviors (Leith & Baumeister, 1996). Ego threat is also linked to increased alcohol use (Baumeister, 1997). Indeed, research suggests that increased alcohol consumption may be specific to incidents that relate to contingent domains, such as others' approval (Baumeister, 1997). Finally, lack of self-regulation has even been linked to increased vulnerability to suicide (Vohs & Baumeister, 2000).

In sum, the pursuit of self-esteem is triggered by threats in domains on which self-worth is staked. The pursuit of self-esteem is characterized by self-centered preoccupation with one's worth and value, intense emotional responses to success and failure, and emotional and behavioral dysregulation. In the next section, we examine the impact on others of frequently used strategies for pursuing self-esteem. Specifically, we explore how self-preoccupation, emotional dysregulation, and behavioral dysregulation can cause harm, misfortune, and destruction for others; we also consider individual differences in people's strategies for pursuing self-esteem.

INTERPERSONAL COSTS OF EVERYDAY STRATEGIES FOR PURSUING SELF-ESTEEM

Thus far we have considered how people generally respond to threats to domains of contingency: They experience drops in self-esteem and increases in negative affect, become highly preoccupied with the self, and are motivated to maintain, protect, and enhance their self-esteem. Repairing self-esteem can take many forms, such as distancing the self from others, making downward social comparisons, stereotyping and derogating out-groups, and seeking reassurance from others. These are but a few of the many self-protective and self-enhancing responses to self-esteem threat that have been well-documented in research and appear to be ubiquitous. Although these strategies may temporarily relieve the anxiety created by failure in contingent domains, even these run-of-the-mill ways of pursuing self-esteem can have enduringly harmful and destructive ripple effects on others and society.

Distancing Self from Others

When people are outperformed by a close other in a domain that is central to their self-concept, they are likely either to diminish the relevance of the domain or distance themselves from the other (Tesser, 1988). For example, Pleban and Tesser (1981) conducted a study in which college students individually competed against another student, who was actually a confederate, on a series of general knowledge questions. The questions were rigged so that some participants were asked questions on topics that were highly self-relevant to their self-concept and that the confederate was able to answer correctly. The researchers found that participants in this condition distanced themselves more from the confederate, saying that they would not want to work with him or her in the future.

Distancing from others may also take the form of withholding help to others who outperform the self in domains that are relevant to the self-concept. Tesser and Smith (1980) conducted a study in which participants were asked to play a game of Password with both a friend and a stranger, and were instructed to give clues to the other person to help him or her guess a word. Some of the participants were told that the game was highly correlated with their intelligence and leadership skills. Under these conditions, participants were less likely to be helpful toward their friend. One explanation for this finding is that participants in the ego-threat condition did not want their friends to outshine them on a task that was highly relevant to their self-concept. In contrast, when the task was not self-relevant, people gave more difficult clues to the strangers than to their friends. Both response modes are costly to others: When people pursue self-esteem goals, they distance themselves from others and become competitive, withholding information from others in order to protect and maintain their self-worth. This research illustrates how, when people pursue self-esteem, life can easily turn into a zero-sum game: One person's success may be a threat to another person's self-worth, especially if that person is close to him or her. Thus, instead of helping those to whom we are close and promoting mutually supportive and caring relationships, the pursuit of self-esteem leads us to exactly the opposite: competition, distancing from others, and withholding of assistance that could support the other person in his or her endeavors.

Downward Social Comparisons

Following threats in domains of contingency, people tend to actively seek out information about others who also did poorly (Pyszczynski, Greenberg, & Laprelle, 1985; Wood, Giordano-Beech, & Ducharme, 1999) and compare themselves with others who are less fortunate (Aspinwall & Taylor, 1993; Beauregard & Dunning, 1998; Crocker & Schwartz, 1985; Wills, 1981; Wood et al., 1999). Comparisons with worse-off others reduce anxiety and enhance people's self-esteem and mood (Gibbons, 1986; Morse & Gergen, 1970). However, this self-enhancement strategy may come at a price to others. For example, following threats in contingent domains, people are more likely to remember negative information about others, even information that is unrelated to the domain of the threat (Crocker, 1993). Engaging in downward comparisons also creates distance between the self and others. In this context, others are merely seen as a means to achieving the goal of protecting and enhancing self-esteem. Thus, although focusing on others' shortcomings may repair people's threatened self-esteem temporarily, it is likely to have a detrimental impact on others in the long run by making them feel unsupported and disconnected.

Prejudice and Derogation

Prejudice toward and derogation of out-groups are extremely common but destructive human behaviors, often triggering hostility and aggression that result in intergroup conflict and violence (Brewer & Brown, 1998). How do outgroup prejudice and derogation relate to the pursuit of self-esteem? When people experience a threat to their self-concept, they become motivated to repair their self-esteem—an activity they pursue by favoring the groups to which they belong and derogating outgroup members. For example, research has shown that people who receive a threat to their self-esteem are more likely to show ingroup favoritism (Crocker, Thompson, McGraw, & Ingerman, 1987), automatically stereotype others (Fein & Spencer, 1997; Spencer & Fein, 1994; Spencer, Fein, Wolfe, Fong, & Dunn, 1998), and perceive and recall members of their own group as possessing more favorable qualities, traits, and abilities than members of other groups (Brewer & Brown, 1998).

The pursuit of self-esteem via derogation of outgroup members has high costs for targets of prejudice. For example, African Americans who experience prejudice and discrimination are likely to have poorer mental and physical health outcomes that are often associated with higher mortality rates among this population (Jackson et al., 1996; LaVeist, Sellers, & Neighbors, 2001; Neighbors, Jackson, Broman, & Thompson, 1996). Furthermore, targets of prejudice and derogation are likely to pursue their own self-esteem by questioning their identity and self-worth (Crocker, Major, & Steele, 1998; Cross & Fhagen-Smith, 2001; Jones, 1986). For example, African American students who are rejected by white students may become preoccupied with attempting to discern whether they deserved the rejection personally or whether it could be attributed to the other person's prejudices (Crocker, Voelkl, Testa, & Major, 1991; Major & Crocker, 1993). In sum, when threatened, people try to protect and restore their self-esteem by derogating others, which can impose costs on the targets of prejudice and also create ripple effects by triggering others' self-esteem concerns.

Overall, this research shows how the everyday pursuit of self-esteem, triggered by threats to the self in domains on which self-worth is staked, leads to attempts to maintain, protect, and enhance self-esteem at the expense of others. Although some of these efforts may seem innocuous—what, after all, is so bad about restoring one's sense of self-worth after failing a test by focusing on others who did worse?—they all have the consequence of creating distance, feeding competition, and undermining a sense of common humanity. Even the seemingly innocuous strategy of comparing oneself to worse-off others to restore a sense of well-being can have the unintended effect of diminishing the humanity of the downward comparison target, making it easier to commit acts of harm or violence against them.

AGGRESSION, VIOLENCE, AND THE PURSUIT OF SELF-ESTEEM

Aggression and violence are more extreme and dramatic examples of the harm and destruction that can result from the pursuit of self-esteem (Baumeister, Smart, & Boden, 1996). Perceived threats to the ego produce negative affect (e.g., anger, frustration, shame, humiliation), which, in turn, can interfere with emotional regulation by increasing the propensity to react aggressively when confronted with negative feedback. Anger, hostility, and aggression are positively related, and the emotional dysregulation that accompanies threats to the self has been identified as an important factor in the etiology of aggressive behavior. In particular, some types of aggression (e.g., reactive, hostile aggression) may be due partly to an inability to control angry emotions. Other forms of aggression (e.g., proactive, instrumental aggression) seem related to an inability to feel empathy for others and a lack of anxiety about the use of aggression. Because the pursuit of self-esteem is related to both emotional and behavioral dysregulation, as well as to preoccupation with the self and lower empathy, both types of aggression may increase when people pursue self-esteem (Baumeister, Bushman, & Campbell, 2000; Bushman & Baumeister, 1998; Park & Crocker, 2002). Thus, although increased aggression and hostility may make people feel better following ego threat (Bushman, Baumeister, & Phillips, 2001), this enhanced sense of self often occurs at the expense of innocent third parties (Bushman & Baumeister, 1998).

Emotional dysregulation is linked to the occurrence of violence and aggression in both laboratory and real-world situations (Baumeister et al., 1993). Research has shown, however, that although people engage in aggressive behaviors to regulate negative affect and to feel better about themselves, aggressive behaviors do not actually discharge or eliminate angry or hostile feelings; ironically, people report a *more intense* negative mood (Bushman et al., 2001).

The domains in which people stake their self-worth and the ways in which they pursue self-esteem may affect the frequency of aggressive behavior, independent of emotional regulation. People whose self-worth is based on internal sources, such as religious beliefs or virtue, may inhibit hostile, harmful, or aggressive behavior even when they experience emotional dysregulation; the translation of anger into physical violence depends on normative beliefs and social mores that condone the use of violence as a viable response (Berkowitz, 1993). However, people who stake their self-worth on these internal sources may respond to threat with more socially acceptable forms of indirect aggression. Consistent with this view, internal contingencies of self-worth are associated with lower self-reported physical aggression but not lower verbal aggression, hostility, or anger (after controlling for level of self-esteem and socially desirable responding; Crocker, Sommers, & Luhtanen, in press). Externally based contingencies of self-worth, on the other hand, are strongly associated with hostility (Crocker et al., in press).

Domestic Violence

One extremely harmful form of aggression that appears to result, in part, from the pursuit of self-esteem, is domestic violence. Research has documented the self-perpetuating nature of domestic violence. Many abusive men either have witnessed violence in their family of origin or been the victim of child abuse and experienced parental rejection (Mischel & Shoda, 1995); domestic violence is highly correlated with child abuse (Osofsky, 1999).

Infants who are maltreated either through exposure to abuse or as a direct victim of abuse are more likely to experience insecure relationships with caregivers (Kaufman & Henrich, 2000). As a result of their unmet needs, attachment relationships are compromised, leaving these individuals with a pattern of sensitivity to rejection, insecure attachment styles, and unsatisfying relationships (Feldman & Downey, 1994). Insecure attachment is also implicated in tendencies to inhibit or exaggerate negative emotions and other emotional regulation problems (Kaufman & Henrich, 2000). Unmet attachment needs, anxiety, and rejection fears are thus hypothesized to be important factors in the occurrence of domestic violence (Downey, Feldman, & Ayduk, 2000; Mischel & Shoda, 1995), which is used as a coping strategy to feel better following felt rejection (Bushman et al., 2001). Abusive men seek attention from their spouse through an interaction pattern of low-level conflict that, at times, erupts into violence (Gottman, Jacobson, Rushe, & Shortt, 1995), or they use aggression to maintain the spouse's closeness and control her behavior. In other words, it seems that abusive men use defensive strategies to cope with an excessive need for reassurance and approval.

Domestic violence is clearly linked to behavioral and emotional dysregulation and the inability to cope with emotion in the context of interpersonal relationships with significant others. At the physiological level, behavioral regulation patterns indicate that most abusive men experience heart rate increases and other signs of emotional arousal during conflict-laden discussions. Abusive men who experience increased physiological arousal may also rely more on a self-regulatory style that is impulsive, based on emotions, fears, and passions (Metcalfe & Mischel, 1999) that undermine self-control. A smaller subgroup of abusive men who are the most violent display decreased physiological arousal under conditions of low-level conflict with a significant other. This group of men is also more likely to use violence against others as well as their domestic partner (Gottman et al., 1995).

Domestic violence causes tremendous harm to the victim, the perpetrator, and others. Women in abusive relationships report lower levels of self-esteem, increased depression, and high levels of post-traumatic stress disorder (PTSD). Research suggests that domestic violence and its psychological consequences can compromise women's abilities to parent adequately (Levendosky & Graham-Bermann, 2000), and children who witness domestic violence show increased levels of anxiety and depression (Graham-Berman, 1996) and signs of PTSD (Graham-Bermann, 1998). Children who witness abuse in the home are also more aggressive themselves, suggesting that domestic violence contributes to cross-generational violence (McCloskey, Figueredo, & Koss, 1995). Indeed, parental reports of childhood aggression and adulthood aggression significantly predict aggression among their children (Huesmann et al., 2002).

We do not mean to suggest that all domestic violence and its consequences are caused by the pursuit of self-esteem. Yet it seems clear that early experiences resulting in unmet attachment needs and sensitivity to rejection create adults whose sense of self-worth is based on others' approval and who simultaneously expect and react to perceived rejection with anger, aggression, and violence.

Intergroup Violence

Domestic violence is a form of interpersonal violence that has high social costs. Similarly, intergroup violence that occurs within and between racial, ethnic, and national groups also has grave consequences. Many aggressive subcultures exist within our society, such as delinquent groups (Tedeschi & Felson, 1994). One subculture of violence in American society is that of criminal gangs. Typically, gangs have strict rules of conduct and rigid standards that guide gang membership. Gang-related violence is noteworthy because of its reliance on social influence, which guarantees that gang members meet group standards of behavior (Berkowitz, 1993). Violent behavior and criminal activity may be used to prove masculinity; youth who are susceptible to influence from gangs may be unusually high in the need to gain approval from others. Adolescents who join gangs may then use gang membership as a defensive strategy to protect against potential ego threats that are present in their dangerous neighborhoods, and gang membership may increase self-esteem and serve other self-protective functions (Baumeister et al., 1996).

The crime and violence that accompany some types of gang membership have costs in the form of crime enforcement and the psychological repercussions to others living in unsafe neighborhoods (Raviv et al., 2002; Raviv, Raviv, Shimoni, Fox, & Leavitt, 1999). Neighborhood disorder and exposure to violence have been shown to predict adolescents' actual feeling of irritability and dejection in response to a potentially threatening or provocative situation (Ewart & Suchday, 2002). Children living in areas with moderate crime levels also show increased levels of behavioral problems when compared to children living in areas with less crime (Plybon & Kliewer, 2001).

INDIVIDUAL DIFFERENCES IN THE PURSUIT OF SELF-ESTEEM

We have explored both run-of-the-mill strategies for pursuing self-esteem in response to threats in domains of contingency—strategies that, in the end, diminish or harm others—and more extreme forms of aggression and violence, such as domestic and gang violence, that can result from the pursuit of self-esteem. It is important to note that, although domestic violence and gang violence are relatively rare, the everyday strategies we reviewed are remarkably robust and frequently used and have been demonstrated in hundreds of studies. No one should presume that he or she is immune from using these strategies to restore a sense of self-worth when threatened in a domain on which self-worth is staked. At the same time, as the research on domestic violence demonstrates, people differ in the frequency with which they are caught in the pursuit of self-esteem and in the particular strategies they favor, and consequently, the harm their pursuit of self-esteem inflicts on others.

Fragile Egotism

In general, people are more likely to pursue self-esteem if their self-esteem is fragile. Fragile self-esteem is unstable or contingent and therefore easily threatened by criticism, rejection, or other negative events. Consequently, the sense of self needs to be defended and bolstered more often (Baumeister et al., 1996; Deci & Ryan, 1995; Kernis, in press). People whose sense of self-worth depends on external validation, achievements, or accomplishments are more easily and frequently captured by the question of whether they are wonderful or worthless and, hence, more susceptible to the pursuit of self-esteem. In fact, there appear to be two general styles of pursuing self-esteem: one more characteristic of people with self-esteem that is high and fragile, and one more characteristic of people with self-esteem that is low and fragile.

High, Unstable Self-Esteem

Self-esteem that is both high and fragile conveys a sense of superiority— the sense of being wonderful and worthy *because* one is better than others in domains on which self-worth is staked. Yet this type of high self-esteem is vulnerable because it depends on one's accomplishments; therefore, a failure, setback, or criticism has the potential to puncture or deflate one's self-worth. Along these lines, research has shown that praise or acceptance for one's accomplishments leads to defensiveness, whereas praise or acceptance of one's intrinsic qualities does not (Schimel, Arndt, Pyszczynski, & Greenberg, 2001). To sustain the feeling of being wonderful and worthy and avoid feelings of worthlessness, people with high and fragile self-esteem, who generally believe they possess positive qualities and competencies (Blaine & Crocker, 1993), respond to ego threat with defensiveness, making excuses, blaming others (Kernis, Cornell, Sun, Berry, & Harlow, 1993; Kernis, Grannemann, & Barclay, 1989; Kernis & Waschull, 1995; Vohs & Heatherton, 2001), and by displaying antagonism, anger, hostility, and aggression, more than do people with high and stable self-esteem or people with low self-esteem (Kernis et al., 1989).

The consequences of fragile egotism are reflected in several areas of research, most notably in the work on high, unstable self-esteem (Kernis, Paradise, Whitaker, Wheatman, & Goldman, 2000; Kernis & Waschull,

1995; Kernis et al., 1998); narcissism (Morf, 1994; Morf & Rhodewalt, 1993, 2001; Rhodewalt & Morf, 1995); and the combination of high and contingent self-worth (Luhtanen & Crocker, 2002; Park & Crocker, 2002). Although there are unique features of each of these forms of fragile egotism, they all share the factor of positive self-views that are vulnerable to threat.

Work by Kernis and Waschull (1995) suggests that people with high, unstable self-esteem are highly ego-involved in events and, hence, easily triggered into pursuing self-esteem. Kernis distinguishes between high, unstable self-esteem—that is, fragile feelings of self-worth that fluctuate in response to positive and negative events—and high, stable self-esteem that is less volatile and less susceptible to the ups and downs in state self-esteem and mood associated with successes and failures. People with high but unstable self-esteem are more defensive and more likely to express anger, hostility, and aggression toward others when confronted with an ego threat (Baumeister et al., 1996; Kernis et al., 1989). In sum, when self-esteem is high and unstable, people are easily triggered into pursuing self-esteem, often at the expense of others' well-being.

Narcissism

Narcissists have *exaggeratedly* positive or inflated, yet fragile, self-views (Raskin & Terry, 1988). Studies suggest that narcissists' unstable self-esteem stems from their extremely positive self-views, coupled with extreme fears of being found worthless (Morf & Rhodewalt, 2001; Rhodewalt, Madrian, & Cheney, 1998; Rhodewalt & Morf, 1995). When their fragile self-esteem is threatened, narcissists may easily be triggered into protecting, maintaining, and enhancing their self-esteem, often at the expense of others. In order to sustain their exaggeratedly positive self-views, narcissists constantly seek external self-validation in the form of attention and admiration from others (Rhodewalt & Morf, 1995). Consequently, their self-views can be easily challenged by external agents or events. Consistent with this view, narcissists' self-esteem fluctuates from day to day in response to whether their social interactions are positive or negative (Rhodewalt et al., 1998).

When threatened, narcissists respond with intensely negative emotions: "They live on an interpersonal stage with exhibitionistic behavior and demands for attention and admiration but respond to threats to self-esteem with feelings of rage, defiance, shame, and humiliation" (Morf & Rhodewalt, 2001, p. 4). Furthermore, narcissists respond to ego threat with aggression against others (Baumeister et al., 2000; Bushman & Baumeister, 1998). For example, Bushman and Baumeister (1998) conducted a study in which participants had the opportunity to aggress against someone who had insulted them, someone who had praised them, or against a neutral third person. They found that the combination of high self-esteem, narcissism, and insult resulted in the highest levels of aggression; high levels of narcissism predicted increased aggression, especially in instances when negative feedback was received (Bushman & Baumeister, 1998). Building on this research, Kirkpatrick and colleagues identified narcissism as a significant, positive predictor of aggression when these subjects were placed in conditions of ego threat (Kirkpatrick, Waugh, Valencia, & Webster, 2002).

Narcissistic tendencies are also linked to bullying behavior. Salmivalli (2001) reports that bullying behavior is most typical of adolescent boys who have a "defensive" style of self-esteem, defined as needing to be the center of attention, thinking too highly of oneself, and demonstrating inability in facing criticism. Indeed, the construct proposed by Salmivalli seems to closely mirror the model of narcissism used in previous studies by Bushman and Baumeister (1998), thus providing further evidence for a connection between narcissistic personality traits and aggressive behavior.

In sum, research suggests that narcissists tend to focus more on the self and on protecting their fragile self-esteem than on relating to others or enhancing the quality of their relationships with others. When narcissists experience an ego threat, they are likely to react with anger, hostility, and aggression toward others. This reaction may temporarily relieve anxiety but ultimately deter them from building close, mutually caring and supportive relationships with others. Even in the absence of ego threat, narcissists tend to focus more on self-enhancement than on their relationships. For example, although both narcissists and high self-esteem people see themselves as better than average on agential traits such as intellectual ability, narcissists do not believe that they are better than average on communal traits such as agreeableness or morality (Campbell, Rudich, & Sedikedes, 2002). Unlike high self-esteem individuals, narcissists rate themselves as superior to their romantic partners. Furthermore, narcissists tend to endorse more external contingencies of self-worth, such as appearance and outdoing others in competition (Crocker, Luhtanen, Cooper, & Bouvrette, in press), consistent with their insatiable need for external validation and admiration from others (Morf, 1994; Morf & Rhodewalt, 1993, 2001).

High and Contingent Self-Esteem

Another form of fragile egotism can be found among people who have high self-esteem that is highly contingent. High self-esteem people react to ego threat in ways that enhance their self-esteem, such as dismissing the validity of a test on which they perform poorly (Schlenker, Weigold, & Hallam, 1990), seeking out feedback about their abilities and competencies, and becoming more independent in their self-views (Vohs & Heatherton, 2001). These responses to ego threats have consequences for how high versus low self-esteem people interact with others. For example, high self-esteem people who received failure feedback on a test of intellectual ability were rated as more antagonistic (i.e., arrogant, fake, uncooperative, rude, and unfriendly) and were liked less by their interaction partners than low self-esteem people who received failure feedback or high self-esteem people who were not threatened (Heatherton & Vohs, 2000). Thus, when high self-esteem people are threatened, they respond to ego threats in ways that compromise their ability to form and maintain close, mutually caring, supportive relationships with others. In contrast, low self-esteem people seek self-esteem via a different route: by focusing more on their relationships and striving to be interpersonally responsive and likable (Park & Crocker, 2003; Vohs & Heatherton, 2001).

This tendency for high self-esteem people to become antagonistic and unlikable, however, appears to be true only when they are threatened in domains of contingency (Park & Crocker, 2002). In a study described previously, Park and Crocker (2003) showed that high self-esteem students whose self-worth was staked on their academic performance responded to an academic threat by becoming defensive and preoccupied with self-evaluative thoughts. In an interaction with other students who were describing a personal problem, high self-esteem and academically contingent students who had failed a GRE (Graduate Record Exam) rated themselves as preoccupied, unsupportive, and unempathic; the students with the problems also rated these threatened students as preoccupied, unsupportive, and unempathic, and did not much like them or want to interact with or tell another problem to them. In sum, the form of fragile egotism seen in people whose self-worth is high but contingent is associated with self-centered thoughts, defensiveness, and lowered capability for providing emotional support to others.

Low and Fragile Self-Esteem

People with low self-esteem—those with less positive views of themselves—tend to self-enhance indirectly by focusing on their social qualities and relationships, seeking interpersonal feedback, and becoming more interdependent in their self-construals (Baumeister et al., 1989; Brown et al., 1988; Schuetz & Tice, 1997; Tice, 1991; Vohs & Heatherton, 2001). Low self-esteem is associated with external and interpersonal contingencies of self-worth; people with low and fragile self-esteem tend to base their self-esteem on others' approval and their physical appearance (Crocker, Luhtanen, et al., 2002). Because they are unsure of their abilities, using the strategy of directly defending against threat by blaming others or discrediting the threat is more difficult for them (Blaine & Crocker, 1993). Instead, people with fragile, low self-esteem attempt to bolster their self-esteem by

seeking reassurance and approval from others. Like high self-esteem people, their pursuit of self-esteem involves the use of others to validate their
self-worth, but rather than derogating others and becoming hostile or antagonistic, people with fragile, low self-esteem become dependent and
needy of approval and reassurance. Yet, because they doubt themselves,
they rarely feel truly reassured that others care for them or value them in
spite of their shortcomings. Although this strategy for pursuing self-esteem
may appear to be less harmful and destructive than the hostility of high,
unstable self-esteem people, several lines of research indicate that it wreaks
its own form of harm and destruction, particularly self-esteem that is contingent on approval and regard from others. In particular, research on low
self-esteem, insecure attachment styles, and rejection sensitivity all share
the common theme of low and interpersonally contingent, fragile self-
esteem.

As noted, people with low self-esteem tend to base their self-esteem on
others' approval and regard or on superficial aspects of the self, such as
appearance, that require validation from others. Low self-esteem is also
strongly associated with self-esteem instability (Kernis et al., 1989). Thus,
it seems likely that most people with low self-esteem also have fragile self-
esteem. Murray and colleagues explored the interpersonal consequences of
low self-esteem in romantic relationships. In a study of the way that people
interact with their partner following threats to the self (Murray, Holmes,
& Griffin, 2000), they found that people with low self-esteem regulate
perceptions of their partner and the quality of their relationships in a self-
protective manner. Specifically, when low self-esteem people experience
self-doubt, they display less confidence in the quality of their relationship,
perceive less supportiveness in their partner, and distance themselves from
their partner. In contrast, high self-esteem people use their relationship as
a self-affirmation and have increased confidence in their partner following
threat.

People who are either low in self-esteem or depressed tend to repair
self-esteem by seeking reassurance from others (Joiner, 1994; Joiner,
Metalsky, Katz, & Beach, 1999). Research by Joiner and colleagues has
shown that seeking reassurance from others makes people feel good about
themselves and decreases their anxiety (Joiner, Alfano, & Metalsky, 1992;
Joiner, Katz, & Lew, 1999; Joiner, Metalsky, Gencoz, & Gencoz, 2001;
Joiner, Metalsky, et al., 1999; Katz, Beach, & Joiner, 1998). For example,
college students who experienced negative life events were more likely to
seek reassurance from others to deal with increases in anxiety and decreases in self-esteem (Joiner et al., 1999). However, seeking reassurance
from others may ultimately backfire because people who are contingent on
others' approval may burden others by putting them in the position of
constantly having to reassure them, which can become mentally and emotionally draining for others and result in rejection (Joiner et al., 1992).

Thus, people who are highly contingent on the approval of others are in the position of constantly taking from others, rather than giving and contributing to the relationship, and ultimately they damage the relationship.

Insecure Attachment Styles

According to attachment theory, people possess working models, or internal representations, of the attachment relationships that they experienced throughout their lives, beginning with the early caretaker–child relationship (Bowlby, 1969, 1973, 1980). People differ in the types of working models they have of themselves and of others (Ainsworth, Blehar, Waters, & Wall, 1978). Insecurely attached people are uncertain about whether others will "be there" for them in times of need, have lower self-esteem, and are more reliant on external validation of self-worth (Bartholomew & Horowitz, 1991; Griffin & Bartholomew, 1994). The preoccupied attachment style (Bartholomew, 1990)—a type of insecure attachment in which people possess a negative model of the self and a positive model of others—is negatively correlated with self-esteem and positively correlated with basing self-worth on appearance and others' approval (Park, Crocker, & Mickelson, in press).

Because people with insecure attachment styles lack a sense of a "secure base," they (1) are more likely to experience shame and fear negative evaluation from others (Mikulincer, 1998; Wagner & Tangney, 1991); (2) are more anxious and hostile than securely attached people (Kobak & Sceery, 1988); and (3) deal with stressful events by mentally ruminating on negative thoughts, memories, and affect, rather than engaging in more active, problem-focused coping strategies (Kobak & Sceery, 1988; Shaver & Hazan, 1993).

These characteristics lead insecurely attached people to experience high levels of emotional distress and act in ways that undermine their relationships with others (Collins, 1996; Kobak & Hazan, 1991). For example, Collins and Feeney (2000) found that whereas securely attached individuals in intimate relationships were more effective support seekers and caregivers in their intimate relationships, insecurely attached individuals were less effective in seeking support and in caring for their partners. Indeed, people with a preoccupied attachment style crave constant reassurance from their partners (Bartholomew, 1990), worrying that their partners will not want to be as close as they would like them to be (Collins & Read, 1990; Feeney & Noller, 1990; Simpson, Rholes, & Nelligan, 1992). In sum, people with insecure, and especially preoccupied, attachment styles pursue self-esteem by seeking validation from others, yet they are deficient in their ability to provide support to others.

Rejection Sensitivity

Rejection sensitivity is associated with low self-esteem, neuroticism, and insecure attachment styles (Downey & Feldman, 1996). People who are high in rejection sensitivity anxiously expect, readily interpret, and overreact to signs of rejection (Downey & Feldman, 1996; Downey et al., 2000; Downey, Freitas, Michaelis, & Khouri, 1998; Feldman & Downey, 1994). Even when the other person's behavior is ambiguous, people high in rejection sensitivity are more likely to expect and perceive intentional rejection than people low in rejection sensitivity (Downey & Feldman, 1996). Heightened concerns about rejection, in turn, can have deleterious consequences for interpersonal relationships. For example, people who are highly rejection sensitive in romantic relationships are more likely to perceive their partner's insensitive behavior as intentional rejection and are more insecure and unhappy about their relationships than less rejection-sensitive people (Downey & Feldman, 1996).

Why are highly rejection-sensitive people dissatisfied with their relationships? Downey and colleagues (2000) found that highly rejection-sensitive people react in destructive ways that undermine the relationship when faced with the threat of real or perceived rejection. Among highly rejection-sensitive women, anticipated rejection leads to increased hostility and decreased supportiveness toward their partners; among highly rejection-sensitive men, the possibility of rejection leads to increased jealousy, possessiveness, and a desire to control their partners (Downey et al., 2000). These maladaptive responses to rejection may contribute to a self-fulfilling prophecy that gradually undermines the quality of a relationship. Not surprisingly, research has shown that highly rejection-sensitive people are more likely to be in relationships that terminate, compared to people who are low in rejection sensitivity (Downey et al., 1998). Thus, highly rejection-sensitive people's expectation of, interpretation of, and reaction to real or perceived rejection ultimately leads them to create situations in which they experience exactly what they do not want.

In sum, research suggests that people with high, fragile self-esteem pursue self-esteem through different strategies than do people with low, fragile self-esteem. When threatened, people with high, fragile self-esteem respond by directly defending against the threat and become angry, hostile, antagonistic—and, consequently, less likable. People with low, fragile self-esteem tend to seek reassurance from others that they are still loveable or valued. Initially, at least with strangers, they become more likeable (Heatherton & Vohs, 2000). Yet their need for reassurance seems insatiable, and they readily perceive rejection and lack of approval from others, to which they respond by distancing themselves or expressing anger, ultimately destroying their relationships with this corrosive pattern.

The pursuit of self-esteem is not restricted to people who feel worthless or to those who have high self-esteem; both high and low self-esteem can be associated with the pursuit of self-esteem, although the strategies each group uses to maintain and protect self-esteem in the face of threats differs. Beyond mere level of self-esteem, research suggests that the pursuit of self-esteem is linked to fragile self-worth, unstable and contingent self-esteem, and especially self-esteem that requires external validation.

CONCLUDING THOUGHTS

The notions that the pursuit of self-esteem is a fundamental need and that seeking self-esteem is inherently good are central assumptions in our Western, individualistic culture. Protecting and enhancing self-esteem is viewed as a primary goal, directing much social behavior (Baumeister et al., 1993). Yet, as we have emphasized throughout, the pursuit of self-esteem can cause harm and destruction. Others suffer when our ability to relate to them is compromised by the pursuit of self-esteem in the face of real or perceived ego threat. Events that are perceived as self-threatening initiate coping strategies aimed at repairing the self by distancing self from others, making downward comparisons, preoccupation with the self, expressing less empathy and supportiveness toward others' problems, prejudice toward and derogation of outgroups, antagonism, anger, hostility, and blame, and in the extreme, violence and aggression toward others. We argue that these strategies, although they temporarily relieve anxiety and negative affect, are ultimately counterproductive. They do not fulfill the fundamental human need for relatedness—for close, mutually caring and supportive relationships with others (Deci & Ryan, 2000). Instead, they create distance, competition, and lack of safety for others. When people are invested in protecting, maintaining, and enhancing self-worth, they ultimately focus on themselves at the expense of others. Over time, the costs to others accumulate, resulting in conflict, aggression, and violence toward others. Although the harm is easier to see when we examine more extreme and unusual strategies for pursuing self-esteem, such as domestic and gang violence, it is just as real for the everyday strategies we all use to protect our self-esteem from threat. The everyday strategies, such as making downward comparison or derogating others, may, in fact, be more pernicious, precisely because they are so frequent and the harm so subtle.

Can the Pursuit of Self-Esteem Lead to Good Instead of Evil?

In this chapter we have focused on the harmful ways people pursue self-esteem, from everyday, run-of-the-mill self-protective strategies, such as making downward comparisons, to more extreme and devastating behaviors, such as domestic and gang violence. But does the pursuit of self-esteem *always* lead to these harmful and destructive consequences? Are people just as likely to do good, to help or benefit others, in the pursuit of self-esteem?

Although it is not our focus here, we certainly agree that many good works, from charitable contributions to helping behaviors, are done for the sake of self-esteem (Pyszczynski, Greenberg, & Goldenberg, 2003). Although space constraints preclude an extensive discussion of these findings, our research consistently supports the conclusion that basing self-esteem on internal sources, especially being a virtuous person, is related to less destructive and more constructive behavior (Crocker, Luhtanen, Cooper, & Bouvrette, in press; Crocker et al., 2003). College students whose self-esteem is based on being virtuous, for example, spend more time in volunteer activities, get higher grades, and drink less alcohol in their freshman year of college than students who base their self-worth on external contingencies, such as their appearance (Crocker & Luhtanen, 2003; Crocker, Luhtanen, et al., 2002; Luhtanen & Crocker, 2002).

Yet, we suspect that even when people pursue self-esteem by being virtuous, subtle costs and harm to others may result. When good works and noble deeds are done for the sake of self-esteem, the focus is on the self, not on whether the good deed is actually helpful to, or appreciated by, the other. Thus, good deeds done for the sake of self-esteem may create a sense of superiority and distance, with the helper feeling superior to the beneficiary. For example, consider a person who bakes cookies and delivers them daily to the old and infirm in her town; although this is a good deed, it is not always appreciated. She delivers cookies, whether they are wanted or not, in order to feel morally virtuous, not because this act will truly help others in need. Those who receive unwanted deliveries of cookies may feel patronized and resent the clear expectation that they express their "gratitude" to boost the self-esteem of the do-gooder. Indeed, research shows that receiving help can sometimes be harmful to the recipient (Nadler & Fisher, 1986; Nadler, Fisher, & Streufert, 1976; Schneider, Major, Luhtanen, & Crocker, 1996). We suspect that such harm is most likely to occur when help is offered to raise the self-esteem of the help-giver by "proving" his or her moral virtue and superiority.

Responsibility and Choice

Despite our account of harm and destruction—forms of evil that result from the pursuit of self-esteem—we do not consider people who cause harm to others in the pursuit of self-esteem to be evil in the sense of wicked; we do not think that people typically intend to hurt others when they engage in downward comparisons, derogation of others, or self-distancing behaviors. Except in the extreme case of aggression and violence, the harm that is done to others is often subtle and difficult to see, especially if one is not looking for it. In our view, the pursuit of self-esteem, although related to early attachment experiences and dispositional qualities such as narcissism and rejection sensitivity, is typically triggered by situations—specifically, threats to the self in domains in which self-worth has been staked.

At the same time, we do not believe that the perpetrators of these acts are simply innocent victims of their need for self-esteem. In contrast to many other researchers, we do not consider self-esteem to be a fundamental human need. Instead, we propose that people have a choice, at every moment, whether to take the action that makes them *feel* good about themselves in the short term, or the action that will *be* good in the long run for both others and the self. Consequently, our inclination is to consider people responsible for the harm they do to others in the pursuit of self-esteem. One of the goals of our research is to illuminate the costs of pursuing self-esteem and help people understand those costs as well as the real choices available to them. At each moment, we have a choice whether to engage in behaviors that protect and maintain our self-esteem (at the expense of others) or to shift to goals that include others, as well as the self; often, these are goals of building, giving, contributing, or creating something larger than the self (Crocker, 2002; Crocker & Park, in press). In our view, goals that include others are not only better for others as well as the self, but they are also more likely to create what we really want in our lives—mutually supportive connections with others, openness to learning, and a feeling of being the agent of our lives.

ACKNOWLEDGMENTS

All authors contributed equally to this chapter; order of authorship was determined alphabetically. The research reported in this chapter was supported by National Institute of Mental Health Grant Nos. R01 MH58869-01 and K02 MH01747-01. We are grateful to Charles Behling for his helpful comments on an earlier draft of this chapter, and to Noah Nuer, Carole Levy, and the staff of Learning as Leadership, Inc., for inspiring our work on the costs of pursuing self-esteem.

REFERENCES

Ainsworth, M. D. S., Blehar, M. C., Waters, E., & Wall, S. (1978). *Patterns of attachment: A psychological study of the Strange Situation.* Hillsdale, NJ: Erlbaum.

Allport, G. W. (1955). *Becoming.* New Haven, CT: Yale University Press.

Aspinwall, L. G., & Taylor, S. E. (1993). Effects of social comparison direction, threat, and self-esteem on affect, self-evaluation, and expected success. *Journal of Personality and Social Psychology, 64,* 708–722.

Bartholomew, K. (1990). Avoidance of intimacy: An attachment perspective. *Journal of Social and Personal Relationships, 7,* 147–178.

Bartholomew, K., & Horowitz, L. M. (1991). Attachment styles among young adults: A test of a four-category model. *Journal of Personality and Social Psychology, 61,* 226–244.

Baumeister, R. F. (1997). Esteem threat, self-regulatory breakdown, and emotional distress as factors in self-defeating behavior. *Review of General Psychology, 1,* 145–174.

Baumeister, R. F. (1998). The self. In D. T. Gilbert, S. T. Fiske, & G. Lindzey (Eds.), *Handbook of social psychology* (4th ed., Vol. 2, pp. 680–740). New York: McGraw-Hill.

Baumeister, R. F. (1999). Low self-esteem does not cause aggression. *APA Monitor, 30*(No. 1 January), 7.

Baumeister, R. F., Bushman, B. J., & Campbell, W. K. (2000). Self-esteem, narcissism, and aggression: Does violence result from low self-esteem or from threatened egotism? *Current Directions in Psychological Science, 9,* 141–156.

Baumeister, R. F., Campbell, J. D., Krueger, J. I., & Vohs, K. D. (2003). Does high self-esteem cause better performance, interpersonal success, happiness, or healthier lifestyles? *Psychological Science in the Public Interest, 4,* 1–44.

Baumeister, R. F., Heatherton, T. F., & Tice, D. M. (1993). When ego threats lead to self-regulation failure: Negative consequences of high self-esteem. *Journal of Personality and Social Psychology, 64,* 141–156.

Baumeister, R. F., Smart, L., & Boden, J. M. (1996). Relation of threatened egotism to violence and aggression: The dark side of high self-esteem. *Psychological Review, 103,* 5–33.

Baumeister, R. F., Tice, D. M., & Hutton, D. G. (1989). Self-presentational motivations and personality differences in self-esteem. *Journal of Personality, 57,* 547–579.

Beauregard, K. S., & Dunning, D. (1998). Turning up the contrast: Self-enhancement motives prompt egocentric contrast effects in social judgments. *Journal of Personality and Social Psychology, 74,* 606–621.

Benson, P. L., Galbraith, J., & Espeland, P. (1998). *What kids need to succeed: Proven, practical ways to raise good kids.* Minneapolis, MN: Free Spirit.

Berkowitz, L. (1993). *Aggression: Its causes, consequences, and control.* New York: McGraw-Hill.

Blaine, B., & Crocker, J. (1993). Self-esteem and self-serving biases in reactions to positive and negative events: An integrative review. In R. F. Baumeister (Ed.), *Self-esteem: The puzzle of low self-regard* (pp. 55–85). Hillsdale, NJ: Erlbaum.

Bowlby, J. (1969). *Attachment and loss: Vol. 1. Attachment.* New York: Basic Books.

Bowlby, J. (1973). *Attachment and loss: Vol. 2. Separation: Anxiety and anger.* New York: Basic Books.

Bowlby, J. (1980). *Attachment and loss: Vol. 3. Loss: Sadness and depression.* New York: Basic Books.

Branden, N. (1994). *The six pillars of self-esteem*. New York: Bantam.

Brewer, M. B., & Brown, R. (1998). Intergroup relations. In D. T. Gilbert, S. T. Fiske, & G. Lindzey (Eds.), *Handbook of social psychology* (4th ed., Vol. 2). Boston: McGraw-Hill.

Brown, J. D., Collins, R. L., & Schmidt, G. W. (1988). Self-esteem and direct versus indirect forms of self-enhancement. *Journal of Personality and Social Psychology, 55,* 445–453.

Bushman, B. J., & Baumeister, R. F. (1998). Threatened egotism, narcissism, self-esteem, and direct and displaced aggression: Does self-love or self-hate lead to violence? *Journal of Personality and Social Psychology, 75,* 219–229.

Bushman, B. J., Baumeister, R. F., & Phillips, C. M. (2001). Do people aggress to improve their mood? Catharsis beliefs, affect regulation opportunity, and aggressive responding. *Journal of Personality and Social Psychology, 81,* 17–32.

Campbell, W. K., Rudich, E. A., & Sedikedes, C. (2002). Narcissism, self-esteem, and the positivity of self-views: Two portraits of self-love. *Personality and Social Psychology Bulletin, 28,* 358–368.

Collins, N. L. (1996). Working models of attachment: Implications for explanation, emotion, and behavior. *Journal of Personality and Social Psychology, 71,* 810–832.

Collins, N. L., & Feeney, B. (2000). A safe haven: An attachment theory perspective on support seeking and care giving in close relationships. *Journal of Personality and Social Psychology, 78,* 1053–1073.

Collins, N. L., & Read, S. J. (1990). Adult attachment, working models, and relationship quality in dating couples. *Journal of Personality and Social Psychology, 58,* 644–663.

Cooper, M. L., Agocha, V. B., & Sheldon, M. S. (2000). A motivational perspective on risky behaviors: The role of personality and affect regulatory processes. *Journal of Personality, 68,* 1059–1088.

Cooper, M. L., Frone, M. R., Russell, M., & Mudar, P. (1995). Drinking to regulate positive and negative emotions: A motivational model of alcohol use. *Journal of Personality and Social Psychology, 69,* 990–1005.

Cooper, M. L., Shapiro, C. M., & Powers, A. M. (1998). Motivations for sex and risky sexual behavior among adolescents and young adults: A functional perspective. *Journal of Personality and Social Psychology, 75,* 1528–1558.

Crocker, J. (1993). Memory for information about others: Effects of self-esteem and performance feedback. *Journal of Research in Personality, 27,* 35–48.

Crocker, J. (2002). The costs of seeking self-esteem. *Journal of Social Issues, 58,* 597–615.

Crocker, J., Karpinski, A., Quinn, D. M., & Chase, S. (in press). When grades determine self-worth: Consequences of contingent self-worth for male and female engineering and psychology majors. *Journal of Personality and Social Psychology.*

Crocker, J., & Luhtanen, R. K. (2003). Level of self-esteem and contingencies of self-worth: Unique effects on academic, social, and financial problems in college freshmen. *Personality and Social Psychology Bulletin, 29,* 701–712.

Crocker, J., Luhtanen, R., Cooper, M. L., & Bouvrette, S. A. (in press). Contingencies of self-worth in college students: Measurement and theory. *Journal of Personality and Social Psychology.*

Crocker, J., Major, B., & Steele, C. M. (1998). Social stigma. In D. Gilbert, S. T. Fiske, & G. Lindzey (Eds.), *Handbook of social psychology* (4th ed., Vol. 2, pp. 504–553). New York: McGraw-Hill.

Crocker, J., & Park, L. E. (in press). The costly pursuit of self-esteem. *Psychological Bulletin.*

Crocker, J., & Schwartz, I. (1985). Prejudice and ingroup favoritism in a minimal intergroup situation: Effects of self-esteem. *Personality and Social Psychology Bulletin, 11,* 379–386.

Crocker, J., Sommers, S. R., & Luhtanen, R. K. (2002). Hopes dashed and dreams fulfilled: Contingencies of self-worth and admissions to graduate school. *Personality and Social Psychology Bulletin, 28,* 1275–1286.

Crocker, J., Sommers, S. R., & Luhtanen, R. K. (in press). Contingencies of self-worth: Progress and prospects. *European Review of Social Psychology.*

Crocker, J., Thompson, L., McGraw, K., & Ingerman, C. (1987). Downward comparison, prejudice, and evaluation of others: Effects of self-esteem and threat. *Journal of Personality and Social Psychology, 52,* 907–916.

Crocker, J., Voelkl, K., Testa, M., & Major, B. M. (1991). Social stigma: Affective consequences of attributional ambiguity. *Journal of Personality and Social Psychology, 60,* 218–228.

Crocker, J., & Wolfe, C. T. (2001). Contingencies of self-worth. *Psychological Review, 108,* 593–623.

Cross, W. J., & Fhagen-Smith, P. (2001). Patterns of African-American identity development: A life-span perspective. In C. L. Wijeyesinghe & B. W. I. Jackson (Eds.), *New perspectives on racial identity development* (pp. 243–270). New York: New York University Press.

Dawes, R. M. (1994). *House of cards: Psychology and psychotherapy built on myth.* New York: Free Press.

Deci, E. L., & Ryan, R. M. (1995). Human autonomy: The basis for true self-esteem. In M. H. Kernis (Ed.), *Efficacy, agency, and self-esteem* (pp. 31–49). New York: Plenum Press.

Deci, E. L., & Ryan, R. M. (2000). The "what" and "why" of goal pursuits: Human needs and the self-determination of behavior. *Psychological Inquiry, 11,* 227–268.

Downey, G., & Feldman, S. (1996). Implications of rejection sensitivity for intimate relationships. *Journal of Personality and Social Psychology, 70,* 1327–1343.

Downey, G., Feldman, S., & Ayduk, O. (2000). Rejection sensitivity and male violence in romantic relationships. *Personal Relationships, 7,* 45–61.

Downey, G., Freitas, A. L., Michaelis, B., & Khouri, H. (1998). The self-fulfilling prophecy in close relationships: Rejection sensitivity and rejection by romantic partners. *Journal of Personality and Social Psychology, 75,* 545–560.

Epstein, S. (1985). The implications of cognitive–experiential self-theory for research in social psychology and personality. *Journal for the Theory of Social Behavior, 15,* 283–310.

Ewart, C. K., & Suchday, S. (2002). Discovering how urban poverty and violence affect health: Development and validation of a neighborhood stress index. *Health Psychology, 21,* 254–262.

Feeney, J. A., & Noller, P. (1990). Attachment style as a predictor of adult romantic relationships. *Journal of Personality and Social Psychology, 58,* 281–291.

Fein, S., & Spencer, S. J. (1997). Prejudice as self-image maintenance: Affirming the self through derogating others. *Journal of Personality and Social Psychology, 73,* 31–44.

Feldman, S., & Downey, G. (1994). Rejection sensitivity as a mediator of the impact of childhood exposure to family violence on adult attachment behavior. *Development and Psychopathology, 6,* 231–247.

Gibbons, F. X. (1986). Stigma and interpersonal relationships. In S. C. Ainlay, G. Becker, & L. M. Coleman (Eds.), *The dilemma of difference* (pp. 123–156). New York: Plenum Press.

Glennon, W. (1999). *200 ways to raise a girl's self-esteem: An indispensible guide for parents, teachers, and other concerned caregivers.* Berkeley, CA: Conari Press.

Goode, E. (2002, October 1, 2002). Deflating self-esteem's role in society's ills. *The New York Times,* pp. D1–D6.

Gottman, J. M., Jacobson, N. S., Rushe, R. H., & Shortt, J. W. (1995). The relationship between heart rate reactivity, emotionally aggressive behavior, and general violence in batterers. *Journal of Family Psychology, 9,* 227–248.

Graham-Berman, S. A. (1996). Family worries: Assessment of interpersonal anxiety in children from violent and nonviolent families. *Journal of Clinical Child Psychology, 25,* 280–287.

Graham-Bermann, S. A. (1998). The impact of woman abuse on children's social development. In G. W. Holden (Ed.), *Children exposed to marital violence: Theory, research, and applied issues* (pp. 21–54). Washington, DC: American Psychological Association.

Greenberg, J., Pyszczynski, T., & Solomon, S. (1986). The causes and consequences of the need for self-esteem: A terror management theory. In R. F. Baumeister (Ed.), *Public self and private self* (pp. 189–207). New York: Springer-Verlag.

Griffin, D., & Bartholomew, K. (1994). Models of self and other: Fundamental dimensions underlying measures of adult attachment. *Journal of Personality and Social Psychology, 67,* 430–445.

Heatherton, T. F., & Ambady, N. (1993). Self-esteem, self-prediction, and living up to commitments. In R. F. Baumeister (Ed.), *Self-esteem: The puzzle of low self-regard* (pp. 131–141). New York: Plenum Press.

Heatherton, T. F., & Vohs, K. D. (2000). Interpersonal evaluations following threat to self. *Journal of Personality and Social Psychology, 78,* 725–736.

Huesmann, L. R., Dubow, E. F., Eron, L. D., Boxer, P., Slegers, D., & Miller, L. S. (2002, April). *Continuity and discontinuity of aggressive behavior across three generations.* Paper presented at the Society for Life History Research on Psychopathology, New York.

Jackson, J. S., Brown, T. N., Williams, D. R., Torres, M., Sellers, S. L., & Brown, K. (1996). Racism and the physical and mental health status of African-Americans: A thirteen year national panel study. *Ethnicity and Disease, 6,* 132–147.

James, W. (1890). *The principles of psychology* (Vol. 1). Cambridge, MA: Harvard University Press.

Joiner, T. E. (1994). Contagious depression: Existence, specificity to depressed symptoms, and the role of reassurance seeking. *Journal of Personality and Social Psychology, 67,* 287–296.

Joiner, T. E., Alfano, M. S., & Metalsky, G. I. (1992). When depression breeds contempt: Reassurance seeking, self-esteem, and rejection of depressed college students by their roommates. *Journal of Abnormal Psychology, 101,* 165–173.

Joiner, T. E., Katz, J., & Lew, A. (1999). Harbingers of depressotypic reassurance seeking: Negative life events, increased anxiety, and decreased self-esteem. *Personality and Social Psychology Bulletin, 25,* 630–637.

Joiner, T. E., Metalsky, G. I., Gencoz, F., & Gencoz, T. (2001). The relative specificity of excessive reassurance-seeking to depressive symptoms and diagnoses among clinical samples of adults and youth. *Journal of Psychopathology and Behavioral Assessment, 23,* 35–41.

Joiner, T. E., Metalsky, G. I., Katz, J., & Beach, S. R. H. (1999). Depression and excessive reassurance-seeking. *Psychological Inquiry, 10,* 269–278.

Jones, J. M. (1986). Racism: A cultural analysis of the problem. In J. F. David & S. L. Gartner (Eds.), *Prejudice, discrimination, and racism* (pp. 279–314). San Diego, CA: Academic Press.

Katz, J., Beach, S. R. H., & Joiner, T. E. (1998). When does partner devaluation predict emotional distress? Prospective moderating effects of reassurance-seeking and self-esteem. *Personal Relationships, 5,* 409–421.

Kaufman, J., & Henrich, C. (2000). Exposure to violence and early childhood trauma. In C. H. Zeanah (Ed.), *Handbook of infant mental health* (2nd ed., pp. 195–207). New York: Guilford Press.

Kernis, M. H. (in press). Toward a conceptualization of optimal self-esteem. *Psychological Inquiry.*

Kernis, M. H., Cornell, D. P., Sun, C.-R., Berry, A., & Harlow, T. (1993). There's more to self-esteem than whether it is high or low: The importance of stability of self-esteem. *Journal of Personality and Social Psychology, 65,* 1190–1204.

Kernis, M. H., Grannemann, B. D., & Barclay, L. C. (1989). Stability and level of self-esteem as predictors of anger arousal and hostility. *Journal of Personality and Social Psychology, 56,* 1013–1023.

Kernis, M. H., Paradise, A. W., Whitaker, D. J., Wheatman, S. R., & Goldman, B. N. (2000). Master of one's psychological domain? Not likely if one's self-esteem is unstable. *Personality and Social Psychology Bulletin, 26,* 1297–1305.

Kernis, M. H., & Waschull, S. B. (1995). The interactive roles of stability and level of self-esteem: Research and theory. In M. P. Zanna (Ed.), *Advances in experimental social psychology* (Vol. 27, pp. 93–141). San Diego, CA: Academic Press.

Kernis, M. H., Whisenhunt, C. R., Waschull, S. B., Greenier, K. D., Berry, A. J., Herlocker, C. E., & Anderson, C. A. (1998). Multiple facets of self-esteem and their relations to depressive symptoms. *Personality and Social Psychology Bulletin, 24,* 657–668.

Kirkpatrick, L. A., Waugh, C. E., Valencia, A., & Webster, G. D. (2002). The functional domain specificity of self-esteem and the differential prediction of aggression. *Journal of Personality and Social Psychology, 82,* 756–767.

Kobak, R. R., & Hazan, C. (1991). Attachment in marriage: Effects of security and accuracy of working models. *Journal of Personality and Social Psychology, 60,* 861–869.

Kobak, R. R., & Sceery, A. (1988). Attachment in late adolescence: Working models, affect regulation, and representations of self and others. *Child Development, 59,* 135–146.

LaVeist, T. A., Sellers, R., & Neighbors, H. W. (2001). Perceived racism and self and system blame attribution: Consequences for longevity. *Ethnicity and Disease, 11,* 711–721.

Leary, M. R., & Baumeister, R. F. (2000). The nature and function of self-esteem: Sociometer theory. In M. Zanna (Ed.), *Advances in experimental social psychology* (Vol. 32, pp. 1–62). San Diego, CA: Academic Press.

Leary, M. R., & Downs, D. L. (1995). Interpersonal functions of the self-esteem motive: The self-esteem system as sociometer. In M. H. Kernis (Ed.), *Efficacy, agency, and self-esteem* (pp. 123–144). New York: Plenum Press.

Leith, K. P., & Baumeister, R. F. (1996). Why do bad moods increase self-defeating behavior? Emotion, risk-taking, and self-regulation. *Journal of Personality and Social Psychology, 71,* 1250–1267.

Levendosky, A. A., & Graham-Bermann, S. A. (2000). Behavioral observations of parenting in battered women. *Journal of Family Psychology, 14,* 80–94.

Luhtanen, R. K., & Crocker, J. (2002). *Fragile self-esteem and alcohol use in college students.* Unpublished manuscript, University of Michigan, Ann Arbor.

Major, B., & Crocker, J. (1993). Social stigma: The consequences of attributional ambiguity. In D. M. Mackie & D. L. Hamilton (Eds.), *Affect, cognition, and stereotyping: Interactive processes in group perception* (pp. 345–370). New York: Academic Press.

Maslow, A. H. (1968). *Motivation and personality.* New York: Harper & Row.

McCloskey, L. A., Figueredo, A. J., & Koss, M. P. (1995). The effects of systemic family violence on children's mental health. *Child Development, 66,* 1239–1261.

McElherner, L. N., & Lisovskis, M. (1998). *Jumpstarters: Quick classroom activities that develop self-esteem, creativity, and cooperation.* Minneapolis, MN: Free Spirit.

Mecca, A. M., Smelser, N. J., & Vasconcellos, J. (1989). *The social importance of self-esteem.* Berkeley: University of California Press.

Metcalfe, J., & Mischel, W. (1999). A hot/cool system analysis of delay of gratification: Dynamics of willpower. *Psychological Review, 106,* 1–17.

Mikulincer, M. (1998). Adult attachment style and individual differences in functional versus dysfunctional experiences of anger. *Journal of Personality and Social Psychology, 74,* 513–524.

Miller, P. J. (2001, April). *Self-esteem as folk theory: A comparison of ethnographic interviews.* Paper presented at the annual meeting of the Society for Research in Child Development, Minneapolis, MN.

Mischel, W., & Shoda, Y. (1995). A cognitive-affective system theory of personality: Reconceptualizing situations, dispositions, dynamics, and invariance in personality structure. *Psychological Review, 102,* 246–268.

Morf, C. C. (1994). Interpersonal consequences of narcissists' continual effort to maintain and bolster self-esteem. *Dissertation Abstracts International, 55,* 2430B.

Morf, C. C., & Rhodewalt, F. (1993). Narcissism and self-evaluation maintenance: Explorations in object relations. *Personality and Social Psychology Bulletin, 19,* 668–676.

Morf, C. C., & Rhodewalt, F. (2001). Unraveling the paradoxes of narcissism: A dynamic self-regulatory processing model. *Psychological Inquiry, 12,* 177–196.

Morse, S., & Gergen, K. (1970). Social comparison, self-consistency, and the concept of self. *Journal of Personality and Social Psychology, 16,* 148–156.

Muraven, M., Tice, T. M., & Baumeister, R. F. (1998). Self-control as a limited resource: Regulatory depletion patterns. *Journal of Personality and Social Psychology, 74,* 774–789.

Murray, S. L., Holmes, J. G., & Griffin, D. W. (2000). Self-esteem and the quest for felt security: How perceived regard regulates attachment processes. *Journal of Personality and Social Psychology, 78,* 478–498.

Nadler, A., & Fisher, J. D. (1986). The role of threat to self-esteem and perceived control in recipient reaction to help: Theory, development, and empirical validation. In L. Berkowitz (Ed.), *Advances in experimental social psychology* (Vol. 19, pp. 81–121). Orlando, FL: Academic Press.

Nadler, A., Fisher, J. D., & Streufert, S. (1976). When helping hurts: Effects of donor–recipient similarity and recipient self-esteem on reactions to aid. *Journal of Personality, 44,* 392–409.

Neighbors, H. W., Jackson, J. S., Broman, C., & Thompson, E. (1996). Racism and the mental health of African Americans: The role of self and system blame. *Ethnicity and Disease, 6,* 167–175.

Osofsky, J. D. (1999). The impact of violence on children. *Future of Children, 9,* 33–49.

Park, L. E., & Crocker, J. (2003, January). *Thinking of me: Contingencies of self-worth and failure.* Poster session at the annual meeting of the Society for Personality and Social Psychology, Los Angeles.

Park, L. E., & Crocker, J. (2002). *The interpersonal costs of seeking self-esteem.* Unpublished manuscript, University of Michigan, Ann Arbor.

Park, L. E., Crocker, J., & Mickelson, K. (2003). *Attachment styles and contingencies of self-worth.* Manuscript under review.

Pleban, R., & Tesser, A. (1981). The effects of relevance and quality of another's performance on interpersonal closeness. *Social Psychology Quarterly, 44,* 278–285.

Plybon, L. E., & Kliewer, W. (2001). Neighborhood types and externalizing behavior in urban school-age children: Tests of direct, mediated, and moderated effects. *Journal of Child and Family Studies, 10,* 419–437.

Pyszczynski, T., & Greenberg, J. (1987). Self-regulatory perseveration and the depressive self-focusing style: A self-awareness theory of reactive depression. *Psychological Bulletin, 102,* 122–138.

Pyszczynski, T., Greenberg, J., & Goldenberg, J. (2003). Freedom versus fear: On the defense, growth, and expansion of the self. In M. R. Leary & J. P.

Tangney (Eds.), *Handbook of self and identity* (pp. 314–343). New York: Guilford Press.

Pyszczynski, T., Greenberg, J., & Laprelle, J. (1985). Social comparison after success and failure: Biased search for information consistent with a self-serving conclusion. *Journal of Experimental Social Psychology, 21,* 195–211.

Pyszczynski, T., Holt, K., & Greenberg, J. (1987). Depression, self-focused attention, and expectancies for positive and negative future life events for self and others. *Journal of Personality and Social Psychology, 52,* 994–1001.

Raskin, R., & Terry, H. (1988). A principal-components analysis of the Narcissitic Personality Inventory and further evidence of its construct validity. *Journal of Personality and Social Psychology, 54,* 890–902.

Raviv, A., Erel, O., Fox, N. A., Leavitt, L. A., Raviv, A., Dar, I., Shahinfar, A., & Greenbaum, C. W. (2002). Individual measurement of exposure to everyday violence among elementary school children across various settings. *Journal of Community Psychology, 20,* 1–23.

Raviv, A., Raviv, A., Shimoni, H., Fox, N. A., & Leavitt, L. A. (1999). Children's self-report of exposure to violence and its relation to emotional distress. *Journal of Applied Developmental Psychology, 20,* 337–353.

Rhodewalt, F., Madrian, J. C., & Cheney, S. (1998). Narcissism, self-knowledge organization, and emotional reactivity: The effect of daily experiences on self-esteem and affect. *Personality and Social Psychology Bulletin, 24,* 75–87.

Rhodewalt, F., & Morf, C. C. (1995). Self and interpersonal correlates of the Narcissistic Personality Inventory: A review and new findings. *Journal of Research in Personality, 29,* 1–23.

Rogers, C. R. (1961). *On becoming a person.* Boston: Houghton Mifflin.

Rosenberg, M. (1979). *Conceiving the self.* New York: Basic Books.

Salmivalli, C. (2001). Feeling good about oneself, being bad to others? Remarks on self-esteem, hostility, and aggressive behavior. *Aggressive and Violent Behavior, A Review Journal, 6,* 375–393.

Schimel, J., Arndt, J., Pyszczynski, T., & Greenberg, J. (2001). Being accepted for who we are: Evidence that social validation of the intrinsic self reduces general defensiveness. *Journal of Personality and Social Psychology, 80,* 35–52.

Schlenker, B. R., Weigold, M. F., & Hallam, J. R. (1990). Self-serving attributions in social context: Effects of self-esteem and social pressure. *Journal of Personality and Social Psychology, 58,* 855–863.

Schneider, M. E., Major, B., Luhtanen, R., & Crocker, J. (1996). When help hurts: Social stigma and the costs of assumptive help. *Personality and Social Psychology Bulletin, 22,* 201–209.

Schuetz, A., & Tice, D. M. (1997). Associative and competitive indirect self-enhancement in close relationships moderated by trait self-esteem. *European Journal of Social Psychology, 27,* 257–273.

Seligman, M. E. P. (1998). The American way of blame. *APA Monitor, 29,* 4.

Shaver, P. R., & Hazan, C. (1993). Adult romantic attachment: Theory and evidence. In D. Perlman & W. Jones (Eds.), *Advances in personal relationships* (Vol. 4, pp. 29–70). London: Kingsley.

Simpson, J. A., Rholes, W. S., & Nelligan, J. S. (1992). Support seeking and support giving within couples in an anxiety-provoking situation: The role of attachment styles. *Journal of Personality and Social Psychology, 62,* 434–446.

Slater, L. (2002, February 3). The trouble with self-esteem. *The New York Times,* Section 6, pp. 44–47.

Smith, C. A., & Ellsworth, P. C. (1985). Patterns of cognitive appraisal in emotion. *Journal of Personality and Social Psychology, 48,* 813–838.

Solomon, S., Greenberg, J., & Pyszczynski, T. (1991). A terror-management theory of social behavior: The psychological functions of self-esteem and cultural worldviews. In M. P. Zanna (Ed.), *Advances in experimental social psychology* (Vol. 24, pp. 91–159). San Diego, CA: Academic Press.

Spencer, S. J., & Fein, S. (1994). *The effect of self-image threat on stereotyping.* Paper presented at the annual meeting of the Eastern Psychological Association, Providence, RI.

Spencer, S. J., Fein, S., Wolfe, C. T., Fong, C., & Dunn, M. A. (1998). Automatic activation of stereotypes: The role of self-image threat. *Personality and Social Psychology Bulletin, 24,* 1139–1152.

Steele, C. M. (1988). The psychology of self-affirmation: Sustaining the integrity of the self. In L. Berkowitz (Ed.), *Advances in experimental social psychology* (Vol. 21, pp. 261–302). New York: Academic Press.

Tangney, J. P., Wagner, P. E., Hill-Barlow, D., Marschall, D. E., & Gramzow, R. (1996). Relation of shame and guilt to constructive versus destructive responses to anger across the lifespan. *Journal of Personality and Social Psychology, 70,* 797–809.

Taylor, S. E., & Brown, J. D. (1988). Illusion and well-being: A social-psychological perspective on mental health. *Psychological Bulletin, 103,* 193–210.

Tedeschi, J. T., & Felson, R. (1994). *Aggression and coercive actions: A social interactionist perspective.* Washington, DC: American Psychological Association.

Tesser, A. (1988). Toward a self-evaluation maintenance model of social behavior. In L. Berkowitz (Ed.), *Advances in experimental social psychology* (Vol. 21, pp. 181–227). San Diego, CA: Academic Press.

Tesser, A., & Smith, J. (1980). Some effects of friendship and task relevance on helping: You don't always help the one you like. *Journal of Experimental Social Psychology, 16,* 582–590.

Tice, D. M. (1991). Esteem protection or enhancement? Self-handicapping motives and attributions differ by trait self-esteem. *Journal of Personality and Social Psychology, 60,* 711–725.

Tice, D. M., & Bratslavsky, E. (2000). Giving in to feel good: The place of emotion regulation in the context of general self-control. *Psychological Inquiry, 11,* 149–159.

Tice, D. M., Bratslavsky, E., & Baumeister, R. F. (2001). Emotional distress regulation takes precedence over impulse control: If you feel bad, do it! *Journal of Personality and Social Psychology, 80,* 53–67.

Vohs, K. D., & Baumeister, R. F. (2000). Escaping the self consumes regulatory resources: A self-regulatory model of suicide. In T. Joiner & M. D. Rudd (Eds.), *Suicide science: Expanding the boundaries* (pp. 33–41). Norwell, MA: Kluwer.

Vohs, K. D., & Heatherton, T. F. (2001). Self-esteem and threats to self: Implications for self-construals and interpersonal perceptions. *Journal of Personality and Social Psychology, 81,* 1103–1118.

Wagner, P. E., & Tangney, J. (1991). *Affective styles, aspects of the self, and psychological symptoms.* Unpublished manuscript, George Mason University, Fairfax, VA.

Walden, T. A., & Smith, M. C. (1997). Emotion regulation. *Motivation and Emotion, 21,* 7–25.

Weiner, B. (1985). An attributional theory of achievement motivation and emotion. *Psychological Review, 92,* 548–573.

Wills, T. A. (1981). Downward comparison principles in social psychology. *Psychological Bulletin, 90,* 245–271.

Wood, J. V., Giordano-Beech, M., & Ducharme, M. J. (1999). Compensating for failure through social comparison. *Personality and Social Psychology Bulletin, 25,* 1370–1386.

CHAPTER 12

THE MANY FACES OF LIES

BELLA M. DePAULO

It is rarely difficult to interest the American public in the topic of lying. Occasionally, though, the interest becomes obsessive. The talking heads on television start screaming, every newspaper and magazine is stuffed with stories, it is the buzz around the water cooler and the dinner table, and for a while, it seems that no one can get enough of it. One profoundly important instance of this national preoccupation with lying occurred as the Watergate story unfolded and a stunned citizenry learned that a massive campaign of lies, crimes, evasions, and cover-ups could be orchestrated from the highest office in the land. The Watergate scandal may have marked the end of American political innocence, but it did not mark the beginning or the end of lying in public life.

Lying famously reemerged as political spectacle in the fall of 1998, when President Bill Clinton, under increasing suspicion of having had an affair with the young intern Monica Lewinsky, looked into the camera and sternly declared, "I did not have sexual relations with that woman, Miss Lewinsky."

At that time, one of the nightly television programs hosting impassioned discussions of the issues of the day was *Hardball with Chris Matthews*. I sat next to former Connecticut Governor Lowell Weicker as he insisted that "one thing that really has to be thrown out with the rest of the garbage here is people that think that all politicians lie. They do not." Referring to Clinton's response to his accusers, Weicker added, "If we accept what's going on here we'll admit that lying is a normal part of life in this country."

In so proclaiming, former Governor Weicker revealed two fundamental beliefs about lying. The first is that people can be separated into those who lie and those who do not. The second is that lying is abnormal, unacceptable, and wrong. Many ordinary citizens share these beliefs with Governor Weicker. A long line of philosophers and theologians over the centuries has also weighed in with dark views of liars and their lies. A contemporary example is the philosopher Sissela Bok (1978), who proclaimed, "Deceit and violence—these are two forms of deliberate assault on human beings. Both can coerce people into acting against their will" (p. 19).

What was not clear when I first started studying lying as a graduate student in the mid-1970s was whether, from a scientific perspective, either of Weicker's assumptions was true. There were, of course, plenty of writings about lying in the professional literature and the popular press. In addition to philosophers and theologians, anthropologists, sociologists, political scientists, educators, and scholars from many other disciplines also had their say. Within my own field of experimental social psychology, there was a growing stack of published reports on clues to deception and laypersons' obliviousness to many of the lies that other people tell them (reviewed early on by DePaulo, Zuckerman, & Rosenthal, 1980, and Zuckerman, DePaulo, & Rosenthal, 1981; then later by many others—e.g., DePaulo et al., 2003; Vrij, 2000—as the literature continued to grow). But no one had yet laid an empirical glove on the more fundamental questions about the nature of lying in everyday life. How often do people lie? To whom do they tell their lies? Do people lie more often about some topics than about others? Do certain kinds of people lie more often than other kinds of people?

I began my research on lying in everyday life with a bias—my belief that telling the whole truth is neither possible nor desirable, even if it *were* possible. Even the simplest of questions (e.g., "So, what did you do today?") can be answered in any number of ways, in any level of detail. That means that all of our presentations of self in everyday life are necessarily edited in some way (Goffman, 1959; Schlenker, 2003). When we are interacting truthfully, we choose the aspects of ourselves to present that are most relevant to the ongoing conversation and our current goals, without any attempt to mislead. Deceptive interactions are often motivated by the same goals as truthful ones. For example, we may want to exchange pleasantries or opinions, create particular impressions of ourselves, reassure others, win friends, or influence people. When these goals can be accomplished without misleading anyone—for example, when the impressions of ourselves that we want to convey are consistent with what we really do think of ourselves, or when the targets of our influence attempts have no reason to want to resist those attempts—then there is no need to deceive. Under less auspicious conditions, however—for example, when we want to claim familiarity with the topic of discussion when, in fact, we have none, or when the targets of a sales pitch would turn and run if they knew the truth—then it becomes tempting to lie. From this perspective, I expected lying to be a part of everyday life, rather than an extraordinary event. But I still needed the data to show it.

I set out with my students and colleagues to conduct some of the first studies about the place of lying in day-to-day life (DePaulo & Kashy, 1998; DePaulo, Kashy, Kirkendol, Wyer, & Epstein, 1996; Kashy & DePaulo, 1996; see also Camden, Motley, & Wilson, 1984; Lippard, 1988). In our wildest dreams, we wanted to recruit a nationally representative random sample of Americans. But considering that we were going to ask the participants to write down all of their lies, every day for a week and turn them in to a team of psychologists, we realized immediately (clever researchers that we were) that we would have to begin more modestly. We sought instead to recruit two very different samples of participants, neither of them representative of any definable group, and look for patterns of results across the two samples that might suggest the beginnings of some generalizable understandings about lying.

The first group was comprised of 77 college students—30 men and 47 women—who received partial course credit for participating in our study. The second sample was comprised of 30 men and 40 women recruited from the community, who responded to advertisements posted at a local community college or to letters we sent to people whose names we selected randomly from the telephone directory or from lists of people enrolled in continuing education courses. These participants were paid for their time. As we had hoped, the community members were very different, demographically, from the college students. They ranged in age from 18 to 71, and a third of them had no more than a high school education. Most were employed, more than half were married, and nearly half had children.

In a lengthy introductory session, we explained to participants that "a lie occurs any time you intentionally try to mislead someone." We asked them to record any deliberate attempts to mislead, whether verbal or nonverbal. Motive was not to be considered; they were to record even those lies they told for a "good reason." We gave them little notebooks to carry with them at all times, so that they could easily make a note of their lies soon after they told them.

The most important entries in the diaries that participants turned in to us were their descriptions, in their own words, of the lies they had told and their reasons for telling them. For each of their lies, the participants also completed a set of rating scales indicating, for example, how they felt about telling the lie, how much they planned the lie, and the degree to which they regarded the lie as serious. They also recorded the initials of the persons to whom they told their lies.

We tried to create conditions that would encourage participants to tell us all of their lies. For example, we asked them not to include their names on any of their materials. Instead, we collated the materials using identification numbers of the participants' own choosing. We also noted that if there were any lies or reasons for lying that they did not wish to describe, even anonymously, then they could simply write "rather not say." That way, we could count the lie without needing to know its precise content. Participants rarely used that option.

It is difficult to make sense of the number of lies people report without also knowing about the number of opportunities they have to tell lies. If, for instance, participants reported telling more lies to friends than acquaintances, we would want to know whether this difference occurred simply because participants interacted with friends so much more often than they interacted with acquaintances. Therefore, we also asked participants to keep records of all of their social interactions, regardless of whether they had told any lies during those interactions. (To keep the task manageable, we only asked them to record interactions that lasted at least 10 minutes.) Our most important measure of lying was the number of lies told per social interaction.

HOW OFTEN DO PEOPLE LIE?

By the end of the week, the 147 participants had recorded a total of 1,535 lies in their diaries (see Table 12.1): two lies per day for the college students, or one lie in every three of their social interactions; and one lie per day for the people in the community, or one lie in every five of their social interactions. Of all of the different people with whom they interacted over the course of the week, the college students lied at least once to 38%, and the community members lied to 30%.

TABLE 12.1. Number of Everyday Lies, Social Interactions, and Interaction Partners

	College (N = 77)	Community (N = 70)
Total number of lies (across all participants)	1,058	477
Mean number of social interactions per day	6.6	5.8
Mean number of lies per day	2	1
Mean number of lies per social interaction	0.3	0.2
Mean number of interaction partners	15	14
Percent of partners to whom at least one lie was told	38	30
Number of participants who told no lies	1	6

Note. From DePaulo et al. (1996). Copyright 1996 by the American Psychological Association. Adapted by permission.

Of the 77 college students, only one claimed to have not told a single lie. Of the 70 people from the community, only six claimed complete honesty during that 1 week. I thought I knew how many people could make that claim if they recorded their lies for a much longer period of time. And, although the participants in these studies were not politicians, I knew I had a response to Governor Weicker's insistence that we should throw out with the rest of the garbage the idea that all politicians lie. Indeed. We should replace it with the presumption that *all people* lie.

But were Governor Weicker and so many others correct in implying that lying is wrong and unacceptable? Is it reasonable to construe lying as one of the "forms of deliberate assault upon human beings," as did Bok? To consider these question in an informed way, it is important to look closely at the specifics of the lies that people tell.

WHAT DO PEOPLE LIE ABOUT?

The contents of the everyday lies that we collected fit into five categories (see Table 12.2). People lied about (1) their feelings and opinions; (2) their actions, plans, and whereabouts; (3) their knowledge, achievements, and failings; (4) explanations for their behaviors; and (5) facts and personal possessions.

Of these five topics of lies, the lies about feelings and opinions were the most commonplace for both the college students and the members of the community. Some of the lies in this category that participants recorded in their diaries included the following:

TABLE 12.2. Contents of Everyday Lies: Percentages in Each Category

	College	Community
Feelings and opinions	37	30
Actions, plans, and whereabouts	27	28
Knowledge, achievements, and failings	16	17
Explanations for behaviors	10	11
Facts, personal possessions	9	15

Note. Entries are the percentage of all lies that fit into each category (e.g., of all of the lies told by the college students, what percentage were lies about feelings and opinions?). For the college students, the standard deviations were 26 for feelings and for actions, 17 for knowledge, 15 for explanations, and 13 for facts. For the community members, the standard deviations were 30 for feelings, 27 for actions, 25 for knowledge, 15 for explanations, and 23 for facts. From DePaulo et al. (1996). Copyright 1996 by the American Psychological Association. Adapted by permission.

"I told him I missed him and thought about him every day when I really don't think about him at all."

"I told her that she looked good when I thought that she looked like a blimp."

"Exaggerated how hurt I was by a comment."

"Took sides with her when I really thought she was also at fault."

"I was asked whether it bothered me that I am the only one left in the infertility support group who is still trying to get pregnant, and I said no."

Aside from lying about their feelings, both the college students and the community members lied most often about their actions, plans, and whereabouts. Here are some examples of such lies:

"Lied about where I had been. Didn't tell them all of the places."

"Told the person collecting for the Heart Association that I had already given that day."

"Said I had been true to my girl."

"Said I sent the check this morning."

Lies about knowledge or lack of knowledge, achievements and accomplishments, and failings and shortcomings also appeared frequently in participants' diaries. Examples included the following:

"Led him to believe I had been a daring ski jumper."

"Tried to appear knowledgeable about operating room procedures when I only knew a little about them."

"I told him I had done poorly on my calculus homework when I had aced it. "

"I said I had gained 5 pounds this weekend and was fat."

Lies about the reasons or explanations for actions accounted for about 10% of all of the lies told by the college students and community members. Here are some examples:

"I told everyone at work I was late because I had car trouble."

"Told her I had to quit because my parents want me to."

"Told professor I shouldn't be disturbed while typing due to needing to keep a rhythm. Said I was eccentric that way."

"I told him I didn't take out our garbage because I didn't know where to take it."

Finally, lies about facts and possessions were the least commonplace among the college students, but the community members told such lies more often than they told lies about the reasons or explanations for their behaviors. Examples included the following:

"I said that I did not have change for a dollar."
"I told him my motorcycle belonged to my sister."
"I told him my father was an ambassador."

The lies presented so far are just a sampling of the hundreds of lies participants recorded in their diaries, but they are not unrepresentative of the entire pack of lies that we collected. There was a smattering of lies more serious than these, but they were the exceptions. I present many more of our findings before returning to the question of the acceptability of lying. My first impression upon reading all of the diaries, though, was that it would be a stretch to equate these kinds of lies with violence or evil.

HOW DO LIARS JUSTIFY THEIR LIES?

Our participants seemed untroubled by their lies. Although they did report feeling a bit more distressed while telling their lies than they had felt a moment before the lie was conveyed, they rated their overall levels of discomfort as low. They did not put much planning into their lies, they generally did not regard their lies as serious, and they claimed that it was not all that important to them to avoid getting caught telling their lies. Participants thought that the targets of their lies were fooled by the lies at the time that they heard them. A week later participants reported that, so far as they knew, most of their lies remained undetected. At that point, the participants also noted that if they could relive the interaction in which they had told their lies, they would still tell more than 70% of them. In fact, participants even suggested that they were protecting their targets (as well as themselves) with their lies, by claiming that both they and their targets would have felt worse if the truth had been told instead of the lie (see Table 12.3).

Participants' claims about protecting the targets of their lies were recorded on the rating scales we provided. Even more telling indications of the ways in which participants justified their lies were their open-ended descriptions of their reasons for telling each of their lies. Potentially, these reasons could be coded into innumerable categories, and at first, we preserved many distinctions. Ultimately, however, our judgments were consistent with those of scholars dating back centuries, who underscored the distinction between self-serving motives and other-oriented motives as the most important one.

Self-centered lies are told to protect or enhance the liar psychologically, or to protect or promote the liar's interests. Self-centered lies told for

TABLE 12.3. Participants' Descriptions of Their Everyday Lies

Description	College	Community
Discomfort before the lie	3.6	4.1
Discomfort during the lie	4.1	4.7
Discomfort after the lie	4.0	4.5
Planning of the lie	3.0	3.1
Seriousness of the lie	3.3	3.1
Importance of not getting caught	4.0	4.1
Target seemed to believe the lie	6.7	6.8
Liar is protecting the target	5.8	6.0
Liar is protecting him- or herself	5.5	5.5
Was the lie discovered? (%)		
No	59	57
Yes	23	15
Don't know	16	23
Would the liar tell the lie again? (% yes)	73	82

*Note.*The first nine items were rated on 9-point scales, with higher ratings indicating more of the quality. All ratings were made by the liars (participants). The percentages in the three sub-categories of discovery (no, yes, don't know) do not sum to 100 because the percentages were computed for each participant and then averaged across participants. From DePaulo et al. (1996). Copyright 1996 by the American Psychological Association. Adapted by permission.

psychological reasons are often told to protect the liars from embarrassment, disapproval, conflict, or from getting their feelings hurt. The more instrumentally oriented self-centered lies are told in the service of the liar's personal gain or convenience. Here are some examples of self-serving lies and the corresponding reasons for the lies recorded in participants' diaries:

> *Lie:* "Lied about why we moved back to Virginia. I said we decided for my husband to leave his last job. Actually, he was fired."
> *Reason:* "Embarrassment."

> *Lie:* "Saw some people while running. They were impressed with my running. I appeared nonchalant, while actually I was quite proud."
> *Reason:* "To impress them."

> *Lie:* "Told her I couldn't babysit for her because I had to go somewhere."
> *Reason:* "Did not want to babysit. Her kids are brats."

Other-oriented lies are the complement of self-centered lies. They are also told for reasons of psychological protection or advantage, but the person protected or advantaged is not the liar. Liars telling other-oriented lies are trying to spare other people from embarrassment, disapproval, conflict, of from getting their feelings hurt. They also tell such lies in the service of other people's gain or convenience. At least from the liars' point of view, these are kindhearted, altruistic lies. Here are some examples:

Lie: "Told her she looked well, voice sounded good, when, in fact, she looks less well than a few weeks ago."
Reason: "Not to add worry as she undergoes chemotherapy treatments."

Lie: "After sex, I pretended to have experienced orgasm."
Reason: "Didn't want to hurt my husband."

Lie: "I told her she should have a lot of confidence because she was pretty."
Reason: "Because she was in a depressed state because she had broken up with her boyfriend."

Are these liars also serving their own interests with their lies? Overall, the participants in both samples were about twice as likely to tell lies that were self-serving than to tell lies that were other-oriented (see Table 12.4). However, this disproportionate number of self-serving lies occurred only when men were involved as liars or targets. When women lied to other women, they were just as likely to tell kindhearted lies as self-serving ones.

TABLE 12.4. Reasons for Telling Everyday Lies: Percentages in Each Category

| | College | | Community | |
Liars and targets of lies	Self-centered	Other-oriented	Self-centered	Other-oriented
Men lying to men	66	8	57	19
Men lying to women	58	18	51	23
Women lying to men	50	22	59	18
Women lying to women	35	35	43	42
Overall	45	26	57	24

Note. Entries are percentages within each category (e.g., among men lying to men in the college student sample, 66% of the lies were self-centered and 8% were other-oriented). Not included in the table are the percentages of lies that were neither self-centered nor other-oriented. From DePaulo et al. (1996). Copyright 1996 by the American Psychological Association. Adapted by permission.

WHAT KINDS OF PEOPLE TELL LIES MOST READILY?

I have claimed that Governor Weicker was wrong in suggesting that people could be tossed into one of two moral bins, one for the people who are honest and the other for the liars. However, I do think that people can be placed on a continuum of readiness to lie. Over the course of the week of self-observation, the college students told up to 46 lies, and the community members told as many as 30. Perhaps, then, the people who lie more readily than others are the ones who should be thrown out with the garbage.

Debby Kashy and I did think that the people who told a greater number of lies might, indeed, be different kinds of people than those who told fewer lies, so to test our hypothesis, we asked the participants in both samples to complete a variety of personality scales before they recorded any of their lies. To test the dark view of liars as unsavory sorts, we included two scales measuring Manipulativeness, Machiavellianism (Christie & Geis, 1970), and Social Adroitness (Jackson, 1976), as well as a scale assessing the converse characteristic of Responsibility (Jackson, 1976). If people who lie more readily than others are, in fact, willing and able schemers, then we should find that manipulative people tell relatively more lies and responsible people tell fewer. Our self- presentational perspective is a bit less damning. Rather than claiming that people who lie a lot are people who do not care about others, we instead maintain that they do care, perhaps a bit too much. What they care about is what other people think of them. To test this hypothesis, we included scales measuring Public Self-Consciousness (Fenigstein, Scheier, & Buss, 1975) and Other- Directedness (Briggs, Cheek, & Buss, 1980). We also thought that people who tell a lot of lies might be especially sociable, because some of the goals that motivate lying, such as making a good impression and flattering others, may be especially important to people who like to spend a lot of time with others. Therefore, we also included scales assessing Extraversion (Briggs et al., 1980) and Social Participation (Jackson, 1976).

Our results showed that liars come in all of the predicted varieties (see Table 12.5). People who tell many lies are, in fact, more manipulative and irresponsible than people who tell few lies. Frequent liars also care deeply about what other people think of them, and they are more extraverted.

RUSH LIMBAUGH FINDS THE ROOT
OF OUR SOCIETY'S MORAL DECAY, AND I'M IT

One day in the summer of 1998, the conservative and highly opinionated talk show host, Rush Limbaugh, opened a segment of his television show with the following proclamation:

TABLE 12.5. Personality Correlates of the Rate of Telling Everyday Lies

	College		Community		
Personality characteristic	r	p	r	p	Combined p
Manipulativeness					
Machiavellianism	.12	.31	.23	.06	.039
Social adroitness	.30	.01	.24	.05	.001
Responsibility	−.16	.17	−.16	.20	.058
Concern with self-presentation					
Public self-consciousness	.12	.29	.26	.03	.023
Other-directedness	.08	.51	.40	.001	.004
Sociability					
Social participation	.10	.39	.14	.24	.150
Extraversion	.18	.11	.20	.10	.023

Note. From Kashy & DePaulo (1996). Copyright 1996 by the American Psychological Association. Adapted by permission.

"I made a prediction not long ago in the heat of one of the controversies surrounding the president. I said, look, over the course of this year we're going to hear how everybody lies, it ain't any big deal. Therefore, Clinton is nothing special. And I'm making a joke! I make joke predictions about these people all the time. And they come true!"

He then held up an issue of the *Journal of Personality and Social Psychology,* in which one of my diary studies was published, and elicited derisive laughter from his studio audience as he quoted me as saying, "Most people think lying is manipulative and exploitative . . . but those lies are not the most common ones. More often, people lie to enhance their self-esteem, to get others to like them or respect them and to spare other's feelings. . . . Being honest all the time is not a great idea because the truth often hurts." Actually, he had the wrong issue of the journal, and those words never appeared in it, but as a paraphrase of what I really did think, it was close enough.

Continuing, he added, "I don't know if this is coordinated with the Clinton administration, I doubt that it is. But this is just the classic example of the moral decay and the evaporating fiber of our society. . . . It's what Moynihan called 'defining deviancy down.' We got all sorts of problems out there, and after fighting them for years and years and we decide we can't solve it, we'll just say, hey, that's normal!"

Lowell Weicker wanted to toss me out with the rest of the garbage for believing that all politicians lie. Now Rush Limbaugh was holding me up as a classic example of the moral decay and evaporating fiber of society. It was turning out to be a rough year.

Much as I dislike Rush Limbaugh and virtually all of his opinions, I must admit that the question he raised is not unfair. If everyone lies (as I believe they do), then does that mean that lying is acceptable?

IS IT OK TO LIE?

The question of whether it is acceptable to lie is a difficult one for someone such as myself who has worked for several decades as a social scientist. I like to answer questions with data, and this question demands something more. I will get to that something more, but first, I want to see whether I can squeeze some hints out of the data my colleagues and I have collected. (Because the studies I have described so far are not experiments, hints are all they can provide.)

One way to approach the acceptability issue is to ask whether lying seems to be linked to good or bad outcomes. The diary studies offer some tentative answers to this question. The participants in those studies recorded all of their social interactions, regardless of whether or not they had lied during those interactions. They also rated the pleasantness and meaningfulness of each of their interactions. Participants generally described their interactions as pleasant, and as slightly more meaningful than superficial. However, these positive qualities were less in evidence in social interactions in which the participant had lied than in those in which the participant had told only the truth. In this way, then, the little lies of everyday life did seem to leave a bit of a smudge.

The participants in the diary studies also noted that they felt a bit more uncomfortable while they were telling their lies than they had just beforehand. Again, levels of discomfort were reported to be slight, even when participants were lying. But the faint stain left by the lies was still discernible.

There was another hint from the diary studies that participants were not completely at ease with the telling of their lies, however mundane those lies may have been. Participants seemed to shy away from telling their lies in face-to-face interactions. When we looked at the percentage of all conversations in which no lies were told that were conducted face-to-face, and compared it to the percentage of all dishonest conversations that were conducted face-to-face, more of the honest conversations than the dishonest ones were in person. However, when we looked at a more distant modality (i.e., telephone), we found the opposite: A greater percentage of the dishonest conversations than of the honest ones took place out of sight of the other person.

If people are not completely at ease with the telling of even the little lies of everyday life, then we might find that they allot their lies accordingly, doling out fewer to the people they care about the most. That is, in fact, what we did find. Both the college students and the community members reported telling fewer everyday lies (per social interaction) to the people to whom they felt closer (DePaulo & Kashy, 1998).

We found that closeness was linked to lower rates of lying when we averaged across all of the different kinds of everyday lies that our participants had told. When people talk about issues of honesty, however, they often distinguish between their altruistic lies and their self- serving lies. In fact, in our introductory sessions with our participants in the diary studies, in which we tried to explain to them what kinds of communications should count as lies, we found that it was especially important to underscore the point that altruistic lies are indeed lies. Those participants, like so many other people with whom I have had engaging conversations about lying, sometimes argue that if they told a lie for a good reason, then it was not really a lie. Although I disagree with them on definitional issues, I do think it is worthwhile to ask whether people are as reluctant to tell altruistic lies as self-serving ones to the people they care about the most.

They are not. When we looked separately at the rates of telling self-serving compared to altruistic lies, we found, for example, that people told fewer self-serving lies to friends than to acquaintances or strangers (the same pattern we had found when we did not distinguish among types of lies) but that they told more altruistic lies to friends than to acquaintances or strangers. It is to our close relationship partners, then, that we are especially likely to claim, falsely but reassuringly, that they did the right thing and we know just how they feel. We are relatively more likely to tell puffed up tales of our own accomplishments or devious untruths designed to dodge obligations and unpleasantries to those outside of our close social circles.

All of the suggestions I have offered so far about the nature and acceptability of lying have been based solely on my studies of lying in everyday life. In those diary studies, participants described each of their lies and reasons for telling their lies in just a sentence or so. Most of the lies they recorded did seem to be of little moral consequence, perhaps undeserving of any extended discourse. But interspersed here and there in the diaries were some lies that seemed much more ominous, and I wanted to know a whole lot more about those.

ARE SERIOUS LIES DIFFERENT FROM EVERYDAY LIES?

The next set of studies focused specifically on the most serious lies people had told during their lives. My colleagues Matthew Ansfield, Susan Kirkendol, Joe Boden, and I wanted people to tell us, in their own words, about the most serious lie anyone ever told to them and the most serious lie they had ever told to anyone else. (We let them make their own judgments as to seriousness.) Then we wanted them to answer a long series of questions about the experiences they described. As with the study of every-day lies, we would have loved to recruit a random sample of Americans to participate, but we were no more deluded about the prospects this time than we were the first time. We recruited college students, who described 128 serious lies, and people from the community, who described 107 such lies (DePaulo, Ansfield, Kirkendol, & Boden, in press). Once again, the community members were, demographically, a more diverse set of people than were our college students. They ranged in age from 19 to 84. Sixty percent were married, 90% were employed, and 29% had no more than a high school education.

The 235 serious lies seemed to us to cover a wide spectrum of serious-ness, but there was little doubt that these lies, on the whole, were far more serious than were most of the lies described in the diary studies. By their own ratings, the participants agreed. The mean rating on a 9-point scale (with 9 indicating greatest seriousness) was 6.8 for these serious lies, com-pared to 3.2 for the everyday lies.

The content of the serious lies was telling, too. In categorizing the lies by content, we did not try to retain the same categories used in the every-day lies studies, but instead used the categories that emerged from the data. We identified eight content categories (see Table 12.6). Among the most common varieties of serious lies were lies about affairs or other forms of romantic cheating. These ranged from a lie about time spent with a former girlfriend to a lie maintained by a clergyman, professor of reli-gion, and father of five about an affair with a secretary that lasted 15 years. Nearly as common as lies about affairs were lies about misdeeds, such as the lies told by the participant who denied giving out drugs on a high school field trip, then lied on his college application about having been suspended for it. Other serious lies concerned feelings or personal facts (e.g., a lie about a miscarriage); forbidden socializing (e.g., describing plans to spend the night babysitting instead of attending the forbidden

TABLE 12.6. Content of the Serious Lies: Percentages in Each Category

	College	Community
Affairs	23	22
Misdeeds	20	23
Personal facts or feelings	21	16
Forbidden socializing	15	6
Money, job	2	21
Death, illness, injury	9	3
Identity	4	7
Violence, danger	6	4

school dance); money or jobs (e.g. , investing money in the stock market after promising to save it for a down payment on a home); death, illness, or injury (e.g., a parent or grandparent's serious illness is misrepresented to a teenager); identity (e.g., lies about frequenting a bar for gay men); and violence or danger (e.g., a lie told by a commanding officer who claimed that there were no enemy in a village he knew to be heavily defended). Even when the categories were similar across the two sets of studies, the specific entries in those categories were markedly different. In the everyday lies studies, for example, the category of lies about feelings included the lies told to hide the offense taken at a casual comment, and feelings of fatigue feigned to excuse an early departure from a boring party. In the serious lies studies, the category was more likely to include the lie of professing love in the wedding vows.

We were able to sort the serious lies into the same two broad categories of motives—self-centered and other-oriented—that we had used to classify the everyday lies. The proportions of these two kinds of motives, however, were vastly different in the two sets of studies. Whereas about 25% of the everyday lies could be categorized as kindhearted (or other-oriented), only 10% of the serious lies fit the same description. The other 90% of the serious lies were self-serving (compared to about half of the everyday lies; the other everyday lies were neither kindhearted nor self-serving).

I noted earlier that in our studies of everyday lies, we found that people are reluctant to tell their boastful, though largely inconsequential, self-serving lies to the targets of their fondest affections. Perhaps it should then follow that people will also want to spare those close relationship partners from the most serious and shattering lies. Maybe the most hurtful lies are volleyed at the most despised persons known to the liars. Before my coauthors and I had collected people's stories about their most serious lies, some colleagues had argued for that possibility, citing, for example, the vicious lies told by cutthroat competitors in the workplace. We did find a few such lies in the stories we gathered, but they were far outnumbered by the serious lies hurled to and from the closest of relationship partners. Nearly two-thirds of the most serious lies that participants recounted were told either to or by parents, spouses or other romantic partners, best friends, or children.

Why spare the people we care about from the usually insignificant self-serving lies of everyday life while stunning them with the most serious ones? A big part of the answer, I think, can be found in what it is that people are trying to hide with their lies. In the everyday lies studies, participants filled their diaries with ordinary concerns, such as failing to win the enthusiastic praise of a teacher or finding themselves out of the loop about an interesting new development at work. Hiding such minor setbacks, or feelings about them, from a close relationship partner would probably be a greater threat to the relationship than would telling the truth about them. Owning up to them could even add to the feelings of closeness in the relationships.

The truths that are hidden by serious lies, however, are made of sterner stuff. The lies that our participants regarded as the most serious ones in their lives were often told to conceal matters such as affairs, car accidents, excessive drinking, shoplifting, and injuring a child in a fit of rage. Admitting these truths could threaten valued relationships, including relationships with the persons to whom the truths are acknowledged. These truths, if revealed, could also endanger the liar's reputation and livelihood.

Lies are told to close friends, lovers, parents, and children, and by presidents to the entire American public, not because the liars do not care about the targets of their lies or what those targets think of them, but because they *do*. In fact, the higher the expectations of others for our own virtuous behavior and the more important it is to us to maintain our honor in their eyes, the more likely it may be that we will lie to them to cover our failings (cf. Millar & Tesser, 1988).

We say that we do not want the most important persons in our lives to lie to us. More to the point, I think, is that we want them to refrain from behaving in ways that would tempt them to lie to us (cf. McCornack & Levine, 1990). We want the people we care most about to be people who do not cheat, do not make promises they cannot honor, do not claim more than they deserve, and do not squander our investments or our trust. We want them to be free of the frailties that make all of us human. This is a wish that can never come true.

We can try to behave in ways that bring out the best in others, so that they will be tempted to lie only infrequently. When they do fall short of our expectations, though, their honesty in admitting as much may depend on the reactions they expect from us (cf. Saxe, 1991). If we characteristically play the role of the wounded victim or the enraged tyrant, they may well be hesitant to own up to the truth. We can thereby protect ourselves from hearing about their bad behavior at the cost of being the target of their lies. The challenge is to be sufficiently understanding of ordinary human failings that others can admit to them, while still maintaining standards of integrity and discernment.

SHOULD WE REFRAIN FROM TELLING EVEN KINDHEARTED LIES?

Morally, the domain of serious lies is, in many ways, the least ambiguous. Personally, I know I would like to avoid behaving in ways that would tempt me to tell serious lies, and I would like others to do the same. Most often, we do succeed. Lies that people regard as serious seem to be told infrequently.

The little self-serving lies of everyday life are a bit stickier. They are just so easy to tell—but not quite as easy to justify. Feeling embarrassed about sleeping through your alarm? Say you got stuck in traffic. Did you get caught saying something controversial or just downright stupid? Clarify what you "really" meant. Questions from my research life about the acceptability of these kinds of lies have set up shop in the rest of my life and will not go away. I used to tell these kinds of lies without a whole lot of thought or regret. Now, I more often catch myself before I do, and I tell the truth instead. Sometimes I will admit to embarrassing truths even before I am backed into a comer. A few years before I started my diary studies, during a semester when I was teaching a graduate course in research methods, I called my dentist to tell him about an especially bad toothache. He asked me if the gum was swollen. I touched it and answered that I was not sure. He then suggested that I touch the gum on the other side of my mouth for comparison. Then I died of humiliation. Or would have, had he known that I taught a graduate course in research methods. I remember thinking how mortified I would have felt if any of the students in my course overheard that conversation. Now when I teach that course, I tell that story on the first day. It usually gets a laugh. But telling those kinds of truths does have its costs. The students may conclude that I am, indeed, stupid. So in these kinds of situations, in which I am tempted to tell a small self-serving lie, neither the truth nor the lie automatically wins. It is always a battle.

For a while, I had similar internal skirmishes over the telling of altruistic lies. Compared to the time in my life that preceded my career as a scholar of lying, I became much more aware of my inclination to say something untrue in order to spare someone else's feelings. I also saw more clearly that it was I who was presuming to know what the other person would want to hear. This particular lesson was hard to escape. Bok emphatically underscored the differences between the liar's point of view and that of the target of lies in her philosophical writings on lying (Bok, 1978), and Anne Gordon and Art Miller built a similar argument with data (Gordon & Miller, 2000). So I tried to figure out how to tell tactful truths instead of reassuring lies. In the midst of this personal honesty project, my mother wanted to give me a ring of hers that was beautiful but too ornate for my own tastes. I told her, truthfully, that I thought it was beautiful but that because it was so ornate, I did not think I would wear it very often. My mother successfully survived the adolescent years (and all of the other ones) of her four children, so I doubt that she was scarred by my rejection of her ring. But the memory still bothers me. I continue to be more aware of my supposedly altruistic lies than I was in my preresearch life, but I probably do not tell them any less readily than I did then. I am a fan of David Nyberg and his wonderful book, *The Varnished Truth*. In a chapter entitled, "Truth-Telling Is Morally Overrated," he poses these questions: "Your two closest friends offer to tell you, with unchecked candor and without regard for your feelings, everything they think about you. Would you want them to do it? These two friends ask you to do the same for them. Would you?" (1993, pp. 8–9). Case closed.

Not everyone agrees. When I tell people that I study lying, some reply, with great pride, that they simply do not lie. Some will back off from that claim once I explain that any communication meant to mislead is a lie, even if, ironically, it is literally true. A few others offer concessions when I add that there are no exemptions for good intentions, that altruistic lies are still lies. For those who do not concede even then, I might tell my story about the ring. If that fails, I bring up the lie (described earlier) told to the person undergoing chemotherapy treatments. Would they really tell that person that she looks less well than she had 2 weeks before? They try to convince me of the value of being the person others know they really can trust to tell them the truth. It is a standoff. After a few such conversations, it became clear to me that it was time to collect some data.

Kathy Bell and I tried to recreate in the laboratory just the sort of situation that would cast participants into a lie-telling dilemma: one in which they might not want to lie, but telling the truth could hurt another person's feelings (Bell & DePaulo, 1996; DePaulo & Bell, 1996; see also Bavelas, Black, Chovil, & Mullett, 1990). We brought a participant into a room we had set up like an art gallery. The participant, with no one else present, was asked to look at the paintings and choose the two he or she liked the most and the least. Then the participant was asked to write down what he or she liked and disliked about each of the four paintings. Only after completing this task did the participant learn that he or she would then discuss some of the paintings in the gallery with a woman who was introduced as an art student (but who, in two of the three studies, was actually a confederate). We also told each participant that we would never show the art student the comments written about the paintings, and, in fact, we never did.

The most telling moment occurred when the art student referred to one of the two paintings the participant disliked the most, and said, "This is one that I did. What do you think of it?" In each session, the art student also claimed that one of the participant's favorite paintings was her own work. The participant's other two choices (one liked and one disliked painting) were attributed to other artists and were also discussed.

The first question we wanted to address was how often the participants would tell outright lies. In the psychologically easy situation, in which the art student claimed to have created a painting that was one of the participant's favorites, we did not expect any of the participants to do anything so perverse as to claim that they disliked the painting. And, in fact, no one did. Nor did anyone claim to dislike the painting they really liked when it was created by a different artist. Instead, about 80% of the participants honestly and explicitly stated that they liked the painting that they really did like, regardless of whether it was the art student's work or the creation of a different artist (see Table 12.7).

But what about the more interesting situation in which participants really disliked the artist's work? If the participants were to be as forthcoming about their feelings toward the disliked paintings as they were about their feelings about the paintings they liked, then they should honestly and explicitly say, about 80% of the time, that they disliked the paintings. Instead, when the paintings the participants disliked were the art student's own work, they only admitted explicitly to disliking the work half that often. Sixteen percent of the time, they told a bald-faced lie: They explicitly claimed to like the painting of the art student's that they actually disliked.

The 16% of participants who told an outright lie about the painting they disliked to the creator of the painting who was sitting right in front of them were the only participants to tell blatant lies. In a sense, then, maybe all of those people who insist that they would not lie in this situation (or any other) are correct—if, and only if, lying is defined very narrowly as explicitly stating the exact opposite of what you really believe is so. But I think that any communications deliberately designed to mislead should count as lies, and by that criterion, there appeared to be plenty. The participants in the art studies seemed to find ways to mislead the artist that could be defended as truthful. In short, they were trying to get by on technicalities.

The strategy we least anticipated is one we now think of as conveying positive evaluations by implication. Participants seemed to use what they said or did not say about the other artist's work, relative to what they said or did not say about the present artist's work, to imply a relatively positive evaluation of the present artist's work. Here is an example of what I mean: I have already noted that only 40% of the participants explicitly admitted

TABLE 12.7. Percent Who Explicitly Said That They Liked or Disliked the Paintings

	Disliked paintings		Liked paintings	
	Professed liking	Professed disliking	Professed liking	Professed disliking
Not special (other artists' work)	0	64	83	0
Special (artist's own work)	16	40	79	0

Note. Entries are from DePaulo and Bell (1996), the condition in which participants received no special instructions as to honesty. Copyright 1996 by the American Psychological Association. Adapted by permission.

that they disliked a painting that was the artist's own work. In comparison, 64% of them explicitly said that they disliked a painting that was the work of a different artist. Analogously, whereas 16% of the participants told a kindhearted, outright lie about a painting they disliked that was the work of the artist right in front of them (claiming that they liked it), no one did the same when the painting had been created by some other artist. Many of the artists who may be wondering what the participant really does think of their paintings can say to themselves, "Well, she said that she disliked the other painting that I did not create, and she did not say that she disliked mine." The artists can then infer that the participant likes their work, but the participant lets herself off the moral hook on the technicality that she did not actually make such a statement.

The strategy Kathy Bell and I did expect participants to use was to exaggerate or understate the aspects of the paintings that they really did like or dislike. In fact, that is why we asked participants to write down the aspects they liked and disliked before they even knew they would be meeting an art student—so we would have the evidence we needed to catch them in the act. (Also, less interestingly, we wanted to be sure they listed equal numbers of liked and disliked aspects of the paintings that would be described as the artist's own work, compared to the paintings to be described as the work of another artist. Fortunately, they did.) When participants discussed paintings they disliked that were not created by the artist with whom they were interacting, they mentioned an average of four aspects they liked and five they disliked. They thereby indicated that they disliked those paintings more than they liked them. However, when the paintings they disliked were the work of the artist in the room, participants mentioned only three disliked aspects but twice as many liked ones. This strategy of amassing misleading evidence also nicely fits the criterion of defensibility, at least in participants' minds. They could tell themselves that they were not lying when they mentioned all of those liked aspects of the paintings they disliked; after all, there were some aspects of the disliked paintings that they really did like. They could also reassure themselves that there was nothing dishonest about not mentioning all of the aspects of the paintings that they disliked; after all, they were not claiming to like those aspects, they were simply refraining from mentioning them. I don't buy it. By mentioning so many more liked than disliked aspects of the paintings they actually disliked when they were the artist's own work, at the same time that they mentioned more disliked than liked aspects when the paintings they disliked were the work of another artist, the participants were, I believe, deliberately trying to mislead the artist. They were subtly lying.

There are many interesting implications of the ways in which participants handled the sticky situation we created for them, as they interacted with the art students. Here I mention two of my favorites. First, I think the participants' strategy was quite impressive and far more imaginative than any of my conversationalists and I ever dreamed up, as we argued over whether anyone ever really negotiates such situations without lying. I think what the participants did was to give the artist the choice as to what to believe. If the artist wanted to believe that the participant really did like her painting (the one the participant actually disliked), she could note that the participant mentioned twice as many aspects she liked about the painting than ones she disliked. She might also notice that the participant never explicitly said that she disliked the painting, when she may have done so when discussing one of the other paintings (the disliked one painted by the other artist). However, if the artist were willing to hear what the participant really did think, she could have figured it out; she could have noticed, for example, that even though the participant did not explicitly say that she disliked the painting, she did not say that she liked it, either. Chances are, the artist did hear the participant say quite explicitly that she did like two of the other paintings that were discussed (the two she really did like). Furthermore, the lopsided listing of six liked aspects compared to only three disliked aspects would not have been so convincing when compared to the even more lopsided listings ticked off in the descriptions of the paintings the participant really did like. In those discussions, the participant described even more liked aspects and even fewer disliked ones.

The second implication concerns our understanding of former President Clinton's infamous denial: "1 did not have sexual relations with that woman, Miss Lewinsky." Rush Limbaugh notwithstanding, I have never had any conversations with President Clinton, nor have I ever coordinated my research with him. But I do have a guess as to what he was doing with that statement. He was saying that only a particular act "counts" as sexual relations, and he did not perform that act with Monica Lewinsky. Therefore, his statement was defensible as the truth, and he was not lying. This sort of verbal ploy has since been dubbed *Clintonesque,* but I think it is *humanesque.* In spirit, it is no different from the strategy used by the participants in the art study who mentioned twice as many aspects they liked than aspects they disliked when discussing a painting they disliked with the artist who had created it. Both Clinton and the participants in the art studies were deliberately misleading their audiences. In my eyes, they were all lying, but in theirs, they were not.

IT IS NOT JUST ABOUT LYING

With our cynical words and our soft hearts, we seem to cry out for honesty from our political leaders. There is a popular joke about how we can tell when politicians are lying ("they are moving their lips") that may have been mildly amusing the first time but by now is more like a cliché. We sneer at that witticism at the same time that we fall for the movies and television shows about the fictional candidates and leaders who really do tell the truth.

But consider this snapshot from the aftermath of the presidential election of the year 2000. That, of course, was the election that was not definitively decided until months after Election Day. Vice President Al Gore won the popular vote, but Governor George W. Bush was declared the winner of the critical electoral vote after legal brawls clamored all the way to the U.S. Supreme Court.

Just days after the resolution of the long, bitter, contentious, and still-controversial process, Richard Gephardt, the leader of the House Democrats, appeared on the widely watched NBC Sunday morning news program *Meet the Press*. Here is an excerpt from that show (in Barry, 2000, p. 4):

> "So George W. Bush is the legitimate 43rd president of the United States?" asked the host, Tim Russert.
>
> "George W. Bush is the next president of the United States," Mr. Gephardt answered.
>
> "But is he legitimate?" Mr. Russert pressed. "Is he?"
>
> After some momentary filibustering, Mr. Gephardt answered: "He is the president of the United States."

Days later, Gephardt clarified what he really believed—that Bush was indeed a legitimate president (Barry, 2000). I do not believe that he really felt that way. But the pressure was on. Tim Russert was pushing him, and then public sentiment was doing the same. What they were pushing him to do was to lie. Lie so the nation can heal. Lie so we can all move forward.

The same public that snickers at the joke about the politicians moving their lips, the same public that laps up fanciful tales of political candidates who cannot tell a lie, was now insisting that Gephardt do just that.

Are we all just hypocrites or intellectual lightweights who cannot keep straight what it is that we really *do* want? I don't think so. It is easy to condemn lying when we ponder it as if it were an independent moral issue, in a world apart from all others. But it is not. Yes, we care about honesty. And we should. But we also care about healing, and we *should* care about that, too. We can disagree about whether a particular lie or a particular truth will mend our wounds, but we are likely to agree that somehow, our wounds should be tended so that we can face the future with less pain.

When people tell even more altruistic lies to their friends and intimates than to acquaintances and strangers, I do not think they are (just) saying that certain kinds of lies really are acceptable, and even worthy, when told to the people they love. I think they are saying that sometimes other values matter more than scrupulous honesty. Showing that we care about other people's feelings, that important people in our lives have earned our loyalty, and that we value the sentiments that motivate their ill-conceived attempts at kindness (e.g., the disappointing gifts) are all, to some people, legitimate contenders for the moral high ground. We can argue about whether those other values really do trump the value of honesty. In doing so, we have already won, by opening our minds.

REFERENCES

Barry, D. (2000, December 24). Smile. It's transition time. *The New York Times,* Section 4, pp. 1, 4.

Bavelas, J. B., Black, A., Chovil, N., & Mullett, J. (1990). *Equivocal communication.* Newbury Park, CA: Sage.

Bell, K. L., & DePaulo, B.M. (1996). Liking and lying. *Basic and Applied Social Psychology, 18,* 243–266.

Bok, S. (1978). *Lying: Moral choice in public and private life.* New York: Pantheon.

Briggs, S. R., Jr., Cheek, J. M., & Buss, A. H. (1980). An analysis of the Self-Monitoring Scale. *Journal of Personality and Social Psychology, 38,* 679–686.

Camden, C., Motley, M. T., & Wilson, A. (1984). White lies in interpersonal communication: A taxonomy and preliminary investigation of social motivations. *Western Journal of Speech Communication, 48,* 309–325.

Christie, R., & Geis, F. L. (1970). *Studies in Machiavellianism.* New York: Academic Press.

DePaulo, B. M., Ansfield, M. E., Kirkendol, S. E., & Boden, J. M. (in press). Serious lies. *Basic and Applied Social Psychology.*

DePaulo, B. M., & Bell, K. L. (1996). Truth and investment: Lies are told to those who care. *Journal of Personality and Social Psychology, 71,* 703–716.

DePaulo, B. M., & Kashy, D. A. (1998). Everyday lies in close and casual relationships. *Journal of Personality and Social Psychology, 74,* 63–79.

DePaulo, B. M., Kashy, D. A., Kirkendol, S. E., Wyer, M. M., & Epstein, J. A. (1996). Lying in everyday life. *Journal of Personality and Social Psychology, 70,* 979–995.

DePaulo, B. M., Lindsay, J. J., Malone, B. E., Muhlenbruck, L., Charlton, K., & Cooper, H. (2003). Cues to deception. *Psychological Bulletin, 129,* 74–118.

DePaulo, B. M., Zuckerman, M., & Rosenthal, R. (1980). Detecting deception: Modality effects. In L. Wheeler (Ed.), *The review of personality and social psychology* (pp. 125–162). Beverly Hills, CA: Sage.

Fenigstein, A., Scheier, M. F., & Buss, A. H. (1975). Public and private self- consciousness: Assessment and theory. *Journal of Consulting and Clinical Psychology, 43,* 522–527.

Goffman, E. (1959). *The presentation of self in everyday life.* Garden City, NY: Doubleday/Anchor Books.

Gordon, A. K., & Miller, A. G. (2000). Perspective differences in the construal of lies: Is deception in the eye of the beholder? *Personality and Social Psychology Bulletin, 26,* 46–55.

Jackson, D. N. (1976). *Jackson Personality Inventory*. Port Huron, MI: Research Psychologists Press.

Kashy, D. A., & DePaulo, B. M. (1996). Who lies? *Journal of Personality and Social Psychology, 70,* 1037–1051.

Lippard, P. V. (1988). "Ask me no questions, I'll tell you no lies": Situational exigencies for interpersonal deception. *Western Journal of Speech Communication, 52,* 91–103.

McCornack, S. A., & Levine, T. R (1990). When lies are uncovered: Emotional and relational outcomes of discovered deception. *Communication Monographs, 57,* 119–138.

Millar, K. U., & Tesser, A. (1988). Deceptive behavior in social relationships: A consequence of violated expectations. *Journal of Psychology, 122,* 263–273.

Nyberg, D. (1993). *The varnished truth*. Chicago: University of Chicago Press.

Saxe, L. (1991). Lying. *American Psychologist, 46,* 409–415.

Schlenker, B. R. (2003). Self-presentation. In M. R. Leary & J. P. Tangney (Eds.), *Handbook of self and identity* (pp. 492–518). New York: Guilford Press.

Vrij, A. (2000). *Detecting lies and deceit*. Chichester, UK: Wiley.

Zuckerman, M., DePaulo, B. M., & Rosenthal, R. (1981). Verbal and nonverbal communication of deception. In L. Berkowitz (Ed.). *Advances in experimental social psychology* (Vol. 14, pp. 1–59). New York: Academic Press.

CHAPTER 13

A Moral-Emotional Perspective on Evil Persons and Evil Deeds

JUNE PRICE TANGNEY
JEFF STUEWIG

Shame and guilt are generally regarded as moral emotions in that they motivate people to do good and to avoid doing evil. Contemporary research, however, has suggested that shame and guilt are not equally moral, nor adaptive, emotions. In this chapter, we reexamine some of our previous conclusions about the maladaptive nature of shame. In normal populations, guilt is clearly the moral emotion of choice, whereas shame has been associated with substantial hidden costs. However, based on our recent research with incarcerated offenders, we suspect that shame may not be all bad, in all contexts. For example, feelings of shame may frequently provoke self-loathing, denial, and defense, but the capacity to experience shame may be preferable to the complete absence of moral emotional experience presumed to be characteristic of psychopaths.[1] In extreme popu-

---

[1] The term *sociopath* is sometimes used instead of *psychopath*. The term of choice sometimes reflects the belief about the origins of the condition; other times it reflects habit or training. Criminologists and sociologists often use the word *sociopath* because they believe that social forces create the condition. Those who take a more psychological, biological, and genetic approach may use the term *psychopath*. Essentially, however, the traits and behaviors that describe these individuals are the same no matter which term is used. Researchers using Hare's PCL-R use the term *psychopath* to refer to individuals who score at or above a specified cutoff.

lations, the mere existence of any sort of self-evaluative emotion may offer a ray of hope for rehabilitation and redemption. We conclude with a discussion of the clinical and policy implications of recent research on moral emotions and psychopathy.

CONTRASTING THE SHAME AND GUILT EXPERIENCES

The terms *shame* and *guilt* are often used interchangeably. It is not uncommon, for example, to hear people refer to "feelings of shame and guilt" or "the effects of shame and guilt" without making any distinction between the two. Recently, however, there has been an increase in research examining how they may differ. One idea is that shame and guilt differ in the *types* of events that elicit them. Analyses of personal shame and guilt experiences provided by children and adults revealed few, if any, "classic" shame-inducing or guilt-inducing situations (Tangney, 1992; Tangney et al., 1994). Most types of events (e.g., lying, cheating, stealing, failing to help another, disobeying parents, etc.) are cited by some people in connection with feelings of shame and by other people in connection with guilt. Similarly, Keltner and Buswell (1996) reported a high degree of overlap in the types of events that cause shame and guilt.

Another line of thought is that shame and guilt differ along the self versus behavior dimension. According to Lewis (1971), shame involves a negative evaluation of the global self, whereas guilt involves a negative evaluation of a specific behavior. Although this distinction may, at first glance, appear rather subtle, this differential emphasis on self ("*I* did that horrible thing") versus behavior ("I *did* that horrible *thing*") sets the stage for very different emotional experiences and very different patterns of motivations and subsequent behavior.

In brief, shame is an acutely painful emotion that is typically accompanied by a sense of "shrinking" or "smallness," and by a sense of worthlessness and powerlessness. Although shame does not necessarily involve the presence of an actual observing audience to witness one's shortcomings, imagery or "self-talk" of how one's defective self would appear to others is often present. Not surprisingly, shame often leads to a desire to escape or hide—to sink into the floor and disappear.

Guilt, in contrast, is typically a less painful, devastating experience because the focus is on the specific behavior, not the entire self. One's core identity or self-concept is not under attack. Instead of feeling defensive, people experiencing guilt are focused on the act and its consequences; they feel tension, remorse, and regret over the "bad thing done." People feeling guilt often ruminate obsessively over their action, wishing they had behaved differently or could somehow undo the harm that was done. Rather than motivating avoidance and defense, guilt motivates reparative behavior: confession, apology, and attempts to fix the situation.

This distinction between shame and guilt has been supported by studies employing a range of methodologies, including qualitative case study analyses (Lewis, 1971; Lindsay-Hartz, 1984; Lindsay-Hartz, DeRivera, & Mascolo, 1995), content analyses of shame and guilt narratives (Ferguson, Stegge, & Damhuis, 1990; Tangney, 1992; Tangney, Marschall, Rosenberg, Barlow, & Wagner, 1994), participants' quantitative ratings of personal shame and guilt experiences (e.g., Ferguson, Stegge, & Damhuis, 1991; Tangney, 1993; Tangney, Miller, Flicker, & Barlow, 1996; Wallbott & Scherer, 1988, 1995; Wicker, Payne, & Morgan, 1983), and analyses of participants' counterfactual thinking (Niedenthal, Tangney, & Gavanski, 1994).

GUILT IS GOOD, SHAME IS BAD?

Over the past decade and a half, research from our laboratory has emphasized the generally adaptive nature of guilt, in contrast to the generally maladaptive nature of shame. One of the consistent themes emerging from our research, and that of others, is that shame and guilt are not equally "moral" emotions. On balance, guilt appears to be the more adaptive emotion, benefiting individuals and their relationships in a variety of ways (Baumeister, Stillwell, & Heatherton, 1994, 1995a, 1995b; Tangney, 1991, 1995). Here, we summarize three sets of findings that suggest that guilt is the more moral, adaptive emotion.

Hiding versus Amending

First, research consistently shows that shame and guilt lead to contrasting motivations or "action tendencies" (Ferguson et al., 1991; Lewis, 1971; Lindsay-Hartz, 1984; Tangney, 1993; Tangney, Miller, et al., 1996; Wallbott & Scherer, 1995; Wicker et al., 1983). As noted, shame has been associated with attempts to deny, hide, or escape the shame-inducing situation, whereas guilt has been associated with the reparative actions of confessing, apologizing, undoing. For example, when people are asked to describe and rate personal shame and guilt experiences anonymously (Tangney, 1993; Tangney, Miller, et al., 1996), their ratings indicate that they feel more compelled to hide from others and less inclined to admit what they had done when feeling shame as opposed to guilt. Taken together, findings across studies suggest that guilt motivates people in a constructive, proactive, future-oriented direction, whereas shame motivates people toward separation, distance, and defense.

Other-Oriented Empathy

Second, there appears to be a special link between guilt and empathy. Empathy is a highly valued, prosocial emotional process that motivates altruistic, helping behavior, fosters close interpersonal relationships, and inhibits antisocial behavior and aggression (Eisenberg, 1986; Eisenberg & Miller, 1987; Feshbach, 1978, 1984, 1987; Feshbach & Feshbach, 1969, 1982, 1986). Research indicates that feelings of shame disrupt the ability to make an empathic connection, whereas guilt and empathy go hand-in-hand. This differential relationship of shame and guilt to empathy has been observed at the levels of both emotion traits (i.e., dispositions) and emotion states.

Studies of emotion traits focus on *individual differences.* When faced with failures or transgressions, to what degree is a person inclined to feel shame and/or guilt? To assess proneness to shame and proneness to guilt, we use a scenario-based method in which respondents are presented with a series of situations often encountered in daily life. Each scenario is followed by responses that capture phenomenological aspects of shame, guilt, and other theoretically relevant experiences (e.g., externalization, pride). For example, in the adult version of our Test of Self-Conscious Affect (TOSCA; Tangney, Wagner, & Gramzow, 1989), participants are asked to imagine the following scenario: "You make a big mistake on an important project at work. People were depending on you and your boss criticizes you." People then rate their likelihood of reacting with a shame response ("You would feel like you wanted to hide"), a guilt response ("You would think 'I should have recognized the problem and done a better job' "), and so forth. Responses across the scenarios capture affective, cognitive, and motivational features associated with shame and guilt, respectively, as described in the theoretical, phenomenological, and empirical literature. (See Tangney [1996] and Tangney & Dearing [2002] for a summary of research supporting the reliability and validity of the TOSCA and the more recent TOSCA-3.)

Researchers have consistently demonstrated that shame proneness and guilt proneness are differentially related to the ability to empathize (Leith & Baumeister, 1998; Tangney, 1991, 1994, 1995; Tangney & Dearing, 2002; Tangney, Wagner, Burggraf, Gramzow, & Fletcher, 1991), a finding that is remarkably consistent across various ages and demographic groups. In general, guilt-prone individuals tend to show high levels of empathy. Proneness to guilt consistently correlates with measures of perspective taking and empathic concern. In contrast, shame proneness has been associated with an impaired capacity for other-oriented empathy and a propensity for problematic, "self-oriented" personal distress responses.

Individual differences aside, similar findings are obtained when considering the emotion states of shame and guilt "in the moment." For example, when people described their personal guilt experiences, they conveyed greater empathy for others compared to their descriptions of personal shame experiences (Leith & Baumeister, 1998; Tangney et al., 1994). In another study, Marschall (1996) found that people induced to feel shame subsequently reported less empathy for a disabled student. The effect was most pronounced among low shame-prone individuals. Consistent with the dispositional findings (Tangney, 1991, 1995), shame-prone participants were fairly unempathic across conditions (i.e., regardless of whether or not they had just been shamed in the laboratory). But among low shame-prone participants, who have a higher capacity for empathy, in general, the shame induction had the apparent effect of "short-circuiting" an empathic response. In short, as a result of the shame induction, low shame-prone people were rendered relatively unempathic—that is, more like their shame-prone peers.

Why does shame, but not guilt, interfere with other-oriented empathy? In focusing on a bad *behavior* (as opposed to a bad *self*), people experiencing guilt are relatively free of the egocentric, self-involved process of shame. Instead, their focus on a specific behavior is likely to highlight the consequences of that behavior for distressed others, further facilitating an empathic response (Tangney, 1991, 1995). In contrast, the painful self-focus of shame is apt to "derail" the empathic process. As indicated by content analyses of autobiographical accounts of shame and guilt experiences, the shamed individual is inclined to focus on him- or her*self,* as opposed to the harmed other (Tangney et al., 1994).

Anger and Aggression

Third, research has shown a link between shame and anger, again observed at both the dispositional and state levels. Lewis (1971) first speculated on the dynamics between shame and anger (or humiliated fury), based on her clinical case studies, noting that clients' feelings of shame often preceded their expressions of anger and hostility in the therapy room. More recent empirical research has supported her claim. Studies of children, adolescents, college students, and adults have consistently shown that proneness to shame is positively correlated with feelings of anger and hostility and an inclination to externalize blame (Tangney, 1994, 1995; Tangney, Wagner, Fletcher, & Gramzow, 1992; Tangney et al., 1991).

Not only are shame-prone individuals more prone to externalizing their feelings of blame and anger than their non-shame-prone peers, but once angered, they are also more likely to handle and express their anger in a destructive fashion. For example, in a cross-sectional developmental study of children, adolescents, college students, and adults (Tangney, Wagner, et al., 1996), proneness to shame was consistently correlated with malevolent intentions and a propensity to engage in direct physical, verbal, and symbolic aggression (e.g., shaking a fist), indirect aggression (e.g., harming something important to the target, talking behind the target's back), all manner of displaced aggression, self-directed aggression, and anger held in (a ruminative unexpressed anger). Not surprisingly, shame-prone individuals reported that their anger typically results in negative long-term consequences for themselves and for their relationships with others.

In contrast, guilt-proneness was generally associated with more constructive means of handling anger. Proneness to "shame-free" guilt was positively correlated with constructive intentions and negatively correlated with direct, indirect, and displaced aggression. Instead, relative to non-guilt-prone persons, guilt-prone individuals are inclined to engage in constructive behavior, such as nonhostile discussion with the target of their anger, and direct corrective action. Moreover, guilt-prone individuals reported that their anger typically results in positive long-term consequences. The relationship of shame and guilt to these anger-related dimensions are remarkably robust, holding across demographically diverse samples and when controlling for the influence of social desirability.

Shame and anger have been similarly linked at the situational level, too. For example, Wicker and colleagues (1983) found that college students reported a greater desire to punish others involved in personal shame versus guilt experiences. Tangney, Miller, and colleagues (1996) found a similar trend among college students, who reported more feelings of anger in connection with narrative accounts of shame versus guilt experiences. Finally, in a study of specific real-life episodes of anger in romantically involved couples, shamed partners were significantly angrier, more likely to engage in aggressive behavior, and less likely to elicit conciliatory behavior from their perpetrating significant other (Tangney, 1995). Not only were shamed partners more aggressive, but when they confronted their partners, the partners in turn responded with anger, resentment, defiance, and denial, leading to increasingly hostile situations. Not surprisingly, on balance, couples reported more negative long-term consequences for anger episodes involving partner shame than those not involving shame. In short, these data provide a powerful empirical example of the shame–rage spiral described by Lewis (1971) and Scheff (1987), in which (1) partner shame leads to feelings of rage (2) and destructive retaliation, which then (3) sets into motion anger and resentment in the perpetrator (4) as well as expressions of blame and retaliation in kind, (5) which is likely to further shame the initially shamed partner, and so forth—without any constructive resolution in sight.

The findings converge from a broad range of studies using multiple methods, diverse samples, and multiple contexts: Shame and anger go hand-in-hand. More specifically, desperate to escape painful feelings of shame, shamed individuals may be inclined to react defensively and "turn the tables," externalizing blame and anger onto a convenient scapegoat. There may be short-term gain in blaming someone else and feeling indignant anger, if only because such anger can serve to reactivate the "self" and reignite some sense of control and superiority. Unfortunately, the long-term costs are often steep. Friends, acquaintances, and loved ones alike are apt to be truly puzzled and hurt by what appear to be irrational bursts of anger, coming seemingly out of the blue. In general, the ways in which shame-prone individuals manage anger pose real challenges for close, ongoing relationships.

IS THERE A TRADE-OFF?
DOES GUILT ENHANCE RELATIONSHIPS
BUT COMPROMISE INDIVIDUAL ADJUSTMENT?

The research reviewed so far suggests that guilt is, on balance, the more "moral" or adaptive emotion—at least, when considering social behavior and interpersonal adjustment. But are there hidden costs for the individual? Does the tendency to experience guilt ultimately lead to increases in anxiety and depression or to decreases in self-esteem? Is shame perhaps less problematic for intrapersonal as opposed to interpersonal adjustment?

The empirical data present a clear answer in the case of shame. Researchers consistently find that proneness to shame is related to a whole host of psychological symptoms, including depression, anxiety, eating disorder symptoms, subclinical psychopathy, and low self-esteem (Allan, Gilbert, & Goss, 1994; Brodie, 1995; Cook, 1988, 1991; Gramzow & Tangney, 1992; Harder, 1995; Harder, Cutler, & Rockart, 1992; Harder & Lewis, 1987; Hoblitzelle, 1987; Sanftner, Barlow, Marschall, & Tangney, 1995; Tangney, 1993; Tangney, Burggraf, & Wagner, 1995; Tangney & Dearing, 2002; Tangney et al., 1991; Tangney, Wagner, & Gramzow, 1992). This relationship appears to be robust across a range of measurement methods and across diverse age groups and populations. In concurrence with the clinical literature, empirical research finds overall that people who frequently experience feelings of shame about the self are correspondingly more vulnerable to a range of psychological problems.

The findings for guilt and psychopathology are less clear cut. The traditional view is that guilt plays a significant role in psychological symptoms. At least as early as Freud (1909/1955, 1917/1957, 1923/1961), clinical theory and case studies made frequent reference to a maladaptive guilt characterized by chronic self-blame and obsessive rumination over one's transgressions (Blatt, 1974; Ellis, 1962; Freud, 1924/1961; Hartmann &

Loewenstein, 1962; Rodin, Silbertstein, & Striegel-Moore, 1984; Weiss, 1993). More recent theory and research, in contrast, has emphasized the adaptive functions of guilt, particularly for interpersonal behavior (Baumeister et al., 1994, 1995a; Hoffman, 1982; Tangney, 1991, 1994, 1995; Tangney, Wagner, Fletcher, & Gramzow, 1992; Tangney & Dearing, 2002).

Attempting to reconcile these perspectives, Tangney and colleagues (1995) argued that once the critical distinction between shame and guilt is made, there is no compelling reason to expect guilt over specific behaviors to be associated with poor psychological adjustment. Rather, guilt is most likely to be maladaptive when it becomes fused with shame. When a person begins with a guilt experience ("Oh, look at what a horrible *thing* I have *done*") but then magnifies and generalizes the event to the self (". . . and aren't I a horrible *person*"), many of the advantages of guilt are lost. Not only is the person faced with tension and remorse over a specific behavior that needs to be fixed, but he or she is also saddled with feelings of contempt and disgust for a bad, defective self. Ultimately, it is the shame component of this sequence—not the guilt component—that poses the problem. In the case of guilt (about a specific behavior), there are typically a multitude of paths to redemption. Having transgressed, a person feeling guilt (1) often has the option of changing the objectionable behavior or even better yet, (2) has an opportunity to repair the negative consequences, or at the very least, (3) can extend a heart-felt apology. Even in cases where direct reparation or apology is not possible, the person can resolve to do better in the future. In contrast, a self that is defective at its core is much more difficult to transform or amend. When the problem is internal, stable, and global, then we have trouble. Shame—and, in turn, shame-fused guilt—offers little opportunity for redemption. Thus, it is guilt *with an overlay of shame* that most likely leads to the interminable painful rumination and self-castigation so often described in the clinical literature.

The empirical results are quite consistent with this view. Studies employing adjective checklist-type (and other globally worded) measures of shame and guilt find that both shame-prone and guilt-prone styles are associated with psychological symptoms (Harder, 1995; Harder et al., 1992; Harder & Lewis, 1987; Jones & Kugler, 1993; Meehan et al., 1996). On the other hand, when the measures used are sensitive to Lewis's (1971) distinction between shame about the self versus guilt about a specific behavior (e.g., scenario-based methods, such as the TOSCA, assessing shame proneness and guilt proneness with respect to specific situations), the experience of "shame-free" guilt is essentially unrelated to psychological symptoms. Numerous independent studies converge: Guilt-prone children, adolescents, and adults are not at increased risk for depression, anxiety, low self-esteem, etc. (Burggraf & Tangney, 1990; Gramzow & Tangney, 1992; Mclaughlin, 2002; Quiles & Bybee, 1997; Schaefer, 2000; Tangney, 1994;

Tangney et al., 1991, 1995; Tangney & Dearing, 2002; Tangney, Wagner, & Gramzow, 1992).

In short, there does not appear to be a substantial personal cost for the interpersonally beneficial effects of guilt. Guilt is the moral emotion of choice at multiple levels, when considering the individual, relationships, and society at large.

Linking Moral Emotions to Risky, Illegal, and Otherwise Inadvisable Behavior

Beyond psychological adjustment, what are the implications of shame and guilt experiences for the commission of immoral *behavior* in the form of various transgressions, risky behaviors, and other ill-advised deeds? There is the widely held assumption that because shame is so painful, at least it motivates people to avoid "doing wrong" and thereby decreases the likelihood of transgression and impropriety (Barrett, 1995; Ferguson & Stegge, 1995; Kahan, 1997; Zahn-Waxler & Robinson, 1995). As it turns out, there is virtually no direct evidence supporting this presumed adaptive function of shame. To the contrary, recent research with nonclinical samples suggests that shame may even make matters worse.

In a study of college undergraduates, self-reported moral behaviors (assessed by the Conventional Morality Scale; Tooke & Ickes, 1988) were substantially positively correlated with proneness to guilt, but unrelated to proneness to shame (Tangney, 1994). For example, compared to their less guilt-prone peers, guilt-prone individuals were more likely to endorse such items as "I would not steal something I needed, even if I were sure I could get away with it," "I will not take advantage of other people, even when it's clear that they are trying to take advantage of me," and "Morality and ethics don't really concern me" (reversed). In other words, results from this study suggest that guilt *but not shame* motivates people to choose the "moral paths" in life.

The notion that shame and guilt are differentially related to "moral behavior" is further supported by research on drug and alcohol abuse, aggression, and delinquency. In samples of children, adolescents, college students, and adults, shame proneness has been positively related to aggression and delinquency (Ferguson et al., 1999; Tangney, Wagner, Hill-Barlow, Marschall, & Gramzow, 1996; Tibbetts, 1997). In a longitudinal study, Stuewig and McCloskey (2002) found that those high in delinquency and shame proneness at age 15 were more likely to be arrested subsequently for a violent act (according to juvenile court records), compared to those who were high in delinquency and low in shame. Similarly, proneness to problematic feelings of shame have been linked to substance use and abuse (Dearing & Tangney, 2002; Meehan et al., 1996; O'Connor, Berry, Inaba, Weiss, & Morrison, 1994).

Proneness to "shame-free" guilt, on the other hand, does not show the same positive link to aggression, delinquency, and substance abuse. In fact, guilt proneness has been negatively related to alcohol and drug problems (Dearing & Tangney, 2002) and negatively related (Merisca & Bybee, 1994; Stuewig & McCloskey, 2002; Tangney, Wagner, Hill-Barlow, Marschall, & Gramzow, 1996) or inconsistently related (Ferguson, Stegge, Miller, & Olsen, 1999) to aggression and delinquency.

The most direct evidence linking moral emotions with moral behavior comes from our ongoing longitudinal family study of moral emotions. In this study, 380 children and their parents and their grandparents were initially studied when the children were in the fifth grade. Children were recruited from public schools in an ethnically and socioeconomically diverse suburb of Washington, DC. (Sixty percent of the sample is white, 31% black, and 9% other. Most children generally came from low- to moderate-income families. The typical parents had attained a high school education.) The sample was followed up when the index children were 18–19 years old. At that time they participated in an in-depth social and clinical history interview, assessing their emotional and behavioral adjustment across all major life domains. Analyses of these extensive interviews show that moral emotional style in the fifth grade predicts critical "bottom line" behaviors in young adulthood, including substance use, risky sexual behavior, involvement with the criminal justice system, and suicide attempts.

More specifically, shame proneness assessed in the fifth grade predicted later risky driving behavior, earlier initiation of alcohol use, drug use of various kinds, suicide attempts, and a lower likelihood of practicing "safe sex." In contrast, guilt-prone fifth graders were less likely to make suicide attempts, use heroin or marijuana, drive under the influence, and they began drinking at a later age. Compared to peers who experienced guilt infrequently in fifth grade, these guilt-prone children were, in adolescence, less likely to be arrested and convicted. Furthermore, they had fewer sexual partners and were more likely to practice "safe sex." These links between early moral emotional style and subsequent behavioral adjustment held when controlling for family income and mothers' education. Thus, this is not simply an SES (socioeconomic status) effect. Equally important, the effects largely remained even when controlling for children's anger in fifth grade. Thus, these findings do not simply reflect the fact that badly behaved children are inclined to become badly behaved adults.

In short, the capacity for guilt may foster a lifelong pattern of generally following a moral path, motivating individuals to accept responsibility and take reparative action in the wake of the inevitable, if only occasional, failure or transgression. In contrast, there is virtually no direct evidence supporting this presumed adaptive function in the case of shame. To the contrary, recent research with nonclinical samples has linked shame with a range of illegal, risky, or otherwise problematic behaviors.

EVIL DEEDS VERSUS EVIL PERSONS?

Thus far, most of the research discussed has focused on the *average* person's feelings of shame and guilt in response to the failures and transgressions of life. At the heart of this "self versus behavior" approach to moral emotions is the notion that bad (even evil) deeds do not necessarily imply that the perpetrator is a bad (evil) person. Because the vast majority of our research on moral emotions has been conducted on normal, nonclinical, nonidentified participants (e.g., college students, elementary school children and their parents and grandparents, airport travelers, etc.), we have generally taken as a given the reality of the "fundamentally good person." Our assumption has been that people's shame reactions typically reflect an overreaction—an unduly harsh assessment of the self based on cognitive distortions inherent in "I did a bad deed, therefore I'm a bad person." In fact, we have reasoned elsewhere that shame is often psychologically problematic, in part, because the leap from "doing a bad thing" (guilt) to "being a bad person" (shame) is typically unwarranted. Good people do not need (or deserve) to feel much shame—at least, not nearly as much as they typically do.

Are there evil *people* in the world? This is a question we have mulled over a great deal in preparing this chapter and in reflecting on our recent research experience with incarcerated inmates. In studying evil, social psychologists have long emphasized "the power of the situation." Classics such as Zimbardo's prison study and Milgram's obedience studies serve to remind us that given certain circumstances, the "situation" can induce ordinary, even good, people to commit very destructive deeds. But based on our recent research experience with incarcerated inmates, we have come to appreciate the importance of individual differences as well. Our tentative conclusions are:

1. There *are* some people whom many would describe as "evil." There exists a costly but reliable and valid measure (discussed in the following material) with which to identify them. Fortunately, even in jails and prisons, such people are a clear minority. For this small group, effective treatments have yet to be found.
2. The vast majority of prison inmates are not evil. These are people who *have* the capacity for moral emotions. They may engage in bad (even evil) deeds, but they are not bad evil people. The potential for intervention is present.

ASSESSMENT OF EVIL

Evil is a strong word when applied to behaviors, but even more so when applied to persons. Many people are uncomfortable with the notion of identifying or labeling others as evil. For some, the concern is the strong value judgment inherent in the term. For others, the concern is the heavy religious connotations associated with the notion of *evil*. Still others worry that the term is damning, implying an intractable trait with no hope for redemption. "What do we gain by using the term *evil* at all?" asked one of our graduate students. "How does it help us to better understand human behavior to develop an index of evil?"

No question about it, *evil* is a hot term—emotionally loaded, morally judgmental, full of brimstone and fire. But it is a construct that has been with us—often, centrally so—throughout human history. It is a deeply entrenched construct that will not go away. Precisely because it is such an emotionally "hot" construct, it may be especially important to develop objective measures, based in rational methods, preferably using "cooler" terminology.

Measures of "evil" are especially relevant in judicial contexts. For example, in making sentencing decisions, judges and juries are often asked by statute to consider the degree to which crimes are "heinous," "cruel," "wantonly vile," or "inhuman." In some cases, such determinations can be a life-or-death matter. Death penalty statutes, in particular, cite numerous aggravating circumstances that can be referred to when arguing a case.

The problem is that terms such as *heinous, cruel,* and *wantonly vile* are ambiguous in their definitions and are apt to have different meanings to different people. What is cruel to one person may not be cruel to another. For centuries, judges and juries have had to rely on their personal definitions and intuitions to make such decisions—leaving decision makers vulnerable to personal, emotional, and idiosyncratic biases. To address this problem, Welner (1998) has attempted to develop a more objective procedure to measure the degree of depravity, or evil, inherent in a broad range of crimes. Drawing on relatively "cool" conceptualizations, Welner's Depravity Scale considers intent (e.g., evidence of planning), nature of offense (e.g., degree of victim's suffering), and the perpetrator's behavior around the time of the event (e.g., indifference), using strict criteria in order to lessen the amount of subjectivity that typically has pervaded courtrooms when evil acts are evaluated. We may still bristle at the notion of assigning an "evil" score to a particular transgression. Nevertheless, a process based on careful thought, state-of-the-art theory, and hard data may be far preferable to the practice of allowing individuals to "wing it," using their own idiosyncratic basis for judging evil.

Welner's (1998) method is designed to provide an index of evil in reference to specific acts or crimes. Evil can also be conceptualized at the personological level, and it is here that even greater ethical dilemmas and concerns arise. Psychologists studying criminal behavior have identified a subgroup of offenders who really do appear to embody the characteristics that most people would ascribe to "evil" persons. According to Robert Hare, one of the leading authorities on psychopathy, "Psychopaths are social predators who charm, manipulate, and ruthlessly plow their way through life, leaving a broad trail of broken hearts, shattered expectations, and empty wallets. Completely lacking in conscience and in feelings for others, they selfishly take what they want and do as they please, violating social norms and expectations without the slightest sense of guilt or regret" (Hare, 1999, p. xi). These behaviors are not a passing phase but a personality style presumed to be *pervasive* and *longstanding*.

The most extreme examples of psychopathy are those who have become infamous. Ted Bundy, John Wayne Gacy, and Richard Ramirez were all psychopaths as well as serial killers. But the majority of psychopaths are not serial killers; they might kill but only when it serves their interest. Many psychopaths perpetrate confidence scams, deal drugs, and commit a variety of other criminal acts. They are often impulsive and reckless, unconcerned about who they hurt, focused more on instant gratification than on any sort of criminal plotting.

The "gold standard" for assessing psychopathy is Hare's Psychopathy Checklist—Revised (PCL-R; Hare, 1991). The PCL-R yields a total Psychopathy score as well as scores on two related factors.[2] Factor 1 assesses the "selfish, callous and remorseless use of others." It taps a personality style defined by people who are glib and superficial, egocentric and grandiose, deceitful and manipulative, display shallow emotions, and are lacking in feelings of remorse or guilt as well as the capacity to empathize with others. Factor 2 assesses a "chronically unstable and antisocial lifestyle," focusing more directly on criminal and other problematic behaviors. People who score high are impulsive, have poor behavior controls, need excitement, lack responsibility, displayed behavior problems early in life, and have persisted in antisocial behavior as adults.

Although measured on a continuum (20 items, 3-point scale from 0 = not present to 2 = definitely present for each item), PCL-R scores are thought by many to reflect an underlying dichotomy. Persons who score 30 or higher on the PCL-R are thought to present a qualitatively distinct characterological disorder known as psychopathy (Harris, Rice, & Quinsey, 1994). From this perspective, psychopathy is a discrete category or "taxon" (see also Hare, 1996; Meehl, 1992, 1995).

---

[2]Psychopathy is different from the DSM-IV diagnosis of antisocial personality disorder (APD). Psychopathy is defined by a cluster of personality traits as well as antisocial behaviors. APD, on the other hand, is diagnosed using a checklist of antisocial and criminal behaviors. Although most criminals can be diagnosed as having APD, only a small subgroup are true psychopaths.

The good news is that psychopaths are relatively rare, comprising approximately 1% of the general population, 15% of local jail inmates, and 25% of state and federal prison inmates (Bodholdt, Richards, & Gacono, 2000; Hare, 1991, 1996). The bad news is that this very small proportion of the general population accounts for the majority of our nation's crime and associated heartache (Wolfgang, Figlio, & Sellin, 1972). According to Hare (1999) about 20% of male and female prison inmates are psychopaths, yet they are responsible for more than 50% of the serious crimes committed. In addition, they are largely violent in that they commit twice as many violent and aggressive acts, both in and out of prison, as do other criminals. In fact, 44% of the offenders who killed a law enforcement officer on duty were psychopaths (Federal Bureau of Investigations, as cited in Hare, 1999). There truly are a small number of remarkably destructive people perpetrating the majority of this world's evil deeds.

We wish to emphasize that use of the PCL-R to assess psychopathy—or "evil"—does not imply any particular etiology of this construct. The PCL-R is "descriptive": It measures certain traits and behaviors that are considered to be indicative of psychopathy. It contains no implications as to the root cause of psychopathy, which could be genetics, bad parents, bad childhood, impaired superego, the devil, a "disorder of emotion" caused by brain dysfunction, or just bad luck (Blair, 1995, 2001, 2002; Blair, Colledge, Murray, & Mitchell, 2001; Karpman, 1948; Mealey, 1995a, 1995b; Porter, 1996; Weiler & Widom, 1996). The jury's still out on the causes of psychopathy, but in order to answer the all-important etiology question, we need a reasonably objective, repeatable (e.g., reliable and valid) method for measuring characteristics associated with evil. A descriptive scientific index is a prerequisite.

Use of the PCL-R to assess psychopathy is not cheap. It requires an average 6 hours of time from a specially trained clinician, including client interview, records review, scoring, and interpretation. But if one is interested in quantifying "evil" by using strict, empirically-derived criteria in order to minimize subjectivity (Hare, 1991); if one is interested in predicting recidivism (Harris, Rice, & Quinsey, 1993; Hart, Kropp, & Hare, 1988; Serin & Amos, 1995); or if one is interested in identifying the root causes of psychopathy in order to effectively intervene, the PCL-R is clearly the instrument of choice.

SHAME, GUILT, EMPATHY, AND THE PSYCHOPATH

Just what does the moral emotional profile of the psychopath look like? There is surprisingly little systematic data on the moral reasoning or moral emotions of psychopaths. Psychologists and criminologists alike often assume that psychopaths lack any real capacity for moral emotions. According to both clinical and theoretical accounts, psychopaths lack a sense of remorse and guilt and, more generally, are unable to empathize with others (Cleckley, 1941; Rogers & Bagby, 1994; Samenow, 1984, 1989). In fact, impaired empathy and an absence of guilt are two of 20 criteria that define psychopathy, as measured by the PCL-R (Hare, 1991). But researchers have yet to systematically measure and evaluate the psychopath's capacity for experiencing guilt and empathy. Even less is known about the experience of shame in psychopaths or in incarcerated offenders more generally. Are psychopaths literally "shameless," lacking the capacity for yet a third moral–emotional experience? Or are psychopaths, in contrast, unusually and acutely sensitive to feelings of shame and humiliation—feelings so painful that they turn to delinquent, aggressive, interpersonally exploitative behavior as an escape?

We recently began a prospective study of moral emotions and criminal recidivism and rehabilitation at a large, urban, county adult detention center. Based on analyses of the first 143 male participants enrolled in the study, it is not possible to draw any firm conclusions about the moral emotions of psychopaths. Only 29 (20%) meet PCL-R criteria for psychopathy.[3] (Once completed, the project should include a substantial subsample of psychopaths—approximately 135, given a target total sample of 900 general population inmates.) Initial analyses of the first 143 general population inmates showed virtually no correlation between the PCL-R scores (measured on a continuum) and baseline measures of shame proneness and various dimensions of empathy. However, total PCL-R scores were negatively correlated with the propensity to experience guilt ($r = -.19$, $p < .05$. This appears to be largely due to Factor 2 (i.e., antisocial lifestyle) ($r = -.22$, $p = .01$), consistent with numerous other studies showing a link between guilt and "good" behavior. Factor 1 (i.e., parasitic personality style) showed no consistent relationship to self-reported shame, guilt, or empathy (perhaps owing to the differential validity of these measures among those high on psychopathy).

---

[3] For this study we used the Screening Version of the Psychopathy Checklist (PCL:SV; Hart, Cox, & Hare, 1995). The PCL:SV is a 12-item measure of psychopathy derived from the 20-item PCL-R. Like the longer version, it consists of the same two factors, each containing six items. (The PCL:SV manual refers to the subscales as Part 1 and Part 2, paralleling the PCL-R's Factor 1 and Factor 2. In describing our PCL:SV, we employ the more familiar term *Factor* to avoid confusion among readers not acquainted with the PCL:SV, specifically.) The screening version has excellent concurrent validity with the PCL-R. Across five different samples, the weighted mean correlation between total scores on the two versions was .80 (.67 and .68 for Factors 1 and 2, respectively). In addition, it has shown good internal consistency, with a weighted mean Cronbach's alpha across 11 studies of .84 for the total scale (.81 for Factor 1 and .75 for Factor 2). Although no formal test–retest reliability was reported for the screening version, the PCL-R was found to have a 1-month reliability of .94. Using the Spearman–Brown formula, they estimate the test–retest reliability for the screening version at about .90 (Hart et al., 1995).

One very real possibility is that psychopaths are unwilling or unable to accurately report their experiences of shame or guilt. That is, their self-reports of moral emotions may be differentially invalid. Psychopathic participants may tell the truth ("I feel no guilt") or they might lie ("Oh, I was so sorry") in order to give the most socially desirable response or just for the hell of it (pathological lying is one of the items on the PCL-R). The notion here is that above a certain point on the psychopathy scale, self-reported moral emotions (and, indeed, other socially desirable characteristics as well) may be basically meaningless.[4] As our sample grows, we will be able to empirically test this "differential validity" hypothesis by examining the degree to which psychopathy moderates already established relationships of shame with other key variables (e.g., empathy, aggression).

Another possibility is that there are distinct subtypes of psychopathy (Brodie, 1995; Mealey, 1995a; Schmitt & Newman, 1999). Paralleling Brodie's (1995) distinction between isolative versus interactive sociopaths, some individuals who score high on Factor 1 may be inordinately sensitive to feelings of shame and humiliation, whereas others may be literally "shameless," lacking the capacity to feel any sort of negative self-directed emotion. Along similar lines, Schmitt and Newman (1999) distinguished between "high anxious" and "low anxious" psychopaths. Such differences would have important implications for intervention.

THE NONPSYCHOPATHIC INMATE

Perhaps the most important single finding in the literature on psychopathy is that the vast majority of inmates are potentially reachable. Based on empirically derived Hare (1991, 1996) criteria, approximately 85% of local jail inmates (75% of inmates in state or federal prisons) are *not psychopaths;* they do not show the combination of behavioral and personality characteristics that mark the true psychopath.

Our guess is that an important part of what sets psychopaths apart from nonpsychopaths is that the latter have some capacity for moral emotions. They may engage in bad (even evil) deeds, but they are not bad evil people. When they do commit bad acts, they know they have done something bad, and they feel bad about it (even if they do not readily acknowledge these feelings to others). The key question to explore regarding this large majority of current and future inmates is, What *kind* of moral emo-

---

[4]Similarly, in the criminology literature, Gottfredson and Hirschi (1990) suggested that self-report questionnaires have differential validity depending on the degree of criminality (i.e., degree of self-control) of the individual. In one test of this theory, using item-response theory models, Piquero, MacIntosh, and Hickman (2000) found that "one's level of self-control influences self-report responses" (p. 897).

tion(s) do they feel? Are they inclined to feel *guilt* about their specific misdeeds and feel a proactive press to repair and make amends to the harmed person? Or are they likely to feel *shame* as a person? Shame leads to denial, defense, and retaliation in response to the mistaken notion that because they did bad (even evil), they *are* bad, evil persons.

In normal populations, shame is not a preferred response in psychological terms. It is a moral emotion that can sometimes go haywire, making matters worse (read *more evil*) than they might otherwise have been. As noted, feelings of shame frequently provoke self-loathing, denial, defensiveness, externalization of blame, and hostile aggression. But the capacity to experience shame may be preferable to the complete absence of moral–emotional experience presumed to be characteristic of psychopaths. In extreme populations, the mere existence of any sort of self-evaluative emotion may offer a ray of hope for rehabilitation and redemption. In short, shame can serve as a starting point—a hook—with the ultimate treatment goal of transforming maladaptive shame into adaptive guilt.

IMPLICATIONS FOR TREATMENT AND POLICY

Although research on moral emotions and moral behavior is still in its infancy, particularly as it pertains to antisocial behavior and criminal recidivism, the theory and research reviewed here already have a number of direct treatment and policy implications.

Treatment Implications

For most of the past century the predominant model in the field of corrections was one of rehabilitation. This perspective changed during the 1970s and 1980s, when the concept of "nothing works" gained ground based on several reviews of the treatment literature (Martinson, 1974; Sechrest, White, & Brown, 1979). Recently, due to the development of more sophisticated methods, such as meta-analysis, and tighter control over program implementation, studies have begun to show that rehabilitation *can* effectively change some offenders (Cecil, Drapkin, MacKenzie, & Hickman, 2000; Cullen & Gendreau, 2000; MacKenzie, 2000; Wilson, Gallagher, & MacKenzie, 2000). There is now a call for more "evidence-based" corrections' models (Farrington, Petrosino, & Welsh, 2001; MacKenzie, 2001). As Cullen and Gendreau (2001) state, we need to now move from "nothing works" to "what works." An even more important question may be "*What* works with *whom*?" In the search for "what works," criminologists and forensic psychologists now emphasize that a "one-size-fits-all" approach is not terribly effective when designing treatment for criminal offenders. What is needed is a better understanding of the key moderators of response to treatment—an understanding of *what* works for *whom*. Based on a comprehensive meta-analysis of four decades of correctional research, Andrews and colleagues (1990) identified three elements—risk, need, and responsivity—as the variables most strongly linked to successful outcome.

In the search for factors that predict treatment effectiveness, another especially promising candidate is psychopathy, which is related to important personality characteristics, broad patterns of behavior, and fundamental motivations. It follows that different types of treatment may be better suited for individuals high versus low in psychopathy.

From our perspective, restorative justice-inspired programs may be especially well suited for low psychopathic, high shame-prone individuals. *Restorative justice* is a philosophical framework that calls for active participation by the victim, the offender, and the community toward achieving the goal of repairing the fabric of the community (Braithwaite, 1989, 2000). For example, the "Impact of Crime" workshop implemented in Fairfax County, Virginia's Adult Detention Center emphasizes principles of community, personal responsibility, and reparation. Utilizing cognitive restructuring techniques, case workers and group facilitators challenge common distorted ways of thinking about crime, victims, and locus of responsibility. As inmates grapple with issues of responsibility, the question of blame inevitably arises, as do the emotions of self-blame. Upon reexamining the causes of their legal difficulties and revisiting the circumstances surrounding their offense and its consequences, many inmates experience new feelings of shame or guilt, or both. Another important feature of the restorative justice approach is its "guilt-inducing, shame-reducing" philosophy. In early stages of treatment, offenders may feel a predominance of shame, focusing on themselves rather than the plight of their victims. Although not optimal, in themselves, feelings of shame can serve as a therapist's "hook," yielding intense feelings that can be processed, transformed, and harnessed as the more "adaptive" feelings of guilt. In the long term, restorative justice approaches (e.g., Maruna, 2001) encourage offenders to take responsibility for their behavior, acknowledge negative consequences, feel guilt for having *done* the wrong thing, empathize with their victims, and act to make amends. But they are ultimately discouraged from feeling shame about *themselves*.

These ideas can also be incorporated into existing jail and prison programs. Therapists and group facilitators can help inmates develop a more adaptive moral emotional style by (1) educating offenders about the distinction between feelings of guilt about specific behaviors versus feelings of shame about the self, (2) encouraging appropriate experiences of guilt and emphasizing associated constructive motivations to repair or make amends, and (3) helping offenders recognize and modify maladaptive shame experiences, in addition to (4) using inductive and educational strategies that foster a capacity for perspective taking and other-oriented empathy.

Such programs may be of little benefit to psychopaths, however, who lack the basic building blocks of an effective moral motivational system (Gacono, Nieberding, Owen, Rubel, & Bodholdt, 2001; Kernberg, 1998). In fact, evidence suggests that corrections-based treatment is less effective for inmates high on psychopathy (Harris, Rice, & Cormier, 1991; Ogloff, Wong, & Greenwood, 1990) or high on Factor 1 (Hare, Clark, Grann, & Thornton, 2000). In fact, programs incorporating a significant empathy-training component may be *contraindicated* for psychopaths (Rice, Harris, & Cormier, 1992). A one-size-fits-all approach may be simpler in implementation, but ultimately it may represent an inefficient use of resources. Inmates unlikely to benefit from certain programs (e.g., psychopaths in restorative justice programs) take up precious space and, at the same time, do not have the opportunity to benefit from alternative treatments specifically designed with their unique characteristics and needs in mind.

Moreover, treatment efficacy may be substantially enhanced by treating psychopaths and nonpsychopaths in separate groups. Owing to their unique personality traits, psychopaths are particularly likely to disrupt and undermine the treatment process, especially in groups (Hare, 1999). They are detrimental to the therapeutic milieu, they monopolize group time, and they discourage others from participating by mocking, intimidating, or threatening those who do attempt to benefit from the treatment. Perhaps equally important, they often model poor attitudes and behavior, using their substantial charm and persuasive ability to derail constructive therapeutic interactions and prosocial messages.

Many prisons in England, Canada, and the United States have adopted a "no treatment" policy for psychopaths, a policy upheld by the U.S. Supreme Court. Yet because we have not had success so far in treating psychopaths does not mean that they are untreatable. We need to work at developing and testing psychopathy-specific interventions (Hare, 1996, 1999). Many previous studies suffered from methodological weaknesses (e.g., weak implementation of the intervention, no control group, excessive attrition, and no random assignment). Not only are interventions improving, but so are the methods used in evaluating such programs. In fact, recently there has been some evidence that treatment decreased the risk of subsequent violence in a group of psychopaths drawn from a civil psychiatric patient population (Skeem, Monahan, & Mulvey, 2002). Although this is just one study, and it needs to be replicated, it does offer a ray of hope. Hare (1996) recommends cognitive-behavioral treatment that is less concerned with empathy and more focused on teaching such individuals to take responsibility for their behavior. In addition, psychopaths should remain under intensive supervision both inside an institution and out in the community. Finally, if psychopathy is truly biologically based, as some recent research indicates (Blair, 1995, 2001, 2002; Blair et al., 2001, 2002; Kiehl et al., 2001), a psychopharmacological treatment model is not out of the realm of possibility. With the advent of "designer" pharmaceuticals, we have seen dramatic advances in treating depression by targeting highly specific neurotransmitter processes. It is conceivable that scientists will one day provide society with the option of treating psychopathic offenders with antipsychopathic pharmocotherapy.

Implications for Jail and Prison Policies

Theory and research on moral emotions have implications for more general jail/prison policies and procedures. Aspects of the incarceration experience itself may provoke feelings of shame and humiliation (Dunnegan, 1997; Gilligan, 1996; Smith, 1992), and it has been suggested that, particularly when punishment is perceived as unjust, such feelings of shame can lead to defiance and, paradoxically, an *increase* in criminal behavior (Sherman, 1993). This outcome is especially troubling in light of Indermaur's (1994) finding that fully 90% of offenders view their sentences as unfair! Knowledge of the relative pros and cons of the different moral emotions can help inform correctional officials as they make policy decisions about specific practices (e.g., the manner in which strip searches are conducted, how inmates are addressed), or more general aspects of the jail/prison environment (e.g., "direct supervision" models of incarceration that place deputies in common living areas, as opposed to monitoring inmates down long corridors of peepholes) to minimize the potential for humiliation.

Implications for Judicial Policy

A third important area where basic research on moral emotions has immediate implicit applications concerns judicial sentencing practices. As it becomes clear that imprisonment is both extremely costly and ineffective at reducing crime (Andrews et al., 1990; Bonta, 1996), judges understandably have begun to search for creative alternatives to traditional sentences. The trend toward "shaming sentences" has gained a good deal of momentum in recent years. Judges across the country are sentencing offenders to parade around in public carrying signs broadcasting their crimes, to post signs on their front lawns warning neighbors of their vices, and to display, for example, "drunk driver" bumper stickers on their cars. Other judges have focused on sentencing alternatives based on a restorative justice model (e.g., community service and other forms of reparation), which seem to be designed—at least, implicitly—to elicit feelings of guilt for the offense and its consequences, rather than feelings of shame and humiliation about the self. In seeking less costly and potentially more effective alternatives, judges have been operating in an empirical vacuum. Regarding shaming sentences, in particular, there exist no systematic data on the effectiveness or nonmonetary costs of such efforts to publicly humiliate offenders, but our findings strongly argue that this approach is a misguided approach to alternative sentencing. Rather than encouraging people to accept responsibility and make reparations, shame often provokes anger, aggression, denial, and externalization of blame.

SUMMARY AND CONCLUSIONS

Recent research indicates that, in normal populations, guilt is the more "moral" adaptive emotion, whereas shame carries with it substantial hidden costs. Our recent research with incarcerated offenders, however, has caused us to reexamine some of our assumptions about the presumably maladaptive nature of shame. Although shame is not an optimal response to one's failures and transgressions, the capacity to experience shame may be preferable to the complete absence of moral emotion presumed to be characteristic of psychopaths. Psychopaths are the sort of people whom many would describe as "evil"; there exists a costly but reliable and valid measure to identify them. Fortunately, even in jails and prisons, psychopaths are a clear minority. By differentiating psychopathic from nonpsychopathic offenders, more effective treatments can be designed specific to each group's unique characteristics. At the same time, interventions with nonpsychopathic inmates may be enhanced by delivering treatment separately from their psychopathic peers.

REFERENCES

Allan, S., Gilbert, P., & Goss, K. (1994). An exploration of shame measures: II. Psychopathology. *Personality and Individual Differences, 17,* 719–722.

Andrews, D. A., Zinger, I., Hoge, R. D., Bonta, J., Gendreau, P., & Cullen, F. T. (1990). Does correctional treatment work? A clinically relevant and psychologically informed meta-analysis. *Criminology, 28,* 369–403.

Barrett, K. C. (1995). A functionalist approach to shame and guilt. In J. P. Tangney & K. W. Fischer (Eds.), *Self-conscious emotions: The psychology of shame, guilt, embarrassment, and pride* (pp. 25–63). New York: Guilford Press.

Baumeister, R. F., Stillwell, A. M., & Heatherton, T. F. (1994). Guilt: An interpersonal approach. *Psychological Bulletin, 115,* 243–267.

Baumeister, R. F., Stillwell, A. M., & Heatherton, T. F. (1995a). Interpersonal aspects of guilt: Evidence from narrative studies. In J. P. Tangney & K. W. Fischer (Eds.), *Self-conscious emotions: The psychology of shame, guilt, embarrassment, and pride* (pp. 255–273). New York: Guilford Press.

Baumeister, R. F., Stillwell, A. M., & Heatherton, T. F. (1995b). Personal narratives about guilt: Role in action control and interpersonal relationships. *Basic and Applied Social Psychology, 17,* 173–198.

Blair, R. J. R. (1995). A cognitive developmental approach to morality: Investigating the psychopath. *Cognition, 57,* 1–29.

Blair, R. J. R. (2001). Neuro-cognitive models of aggression, the antisocial personality disorders and psychopathy. *Journal of Neurology, Neurosurgery and Psychiatry, 71,* 727–731.

Blair, R. J. R. (2002). A neuro-cognitive model of the psychopathic individual. In T. Robbins & M. Ron (Eds.), *Disorders of brain and mind II.* Cambridge, UK: Cambridge University Press.

Blair, R. J. R., Colledge, R., Murray, L., & Mitchell, D. G. (2001). A selective impairment in the processing of sad and fearful expressions in children with psychopathic tendencies. *Journal of Abnormal Child Psychology, 29*(6), 491–498.

Blair, R. J. R., Mitchell, D. G. V., Richell, R. A., Kelly, S., Leonard, A., Newman, C., & Scott, S. K. (2002). Turn a deaf ear to fear: Impaired recognition of vocal affect in psychopathic individuals. *Journal of Abnormal Psychology, 111,* 682–686.

Blatt, S. (1974). Levels of object representation in anaclitic and introjective depression. *Psychoanalytic Study of the Child, 29,* 107–157.

Bodholdt, R. H., Richards, H. R., & Gacono, C. B. (2000). Assessing psychopathy in adults: The psychopathy checklist—revised and screening version. In C. B. Gacono (Ed.), *The clinical and forensic assessment of psychopathy: A practitioner's guide* (pp. 55–86). Mahwah, NJ: Erlbaum.

Bonta, J. (1996). Risk-needs assessment and treatment. In A. T. Harland (Ed.), *Choosing correctional options that work: Defining the demand and evaluating the supply* (pp. 18–32). Thousand Oaks, CA: Sage.

Braithwaite, J. (1989). *Crime, shame, and reintegration.* Melbourne: Cambridge University Press.

Braithwaite, J. (2000). Shame and criminal justice. *Canadian Journal of Criminology, 42,* 281–298.

Brodie, P. (1995). *How sociopaths love: Sociopathy and interpersonal relationships.* Unpublished doctoral dissertation, George Mason University, Fairfax, VA.

Burggraf, S. A., & Tangney, J. P. (1990, June). *Shame-proneness, guilt-proneness, and attributional style related to children's depression.* Poster presented at the annual meeting of the American Psychological Society, Dallas, TX.

Cecil, D. K., Drapkin, D. A., MacKenzie, D. L., & Hickman, L. J. (2000). The effectiveness of adult basic education and life-skills programs in reducing recidivism: A review and assessment of the research. *Journal of Correctional Education, 51,* 207–226.

Cleckley, H. (1941). *The mask of sanity.* St. Louis, MO: Mosby.

Cook, D. R. (1988, August). *The measurement of shame: The Internalized Shame Scale.* Paper presented at the annual meeting of the American Psychological Association, Atlanta, GA.

Cook, D. R. (1991). Shame, attachment, and addictions: Implications for family therapists. *Contemporary Family Therapy, 13,* 405–419.

Cullen, F., & Gendreau, P. (2000). Assessing correctional rehabilitation: Policy, practice and prospects. In J. Horney, J. Martin, D. L. MacKenzie, R. Peterson, & D. Rosenbaum (Eds.), *Policies, processes and decisions of the criminal justice system.* Washington, DC: National Institute of Justice, U.S. Department of Justice.

Cullen, F., & Gendreau, P. (2001). From nothing works to what works: Changing professional ideology in the 21st century. *The Prison Journal, 81,* 312–337.

Dearing, R. L., & Tangney, J. P. (2002, June). *The differential relationship of college student alcohol problems to shame-proneness, guilt-proneness, and externalization of blame.* Poster session at the annual meeting of the Research Society on Alcoholism, San Francisco.

Dunnegan, S. W. (1997). Violence, trauma and substance abuse. *Journal of Psychoactive Drugs, 29,* 345–351.

Eisenberg, N. (1986). *Altruistic cognition, emotion, and behavior.* Hillsdale, NJ: Erlbaum.

Eisenberg, N., & Miller, P. A. (1987). Empathy, sympathy, and altruism: Empirical and conceptual links. In N. Eisenberg & J. Strayer (Eds.), *Empathy and its development* (pp. 292–316). New York: Cambridge University Press.

Ellis, A. (1962). *Reason and emotion in psychotherapy.* New York: Lyle Stuart.

Farrington, D. P., Petrosino, A., & Welsh, B. C. (2001). Systematic reviews and cost–benefit analyses of correctional interventions. *The Prison Journal, 81,* 338–358.

Ferguson, T. J., & Stegge, H. (1995). Emotional states and traits in children: The case of guilt and shame. In J. P. Tangney & K. W. Fischer (Eds.), *Self-conscious emotions: The psychology of shame, guilt, embarrassment, and pride* (pp. 174–197). New York: Guilford Press.

Ferguson, T. J., Stegge, H., & Damhuis, I. (1990). Guilt and shame experiences in elementary school-age children. In R. J. Takens (Ed.), *European perspectives in psychology* (Vol. 1, pp. 195–218). New York: Wiley.

Ferguson, T. J., Stegge, H., & Damhuis, I. (1991). Children's understanding of guilt and shame. *Child Development, 62,* 827–839.

Ferguson, T. J., Stegge, H., Miller, E. R., & Olsen, M. E. (1999). Guilt, shame, and symptoms in children. *Developmental Psychology, 35,* 347–357.

Feshbach, N. D. (1978). Studies of empathic behavior in children. In B. A. Maher (Ed.), *Progress in experimental personality research* (Vol. 8, pp. 1–47). New York: Academic Press.

Feshbach, N. D. (1984). Empathy, empathy training, and the regulation of aggression in elementary school children. In R. M. Kaplan, V. J. Konenci, & R. Novoco (Eds.), *Aggression in children and youth.* The Hague, Netherlands: Nijhoff.

Feshbach, N. D. (1987). Parental empathy and child adjustment/maladjustment. In N. Eisenberg & J. Strayer (Eds.), *Empathy and its development* (pp. 271–291). New York: Cambridge University Press.

Feshbach, N. D., & Feshbach, S. (1969). The relationship between empathy and aggression in two age groups. *Developmental Psychology, 1,* 102–107.

Feshbach, N. D., & Feshbach, S. (1982). Empathy training and the regulation of aggression: Potentialities and limitations. *Academic Psychology Bulletin, 4,* 399–413.

Feshbach, N. D., & Feshbach, S. (1986). Aggression and altruism: A personality perspective. In C. Zahn-Waxler, E. M. Cummings, & R. Iannotti (Eds.), *Altruism and aggression: Biological and social origins* (pp. 189–217). Cambridge, UK: Cambridge University Press.

Freud, S. (1955). Notes upon a case of obsessional neurosis. In J. Strachey (Ed. & Trans.), *The standard edition of the complete psychological works of Sigmund Freud* (Vol. 10, pp. 155–318). London: Hogarth Press. (Original work published 1909)

Freud, S. (1957). Mourning and melancholia. In J. Strachey (Ed. & Trans.), *The standard edition of the complete psychological works of Sigmund Freud* (Vol. 14, pp. 243–258). London: Hogarth Press. (Original work published 1917)

Freud, S. (1961). The dissolution of the Oedipus Complex. In J. Strachey (Ed. & Trans.), *The standard edition of the complete psychological works of Sigmund Freud* (Vol. 19, pp. 173–182). London: Hogarth Press. (Original work published 1924)

Freud, S. (1961). The id and the ego. In J. Strachey (Ed. & Trans.), *The standard edition of the complete psychological works of Sigmund Freud* (Vol. 19, pp. 12–66). London: Hogarth Press. (Original work published 1923)

Gacono, C. B., Nieberding, R .J., Owen, A., Rubel, J., & Bodholdt, R. (2001). Treating conduct disorder, antisocial, and psychopathic personalities. In J. Ashford, B. Sales, & W. Reid (Eds.), *Treating adult and juvenile offenders with special needs* (pp. 99–129). Washington, DC: American Psychological Association.

Gilligan, J. (1996). Exploring shame in special settings: A psychotherapeutic study. In C. Cordess & M. Cox (Eds.), *Forensic psychotherapy: Crime, psychodynamics and the offender patient: Vol. 2. Mainly practice* (pp. 475–489). London: Kingsley.

Gottfredson, M. R., & Hirschi, T. (1990). *A general theory of crime.* Palo Alto, CA: Stanford University Press.

Gramzow, R., & Tangney, J. P. (1992). Proneness to shame and the narcissistic personality. *Personality and Social Psychology Bulletin, 18,* 369–376.

Harder, D. W. (1995). Shame and guilt assessment, and relationships of shame- and guilt-proneness to psychopathology. In J. P. Tangney & K. W. Fischer (Eds.), *Self-conscious emotions: The psychology of shame, guilt, embarrassment, and pride* (pp. 368–392). New York: Guilford Press.

Harder, D. W., Cutler, L., & Rockart, L. (1992). Assessment of shame and guilt and their relationship to psychopathology. *Journal of Personality Assessment, 59,* 584–604.

Harder, D. W., & Lewis, S. J. (1987). The assessment of shame and guilt. In J. N. Butcher & C. D. Spielberger (Eds.), *Advances in personality assessment* (Vol. 6, pp. 89–114). Hillsdale, NJ: Erlbaum.

Hare, R. D. (1991). *The Hare Psychopathy Checklist—Revised.* Toronto: Multi-Health Systems.

Hare, R. D. (1996). Psychopathy: A clinical construct whose time has come. *Criminal Justice and Behavior, 23,* 25–54.

Hare, R. D. (1999). *Without conscience: The disturbing world of the psychopaths among us.* New York: Guilford Press.

Hare, R. D., Clark, D., Grann, M., & Thornton, D. (2000). Psychopathy and the predictive validity of the PCL-R: An international perspective. *Behavioral Sciences and the Law, 18*, 623–645.

Harris, G. T., Rice, M. E., & Cormier, C. A. (1991) Psychopathy and violent recidivism. *Law and Human Behavior, 15*, 625–637.

Harris, G. T., Rice, M. E., & Cormier, C. A. (1994). Psychopaths: Is a therapeutic community therapeutic? *Therapeutic Communities, 15*, 283–299.

Harris, G. T., Rice, M. E., & Quinsey, V. L. (1993). Violent recidivism of mentally disordered offenders: The development of a statistical prediction instrument. *Criminal Justice and Behavior, 20*, 315–335.

Harris, G. T., Rice, M. E., & Quinsey, V. L. (1994). Psychopathy as a taxon: Evidence that psychopaths are a discrete class. *Journal of Consulting and Clinical Psychology, 62*, 387–397.

Hart, S. D., Cox, D. N., & Hare, R. D. (1995). *The Hare Psychopathy Checklist—Screening Version*. Toronto: Multi-Health Systems.

Hart, S. D., Kropp, P. R., & Hare, R. D. (1988). Psychopathy and conditional release from prison. *Journal of Consulting and Clinical Psychology, 56*, 227–232.

Hartmann, E., & Loewenstein, R. (1962). Notes on the superego. *Psychoanalytic Study of the Child, 17*, 42–81.

Hoblitzelle, W. (1987). Attempts to measure and differentiate shame and guilt: The relation between shame and depression. In H. B. Lewis (Ed.), *The role of shame in symptom formation* (pp. 207–235). Hillsdale, NJ: Erlbaum.

Hoffman, M. L. (1982). Development of prosocial motivation: Empathy and guilt. In N. Eisenberg-Berg (Ed.), *Development of prosocial behavior* (pp. 281–313). New York: Academic Press.

Indermaur, D. (1994). Offenders' perceptions of sentencing. *Australian Psychologist, 29*, 140–144.

Jones, W. H., & Kugler, K. (1993). Interpersonal correlates of the Guilt Inventory. *Journal of Personality Assessment, 61*, 246–258.

Kahan, D. M. (1997). Ignorance of law is an excuse—but only for the virtuous. *Michigan Law Review, 96*, 127–154.

Karpman, B. (1948). Conscience in the psychopath: Another version. *American Journal of Orthopsychiatry, 18*, 455–491.

Keltner, D., & Buswell, B. N. (1996). Evidence for the distinctness of embarrassment, shame, and guilt: A study of recalled antecedents and facial expressions of emotion. *Cognition and Emotion, 10*, 155–171.

Kernberg, O. F. (1998). The psychotherapeutic management of psychopathic, narcissistic, and paranoid transferences. In T. Millon, E. Simonsen, M. Birket-Smith, & R. D. Davis (Eds.), *Psychopathy: Antisocial, criminal, and violent behavior* (pp. 372–392). New York: Guilford Press.

Kiehl, K. A., Smith, A. M., Hare, R. D., Mendrek, A., Forster, B. B., Brink, J., & Liddle, P. F. (2001). Limbic abnormalities in affective processing by criminal psychopaths as revealed by functional magnetic resonance imaging. *Biological Psychiatry, 50*, 677–684.

Leith, K. P., & Baumeister, R. F. (1998). Empathy, shame, guilt, and narratives of interpersonal conflicts: Guilt-prone people are better at perspective taking. *Journal of Personality, 66*, 1–37.

Lewis, H. B. (1971). *Shame and guilt in neurosis*. New York: International Universities Press.

Lindsay-Hartz, J. (1984). Contrasting experiences of shame and guilt. *American Behavioral Scientist, 27,* 689–704.

Lindsay-Hartz, J., de Rivera, J., & Mascolo, M. F. (1995). Differentiating shame and guilt and their effects on motivation. In J. P. Tangney & K. W. Fischer (Eds.), *Self-conscious emotions: Shame, guilt, embarrassment, and pride* (pp. 274–300). New York: Guilford Press.

MacKenzie, D. L. (2000). Evidence based corrections: Identifying what works. *Crime and Delinquency, 46,* 457–471.

MacKenzie, D. L. (2001). Corrections and sentencing in the 21st century: Evidence based corrections and sentencing. *The Prison Journal, 81,* 299–312.

Marschall, D. E. (1996). *Effects of induced shame on subsequent empathy and altruistic behavior*. Unpublished master's thesis, George Mason University, Fairfax, VA.

Martinson, R. (1974). What works? Questions and answers about prison reform. *Public Interest, 35,* 22–54

Maruna, S. (2001). *Making good: How ex-convicts reform and rebuild their lives*. Washington, DC: American Psychological Association.

McLaughlin, D. E. (2002). Posttraumatic stress disorder symptoms and self-conscious affect among battered women. *Dissertation Abstract International, 62,* 4470B.

Mealey, L. (1995a). Primary sociopathy (psychopathy) is a type, secondary is not. *Behavioral and Brain Sciences, 19,* 579–599.

Mealey, L. (1995b). The sociobiology of sociopathy: An integrated evolutionary model. *Behavioral and Brain Sciences, 19,* 523–540.

Meehan, M. A., O'Connor, L. E., Berry, J. W., Weiss, J., Morrison, A., & Acampora, A. (1996). Guilt, shame, and depression in clients in recovery from addiction. *Journal of Psychoactive Drugs, 28,* 125–134.

Meehl, P. E. (1992). Factors and taxa, traits and types, differences of degree and differences in kind. *Journal of Personality, 60,* 117–174.

Meehl, P. E. (1995). Bootstraps taxometrics: Solving the classification problem in psychopathology. *American Psychologist, 50,* 266–275.

Merisca, R., & Bybee, J. S. (1994, April). *Guilt, not moral reasoning, relates to volunteerism, prosocial behavior, lowered aggressiveness, and eschewal of racism*. Poster presented at the annual meeting of the Eastern Psychological Association, Providence, RI.

Niedenthal, P. M., Tangney, J. P., & Gavanski, I. (1994). "If only I weren't" versus "If only I hadn't": Distinguishing shame and guilt in counterfactual thinking. *Journal of Personality and Social Psychology, 67,* 585–595.

O'Connor, L. E., Berry, J. W., Inaba, D., Weiss, J., & Morrison, A. (1994). Shame, guilt, and depression in men and women in recovery from addiction. *Journal of Substance Abuse Treatment, 11,* 503–510.

Ogloff, J. R, Wong, S., & Greenwood, A. (1990). Treating criminal psychopaths in a therapeutic community program. *Behavioral Sciences and the Law, 8,* 181–190.

Piquero, A. R., MacIntosh, R., & Hickman, M. (2000). Does self-control affect survey response? Applying exploratory, confirmatory, and item response theory analysis to Grasmick et al.'s self-control scale. *Criminology, 38,* 897–930.

Porter, S. (1996). Without conscience or without active conscience? The etiology of psychopathy revisited. *Aggression and Violent Behavior, 1,* 179–189.

Quiles, Z. N., & Bybee, J. (1997). Chronic and predispositional guilt: Relations to mental health, prosocial behavior and religiosity. *Journal of Personality Assessment, 69,* 104–126.

Rice, M. E., Harris, G. T., & Cormier, C. A. (1992). An evaluation of a maximum security therapeutic community for psychopaths and other mentally disordered offenders. *Law and Human Behavior, 16,* 399–412.

Rodin, J., Silberstein, L., & Striegel-Moore, R. (1984). Women and weight: A normative discontent. In *Nebraska Symposium on Motivation* (Vol. 32, pp. 267–307). Lincoln: University of Nebraska Press.

Rogers, R., & Bagby, R. M. (1994). Dimensions of psychopathy: A factor analytic study of the MMPI Antisocial Personality Disorder Scale. *International Journal of Offender Therapy and Comparative Criminology, 38,* 297–308.

Sanftner, J. L., Barlow, D. H., Marschall, D. E., & Tangney, J. P. (1995). The relation of shame and guilt to eating disorders symptomatology. *Journal of Social and Clinical Psychology, 14,* 315–324.

Samenow, S. E. (1984). *Inside the criminal mind.* New York: Crown.

Samenow, S. E. (1989). *Before it's too late: Why some kids get into trouble and what parents can do about it.* New York: Crown.

Schaefer, D. A. (2000). The difference between shame-prone and guilt-prone persons on measures of anxiety, depression and risk of alcohol abuse. *Dissertation Abstracts International, 60,* 2389B.

Scheff, T. J. (1987). The shame–rage spiral: A case study of an interminable quarrel. In H. B. Lewis (Ed.), *The role of shame in symptom formation* (pp. 109–149). Hillsdale, NJ: Erlbaum.

Schmitt, W., & Newman, J. (1999). Are all psychopathic individuals low-anxious? *Journal of Abnormal Psychology, 108,* 353–358.

Sechrest, L., White, S. O., & Brown, E. D. (Eds.). (1979). *The rehabilitation of criminal offenders: Problems and prospects.* Washington, DC: National Academy of Sciences.

Serin, R. C., & Amos, N. L. (1995). The role of psychopathy in the assessment of dangerousness. *International Journal of Law and Psychiatry, 18,* 231–238.

Sherman, L. W. (1993). Defiance, deterrence, and irrelevance: A theory of the criminal sanction. *Journal of Research in Crime and Delinquency, 30,* 445–473.

Skeem, J. L., Monahan, J., & Mulvey, E. P. (2002). Psychopathy, treatment involvement, and subsequent violence among civil psychiatric patients. *Law and Human Behavior, 26,* 577–603.

Smith, J. S. (1992). Humiliation, degradation and the criminal justice system. *Journal of Primary Prevention, 12,* 209–222.

Stuewig, J., & McCloskey, L. (2002). *Do shame and guilt predict antisocial behavior in late adolescence? Findings from a prospective study.* Paper presented at the annual meeting of the American Society of Criminology, Chicago.

Tangney, J. P. (1991). Moral affect: The good, the bad, and the ugly. *Journal of Personality and Social Psychology, 61,* 598–607.

Tangney, J. P. (1992). Situational determinants of shame and guilt in young adulthood. *Personality and Social Psychology Bulletin, 18,* 199–206.

Tangney, J. P. (1993). Shame and guilt. In C. G. Costello (Ed.), *Symptoms of depression* (pp. 161–180). New York: Wiley.

Tangney, J. P. (1994). The mixed legacy of the super-ego: Adaptive and maladaptive aspects of shame and guilt. In J. M. Masling & R. F. Bornstein (Eds.), *Empirical perspectives on object relations theory* (pp. 1–28). Washington, DC: American Psychological Association.

Tangney, J. P. (1995, September). Tales from the dark side of shame: Further implications for interpersonal behavior and adjustment. In R. Baumeister & D. Wegner (Chairs), *From bad to worse: Problematic responses to negative affect.* Paper presented at symposium conducted at the annual meeting of the Society for Experimental Social Psychology, Washington, DC.

Tangney, J. P. (1996). Conceptual and methodological issues in the assessment of shame and guilt. *Behaviour Research and Therapy, 34,* 741–754.

Tangney, J. P., Burggraf, S. A., & Wagner, P. E. (1995). Shame-proneness, guilt-proneness, and psychological symptoms. In J. P. Tangney & K. W. Fischer (Eds.), *Self-conscious emotions: The psychology of shame, guilt, embarrassment, and pride* (pp. 343–367). New York: Guilford Press.

Tangney, J. P., & Dearing, R. (2002). *Shame and guilt.* New York: Guilford Press.

Tangney, J. P., Marschall, D. E., Rosenberg, K., Barlow, D. H., & Wagner, P. E. (1994). *Children's and adults' autobiographical accounts of shame, guilt and pride experiences: An analysis of situational determinants and interpersonal concerns.* Unpublished manuscript.

Tangney, J. P., Miller, R. S., Flicker, L., & Barlow, D. H. (1996). Are shame, guilt and embarrassment distinct emotions? *Journal of Personality and Social Psychology, 70,* 1256–1269.

Tangney, J. P., Wagner, P. E., Hill-Barlow, D. H., Marschall, D. E., & Gramzow, R. (1996). The relation of shame and guilt to constructive vs. destructive responses to anger across the lifespan. *Journal of Personality and Social Psychology, 70,* 797–809.

Tangney, J. P., Wagner, P. E., Burggraf, S. A., Gramzow, R., & Fletcher, C. (1991, June). *Children's shame-proneness, but not guilt-proneness, is related to emotional and behavioral maladjustment.* Poster presented at the annual meeting of the American Psychological Society, Washington, DC.

Tangney, J. P., Wagner, P. E., Fletcher, C., & Gramzow, R. (1992). Shamed into anger? The relation of shame and guilt to anger and self-reported aggression. *Journal of Personality and Social Psychology, 62,* 669–675.

Tangney, J. P., Wagner, P., & Gramzow, R. (1989). *The Test of Self-Conscious Affect (TOSCA).* Fairfax, VA: George Mason University.

Tangney, J. P., Wagner, P. E., & Gramzow, R. (1992). Proneness to shame, proneness to guilt, and psychopathology. *Journal of Abnormal Psychology, 103,* 469–478.

Tibbetts, S. G. (1997). Shame and rational choice in offending decisions. *Criminal Justice and Behavior, 24,* 234–255.

Tooke, W. S., & Ickes, W. (1988). A measure of adherence to conventional morality. *Journal of Social and Clinical Psychology, 6,* 310–334.

Wallbott, H. G., & Scherer, K. R. (1988). How universal and specific is emotional experience? Evidence from 27 countries and five continents. In K. R. Scherer (Ed.), *Facets of emotion: Recent research* (pp. 31–56). Hillsdale, NJ: Erlbaum.

Wallbott, H. G., & Scherer, K. R. (1995). Cultural determinants in experiencing shame and guilt. In J. P. Tangney & K. W. Fischer (Eds.), *Self-conscious emotions: The psychology of shame, guilt, embarrassment, and pride* (pp. 465–487). New York: Guilford Press.

Weiler, B., & Widom, C. (1996). Psychopathy and violent behaviour in abused and neglected young adults. *Criminal Behaviour and Mental Health, 6,* 253–271.

Weiss, J. (1993). *How psychotherapy works.* New York: Guilford Press.

Welner, M. (1998). Defining evil: A depravity scale for today's courts. *The Forensic Echo, 2*(6), 4–12.

Wicker, F. W., Payne, G. C., & Morgan, R. D. (1983). Participant descriptions of guilt and shame. *Motivation and Emotion, 7,* 25–39.

Wilson, D. B., Gallagher, C., & MacKenzie, D. L. (2000). A meta-analysis of corrections-based education, vocation, and work programs for adult offenders. *Journal of Research in Crime and Delinquency, 37,* 347–368.

Wolfgang, M., Figlio, R., & Sellin, T. (1972). *Delinquency in a birth cohort.* Chicago: University of Chicago Press.

Zahn-Waxler, C., & Robinson, J. (1995). Empathy and guilt: Early origins of feelings of responsibility. In J. P. Tangney & K. W. Fischer (Eds.), *Self-conscious emotions: The psychology of shame, guilt, embarrassment, and pride* (pp. 143–173). New York: Guilford Press.

PART IV

THE POSSIBILITIES
FOR KINDNESS

CHAPTER 14

BENEFITS AND LIABILITIES OF EMPATHY-INDUCED ALTRUISM

C. DANIEL BATSON
NADIA AHMAD
E. L. STOCKS

One of life's lessons is that nothing is all good. Even chocolate cake has calories and cholesterol. This lesson makes us leery of terms such as *good* and *evil*, value assessments that present pure opposites. Has anyone ever seriously and sanely admitted to being evil? People admit to misbehavior, to moral shortcomings, even to crimes, but not to evil. Yet with increasing frequency political leaders and pundits are ready to apply this label to others with phrases such as "the Evil Empire," "the Great Satan," "a war between the forces of good and the forces of evil." These labels are applied not simply to point out the others' shortcomings but to justify totally dismissing the others' point of view and agenda. Talk of good and evil is used to imply the speaker's own innocence, virtue, and license to punish, even to kill. Not surprisingly, those who bandy charges of evil are often seen as the very incarnation of evil by the targets of their epithets. To avoid fanning these flames of moral one-upsmanship that blind more than illumine, we shall speak not of good and evil, but of benefits and liabilities.

Most people, if asked, would probably say that altruism is all good. But having learned life's lesson that nothing is all good, they might also quickly add that altruism does not really exist; it is too good to be true. We believe that there is now rather clear evidence that each of these answers is wrong. Altruism does exist, but it is not all good. Like chocolate cake, it brings liabilities as well as benefits.

THE EMPATHY–ALTRUISM HYPOTHESIS

Why do people do what they do—especially what they do for others? In Western thought, the most common answer to this question about the nature of human motivation is: self-interest. People do what they do, including everything they do for others, in order to benefit themselves; benefiting others is only an instrumental goal on the way to the ultimate goal of self-benefit. This is the dominant view in philosophy, biology, psychology, economics, and the social sciences (see Mansbridge, 1990).

Over the past 25 years, our colleagues and we have explored the possibility that the repertoire of human motivation is not limited to self-interest. Specifically, we have looked at whether altruistic motivation may be produced by empathic emotion. We have called this possibility the *empathy–altruism hypothesis* (Batson, 1987, 1991).

To explain what we mean by this hypothesis, some definitions may be useful. We define *empathy* as *an other-oriented emotional response elicited by and congruent with the perceived welfare of another*. If the other is in need, empathy includes feelings of sympathy, compassion, tenderness, and the like. We define *altruism* as *a motivational state with the ultimate goal of increasing another's welfare*. Altruism is contrasted with *egoism*, which we define as *a motivational state with the ultimate goal of increasing one's own welfare*. The empathy–altruism hypothesis states that empathic emotion (as defined) produces altruistic motivation (as defined) to benefit the person for whom the empathy is felt.

Note that these definitions have some important implications. First, we use the term *altruism* to refer to motivation, not behavior. Helping behavior may or may not be altruistically motivated; altruistic motivation may or may not evoke helping behavior. Second, altruism is a motivational state, not a disposition. Following Kurt Lewin (1951), we focus on motivation as a goal-directed psychological force in a given situation. Third, for a motive to be altruistic, the desire to benefit the other must be an ultimate goal, not an instrumental goal en route to some other goal. Fourth, we do not assume that a person is limited to one motive at a time. A person can be both egoistically and altruistically motivated at the same time—and may have motives other than these two as well. The empathy–altruism hypothesis claims, however, that the motivation produced by empathy is altruistic. Finally, there may be sources of altruistic motivation other than empathy. In this chapter, however, we limit our analysis to empathy-induced altruism.

Over 30 experiments have now been conducted to test the empathy–

altruism hypothesis against various egoistic alternatives, that is, against hypotheses claiming that the motivation produced by empathy is directed toward the ultimate goal of obtaining some self-benefit (see Batson, 1991, 1998, for partial reviews). With remarkable consistency, results of these experiments have supported the empathy–altruism hypothesis, leading to the tentative conclusion that it is true (Batson, 1991). This tentative conclusion has, in turn, led to the suggestion that we psychologists need to change our view of human motivation and, indeed, of human nature. If the human motivational repertoire is not limited to self-interest—if one person can have the welfare of another as an ultimate goal—then humans are more social creatures than even our most social social-psychological theories have suggested.

In this chapter, we do not want to discuss the research that has led to these rather sweeping conceptual conclusions. Instead, we want to consider more practical implications of the empathy–altruism hypothesis. Our analysis focuses first on some of the potential social benefits of empathy-induced altruism. Then we consider some of the liabilities.

SOME BENEFITS OF EMPATHY-INDUCED ALTRUISM

More, More Sensitive, and Less Fickle Help

Perhaps the least surprising benefit of knowing that empathic emotion produces altruistic motivation is that inducing empathy should lead to more help for those in need. Even before we knew that the motivation produced by empathy was altruistic, there was much evidence that increased empathy led to increased helping (see Eisenberg & Miller, 1987, for a review). But now, knowing that the motivation is altruistic, we have reason to believe that empathy not only leads to more help; it should lead to more sensitive and less fickle help as well.

There are, of course, egoistic motives for helping. We may help someone in need in order to gain rewards, including social and self-rewards (e.g., praise and self-approval). We may help in order to avoid punishment, including social and self-punishments (e.g., censure and self-castigation). We may help in order to reduce our own distress caused by witnessing someone else in distress. These various egoistic motives for helping are certainly important (Batson, 1991; Schroeder, Penner, Dovidio, & Piliavin, 1995), but often they are not enough to create a more caring, humane society, in which people are more responsive to each other's needs. Empathy-induced altruistic motivation may be a key resource.

Because altruistic motivation is directed toward the goal of enhancing the welfare of the person in need rather than enhancing one's own welfare, it is likely to motivate behavior that is more sensitive and responsive to the victim's actual need. The egoistic goals of gaining rewards and avoiding punishments can often be reached even if the help offered does not end the needy individual's suffering. As the saying goes, "It's the thought that counts." In contrast, the altruistic goal is to end the needy individual's suffering. When motivation is altruistic, it is the result, not the thought, that counts. Experimental evidence supports this reasoning. Unlike those feeling little empathy, empathically aroused individuals tend to feel good if, and only if, the other's need is relieved (Batson et al., 1988; Batson & Weeks, 1996).

A particularly effective demonstration of the sensitivity that characterizes helping evoked by empathy comes from an experiment by Sibicky, Schroeder, and Dovidio (1995). Participants either were or were not induced to feel empathy for a person in need. In addition to the typical condition in which helping would benefit this person, Sibicky et al. added a condition in which helping would provide this person with a short-term benefit but could be detrimental in the long term. Based on the empathy–altruism hypothesis, these researchers predicted that participants induced to feel empathy would help significantly less when doing so could be detrimental in the long term. Results supported this prediction. In contrast, those not induced to feel empathy did not help significantly less in the new condition. Sibicky et al. concluded that empathy enhances sensitivity to the needs of others, prompting consideration of the long-term consequences that one's helping efforts may have for the person in need.

In addition to producing more sensitive helping, altruistic motivation is also likely to be less fickle than egoistic motivation. Research indicates that individuals experiencing relatively low empathy and, hence, a relative predominance of egoistic over altruistic motives are far less likely to help when they can easily escape exposure to the victim's need without helping, or when they can easily justify to themselves and others a failure to help (Batson, Duncan, Ackerman, Buckley, & Birch, 1981; Batson et al., 1988; Toi & Batson, 1982). The practical implications of these findings are more than a little troubling. Easy escape and high justification for not helping are common characteristics of many of the helping situations we face in life. Amidst the blooming, buzzing confusion of our lives, we can almost always find a way to direct attention elsewhere or to convince ourselves that inaction is justified. Given this fact, the practical potential of empathy-induced altruistic motivation looks promising indeed. In the research just cited, individuals experiencing relatively high empathy showed no noticeable decrease in readiness to help under conditions of easy escape and high justification.

Less Aggression

A second possible practical benefit of the empathy–altruism relationship is inhibition of aggression. To the degree that feeling empathy for someone produces altruistic concern to maintain or increase that person's welfare, then feeling empathy should inhibit any inclination to aggress against or harm that person. Empathic feelings should not, of course, inhibit all aggressive impulses, only those directed toward the target of empathy. Indeed, it is easy to imagine *altruistic aggression,* in which empathy for Person A leads to increased aggression toward Person B, if B is perceived to be a threat to A's welfare.

In apparent support of the idea that empathy can inhibit aggression, Miller and Eisenberg (1988) concluded from a meta-analysis of approximately 50 studies that "empathy is negatively related to aggression, externalizing [i.e., threatening, attacking, and fighting, as well as general disobedience], and antisocial behaviors" (p. 338). However, a closer look at the studies reviewed by Miller and Eisenberg, and at their meta-analysis, suggests the need for a more guarded conclusion.

First, as Miller and Eisenberg noted, the negative relation between empathy and aggression was often weak, overall providing "modest but not entirely consistent support for the notion that empathic responsiveness may be an inhibitor of aggression" (p. 339). Second, the clearest evidence of inhibition was found in studies using self-report questionnaire measures of a general personality disposition of empathy. There is reason to believe that questionnaire measures of dispositional empathy assess individuals' desire to present themselves as nice, sensitive, caring people more than these measures assess true empathic responsiveness (Batson, Bolen, Cross, & Neuringer-Benefiel, 1986). Thus, the lower aggression associated with these measures may not be the result of empathy; instead it may result from a desire to be, or appear to be, nice.

Third, in virtually all of the studies reviewed by Miller and Eisenberg, empathy was assessed toward someone other than the target of aggression. To find that reporting empathy toward Person A is associated with displaying less aggression toward Person B may indicate a general disposition toward empathy that produces a general inhibition of aggression. Alternatively, this relation may, once again, indicate a desire to be, or appear to be, nice. Such a desire could easily reflect egoistic motivation to avoid social and self-censure or to gain social and self-rewards. It may not be a product of empathy-induced altruistic motivation at all.

Miller and Eisenberg did report four studies in which empathy toward the target of potential aggression was manipulated via perceived similarity or via perspective-taking instructions. Unfortunately, the evidence from these studies is inconclusive. Eliasz (1980) reported a study that failed to find a negative relation between empathy and aggression. However, before the empathy manipulation, participants in this study received a negative evaluation from the victim, which was included to provoke anger and aggression. This ordering of events may have prevented empathy from ever developing. Each of the other three studies reported that induced empathy significantly inhibited harming the target of empathy (all three were, however, unpublished dissertation studies).

Subsequent to the Miller and Eisenberg review, Richardson, Hammock, Smith, Gardner, and Signo (1994, Study 2) found that male undergraduates who were induced to feel empathy for a target before the target aggressed against them aggressed no less in return than male undergraduates not induced to feel empathy. Perhaps, however, the target's subsequent aggression eliminated empathy. We cannot know if empathy still existed, because no measures of empathic feelings were taken in this study.

In the one study reported by Miller and Eisenberg, in which self-reported empathic concern for the target of aggression was assessed (Gaines, Kirwin, & Gentry, 1977), the inhibition effect was highly significant. Unfortunately, the causal relationship was unclear in this study because assessment of empathy was based on retrospective self-reports obtained after the opportunity to harm the victim. Those who harmed the victim less may have inferred that they felt more empathic concern, rather than empathy inhibiting an impulse to aggress.

Three more recent lines of research provide clearer support for the idea that empathy-induced altruistic motivation can inhibit aggression. First, research on forgiveness has suggested that a necessary step in the forgiveness process is to replace feelings of anger toward a harm-doer with empathic feelings (McCullough, Worthington, & Rachal, 1997; Worthington, 2001). Of course, replacing feelings of anger with empathic feelings is often easier said than done.

Second, Milner, Halsey, and Fultz (1995) examined the empathic responsiveness of mothers while they watched videotaped segments of an infant who was smiling, was looking around, or was crying. The mothers were in two matched groups, those identified as being at high risk of physically abusing a child and those identified as being at low risk. On average, the high-risk mothers showed no reliable change in empathy across the infant conditions, whereas low-risk mothers showed a highly significant increase in empathy while watching the crying infant. Rather than empathy, high-risk mothers reported feeling more personal distress and hostility while watching the crying infant (see Frodi & Lamb, 1980, for parallel physiological data). These responses of the high-risk mothers are congruent with clinical reports that physical child abusers experience less empathy and more hostility in response to a crying child. Also related is the finding that clinical interventions aimed at increasing empathy reduce the reported likelihood of abuse, rape, and sexual harassment on the part of men identified as being at high risk for committing sexual assaults (Schewe & O'Donohue, 1993).

Third, in an intriguing and ambitious set of experiments, Harmon-Jones, Vaughn, Mohr, Sigelman, and Harmon-Jones (2001) sought to assess the effect of empathy on anger-related left frontal cortical electroencephalographic (EEG) activity. In their key experiment, undergraduate men and women were induced to experience either low or high empathy for another student, and then this other student either did or did not insult them. EEG activity was recorded immediately after the insult occurred (or did not). As predicted based on the empathy–altruism hypothesis, relative left-frontal cortical EEG activity that is typically increased by insult—and was increased in the low-empathy condition—was inhibited in the high-empathy condition. This experiment provides perhaps the clearest evidence that empathy can directly inhibit aggression, at least when the empathy is present *before* the provocation to aggress arises.

More broadly, empathy may be effective in counteracting a particularly subtle and insidious form of hostility—blaming the victims of injustice. In his classic work on the just-world hypothesis, Melvin Lerner (1970) found that research participants were likely to derogate a person whom they perceived to be an innocent victim of suffering. This derogation presumably served to maintain the research participants' belief that people get what they deserve and deserve what they get. Protecting one's belief in a just world in this way can lead to what William Ryan (1971) called *blaming the victim*. He suggested that we are likely to react to the victims of unjust discrimination and oppression in our society by unconsciously blaming them: If they have less, they must deserve less; that is, they must be less deserving. Ryan noted that the prototypical victim blamer is the middle-class person who is fairly comfortable financially. By blaming the victims of poverty and social injustice, middle-class persons can reconcile their own relative advantage with their belief that the world is just.

Derogation and blaming the victim are all-too-common alternatives to caring about the suffering of others. These alternatives can lead to smug acceptance of one's own advantage and of others' pain as being just and right. But empathy-induced altruism may counteract this tendency. In an important follow-up to Lerner's classic experiments, Aderman, Brehm, and Katz (1974) found that perspective-taking instructions designed to evoke empathy eliminated derogation of an innocent victim.

Increased Cooperation in Conflict Situations

There is also evidence that empathy-induced altruistic motivation can increase cooperation in conflict situations. Paradigmatic of such situations is the one-trial "prisoner's dilemma." In this dilemma, it is always in one's own best interest to defect (compete) regardless of what the other person does. Accordingly, game theory and the theory of rational choice both predict no cooperation in a one-trial prisoner's dilemma because each theory assumes that only one motive exists: self-interest. The empathy–altruism hypothesis predicts, however, that if one person in such a dilemma is induced to feel empathy for the other, then for this person two motives exist: self-interest *and* empathy-induced altruism. Although self-interest can be best satisfied by defecting, altruism can be best satisfied by cooperating. So the empathy–altruism hypothesis predicts that empathy should lead to motivational conflict and to increased cooperation. Batson and Moran (1999) reported an experiment in which they found precisely these results.

In a subsequent experiment, Batson and Ahmad (2001) tried an even more stringent test of the ability of empathy to increase cooperation in a conflict situation. Rather than the standard one-trial prisoner's dilemma, in which participants make their decisions simultaneously without knowing what the other has done, Batson and Ahmad altered the procedure so that when each of the female research participants made her decision, she knew that the other participant had already defected. Thus, she knew that if she cooperated, the other participant would receive a very high payoff and she would receive nothing; if she defected, the other participant would receive the same moderate payoff as she. Predictions for behavior in this situation from game theory, from the theory of rational choice, and even from theories of justice and social norms are clear and obvious. There is no longer a dilemma at all; the only rational thing to do is to defect. Not only will defection maximize one's own outcome, but it will also satisfy the norms of fairness and distributive justice. Moreover, there is no longer any need to fear feeling guilty about having taken advantage of the other, should one defect and the other cooperate, as can happen in a simultaneous decision dilemma. The other has already defected. Not surprisingly, in the very few previous studies that have bothered to look at responses in such a situation, the proportion of participants cooperating has been extremely low (around 5%).

The empathy–altruism hypothesis predicts, however, that if one participant is induced to feel empathy for the other in such a situation, then for this participant a dilemma remains: Self-interest and fairness counsel defection, but empathy-induced altruism counsels cooperation. Once again, results were as predicted by the empathy–altruism hypothesis. In the absence of empathy, cooperation was extremely low (around 5%); when empathy was induced prior to the defection, cooperation rose to 45%. Empathy-induced altruism was not strong enough to override other motives (i.e., self-interest, retribution, justice) for all participants induced to feel empathy, but it was strong enough to do so for almost half.

Results of these two experiments suggest that empathy-induced altruism adds complexity—and hope—to conflict situations. When one feels empathy for the other, one's interest lies not only in maximizing one's own gain but also in maximizing the other's gain. Insofar as we know, the idea of using empathy to increase cooperation had not even been considered in any of the over 2,000 prisoner's dilemma studies previously conducted. Yet this technique seems to be far more effective than most other techniques that have been suggested for increasing cooperation in one-trial dilemmas. This technique is quite different from techniques that rely on forcing reciprocity by using, for example, a tit-for-tat strategy (Axelrod & Hamilton, 1981; Trivers, 1971); such techniques apply only to iterated dilemmas and assume that all motivation for social cooperation is egoistic in nature.

Might the introduction of empathy-induced altruism be worth pursuing in business or political negotiations? In these situations, is allowing oneself to feel concern for the other's welfare too big a risk to take? Think, for example, of negotiations between management and labor, between Catholics and Protestants in Northern Ireland, between the Palestinians and Israelis, between Pakistanis and Indians. Empathy-induced altruism might prompt one to give ground. But it might also produce a better outcome for all. It might even save lives.

Empathy-induced altruism may already be used to reduce social conflict more often than is realized. The empathy–altruism hypothesis suggests that a key strategy for counteracting social tension and hostility is to establish personalizing contact between members of the conflicting groups. By *personalizing contact* we refer to interaction in which members of one group are led to deal with members of the other group on a personal, individual basis, not simply as one of *them*. Such contact should encourage empathy for members of the outgroup in two ways. First, it should increase the likelihood of accurately perceiving the other's needs—his or her hopes and fears. Second, it should increase the likelihood of taking the other's perspective. These conditions are precisely the two that have been hypothesized to be necessary and sufficient to evoke empathy (Batson, 1987).

As Stephan and Finlay (1999) pointed out, the induction of empathy is often an explicit component of techniques used in conflict resolution workshops. Participants are encouraged to express their feelings, their hopes and fears, and to actively adopt the perspective of those on the other side of the conflict (Burton, 1986, 1987; Fisher, 1994; Kelman, 1990; Kelman & Cohen, 1986; Rouhana & Kelman, 1994). These efforts should affect perception of the other as in need and foster adoption of the other's perspective—the two key conditions for empathy.

Beyond encouragement, how can personalizing contact among individuals on opposite sides of a conflict be facilitated? Obviously, it is not easy. More is required than simply bringing the antagonists together. Indeed, mere contact is likely to invite further hostility and aggression. One structural technique that has proved especially effective in creating personalizing contact and thereby reducing intergroup conflict and hostility is to introduce superordinate goals (Sherif, Harvey, White, Hood, & Sherif, 1961). *Superordinate goals* are ones that both parties in conflict want to reach but can reach only if they join forces and work together. When a superordinate goal is introduced, potential antagonists find themselves united in the effort to reach the common goal—strange bedfellows, perhaps, but bedfellows nonetheless.

Think of the psychological consequences. To work together toward a common goal, members of one group must attend to and understand what members of the other group value, want, and need. Moreover, to coordinate efforts in pursuit of the goal, members of each group must attend to the perspective of those in the other group. The combined effect of these two consequences should be an increased likelihood of feeling empathy for members of the outgroup. Note that these empathy effects do not require that group members give up their group identity in order for superordinate goals to be effective.

A classic demonstration of the effectiveness of superordinate goals in reducing intergroup conflict was provided by Sherif and colleagues (1961). In their Robber's Cave experiment, superordinate goals were used to eliminate the open hostility that had erupted between competing groups of 12- to 14-year-old boys at a summer camp. This experiment dramatically demonstrated the effectiveness of superordinate goals but revealed little about the psychological process through which they work.

More revealing of the underlying psychological process is the use of superordinate goals in the Jigsaw Classroom. The Jigsaw Classroom is a learning technique developed by Aronson and his colleagues to try to overcome racial tension and animosity in desegregated schools (Aronson, Blaney, Stephan, Sikes, & Snapp, 1978). In such a classroom, students are placed in racially mixed groups (ideally, five to six students per group), and each group is given a learning task. Within a group, each member is given one, but only one, part of the information the group needs to complete the task. As a result, the group must rely on the contribution of each member to succeed.

Aronson and colleagues (1978) reported that liking for fellow group members increased as a result of the jigsaw experience; so did helping. Unfortunately, Aronson and colleagues did not report the effect specifically on interracial liking. In an earlier award-winning study, Weigel, Wiser, and Cook (1975) did report the effects of interdependent, ethnically mixed (European, African, and Mexican American) student work groups on cross-ethnic liking, conflict, and helping. Results of that study indicated that working together in interdependent groups significantly increased both cross-ethnic liking and helping behavior and reduced cross-ethnic conflict (see also Johnson & Johnson, 1987).

Why does cooperative interaction in jigsaw groups increase liking and helping? Aronson and colleagues (1978) suggested that empathy was "one of the crucial mechanisms underlying the effects" (p. 118; see also Aronson & Bridgeman, 1979). Supporting this suggestion, Bridgeman (1981), in dissertation research under Aronson's direction, found that students from a jigsaw classroom were better at a perspective-taking task than were students from a traditional classroom. The task tested students' ability to adopt the perspective of characters in brief stories, seeing the story situation from the character's rather than their own point of view. Results of this study indicated that the perspective-taking abilities learned in the jigsaw groups generalized to use in other situations as well. This finding suggests that the ability of empathy-induced altruism to increase cooperation may extend to conflict situations beyond the one in which empathy is initially induced.

Improving Attitudes toward, and Action on Behalf of, Stigmatized Groups

Is it possible that empathy-induced altruism might be used to improve attitudes toward, and action on behalf of, stigmatized groups? Moreover, might this improvement be achieved even without organizing conflict-resolution workshops or introducing superordinate goals? There is reason to think so. Batson and colleagues (1997) outlined a three-step model of how to use empathy to improve attitudes:

Step 1. Inducing someone to adopt the perspective of a stigmatized person should increase empathy for that person.

Step 2. Feeling empathy for that person should lead to increased valuing of his or her welfare.

Step 3. Valuing of this person's welfare should generalize to valuing the welfare of the stigmatized group as a whole, producing more positive beliefs about, feelings toward, and concern for the group.

This model raises two questions: Can perspective taking be used to arouse empathy for a member of a stigmatized group? If so, will the concern evoked by this empathy generalize to the group as a whole, as claimed? The answer to each of these questions seems to be yes—if membership in the stigmatized group is a salient aspect of the need for which the empathy is induced.

In a series of experiments, Batson and colleagues (1997) successfully used perspective-taking instructions to induce empathy for an individual group member, thereby improving attitudes toward people with AIDS, toward the homeless, and even toward convicted murderers serving life sentences. Especially interesting were results of the effect of inducing empathy for a convicted murderer on attitudes toward murderers. When attitudes were assessed in the laboratory immediately after the empathy induction, there was only a nonsignificant trend for those induced to feel empathy to report more positive attitudes than those not induced to feel empathy. But when attitudes were assessed in an unrelated telephone interview over a week later, those who had been induced to feel empathy for the convicted murderer in the lab reported significantly more positive attitudes than those who had not. Apparently, participants induced to feel empathy resisted letting these feelings influence their attitudes toward convicted murderers measured immediately, when they were aware of the influence. Later, with their guard down, the shift in their attitudes surfaced. Long-term effects of empathy-induced attitude change were also reported by Clore and Jeffrey (1972).

In related research, it has been found that inducing empathy for a member of a racial or ethnic minority can improve attitudes toward the minority group (Dovidio, Gaertner, & Johnson, 1999; Finlay & Stephan, 2000; Vescio, Sechrist, & Paolucci, 2003), and inducing empathy for a gay man can improve attitudes toward homosexuals (Vescio & Hewstone, 2001). Moreover, effects of participation in the role-play simulations of discrimination often used in educational settings, such as the "blue eyes–brown eyes" simulation developed by Elliott (Peters, 1987), have been interpreted by some as being a result of empathy (e.g., Byrnes & Kiger, 1990). Underscoring the broad applicability of empathy-induced attitude change, Shelton and Rogers (1981) found that inducing empathy for whales led to more positive attitudes, expressed as intention to help save whales. Schultz (2000) found that empathy induced for animals being harmed by pollution improved attitudes toward protecting the natural environment.

Do these more positive attitudes manifest themselves in action on behalf of the group? Batson, Chang, Orr, and Rowland (2002) provided evidence that they do. These researchers found that inducing empathy for a member of a stigmatized group (in this case, abusers of hard drugs) led to increased helping of the stigmatized group. Importantly, the increase in helping occurred even when it was clear that this help would not benefit the specific individual (a convicted heroin addict and dealer) who was the target of the empathy induction. It appears that those induced to feel empathy are willing to put their money where their mouth is.

There are practical reasons to use empathy to improve attitudes—and action—on behalf of the disadvantaged, downtrodden, and stigmatized of society. The induction of empathy through perspective taking is likely to be easier than trying to improve attitudes through other methods, such as trying to orchestrate personalizing contact. First, as novels, movies, and documentaries show, it is relatively easy to induce empathy for a member of a stigmatized group. Second, this empathy can be induced in low-cost, low-risk situations. Rather than the elaborate arrangements often required to create direct, cooperative, personal contact, we can be led to feel empathy for a member of a stigmatized group as we sit comfortably in our own home. Third, empathy-inducing experiences can be controlled to ensure that they are positive far more readily than can live, face-to-face, direct contact.

LIABILITIES OF EMPATHY-INDUCED ALTRUISM

Not all of the implications of the empathy–altruism hypothesis are positive. We turn now to some of the negative implications.

It May Be Harmful

Viewed from the perspective of personal survival and narrow self-interest, altruistic motivation is potentially dangerous. As evolutionary biologists are fond of reminding us (e.g., Dawkins, 1976), altruism may incline one to incur costs in time and money that can be seriously damaging, even life threatening. When 28-year-old Lenny Skutnik was asked why he dove into the ice-strewn Potomac River to rescue a drowning plane-crash victim, he said, "I just did what I had to do." We do not know the extent to which the motivation that impelled Skutnik's action was altruistic, but we do know that whatever made him leave the safety of his car very nearly cost him his life.

Not only can altruism be harmful to the person doing the helping, at times, it can also be harmful to the person receiving the help. There is no reason to assume that altruistic motivation will always be accompanied by wisdom. Genuine concern for another's welfare may lead to provision of help that unintentionally humiliates or suffocates the recipient. Balzac, one of our most astute observers of the human condition, graphically portrayed this irony in his classic novel *Pere Goriot* (1834/1962). Goriot's selfless love spoiled his daughters, drove them from him, and, ultimately, destroyed both them and him. Balzac's message: Altruism may be part of human nature, but it, like aggression, must be held carefully in check. It is potentially destructive.

Graham Hancock made a similar point in his scathing indictment of international aid programs in *Lords of Poverty* (1989). He condemned the efforts of such esteemed agencies as the World Bank, UNICEF, UNESCO, the United Nations Development Organization, the United Nations Food and Agriculture Organization (FAO), the European Development Fund, and AID. Many people would admit that the aid efforts of these organizations are less successful than one might wish. Hancock's attack was more fundamental; he claimed that international aid is nothing more than a transaction between bureaucrats and autocrats, in which corruption and self-defeating dependency are inevitable.

To justify his attack, Hancock cited numerous examples, including the aid-financed dam in Guatemala that led to a 70% rise in residential electricity prices; the Sudanese sugar refinery that turned out sugar sold in the Sudan at significantly higher prices than imported sugar; and the World Bank resettlement schemes in Brazil and Indonesia that have destroyed rain forests, contributed to the greenhouse effect, obliterated native cultures, and often left settlers poorer than before the "aid." Such examples are not the whole story about international aid, but they are too numerous and too tragic not to sensitize us to inherent dangers in the best-intentioned relief efforts. They highlight the danger of acting on motives, even altruistic ones, evoked by concern for the suffering of others when one does not fully understand the situation in which these others live. And one can never fully understand.

Even when helping is clearly appropriate, empathy-induced altruism can, at times, make matters worse. This is especially true when the behavior needed to relieve a person's suffering requires a light and delicate touch. Think, for example, of the work of a surgeon. It is no accident, argues neurophysiologist Paul MacLean (1967), that surgeons are prohibited from operating on close kin or friends. The problem is not that they feel no empathic concern for these people; quite the opposite. They feel much empathy and so, presumably, much altruistic motivation. Too much. When operating on one's sister rather than on "a patient," extreme empathic concern and desire to relieve her suffering may cause a normally steady hand to shake. Empathy-induced altruistic motivation may cost the sister her life.

Chilling testimony to another circumstance in which empathy-induced altruism can cause harm was offered by survivors of the death camps in Nazi Europe. In the camps, members of the underground could not save everyone. At times, they were faced with the dilemma of having to decide who would live and who would die. Survivors reported that empathic feelings interfered with making such decisions:

> Compassion was seldom possible, self-pity never. Emotion not only blurred judgment and undermined decisiveness, it jeopardized the life of everyone in the underground. . . . Hard choices had to be made and not everyone was equal to the task, no one less than the kind of person whose goodness was most evident, most admired, but least available for action. (Des Pres, 1976, pp. 153–154, from Kogon, 1953, p. 278)

Not All Needs Are Well Suited to Empathy-Induced Altruism

Many of the pressing social problems we face today do not involve personal needs of the sort likely to evoke empathy. Empathic feelings are usually felt by individuals for individuals (including individualized members of other species—recall the research cited earlier on inducing empathy for whales and other animals in distress). But many of our problems, such as environmental contamination, nuclear proliferation, and overpopulation, are global. These problems are not limited to personal needs of the sort that evoke empathy; they are broader and more abstract. It is difficult, if not impossible, to feel empathy for an abstract concept such as *the environment, world population,* or *the planet,* although personalizing metaphors such as "Mother Earth" may move us in that direction.

Not only is it difficult to evoke empathy for these pressing global needs, but also many of these needs cannot be effectively addressed with a personal helping response. Issues such as environmental contamination, nuclear proliferation, and overpopulation must be addressed, at least in part, in political arenas and through institutional and bureaucratic structures. The process is long and slow; it is not the sort for which emotion-based motivation, such as empathy-induced altruism, is likely to be very effective. Emotions, including empathy, diminish over time.

The less personal, long-term, large-group nature of these global needs and their possible remedies led Garrett Hardin (1977) to question the usefulness of empathy-induced altruism as a potent force in addressing them:

> Is pure altruism possible? Yes, of course it is—on a small scale, over the short term, in certain circumstances, and within small, intimate groups. In familylike groups one should be able to give with little thought "of nicely calculated less or more." But only the most naive hope to adhere to a noncalculating policy in a group that numbers in the thousands (or millions!), and in which many preexisting antagonisms are known and many more suspected. . . .
>
> When those who have not appreciated the nature of large groups innocently call for "social policy institutions [to act] as agents of altruistic opportunities," they call for the impossible. In large groups social policy institutions necessarily must be guided by what I have called the Cardinal Rule of Policy: *Never ask a person to act against his own self-interest.* (pp. 26–27, emphasis in original)

Because empathy diminishes over time, empathy-induced altruism may not be sufficient to sustain the kind of long-term helping efforts often required of community-action volunteers (see Omoto & Snyder, 1995). Empathy-induced altruism may be effective in initiating volunteer action, but other motives may be needed if a volunteer is to continue for the long haul.

Empathy Avoidance

As we are using the term, *altruism* refers to a motive with the ultimate goal of increasing another's welfare. What if we do not want to be altruistically motivated? After all, altruistic motivation can cost us—it can lead us to spend time, money, and energy on behalf of others. If we know that feeling empathy produces altruistic motivation, then we may seek *to avoid feeling empathy.* The knowledge that empathy produces altruism may arouse an egoistic motive to avoid the emergence of empathy and the resulting altruistic motive. This egoistic motive might be aroused, for example, when we see a homeless person on the street or hear about the plight of refugees or see news footage of the ravages of famine. This motive may lead us to turn our head, cross the street, switch channels.

When does empathy avoidance occur? Shaw, Batson, and Todd (1994) suggested that it can occur when, prior to exposure to a person in need, we are aware that (1) we will be asked to help this person, and (2) we know that helping will be costly.

Shaw and colleagues (1994) tested the idea that these two conditions produce empathy avoidance by asking undergraduate men and women to choose which of two audiotaped versions of a homeless man's appeal for help they wished to hear: a high-impact version (designed to evoke emotion and induce empathy) or a low-impact version (designed to be objective and nonemotional). Before making their choice, some participants were told that after listening to the appeal, they would be given a chance to decide whether they wished to volunteer to help the homeless man. Of these participants, half were told that volunteering involved low cost (spending 1 hour preparing letters to send to potential contributors), and half were told that volunteering involved high cost (three 1½-hour meetings face-to-face with the man). As expected based on the conditions specified for empathy avoidance, those participants told that they would be asked to help and that helping involved high cost were significantly less likely to choose to listen to the high-impact version of the homeless man's appeal than were participants given only one of these pieces of information.

Empathy avoidance does, then, seem to exist. At times, our potential to experience empathy-induced altruism—and our awareness of this potential—may lead us to turn away from those in need. Empathy avoidance may be a factor in the experience of *burnout* among those who work in the helping professions (Maslach, 1982). However, the conditions for empathy avoidance among helping professional may not be the same as those specified by Shaw and colleagues (1994). Among professionals, empathy-avoidance is more likely to be due to the perceived impossibility of providing effective help than to the perceived cost of helping. Aware of the impossibility of helping effectively, some welfare case workers—or therapists and counselors, or nurses caring for terminal patients (Stotland, Mathews, Sherman, Hansson, & Richardson, 1978)—may try to avoid feeling empathy in order to avoid the resulting altruistic motivation. They may turn their clients or patients into objects and treat them accordingly. Other professional helpers may, over time, find that their ability to feel empathy is exhausted, leading to what has sometimes been called *compassion fatigue*. For them, the debilitating factor is the sheer number of people in need. There are limits to how often we can draw from the emotional well.

It also seems likely that a person may be motivated to avoid empathy when preparing to act in a way that harms someone else. Indeed, empathy avoidance may help explain why the evidence that empathy inhibits aggression is so weak when an incentive to aggress, such as an insult, precedes the empathy induction. The desire to retaliate may evoke empathy avoidance.

Consistent with this suggestion, Worchel and Andreoli (1978) reported an experiment in which undergraduate men who anticipated having to reward another research participant selectively recalled individuating, personalizing information about the other. As previously noted, this kind of information stimulates empathy. In contrast, men who were insulted by the other participant or who anticipated having to shock him selectively recalled deindividuating, depersonalizing information (Zimbardo, 1970). This kind of information inhibits awareness of need and perspective taking and, hence, empathy. Also relevant, Zimbardo, Banks, Haney, and Jaffe (1973) reported that the "guards" in their prison simulation study employed various deindividuating strategies, which seemed to make it easier for them to mistreat the "prisoners." These strategies may have been used, at least in part, to allow the guards to avoid feeling sorry for the prisoners. In a far more extreme example of this same process, the commandant of Auschwitz, Rudolf Hoess, reported that he "stifled all softer emotions," lest he become unable to carry out his assignment—the systematic extermination of 2.9 million people (Hoess, 1959; quoted by Dawes, van de Kragt, & Orbell, 1990). Empathy avoidance can, it seems, contribute to devastating consequences.

Empathy-Induced Altruism as a Source of Immoral Action

One of the more surprising implications of the empathy–altruism hypothesis—at least for many people—is that empathy-induced altruism can lead to immoral action. This implication is surprising because many people equate altruism with morality. The empathy–altruism hypothesis does not. In this hypothesis, altruism refers to a motivational state with the ultimate goal of increasing another's welfare. What is morality? The dictionary gives the following as the first two definitions: (1) "Of or concerned with principles of right conduct." (2) "Being in accord with such principles." Typically, moral principles are universal and impartial—for example, principles of fairness or justice. Given these definitions of altruism and morality, altruism stands in the same relation to morality as does egoism. An egoistic desire to benefit myself may lead me to put my needs and interests unfairly in front of the parallel needs and interests of others. An altruistic desire to benefit another may lead me to put that person's needs and interests unfairly in front of the parallel needs and interests of others. Each action violates the moral principle of fairness. Egoism, altruism, and morality are three independent motives, each of which may conflict with another.

To test this derivation from the empathy–altruism hypothesis, Batson, Klein, Highberger, and Shaw (1997) conducted two experiments. Results of each experiment supported the proposal that empathy-induced altruism can lead us to act in a way that violates the moral principle of fairness. In each, participants were asked to make a decision regarding resource allocation that affected the welfare of other individuals. Participants who were not induced to feel empathy for one of the other individuals tended to adhere strictly to a principle of fairness; participants who were induced to feel empathy were significantly more likely to violate this principle, allocating resources preferentially to the individual for whom empathy was felt. This allocation occurred even though high-empathy participants who showed partiality agreed with other participants that acting with partiality in this situation was less fair and less moral than acting impartially. Overall, results suggested that empathy-induced altruism and the desire to uphold a moral principle of fairness are independent motives that can, at times, conflict.

We might, of course, ask whether empathy-induced immorality occurs outside the lab. It appears that it does. For example, there is reason to believe that the altruistic motivation produced by empathy can lead to partiality in our decisions, both individually and as a nation, about who among the many in need will get our assistance. A decade ago *Time* magazine essayist Walter Isaacson (1992) commented on the photogenics of disaster. He raised the possibility that the decisions to intervene in Somalia but to ignore the Sudan occurred because those suffering in Somalia proved more photogenic, evoking empathy and altruism in a way that those in the Sudan did not.

The power of empathy-induced altruism to override moral motivation is, however, only half the story. A more positive implication of recognizing the independence of these two prosocial motives is that one can think about using them in concert. Consider the moral motive of justice. Justice is a powerful motive but vulnerable to rationalization; it is easily co-opted (Lerner, 1980; Solomon, 1990). Empathy-induced altruism also is a powerful motive but limited in scope; it produces partiality. If empathy could be evoked for the victims of injustice, perhaps these two motives can be made to work together rather than at odds. Desire for justice may provide perspective and reason; empathy-induced altruism may provide emotional "fire" and a push toward ending victims' suffering, preventing rationalization and derogation.

A combination of this sort occurred, we believe, among some rescuers of Jews in Nazi Europe. A careful look at data collected by Oliner and Oliner (1988) and their colleagues suggests that involvement in rescue activity frequently began with concern for a specific individual or individuals for whom compassion was felt—often individuals known previously. This initial involvement subsequently led to further contacts and rescue activity, which led to a concern for justice that extended well beyond the bounds of the initial target of empathy.

However difficult it may be in practice, coordinating altruism and justice by inducing empathy for the victims of injustice is theoretically straightforward. Yet this strategy is not the only possibility. The story of wise King Solomon presents a far subtler example of the use of empathy-induced altruism—and the partiality it induces—in the service of justice. Recall that two women were brought to Solomon for judgment. One claimed that when the other's infant son had died, the bereft mother switched her dead son for the first woman's live one. The other woman claimed that the dead son was the first woman's, and the live son was hers.

> So the king [Solomon] said, "Bring me a sword," and they brought a sword before the king. The king said, "Divide the living boy in two; then give half to the one, and half to the other." But the woman whose son was alive said to the king—because compassion for her son burned within her—"Please, my lord, give her the living boy; certainly do not kill him!" The other said, "It shall be neither mine nor yours; divide it." Then the king responded: "Give the first woman the living boy; do not kill him. She is his mother." (1 Kings 3:24–27 New Revised Standard Version)

Thus, it is said, did Solomon "execute justice" (1 Kings 3:28—presumably, pun intended). Had Solomon turned to a social psychologist for advice, it is doubtful he would have received so complex and successful an orchestration of prosocial motives. Clearly, we still have a long way to go before we fully understand how empathy-induced altruism and moral motives can compete *and* cooperate. To recognize that empathy-induced altruism can, at times, lead to immoral action is a first step.

Empathy-Induced Altruism as a Threat to the Common Good

Not only does the empathy–altruism hypothesis predict that empathy-induced altruism can lead a person to act immorally, but it also predicts that it can lead a person to act against the common good in a social dilemma. A *social dilemma,* of which the one-trial prisoner's dilemma (discussed earlier) is a special case, arises when (1) a person has a choice about how to allocate scarce resources (e.g., time, money, energy), and regardless of what others do, (2) to allocate the resources to the group would be best for the group as a whole, but (3) to allocate the resources to a single individual (self or another group member) would be best for that individual, and yet (4) if all allocations are made to separate individuals, each individual would be worse off than if all allocations are made to the group. Examples of social dilemmas abound in modern society. They face us each time we decide whether to recycle, car pool, vote, contribute to public TV, contribute to the local symphony, and so on.

In our list of the conditions for a social dilemma, we mentioned the possibility that the person could allocate resources to another individual in the group. Interestingly, in the research on and discussions of social dilemmas, this possibility had never even been considered. Guided by the assumption of universal egoism that underlies game theory, it was taken for granted that the only individual to whom one would allocate scarce resources would be oneself. In contrast, the empathy–altruism hypothesis predicts that if we feel empathy for another member of the group, then we will be altruistically motivated to benefit that person. Moreover, the empathy–altruism hypothesis predicts that this empathy-induced altruistic motivation can harm the common good if a social dilemma arises in which the allocator has an opportunity to allocate resources to this individual (as well as to self or to the group as a whole). Under these conditions, rather than the two motives traditionally assumed to conflict in a social dilemma—egoism and collectivism (motivation with the ultimate goal of increasing a group's welfare)—three motives are in play: egoism, altruism, and collectivism. If the egoistic and altruistic motives are stronger than the collectivistic motive, the common good will suffer.

How often do these conditions arise? Frequently. Indeed, it is hard to think of a real-world social dilemma in which they are not present. They arise every time we try to decide whether to spend our time or money—or whether to appropriate scarce common resources—to benefit ourselves, the community, or another individual about whom we especially care. A father may resist contributing to public TV, not to buy himself a new shirt but because he feels for his daughter, who wants new shoes. An executive may retain an ineffective employee for whom he or she feels compassion to the detriment of the company. Whalers may kill to extinction and loggers clear-cut, not out of personal greed but to provide for their families.

To test whether empathy-induced altruism could indeed hurt the common good in a social dilemma, Batson, Batson, and colleagues (1995) ran two studies. In each, undergraduate participants faced a dilemma in which they could choose to benefit themselves, the group, or one or more other group members as individuals. In Study 1, empathy for another group member was induced through experimental manipulation; in Study 2, the level of empathic response was determined by self-report. In each study, participants who experienced high empathy allocated more resources to the person for whom they felt empathy, reducing the overall collective good. These results suggest the importance of considering self-interest, collective interest, and other interest (i.e., empathy-induced altruism) as three distinct motives, all of which may operate in a social dilemma.

Can altruism seriously threaten the common good? Most people would say that altruism, even if it exists, is weak compared to self-interest (i.e., egoism). After all, we feel our own needs directly; we feel for another's needs only vicariously. We would suggest that empathy-induced altruism can indeed be a serious threat. In fact, when action taken is public, altruism can be a more serious threat to the common good than is self-interest. We make this suggestion because there are clear social norms and sanctions to inhibit pursuit of self-interests at the expense of what is fair and best for all (Kerr, 1995). *Selfish* and *greedy* are stinging epithets. Norms and sanctions against showing concern for another's interests, even if doing so diminishes the common good, are far less clear. Although philosophers have long debated the morality of showing partiality (Kant, 1785/1898; Nagel, 1991; Rawls, 1971), to show favoritism toward another individual, especially an individual in need, is not likely to be called selfish or greedy. One may be accused of being "naive," "a pushover," "soft," or "a bleeding heart," but these terms carry an implicit charge of weakness, not greed.

To test the idea that when behavior is public, altruism can be a more serious threat to the common good than is egoism, Batson and colleagues (1999) conducted two experiments using a modified dilemma situation. In each experiment, some participants chose between allocation of resources to the group as a whole or to themselves alone (egoism condition). Some chose between allocation to a group of which they were not a member or to a member of this group for whom they were induced to feel empathy (altruism condition). Finally, some chose between allocation to a group of which they were not a member or to a member of this group for whom they were not induced to feel empathy (baseline condition). When the decision was private, allocation to the group was significantly—and similarly—lower in the egoism and altruism conditions compared to the baseline. However, when the decision was public, allocation to the group was significantly lower only in the altruism condition. These results indicate, first, that both egoism and altruism can be potent threats to the common good and, second, that anticipated social evaluation is a powerful inhibitor of the egoistic but not the altruistic threat. These results have wide-ranging implications. How do whalers and loggers stand up to the public outcry about overdepletion of natural resources? Easily; they are using these resources not for themselves but to care for their families.

If altruism is such a threat, why are there no sanctions against it, such as there are against egoism? We can only speculate, but it may be that society makes one or both of two assumptions: (1) Altruism is always a good thing; it is always on our side. (2) Altruism is weak. As we said at the outset, there is now rather clear evidence that each of these assumptions is wrong.

SUMMARY AND CONCLUSION

This chapter provides an overview of recent research concerning the practical implications of the empathy–altruism hypothesis. This hypothesis states that empathic emotion produces motivation with an ultimate goal of increasing another's welfare. It may seem that if this hypothesis is true— and there is now strong evidence that it is—then the implications are uniformly positive. We presented a conceptual analysis and review of research to suggest that the implications are more mixed.

On the one hand, empathy-induced altruism does offer important benefits:

1. It can lead to more, more sensitive, and less fickle help for those in need.
2. It can probably also lead to less aggression (e.g., less child abuse).
3. It can lead to increased cooperation in conflict situations.
4. Finally, inducing empathy for a member of a stigmatized group has been found to lead to improved attitudes toward, and to increased action on behalf of, the group as a whole.

On the other hand, empathy-induced altruism may, at times, be a liability:

1. It can cause harm to the altruistically motivated individual, to the targets of altruism, and to third parties.
2. It is more suited to addressing some needs than others.
3. Aware of the potential for empathy to induce altruistic motivation, people may be egoistically motivated to avoid feeling empathy, turning a blind and callous eye to those in need (e.g., the homeless).
4. Empathy-induced altruistic motivation can also lead to immoral action by prompting us to show partiality toward those for whom we especially care, even though fairness dictates impartiality.
5. Finally, empathy-induced altruistic motivation can lead us to act against the common good in social dilemmas. Indeed, at times it may pose a more serious threat to the common good than does self-interested egoism, because there are clear social sanctions against self-interest but not against altruism.

In sum, empathy-induced altruism is not evil, but neither is it all good.

REFERENCES

Aderman, D., Brehm, S. S., & Katz, L. B. (1974). Empathic observation of an innocent victim: The just world revisited. *Journal of Personality and Social Psychology, 29,* 342–347.

Aronson, E., Blaney, N., Stephan, C., Sikes, J., & Snapp, M. (1978). *The jigsaw classroom.* Beverly Hills, CA: Sage.

Aronson, E., & Bridgeman, D. (1979). Jigsaw groups and the desegregated classroom: In pursuit of common goals. *Personality and Social Psychology Bulletin, 5,* 438–446.

Axelrod, R., & Hamilton, W. D. (1981). The evolution of cooperation. *Science,*
211, 1390–1396.

Balzac, H. de (1962). *Pere Goriot* (H. Reed, Trans.). New York: New American
Library. (Original work published 1834)

Batson, C. D. (1987). Prosocial motivation: Is it ever truly altruistic? In L.
Berkowitz (Ed.), *Advances in experimental social psychology* (Vol. 20, pp.
65–122). New York: Academic Press.

Batson, C. D. (1991). *The altruism question: Toward a social-psychological an-*
swer. Hillsdale, NJ: Erlbaum.

Batson, C. D. (1998). Altruism and prosocial behavior. In D. T. Gilbert, S. T.
Fiske, & G. Lindzey (Eds.), *The handbook of social psychology* (4th ed., Vol.
2, pp. 282–316). Boston: McGraw-Hill.

Batson, C. D., & Ahmad, N. (2001). Empathy-induced altruism in a prisoner's dilemma II: What if the target of empathy has defected? *European Journal of*
Social Psychology, 31, 25–36.

Batson, C. D., Ahmad, N., Yin, J., Bedell, S. J., Johnson, J. W., Templin, C. M., &
Whiteside, A. (1999). Two threats to the common good: Self-interested egoism and empathy-induced altruism. *Personality and Social Psychology Bulle-*
tin, 25, 3–16.

Batson, C. D., Batson, J. G., & Todd, R. M., Brummett, B. H., Shaw, L. L., &
Aldeguer, C. M. R. (1995). Empathy and the collective good: Caring for one
of the others in a social dilemma. *Journal of Personality and Social Psychol-*
ogy, 68, 619–631.

Batson, C. D., Bolen, M. H., Cross, J. A., & Neuringer-Benefiel, H. E. (1986).
Where is the altruism in the altruistic personality? *Journal of Personality and*
Social Psychology, 50, 212–220.

Batson, C. D., Chang, J., Orr, R., & Rowland, J. (2002). Empathy, attitudes, and
action: Can feeling for a member of a stigmatized group motivate one to help
the group? *Personality and Social Psychology Bulletin, 28,* 1656–1666.

Batson, C. D., Duncan, B., Ackerman, P., Buckley, T., & Birch, K. (1981). Is empathic emotion a source of altruistic motivation? *Journal of Personality and*
Social Psychology, 40, 290–302.

Batson, C. D., Dyck, J. L., Brandt, J. R., Batson, J. G., Powell, A. L., McMaster,
M. R., & Griffitt, C. (1988). Five studies testing two new egoistic alternatives
to the empathy–altruism hypothesis. *Journal of Personality and Social Psy-*
chology, 55, 52–77.

Batson, C. D., Klein, T. R., Highberger, L., & Shaw, L. L. (1995). Immorality
from empathy-induced altruism: When compassion and justice conflict. *Jour-*
nal of Personality and Social Psychology, 68, 1042–1054.

Batson, C. D., & Moran, T. (1999). Empathy-induced altruism in a prisoner's dilemma. *European Journal of Social Psychology, 29,* 909–924.

Batson, C. D., Polycarpou, M. P., Harmon-Jones, E., Imhoff, H. J., Mitchener,
E. C., Bednar, L. L., Klein, T. R., & Highberger, L. (1997). Empathy and
attitudes: Can feeling for a member of a stigmatized group improve feelings
toward the group? *Journal of Personality and Social Psychology, 72,* 105–
118.

Batson, C. D., & Weeks, J. L. (1996). Mood effects of unsuccessful helping: Another test of the empathy–altruism hypothesis. *Personality and Social Psychology Bulletin, 22,* 148–157.

Bridgeman, D. L. (1981). Enhanced role-taking through cooperative interdependence: A field study. *Child Development, 52,* 1231–1238.

Burton, J. W. (1986). The procedures of conflict resolution. In E. E. Azar & J. W. Burton (Eds.), *International conflict resolution: Theory and practice* (pp. 92–116). Boulder, CO: Reiner.

Burton, J. W. (1987). *Resolving deep-rooted conflict.* Lanham, MD: University Press of America.

Byrnes, D. A., & Kiger, G. (1990). The effect of a prejudice-reduction simulation on attitude change. *Journal of Applied Social Psychology, 20,* 341–356.

Clore, G. L., & Jeffrey, K. M. (1972). Emotional role playing, attitude change, and attraction toward a disabled person. *Journal of Personality and Social Psychology, 23,* 105–111.

Dawes, R., van de Kragt, A. J. C., & Orbell, J. M. (1990). Cooperation for the benefit of us—not me, or my conscience. In J. J. Mansbridge (Ed.), *Beyond self-interest* (pp. 97–110). Chicago: University of Chicago Press.

Dawkins, R. (1976). *The selfish gene.* New York: Oxford University Press.

Des Pres, T. (1976). *The survivor: An anatomy of life in the death camps.* New York: Washington Square Press.

Dovidio, J. F., Gaertner, S. L., & Johnson, J. D. (1999, October). *New directions in prejudice and prejudice reduction: The role of cognitive representations and affect.* Paper presented at the annual meeting of the Society of Experimental Social Psychology, St. Louis, MO.

Eisenberg, N., & Miller, P. A. (1987). Empathy and prosocial behavior. *Psychological Bulletin, 101,* 91–119.

Eliasz, H. (1980). The effect of empathy, reactivity, and anxiety on interpersonal aggression intensity. *Polish Psychological Bulletin, 11,* 169–178.

Finlay, K. A., & Stephan, W. G. (2000). Reducing prejudice: The effects of empathy on intergroup attitudes. *Journal of Applied Social Psychology, 30,* 1720–1737.

Fisher, R. (1994). General principles for resolving intergroup conflict. *Journal of Social Issues, 50,* 47–66.

Frodi, A. M., & Lamb, M. E. (1980). Child abusers' responses to infant smiles and cries. *Child Development, 51,* 238–241.

Gaines, T., Kirwin, P. M., & Gentry, W. D. (1977). The effect of descriptive anger expression, insult, and no feedback on interpersonal aggression, hostility, and empathy motivation. *Genetic Psychology Monographs, 95,* 349–367.

Hancock, G. (1989). *Lords of poverty: The power, prestige, and corruption of the international aid business.* New York: Atlantic Monthly Press.

Hardin, G. (1977). *The limits of altruism: An ecologist's view of survival.* Bloomington: Indiana University Press.

Harmon-Jones, E., Vaughn, K., Mohr, S., Sigelman, J., & Harmon-Jones, C. (2001). *The effects of empathy on anger-related left frontal cortical activity and hostile attitudes.* Unpublished manuscript, University of Wisconsin, Madison.

Hoess, R. (1959). *Commandant at Auschwitz: Autobiography.* London: Weidenfeld & Nicholson.

Isaacson, W. (1992, December 21). Sometimes, right makes might. *Time,* p. 82.

Johnson, D. W., & Johnson, R. T. (1987). *Learning together and alone: Cooperative, competitive, and individualistic learning.* Englewood Cliffs, NJ: Prentice-Hall.

Kant, I. (1898). Fundamental principles of the metaphysic of morals. In *Kant's critique of practical reason and other works on the theory of ethics* (4th ed., T. K. Abbott, Trans.). New York: Longmans, Green. (Original work published 1785)

Kelman, H. C. (1990). Interactive problem-solving: A social psychological approach to conflict resolution. In J. W. Burton & F. Dukes (Eds.), *Conflict: Readings in management and resolution* (pp. 199–215). New York: St. Martin's Press.

Kelman, H. C., & Cohen, S. P. (1986). Resolution of international conflict: An interactional approach. In S. Worchel & W. G. Austin (Eds.), *Psychology of intergroup relations* (pp. 323–432). Chicago: Nelson Hall.

Kerr, N. L. (1995). Norms in social dilemmas. In D. A. Schroeder (Ed.), *Social dilemmas: Perspectives on individuals and groups* (pp. 31–47). Westport, CT: Praeger.

Kogon, E. (1953). *The theory and practice of hell* (H. Norden, Trans.). New York: Farrar, Straus.

Lerner, M. J. (1970). The desire for justice and reactions to victims. In J. Macaulay & L. Berkowitz (Eds.), *Altruism and helping behavior* (pp. 205–229). New York: Academic Press.

Lerner, M. J. (1980). *The belief in a just world: A fundamental delusion.* New York: Plenum Press.

Lewin, K. (1951). *Field theory in social science.* New York: Harper.

McCullough, M. E., Worthington, E. L., Jr., & Rachal, K. C. (1997). Interpersonal forgiving in close relationships. *Journal of Personality and Social Psychology, 73,* 321–336.

MacLean, P. D. (1967). The brain in relation to empathy and medical education. *Journal of Nervous and Mental Disease, 144,* 374–382.

Mansbridge, J. J. (Ed.). (1990). *Beyond self-interest.* Chicago: University of Chicago Press.

Maslach, C. (1982). *Burnout: The cost of caring.* Englewood Cliffs, NJ: Prentice-Hall.

Miller, P. A., & Eisenberg, N. (1988). The relation of empathy to aggressive and externalizing/antisocial behavior. *Psychological Bulletin, 103,* 324–344.

Milner, J. S., Halsey, L. B., & Fultz, J. (1995). Empathic responsiveness and affective reactivity to infant stimuli in high- and low-risk for physical child abuse mothers. *Child Abuse and Neglect, 19,* 767–780.

Nagel, T. (1991). *Equality and partiality.* New York: Oxford University Press.

New revised standard version of the Bible. (1991). New York: Oxford University Press.

Oliner, S. P., & Oliner, P. M. (1988). *The altruistic personality: Rescuers of Jews in Nazi Europe.* New York: Free Press.

Omoto, A. M., & Snyder, M. (1995). Sustained helping without obligation: Motivation, longevity of service, and perceived attitude change among AIDS volunteers. *Journal of Personality and Social Psychology, 68,* 671–686.

Peters, W. (1987). *A class divided: Then and now.* New Haven, CT: Yale University Press.

Rawls, J. (1971). *A theory of justice.* Cambridge, MA: Harvard University Press.

Richardson, D. R., Hammock, G. S., Smith, S. M., Gardner, W., & Signo, M. (1994). Empathy as a cognitive inhibitor of interpersonal aggression. *Aggressive Behavior, 20,* 275–289.

Rouhana, N. N., & Kelman, H. C. (1994). Promoting joint thinking in international conflicts: An Israeli–Palestinian continuing workshop. *Journal of Social Issues, 50,* 157–178.

Ryan, W. (1971). *Blaming the victim.* New York: Random House.

Schewe, P. A., & O'Donohue, W. (1993). Sexual abuse with high-risk males: The roles of victim empathy and rape myths. *Violence and Victims, 8,* 339–351.

Schroeder, D. A., Penner, L. A., Dovidio, J. F., & Piliavin, J. A. (1995). *The psychology of helping and altruism: Problems and puzzles.* New York: McGraw-Hill.

Schultz, P. W. (2000). Empathizing with nature: The effects of perspective taking on concern for environmental issues. *Journal of Social Issues, 56,* 391–406.

Shaw, L. L., Batson, C. D., & Todd, R. M. (1994). Empathy avoidance: Forestalling feeling for another in order to escape the motivational consequences. *Journal of Personality and Social Psychology, 67,* 879–887.

Shelton, M. L., & Rogers, R. W. (1981). Fear-arousing and empathy-arousing appeals to help: The pathos of persuasion. *Journal of Applied Social Psychology, 11,* 366–378.

Sherif, M., Harvey, O. J., White, B. J., Hood, W. E., & Sherif, C. W. (1961). *Intergroup conflict and cooperation: The Robber's Cave experiment.* Norman: University of Oklahoma Book Exchange.

Sibicky, M. E., Schroeder, D. A., & Dovidio, J. F. (1995). Empathy and helping: Considering the consequences of intervention. *Basic and Applied Social Psychology, 16,* 435–453.

Solomon, R. C. (1990). *A passion for justice: Emotions and the origins of the social contract.* Reading, MA: Addison-Wesley.

Stephan, W. G., & Finlay, K. (1999). The role of empathy in improving intergroup relations. *Journal of Social Issues, 55,* 729–743.

Stotland, E., Mathews, K. E., Sherman, S. E., Hansson, R. O., & Richardson, B. Z. (1978). *Empathy, fantasy, and helping.* Beverly Hills, CA: Sage.

Toi, M., & Batson, C. D. (1982). More evidence that empathic emotion is a source of altruistic motivation. *Journal of Personality and Social Psychology, 43,* 281–292.

Trivers, R. L. (1971). The evolution of reciprocal altruism. *Quarterly Review of Biology, 46,* 35–57.

Vescio, T. K., & Hewstone, M. (2001). *Empathy arousal as a means of improving intergroup attitudes: An examination of the affective supercedent hypothesis.* Unpublished manuscript, Pennsylvania State University, State College.

Vescio, T. K., Sechrist, G. B., & Paolucci, M. P. (2003). Perspective taking and prejudice reduction: The mediational role of empathy arousal and situational attributions. *European Journal of Social Psychology, 33,* 455–472.

Weigel, R. H., Wiser, P. L., & Cook, S. W. (1975). The impact of cooperative learning experiences on cross-ethnic relations and attitudes. *Journal of Social Issues, 31,* 219–244.

Worchel, S., & Andreoli, V. (1978). Facilitation of social interaction through deindividuation of the target. *Journal of Personality and Social Psychology, 36,* 549–556.

Worthington, E. L., Jr. (2001). Unforgiveness, forgiveness, and reconciliation and their implications for societal interventions. In R. G. Helmick & R. L. Petersen (Eds.), *Forgiveness and reconciliation: Religion, public policy, and conflict transformation* (pp. 161–182). Philadelphia: Templeton Foundation Press.

Zimbardo, P. G. (1970). The human choice: Individuation, reason, and order versus deindividuation, impulse, and chaos. In W. J. Arnold & D. Levine (Eds.), *Nebraska symposium on motivation, 1969* (Vol. 17, pp. 237–307). Lincoln: University of Nebraska Press.

Zimbardo, P. G., Banks, W. C., Haney, C., & Jaffe, D. (1973, April 8). The mind is a formidable jailer: A Prandelian prison. *The New York Times Magazine,* Section 6, pp. 38–60.

CHAPTER 15

EMPATHY-RELATED RESPONDING

Moral, Social, and Socialization Correlates

NANCY EISENBERG
CARLOS VALIENTE
CLAIRE CHAMPION

We have been studying, to some degree or another, empathy-related responding for 25 years. Initially, our interest in empathy was based on its purported role in moral development, especially prosocial behavior. Later, based on what we had learned in the first decade of research, we viewed it in a larger context—as a capacity related to social competence more broadly and in the context of children's developing capacity for regulating their emotions, including vicariously induced emotion. In addition, because of our interest in the socialization of both moral behavior and emotional responding, our research program has included the assessment of parental characteristics and behaviors related to empathy-related responding.

In this chapter, we provide an overview of our program of research on empathy-related responding in the context of some other related work. In our view, empathy-related responding, especially sympathy, is the basis of much prosocial interpersonal behavior. We start with a discussion of definitions and critical concepts, then examine the relation of empathy-related responding to prosocial behavior and the possible role of empathy in the continuity of prosocial behavior over time. We also touch briefly on the relations of empathy-related responding to social competence, aggression, and prosocial moral reasoning. Next, we discuss the socialization of empathy-related responding, and finally, we describe how this research relates to our broader perspective on morality.

CONCEPTUAL AND METHODOLOGICAL ISSUES

The topic of empathy-related responding has been discussed by philosophers for centuries. Over the centuries, numerous philosophers and, more recently, psychologists have suggested that empathy-related processes motivate prosocial behavior (Blum, 1980; Hoffman, 1982; Hume, 1777/ 1966; Staub, 1979)—that people who experience others' emotions are likely to engage in prosocial behavior. However, in 1982 Underwood and Moore published a review in which they found, contrary to most theory, *no* empirical relation between empathy and prosocial behavior such as helping and sharing. This finding was intriguing, so we took a closer look at the data. Upon careful consideration of this literature, it became clear that most of the work before 1982 had been conducted with children using measures that were problematic and that there were conceptual problems with most of the existing research (Eisenberg & Miller, 1987).

In regard to conceptual problems, most investigators had not differentiated between different types of empathy-related responding that would be expected to involve different affective motivations. Batson (1991), a social psychologist, first differentiated between empathy and personal distress in the late 1970s. Making yet one more distinction (between empathy and sympathy), we (Eisenberg & Fabes, 1998; Eisenberg, Shea, Carlo, & Knight, 1991) define *empathy* as an affective response that stems from the apprehension or comprehension of another's emotional state or condition, and which is similar to what the other person is feeling or would be expected to feel. Thus, if someone views a sad person and consequently feels sad, that person is experiencing empathy.

In most situations, especially after infancy, empathy is likely to evolve into either sympathy or personal distress (or both). *Sympathy* is defined as an emotional response stemming from the apprehension of another's emotional state or condition, which is not the same as the other's state or condition but consists of feelings of sorrow or concern for the other. Thus, if a girl sees a sad peer and feels concern for the peer, she is experiencing sympathy. Such a sympathetic reaction often is based on empathic sadness, although sympathy also may be based on cognitive perspective taking or accessing information from memory that is relevant to the other's experience. However, empathy also can lead to personal distress. *Personal distress* is a self-focused, aversive affective reaction to the apprehension of another's emotion (e.g., discomfort, anxiety). Personal distress sometimes may stem from empathy, primarily if the empathic response is experienced as too arousing. However, it is possible that personal distress sometimes stems from other processes (e.g., guilt) or from retrieving certain information from mental storage.

These conceptual nuances become important when attempting to predict prosocial behavior (i.e., voluntary behavior intended to benefit another), including altruism (i.e., those prosocial behaviors motivated by other-oriented or moral concerns/emotion rather than concrete or social rewards or the desire to reduce aversive affective states; Eisenberg, 1986), as well as other outcomes from empathy-related responding. For example, sympathy and personal distress are expected to result in different motivations and, consequently, different behavior. Batson (1991) hypothesized that a sympathetic emotional reaction is associated with the desire to reduce the other person's distress or need and therefore is likely to lead to altruistic behavior. Sympathy would not be expected to relate to prosocial behaviors motivated by factors such as personal gain, social approval, or the desire to alleviate one's own feelings of guilt, shame, or distress. In contrast, because personal distress is an aversive experience, it is believed to be associated with the motivation to reduce one's own distress. Consequently, personal distress is expected to result in the desire to avoid contact with the needy or distressed other if possible. People experiencing personal distress would be expected to assist only when helping is the easiest way to reduce the helper's own distress. Given the differences in the hypothesized motivational bases and behaviors stemming from sympathy and personal distress, the lack of differentiation between them (as well as among prosocial behaviors with different motivations) in many studies likely prevented researchers and reviewers from finding a clear relation between empathy-related responding and other-oriented prosocial behavior

In addition, as mentioned earlier, there were methodological problems in many of the early studies on empathy, especially those conducted with children, that muddied the pattern of empirical findings. Recall that Underwood and Moore (1982) found no relation between measures of empathy and prosocial responding. However, when Eisenberg and Miller (1987) reexamined the relation between empathy and prosocial behavior, they included studies with children and adults and divided the studies into groups based on the manner in which empathy (which usually was not differentiated from sympathy or personal distress) was assessed. Self-report indices of empathy used with younger children were unrelated to prosocial behavior, whereas most other types of indices (e.g., facial indices used with children, physiological indices, self-report indices used with older children and adults, experimental manipulations) were significantly associated with prosocial responding.

Most obvious from this review and other work we did on the topic were the problems with self-report indices of emotional responding for younger children. The commonly used picture-story indices of empathy, in

which children are exposed to brief hypothetical scenarios involving protagonists in emotion-evoking stories and are then asked how they themselves feel, frequently have been criticized. The brief scenarios may be too
short to elicit an emotional response; demand characteristics are strong;
and the children are expected to change emotions every few minutes in response to a new story. In addition, gender differences on these indices vary
as a function of sex of the experimenter, with children scoring higher if interviewed by same-sex adults (see Eisenberg & Lennon, 1983). The fact
that younger children's self-reported empathic reactions to others in experimental settings (usually involving videotapes of distressed or needy others) were unrelated to prosocial behavior suggests that children may have
difficulty assessing or reporting their own emotional reactions. Moreover,
most self-report measures with children do not differentiate between sympathy and personal distress, which could undermine the reported relation
between these two variables and children's prosocial behavior.

We do not mean to argue against the use of self-report measures, at
least with older children and adults. Despite the demand characteristics of
self-report indices and other shortcomings, they do have a place in the
work on vicarious emotional responding, in part because it is difficult to
assess internal emotional states in other ways, and self-reports can be used
to differentiate between older children's and adults' response of sympathy
versus personal distress. Thus, we would argue that self-report indices
should not be dismissed, but are best used in combination with other types
of indices.

EMPIRICAL FINDINGS ON THE RELATION
OF EMPATHY-RELATED RESPONDING
TO PROSOCIAL BEHAVIOR

Recall that Batson predicted that sympathy would be positively related to
altruistic behavior, whereas personal distress would be negatively related.
In a series of primarily experimental studies in which he apparently induced either sympathy or personal distress, he obtained some support for
these predictions. However, Batson, Bolen, Cross, and Neuringer-Benefiel
(1986) did not find that dispositional differences in sympathy predicted altruism after controlling for variables that they believed might reflect
nonaltruistic motives; indeed, Batson has argued that there may not be a
prosocial personality. His view appears to be that sympathy or personal
distress can be induced in anyone and that individual differences in
dispositional empathy-related responding are not very predictive of altruism. Our view, in contrast, is that there are individual differences in people's empathy-related responding and prosocial tendencies—differences
that are somewhat stable over time.

Situational Empathy-Related Responding and Prosocial Behavior

The experimental methods and self-report measures Batson used generally were inappropriate for use with children. Thus, Eisenberg, Fabes, and their students began a series of studies designed to develop alternative methods of assessing empathy-related responding and to examine the relations of sympathy and personal distress to children's prosocial behavior. Unlike Batson, our goal was not to prove that there is such a thing as pure altruism; we sought to examine the relations of situational and dispositional empathy-related responding to prosocial behavior, especially those responses that were likely to be based on concern for another.

In this work we used self-report, facial, and physiological markers of sympathy and personal distress to measure responses in situations likely to induce a reaction akin to sympathy or personal distress (e.g., a film). Children and adults tended to exhibit facial concerned attention in sympathy-inducing contexts and distress in situations believed to elicit personal distress, and older children's and adults' self-reports also were somewhat consistent with the emotional context (Eisenberg, Fabes, et al., 1988; Eisenberg, Fabes, Schaller, Miller, et al., 1991; Eisenberg, Schaller, et al., 1988; see also Eisenberg & Fabes, 1990, for a review). In two studies (Eisenberg, Fabes, et al., 1988; Eisenberg, Schaller, et al. 1988), younger children's self-reports of sympathy and personal distress were less differentiated and contextually appropriate than those of older children and adults, although, in general, verbal reports of emotion in the evocative situations were consistent with the context (i.e., sympathy or distress inducing) at all ages. Moreover, study participants exhibited higher heart rate (HR) and skin conductance (SC) in the distressing situations. We suggested that HR acceleration might reflect distress, whereas HR deceleration might reflect interest in, and processing of, information coming from external stimuli—in this case, the sympathy-inducing stimulus. HR acceleration also has been linked to the processing of information that is internal rather than outside of the self, suggesting the possibility that it taps a self-focus. SC may be a purer measure of emotional arousal than HR and, consequently, a more direct measure of personal distress. High SC is more likely to accompany anxiety than sadness (which is involved in empathic feelings) and is expected to result in an aversive state and the desire to avoid/reduce the situation rather than confront the other's distress (Eisenberg & Fabes, 1990; Fabes, Eisenberg, Karbon, Troyer, & Switzer, 1994).

Once we obtained validation of our measures of sympathy and personal distress, we examined the relation of children's and adults' sympathy or personal distress to helping or sharing with needy/distressed individuals (or others like them) when it was easy to avoid contact with the needy other. For example, children would view a film of injured children who were talking about their experiences in the hospital. Typically we would measure HR and/or SC while the children watched the film, taped and coded their facial reactions to the film, and asked them to rate how they felt during the film when the film was over. A little later, they had the opportunity to assist the child (or children) in the film (or others like him or her) by doing one of a variety of tasks (in different studies), including donating part of a payment or doing a boring task to help the needy or distressed children rather than playing with attractive toys. Using this multimethod approach, we have found, as predicted by many theorists, links between empathy-related responding and prosocial behavior.

Self-Report Indices of Empathy-Related Responding

Findings using self-report instruments are mixed. In one study, we found that after controlling for age, children's reports of positive mood to an empathy-inducing film (about injured children in the hospital) were negatively related with prosocial behavior (i.e., helping). In addition, girls' report of negative mood and boys' report of sympathy and distress were positively related with prosocial behavior (i.e., helping; Fabes, Eisenberg, & Miller, 1990). Boys' reports of positive mood also were negatively correlated with the amount of donating behavior, whereas adults' reports of sympathy and personal distress (marginally for the latter) both predicted high levels of helping (Eisenberg et al., 1989). Furthermore, in a study with preschoolers, reports of sad reactions (e.g., by pointing to pictures of facial expressions) to an empathy-inducing film were positively related to helping the distressed children in the film, whereas reports of happy responses were negatively related. However, reports of feeling "sorry" for the children were unrelated to helping (Miller, Eisenberg, Fabes, & Shell, 1996). Indeed, the pattern of findings is not always as expected. In a study of kindergarteners and second graders, reported sympathetic reactions to a film were unrelated to helping of the needy children in the film (Fabes, Eisenberg, Karbon, Bernzweig, et al., 1994). Furthermore, reported empathy-related responding was not significantly related to helping in a study of preschoolers (Eisenberg et al., 1990) or to mother-reported helpfulness in a study of third and sixth graders; Fabes, Eisenberg, & Eisenbud, 1993).

In summary, findings in experimental situations provide some support for the relation of self-reported sympathy/empathy to prosocial behavior. It is likely that associations are clearer and stronger as children mature because reports of empathy-related emotion become more differentiated and appropriate to the situation with age (Eisenberg, Fabes, et al., 1988). In addition, the finding that personal distress is sometimes positively related to prosocial behavior (i.e., helping) is counter to theory and may be due to the difficulty in differentiating between distress for others and self-related distress when using self-report measures (Eisenberg et al., 1989; Fabes et al., 1990). Finally, positive correlations between adults' reports of sympathy and personal distress and indices of social desirability suggest that self-reports of empathy-related responding sometimes may not reflect the true emotions felt during the viewing of the movie (Eisenberg et al., 1989), although social desirability does not seem to be substantially related to younger children's reports of situational empathy-related responding (Eisenberg, Fabes, Schaller, Carlo, & Miller, 1991).

Physiological Indices of Empathy-Related Responding

As noted, HR and SC are the two indices of empathy-related emotions and personal distress that we have used in our laboratory to predict prosocial behavior. We view HR deceleration as an indirect marker of sympathy and HR acceleration as an index of personal distress; SC arousal is viewed as a marker of personal distress (Eisenberg & Fabes, 1991). Across several studies using HR or SC as markers of empathy-related responding, we have found support for the hypothesis that sympathy and personal distress are differentially related to prosocial behavior (Eisenberg & Fabes, 1990).

In an early study, HR was measured as children (second and fifth graders) and adults watched an empathy-inducing movie. For the most sympathy-inducing part of the movie, HR deceleration was found to be positively related with helping behavior (i.e., helping the mother or the children injured in the movie; Eisenberg et al., 1989). In a second study, 4- and 5-year-olds were placed in a similar situation but with a simpler version of the movie and a different request for helping behavior (i.e., packing crayons for hospitalized children). Similar results were found for the most sympathy-inducing portion of the movie: Helpers exhibited HR deceleration, whereas nonhelpers tended to exhibit HR acceleration. However, HR recorded during the distress portion of the movie did not relate to prosocial behavior (Eisenberg et al., 1990). In a third study involving third and sixth graders and similar procedures, HR acceleration (versus deceleration) while the children viewed the most empathy-inducing portion of the film was associated with low donating (Eisenberg & Fabes, 1990). Using a more life-like paradigm, HR responding in response to a crying baby (acceleration vs. deceleration) was negatively related to the quality (but not quantity) of comforting behavior displayed by young elementary school children in one study (Fabes, Eisenberg, Karbon, Troyer, et al., 1994) but was unrelated to helping in another (Eisenberg et al., 1993).

In a study with kindergartners and second graders, in addition to showing a movie and monitoring children's HR, we measured SC. SC was inversely related to helping behavior and positively correlated with facial distress. SC reactivity accounted for a significant amount of the variance in helping behavior, above and beyond all other predictors (i.e., facial indices; Fabes, Eisenberg, Karbon, Bernzweig, et al., 1994). In another study with kindergartner to third graders, SC collected during the distress portion of the movie was related negatively to teachers' reports of children's prosocial behavior (Holmgren, Eisenberg, & Fabes, 1998). Similarly, third- and sixth-grade boys' (but not girls') SC in response to an empathy-inducing film was negatively related to mothers' ratings of girls' (but not boys') helpfulness (Fabes et al., 1993). Thus, SC—believed to be an indicator of personal distress—has been linked not only to low prosocial responding in an empathy-inducing context, but with low levels of dispositional prosocial behavior. Consequently, our findings with physiological measures support a link between empathy-related responding and prosocial behavior as well as the distinction between sympathy and personal distress.

Facial Indices of Empathy-Related Emotions

In several studies, we have found a relation between empathy-related facial responding and prosocial behavior, although the strength of this relation appears to be stronger for boys than for girls. For example, in a study with 4- and 5-year-olds, boys' facial sadness was positively related to helping, whereas their facial distress was negatively correlated; no findings were obtained for girls (Eisenberg et al., 1990). In a study involving third and sixth graders, boys', but not girls', facial expressions of concerned attention while watching an empathy-inducing film were related to helping handicapped children, such as the one shown in the film. In addition, facial expressions of happiness during the movie were negatively related to boys' prosocial behavior (Eisenberg & Fabes, 1990). Similarly, boys', but not girls', facial expressions of concerned attention and sadness were positively related to helping in a study of second and fifth graders (Fabes et al., 1990).

In other studies, there were no sex differences in findings for facial empathy-related responding, or they were not examined. In one such study, facial expressions of concerned attention (but not distress) were positively related to helpfulness among second graders but not kindergartners (sex differences were not reported; Fabes, Eisenberg, Karbon, Bernzweig, et al., 1994). Similar relations between facial reactions and helping have been found for adults, with the findings holding for both sexes (Eisenberg et al., 1989). In other studies assessing children's empathy-related reactions to, and helping of, a crying infant, facial distress during crying was unrelated to young elementary school children's helping in one study (Fabes, Eisenberg, Karbon, Troyer, et al., 1994) and was negatively related to helping in another (Eisenberg et al., 1993). Furthermore, preschoolers' facial concern/worry in response to simulated injuries by adults (a mother and an experimenter) was found to be positively related to attempts to help the adults, whereas their distressed reactions were neg-atively related (Miller et al., 1996). In contrast, facial measures of sympa-thy or distress in response to one specific film sometimes have not shown a consistent pattern of relations to measures of dispositional prosocial be-havior outside of the empathy-inducing setting (e.g., Eisenberg et al., 1990; Fabes et al., 1993; cf. Miller et al., 1996).

In summary, relations between empathy-related responding in spe-cific situations and prosocial behavior have been found using a variety of instruments that measure vicarious emotional responding. Overall, these findings show that markers of sympathy and personal distress pre-dict when people assist in a given context (Eisenberg & Fabes, 1990, 1991). It is important to remember that the studies just reviewed in-volved situationally induced reactivity in the laboratory. In other studies that are discussed shortly, more dispositional measures of empathy-related responding were used, such as self- or other-report questionnaires or laboratory assessments involving the average of responses to more than one empathy-inducing film. In these studies, these more general measures of empathy-related responding often have been examined as correlates of prosocial behavior in another setting that is directed toward someone who was not the target of the study participants' empathy-related responding.

Young Children's Naturally Occurring Prosocial Behavior: Relations to Other-Oriented Moral Reasoning and Dispositional Empathy-Related Responding

In several studies, we examined the relations of preschoolers' naturally oc-curring prosocial behaviors in the preschool classroom to indices of other-orientation, including the children's other-oriented moral reasoning and empathy-related responding. In one study, children's prosocial behaviors were coded as occurring spontaneously (i.e., without a peer's verbal or nonverbal request) or in response to a request, and as helping or sharing (little comforting was observed). Helping behaviors generally were low in cost, such as reaching for paints for someone or tying a peer's apron. Shar-ing was higher cost, in that it required giving up an object or space in the child's possession. We found that spontaneous sharing, but not the other types of prosocial behavior, was related to preschoolers' references to oth-ers' needs in the assessment of their prosocial moral reasoning (Eisenberg-Berg & Hand, 1979). In another study, preschoolers' spontaneous sharing was not related to need-oriented reasoning but was negatively related to children's hedonistic (i.e., selfish) reasoning. Moreover, as in the other study, compliant prosocial behaviors were unrelated to moral reasoning (Eisenberg, Pasternack, Cameron, & Tryon, 1984). Thus, children's em-pathic concerns when reasoning about hypothetical moral dilemmas appeared to be associated with prosocial behaviors that were likely to be other-oriented—that is, did not simply reflect compliance with a request—and had a cost.

In addition, we found that young children's costly (i.e., spontaneous) prosocial behaviors tended to be associated with dispositional sympathy, whereas high levels of compliant prosocial behaviors in children of that age were linked to nonassertiveness and proneness to personal distress (Eisenberg et al., 1984, 1990; Eisenberg, Cameron, Tryon, & Dodez, 1981). For example, Eisenberg, McCreath, and Ahn (1988) found that preschoolers' expressions of sadness/concern (averaged) in response to two different videotapes of distressed children were positively related to children's prosocial behavior that was spontaneously emitted (rather than requested). In addition, for girls only, facial concern/sadness was positively related to requested prosocial behaviors. Anxious expressions in response to the films were related to frequency, but not proportion, of compliance with peers' requests for prosocial actions; children high in frequency of performing compliant prosocial behaviors also were frequent targets of peers' requests for sharing or helping. In another study in which only naturally occurring compliant prosocial behavior in the preschool was observed (spontaneous prosocial behavior were very infrequent), preschoolers' facial concern in reaction to two empathy-inducing films was negatively related to their compliant prosocial behavior (Eisenberg et al., 1990). Thus, children prone to personal distress seemed to assist others relatively frequently only because they were asked more often to do so (and did not seem assertive enough to say "no"), not for other-oriented reasons. Moreover, helping behaviors in this context (e.g., handing another child a block) tend to be low cost and may be indicative of children's sociability (Eisenberg-Berg & Hand, 1979), as well as compliance (if the helping is requested).

The Relation of Empathy-Related Responding to the Long-Term Prediction of Prosocial Dispositions

In our work on prosocial behavior, we have found that there is considerable intraindividual consistency over time in the types of prosocial behaviors that are likely to be other-oriented in origin and that sympathy or empathy may play a role in this consistency. We have conducted a 23-year study of prosocial moral reasoning and prosocial responding. The initial assessment involved the preschool sample, for which we found a relation between needs-oriented (empathic) moral reasoning and spontaneous sharing behavior (Eisenberg-Berg & Hand, 1979). As we followed up this sample over time, we found that spontaneous sharing, as assessed naturalistically in one of our preschool studies, predicted prosocial behavior and values/beliefs across childhood and into early adulthood.

A number of prosocial constructs were assessed every 2 years from the age of 9–10 to early adulthood. In late childhood and adolescence, some behavioral measures of helping or sharing were obtained. Mothers' reports of children's prosocial behaviors were obtained in adolescence, whereas friends reported on sympathy and prosocial tendencies in early adulthood. Eisenberg and colleagues (1999) found that spontaneous sharing was at least marginally correlated with costly donating at ages 9–10 and 11–12, self-reported helping at ages 15–16, self-reported consideration for others at ages 19–20, a self-report prosocial aggregate measure at ages 21–22 and 23–24; mothers' reports of helpfulness at ages 15–16 and 17–18; costly helping at age 17–18, sympathy at ages 13–14, 15–16, 17–18, 19–20, 21–22, perspective taking at ages 17–18, 19–20, and 21–22, and friends' reports of sympathy at ages 19–20, 21–22, and 23–24. Spontaneous sharing generally was unrelated to self-reported empathy in childhood, self-reported personal distress, and low-cost helping, and adult friends' reports of perspective taking or prosocial behavior (although it was related to reports of sympathy). Thus, spontaneous sharing in preschool was fairly consistently related to self-reports of prosocial responding and sympathy in late childhood, adolescence, and early adulthood, and sometimes predicted actual prosocial behavior and mothers' reports thereof. There were relatively few relations between the other types of prosocial behavior and later measures of prosocial responding, although preschoolers higher in compliant sharing reported being relatively helpful in adolescence. Of particular interest, reported sympathy generally tended to mediate the relations of preschoolers' spontaneous sharing with their prosocial tendencies in adulthood.

When the study participants were ages 25–26, we again examined the relations of preschool prosocial behavior to later prosocial dispositions (Eisenberg et al., 2002). Consistent with prior findings (although the correlation was only marginally significant 2 years prior), self-reported prosociality was positively related to observed preschoolers' spontaneous sharing. It also was positively related to compliant sharing. Moreover, friends' reports of prosociality were marginally but positively related to spontaneous sharing in preschool (the three correlations mentioned here ranged from .35 to .37).

It is also interesting to look in the other direction: from measures of prosociality in the mid-20s back to measures of earlier prosocial tendencies. Individual measures of self-reported prosociality were nearly always substantially related to the same or similar measures from up to 16 years earlier. For example, reports of helping at ages 21–22, 23–24, and 25–26 on a short version of Rushton, Chrisjohn, and Fekken's (1981) self-report prosocial behavior scale were significantly related to reports on the longer version of the scale at ages 13–14, 15–16, and 17–18 (rs ranged from .46 to .74). Similarly, sympathy scores on Davis's self-report measure (Davis,

1994) at ages 21–22, 23–24, and 25–26 were positively related to empathy on Bryant's (1982) empathy scale at ages 11–12 (rs ranged from .47 to .59) and 13–14 (rs ranging from .59 to .74). Sympathy at age 23–24 also was related to self-reported empathy at 9–10 years of age (r = .49). In addition, self-reported prosocial dispositions at ages 21–22 or older usually were at least marginally, positively related to mothers' reports of participants' prosocial behavior in adolescence. Furthermore, all correlations between the measures of sympathy at the three assessments when the participants were in their 20s and those at ages 15–16, 17–18, or 19–20 were significant (they ranged from .47 to .79). These relations changed relatively little when controlling for social desirability in adulthood. Moreover, partly because the sample size was small, we checked carefully to see if the findings were due to highly skewed variables or outliers; they were not.

Overall, there were many more significant correlations than would be expected by chance between adults' prosocial dispositions and self-reported prosociality/helping, empathy, sympathy, and perspective taking in late childhood and adolescence. Thus, there was strong evidence of intraindividual consistency in prosocial dispositions over time, including empathy-related responding.

There also were numerous relations between measures of prosocial moral judgment in adulthood and measures of sympathy or empathy at younger ages, including some with empathy reported at ages 9–10 or 11–12. Five of nine correlations with measures of self-reported empathy at ages 9–10, 11–12, and 13–14 were significant, and five of six were significant with 15–16- and 17–18-year-olds' reports of sympathy. These findings are consistent with the view that empathy-related responding contributes to moral reasoning (and, perhaps, vice versa). We return to this issue shortly (Eisenberg et al., 2002).

THE RELATIONS OF EMPATHY-RELATED RESPONDING TO SOCIAL COMPETENCE AND ANTISOCIAL BEHAVIOR

As might be expected if sympathy were a causal factor in prosocial behavior, empathy-related responding has been related not only to prosocial behavior, but also to social competence and adjustment. In a meta-analytic review, Eisenberg and Miller (1987) found that empathy-related responding was weakly but positively related to various measures of social competence. Similarly, in a different meta-analysis, Miller and Eisenberg (1988) found modest relations between most measures of empathy-related responding and low levels of antisocial behavior. However, in most of the early studies included in these meta-analyses, sympathy and personal distress generally were not differentiated; this omission could have reduced the strength of obtained relations. More recently, we have obtained empirical evidence indicating that sympathy is related not only to social competence, but also to children's adjustment and to children's and adults' self-regulation.

For example, in a longitudinal study, we found that 6- to 8-year-olds' dispositional sympathy, as assessed by teachers' reports, was significantly correlated with children's teacher-rated social skills 2 years earlier, concurrent teacher ratings of nonaggressive/socially appropriate behavior and prosocial/socially competent behavior, mothers' ratings of low levels of concurrent externalizing problems, and children's socially competent responses in a puppet game in which they acted out how they would respond in various hypothetical social conflict situations. Children's self-reported dispositional sympathy was related to teachers' ratings of their social skills 2 years earlier, peers' reports of sociometric status 2 years' prior, and children's socially constructive responses on Bryant's puppet task (1982). Four years later, when the children were 10–12 years old, teachers' reports of students' dispositional sympathy significantly related to teachers' reports of social competence concurrently and 2, 4, and 6 years earlier, as well as with same-sex peers' reports of social status 8 years earlier. Similarly, primary care-giving parents' (usually mothers') reports of children's dispositional sympathy were negatively related to mothers' and/or fathers' reports of externalizing problems (e.g., aggression, stealing) 2, 4, and 6 years before, especially for boys (Murphy, Shepard, Eisenberg, Fabes, & Guthrie, 1999). Moreover, at all three times that sympathy was assessed in this study, parents', children's, and/or teachers' reports of children's dispositional sympathy significantly related to concurrent and/or antecedent levels of regulation and low negative emotionality, often across 2 or more years of time (Eisenberg, Fabes, Murphy, et al., 1996; Eisenberg, Fabes, et al., 1998; Murphy et al., 1999; see also Eisenberg et al., 1994).

In a study of third graders in Indonesia, we obtained similar relations between teachers' or parents' reports of children's sympathy and their reports of low externalizing problems, high popularity, and regulation. Moreover, teachers' (but not parents') reports of children's sympathy were significantly related to parents' and teachers' reports of popularity, regulation, and low externalizing negatively related to peers' reports of children's fighting, and positively related to peers' reports of children's social status (parents' reports of children's sympathy were correlated only with their reports of low externalizing behavior and high popularity and regulation; Eisenberg, Liew, & Pidada, 2001). Furthermore, using a situational measure of empathy-related responding (i.e., reactions to evocative slides) rather than adults' reports in a U.S. sample, we found a relation between children's empathy (measured via facial and reported reactions to emotionally evocative slides) and their low externalizing problems and high social competence (Zhou et al., 2002). In particular, empathy in response to negative slides was predictive of antisocial behavior, even when controlling for levels of empathy and problem behaviors 2 years prior.

EMPATHY-RELATED RESPONDING
AND MORAL REASONING

As suggested, empathy-related responding may contribute to the development of reasoning about prosocial moral dilemmas, or what we have called prosocial moral reasoning: that is, reasoning about moral dilemmas in which one person's needs or desires conflict with those of others in a context in which the role of prohibitions, authorities' dictates, and formal obligations is minimal (Eisenberg, Carlo, Murphy, & VanCourt, 1995; Eisenberg-Berg, 1979). Moral judgment has been associated with moral behavior, including prosocial behavior; thus, associations of empathy-related responding to moral judgment suggest another pathway through which empathy-related responding may affect moral behavior. Work on prosocial moral reasoning is an outgrowth of the larger body of work on moral judgment, based on Kohlberg's (1981) pioneering theory and research.

The roles of cognition and affect in morality—including moral reasoning—have been debated for many years. Cognitive developmental theorists (e.g., Kohlberg, 1969) have claimed that cognition and rationality are central to morality, and that the capabilities for complex perspective taking (i.e., cognitively taking the perspective of another) and understanding abstract concepts are associated with, and underlie, advances in moral reasoning and in quality of prosocial behavior (Colby, Kohlberg, Gibbs, & Lieberman, 1983; Underwood & Moore, 1982). Others have asserted that affect, especially empathy-related responding, often functions as a motive for other-oriented moral behavior and can influence individuals' moral reasoning (Eisenberg, 1986; Haidt, 2001). As discussed, people who experience sympathy are expected to be motivated to consider and respond to others' needs, even if there is a moderate cost of doing so (Batson, 1991; Hoffman, 2000). Moreover, Hoffman (1987) has argued that sympathy/empathy stimulates the development of internalized moral reasoning that reflects concern for others' welfare, whereas Eisenberg (1986) suggested that sympathy primes the use of preexisting other-oriented moral cognitions. Based on such theoretical assertions, we have hypothesized that not only are empathy-related responding and prosocial moral reasoning related, but that prosocial moral reasoning sometimes might mediate the relation of sympathy to prosocial behavior.

We have obtained support for the association between sympathy and prosocial or care-oriented moral reasoning in several studies. Skoe, Eisenberg, and Cumberland (2002) found links between adults' reports of experiencing sympathy when resolving moral conflicts and their care-related moral reasoning, especially when discussing real-life dilemmas. In addition, reports of feelings of sympathy were related to ratings of the importance of a real-life or hypothetical moral dilemma.

Moreover, in the longitudinal study of prosocial moral reasoning already discussed (Eisenberg et al., 1999, 2002), we have repeatedly found correlations between reported sympathy and higher-level prosocial moral reasoning and/or the greater use of empathy-related types of moral reasoning or lesser use of hedonistic reasoning, from early adolescence into adulthood (Eisenberg et al., 1987, 1995; Eisenberg, Miller, Shell, McNalley, & Shea, 1991). Similar relations were obtained in other samples in the United States (Carlo, Eisenberg, & Knight, 1992; Eisenberg-Berg & Mussen, 1978) and in Brazil (Eisenberg, Zhou, & Koller, 2001).

In a recent study of adolescents in Brazil, we (Eisenberg, Zhou, & Koller, 2001) also obtained some initial support for the notion that prosocial moral reasoning mediates the relation of sympathy to prosocial behavior. In a structural equation model, sympathy (as well as cognitive perspective taking) predicted adolescents' level of prosocial moral reasoning, which, in turn, predicted their self-reported prosocial behavior (this measure correlated substantially with peer-reported prosocial behavior in another sample). In addition, sympathy laid a direct path to prosocial behavior. Thus, sympathy may contribute to prosocial behavior directly as well as through its effects on prosocial moral reasoning. A model with a direct path added from perspective taking to prosocial behavior did not fit the data as well, and that added path was not significant.

SOCIALIZATION CORRELATES
OF EMPATHY-RELATED RESPONSES

Due, in part, to the role of children's empathy-related responses in their prosocial and antisocial development, identifying the socialization factors that might promote or inhibit children's empathy-related responses, has been an important focus of our work. When my colleagues and I began this work, there was limited research and theory on the relation of parents' characteristics and behaviors to their children's empathy-related responses. More recently, considerable empirical (e.g., Eisenberg et al., 1992; Halberstadt, Crisp, & Eaton, 1999; Zhou et al., 2002) and theoretical (Denham, 1998; Eisenberg, Cumberland, & Spinrad, 1998) attention has been given to the socialization of children's experience, expression, and regulation of emotion, including their empathy-related responding. Most of our work on the socialization of empathy-related responses has focused on relations between children's empathy-related reactions or dispositional sympathy and (1) parents' empathy-related responses, (2) parents' expressivity, (3) parental warmth and support, and (4) emotion-related parenting practices.

Parents' Empathy-Related Responses

It is logical to predict associations between parents' and their offspring's empathy-related responses. Although limited support for this hypothesis was found in some studies (Kalliopuska, 1984; Strayer & Roberts, 1989), others found significant relations (Trommsdorff, 1991) or constructs complex patterns of relations (Barnett, King, Howard, & Dino, 1980). One limitation of these data is that the constructs of sympathy, empathy, and personal distress generally were not differentiated. When sympathy and personal distress were differentiated, generally the hypothesized relations were found. For example, in a series of studies, we found that mothers' sympathy tended to be positively related to daughters', but not sons', sympathy and negatively related to daughters', but not sons', personal distress (Eisenberg, Fabes, Schaller, Carlo, et al., 1991; Eisenberg & McNally, 1993; Fabes et al., 1990). However, mothers' sympathy was positively related to sons' dispositional sympathy in one study (Eisenberg et al., 1992). Likewise, fathers' sympathy was positively related to sons' sympathy in another study (Eisenberg, Fabes, Schaller, Carlo, et al., 1991). In addition, mothers' personal distress related negatively to daughters' sympathy and positively to their facial distress or inappropriate positive affect when viewing empathy-inducing films (Eisenberg et al., 1992; Fabes et al., 1990). Finally, mothers who exhibited facial distress and heart-rate acceleration (an index of distress) during empathy-inducing films had children who tended to exhibit these same reactions (Eisenberg et al., 1992). Based on these data, it appears that there are significant relations between parents' and children's empathy-related responses, but the relations are most prominent for same-sex parent–child dyads.

Parents' Expressivity

It is often hypothesized that children's willingness to express and, to some degree, experience emotions is related to parents' expression of emotion. Indeed, parents' expressivity has been related to children's tendencies to express emotions similar in valence (positive vs. negative) to those of their parents (Halberstadt et al., 1999). Parental expressivity may be related to children's empathy-related responses because (1) children in expressive families learn that it is acceptable to experience and express emotions, (2) parental expression of some emotions (e.g., positive ones and perhaps "softer" negative ones) is correlated with parental warmth, which appears to be related to children's empathy (Barnett, 1987; Zhou et al., 2002), and/or (3) parents and children share genetic predispositions for emotionality.

Data from several studies support the premise that parents' expressivity is related to children's empathy-related responses. For example, in a study of adults, young women's, but not men's, reports of their parents' expression of positive emotion were positively related to their sympathy, sadness, and distress in response to a sympathy-inducing film, and marginally, negatively related to their heart-rate reactions to the film (Eisenberg, Fabes, Schaller, Miller, et al., 1991). Eisenberg and McNally (1993) also found that mothers' positive emotional communication related positively to adolescent girls' reported sympathy, positively to boys' and girls' perspective taking, and negatively to boys' reported personal distress. Mothers' positive facial expressivity also appears to relate positively to children's facial and self-reported empathy with positive and negative emotions (Zhou et al., 2002). In contrast, in Java, Indonesia, no significant relation was found between parents' (mostly mothers') positive expressivity in the family and children's dispositional sympathy, perhaps because the expression of intense emotions, even positive ones, is viewed more negatively in Java (Eisenberg, Liew, et al., 2001).

Negative parental expressivity also has been found to relate to children's empathy-related responses. For example, Eisenberg, Fabes, Schaller, Miller, and colleagues (1991) found that parents' negative submissive expressivity (i.e., softer, less assertive negative emotions such as loss) was positively correlated with female undergraduates' reported sympathy, sadness, and distress; negative dominant expressivity (e.g., anger, hostility) was marginally correlated with low levels of skin conductance during a distressing film (indicating less empathic responsivity). In a study of younger children, mothers' expression of negative submissive emotion related positively to girls' facial expressions of concerned attention (an index of sympathy), whereas mothers' expression of negative dominant emotion was associated with girls' facial distress, facial sadness (but only for young girls), and low levels of boys' facial expressions of concern (Eisenberg et al., 1992). Similar relations between negative dominant expressivity and facial distress were recently found for a total sample of boys and girls (Valiente et al., 2002). Moreover, in an Indonesian sample, parents' (mostly mothers') reports of the expression of negative submissive and dominant emotion in the family were negatively related to third-graders' dispositional sympathy (Eisenberg, Liew, et al., 2001). Although not all findings are consistent, at this time it appears that positive expressivity relates to high levels of sympathy and to low levels of personal distress, whereas negative expressivity, especially negative dominant expressivity, is positively related to personal distress and negatively related to sympathetic responses. Parental negative submissive emotion has been positively related to empathy/sympathy in the United States but negatively related in Indonesia, perhaps partly because the expression of negative emotion is viewed more negatively in Indonesia than in North America.

Parental Warmth and Support

Theorists have argued that parents' warmth promotes children's sympathy by fostering security and self-regulation, which would be expected to allow children to consider and respond to others' feelings (Hoffman, 2000; Radke-Yarrow, Zahn-Waxler, & Chapman, 1983; Staub, 1979). Consistent with this view, attachment theorists have noted that parental warmth is a key component in the development of a secure parent–child relationship, and a secure parent–child relationship has been linked to young children's sympathy (Waters, Wippman, & Sroufe, 1979) and prosocial responding in the preschool years (Iannotti, Cummings, Pierrehumbert, Milano, & Zahn-Waxler, 1992; Kestenbaum, Farber, & Sroufe, 1989).

Findings pertaining to the relation between parental warmth and children's empathy-related responses are mixed. Although some researchers have found that warm and empathetic (Trommsdorff, 1991; Zahn-Waxler, Radke-Yarrow, & King, 1979) and nonpunitive and affectionate (Eisenberg-Berg & Mussen, 1978) parenting sometimes relate to higher levels of children's empathy/sympathy, others have not found such a relation (Eisenberg, Fabes, Schaller, Carlo, et al., 1991; Iannotti et al., 1992; Janssens & Gerris, 1992) or the relations were dependent on the child's age (Fabes, Eisenberg, Karbon, Bernzweig, et al., 1994). However, parents' abuse of their children has been associated with low levels of children's empathetic responding (Main & George, 1985; see also Miller & Eisenberg, 1988).

It is likely that relations of parental warmth to sympathy and/or prosocial behavior are moderated by other parenting behaviors or child characteristics. For example, nurturant care giving seems to foster more sympathy and altruism in children when caregivers model prosocial behavior (Yarrow, Scott, & Waxler, 1973). Moreover, although mothers' and fathers' support generally was not related to 7- to 10-year olds' empathy, mothers' (but not fathers') support during stressful times predicted girls' empathy concurrently, and mothers' support during stressful situations at age 10 predicted children's empathy 4 years later (Bryant, 1987). Hastings, Zahn-Waxler, Robinson, Usher, and Bridges (2000) also found that authoritative mothers who displayed low levels of negative affect had children who were described by mothers and teachers as empathetic, interpersonally responsible, and prosocial 2 years later.

In regard to potential mediating processes, parental warmth likely fosters high levels of children's regulatory abilities (Eisenberg, Gershoff, et al.,

2001), which generally have been positively related to sympathy and nega-tively related to personal distress (see Eisenberg, Wentzel, & Harris, 1998). In a recent longitudinal study, Zhou and colleagues (2002) used structural equation modeling to examine one of the processes that may maintain the relations between parental warmth and children's observed and reported empathy in response to viewing evocative slides. At the initial assessment (i.e., time 1), mothers' positive expressivity mediated the rela-tion between warmth and empathy with positive emotions, whereas 2 years later mediation was significant only for empathy with negative emo-tions. Importantly, the later finding remained significant when controlling for the stability of the variables overtime. However, a model predicting parenting from indices of child functioning also fit the data nearly as well as the parent-driven socialization model. Thus, it is likely that there is a bidirectional process in which parenting and children's functioning influence each other as children develop (Maccoby & Martin, 1983).

Emotion-Related Parenting Practices

In a number of studies, investigators have examined the role of parents' re-actions to, and discussion of, emotion in children's empathy-related re-sponses. When parents' reactions to children's emotions are positive and supportive, they may foster an environment wherein children feel free to experience and express emotions (including vicariously induced emotions), and such parents may be more likely to teach their children about emo-tions (which could contribute to the optimal regulation of emotion and sympathy). In contrast, it is believed that children who are negatively sanc-tioned for expressing emotion learn over time to hide their emotional reac-tions but to experience emotions more intensely internally (e.g., physiolog-ically; Buck, 1984). Because personal distress reactions may involve high of levels of empathic arousal (Eisenberg et al., 1994; Hoffman, 1982), in-dividuals who cannot regulate their emotions and who become highly aroused by exposure to others' negative states or emotion are likely to ex-perience personal distress rather than sympathy. In addition, because par-ents' discussion of emotion often relates to others' emotional states (Dunn, Bretherton, & Munn, 1987), it may also foster optimal empathy-related responses (i.e., sympathy) through promoting perspective taking and an understanding of emotion.

There is some support for the notion that parents who are not puni-tive or constraining in regard to their offspring's expression of emotion have children who display high levels of sympathy and low levels of per-sonal distress. For example, Eisenberg, Schaller, and colleagues (1988) found that parental leniency in regard to children's expression of emotions was positively related to children's dispositional empathy, whereas parental restrictiveness was positively related to children's facial distress during a sympathy-inducing film. In another study, boys whose parents were restrictive about the expression of negative emotions that were not harmful to others displayed more distress physiologically and facially, although they reported lower amounts of distress than did other boys. In contrast, mothers' emphasis on controlling emotions that were unlikely to hurt another was positively related to boys' personal distress (assessed by heart-rate acceleration and facial distress; Eisenberg, Fabes, Schaller, Carlo, et al., 1991).

In our laboratory, we have also found evidence that mothers' discussion of emotion sometimes is related to their children's empathy-related responses. For example, mothers who verbally linked the events in an empathy-inducing film to their children's experiences had children who displayed high levels of sadness, distress, and sympathy (Eisenberg et al., 1992). In this same study, boys' reports of sympathy and sadness were positively related to mothers' discussion of their own sadness/sympathy. Using structural equation modeling, we have found that parental linking of another's experience to their child's own experience relates negatively to children's unregulated expressivity (although it was not related to children's empathy with slides about negative events; Eisenberg, Losoya, et al., 2001). Whereas we have found that some types of discussion of negative emotion seem to promote sympathy, Trommsdorff (1995) found that German and Japanese mothers who verbalized or matched their 5-year-old daughters' emotions had daughters that experienced distress rather than empathy when exposed to a peer's sadness. It appears that discussion of emotion that fosters regulation and is not overly focused on negativity (and overly arousing) promotes sympathetic responses.

In summary, existing data generally support the premise that parental socialization is related to children's empathy-related responses. However, many of the relations have been examined only for mothers, and some seem to differ depending on the sex of the child and parent. Currently it is unclear if the relations between parental socialization and children's empathy-related responses change (or remain the same) as children age and if children's temperament (e.g., proneness to experience negative emotions, degree of self-regulation) moderates the relations between socialization practices and children's empathy-related responding. Moreover, although much of our work and the work of others is consistent with the conclusion that the aforementioned aspects of parental socialization lead to children's empathy-related responses, it is likely that the process is bidirectional and partially influenced by genetic factors (Fabes, Eisenberg, Karbon, Bernzweig, et al., 1994; Zahn-Waxler, Robinson, & Emde, 1992).

IMPLICATIONS OF OUR WORK FOR CONCEPTIONS
OF EMPATHY-RELATED AND PROSOCIAL RESPONDING

As is obvious from the review of our research, we believe that the development of empathy-related responding is influenced by socialization in the family (as well as outside the family). What may not be as clear is our belief that empathy-related responding also has a biological basis. In an excellent study of empathy-related responding and prosocial behavior, Zahn-Waxler and colleagues (Zahn-Waxler et al., 1992; Zahn-Waxler, Schiro, Robinson, Emde, & Schmitz, 2001) found evidence for a hereditary basis of sympathetic concern and prosocial behavior (but not self-distress). These findings are consistent with our own work indicating that empathy-related responding and prosocial behavior are associated with individual differences in temperamentally based negative emotionality and emotion-relevant regulation. In brief, we have found that children and adults who are well regulated—who can effortfully modulate their own attention and/or inhibit their behavior when they need to—often are more sympathetic and prosocial (Eisenberg, Fabes, Karbon, et al., 1996; Eisenberg, Fabes, Murphy, et al., 1996; Eisenberg et al., 1997) than those who are not well regulated. Moreover, adults' reports of children's negative emotionality (probably especially anger/frustration) tend to be negatively related to children's dispositional sympathy and children's self-reported sympathy; conversely, facial indices of children's empathic personal distress have been associated with children's adult-reported negative emotionality (Eisenberg, Wentzel, & Harris, 1998; Guthrie et al., 1997). Nonetheless, children who are prone to intense emotions (positive and negative) but are also well regulated tend to be sympathetic (Eisenberg, Fabes, Murphy, et al., 1996).[1]

The important point is that empathy-related responding appears to have a temperamental/personality basis. Thus, we believe there is a constitutional and hereditary basis to empathy-related responding. Nonetheless, numerous developmentalists (including us) believe that temperamen-

---

[1] Adults' self-reported emotionality tends to be positively associated with both sympathy (especially adult-reported proneness to sadness) and personal distress (especially for report of frequent negative emotionality; Eisenberg et al., 1994; Eisenberg, Wentzel, & Harris, 1999). However, in studies with adults, the measures of negative emotionality generally have not included any or many items related to anger/frustration. In contrast, it is likely that adult observers often were especially influenced by displays of children's anger/frustration when rating children's negative emotionality. The combination of the types of negative emotions in adult-report measures of negative emotionality and the fact that the adults (but not children) usually reported on their own affect (and often may have reported on less overt negative emotions than anger, e.g., anxiety) is likely responsible for the different findings for children and adults.

tal tendencies can be influenced by socialization and other environmental factors (Eisenberg, Gershoff, et al., 2001; Rothbart & Bates, 1998). Because of the relation of effortful emotion-relevant regulation to empathy-related responding, and because we believe that such regulation is partly socialized (e.g., Eisenberg, Gershoff, et al., 2001; Eisenberg, Valiente, et al., 2003), we have hypothesized that socializers affect children's sympathy partly through their influence on children's emerging effortful regulation. This effect is in addition to the other numerous (albeit related) ways that parents might influence children's empathy-related responding (e.g., by helping them to notice and understand others' emotional states).

Thus, we view empathy-related responding as based partly on automatic, biologically based processes and partly on the degree to which individuals voluntarily focus attention on others and/or try to control their emotional arousal so that they do not become overly aroused in distressing situations. In addition, whether or not people react to others' emotional states or condition likely depends on the degree to which people generally are oriented toward others, care about them, and hold other-oriented values. We suspect that these tendencies also are based on a combination of hereditary and other more environmentally based factors, and are partly under the control of the individual.

When thinking about the role of human intentionality and responsibility in prosocial tendencies, it is important to differentiate between empathy-related responding and prosocial behavior. Empathy, sympathy, and personal distress are emotional reactions (based partly on cognitions) and thus are sometimes difficult to control and regulate. Empathy often may be a relatively automatic response (although people can purposefully enhance sympathy by processes such as perspective taking). In contrast, prosocial behaviors such as helping, sharing, or consoling others, although sometimes based primarily on emotion, would seem to be under voluntary control more than are empathy-related responses. Indeed, they often are defined as intentional, voluntary behaviors. Even if individuals do not feel sympathy or empathy for another person, they can decide to help another person based on their values or other reasons. Thus, especially after the first few years of life, we believe that people have considerable voluntary control over their prosocial behavior.

Our research is consistent with a complex view of human nature. We believe that some people are, due to hereditary and/or constitutional factors, more predisposed than others to orient and respond to others' emotions and needs. Our research indicates that there are individual differences in empathy-related responding and prosocial behaviors that are somewhat consistent over time (especially after the first few years of life). Put differently, sympathy and prosocial behavior probably "come more naturally" to some people than others. In addition, our research on social-ization is consistent with the view that children's capacity for sympathy (or personal distress) can be enhanced or undermined by parents and other socializers. Further, people's values and moral reasoning likely affect, and are affected by, their empathy-related responding, which, in turn, influ-ences their prosocial behavior. Although values are socialized, individuals also are believed to play an active role in constructing their own values and moral reasoning (e.g., Kohlberg, 1981). Therefore, despite genetic, constitutional, and environmental influences on humans' capacity for sympathy and prosocial behavior, individuals can contribute to the de-velopment of an other-orientation in themselves, and they can choose to assist, or not assist, others in specific situations.

Our theoretical framework and findings have implications for policies related to children. First, prosocial tendencies can be affected by parents and other socializers (some experimental work is consistent with this no-tion; Brestan & Eyberg, 1998). Thus, it is desirable that socializers learn optimal ways to promote sympathetic concern for others, higher-level moral reasoning, and children's knowledge and willingness to help others. There are intervention programs that do just these things, but they are available only to a small number of children. Moreover, because regula-tory skills are partly learned in childhood, we need to know more about how to enhance children's ability to effortfully control their behavior and their willingness to do so for the sake of others. In addition, because indi-vidual differences in children's temperament are related to empathy-related responding, it is important to design interventions/programs that take these differences into account (Eisenberg, Wentzel, et al., 1998). Simi-larly, interventions to promote prosocial behavior may vary in effective-ness, depending on children's preexisting dispositional sympathy and their moral reasoning level (as well as their personality).

The first author's personal values have contributed to her interest in empathy-related responses and to the development of her conceptual framework. As she noted elsewhere (Eisenberg, 1996), her involvement in the civil rights movement and other political activities in the late 1960s and early 1970s initially sparked an interest in the development of human-itarian political attitudes. Early in graduate training, this interest led to re-search on empathy-related responding and prosocial behavior and moral reasoning (i.e., her master's thesis and doctoral dissertation examined humanitarian political attitudes and their relations to prosocial moral reasoning, prosocial behavior, and/or empathy).

Claire Champion is a PhD student at Arizona State University; Carlos Valiente also was a graduate student but is now on the faculty at Arizona State University. At the end of Claire Champion's college education in France (when doing an honor thesis), she came to be interested in people's recognition of facial expressions, which slowly led her to study how people regulate their emotions (the topic of her master's thesis) and the consequences of emotion-related regulation for behaviors such as prosocial behavior or social competence.

Due, in part, to Carlos Valiente's belief that parenting contributes to children's emotional and behavioral adjustment, he has focused on socialization factors that might promote or inhibit children's emotion-related regulation during his graduate training. Stemming from these experiences, he has begun to examine the relations of children's empathy-related responses to both their adjustment and the family context.

ACKNOWLEDGMENTS

Work on this chapter was supported by a grant from the National Institute of Mental Health (No. R01 MH 60838) to Nancy Eisenberg and by a minority fellowship from the American Psychological Association to Carlos Valiente.

REFERENCES

Barnett, M. A. (1987). Empathy and related responses in children. In N. Eisenberg & J. Strayer (Eds.), *Empathy and its development* (pp. 46–162). Cambridge, UK: Cambridge University Press.

Barnett, M. A., King, L. M., Howard, J. A., & Dino, G. A. (1980). Empathy in young children: Relation to parents' empathy, affection, and emphasis on the feelings of others. *Developmental Psychology, 16,* 243–244.

Batson, C. D. (1991). *The altruism question: Toward a social-psychological answer.* Hillsdale, NJ: Erlbaum.

Batson, C. D., Bolen, M. H., Cross, J. A., & Neuringer-Benefiel, H. E. (1986). Where is the altruism in the altruistic personality? *Journal of Personality and Social Psychology, 50,* 212–220.

Blum, L. A. (1980). *Friendship, altruism and morality.* London: Routledge & Kegan Paul.

Brestan, E. V., & Eyberg, S. M. (1998). Effective psychosocial treatments of conduct-disordered children and adolescents: 29 years, 82 studies, and 5,272 kids. *Journal of Clinical Child Psychology, 27,* 180–189.

Bryant, B. K. (1982). An index of empathy for children and adolescents. *Child Development, 53,* 413–425.

Bryant, B. K. (1987). Mental health, temperament, family, and friends: Perspectives on children's empathy and social perspective taking. In N. Eisenberg & J. Strayer (Eds.), *Empathy and its development* (pp. 245–270). Cambridge, UK: Cambridge University Press.

Buck, R. (1984). *The communication of emotion.* New York: Guilford Press.

Carlo, G., Eisenberg, N., & Knight, G. P. (1992). An objective measure of adolescents' prosocial moral reasoning. *Journal of Research on Adolescence, 2,* 331–349.

Colby, A., Kohlberg, L., Gibbs, J., & Lieberman, M. (1983). A longitudinal study of moral judgment. *Monographs of the Society for Research in Child Development, 48*(1–2, Serial No. 200).

Davis, M. H. (1994). *Empathy: A social psychological approach.* Madison, WI: Brown & Benchmark.

Denham, S. A. (1998). *Emotional development in young children.* New York: Guilford Press.

Dunn, J., Bretherton, I., & Munn, P. (1987). Conversations about feeling states between mothers and their young children. *Developmental Psychology, 23,* 132–139.

Eisenberg, N. (1986). *Altruistic emotion, cognition, and behavior.* Hillsdale, NJ: Erlbaum.

Eisenberg, N. (1996). In search of the good heart. In M. R. Merrens & G. G. Brannigan (Eds.), *The developmental psychologists: Research adventures across the lifespan* (pp. 89–104). New York: McGraw Hill.

Eisenberg, N., Cameron, E., Tryon, K., & Dodez, R. (1981). Socialization of prosocial behavior in the preschool classroom. *Developmental Psychology, 17,* 773–782.

Eisenberg, N., Carlo, G., Murphy, B., & Van Court, P. (1995). Prosocial development in late adolescence: A longitudinal study. *Child Development, 66,* 1179–1197.

Eisenberg, N., Cumberland, A., & Spinrad, T. L. (1998). Parental socialization of emotion. *Psychological Inquiry, 9,* 241–273.

Eisenberg, N., & Fabes, R. A. (1990). Empathy: Conceptualization, assessment, and relation to prosocial behavior. *Motivation and Emotion, 14,* 131–149.

Eisenberg, N., & Fabes, R. A. (1991). Prosocial behavior and empathy: A multimethod, developmental perspective. In M. Clark (Ed.), *Review of personality and social psychology: Prosocial behavior* (Vol. 12, pp. 34–61). Newbury Park, CA: Sage.

Eisenberg, N., & Fabes, R. A. (1998). Prosocial development. In W. Damon (Series Ed.) & N. Eisenberg (Vol. Ed.), *Handbook of child psychology: Vol. 3. Social, emotional, and personality development* (5th ed., pp. 701–778). New York: Wiley.

Eisenberg, N., Fabes, R. A., Bustamante, D., Mathy, R. M., Miller, P., & Lindholm, E. (1988). Differentiation of vicariously-induced emotional reactions in children. *Developmental Psychology, 24,* 237–246.

Eisenberg, N., Fabes, R. A., Carlo, G., Speer, A. L., Switzer, G., Karbon, M., & Troyer, D. (1993). The relations of empathy-related emotions and maternal practices to children's comforting behavior. *Journal of Experimental Child Psychology, 55,* 131–150.

Eisenberg, N., Fabes, R. A., Carlo, G., Troyer, D., Speer, A. L., Karbon, M., & Switzer, G., (1992). The relations of maternal practices and characteristics to children's vicarious emotional responsiveness. *Child Development, 63,* 583–602.

Eisenberg, N., Fabes, R. A., Karbon, M., Murphy, B. C., Wosinski, M., Polazzi, L., Carlo, G., & Juhnke, C. (1996). The relations of children's dispositional prosocial behavior to emotionality, regulation, and social functioning. *Child Development, 67,* 974–992.

Eisenberg, N., Fabes, R. A., Miller, P. A., Fultz, J., Mathy, R. M., Shell, R., & Reno, R. R. (1989). The relations of sympathy and personal distress to prosocial behavior: A multimethod study. *Journal of Personality and Social Psychology, 57,* 55–66.

Eisenberg, N., Fabes, R. A., Miller, P. A., Shell, C., Shea, R., & May-Plumlee, T. (1990). Preschoolers' vicarious emotional responding and their situational and dispositional prosocial behavior. *Merrill–Palmer Quarterly, 36,* 507–529.

Eisenberg, N., Fabes, R. A., Murphy, B., Karbon, M., Maszk, P., Smith, M., O'Boyle, C., & Suh, K. (1994). The relations of emotionality and regulation to dispositional and situational empathy-related responding. *Journal of Personality and Social Psychology, 66,* 776–797.

Eisenberg, N., Fabes, R. A., Murphy, B., Karbon, M., Smith, M., & Maszk, P. (1996). The relations of children's dispositional empathy-related responding to their emotionality, regulation, and social functioning. *Developmental Psychology, 32,* 195–209.

Eisenberg, N., Fabes, R. A., Schaller, M., Carlo, G., & Miller, P. A. (1991). The relations of parental characteristics and practices to children's vicarious emotional responding. *Child Development, 62,* 1393–1408.

Eisenberg, N., Fabes, R. A., Schaller, M., Miller, P., Carlo, G., Poulin, R., Shea, C., & Shell, R. (1991). Personality and socialization correlates of vicarious emotional responding. *Journal of Personality and Social Psychology, 61,* 459–470.

Eisenberg, N., Fabes, R. A., Shepard, S. A., Murphy, B. C., Jones, J., & Guthrie, I. K. (1998). Contemporaneous and longitudinal prediction of children's sympathy from dispositional regulation and emotionality. *Developmental Psychology, 34,* 910–924.

Eisenberg, N., Gershoff, E. T., Fabes, R. A., Shepard, S. A., Cumberland, A. J., Losoya, S. H., Guthrie, I. K., & Murphy, B. C. (2001). Mothers' emotional expressivity and children's behavior problems and social competence: Mediation through children's regulation. *Developmental Psychology, 37,* 475–490.

Eisenberg, N., Guthrie, I., Cumberland, A., Murphy, B. C., Shepard, S. A., Zhou, Q., & Carlo, G. (2002). Prosocial development in early adulthood: A longitudinal study. *Journal of Personality and Social Psychology, 82,* 993–1006.

Eisenberg, N., Guthrie, I. K., Fabes, R. A., Reiser, M., Murphy, B. C., Holgren, R., Maszk, P., & Losoya, S. (1997). The relations of regulation and emotionality to resiliency and competent social functioning in elementary school children. *Child Development, 68,* 295–311.

Eisenberg, N., Guthrie, I. K., Murphy, B. C., Shepard, S. A., Cumberland, A., & Carlo, G. (1999). Consistency and development of prosocial dispositions: A longitudinal study. *Child Development, 70,* 1360–1372.

Eisenberg, N., & Lennon, R. (1983). Gender differences in empathy and related capacities. *Psychological Bulletin, 94,* 100–131.

Eisenberg, N., Liew, J., & Pidada, S. U. (2001). The relations of parental emotional expressivity with quality of Indonesian children's social functioning. *Emotion, 1,* 116–136.

Eisenberg, N., Losoya, S., Fabes, R. A., Guthrie, I. K., Reiser, M., Murphy, B., Shepard, S. A., Poulin, R., & Padgett, S. J. (2001). Parental socialization of children's dysregulated expression of emotion and externalizing problems. *Journal of Family Psychology, 15,* 183–205.

Eisenberg, N., McCreath, H., & Ahn, R. (1988). Vicarious emotional responsiveness and prosocial behavior: Their interrelations in young children. *Personality and Social Psychology Bulletin, 14,* 298–311.

Eisenberg, N., & McNally, S. (1993). Socialization and mothers' and adolescents' empathy-related characteristics. *Journal of Research on Adolescence, 3,* 171–191.

Eisenberg, N., & Miller, P. (1987). The relation of empathy to prosocial and related behaviors. *Psychological Bulletin, 101,* 91–119.

Eisenberg, N., Miller, P. A., Shell, R., McNalley, S., & Shea, C. (1991). Prosocial development in adolescence: A longitudinal study. *Developmental Psychology, 27,* 849–857.

Eisenberg, N., Pasternack, J.F., Cameron, E., & Tryon, K. (1984). The relation of quality and mode of prosocial behavior to moral cognitions and social style. *Child Development, 155,* 1479–1485.

Eisenberg, N., Schaller, M., Fabes, R. A., Bustamante, D., Mathy, R. M., Shell, R., & Rhodes, K. (1988). Differentiation of personal distress and sympathy in children and adults. *Developmental Psychology, 24,* 766–775.

Eisenberg, N., Shell, R., Pasternack, J., Lennon, R., Beller, R., & Mathy, R. M. (1987). Prosocial development in middle childhood: A longitudinal study. *Developmental Psychology, 24,* 712–718.

Eisenberg, N., Shea, C. L., Carlo, G., & Knight, G. (1991). Empathy-related responding and cognition: A "chicken and the egg" dilemma. In W. Kurtines & J. Gewirtz (Eds.), *Handbook of moral behavior and development. Vol. 2. Research* (pp. 63–88). Hillsdale, NJ: Erlbaum.

Eisenberg, N., Wentzel, M., & Harris, J. D. (1998). The role of emotionality and regulation in empathy-related responding. *School Psychology Review, 27,* 506–521.

Eisenberg, N., Valiente, C., Morris, A. S., Fabes, R. A., Cumberland, A., Reiser, M., Gershoff, E. T., Shepard, S. A., & Losoya, S. (2003). Longitudinal relations among parental emotional expressivity, children's regulation, and quality of socioemotional functioning. *Developmental Psychology, 39,* 2–19.

Eisenberg, N., Zhou, Q., & Koller, S. (2001). Brazilian adolescents' prosocial moral judgment and behavior: Relations to sympathy, perspective taking, gender-role orientation, and demographic characteristics. *Child Development, 72,* 518–534.

Eisenberg-Berg, N. (1979). The development of children's prosocial moral judgment. *Developmental Psychology, 15,* 128–137.

Eisenberg-Berg, N., & Hand, M. (1979). The relationship of preschooler's reasoning about prosocial moral conflicts to prosocial behavior. *Child Development, 50,* 356–363.

Eisenberg-Berg, N., & Mussen P. (1978). Empathy and moral development in adolescence. *Developmental Psychology, 14,* 185–186.

Fabes, R. A., Eisenberg, N., & Eisenbud, L. (1993). Behavioral and physiological correlates of children's reactions to others in distress. *Developmental Psychology, 29,* 655–663.

Fabes, R. A., Eisenberg, N., Karbon, M., Bernzweig, J., Speer, A. L., & Carlo, G.

(1994). Socialization of children's vicarious emotional responding and pro-social behavior: Relations with mothers' perceptions of children's emotional reactivity. *Developmental Psychology, 30,* 44–55.

Fabes, R. A., Eisenberg, N., Karbon, M., Troyer, D., & Switzer, G. (1994). The relations of children's emotion regulation to their vicarious emotional responses and comforting behavior. *Child Development, 65,* 1678–1693.

Fabes, R. A., Eisenberg, N., & Miller, P. A. (1990). Maternal correlates of children's vicarious emotional responsiveness. *Developmental Psychology, 26,* 639–648.

Guthrie, I. K., Eisenberg, N., Fabes, R. A., Murphy, B. C., Holmgren, R., Maszk, P., & Suh, K. (1997). The relations of regulation and emotionality to children's situational empathy-related responding. *Motivation and Emotion, 21,* 87–108.

Haidt, J. (2001). The emotional dog and its rational tail: A social intuitionist approach to moral judgment. *Psychological Review, 108,* 814–834.

Halberstadt, A. G., Crisp, V. W., & Eaton, K. L. (1999). Family expressiveness: A retrospective and new directions for research. In P. Philippot & R. S. Feldman (Eds.), *The social context of nonverbal behavior: Studies in emotion and social interaction* (pp. 109–155). New York: Cambridge University Press.

Hastings, P. D., Zahn-Waxler, C., Robinson, J., Usher, B., & Bridges, D. (2000). The development of concern for others in children with behavior problems. *Developmental Psychology, 36,* 531–546.

Hoffman, M. L. (1982). Development of prosocial motivation: Empathy and guilt. In N. Eisenberg (Ed.), *The development of prosocial behavior* (pp. 281–313). New York: Academic Press.

Hoffman, M. L. (1987). The contribution of empathy to justice and moral judgment. In N. Eisenberg & J. Strayer (Eds.), *Empathy and its development* (pp. 47–80). Cambridge, UK: Cambridge University Press.

Hoffman, M. L. (2000). *Empathy and moral development: Implications for caring and justice.* Cambridge, UK: Cambridge University Press.

Holmgren, R. A., Eisenberg, N., & Fabes, R. A. (1998). The relations of children's situational empathy-related emotional to dispositional prosocial behaviour. *International Journal of Behavioral Development, 22,* 169–193.

Hume, D. (1966). *Enquiries concerning the human understanding and concerning the principles of morals* (2nd ed.). Oxford, UK: Clarendon Press. (Original work published 1777)

Iannotti, R. J., Cummings, E. M., Pierrehumbert, B., Milano, M. J., & Zahn-Waxler, C. (1992). Parental influences on prosocial behavior and empathy in early childhood. In J. M. A. M. Janssens & J. R. M. Gerris (Eds.), *Child rearing: Influence on prosocial and moral development* (pp. 77–100). Amsterdam: Swets & Zeitlinger.

Janssens, J. M. A. M., & Gerris, J. R. M. (1992). Child rearing, empathy and prosocial development. In J. M. A. M. Janssens & J. R. M. Gerris (Eds.), *Child rearing: Influence on prosocial and moral development* (pp. 57–75). Amsterdam: Swets & Zeitlinger.

Kalliopuska, M. (1984). Relation between children's and parents' empathy. *Psychological Reports, 54,* 295–299.

Kestenbaum, R., Farber, E. A., & Sroufe, L. A. (1989). Individual differences in empathy among preschoolers: Relations to attachment history. *New Directions in Child Development, 44,* 51–64.

Kohlberg, L. (1969). Stage and sequence: The cognitive-developmental approach to socialization. In D. A. Goslin (Ed.), *Handbook of socialization theory and research* (pp. 325–480). New York: Rand McNally.

Kohlberg, L. (1981). *The philosophy of moral development: Moral stages and the idea of justice.* San Francisco: Harper & Row.

Maccoby, E. E., & Martin, J. A. (1983). Socialization in the context of the family: Parent–child interaction. In P. H. Mussen (Series Ed.) & E. M. Hetherington (Vol. Ed.), *Handbook of child psychology: Vol. 4. Socialization, personality, and social development* (4th ed., pp. 1–101). New York: Wiley.

Main, M., & George, C. (1985). Responses of abused and disadvantaged toddlers to distress in agemates: A study in the day care setting. *Developmental Psychology, 21,* 407–412.

Miller, P., & Eisenberg, N. (1988). The relation of empathy to aggression and externalizing/antisocial behavior. *Psychological Bulletin, 103,* 324–344.

Miller, P. A., Eisenberg, N., Fabes, R. A., & Shell, R. (1996). Relations of moral reasoning and vicarious emotion to young children's prosocial behavior toward peers and adults. *Developmental Psychology, 32,* 210–219.

Murphy, B. C., Shepard, S. A., Eisenberg, N., Fabes, R. A., & Guthrie, I. K. (1999). Contemporaneous and longitudinal relations of young adolescents' dispositional sympathy to their emotionality, regulation, and social functioning. *Journal of Early Adolescence, 19,* 66–97.

Radke-Yarrow, M., Zahn-Waxler, C., & Chapman, M. (1983). Prosocial dispositions and behavior. In P. Mussen (Series Ed.) & E. M. Hethering (Vol. Ed.), *Manual of child psychology: Vol. 4. Socialization, personality, and social development* (pp. 469–545). New York: Wiley.

Rothbart, M. K., & Bates, J. E. (1998). Temperament. In W. Damon (Series Ed.) and N. Eisenberg (Vol. Ed.), *Handbook of child psychology: Vol. 3. Social, emotional, and personality development* (pp. 105–176). New York: Wiley.

Rushton, J. P., Chrisjohn, R. D., & Fekken, G. C. (1981). The altruistic personality and the self-report altruism scale. *Personality and Individual Differences, 2,* 1–11.

Skoe, E., Eisenberg, N., & Cumberland, A. (2002). The role of reported emotion in real-life and hypothetical moral dilemmas. *Personality and Social Psychology Bulletin, 28,* 962–973.

Staub, E. (1979). *Positive social behavior and morality: Vol. 2. Socialization and development.* New York: Academic Press.

Strayer, J., & Roberts, W. (1989). Children's empathy and role taking: Child and parental factors, and relations to prosocial behavior. *Journal of Applied Developmental Psychology, 10,* 227–239.

Trommsdorff, G. (1991). Child-rearing and children's empathy. *Perceptual and Motor Skills, 72,* 387–390.

Trommsdorff, G. (1995). Person–context relations as developmental conditions for empathy and prosocial action: A cross-cultural analysis. In T. A. Kindermann & J. Valsiner (Eds.), *Development of person–context relations* (pp. 189–208). Hillsdale, NJ: Erlbaum.

Underwood, B., & Moore, B. (1982). Perspective-taking and altruism. *Psychological Bulletin, 91,* 143–173.

Valiente, C., Eisenberg, N., Shepard, S. A., Fabes, R. A., Cumberland, A. J., Losoya, S. H., & Spinrad, T. L. (2003). *The relations of mothers' negative expressivity to children's experience and expression of negative emotion.* Manuscript submitted for publication.

Waters, E., Wippmann, J., & Sroufe, L. A. (1979). Attachment, positive affect, and competence in the peer group: Two studies in construct validation. *Child Development, 50,* 821–829.

Yarrow, M. R., Scott, P. M., & Waxler, C. Z. (1973). Learning concern for others. *Developmental Psychology, 8,* 240–260.

Zahn-Waxler, C., Radke-Yarrow, M., & King, R. A. (1979). Child rearing and children's prosocial initiations toward victims of distress. *Child Development, 50,* 319–330.

Zahn-Waxler, C., Robinson, J. J., & Emde, R. N. (1992). The development of empathy in twins. *Developmental Psychology, 28,* 1038–1047.

Zahn-Waxler, C., Schiro, K., Robinson, J. L., Emde, R. N., & Schmitz, S. (2001). Empathy and prosocial patterns in young MZ and DZ twins. In R. N. Emde & J. K. Hewitt (Eds.), *Infant to early childhood: Genetic and environmental influences on developmental change* (pp. 141–162). Oxford, UK: Oxford University Press.

Zhou, Q., Eisenberg, N., Losoya, S. H., Fabes, R. A., Reiser, M., Guthrie, I. K., Murphy, B. C., Cumberland, A. J., & Shepard, S. A. (2002). The relations of parental warmth and positive expressiveness to children's empathy-related responding and social functioning: A longitudinal study. *Child Development, 73,* 893–915.

CHAPTER 16

SOCIAL SUPPORT AND BEHAVIOR TOWARD OTHERS

Some Paradoxes and Some Directions

THOMAS ASHBY WILLS

JODY A. RESKO

In this chapter we consider how social relationships provide a context that shapes adolescents' behavior toward others. Although altruism or aggression may be related to the dispositional characteristics of an individual and to the institutional environment in which he or she operates, a person's social relationships can be important factors shaping the orientations that influence behavior toward others in positive or negative directions.

Social support from parents is a major protective factor for adolescents, inversely related to substance use and positively related to psychological well-being (Wills, Blechman, & McNamara, 1996; Wills & Filer, 2001). Here we suggest that a history of supportive relationships within the family is related to patterns of active coping that promote prosocial behavior, whereas social conflict and rejection by parents are related to patterns of maladaptive coping that are conducive to antisocial behavior. We discuss this thesis from the perspective of epidemiological research with representative samples of adolescents and consider how support from peers may have different effects from parental support.

Adolescence is a period of particular relevance for the development of altruistic or aggressive behavior. Between the ages of 11 and 18 years, adolescents go through several major life transitions and shift from a situation in which their social relationships tend to be family-centered to one in which relationships are largely peer-oriented and self-chosen (Brown, Dolcini, & Leventhal, 1997). Though childhood is relevant for shaping social orientations, adolescence is the period when teens build their own social networks; their patterns of coping are now expressed in behavior toward significant persons outside the family, such as teachers, peers, and other community members (Moffitt, 1993a).

In considering the role of social relationships for young people, it is important to recognize that adolescents live in two social worlds: the world of family relationships and the world of peer relationships. Within the general population of adolescents, there is considerable variation in the balance of parent and peer relationships, with some individuals being more involved with family and some being relatively more involved with peers (Wills, Mariani, & Filer, 1996). The social worlds of parent and peers can embody somewhat different values; parents are more likely to value conventional routes to achievement (e.g., studying and getting good grades), whereas peers, on the average, are more likely to accept unconventional or rebellious behavior (Jessor & Jessor, 1977; Steinberg, Lamborn, Dornbusch, & Darling, 1992). Thus the processes that lead some individuals to become detached from the family and involved in deviant peer groups that engage in destructive behaviors (e.g., stealing and fighting) are of central relevance for a developmental model of behavior toward others (Dishion, Patterson, & Griesler, 1994; Thornberry & Krohn, 1997; Wills & Vaughan, 1989).

Adolescent substance use (tobacco, alcohol, and marijuana) is a criterion variable that is of interest not only because of health consequences but also because it is correlated with indices of antisocial behavior (Donovan & Jessor, 1985; Donovan, Jessor, & Costa, 1988). The studies discussed here included measures for understanding how social support is related to a chain of processes that can lead to involvement versus noninvolvement in substance use and other problematic behaviors. This chapter explains the research approach and summarizes findings from this research program, delineating how family and peer support are related to patterns of adaptation. We then discuss what this research means for understanding good and evil in human nature, and implications of the research for promoting altruism and preventing destructive behavior.

SOCIAL SUPPORT AND ADAPTATION IN ADOLESCENCE

Research Approach

The research program uses the approach of social epidemiology by surveying samples of adolescents from the general population and studying how socially significant behaviors are distributed within this population. In the data collection, research staff administer self-report questionnaires to students in a classroom setting, and participants complete the questionnaire in about a 40-minute period. Parents and students are informed about the purpose and nature of the research, and both are informed that they can decline or discontinue participation. Student participants are informed that the data they provide are strictly confidential and will not be reported to their parents or teachers. The studies typically obtain completed questionnaires from around 90% of the eligible population.

We discuss findings from three studies, all conducted in the New York metropolitan area. Study 1 was designed to test stress-coping constructs and their convergence with constructs from problem behavior theory (Jessor & Jessor, 1977; Wills, 1985). Study 2 was focused on the impact of daily "hassles" in adolescents' lives (Wills, 1990), and Study 3 was designed to test a comprehensive model of dispositional and social factors (Tarter & Vanyukov, 1994; Wills & Filer, 1996). The studies were longitudinal, with participants initially surveyed at relatively young ages (seventh grade in Studies 1 and 2, sixth grade in Study 3) and then resurveyed at yearly intervals. We note briefly that directionality of findings has been demonstrated with several types of longitudinal analyses (e.g., Wills & Cleary, 1999; Wills et al., 2001).[1]

Sample sizes have varied across studies from 900 to 1,800 participants. The samples in these studies are diverse in ethnic characteristics, including African Americans (typically about 30% of the sample), Hispanics (25%), Caucasians (35%), and participants of mixed ethnicity (usually about 10% of the sample). Data on parental education and community characteristics show that from a socioeconomic standpoint, the samples are representative of the state population, which is, itself, close to national figures.

Persons unfamiliar with adolescent research sometimes ask whether teenagers are accurate or honest in their responses. This issue has been examined for adolescent substance use in studies that compare self-reports with biochemical indices; these have shown that self-report responses made under confidential conditions are generally valid (e.g., Wills & Cleary, 1997). For psychosocial variables, we obtain ratings by teachers on some of the same characteristics reported by students, such as competence and self-control. Since teachers do not know what students said about themselves on the self-report questionnaires, the teacher ratings represent an independent source of evidence. Results have shown that findings from self-report data are corroborated by these independent teacher ratings (e.g., Wills, Cleary, et al., 2001; Wills, Sandy, Yaeger, & Shinar,

---

[1]For example, parental support is inversely related to change in adolescent substance use over time. It is possible that there may be some reciprocal effects, but the literature is not clear on this issue, and methodological issues are important (see Wills & Cleary, 1999).

2001). Thus the validity of self-reports from adolescents has been supported by several methods.

The theoretical approach in this research has been guided by transactional models of behavioral development, which come from the disciplines of developmental psychology (Rothbart & Ahadi, 1994; Scarr, 1992), personality and clinical psychology (Caspi, 1993; Dishion & Patterson, 1997), and behavioral genetics (Tarter, Moss, & Vanyukov, 1995). These models posit that complex behaviors (such as substance use or aggression) have multiple determinants, so that understanding these behaviors requires attention to the relations among dispositional, environmental, and social factors. Instead of assuming that social support is independent of other domains, we explicitly posit that it is related to factors such as children's temperament, and such covariances are included in the analyses (e.g., Wills, Cleary, et al., 2001). In this approach, an adverse outcome is posited to be the result of a "chain of failures" (Moffitt, 1993b; Wills, Sandy, & Yaeger, 2000). The question is how social support influences exposure to risk factors and protective factors that are more proximal to adolescent substance use.

Parental Support and Patterns of Coping

In the first study the intent was to test a model positing that parental support has ramifications for stress and coping processes. It was predicted that adolescents who feel accepted and supported by family members will demonstrate greater feelings of psychological well-being (Wills, 1991) and more effective coping responses than adolescents who do not feel accepted and supported in the family. Supportive parents provide a base that encourages active approaches to coping (Carver, Scheier, & Weintraub, 1989), and positive relationships within the family environment help to build commitment to mainstream values in the larger social system (Jessor & Jessor, 1977). Thus parental support is expected to have influences beyond its effects on adolescents' psychological well-being.

This study used a functional approach to the assessment of social support by using items that indexed the extent to which the adolescent perceived that parents would be supportive if he or she had a problem or needed advice. Participants were instructed to answer the items in relation to the parent they talked to the most (because there were many single-parent families in the sample). Emotional support was assessed with items such as "When I feel bad about something, my parent will listen" and "If I talk to my parent, I think [he or she] tries to understand how I feel." Instrumental support was assessed with items such as "If I need help with my school work, I can ask my parent about it," and "If I talk to my parent, [he or she] has suggestions about how to handle problems." The subscales are positively correlated and are typically combined in a composite score or latent construct for perceived parental support. Descriptive statistics indicate that adolescents generally tend to perceive a high level of support from parents.

A cohort of adolescents was surveyed four times over the period from 12 to 16 years of age, and findings for parental support were replicated over assessments (summarized in Table 16.1, with notation based on Cohen's definition of effect sizes).[2] Because all analyses included controls for gender, ethnicity, family structure, and parental education, the effects reported here for social support are independent of these demographic attributes. Parental support was related not only to higher self-esteem and perceived control, but also to a pattern of active coping (e.g., problem solving and situation redefinition); this coping pattern is an important protective factor for outcomes that include substance abuse and behavior problems (Dubow & Reid, 1997; Wills & Hirky, 1996). Parental support also had effects for other domains; it was related to less tolerance for deviant behaviors, a known risk factor for adolescent problems (Jessor & Jessor, 1977), and it was related to more academic competence, an important protective factor for adolescents (Hawkins, Catalano, & Miller, 1992). There were smaller, inverse effects of parental support for indices of maladaptive coping and self-derogation.[3] Thus the effects of a supportive family environment extend beyond subjective well-being, which is of interest in its own right, to influences on patterns of attitudes and coping that may have implications for antisocial behavior.

Why does being in a supportive family environment have such generalized effects? Definitive answers to this question have not accumulated, but plausible hypotheses can be posed. The attitudinal approach suggests that positive family relationships provide a reason for young persons to "buy in" to the social system early on. From the standpoint of social cognition, feelings of self-esteem and self-acceptance can generalize to positive perceptions of other persons in the larger social world. The coping–competence perspective suggests that supportive relationships encourage the development of more persistent and effortful patterns of coping, which in turn have long-term payoffs for achievement and adjustment (Wills,

---

[2]A large effect size is a Cohen d of .8, corresponding to standardized regression coefficients around .40. Moderate effect sizes are Cohen d's around .5 (betas in the range of .20 to .30), and small effect sizes are Cohen d's of .2 (betas of .10 to .15).

[3]Examples of tolerance for deviance are responses indicating relative acceptance of behaviors such as "Hitting someone because you didn't like what they said or did," "Shoplifting from a store," or "Marking up public or private property on purpose." Examples of maladaptive coping are responses indicating that when the person has a problem, he or she tends to "Blame and criticize other people," "Give up the attempt to get what you want," "[Not] let others see how bad things are," and "Just wish the problem would go away." Self-derogation is reflected in agreement with items such as "I feel pretty useless at times," "I feel I do not have much to be proud of," and "At times I think I am not as good as other people."

TABLE 16.1. Findings on Social Support, from Study 1

Parent support is related to . . .

Large effect sizes	Moderate effect sizes	Small effect sizes
More active coping	Higher academic competence	Less helpless coping
More positive affect	Less tolerance for deviance	Less avoidant coping
More positive self-regard	Less negative affect	Less self-derogation
More perceived control	Less anger coping	Less substance coping

Blechman, et al., 1996). A supportive family environment also provides a significant stress-buffering effect, helping young persons to deal adaptively with periods of difficulty (Sandler, Miller, Short, & Wolchik, 1989; Wills & Cleary, 1996). Exposure to these kinds of resources on an ongoing basis would serve to reduce the inclination to regard antisocial behavior as desirable or justified.

Support from Different Social Systems

It was previously suggested that adolescents live in two social worlds that can have different value systems. This concept was developed in a second study, conducted over the age range of 12–14 years and exploring the implications of different types of support for adolescents' stress and coping processes. Predictions were based on the notion that although supportive relationships with peers have some desirable effects, the different values and norms of the peer network may tend to reinforce some behaviors that, from a societal standpoint, are maladaptive; hence, separate measures were obtained for parental and peer support. The assessments used the help-seeking approach, asking about the tendency to seek help from others in times of stress (Wills & DePaulo, 1991). The support measures asked participants to rate the extent to which they sought help from parents and from peers when they had a problem. The measures had items such as "I discuss my feelings with a friend I feel close to" and "I discuss my feelings with my mother/father"; alternatively, "I get emotional support from one of my friends" and "I get emotional support from my mother/father." That is, the content of the items was identical for the two measures; only the source of support differed. Distributions again were skewed toward higher scores, and means were similar for parent and peer support seeking. The bottom line: Although adolescents often seek support from peers, they also seek support frequently from parents.

In analyses the parental and peer support measures were entered together so as to control for a positive correlation (around .30) between the two support measures. In addition to demographic controls, analyses of risk factors included a score for recent negative events, and analyses of protective factors included a score for recent positive events; this controls for any correlation of support-seeking patterns with recent experiences. Table 16.2 summarizes findings that were replicated over three assessments. These findings showed the two sources of support to have somewhat different effects. Parental support was related to higher scores on indices of good self-control, a conceptual replication of findings from Study 1. Parental and peer support were independently related to greater feelings of acceptance, optimism, and subjective well-being—evidence suggesting beneficial effects for both types of support. In addition, parental support was positively related to academic competence and inversely related to loneliness; however, peer support had no significant relation to these variables.[4]

What seems most striking in the findings is that peer support sometimes has effects that are the opposite of the effects for parental support. For example, parental support is inversely related to a maladaptive coping syndrome involving indices such as anger, avoidance, and pessimism, whereas peer support has significant positive relations to these indices in some cases. For substance-related variables, such as affiliating with peer substance users and perceiving substance use as a coping mechanism, effect sizes were moderate to small, but it is clear that parental support is inversely related to these variables but peer support is positively related to them. For important dimensions such as subjective distress and risk-taking tendency, parental support is indicated as a protective factor, whereas peer support has small but significant positive relations to these domains. When considering the unique effects of parental and peer support, it is difficult to escape the conclusion that although peer support may contribute to better mood states (cf. Larson, 1983), the effects of adolescent peer networks are not invariably positive. To some extent, though a small one in the general population, peers may support a pattern of avoidance and alienation.

Another type of question concerns transactional effects, tested by considering how social support from a given source buffers the impact of adverse influences, such as peer deviancy. We used peer substance use as an index of deviancy in the peer network and tested whether a given source of support reduced the impact of peer deviancy on the adolescent's behavior. These findings were strong and consistent, indicating that parental support reduced the impact of peer substance use on adolescents' use, whereas peer support had no significant buffering effect. This finding is consistent with studies that have shown no buffering effects of peer support for negative life events (Burke & Weir, 1979; Greenberg, Siegel, & Leitch, 1983; Wills & Vaughan, 1989). All in all, a supportive relationship with parents can reduce the impact of influences for deviant behavior. Relationships with

---

[4]One wave in this study included both perceived-support measures and support-seeking measures. The two types of measures were highly correlated and produced similar results.

TABLE 16.2. Effect Sizes and Directions for Parental
and Peer Support, Study 2

	Parental support	Peer support
Protective factors		
Acceptance	L(+)	L(+)
Subjective well-being	L(+)	M(+)
Optimism	L(+)	M(+)
Good self-control	L(+)	S(+)
Academic competence	M(+)	n.s.
Risk factors		
Loneliness	M(−)	n.s.
Anger coping	M(−)	n.s.
Helpless coping	M(−)	n.s.
Avoidant coping	M(−)	S(+)
Poor self-control	M(−)	S(+)
Subjective distress	M(−)	S(+)
Risk-taking tendency	M(−)	S(+)
Pessimism	S(−)	S(+)
Peer substance use	S(−)	S(+)
Substance use coping	S(−)	S(+)

Note. Analyses based on simultaneous entry of parent and peer support. L, large effect size; M, moderate effect size; S, small effect size; n.s., nonsignificant. (+) indicates positive sign for regression coefficient; (−) indicates negative sign for regression coefficient.

peers may be supportive emotionally, but these do not necessarily have the same effect as parental support.[5]

Do our findings mean that social support from peers is a bad thing? No—support from peers (like support from parents) is related to greater subjective well-being. However, along with support from peers comes involvement with the norms of the peer network, which may be relatively favorable to deviant behaviors such as substance use, and at least neutral to some forms of prosocial behavior. Peer relationships may also present bimodal distributions about behaviors such as studying, with some adolescents valuing this activity and others devaluing it (see Steinberg et al., 1992); such bimodality could account for the nonsignificant overall relation of peer support to academic performance. Note that although peer

---

[5]It is possible that such analyses would have different outcomes if one were indexing the impact of prosocial behavior by peers (e.g., studying hard, participating in school or community activities); peer support could increase the impact of prosocial peers. This type of process has not been well studied and needs to be tested.

support is related to higher scores on dimensions such as acceptance as well as to higher scores on dimensions such as pessimism, such findings are not contradictory, because positive and negative dimensions assessed over reasonable time periods vary with relative independence in the population (cf. Diener, Suh, Lucas, & Smith, 1999; Marshall, Wortman, Kusulas, Heruig, & Vickers, 1992). Overall, teens may have more fun in the peer network but gain less approval for effortful coping, and peers may encourage (or at least not discourage) feelings of anger and alienation.

Two Facets of Family Relationships: Support and Conflict

Adult social relationships typically include aspects of both support and strain (Abbey, Abramis, & Caplan, 1985; Rook, 1984, 1990), as do family relationships for parents and adolescents: Some level of supportive interaction and some level of conflicted interaction is usually present (Barrera, Chassin, & Rogosch, 1993). This recognition leads to the third type of question we asked about social context: What are the relative contributions of family support and conflict? This question was investigated in a third study that used the same measure of functional support administered in Study 1 and also included a scale to measure parent–child conflict. The conflict scale had items such as "I often feel my parents are giving me a hard time" and "I have a lot of arguments with my parents." This scale had inverse but moderate correlations with the support scale, so a score indicating conflict is not merely tapping into an absence of support. The conflict scores had an L-shaped distribution, with the majority of participants showing relatively low levels of conflict while a proportion had higher scores, going up to the top of the scale.

Analyses with simultaneous entry for measures of support and conflict showed a notable symmetry in effects (Table 16.3). Parental support was substantially related to several important protective factors, including academic competence and good self-control, whereas conflict was related to a range of risk factors such as avoidance, risk taking, and poor self-control. This study included Achenbach's (1991) inventory, which includes items about externalizing symptoms during the past month (e.g., "I got into fights," "I hung around with kids who got in trouble") and also includes internalizing symptoms (e.g., "I felt unhappy and sad," "I felt anxious or tense"). (This study did not include a measure of altruistic behavior.) Conflict was related to more antisocial behaviors and more depressive symptoms. Thus, according to our research, support and conflict each have important effects but to different outcomes: Support is related to subjective well-being and good self-control, whereas conflict is related to a range of indices representing poor self-control and a tendency for risky and antisocial behaviors. These findings caution us to consider the internal dynamics of the relationship when considering how social context

TABLE 16.3. Findings on Parental Support and Conflict, with Effect Size and Direction, from Study 3

	Parental support	Parent–child conflict
Protective factors		
Good self-control	L(+)	S(−)
Subjective well-being	L(+)	S(−)
Academic competence	M(+)	M(−)
Risk factors		
Externalizing symptoms	S(−)	L(+)
Internalizing symptoms	S(−)	L(+)
Poor self-control	S(−)	L(+)
Avoidant coping	S(−)	L(+)
Anger coping	S(−)	L(+)
Helpless coping	S(−)	M(+)
Peer substance use	S(−)	M(+)
Risk-taking tendency	S(−)	M(+)
Tolerance for deviance	M(−)	S(+)

Note. Analyses based on simultaneous entry of support and conflict. + indicates positive sign for regression coefficient; − indicates negative sign for regression coefficient; L, large effect size; M, moderate effect size; S, small effect size.

influences aggression. Though adolescents generally rate their parents as supportive, there is a nontrivial level of conflict for part of the population, and the effects of such conflict are a mirror image of the effects for parental support. In short, when the family environment includes a high level of conflict, this can be conducive to aggressive behavior.

Summary

These findings convey several messages about social support in adolescence. The most obvious is that parental supportiveness is a significant protective factor inversely related to aggression, depression, and deviant peer affiliations. What is theoretically striking is the range of effects observed for parental support. It is related not only to indices of subjective well-being but also to patterns of coping and self-control, to developed competencies (e.g., academic competence), to attitudes about deviance and motives for substance use, and to views about the self and the world (i.e., self-esteem and optimism). This evidence implies that parental support operates through multiple pathways for influencing socially significant outcomes. To understand why social support is related to the potential for altruism or aggression, we need to consider the pathways through which parental support operates as well as seek an explanation for why parental supportiveness has such a range of effects.

Another message from the data is that approaching the verbal label *social support* as indicating a necessarily beneficial process could be misleading. Findings show that peer support has some effects that are unarguably beneficial (e.g., greater positive mood) but also some effects that do not appear so beneficial (e.g., more avoidant coping). How can this be? The probable answer is that support from a network serves to enhance the values and norms of that network. For example, if a teen's network of friends has favorable attitudes toward breaking rules and skipping school, then network support could well work toward an undesirable end.[6] Support from a group of antisocial peers may well be experienced as positive by the recipient but can have quite different consequences from the perspective of the larger society. This possibility raises the question of why previously non-antisocial teenagers would affiliate with antisocial peers in the first place, which will be discussed subsequently.

In addition to thinking about the sources of altruistic or destructive behavior in terms of transactions between different networks, we must also consider the profile of processes within a particular relationship. The data show clearly that parents are generally perceived as quite supportive by teenagers; but the existence of strain and conflict in a parent–child relationship cannot be ignored. The data show that higher levels of conflict exist for a part of the population and that conflict in the home is related to a range of undesirable occurrences outside the home. Though the causal interpretation of this observation is not straightforward (as we discuss subsequently), the findings suggest the utility of thinking about the balance of supportive and conflictual elements in a given relationship.

AN INTEGRATED MODEL

As previously noted, the perspective of developmental models is that social support does not exist in isolation. The parent–child relationship is posited to be influenced by factors such as the dispositional characteristics of parents and of children and by the family's background of economic stress (Blackson, Tarter, Loeber, Ammerman, & Windle, 1996; Blackson, Tarter, Martin, & Moss, 1994; Conger, Patterson, & Ge, 1995; Rothbart & Ahadi, 1994). The effects of support are posited to involve multiple pathways, including some mediated effects (i.e., support influences other

---

[6]While driving home one day, I saw a bumper sticker that was a variant of one that says, "My kid is an honor student at _____ school." However, this one said, "My kid beat up your honor student!" It is possible that this parent was a supportive one in some ways, but we can only wonder what values this parent is communicating to his or her children.

variables that are more proximal to outcomes) and some direct effects (i.e., support acts directly on the outcome without going through any intermediates; Uchino, Cacioppo, & Kiecolt-Glaser, 1996; Wills & Cleary, 1996). In order to understand how social support operates in a manner that influences significant outcomes, it is necessary to consider how support is related to other variables in a multivariate system. In this way we can inquire how support processes are involved in a "chain of successes" that leads to desirable outcomes such as positive well-being, and how some aspects of social relationships may be involved in a "chain of failures" that leads to maladaptive and antisocial behavior (Moffitt, 1993b).

The data from Study 3 were used to pursue this perspective and test an integrated model. Standard methods were used to test which of the study variables were implicated in mediating the effects of parental support and conflict, respectively, on three outcomes (Baron & Kenny, 1986; MacKinnon, 1994). A structural model was set up in which parental support and conflict were exogenous (i.e., not influenced by any prior variables) and these were allowed to correlate with children's dispositional characteristics and with an index of external stress on the family. Mediators were identified in the domains of good self-control (e.g., planfulness and problem solving) and poor self-control (e.g., impatience and impulsiveness) as well as the constructs of risk-taking tendency and attitudinal tolerance for deviance, which have been mentioned previously. In the proposed model these mediators were posited to influence developed capacities (such as academic competence), which were then hypothesized to influence exposure to proximal risk factors: negative life events and deviant peer affiliations. The outcome constructs were externalizing symptomatology, internalizing symptomatology, and positive well-being. The model was set up to specify mediated effects of support or conflict through the first domain of variables (i.e., self-control and attitudinal tendencies), and to test statistically for direct effects of support on the outcomes, if such effects existed.

A graphical portrayal of the results (Figure 16.1) shows multiple pathways for the effects of support and conflict. Parental support had protective effects that were mediated through more good self-control and less tolerance for deviance; in addition, part of the effect of support was a direct path to more positive well-being, which did not involve any of the other variables in the model. The "downstream effects" for parental support occurred through paths from good self-control to academic competence (positive in sign) and deviant peer affiliations (negative in sign), as well as an indirect effect from parental support to less tolerance for deviance and consequently, fewer peer affiliations. Note that parental supportiveness was correlated with protective-temperament characteristics of the child, whereas conflict was correlated with difficult-temperament characteristics, such as activity level and irritability (cf. Rothbart & Ahadi,

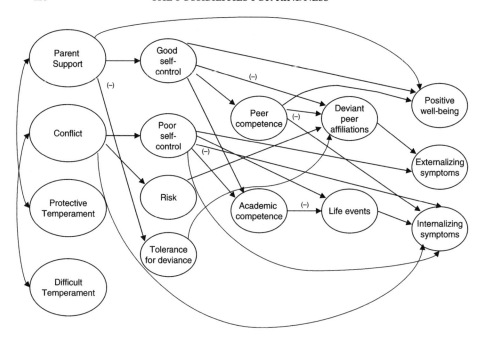

FIGURE 16.1. Model of pathways of parental support and parent–child conflict to three outcomes. Double-headed arrows indicate covariances. Single-headed arrows indicate path effects, like unique effects in multiple regression (i.e., the effect of a given variable on a subsequent one, controlling for effects of other relevant variables in the model). Family life events and its covariances with conflict and support are omitted for illustrative simplicity. Paths are positive in sign unless otherwise noted; (–) indicates inverse paths. Residual correlations among the four sets of endogenous variables (aligned vertically) were included in the model but are omitted from the figure for visual simplicity.

1994). However, the effects indicated for support in the structural model are independent of these correlations and of correlations with family stress.

The effects for conflict involved a different set of pathways, again with both mediated and direct effects. Conflict had a direct effect for depression but indirect effects on aggression, involving pathways from conflict through risk-taking tendency and poor self-control. Poor self-control then had downstream effects for less competence and more negative life events, as well as direct effects for aggression and depression; there was also an indirect effect of conflict through risk-taking tendency to deviant peer affiliations. The integrated model is thus consistent with the perspective outlined previously in showing that (1) social variables have several pathways to outcomes; (2) there are direct effects for support and conflict to outcomes, with opposite meanings (i.e., support related to more well-being, conflict related to more depression); and (3) effects for support and conflict involve different pathways. Thus in studying how social context influences the tendency for altruistic or aggressive behavior, it is necessary to think about multiple pathways to outcomes.

Note that the structural model illustrates some of the paradoxes embedded in the previous discussion. The construct of peer competence (measured through items about perceived popularity and acceptance by peers) had some clearly desirable effects, such as paths to more subjective well-being and less depression. But it also had a path to deviant peer affiliations, which was one of the pathways to externalizing symptomatology. Hence peer support has complex effects that depend, to some extent, on the outcome and are not all protective. The source of support matters, because the norms of various subgroups in the population may be oriented toward divergent goals.

IMPLICATIONS OF THE RESEARCH

We have discussed findings from research conducted with representative samples of adolescents. Parental and peer support were assessed with parallel measures that used comparable items to tap support from different sources. The results were consistent within studies, each with repeated assessments that showed internal replication, and findings on support processes were conceptually replicated across three independent studies. Control variables were included in the analyses, and findings on parental and peer support were independent of gender, ethnicity, family structure, and parental education. So the research provides externally valid findings on how support processes operate in the natural environment with regard to socially significant outcomes.

This research was influenced by developmental models of substance use liability, and the findings illustrate several themes in these models that are highly relevant for the study of altruism and aggression. One is that parental support does not exist in isolation but is related to the dispositional characteristics of children (Rothbart & Ahadi, 1994) and to the background of stress on the family (Conger et al., 1995)—processes that have been observed in all the studies we discussed (e.g., Wills, Cleary, et al., 2001). Another theme is that support not only has antecedents but also has a range of consequences that have a direct bearing on trajectories toward or away from antisocial behavior. Effects of parental support on factors such as self-control and tolerance for deviance act to shape the social environment in which adolescents live. This social environment, once established, may have enduring effects on developmental trajectories (Caspi, 1993; Quinton et al., 1993; Rutter, 1997; Wills, McNamara, et al., 1996).

Another relevant observation is that these processes start young: Problem-prone children have already begun affiliating with likeminded deviant peers by 10–11 years of age (Dishion et al., 1995; Wills & Cleary, 1999; Wills, Gibbons, et al., 2000), which suggests that testing of early preventive interventions would be appropriate. The data illustrate why it is useful to take a multivariate perspective and study how trajectories of behavior unfold over time in response to influences from several domains of variables (Tarter et al., 1995; Wills, Sandy, et al., 2000).

Paradoxical Effects

Our findings suggest what might appear to be a paradoxical view of social support. Parental support is clearly a protective factor. Considering the surprising range of effects observed across several domains (coping and competence, affect and attitudes, beliefs and behaviors), support could be viewed as a strong force for promoting prosocial behavior. But a paradox arises from findings on support sources, which show that although peer support can relate to desirable outcomes, such as subjective well-being, it can also relate to problematic outcomes, such as alienation and anger.

Another paradox arises from the findings in Study 3. The family can be a source of support but it can also be an arena wherein conflict occurs, and there can be blood on the sand. Recalling that participants, for the most part, perceived their parents as moderately to highly supportive, it remains that conflict has adverse effects that occur across a range of behaviors, including destructive outcomes such as stealing and fighting, which are socially significant. Again we are steered in the direction of a mirror-image portrait of the operation of social relationships.

The view we emerge with is that social relationships are neither inherently good or bad in themselves. We can be thankful that family relationships are generally supportive. But when conflict is high and support is low, negative outcomes may occur. In addition, peers are a necessary part of development as young persons eventually attain their independence from the family, and having supportive relationships with peers is a good thing, overall. However, when an adolescent becomes involved in a peer network that encourages deviance, then antisocial behavior is as likely to ensue as prosocial behavior.

What View of Human Nature Does This Work Provide?

In addressing this question, we would emphasize the descriptive data, which show that adolescents generally perceive their parents as supportive. There is reason to believe that this finding is consistent with the perspective of evolutionary psychology: Adults tend to be supportive and nurturant toward their young, fostering strong bonds with them. During the early years of human history, supportive relationships were essential so that parents could teach their children the complex set of skills necessary for survival, even in an apparently simple hunter–gatherer society. There is probably some reciprocity built in by nature; support from parents is likely to be reflected in affection and respect from the offspring, and children's support and loyalty can help the parents to deal with hunger and adversity. In the modern world, with all its new demands, we can see that parents are generally supportive and that most kids turn out well—though they may raise hell for a while (Moffitt, 1993b).

The range of consequences observed for parental support is not inconsistent with the perspective of social evolution. From supportive relationships, children acquire not only emotional well-being but also instrumental and cognitive skills. They learn about views of the world, differences between "tribes," and more abstract concepts such as justice and fairness versus revenge and retribution. Through observation and modeling, children learn different ways to cope with frustration or difficulty. Indeed, what is intriguing about parental support is its linkage with resilience effects (Werner, 1986; Wills, Blechman, et al., 1996; Wills & Cleary, 1996). Also essential to the human species is the ability to persevere in times of difficulty. From the present data it is easy to believe that supportive relationships evolved not just to make people feel good, but also to help them become resilient in times of adversity.

If parents are shaped through evolution to be nurturant, how is it that some individuals evidence conflict and rejection with their children? This is not a theoretical problem for the transactional models. A basic postulate is that personality characteristics are part of the human endowment and that these are normally distributed in the population. Some of these characteristics would conduce toward good relationships with children, but part of the endowment would include dispositional characteristics that may result in less positive relationships, such as a higher level of irritability (Rothbart & Ahadi, 1994), a more active "fight" component in the fight–flight system (Gray, 1991), or an insensitivity to social rewards (Cloninger, Svrakic, & Przybeck, 1993). Developmental models posit that each of these attributes has some adaptive role and that normal variation in these attributes is useful for the species. The problem arises when individuals turn up with particular combinations of these attributes that may not be so adaptive for themselves or others. For example, Cloninger's model postulates that risk for substance abuse arises for a subset of individuals who have high level of novelty seeking, low level of inhibition, and low level of social reward dependence. Each of these attributes may have some adaptive value at moderate levels, but the high–low–low combination has been linked empirically to substance use and abuse in adolescents and adults (Cloninger, Sigvardsson, & Bohman, 1988; Wills, Windle, & Cleary, 1998).

The argument runs that normal variation in personality can result in certain profiles of parent or child characteristics that increase vulnerability for parent–child conflict (see Blackson et al., 1994, 1996). Of course, these are statements of probabilities; the developmental models help to clarify these issues and illustrate how a system generally set up to be nurturing and protective can, at times, generate conflict and vulnerability. Part of our human inheritance is the normal distribution of personality characteristics; the challenge for humans is to deal successfully with all the permutations deriving from this variation.

Do We Need Different Processes to Account for Different Outcomes?

A theoretical issue presented by this work is the paradox of how supportive relationships can lead to bad behavior. Do we need to postulate different processes to account for different outcomes? Our answer is no. As far as anyone can tell, the processes of emotional and instrumental support that operate in peer networks are the same as those that operate elsewhere. Friends may confide about problems, provide reinforcement for successful performance, teach ways to deal with agents of the larger society, and provide sympathy in times of adversity. We could say that the support processes in a group of peers who go out to break windows or beat up undesirables may well be the same processes as in a group of friends who study together to get good grades. The essential difference is what values the peers hold and what behaviors they support. Note that persons who engage in rule breaking are, in essence, taking considerable risks. In doing so they are going into danger, facing a powerful system that has detentions and police and jails; they may need support as much as those who follow more conventional paths. Anyone who takes on risk depends strongly on his or her companions, just as do soldiers who go into combat (see Caputo, 1977; Gray, 1970).

We emphasize this issue because some perspectives suggest that those who commit aggressive actions are young people who have no friends, and their aggression is presumed to be a consequence of isolation and rejection. There is no doubt that adolescents who engage in higher levels of problem behavior can be distinguished on predictor variables; in fact, they differ significantly on family support, anger and hostility, maladaptive coping, and a host of other variables (see Wills, McNamara, et al., 1996). The question is whether or not they have friends. The empirical evidence actually shows that adolescents with high levels of aggression have as many (or more) friends than nonproblem teens and are rated just as central in social networks (Cairns, Cairns, Neckerman, Gest, & Gariepy, 1988; Cairns, Cadwallader, Estell, & Neckerman, 1997; Dishion, Capaldi, Spracklen, & Li, 1995). So the question to focus on is not whether problem-prone teens have friends; it is what view of the world the friends hold and what they talk about favorably when they are together (Dishion, Andrews, & Crosby, 1995).

Another question is why some young people come to affiliate with peers who are known to be overtly aggressive, when aggression is disliked within the general population (Cairns et al., 1997). Is this a paradox that needs to be resolved through positing different processes? It does not seem so, given that similarity/attraction is one of the best-established principles in social psychology (Berscheid, 1985). That young persons who are some-what impulsive and alienated from family begin to hang out with similarly inclined peers is not mysterious. Such relationships may be somewhat more unstable (Dishion et al., 1995) but no less supportive. In addition, such relationships may provide validation for an alienated adolescent's view of the world; namely, that parents cannot be trusted and that adult authorities (such as teachers or police officers) are just out to cause trouble for him or her, conveniently forgetting what the young person might have done to attract the attention of the authorities in the first place. That ado-lescents may adopt this world view as a positive identity and reject conven-tional values could seem puzzling to some, but it does not seem to need separate principles to explain it (cf. Wills, 1992, for social comparison through identity rejection).

Are People Personally Responsible for Their Behavior?

A simple view of human nature that can be derived from the findings is that peoples' propensities for good or evil are shaped by their social rela-tionships. From this it could be argued that children are raised by parents to be good citizens, and if they fail to turn out this way, it is because they had bad parents; accordingly, the parents should be punished. An allied argument is that if antisocial behavior is attributable to hanging around with deviant peers, then the behavior is the result of bad choices by the in-dividual; accordingly, he or she should be held accountable because the peers were not forced on him or her.

So far we have not confronted issues of causal interpretation, and it might be inferred that the relation of parental support to adolescent be-havior necessarily represents a socialization effect. This is not necessarily the case. There is a substantial genetic component to aggressive behavior (Carey & Goldman, 1997), just as there is to substance use and person-ality disorders, in general (Coscina, 1997; McGue, 1999; Plomin, Owen, & McGuffin, 1994; Swan & Carmelli, 1997). For that matter, there is a genetic component to normal temperament and personality factors such as neuroticism and extraversion (Bouchard, 1994; Rothbart, Derryberry, & Posner, 1994). So many of the outcomes discussed in this chapter have a genetic loading. The subtle point is that *correlations* between parental characteristics and adolescent behavior may, to some extent, reflect shared constitutional attributes (e.g., temperament and personality); this concept has been repeatedly demonstrated in behavioral genetic research (e.g., O'Connor, Deter-Deckard, Fulker, Rutter, & Plomin, 1998; Plomin & McClearn, 1993; Rutter et al., 1997). In addition, there is a theoretical basis for believing that genetic characteristics may be related to the types of social relationships in which people engage, perhaps not as a direct effect but rather because temperament and personality characteristics act to steer individuals into different social niches through their influence on the kinds of people whom they find congenial (e.g., Iervolino et al., 2002). So the fact that a parental attribute is related to an adolescent behavior does not necessarily indicate an effect that is entirely attributable to socialization.

The implications in relation to the domain of personal responsibility are therefore more complicated than in the simple view. The evidence on genetic contributions to personality, parenting, and peer affiliations changes many of our traditional questions about attributing behavior to the person versus the situation. But it does not follow that people are powerless before the influence of genetics. Behavioral genetic research shows notable contributions from environmental as well as genetic factors (Plomin et al., 1994), and developmental research shows many factors that moderate the impact of heritable characteristics (e.g., Dick & Rose, 2002; Wills, Sandy, et al., 2001). So the view we end up with is: "Life deals you a hand. If the hand isn't a royal flush, then it's up to you to make the best of it." Obviously young children have less advanced cognitive capacities, so parents ultimately have more moral responsibility for using the hand they got in the most responsible way possible. If parents have an irritable personality or are engaged in substance abuse, they can choose to get treatment. If they have a child who is highly active, they can enlist external sources of support to help them deal with child-rearing responsibilities. And the developmental models point out who is likely to be most at risk, so knowledge is available to agencies that can then target resources to families who need it the most.

Given the power of social groups to influence behavior, the question also arises of whether adolescents are morally blameworthy if they involve themselves with groups of teens who are known to be bad actors. Logically this is a coherent argument, and the literature suggests that everyone knows who the aggressive kids are from an early age (Cairns et al., 1988). There are lots of different people with whom teens could affiliate, so if they choose to hang out with trouble-prone (aggressive and substance-using) peers, are they not simply making a bad choice for which they are culpable? We do not want to discuss whether this is a conscious choice—there is no evidence on this issue—but prefer to emphasize what this argument misses: the large body of evidence showing that adolescents who drift into deviant peer groups are those who are actively rejected by their parents and are not monitored by them (Dishion et al., 1995). Admittedly, there may be qualities in the adolescent that contributed to parental rejection (e.g., difficult temperament, early disruptive behavior); nevertheless, to argue that affiliating with particular peers is a neutral choice would be, we think, contrary to the evidence. Selecting deviant peers appears to occur more through a drift into deviant groups in conditions where parents provide little positive attachment or supervision, where the adolescent him- or herself feels incompetent in important developmental tasks (e.g., doing well in school), and where a heavy load of external stressors accumulates on the family. If a deviant peer group provides a positive identity and emotional support for an adolescent who feels that nobody understands him or her, we could hardly say that this action is counter to basic human needs; furthermore, if the deviant peers are impulsive and fun loving in a way that is similar to the adolescent him- or herself, then the adolescent's attraction can be explained easily in terms of basic social psychology. So we can suggest that troubled adolescents may need counseling and guidance to redirect them away from trouble-prone peer groups and toward other types of rewarding peers and activities (Carroll, 1996), but we find no basis for thinking that their affiliations are mysterious or pathological.

The legal issue of personal responsibility is different from the question of whether the behavior is predictable or understandable. Behavior is shaped by contingencies, and from the societal standpoint, there must be responsibilities. A parent cannot deflect responsibility for failing to supervise his or her children by claiming bad genes, any more than a drunk driver can get off on a charge of vehicular homicide by arguing that he or she had a genetic vulnerability to alcohol. A teenager who fights and steals cannot be excused for this behavior by claiming distant parents or bad friends. So we think the only possible legal argument is that everyone is responsible for their behavior.

The contribution of social psychology is to teach adolescents relevant skills so that development of adverse behavior can be prevented (Sussman & Ames, 2001). For example, prevention programs have been designed to help adolescents make better decisions (Baron & Brown, 1991) and to become involved in positive peer groups that promote prosocial values and staying in school (Eggert, Thompson, Herting, & Randell, 2001). Other theory-based programs have used concepts from social influence theory and social perception theory to teach cognitive and behavioral skills that serve as deterrents to smoking and other problem behavior in high-risk populations (Dent, Sussman, Stacy, & Craig, 1995; Larson & Lochman, 2002; Sussman, Dent, Stacy, & Craig, 1998). Prevention research continues to use this theory base to identify cognitive factors and behavioral-control skills that can be included in primary prevention and health promotion programs (Sussman et al., in press).

Directions for Preventing Destructive Behavior

Our presentation has emphasized that prosocial behavior and destructive behavior in adolescence have multiple determinants. An implication is that there are several points at which interventions (or moderators) could strengthen tendencies for prosocial behavior, for example, through enhancing parental support and through targeting other variables such as competencies and peer affiliations. This is an important implication from the perspective of social policy: Given the range of protective effects observed for parental support, social policies that are "friendly" toward children and families and aimed at making it easier for parents to act supportively are likely to have long-range effects in terms of prosocial behavior.

A converse approach, for averting aggression and depression, can be derived by targeting family conflict and the downstream effects involved in pathways to adverse outcomes. This perspective suggests that preventive interventions could focus on proximal factors such as reinforcement from deviant peers, while also giving attention to more distal factors such as attitudes about deviance and patterns of coping with problems. Prominent among the target approaches are family-centered interventions that aim to enhance parental monitoring of behavior, increase parents' use of positive reinforcement, and resolve the cycles of destructive arguing between parents and adolescents. Such interventions have been found effective for prevention of substance use (Dishion & Kavanaugh, 2001).

From the societal standpoint, if a child is showing early signs of problem behavior and affiliation with trouble-prone companions, then mechanisms should be available so that parents and community agencies can work together to assess children and implement preventive interventions when appropriate. All the arguments—and the research—are on the side of early intervention. School-based interventions afford a window onto academic involvement and peer processes and can be combined with family interventions (Dishion, Kavanaugh, Schneider, Nelson, & Kaufman, 2002). We know the basics of how to implement early preventive interventions that provide cognitive and social supports to high-risk families (Ammerman & Hersen, 1997; Peters & McMahon, 1996), and social-psychological research can help to build on this base.

Regarding future directions, we recommend more research grounded in the perspective of developmental models to provide us with a better understanding of the origins of aggressive behavior. There is a need for research on (1) how the dispositional attributes of children (and parents) are related to the formation of supportive family relationships, (2) the interactions between heredity and environment in shaping social relationships and patterns of coping, and (3) the the effects of these relationships as they are expressed in the world of peers, school, and social institutions. Such studies may need to combine the advantages of psychobiological measures with the external validity of research conducted with community samples (Dick & Rose, 2002; Linnoila, 1997; Wills, Sandy, & Yaeger, 2002). The goal is to understand the chain of variables that leads young people on a trajectory toward prosocial behavior and away from destructive outcomes.

ACKNOWLEDGMENTS

This work was supported by Research Scientist Development Award No. K02 DA00252 from the National Institute on Drug Abuse; by Grant Nos. DA05950, DA08880, and DA12623 from the National Institute on Drug Abuse; and by Grant No. S-184A-00035 from the U.S. Department of Education.

REFERENCES

Abbey, A., Abramis, D. J., & Caplan, R. D. (1985). Effects of different sources of social support and social conflict on emotional well-being. *Basic and Applied Social Psychology, 6*, 111–129.

Achenbach, T. M. (1991). *Manual for the Youth Self-Report and 1991 profile.* Burlington, VT: University of Vermont.

Ammerman, R. T., & Hersen, M. (Eds.). (1997). *Handbook of prevention and treatment with children and adolescents: Intervention in the real world context.* New York: Wiley.

Barerra, M., Jr., Chassin, L., & Rogosch, F. (1993). Effects of social support and conflict on adolescent children. *Journal of Personality and Social Psychology, 64*, 602–612.

Baron, J., & Brown, R.V. (1991). *Teaching decision making to adolescents.* Hillsdale, NJ: Erlbaum.

Baron, R., & Kenny, D. (1986). The moderator–mediator distinction in social-psychological research. *Journal of Personality and Social Psychology, 51*, 1173–1182.

Berscheid, E. (1985). Interpersonal attraction. In G. Lindzey & E. Aronson (Eds.), *Handbook of social psychology* (3rd ed., pp. 413–484). New York: Random House.

Blackson, T. C., Tarter, R. E., Loeber, R., Ammerman, R. T., & Windle, M. (1996). Paternal substance abuse and difficult temperament in fathers and sons, and disengagement from family to deviant peers. *Journal of Youth and Adolescence, 25*, 389–411.

Blackson, T. C. , Tarter, R. E., Martin, C., & Moss, H. (1994). Temperament induced father–son family dysfunction: Etiological implications. *American Journal of Orthopsychiatry, 64*, 280–292.

Bouchard, T. J. (1994). Genes, environment, and personality. *Science, 264,* 1700–1701.

Brown, B. B., Dolcini, M. M., & Leventhal, A. (1997). Transformations in peer relationships in adolescence. In J. Schulenberg, J. Maggs, & I. Hurrelmann (Eds.), *Health risks and developmental transitions during adolescence* (pp. 161–189). New York: Cambridge University Press.

Burke, R. J., & Weir, T. (1979). Helping responses of parents and peers and adolescent well-being. *Journal of Psychology, 102,* 49–62.

Cairns, R. B., Cadwallader, T. W., Estell, D., & Neckerman, H. J. (1997). From groups to gangs: Developmental and criminological perspectives. In D. M. Stoff, J. Breiling, & J. D. Maser (Eds.), *Handbook of antisocial behavior* (pp. 194–204). New York: Wiley.

Cairns, R. B., Cairns, B. D., Neckerman, J. J., Gest, S., & Gariepy, J.-L. (1988). Social networks and aggressive behavior: Peer support or peer rejection? *Developmental Psychology, 24,* 815–823.

Caputo, P. (1977). *A rumor of war.* New York: Ballantine.

Carey, G., & Goldman, D. (1997). The genetics of antisocial behavior. In D. M. Stoff, J. Breiling, & J. D. Maser (Eds.), *Handbook of antisocial behavior* (pp. 243–254). New York: Wiley.

Carroll, M. E. (1996). Reducing drug abuse by enriching the environment with alternative nondrug reinforcers. In L. Green & J. H. Kagel (Eds.), *Advances in behavioral economics* (pp. 37–68). Norwood, NJ: Ablex.

Carver, C. S., Scheier, M. F., & Weintraub, J. K. (1989). Assessing coping strategies: A theoretically based approach. *Journal of Personality and Social Psychology, 56,* 267–283.

Caspi, A. (1993). Why maladaptive behaviors persist: Sources of continuity and change across the life course. In D. C. Funder, R. D. Parke, C. Tomlinson-Keasey, & K. Widaman (Eds.), *Studying lives through time: Personality and development* (pp. 343–376). Washington, DC: American Psychological Association.

Cloninger, C. R., Sigvardsson, S., & Bohman, M. (1988). Childhood personality predicts alcohol abuse in young adults. *Alcoholism: Clinical and Experimental Research, 12,* 494–505.

Cloninger, C. R., Svrakic, D. M., & Przybeck, T. R. (1993). A psychobiological model of temperament and character. *Archives of General Psychiatry, 50,* 975–990.

Conger, R. D., Patterson, G. R., & Ge, X. (1995). A mediational model for the impact of parents' stress on adolescent adjustment. *Child Development, 66,* 80–97.

Coscina, D. V. (1997). The biopsychology of impulsivity. In C. D. Webster & M. A. Jackson (Eds.), *Impulsivity: Theory, assessment, and treatment* (pp. 95–115). New York: Guilford Press.

Dent, C., Sussman, S., Stacy, A., & Craig, S. (1995). Two-year outcomes of Project Toward No Tobacco Use. *Journal of Consulting and Clinical Psychology, 63,* 676–677.

Dick, D. M., & Rose, R. J. (2002). Behavior genetics: What's new, what's next? *Current Directions in Psychological Science, 11,* 70–74.

Diener, E., Suh, E. M., Lucas, R. E., & Smith, H. L. (1999). Subjective well-being: Three decades of progress. *Psychological Bulletin, 125,* 276–302.

Dishion, T. J., Andrews, D., & Crosby, L. (1995). Antisocial boys and their friends: Relationship characteristics and interactional process. *Child Development, 66,* 139–151.

Dishion, T. J., Capaldi, D., Spracklen, K. M., & Li, F. (1995). Peer ecology of adolescent substance use. *Development and Psychopathology, 7,* 803–824.

Dishion, T. J., & Kavanaugh, K. (2001). An ecological approach to family intervention for adolescent substance use. In E. F. Wagner & H. B. Waldron (Eds.), *Innovations in adolescent substance abuse interventions* (pp. 127–142). New York: Pergamon.

Dishion, T. J., Kavanaugh, K., Schneiger, A., Nelson, S., & Kaufman, N. K. (2002). A tiered family-intervention strategy for the public middle-school ecology. *Prevention Science, 3,* 191–202.

Dishion, T. J., & Patterson, G. R. (1997). The timing and severity of antisocial behavior: An ecological framework. In D. M. Stoff, J. Breiling, & J. D. Maser (Eds.), *Handbook of antisocial behavior* (pp. 205–217). New York: Wiley.

Dishion, T. J., Patterson, G. R., & Griesler, P. C. (1994). Peer adaptations in the development of antisocial behavior: A confluence model. In L. R. Huesmann (Ed.), *Aggressive behavior: Current perspectives* (pp. 61–95). New York: Plenum Press.

Donovan, J. E., & Jessor, R. (1985). Structure of problem behavior in adolescence and young adulthood. *Journal of Consulting and Clinical Psychology, 53,* 890–904.

Donovan, J. E., Jessor, R., & Costa, F. M. (1988). Syndrome of problem behavior in adolescence. *Journal of Consulting and Clinical Psychology, 56,* 762–765.

Dubow, E. F., & Reid, G. J. (1997). Risk and resource variables in children's aggressive behavior. In L. R. Huesmann (Ed.), *Aggressive behavior: Current perspectives* (pp. 187–211). New York: Plenum Press.

Eggert, L. L., Thompson, E. A., Herting, J. R., & Randell, B. P. (2001). Reconnecting youth to prevent drug abuse, school dropout, and self-destructive behavior. In E. F. Wagner & H. B. Waldron (Eds.), *Innovations in adolescent substance abuse interventions* (pp. 51–84). New York: Pergamon.

Gray, J. A. (1991). The neuropsychology of temperament. In J. Strelau & A. Angleitner (Eds.), *Explorations in temperament: Perspectives on theory and measurement* (pp. 105–128). New York: Plenum Press.

Gray, J. G. (1970). *The warriors: Reflections on men in battle.* New York: Harper & Row.

Greenberg, M. T., Siegel, J. M., & Leitch, C. J. (1983). The nature and importance of attachment relationships to parents and peers during adolescence. *Journal of Youth and Adolescence, 12,* 373–386.

Hawkins, J. D., Catalano, R. F., & Miller, J. Y. (1992). Risk and protective factors for alcohol and other drug problems in adolescence and early adulthood. *Psychological Bulletin, 112,* 64–105.

Iervolino, A. C., Pike, A., Manke, B., Reiss, D., Hetherington, E. M., & Plomin, R. (2002). Genetic and environmental influences in adolescent peer socialization: Evidence from two genetically sensitive designs. *Child Development,* *73,* 162–174.

Jessor, R., & Jessor, S. (1977). *Problem behavior and psychosocial development.* New York: Academic Press.

Larson, J., & Lochman, J. E. (2002). *Helping schoolchildren cope with anger: A cognitive-behavioral intervention.* New York: Guilford Press.

Larson, R. (1983). Adolescents' daily experiences with family and friends: Contrasting opportunity systems. *Journal of Marriage and the Family, 45,* 739–750.

Linnoila, M. (1997). On the psychobiology of antisocial behavior. In D. M. Stoff, J. Breiling, & J. D. Maser (Eds.), *Handbook of antisocial behavior* (pp. 336–340). New York: Wiley.

MacKinnon, D. P. (1994). Analysis of mediating variables in prevention and intervention studies. In A. Cazares & L. A. Beatty (Eds.), *Scientific methods in prevention research* (pp. 127–153). Rockville, MD: National Institute on Drug Abuse.

Marshall, G. N., Wortman, C. B., Kusulas, J. W., Hervig, L. K., & Vickers, R. W., Jr. (1992). Distinguishing optimism from pessimism. *Journal of Personality and Social Psychology, 62,* 1067–1074.

McGue, M. (1999). The behavioral genetics of alcoholism. *Current Directions in Psychological Science, 8,* 109–115.

Moffitt, T. E. (1993a). Adolescence-limited and life course-persistent antisocial behavior: A developmental taxonomy. *Psychological Review, 100,* 674–701.

Moffitt, T. E. (1993b). The neuropsychology of conduct disorder. *Development and Psychopathology, 5,* 135–151.

O'Connor, T. G., Deter-Deckard, K., Fulker, D., Rutter, M., & Plomin, R. (1998). Genotype–environment correlations in late childhood and early adolescence. *Developmental Psychology, 34,* 970–981.

Peters, R. DeV., & McMahon, R. J. (Eds.). (1996). *Preventing childhood disorders, substance abuse, and delinquency.* Thousand Oaks, CA: Sage.

Plomin, R., & McClearn, G. E. (Eds.). (1993). *Nature, nurture, and psychology.* Washington, DC: American Psychological Association.

Plomin, R., Owen, M. J., & McGuffin, P. (1994). The genetic basis of complex human behaviors. *Science, 264,* 1733–1739.

Quinton, D., Pickles, A., Maughan, B., & Rutter, M. (1993). Partners, peers, and pathways: Assortative pairing and continuities in conduct disorder. *Development and Psychopathology, 5,* 763–783.

Rook, K. S. (1984). The negative side of social interaction: Impact on psychological well-being. *Journal of Personality and Social Psychology, 46,* 1097–1108.

Rook, K. S. (1990). Parallels in the study of social support and social strain. *Journal of Social and Clinical Psychology, 9,* 118–132.

Rothbart, M. K., & Ahadi, S. A. (1994). Temperament and the development of personality. *Journal of Abnormal Psychology, 103,* 55–66.

Rothbart, M. K., Derryberry, D., & Posner, M. J. (1994). A psychobiological approach to the development of temperament. In J. E. Bates & T. D. Wachs (Eds.), *Temperament: Individual differences at the interface of biology and behavior* (pp. 83–116). Washington, DC: American Psychological Association.

Rutter, M. (1997). Antisocial behavior: Developmental psychopathology perspectives. In D. M. Stoff, J. Breiling, & J. D. Maser (Eds.), *Handbook of antisocial behavior* (pp. 115–124). New York: Wiley.

Rutter, M., Dunn, J., Plomin, R., Simonoff, E., Pickles, A., Maughan, B., Ormel, J., Meyer, J., & Eaves, L. (1997). Integrating nature and nurture: Implications of person–environment correlations and interactions for developmental psychopathology. *Development and Psychopathology, 9,* 335–364.

Sandler, I. N., Miller, P., Short, J., & Wolchik, S. A. (1989). Social support as a protective factor for children in stress. In D. Belle (Ed.), *Children's social networks and social supports* (pp. 277–307). New York: Wiley.

Scarr, S. (1992). Developmental theories for the 1990s: Development and individual differences. *Child Development, 63,* 1–19.

Steinberg, L., Lamborn, S. D., Dornbusch, S. M., & Darling, N. (1992). Impact of parenting practices on adolescent achievement: Authoritative parenting, school involvement, and encouragement to succeed. *Child Development, 63,* 1266–1281.

Sussman, S., & Ames, S. L. (2001). *The social psychology of drug abuse.* Philadelphia: Open University Press.

Sussman, S., Dent, C., Stacy, A., & Craig, S. (1998). One-year outcomes of Project Towards No Drug Abuse. *Preventive Medicine, 27,* 632–642.

Sussman, S., Earleywine, M., Wills, T. A., Biglan, A., Dent, C., & Newcomb, M. (in press). Implications of a motivation and decision-making approach for drug abuse prevention. *Substance Use and Misuse* [Special issue].

Swan, G. E., & Carmelli, D. (1997). Behavior genetic investigations of cigarette smoking and related issues in twins. In K. Blum, E. Noble, R. Sparkes, & T. Chen (Eds.), *Handbook of psychiatric genetics* (pp. 387–406). Boca Raton, FL: CRC Press.

Tarter, R. E., Moss, H. B., & Vanyukov, M. M. (1995). Behavior genetic perspective of alcoholism etiology. In H. Begleiter & B. Kissin (Eds.), *Alcohol and alcoholism* (Vol. 1, pp. 294–326). New York: Oxford University Press.

Tarter, R. E., & Vanyukov, M. (1994). Alcoholism as a developmental disorder. *Journal of Consulting and Clinical Psychology, 62,* 1096–1107.

Thornberry, T. P., & Krohn, M. D. (1997). Peers, drug use, and delinquency. In D. M. Stoff, J. Breiling, & J. D. Maser (Eds.), *Handbook of antisocial behavior* (pp. 218–233). New York: Wiley.

Uchino, B. N., Cacioppo, J. T., & Kiecolt-Glaser, J. K. (1996). Social support and physiological processes. *Psychological Bulletin, 119,* 488–531.

Werner, E. E. (1986). Resilient offspring of alcoholics: A longitudinal study from birth to age 18. *Journal of Studies on Alcohol, 47,* 34–40.

Wills, T. A. (1985). Stress, coping, and tobacco and alcohol use in early adolescence. In S. Shiffman & T. A. Wills (Eds.), *Coping and substance use* (pp. 67–94). Orlando, FL: Academic Press.

Wills, T. A. (1990). Stress and coping factors in the epidemiology of substance use. In L. T. Kozlowski, H. M. Annis, H. D. Cappell, F. B. Glaser, M. S. Goodstadt, Y. Israel, H. Kalant, E. M. Sellers, & E. R. Vinglis (Eds.), *Research advances in alcohol and drug problems* (Vol. 10, pp. 215–250). New York: Plenum Press.

Wills, T. A. (1991). Social support and personal relationships. In M. Clark (Ed.), *Review of personality and social psychology* (Vol. 12, pp. 265–289). Newbury Park, CA: Sage.

Wills, T. A. (1992). Social comparison and self-change. In J. D. Fisher, J. Chinsky, Y. Klar, & A. Nadler (Eds.), *Self-change: Social-psychological and clinical perspectives* (pp. 231–252). New York: Springer-Verlag.

Wills, T. A., Blechman, E. A., & McNamara, G. (1996). Family support, coping and competence. In E. M. Hetherington & E. A. Blechman (Eds.), *Stress, coping, and resiliency in children and the family* (pp. 107–133). Hillsdale, NJ: Erlbaum.

Wills, T. A., & Cleary, S. D. (1996). How are social support effects mediated? A test for parental support. *Journal of Personality and Social Psychology, 71,* 937–952.

Wills, T. A., & Cleary, S. D. (1997). Validity of self-reports of smoking by ethnicity in a school sample of urban adolescents. *American Journal of Public Health, 87,* 56–61.

Wills, T. A., & Cleary, S. D. (1999). Peer and adolescent substance use among 6th–9th graders: Latent growth analyses. *Health Psychology, 18,* 453–463.

Wills, T. A., Cleary, S. D., Filer, M., Shinar, O., Mariani, J., & Spera, K. (2001). Temperament related to early-onset substance use. *Prevention Science, 2,* 145–163.

Wills, T. A., & DePaulo, B. M. (1991). Interpersonal analysis of the help-seeking process. In C. R. Snyder & D. R. Forsyth (Eds.), *Handbook of social and clinical psychology* (pp. 350–375). Elmsford, NY: Pergamon.

Wills, T. A., & Filer, M. (1996). Stress-coping model of adolescent substance use. In T. H. Ollendick & R. J. Prinz (Eds.), *Advances in clinical child psychology* (Vol. 18, pp. 91–132). New York: Plenum Press.

Wills, T. A., & Filer, M. (2001). Social networks and social support. In A. Baum, T. A. Revenson, & J. E. Singer (Eds.), *Handbook of health psychology* (pp. 209–234). Mahwah, NJ: Erlbaum.

Wills, T. A., Gibbons, F. X., Gerrard, M., & Brody, G. (2000). Protection and vulnerability processes for early onset of substance use. *Health Psychology, 19,* 253–263.

Wills, T. A., & Hirky, A. E. (1996). Coping and substance abuse. In M. Zeidner & N. S. Endler (Eds.), *Handbook of coping* (pp. 279–302). New York: Wiley.

Wills, T. A., Mariani, J., & Filer, M. (1996). The role of family and peer relationships in adolescent substance use. In G. R. Pierce, B. R. Sarason, & I. G. Sarason (Eds.), *Handbook of social support and the family* (pp. 521–549). New York: Plenum Press.

Wills, T. A., McNamara, G., Vaccaro, D., & Hirky, A. E. (1996). Escalated substance use: A longitudinal grouping analysis. *Journal of Abnormal Psychology, 105,* 166–180.

Wills, T. A., Sandy, J. M., & Yaeger, A. (2000). Temperament and adolescent substance use: An epigenetic approach. *Journal of Personality, 68,* 1127–1152.

Willis, T. A., Sandy, J. M., & Yaeger, A. (2002). Moderators of the relationship between substance use level and problems: Test of a self-regulation model in middle adolescence. *Journal of Abnormal Psychology, 111,* 3–21.

Wills, T. A., Sandy, J. M., Yaeger, A., & Shinar, O. (2001). Family risk factors: Moderation effects for temperament dimensions. *Developmental Psychology, 37,* 283–297.

Wills, T. A., & Vaughan, R. (1989). Social support and substance use in early adolescence. *Journal of Behavioral Medicine, 12,* 321–339.

Wills, T. A., Windle, M., & Cleary, S. D. (1998). Temperament and novelty-seeking in adolescent substance use. *Journal of Personality and Social Psychology, 74,* 387–406.

CHAPTER 17

SACRIFICING TIME AND EFFORT FOR THE GOOD OF OTHERS

The Benefits and Costs of Volunteerism

MARK SNYDER
ALLEN M. OMOTO
JAMES J. LINDSAY

Helping others is a universally recognized virtue, as evidenced by the theme of benevolence and self-sacrifice for the benefit of others within the sacred texts of most of the world's religions (Schroeder, Penner, Dovidio, & Piliavin, 1995). Take, for example, the theme of helping, as it is illustrated in Jesus's parable of the Good Samaritan in the Bible:

> "And who is my neighbor?" Jesus replied, "A man was going down from Jerusalem to Jericho, and he fell among robbers, who stripped him and beat him, and departed, leaving him half dead. Now by chance a priest was going down the road; and when he saw him, he passed by on the other side. So likewise a Levite, when he came to the place and saw him, passed by on the other side. But a Samaritan, as he journeyed, came to where he was; and when he saw him, he had compassion, and went to him and bound his wounds, pouring on oil and wine; then he set him on his own beast and brought him to an inn, and took care of him. And the next day he took out two dennarii and gave them to the innkeeper, saying, 'Take care of him; and whatever more you spend, I will repay you when I come back.' Which of these three, do you think, proved neighbor to him who fell among the robbers?" he said, "The one who showed mercy on him." And Jesus said to him, "Go and do likewise." (Luke 10:29–37, RSV)

Early psychological research on helping behavior focused mainly on situations similar to that faced by the Good Samaritan (Dovidio, 1984; Latané & Darley, 1970). Such situations often involve spontaneous behavior performed in response to an immediate, acute need. Studies on bystander intervention exemplify this type of research. Such investigations often involve individuals who encounter a person—usually a stranger—who is experiencing some distress (e.g., a flat tire, requiring extra change), and a simple act (e.g., assistance with the tire, calling authorities, lending a quarter) will usually provide an immediate solution to the problem at hand. Clearly, situations requiring bystander intervention often are immediately apparent and may produce distress among observer-actors and victims alike. Moreover, those who assist victims in such situations can sometimes place their own lives at risk (e.g., assisting handicapped individuals trapped in the World Trade Center on September 11, 2001; diving into the freezing Potomac River to aid victims of Air Florida Flight 90). The distress and vicarious pride experienced by observers of such noble acts (as well as the dismay when such situations prompt no action) often draw media attention. It is no wonder, then, that such clear, unambiguous helping situations and the psychological factors that contribute to bystanders' actions (or inaction) have received so much attention by the media and social scientists. Indeed, a survey of recently published social psychology textbooks documents the prevalence of this interest in bystander intervention. Almost all textbook discussions of helping behavior focus on the personality and situational factors that influence whether or not bystanders help those in immediate need.

Contrast the parable of the Good Samaritan and the kind of helping that it exemplifies with another form of helping, namely that exemplified by the life story of Agnes Gonxha Bojaxhiu:

> Born August 26, 1910, in Skopje (now in Macedonia), Agnes Gonxha Bojaxhiu was the daughter of Albanian parents—a grocer and his wife. As a public school student she developed a special interest in overseas missions and, by age 12, realized her vocation was aiding the poor. She was inspired to work in India by reports sent home from Jesuit missionaries in Bengal. And at 18, she left home to join a community of Irish nuns with a mission in Calcutta. Here, she took the name "Sister Teresa," after Saint Teresa of Lisieux, the patroness of missionaries. She spent 17 years teaching and being principal of St. Mary's high school in Calcutta. However, in 1946, her life changed forever. After falling ill with suspected tuberculosis she was sent to the town of Darjeeling to recover. "It was in the train I heard the call to give up all and follow him [sic] to the slums to serve him [sic] among the poorest of the poor," she remembered. Two years later, Pope Pius XII granted permission for her to leave her order. (Cable News Network, 1997)

This woman—who later became known as Mother Teresa—would continue to serve the poor of Calcutta and others throughout the world for 50 more years, into her 87th year.

As much as the behavior of modern-day Good Samaritans, such as the heroes of the World Trade Center tragedy and other emergency situations, may captivate the attention of the public, the media, and even social scientists, there are many other heroes who—in the tradition of Mother Teresa—sacrifice much of their time and energy toward helping the needy. Such individual helpers are the volunteers who give of their time on a regular and ongoing basis to provide services and perform good works of many and diverse forms, from handing out pamphlets at health fairs, to teaching English as a second language, to helping the young learn to read, or serving food at a homeless shelter. The conditions that inspire these volunteer activities involve problems that cannot be fixed quickly with a single act. Rather, these helpers must provide their services repeatedly over time in order to produce results. These individuals, their actions, and the contexts in which they volunteer to help are the focus of our concerns here.

In this chapter, we examine volunteerism as a form of helping and prosocial action, drawing on a program of research that examines the psychological factors motivating people to become volunteers and sustaining their volunteer efforts over extended periods of time, as well as the factors that lead to a successful and effective helping relationship. We also examine volunteerism from the broader perspective of the costs and benefits of volunteerism for the volunteers themselves, for the clients whom they serve, for the organizations that utilize volunteer labor, and for society as a whole. Based on this analysis of the costs and benefits of volunteerism, we offer theoretically informed and empirically grounded prescriptions for optimizing the effectiveness of volunteer helping and for ensuring that the help offered by volunteers is, in fact, truly helpful.

WHAT IS VOLUNTEERISM?

Although many definitions of volunteerism have been offered, most include in them the essence of volunteering as "any activity in which time is given freely to benefit another person, group, or organization" (Wilson, 2000, p. 215). As such, volunteerism also falls within the more general domain of helping behaviors. However, whereas many acts of volunteerism are helpful both in their intentions and their impact (e.g., volunteers who provide companionship to the lonely, tutoring to the illiterate, counseling to the troubled), there are also actions that meet this definition but which may be harmful, depending on point of view (Smith, 1981). For example, providing free labor in support of a political candidate is "helpful" in that the volunteer is providing unpaid assistance to a group, but the action also may be perceived as "harmful" by those who dislike the particular candidate. Likewise, a person who freely hands out literature promoting the Ku Klux Klan is engaged in activity intended to benefit a group, but many would argue that this type of service also does not constitute "helping," given the mission of the KKK. A Palestinian youth who straps a bomb to his chest in order to kill Israelis might be considered a volunteer, although the actions of such suicide bombers, whether or not they are actually helpful to their cause, are surely harmful to the victims (as well as the "volunteer") who are injured and killed. And, finally, even the perpetrators of the World Trade Center tragedy of September 11, 2001 can be construed as volunteers working to benefit a cause. They may even have considered the results of their actions as helpful, despite the fact that many others saw them only as harmful acts performed by evildoers. Thus, some refinement of the definition of *volunteer* may be necessary to specify more precisely the ways in which actions are truly voluntary, the extent to which intentions and consequences are helpful or harmful, and to whom they may be helpful or harmful (Smith, 1981).

We find it heuristically useful to identify five defining and characteristic features of volunteerism:

1. The behaviors performed must be voluntary or based on the actor's free will, without bonds of obligation.
2. The act of volunteering, or seeking ways of providing services for others, involves some amount of deliberation.
3. Volunteer services must be delivered over an extended period of time.
4. The decision to volunteer is based entirely on the person's own goals and without expectation of material compensation.
5. Volunteering involves serving those who desire help.

A recurring theme in these features that define volunteerism is the active role of the individual in choosing to volunteer and in charting the course of his or her volunteer action, such that it reflects processes of choice, active decision making, and the influence of personal values and motivations. Let us elaborate on each of these distinguishing features of volunteerism.

The definition of volunteerism that we have adopted excludes instances in which a previous relationship between helper and recipient exists, such as when a person provides care and assistance to an aged parent or a sick spouse. Such relationships often involve a history of helping, receiving help, and reciprocation; helping actions that take place within such relationships may not be truly voluntary but performed in response to the situational pressures and from a sense of obligation flowing from familial or marital relationships. Such helping behaviors that take place within an already existing relationship are more appropriately termed *care giving* (see Omoto & Snyder, 1995).

Those who volunteer must decide not just whether to help, but who to help and when to help and how to help. That is, those who decide to offer their services face a wide variety of social and political causes that could potentially benefit from their efforts (e.g., working on behalf of the environment, volunteering to promote literacy) and organizations that provide opportunities for volunteers (e.g., the Red Cross, Big Brothers/Big Sisters, community-based AIDS service organizations). Moreover, volunteers typically consider the frequency of their service (should it be one or two afternoons a week, 1 day a week?), which types of tasks they wish to perform (should the work involve the provision of direct services to those in need?), and how long they wish to serve (can they make the 6-month-to-a-year commitment often encouraged by volunteer service organizations?). This feature of deliberation—which fosters the helper's meaningful reflection on his or her motivations, values, and other personal attributes—distinguishes volunteerism from bystander intervention, which often occurs in response to emergencies and disasters. The latter type of helping typically involves responses to unforeseen events that offer little opportunity for foresight and advance planning and often demand immediate and instantaneous responses. Helping in such situations is often referred to as spontaneous helping in contrast to the planned helping of volunteerism (e.g., Clary & Snyder, 1991).

As noted, the help provided via volunteerism also differs from the help provided in bystander intervention settings in quantity and duration. Whereas those who offer assistance in response to emergencies may offer their services for minutes or hours, volunteer activities often are sustained over the course of weeks, months, or years and may reflect the outcomes of systematic planning and agenda setting on the part of volunteer helpers. For instance, in one study in which volunteers were tracked from the beginning to the end of their service in community-based AIDS service organizations, the duration of service ranged from 2 to 60+ months, with an average of 16 months (Omoto & Snyder, 1996).

Another feature of volunteerism—providing service without expectation of personal compensation—highlights its self-sacrificial aspect. This characteristic distinguishes volunteers from those employed in the "helping professions," whose provision of help is at least partially, if not largely, a means to an end (i.e., a paycheck). Between the extremes of volunteers and paid helpers lies another class of individuals who receive small amounts of compensation for their services. Missionary work is one example, AmeriCorps and the Peace Corps another. However, because these volunteers receive a modest stipend, scholarship, or money for readjustment following their 1 or 2 years of service to impoverished areas in the

United States and developing countries, they fail to meet traditional definitions of "volunteers." However, it may be that the psychological processes at work within these "quasi-volunteers" (Smith, 1981) are similar to those operating for "true" volunteers.

Finally, volunteers donate their time and efforts to organizations whose missions involve assisting those desiring help. That is, the recipients of volunteer services are very often individuals who have approached service organizations in search of help and assistance. This feature of volunteers excludes those individuals who may provide their services for free but toward arguably "harmful" ends, such as the suicide bombers whose actions are directed toward the destruction of others. Our remaining discussion of volunteers focuses on those individuals whose service is "good" in intention and "good" in consequence.

WHY DO PEOPLE VOLUNTEER?

Despite the effortful, sustained, and nonremunerative aspects of volunteerism, a recent survey revealed that 44% of Americans perform some form of volunteer service, with 30% volunteering at least once a month (Independent Sector, 2001). Given the barriers inherent in volunteering and the frequency with which the behavior occurs, the question of "What motivates people to volunteer?" naturally arises.

To address this question, researchers have explored the motivations that may lie behind volunteerism and the psychological functions that may be served by volunteering (for overviews of relevant theorizing on the motivational foundations of volunteerism, see Snyder, Clary, & Stukas, 2000; Snyder & Omoto, 2000, 2001). These motivationally oriented answers to the questions of "Why do people volunteer?" and "What sustains the actions of volunteers over time?" reflect the spirit of functional theorizing about the purposes served by human thought and action (see Snyder & Cantor, 1998; for similar approaches to attitudes and persuasion, see Katz, 1960; Smith, Bruner, & White, 1956). In the spirit of such functional theorizing, attempts have been made to identify, both conceptually and empirically, the personal and social functions served by volunteerism (e.g., Clary et al., 1998; Omoto & Snyder, 1995).

Theorizing about the Functions of Volunteerism

Surveys have revealed that three out of four Americans consider volunteerism instrumental to creating a better world (e.g., Independent Sector, 1988). Yet, as we have seen, surveys also indicate that it is only some 30% who are engaged in regular volunteering on at least a monthly basis (Independent Sector, 2001). Thus, although 30% of the adult population comprise a substantial volunteer work force, it is, in proportional terms, not nearly as many volunteers as one might expect based on the widespread belief in the positive value of volunteering. This problem of inaction, or the gap caused by actions falling short of beliefs, has long been a topic of inquiry, not only for those examining practical issues such as volunteerism, donating money to charity, or minimizing harmful impact on the natural environment (e.g., Snyder, 1993; Snyder, Omoto, & Smith, in press), but also for those who ponder the theoretical relations between attitudes, intentions, and behavior (Eagly & Chaiken, 1998).

One approach to addressing the issue of inaction is to acknowledge that attitudes, thoughts, feelings, and actions may reflect and fulfill different personal and social functions within individuals (Katz, 1960; Smith et al., 1956; Snyder, 1993). In their treatments of attitudes and persuasion, for example, Smith and colleagues (1956) and Katz (1960) proposed that the same attitudes can be held by different people in service of different psychological purposes or functions.

Just as various psychological functions may underlie people's attitudes and beliefs, diverse functions may underlie and support people's actions as well. Functional theorizing about volunteerism and the research generated by that theorizing (Clary et al., 1998; Omoto & Snyder, 1995; Snyder et al., 2000) has not only proposed sets of functions potentially served by volunteering (e.g., volunteering to express humanitarian values, gain understanding of oneself and others, build and reinforce social contacts, boost and maintain self-esteem, and/or out of concern for one's community), but also some of the dimensions along which these functions vary.

This theorizing has suggested that the functions served by volunteering can be general and common to many forms of volunteering (e.g., the expression of humanitarian concern for those in need could prompt volunteering in many forms) or specific to certain types of volunteers or volunteer settings (e.g., volunteering out of concern for members of one's community may be limited to members of the community in question). Moreover, theorizing about the functional motivations associated with volunteering has suggested, in line with much theorizing about the underpinnings of other forms of helping, that the motivations for helping may vary in the extent to which they are relatively other-oriented (e.g., wanting to provide aid to the needy) or relatively self-oriented (e.g., providing help in order to develop new skills or make new business contacts). Finally, theorizing about volunteering has proposed that the motivational impetus for volunteering may range from concerns about helping specific individuals (e.g., volunteering to be a Big Brother or Big Sister to improve the quality of life of a particular child) to desires to contribute to improving one's community or even society at large (e.g., volunteering in the environmental movement to work for a cleaner world).

Assessing the Functions of Volunteerism

Guided by theorizing about the functions served by volunteering, researchers have developed inventories to empirically identify and measure the diverse functions actually served by volunteering. Some of these inventories have been constructed to be of generic relevance to the field of volunteering (e.g., an inventory developed by Clary et al., 1998, identifies six such functions, each measured reliably by a 5-item scale), whereas other inventories of motivation have been developed for use with specific volunteer populations (e.g., the inventory of motivations for serving as an AIDS volunteer developed by Omoto & Snyder, 1995, which identifies five such motivations, each measured reliably by a 5-item scale). Across different methods of measurement and with data collected from many samples of volunteers who varied in their demographics and the forms of volunteerism in which they were engaged, research with these inventories has revealed distinct sets of motivations that have emerged with noteworthy regularity (e.g., Clary et al., 1998; Okun, Barr, & Herzog, 1998; Omoto & Snyder, 1995).

Examples of the motivations identified and measured by these inventories of motivations for volunteering include the following. First, volunteerism may allow people to express their *values* regarding the welfare of others; in that helping others and giving to the less fortunate are perceived as cherished values within society and are central tenets of many religions and religious orders, it follows that giving time and skills in the service to others allows volunteers to express these internalized values and convictions. Another function appears to involve a quest for *understanding;* people may enter into volunteer situations in order to learn more about a particular social problem, other types of people, or additional skills. For some volunteers, giving their time and labor to service organizations function as part of their membership in a *social* group; for example, fraternities, sororities, youth groups, and fraternal organizations often include voluntary service as part of their mission. As well, some people may volunteer to enhance their *career;* for such people, volunteerism may be instrumental toward the acquisition of career-related skills, business contacts, and experiences to showcase on their résumés. Others may volunteer to reduce their guilt about being more fortunate than others or to help work out personal problems; volunteerism would serve a *protective* function for such people. Still another possible function of volunteer behavior might be that of *enhancing* feelings of self-worth or self-esteem. Finally, volunteering may serve the function of demonstrating concern for particular groups of people, whether it is the residents of one's own neighborhood or community, or the community defined by those affected by particular diseases or other conditions that may place them in need of help and support from others; such volunteering may be motivated by *community concern.*

Research employing these inventories of motivations reveals consider-able variability in the functions served by volunteering (e.g., Clary et al., 1998; Omoto & Snyder, 1993, 1995). Every motivation identified in these inventories is, for some people, their most important motivation for volun-teering and, for other people, their least important motivation, with all gradations in between these extremes. This variability is, of course, to be expected on the basis of functional theorizing, which proposes that, even though many people may appear to be engaging in similar if not identical acts of volunteerism, they may be doing so in response to quite different psychological purposes and motivations.

Furthermore, according to the functional account of volunteerism, this variability in the underlying motivations for volunteerism may be meaningfully linked to critical features of the processes of volunteerism. And, indeed, empirical research has addressed the impact of motivations at critical points in the volunteer process, addressing critical aspects of the antecedents, experiences, and consequences of volunteerism (for reviews of such research, as well as discussions of its theoretical and practical impli-cations, see Snyder et al., 2000, in press; Snyder & Omoto, 2000, 2001). For example, the functional account proposes that the factors that draw people into volunteerism (e.g., recruitment appeals designed to promote volunteering) as well as the factors that sustain people in their volunteer service (e.g., the experiences that people accrue in the course of their vol-unteering) may be meaningfully linked to these motivations. Let us, there-fore, examine research designed to test functionally based hypotheses about the initiation and maintenance of volunteerism.

Can Function-Specific Appeals Effectively Recruit Volunteers?

Given that volunteers offer their service for different reasons, organiza-tions that are dependent on the services of volunteers may be able to build profitably on these differences in their efforts to recruit new volunteers. Specifically, those recruiting appeals that match people's more important motivations should net more volunteers than will appeals with no mention of psychological functions or appeals that mention alternative and less im-portant psychological functions. Clary, Snyder, Ridge, Miene, and Haugen (1994) tested this hypothesis using a series of videotaped advertisements portraying a woman who discussed how her volunteer experience fulfills her personal goals. After completing a measure of the relative strengths of their volunteer functions (i.e., motivations), research participants viewed either a "function-matched" or a "function-mismatched" version of the videotaped advertisement. That is, the advertisement either matched the functions that the participants mentioned for volunteering or they did not. Research participants then evaluated the persuasiveness of the advertise-ment and the likelihood that they would volunteer in the future. The results of this study were consistent with the functional perspective: Participants who viewed functionally matched recruitment messages rated the ads as more appealing and were more likely to volunteer in the future than those who viewed a functionally mismatched advertisement (Clary et al., 1994).

In a related study, Clary and colleagues (1998) examined messages contained in printed brochures instead of video portrayals. After completing the Volunteer Functions Inventory (Clary et al., 1998), research participants evaluated the persuasiveness of six printed volunteer recruitment appeals. Each of the six brochures listed the benefits of volunteering in terms of the psychological function that it fulfilled. When the persuasiveness ratings of the six brochures were regressed on participants' scores for each function measured, the results indicated that the research participants perceived the brochure that matched their motives to be most persuasive.

A pair of field-based studies further tested this matching hypothesis. In the first study, volunteers at an AIDS service organization completed a measure of motivations for AIDS volunteerism and also reviewed three newspaper advertisements written to promote AIDS volunteerism (Omoto, Snyder, & Smith, 1999). One ad had a self-focus appeal (e.g., "Volunteer to feel better about yourself"), another ad was other-focused (e.g., "Volunteer to help people in need"), and the third ad did not appeal to any motivation. Ratings favoring the other-focused ad were successfully predicted by volunteers' other-related motivations but not by their self-focused motivations. Similarly, reactions to the self-focused advertisement were significantly predicted by volunteers' self-oriented motivations but not by their other-oriented motivations. Not only did the match between people's motivations and advertisement content influence the appeal of ads, but another field study (Smith, Omoto, & Snyder, 2001) demonstrated that the match also influenced the likelihood that people would actually respond to such ads. Self-focused, other-focused, and control ads were published in college newspapers, and the researchers tracked the response rates for each ad. The advertisements appeared sequentially in the newspapers of two major universities, and each ad was run for a period of 5 days, followed by a 2-week break. The ads were run in reverse orders at the two universities. Those who responded to the ad were sent a questionnaire that measured, among other things, self-related and other-related motivations to volunteer. Again, consistent with the matching hypothesis, those with other-oriented motivations were more likely than those with self-related motivations to respond to the other-focused ad, although the matching pattern was not as apparent for the self-focused ad. Thus, these investigations provide evidence that people engage in volunteer work to fulfill different psychological functions and that organizations can recruit more volunteers through appealing to these underlying functions.

What Is the Role of Functions in Sustaining Volunteers?

Based on data from a study of AIDS volunteers, in which volunteers were followed over several years of their service, Omoto and Snyder (1995) examined the linkages between volunteers' motives and their duration of service and found a rather intriguing pattern of associations. Although the *values* function received high ratings among volunteers (suggesting that this other-oriented motivation may figure prominently in people's reasons for volunteering; see also Omoto & Snyder, 1993), when it came to predicting who would continue to serve as a volunteer and how long volunteers would serve, it was the relatively self-oriented motivations, such as personal development and esteem maintenance, that served as successful predictors. That is, in the case of AIDS volunteers, concern for others may bring them through the door, but more self-oriented motivations may be what keeps them serving (Omoto & Snyder, 1995; see also Davis, Hall, & Meyer, 2003; Penner & Finkelstein, 1998).

Moreover, not only may the motives that sustain volunteerism be different from those that initiate it, it also appears that a match between one's motivations for volunteering and one's experiences as a volunteer is critical in setting the stage for continuing service as a volunteer. Such a hypothesis was tested directly by Clary and colleagues (1998) using a sample of college students taking part in a mandatory community service program. These research participant volunteers completed the Volunteer Functions Inventory at the beginning of the program and at the end of a semester of participation in the program, at which time they also completed a questionnaire measuring (1) the degree to which each of the six motivations was fulfilled, (2) their satisfaction with the volunteer experience, and (3) their future intentions to volunteer. Consistent with the functional perspective on volunteerism, those volunteer-participants whose initial functions were fulfilled by their experiences reported more satisfaction with their volunteer service and indicated a greater likelihood of continuing to volunteer at the present location or elsewhere in the immediate future (Clary et al., 1998; see also Omoto, Snyder, & Martino, 2000, for a field-based study of hospice volunteers that further demonstrates the importance of matching for volunteer satisfaction).

The importance of volunteer experiences matching volunteers' primary motives for volunteering was also evident in a longitudinal study of AIDS volunteers. In this study volunteers were tracked from their initial inquiries regarding volunteer opportunities through 6 months of service. Those volunteers whose experiences were congruent with their preservice motivations were most committed to sustained service (Crain, Omoto, & Snyder, 1998; O'Brien, Crain, Omoto, & Snyder, 2000).

These results have direct implications for organizations and agencies that are dependent on volunteers to deliver services to clients. Although people seek out volunteer opportunities for a variety of reasons, some other-oriented (e.g., to express their concern for the welfare of others, concern for community) and some self-oriented reasons (e.g., esteem enhancement, understanding, career enhancement), they may discontinue their service if their experiences do not directly match their motivations. Accordingly, those who coordinate volunteer service programs may be able to increase the longevity of service provided by their volunteers as well as the satisfaction and the effectiveness of these volunteers by systematically helping them to recognize the ways in which their experiences as volunteers match with and fulfill the motivations they have expressed for serving as volunteers.

BENEFITS AND COSTS OF VOLUNTEERISM

Some might argue that many volunteer acts are "good" by definition; after all, these are directed at providing services to those in need, and volunteers often provide services that otherwise would not be provided due to lack of public or private funding to pay for such services. Even so, we think it appropriate to ask the question "Who benefits from volunteerism?" and to seek ways to empirically assess the goodness of volunteerism in terms of its demonstrable benefits, if any, to the volunteers themselves, to the recipients of the services they provide, to the organizations within which they volunteer, and to society at large.

Benefits and Costs to Organizations

One obvious way in which agencies "profit" by incorporating volunteers within their operations is the cost savings incurred by enlisting volunteers to perform duties that otherwise would be performed by paid staff. Several methods (ranging from the simple to the complex) have been used to document these cost savings. Two such methods are (1) multiplying the number of volunteer hours by the minimum wage rate, and (2) multiplying by the volunteers' regular pay rate. However, these simple methods can create, respectively, underestimates and overestimates of the true dollar value of volunteers' labor (Dalsimer, 1986; Karn, 1983). More precise values can be estimated by creating different job categories for the volunteers, determining the national average wage for persons in those categories, multiplying the number of service hours performed by volunteers within each job category by the average rate, and adding around 12%—the average amount paid in fringe benefits (Dalsimer, 1986; Karn, 1983). Calculating these precise estimates of cost savings requires some amount of effort among service agency staff; hence, directors and accounting staff at agencies may be reluctant to go through the trouble, unless they can ultimately profit from it (e.g., by demonstrating the increased efficiency of service provision to funding agencies).

Although few service organizations have published the amounts they save by using a volunteer work force, there are some cost savings data available at the national level. Every year, the Independent Sector—a group composed of charitable, educational, religious, and social welfare organizations—estimates the hourly value of volunteer service. These estimates are based on the Bureau of Labor Statistics published reports on the average hourly earnings of all production and nonsupervisory workers on private non-farm payrolls, with 12% added to account for fringe benefits. For 2001, the Independent Sector estimated that for every hour of volunteer service, agencies save about $16.05 (Independent Sector, 2001). Thus, one volunteer working 5 hours each week saves his or her organization $4,173 in a year. With 100 volunteers working the same number of hours, the organization saves over $400,000 annually!

Service organizations and charities may benefit, in ways other than cost savings, from incorporating volunteers within their operations. Most importantly, volunteers serve as effective conduits for expressing the organization's vision, mission, and goals to the general public, including potential financial contributors. Also, volunteers whose attitudes toward the population being served become more favorable can share these positive attitudes with their friends and colleagues. In these ways, service organizations can profit from volunteer involvement both directly (e.g., costs savings) and indirectly (e.g., dissemination of vision, mission, goals, positive attitudes).

There are, however, costs involved in the use of volunteers to provide services, and these costs should be recognized. First, unlike professional service staff who usually begin work at service organizations equipped with specialized knowledge and skills related to service delivery, volunteers often bring little else to the organization other than a desire to do good. The organization must carry the burden of providing volunteers with the skills and knowledge necessary to perform their work. Second, the cost of supervision and coordination is greater when a large number of part-time volunteers is providing services than when services are provided by a smaller number of full-time paid staff (Brudney & Duncombe, 1992). Third, although volunteers often enter their service with a dedication to the cause and the intention of doing good, they may not necessarily feel the same obligation as paid staff to continue providing their services. From the organization's standpoint then, professional staff may be perceived as more capable of providing the consistent service that clients require. Last, the use of volunteers to deliver services may shift liability for client outcomes from the professionally trained service providers to the service organization itself. Directors of service organizations must therefore weigh the certain costs of training and coordinating volunteers, potentially inferior quality and consistency of service, and the potential liability risks against the financial and social benefits of utilizing volunteers.

Moreover, the role of volunteers within organizations may evolve over time. At first, community groups may spring up (in "grassroots" fashion) when needs arise within a given population, as the community tries to "look after its own" until the issue receives enough attention to place it on the public agenda. Such community-based service organizations may begin their tenure with very limited financial resources and, accordingly, be forced to devote much of their resources toward recruiting, training, and placing volunteers into direct service roles. As general awareness of the needs being addressed and the services being provided by these organizations spreads, perhaps with the benefit of the media spotlights directed at them, they may find themselves the beneficiaries of both public and private grants and contributions. However, such grants and bequests may include provisions that (1) specify limits on the percentage of the organizations' financial resources that can be devoted toward indirect costs and administrative overhead, and/or (2) require organizations to demonstrate that services are being utilized and that positive outcomes are occurring. An obvious solution to meeting these provisions, and one adopted by many growing volunteer-based organizations, is to replace volunteers with presumably more reliable (and controllable) paid staff in direct service roles. Volunteers then become relegated to clerical, fund-raising, and one-time-event planning roles.

Benefits and Costs to Recipients of Volunteer Services

In many settings in which volunteers are employed, the effects of volunteers on the recipients of their services are readily apparent. For instance, some volunteers teach adult basic education classes, and their impact is evident when the participants in those programs obtain their high school diplomas. Similarly, the effects of volunteers working with Habitat for Humanity are demonstrated when families move into their new, low-cost homes. Although many service organizations provide data on program utilization and outcomes in their periodic reports to their donors and benefactors and in grant proposals, we know of very few systematic studies of the impact of volunteers on the clients whom they serve. However, studies of the effects of AIDS volunteers on the persons with HIV/AIDS, for whom the volunteers serve as "buddies" and "home helpers" (providing social and emotional support and/or assistance with household tasks) as well as studies of the effectiveness of youth mentoring programs do speak to the question of the potential benefits of volunteerism for the recipients of these services.

Let us first examine relevant data from a study (Omoto & Snyder, 1999) of helping relationships between AIDS volunteers who served as buddies or home helpers in one-to-one helping relationships with persons living with HIV and AIDS (PWAs). Of particular relevance to our current concerns are the effects of these volunteers on the psychological and physical functioning of their client PWAs (Lindsay, Snyder, & Omoto, 2003; see also Crain, Snyder, & Omoto, 2000). In their reports of how their volunteers had affected their lives, these clients stated that having a volunteer made their lives more manageable and less stressful, improved their outlook on life, and increased the amount of support they had for living with HIV. The benefits of being paired with a volunteer were demonstrated on measures of psychological functioning as well. Specifically, PWAs who were paired with volunteer buddies or home helpers appeared less susceptible to the ill effects of avoidant coping than were those PWAs who did not have a buddy/home helper. The data indicate that having an avoidant coping style (i.e., trying to ignore the situation, to "wish it away," or using alcohol/drugs to feel better) has a negative impact on psychological functioning (i.e., more signs of negative psychological functioning, such as depression, anxiety, and fatigue, and fewer signs of positive psychological functioning, such as positive outlook, vigor, and optimism). PWAs with volunteer buddies or home helpers did not show this common relationship between avoidant coping and negative psychological functioning, presumably because PWAs with buddies/home helpers developed more active coping strategies (i.e., seeking out social support, obtaining more information, making a "plan of attack").

There is some evidence that having a volunteer buddy or home helper may lead to better health too. First, those PWAs who were paired with a volunteer indicated that having a volunteer had led to improved physical health. Second, having a volunteer buddy or home helper, when combined with active coping strategies, led to more preventive health behaviors, such as maintaining a good diet, exercising regularly, and getting adequate sleep. Examination of possible volunteer effects on indicators of physical health (e.g., subjective health ratings, health care utilization, number of AIDS-related symptoms) yielded inconsistent results. Thus, PWAs noted improvements in quality of life, psychological functioning, and physical health as a result of participation in the volunteer buddy/home helper program. Although the data suggest that PWAs with a buddy or home helper used more active coping strategies, exhibited better psychological functioning, and took better care of their health, these psychological and behavioral effects may not always have been enough to compensate for the effects of HIV on their immune systems.

In answer to the question "Can volunteers make a difference?", then, an examination of the helping relationships between AIDS volunteers and their client PWAs suggests that the answer is "yes." Further perspective on the question of the effectiveness of volunteers is provided by a recent meta-analysis of the effectiveness of mentoring programs (e.g., Big Brothers/Big

Sisters) on youth outcomes (e.g., school attendance, arrest rates, courses passed, grade point average). Specifically, DuBois, Holloway, Valentine, and Cooper (2002) meta-analyzed the findings from 55 evaluations of such youth mentoring programs. Averaging across all studies, they found that having a mentor had only a small-to-modest effect on youth outcomes. However, when effects of empirically or theoretically sound mentoring models were compared to effects of programs not based on sound models, the results were clear: Those mentoring programs that were based on sound theory and research (e.g., offering parent support and involvement, support groups for mentors, mentor training, mentor supervision) produced strong positive effects, whereas those programs that did not have these foundations yielded very small effects. These results suggest that volunteer programs may benefit their recipients. In order to maximize these benefits, however, programs should be implemented and administered in line with theory-based considerations or data-based "best practices."

Benefits and Costs to Volunteers

Answers to the question about benefits to volunteers are provided by examinations of whether the experience of being a volunteer changes people's thoughts, feelings, and actions. Such changes were apparent among volunteers at several AIDS service organizations, who were tracked over the course of their service as volunteers (Omoto & Snyder, 1996). Following their service, AIDS volunteers reported statistically significant increases in their self-esteem and self-confidence, their knowledge about AIDS and the community affected by AIDS, their sense of control, and their practice of safe sex. These volunteers also claimed that their service led to decreases in their feelings of loneliness and helplessness, perceived personal risk for contracting HIV/AIDS, pity for PWAs, and stress in other areas of their lives. Moreover, these volunteers typically reported high levels of satisfaction throughout their terms of service.

Studies of volunteering in other domains also provide evidence of the beneficial effects of volunteering for the volunteers themselves. Although some of these studies suffer from methodological shortcomings (e.g., selection effects, lack of control groups, and lack of longitudinal approaches; Wilson & Musick, 1999), their findings do suggest that volunteering can produce social, attitudinal, behavioral, psychological, financial, and health improvements in those who serve others. In one study of older volunteers, nearly 85% experienced an overall increase in the size of their network of friends as a result of their service (Morrow-Howell, Kinnevy, & Mann, 1999). Other studies have suggested that volunteering promotes more favorable attitudes toward the client population being served (e.g., Holzberg & Gewirtz, 1963; Holzberg, Gewirtz, & Ebner, 1964; Youniss & Yates,

1997). More generally, participation in volunteer programs may promote feelings of civic obligation and stronger desires to participate in civic affairs (e.g., Riedel, 2002). On a related note, there are indications of linkages between volunteering while in college and later community involvement (e.g., Fendrich, 1993; McAdam, 1988). Furthermore, it appears that antisocial behavior may decline as a function of volunteering: Adolescents who perform volunteer service have been shown to be less likely to become involved in deviant behaviors, such as skipping class, using drugs, getting suspended from school, and becoming involved in the criminal justice system (Allen, Kuperminc, Philliber, & Herre, 1994; Eccles & Barber, 1999; Uggen & Janikula, 1999). The limited available data suggest that, for adults, volunteering has little impact on employment status (e.g., having a job) but may lead to better earning and more prestigious occupation (e.g., having a better-paying job; Wilson & Musick, 1999).

Given the methodological caveats noted above, most of the research examining mental health of volunteers also suggests positive effects. For instance, one meta-analytic review showed a positive association between volunteering among the elderly and life satisfaction (Wheeler, Gorey, & Greenblatt, 1998). Another study indicated a negative relationship between volunteering and depression, but only for those over 65 years of age (Wilson & Musick, 1999). Yet another recent study reported positive relationships between hours spent volunteering and life satisfaction, even after controlling for self-selection and maturation effects (Thoits & Hewitt, 2001). Finally, one review of the service learning literature suggests a multitude of positive psychological effects (Stukas, Clary, & Snyder, 1999). For instance, adolescents and young adults who take part in service learning showed increased personal efficacy, self-esteem, confidence (e.g., Giles & Eyler, 1994, 1998; Williams, 1991; Yates & Youniss, 1996), moral reasoning (Conrad & Hedin, 1981, 1982), problem-solving abilities (e.g., Eyler, Root, & Giles, 1998), empathic understanding (Yogev & Ronen, 1982), general complexity of thought on social issues (Batchelder & Root, 1994), skills on specific tasks (Eyler & Giles, 1997), positive attitudes toward the client population served (Myers-Lipton, 1996; Youniss & Yates, 1997) and school in general (Williams, 1991), social and personal responsibility (e.g., Conrad & Hedin, 1981), altruistic motivation (Yogev & Ronen, 1982), intrinsic work values and importance of career and community involvement (Johnson, Beebe, Mortimer, & Snyder, 1998). In some studies, the effects are facilitated when students' volunteer experiences provide some amount of autonomy, collegiality, reflection, and responsibility (Conrad & Hedin, 1981, 1982; Stukas, Clary, & Snyder, 1999). Moreover, the positive effects may be strongest among students considered "at risk" (e.g., history of discipline problems, poor grades; Follman & Muldoon, 1997).

Volunteering may include physical benefits as well, although research has not revealed health improvements in volunteers, per se. However, studies suggest that volunteering among those who are especially suscepti-ble to health problems—the elderly—may help stave off health problems. In one such study, researchers who tracked elderly respondents over a 4-year period found a higher mortality rate among those who did not volun-teer than those who did, even after controlling for physical health during the initial assessment (Sabin, 1993). The nature of the relationship be-tween the *amount* of volunteering by the elderly and mortality still re-quires elucidation. Some studies suggest a positive linear relationship (Oman, Thoreson, & McMahon, 1999), whereas other studies show greatest longevity among elderly, moderately active volunteers (Musick, Herzog, & House, 1999). Regardless of the form of the relationship, two processes may be at work. First, volunteering often involves expansion of one's social network, which may in turn promote increased physical activ-ity and sources of social support (House, Landis, & Umberson, 1988; Morrow-Howell et al., 1999; Wilson & Musick, 1999). Second, the in-creased activity of older volunteers may decrease the amount of self-absorption that is common among older adults (Oman et al., 1999).

Having presented evidence suggesting that volunteers can benefit from their service, it is also important to recognize that there may be costs involved in volunteering as well. The most obvious costs are financial. Vol-unteers are often required to take time away from work to fulfill their ser-vice, and many volunteer activities may involve out-of-pocket expenses (e.g., transportation costs to and from the volunteer site, costs of the activ-ities involved). Volunteers also may incur psychological and emotional costs. For example, volunteering often requires entering into new and pos-sibly threatening situations (e.g., serving food in an inner-city food kitchen) or coming into contact with people who are sick and suffering (e.g., volunteers who choose to serve as companions to persons with HIV/AIDS befriend people who may die within the volunteer's term of service).

In addition to these possibilities of financial and emotional strain, vol-unteers potentially incur social isolation and possible stigmatization that may come from being a volunteer. For example, volunteers may experi-ence conflicts between spending time as a volunteer and spending time with their friends, family, and other members of their social networks. In-deed, in one study of AIDS volunteers, those who had more extensive so-cial networks were likely to serve as volunteers for shorter periods of time, suggesting that they may have terminated their volunteer service early as one way of resolving the tension between spending time as a volunteer and spending time with members of their social networks (Omoto & Snyder, 1995). Moreover, people who serve as AIDS volunteers often report that they have been made to feel uncomfortable, embarrassed, and even stigma-tized as a result of their service to this population—feelings that may pre-cede the volunteer "burnout" that may be experienced especially among those who do not anticipate the potential stigmatization involved in serving as an AIDS volunteer (e.g., Snyder et al., 1999). To some extent, the feelings of stigmatization experienced by AIDS volunteers may be an instance of the "courtesy stigma" that may accrue to thos who associate with members of stigmatized groups (Goffman, 1963)—an interpretation that is supported by the results of a series of laboratory and field-based studies (Snyder et al., 1999). However, stigmatization does not necessarily occur in all volunteer contexts. Although stigmatization is a common feeling among those who seek help from public and private service agencies (Wyers, 1977), the kind of stigmatization experienced by AIDS volunteers may be unique to volunteers who work for controversial causes or clientele. Put simply, there are likely to be social and psychic costs associated with some forms of volunteerism.

Benefits and Costs to Society

Establishing the benefits of volunteerism to society can be addressed, in part, by considering the statistics published by Independent Sector (2001) on volunteering and contributing to charitable organizations. The rate of volunteerism in America is estimated at about 44% of people over the age of 21 (30%, if looking at frequent volunteer service), and volunteers serve an average of 24 hours per month, with organizations saving about $16.05 per volunteer hour. These numbers suggest a total dollar value of volunteerism to be about $239.2 billion for 2001. For comparison purposes, this dollar amount represents about 55% of the expenditures of the U.S. Department of Health and Human Services for that same period (U.S. Department of Health and Human Services, 2002). Thus, the monetary value of the services provided by volunteers is substantial.

The value of voluntary service in providing needed services, introducing youth to valuable experiences related to social issues, and offering means by which people may utilize their skills has been recognized by policy makers as well. For example, many state legislatures and school boards acknowledge the value of public service by establishing service learning requirements for graduation (Stukas et al., 1999). Initiatives at the federal level also demonstrate the importance of service. In the early 1990s, the U.S. Congress passed the National and Community Service Act and National Service Trust Act, thereby creating the Corporation for National and Community Service and realizing then-President Clinton's vision of a domestic corps of volunteers to provide services in needy areas (e.g., AmeriCorps, Learn and Serve, Senior Corps).

The largest and most publicized of these programs, AmeriCorps, provides health insurance, education awards, and stipends to many of its volunteers to cover their costs of living. Thus, although many of these individuals do not necessarily meet a strict definition of volunteering as giving service without compensation, they do provide needed services for very little financial gain. The effects of this program illustrate the value of volunteerism at the societal level. Evaluations of this program suggest that, overall, members' services are extremely helpful in strengthening communities, improving communication and coordination between service organizations, and enhancing the life skills and civic responsibility among members (Aguirre International, 1999). These benefits complement the gains experienced by those who receive volunteer services.

Beyond the specific programs and services offered, communities in which individuals actively volunteer and work to meet each other's needs send powerful messages to their members. First, these activities provide concrete evidence to people that services are potentially available to individuals in need. Second, because these activities are often public ones, they also may help to instill a norm of reciprocal helping and care giving. In these ways, widespread volunteerism can promote the creation of a caring community environment in which citizens are willing to assume responsibility for assisting those in need.

CONCLUDING COMMENTS

In this chapter, we have examined volunteerism as a form of helping and prosocial action, considering both theoretical and empirical perspectives on the motivational foundations of decisions to become a volunteer and to continue in service as a volunteer. Of particular concern to us have been the benefits and the costs of volunteerism. In this regard, the data are clear: Volunteerism produces benefits for those who receive the services of volunteers, for the volunteers themselves, for the volunteer service organizations, and for society as a whole. From this empirical perspective, then, we can perhaps argue that, based on its demonstrable benefits, volunteerism reflects one of the good sides of human nature—an active, purposeful, agentic side, in which individuals seek out opportunities to act in ways that, at one and the same time, allow them to benefit from and fulfill their own personal motivations and to perform good works for others and for society.

As such, it is quite understandable that societies might seek to promote volunteerism. Indeed, there have been many large-scale media campaigns designed to encourage people to volunteer, and efforts to promote volunteerism can be informed by the results of research on volunteerism (e.g., Snyder & Omoto, 2000, 2001; Snyder et al., in press). As we have discussed, there are also potential costs for those who volunteer and for organizations that rely heavily on volunteers to provide their services and programs. All of these costs need to be appraised realistically and counteracted by organizations dependent on the services of volunteers and by communities and societies seeking to instill cultures of caring as they attempt to promote volunteerism. In fact, greater appreciation and understanding of the benefits and costs of volunteerism may go a long way toward increasing the number and types of prosocial actions—and, ultimately, the degree of goodness in a society.

ACKNOWLEDGMENTS

The preparation of this chapter and the conduction of the research reported in it have been supported by grants from the American Foundation for AIDS Research and the National Institute of Mental Health to Mark Snyder and Allen M. Omoto.

REFERENCES

Aguirre International. (1999). *Making a difference: Impact of AmeriCorps State/ National Direct on members and communities 1994–95 and 1995–96.* San Mateo, CA: Author.

Allen, J. P., Kuperminc, G., Philliber, S., & Herre, K. (1994). Programmatic prevention of adolescent problem behaviors: The role of autonomy, relatedness, and volunteer service in the Teen Outreach Program. *American Journal of Community Psychology, 22,* 617–638.

Batchelder, T. H., & Root, S. (1994). Effects of an undergraduate program to integrate academic learning and service: Cognitive, prosocial cognitive, and identity outcomes. *Journal of Adolescence, 17,* 341–355.

Brudney, J. L., & Duncombe, W. D. (1992). An economic evaluation of paid, volunteer, and mixed staffing options for public services. *Public Administration Review, 52,* 474–481.

Cable News Network. (1997). *Mother Teresa: Angel of mercy* [Online]. Retrieved September 9, 2002, from *http://cnn.com/WORLD/9709/mother.teresa/profile/index.html*

Clary, E. G., & Snyder, M. (1991). A functional analysis of altruism and prosocial behavior: The case of volunteerism. In M. Clark (Ed.), *Prosocial behavior, review of personality and social psychology* (Vol. 12, pp. 119–148). London/ New Delhi: Sage.

Clary, E. G., Snyder, M., Ridge, R. D., Copeland, J., Stukas, A. A., Haugen, J., & Miene, P. (1998). Understanding and assessing the motivations of volunteers: A functional approach. *Journal of Personality and Social Psychology, 74,* 1516–1530.

Clary, E. G., Snyder, M., Ridge, R. D., Miene, P., & Haugen, J. (1994). Matching messages to motives in persuasion: A functional approach to promoting volunteerism. *Journal of Applied Social Psychology, 24,* 1129–1149.

Conrad, D., & Hedin, D. (1981). National assessment of experiential education: Summary and implications. *Journal of Experiential Education, 4,* 6–20.

Conrad, D., & Hedin, D. (1982). The impact of experiential education on adolescent development. *Child and Youth Services, 4,* 57–76.

Crain, A. L., Omoto, A. M., & Snyder, M. (1998, April). *What if you can't always get what you want? Testing a functional approach to volunteerism.* Paper presented at the annual meeting of the Midwestern Psychological Association, Chicago.

Crain, A. L., Snyder, M., & Omoto, A. M. (2000, May). *Volunteers make a difference: Relationship quality, active coping, and functioning among PWAs with volunteer buddies.* Paper presented at the annual meeting of the Midwestern Psychological Association, Chicago.

Dalsimer, J. P. (1986). Financial records and the value of volunteers. *Nonprofit World, 4,* 17–37.

Davis, M. H., Hall, J. A., & Meyer, M. (2003). The first year: Influences on the satisfaction, involvement, and persistence of new community volunteers. *Personality and Social Psychology Bulletin, 29,* 248–260.

Dovidio, J. F. (1984). Helping behavior and altruism: An empirical and conceptual overview. In L. Berkowitz (Ed.), *Advances in experimental social psychology* (Vol. 17, pp. 361–427). Orlando, FL: Academic Press.

Dubois, D. L., Holloway, B. E., Valentine, J. C., & Cooper, H. (2002). Effectiveness of mentoring programs for youth: A meta-analytic review. *American Journal of Community Psychology, 30,* 157–197.

Eagly, A. H., & Chaiken, S. (1998). Attitude structure and function. In D. T. Gilbert, S. T. Fiske, & G. Lindzey (Eds.), *The handbook of social psychology* (Vol. 1, 4th ed., pp. 269–322). Boston: McGraw-Hill

Eccles, J., & Barber, B. (1999). Student council, volunteering, basketball, and marching band: What kind of extracurricular activity matters? *Journal of Adolescent Research, 14,* 10–43.

Eyler, J., & Giles, D. E., Jr. (1997). The importance of program quality in service-learning. In A. S. Waterman (Ed.), *Service-learning: Applications from the research* (pp. 57–76). Mahwah, NJ: Erlbaum.

Eyler, J., Root, S., & Giles, D. E., Jr. (1998). Service-learning and the development of expert citizens: Service-learning and cognitive science. In R. G. Bringle & D. K. Duffy (Eds.), *With service in mind: Concepts and models for service-learning in psychology* (pp. 85–100). Washington, DC: American Association of Higher Education.

Fendrich, J. M. (1993). *Ideal citizens: The legacy of the civil rights movement.* Albany: State University of New York Press.

Follman, J., & Muldoon, K. (1997). Florida learn & serve 1995–96: What were the outcomes? *NASSP Bulletin, 81,* 29–36.

Giles, D. E., Jr., & Eyler, J. (1994). The impact of a college community service laboratory on students' personal, social, and cognitive outcomes. *Journal of Adolescence, 17,* 327–339.

Giles, D. E., Jr., & Eyler, J. (1998). A service-learning research agenda for the next five years. *New Directions for Teaching and Learning, 1,* 65–72.

Goffman, E. (1963). *Stigma: Notes on the management of spoiled identity.* Englewood Cliffs, NJ: Prentice-Hall.

Holzberg, J. D., & Gewirtz, H. (1963). A method of altering attitudes toward mental illness. *Psychiatric Quarterly Supplement, 37,* 56–61.

Holzberg, J. D., Gewirtz, H., & Ebner, E. (1964). Changes in moral judgment and self-acceptance in college students as a function of companionship with hospitalized mental patients. *Journal of Consulting Psychology, 28,* 299–303.

House, J. S., Landis, K. R., & Umberson, D. (1988). Social relationships and health. *Science, 241,* 540–545.

Independent Sector. (1988). *Giving and volunteering in the United States: Findings from a national survey, 1988.* Washington, DC: Author.

Independent Sector. (2001). *Giving and volunteering in the United States: Findings from a national survey.* Washington, DC: Author.

Johnson, M. K., Beebe, T., Mortimer, J. T., & Snyder, M. (1998). Volunteerism in adolescence: A process perspective. *Journal of Research on Adolescence, 8,* 309–332.

Karn, G. N. (1983). The true dollar value of volunteers. *Journal of Volunteer Administration, 1,* 1–19.

Katz, D. (1960). The functional approach to the study of attitudes. *Public Opinion Quarterly, 24,* 163–204.

Latané, B., & Darley, J. M. (1970). *The unresponsive bystander: Why doesn't he help?* New York: Appleton-Century-Crofts.

Lindsay, J. J., Snyder, M., & Omoto, A. M. (2003, May). *Volunteers' impact on psychological and physical functioning of persons living with HIV.* Paper presented at the annual meeting of the American Psychological Society, Atlanta, GA.

McAdam, D. (1988). *Freedom summer.* New York: Oxford University Press

Morrow-Howell, N., Kinnevy, S., & Mann, M. (1999). The perceived benefits of participating in volunteer and educational activities. *Journal of Gerontological Social Work, 32,* 65–80.

Musick, M. A., Herzog, A. R., & House, J. S. (1999). Volunteering and mortality among older adults: Findings from a national sample. *Journal of Gerontology, 54B,* S173–S180.

Myers-Lipton, S. J. (1996). Effect of a comprehensive service-learning program on college students' level of modern racism. *Michigan Journal of Community Service Learning, 3,* 44–54.

O'Brien, L. T., Crain, A. L., Omoto, A. M., & Snyder, M. (2000, May). *Matching motivations to outcomes: Implications for persistence in service.* Paper presented at the annual meeting of the Midwestern Psychological Association, Chicago.

Okun, M. A., Barr, A., & Herzog, A. R. (1998). Motivation to volunteer by older adults: A test of competing measurement models. *Psychology and Aging, 13,* 608–621.

Oman, D., Thoresen, C. E., & McMahon, K. (1999). Volunteerism and mortality among the community-dwelling elderly. *Journal of Health Psychology, 4,* 301–316.

Omoto, A. M., & Snyder, M. (1993). AIDS volunteers and their motivations: Theoretical issues and practical concerns. *Nonprofit Management and Leadership, 4,* 157–176.

Omoto, A.M., & Snyder, M. (1995). Sustained helping without obligation: Motivation, longevity of service, and perceived attitude change among AIDS volunteers. *Journal of Personality and Social Psychology, 68,* 671–686.

Omoto, A. M., & Snyder, M (1996). [*A longitudinal study of AIDS volunteers*].

Unpublished raw data, University of Kansas, Lawrence, and University of Minnesota, Minneapolis.

Omoto, A. M., & Snyder, M. (1999). [*A study of helping relationships between AIDS volunteers and their clients*] Unpublished raw data, University of Kansas, Lawrence, and University of Minnesota, Minneapolis.

Omoto, A. M., Snyder, M., & Martino, S. C. (2000). Volunteerism and the life course: Investigating age-related agendas for action. *Basic and Applied Social Psychology, 22,* 181–198.

Omoto, A. M., Snyder, M., & Smith, D. M. (1999). [*A study of the recruitment of volunteers*]. Unpublished raw data, University of Kansas, Lawrence, and University of Minnesota, Minneapolis.

Penner, L. A., & Finkelstein, M. A. (1998). Dispositional and structural determinants of volunteerism. *Journal of Personality and Social Psychology, 74,* 525–537.

Riedel, E. (2002). The impact of high school community service programs on students' feelings of civic obligation. *American Politics Research, 30,* 499–527.

Sabin, E. P. (1993). Social relationships and mortality among the elderly. *Journal of Applied Gerontology, 12,* 44–60.

Schroeder, D. A., Penner, L. A., Dovidio, J. F., & Piliavin, J. A. (1995). *The psychology of helping and altruism: Problems and puzzles.* New York: McGraw Hill.

Smith, D. H. (1981). Altruism, volunteers, and volunteerism. *Journal of Voluntary Action Research, 10,* 21–36.

Smith, M., Bruner, J., & White, R. (1956). *Opinions and personality.* New York: Wiley.

Smith, D. M., Omoto, A. M., & Snyder, M. (2001, June). *Motivation matching and recruitment of volunteers: A field study.* Paper presented at the annual meeting of the American Psychological Society, Toronto.

Snyder, M. (1993). Basic research and practical problems: The promise of a "functional" personality and social psychology. *Personality and Social Psychology Bulletin, 19,* 251–264.

Snyder, M., & Cantor, N. (1998). Understanding personality and social behavior: A functionalist strategy. In D. Gilbert, S. Fiske, & G. Lindzey (Eds.), *The handbook of social psychology,* (4th ed., vol. 1, pp. 635–679). New York: McGraw-Hill.

Snyder, M., Clary, E. G., & Stukas, A. A. (2000). The functional approach to volunteerism. In G. R. Maio & J. M. Olson (Eds.), *Why we evaluate: Functions of attitudes* (pp. 365–393). Mahwah, NJ: Erlbaum.

Snyder, M., & Omoto, A. M. (2000). Doing good for self and society: Volunteerism and the psychology of citizen participation. In M. Van Vugt, M. Snyder, T. Tyler, & A. Biel (Eds.), *Cooperation in modern society: Promoting the welfare of communities, states, and organizations* (pp. 127–141). London: Routledge

Snyder, M., & Omoto, A. M. (2001). Basic research and practical problems: Volunteerism and the psychology of individual and collective action. In W. Wosinska, R. Cialdini, D. Barrett, & J. Reykowski (Eds.), *The practice of social influence in multiple cultures* (pp. 287–307). Mahwah, NJ: Erlbaum.

Snyder, M., Omoto, A. M., & Crain, A.L. (1999). Punished for their good deeds:

Stigmatization of AIDS volunteers. *American Behavioral Scientist, 42,* 1175–1192.

Snyder, M., Omoto, A. M., & Smith, D. M. (in press). The role of persuasion strategies in motivating individual and collective action. In E. Borgida, J. Sullivan, & E. Reidel (Eds.), *The political psychology of democratic citizenship.* New York: Cambridge University Press.

Stukas, A. A., Jr., Clary, E. G., & Snyder, M. (1999). Service learning: Who benefits and why? *Social Policy Report: Society for Research in Child Development, 13,* 1–19.

Thoits, P. A., & Hewitt, L. N. (2001). Volunteer work and well-being. *Journal of Health and Social Behavior, 42,* 115–131.

Uggen, C., & Janikula, J. (1999). Volunteerism and arrest in the transition to adulthood. *Social Forces, 78,* 331–362.

U. S. Department of Health and Human Services (2002). *FY2003 President's budget for HHS: Budget in brief* [Online]. Retrieved November 13, 2002, from *http://www.hhs.gov/budget/docbudget.htm*

Wheeler, J. A., Gorey, K. M., & Goldblatt, B. (1998). The beneficial effects of volunteering for older volunteers and the people they serve: A meta-analysis. *International Journal of Aging and Human Development, 47,* 69–79.

Williams, R. (1991). The impact of field education on student development: Research findings. *Journal of Cooperative Education, 27,* 29–45.

Wilson, J. (2000). Volunteering. *Annual Review of Sociology, 26,* 215–240.

Wilson, J., & Musick, M. (1999). The effects of volunteering on the volunteer. *Law and Contemporary Problems, 62,* 141–168.

Wyers, N. L. (1977). Shame and public dependency: A literature review. *Journal of Sociology and Social Welfare, 4,* 955–966.

Yates, M., & Youniss, J. (1996). A developmental perspective on community service in adolescence. *Social Development, 5,* 85–111.

Yogev, A., & Ronen, R. (1982). Cross-age tutoring: Effects on tutors' attributes. *Journal of Educational Research, 75,* 261–268.

Youniss, J., & Yates, M. (1997). *Community service and social responsibility in youth.* Chicago: University of Chicago Press.

CHAPTER 18

REDUCING HOSTILITY AND BUILDING COMPASSION

Lessons from the Jigsaw Classroom

ELLIOT ARONSON

> I and the public know
> What all schoolchildren learn,
> Those to whom evil is done
> Do evil in return.
>
> —W. H. Auden

This chapter is more like a story than a scientific essay—a story about converting "evil" into "good"—or, more specifically—hostility into empathy and compassion. If Dickens had not already co-opted the title, this story could be called "A Tale of Two Cities." The cities I write about are Littleton, Colorado, and Austin, Texas.

LITTLETON AND THE LIKE:
EVIL PEOPLE OR EVIL ACTIONS?

Let us begin in Littleton. On April 20, 1999, two Columbine High School seniors, Eric Harris and Dylan Klebold—heavily armed and angry as hell—walked into their school building and went on a killing rampage. By the time they were stopped, 15 people lay dead (including the shooters) and 23 were injured—some with severe wounds. It was the worst massacre of students by students in our nation's history. It was undeniably an evil act. Moreover, it was only one of 18 rampage shootings that took place in our nation's schools just before and after the turn of the millennium.

Some newspaper and TV pundits, in trying to understand the Columbine tragedy, were quick to describe the perpetrators as *evil.* Typical of these analyses is an op-ed piece by one of my favorite columnists, Joanne Jacobs. She asserted that it was idle to try to find reasons for the behavior of Harris and Klebold. According to Jacobs, they committed that act not because they came from broken homes, were zonked out on drugs, or were immersed in violent video games, but simply because they were evil young men. My guess is that her analysis reflects a rather pervasive attitude in this country. That is, when thinking about the concept of evil, most people typically think of particular individuals—individuals who personify evil. Adolph Hitler, Saddam Hussein, and Osama bin Laden would probably make any American's top 10 list of "evil people." They are certainly different from the "good people"—such as Mahatma Gandhi, Albert Schweitzer, and Mother Teresa.

The pervasive belief that all evil acts are committed by a particular type of "evil" person is a form of wishful thinking caused by a need to disassociate. If we can label some people as *evil,* then we do not need to worry about ourselves, our friends, or our relatives committing evil acts— because *we* are not evil people. The solution seems simple enough: All we need to do is develop some sort of "evilness test." Then we can identify, in advance, those people who might commit atrocious acts, remove them from society—and we good people will be safe.

The overwhelming majority of experimental social psychologists would not share this view. From the very first experiment conducted in this field (Triplett, 1898), social psychology researchers have focused attention primarily on the effect of social influence on behavior. At least since Stanley Milgram performed his landmark experiments on obedience (1963), social psychologists have been deeply impressed by the power of the social situation to affect the behavior of ordinary people (like you and me) in extraordinary ways. When two out of three ordinary citizens will deliver potentially lethal shocks to an innocent victim in blind obedience to authority, the concept of "an evil perpetrator" loses its meaning.

The data from countless social-psychological experiments leads us to conclude that, when placed in a powerful social situation, most ordinary human beings can be induced to commit unappetizing actions—actions neither they nor their friends could have predicted. It is clear that Harris and Klebold fit this description to a tee. Neither observations of their day-to-day behavior in school nor a battery of personality tests would have led to the prediction that they were soon to go on a killing rampage (Aronson, 2000). The U.S. Secret Service agrees. The Secret Service conducted an intensive study of 41 student perpetrators of school shootings from

1974 to 2000 and could find no way to distinguish perpetrators from nonperpetrators on the basis of personality, attitudes, or demographics (Vossekuil, Reddy, Fein, Borum, & Modzeleski, 2000). The only factor that differentiated them was gender—but, given that 49% of the population is male, that is hardly a useful piece of information.

Social psychologists have learned that it is not only more accurate to think in terms of evil *actions* than evil people, but it is also more useful because it allows us to specify the social situations likely to produce the behavior in large proportions of the population. Ultimately, this specification might lead us to find ways of changing such provocative situations so that the behavior can be modified. Such an approach, admittedly, is a highly optimistic one. As a social psychologist, I have spent a considerable proportion of my life trying to figure out how to prevent or modify dysfunctional attitudes and behavior (such as prejudice, bullying, and destructive aggression) and to turn the evil actions that result from the attitudes and behavior into humane actions—for example, to turn hostility into compassion.

TAUNTING AND BULLYING AS ROOT CAUSE

In the wake of the Columbine massacre, several media commentators have identified what they regard as one or more possible situational causes to the recent spate of school massacres. The litany is a now-familiar one that includes the ubiquitous presence of hostile aggression in films, TV, and video games; the easy availability of guns in this country; lax or abusive parents; the lack of moral training in schools; and a general disrespect for teachers and other authority figures among today's youngsters.

My own study of the Columbine tragedy and other recent school rampage killings has led me to a different conclusion: Although it is likely that at least some of these factors contributed to these killings, they are not at the root of the problem. Rather, the root cause of the shootings is the poisonous social atmosphere that exists in almost every public school in this country—an atmosphere permeated by daily incidents of exclusion, taunting, bullying, and humiliation. Just about every school in this country consists of social cliques that are rigidly organized into an ironclad hierarchy, with athletes, cheerleaders, "regular guys," "preppies," and class officers at the top. At the bottom of the social pyramid is a much larger group. These are youngsters who are considered to be in the "wrong" race, the "wrong" ethnic group, are shy, dress differently, are too short, too tall, too thin, too fat, too "nerdy," or just do not fit in easily. Interviews with high school and middle school students in all parts of the country have indicated that just about every student in a given school can name the hierarchy of ingroups and outgroups and can identify where each of their classmates falls in that hierarchy (Aronson, 2000; Gibbs, 1999; Lewin, 1999; Tounsend, 1999).

Those youngsters in the relatively small ingroup want to differentiate themselves from the losers, but their behavior typically goes far beyond merely deciding not to associate with them. Usually, their shunning is active rather than passive. In my interviews with high school students, several reported a version of the following scenario:

> "In the cafeteria, I emerge from the food line with my lunch on a tray. I am looking around for a place to sit. Ah, I see a table that is almost half empty. I head over there. Some of the kids see me coming and immediately begin spreading out on the benches, pretending there is no room. I come closer. One of them says, 'Not here, freak!' The others laugh loudly. I turn crimson. I turn around and start looking for another mostly empty table. I spot one and head over there. But the same thing happens. Now, when I look around, the whole room looks hostile. I can't risk that happening again. I walk out of the cafeteria and sit on the steps by myself. Why do they hate me so much? What have I done to them?"

In contrast, getting accepted is seen as a huge reward. For example, at Chaparral High School in Scottsdale, Arizona, the social geography is so clearly mapped out that it looks like an intentional design. But it is not—it is simply the way the students group themselves. Nevertheless, the groupings are clear and inviolable. At lunchtime, the athletes and their closest friends occupy the center table outdoors. In back of that table are some picnic tables occupied by students of slightly less important social status. Here one finds an array of cheerleaders, well-dressed preppies, and members of the student government.

> "You wouldn't dare come sit out here if you didn't know the people," said Lauren Barth, a sophomore cheerleader. "But once you're in with the girls, everyone is really friendly to you. When I made cheerleader, it was like I was just set." (in Lewin, 1999)

Most students do not ever become "just set." Active exclusion is minor compared to the verbal abuse to which many of these youngsters are subjected. When I was very young, there was a ditty that little kids being taunted sometimes chanted, in a singsong voice, to their tormentors: "Sticks and stones / May break my bones, / But names will never hurt me." I fear that claim that "names will never hurt me" is more wishful thinking than real. Names hurt plenty. Kids were chanting it when I was in elementary school some 60 years ago. They are still chanting it today. And the torment often goes beyond name calling and taunting. Some kids are shoved into lockers, others are pushed around or roughed up, some have soft drinks poured on them (Aronson, 2000; Lewin, 1999; Tounsend, 1999).

Exclusion and taunting are extremely widespread in our schools. Even physical bullying is more common than most adults think. Recently, the National Institute of Child Health and Human Development conducted a survey of more than 15,000 U.S. schoolchildren and found that 16% reported that they had been bullied by other youngsters during the past year (National Institutes of Health, 2001). This is undoubtedly an underestimate; the data are based on self-reports, and most children and adolescents are reluctant to admit that they are victims of bullying. My guess is that the actual percentage is a good deal higher.

In most cases, those near the bottom of the social pyramid suffer in silence—but they *do* suffer—retreating further and further from the mainstream. The more they are ignored, excluded, taunted, or bullied, the further away they drift. For a great many youngsters, the high school atmosphere is extremely unpleasant. For some, it is a living hell. Given this kind of social atmosphere, and given the fact that teenagers spend almost half their waking hours imbedded in that atmosphere, it should not be surprising that occasionally, some of these students are driven over the edge.

It is tragic that, in extreme circumstances, "going over the edge" can result in rampage killings, but research has shown that such is often the case outside of the school environment as well. James Gilligan (1992), the director of psychiatric services for the Massachusetts State Prison System, spent over a decade working closely with a wide range of male killers, including rampage killers. He concluded that virtually all rampage killers share an overwhelming sense of shame brought on by rejection and humiliation. According to Gilligan, their violent behavior toward others is an attempt to replace shame with pride, an attempt to gain the respect that they felt was withheld from them. Gilligan's analysis (published several years prior to the Columbine massacre) is eerily confirmed by a videotape Harris and Klebold left behind: "Isn't it fun finally to get the respect that we are going to deserve?" asks Harris, clutching the sawed-off shotgun he was about to use against his classmates. The U.S. Secret Service report is in agreement. Going back to 1974, the Secret Service found that bullying, taunting, and other forms or harassment were found to be at the heart of the overwhelming majority of acts involving targeted lethal school violence in this country (Vossekuil et al., 2000).

Blessedly, going over the edge is rarely lethal among high school students, but the consequences of rejection are always negative. For example, several laboratory experiments by Baumeister, Williams, and their colleagues have demonstrated that exclusion and ostracism produce a wealth of negative behaviors in the target person—including a decrement in cognitive functioning, an increase in aggressiveness, and feelings of sadness (Baumeister, Twenge, & Nuss, 2002; Twenge, Catanese, & Baumeister, 2002; Williams & Zadro, 2001). Outside of the laboratory, in the day-in, day-out school situation, feelings of sadness frequently result in full-scale depression, and the depression sometimes results in the contemplation of, or attempt at, suicide. Recent statistics are chilling: 1 out of 5 teenagers has seriously contemplated suicide; 1 out of 10 has made an attempt at suicide (Goldberg & Connelly, 1999).

Further indication of the prevalence of rejection, humiliation, and taunting in our schools can be found on teenage Internet chat groups. Immediately following the Columbine massacre, hundreds of teenagers wrote to express their feelings and opinions about that tragic incident. Most of the postings were stunning in the their vivid expressions of anguish and unhappiness caused by the social atmosphere of their school. Specifically, these students described how awful it feels to be rejected and taunted by their more popular classmates. A typical Internet posting was written by a 16-year-old girl:

> "Parents need to realize that a kid is not overreacting all the time they say that no one accepts them. Also, all of the popular conformists need to learn to accept everyone else. Why do they shun everyone who is different?"

Another student wrote:

> "It's like in my school, the preppier kids think they're just everything. People are constantly harassing each other because they're different."

Another wrote:

> "It hurts so much to be seen as different but I have learned to get over it and move on. I think that if we had no cliques or at least others weren't looked down on as much, there would not be a problem."

It is striking to note that, several weeks before the contents of the Harris–Klebold videotape were released, many of the teenage writers were already convinced (correctly, as it turned out) that Harris and Klebold must have been driven to their action by experiences of rejection and exclusion similar to their own. I hasten to add that none of these teenagers condoned the shootings; yet their Internet postings revealed a surprisingly high degree of understanding and empathy for the suffering that Harris and Klebold must have endured. While none of the students posting their comments on the Internet expressed any intention of following the lead of Harris and Klebold, some admitted that they had had fantasies of doing similar things. That should make us sit up and take notice—not so that we can track down those kids and hospitalize them (as some have suggested)—but rather, so that we can try to figure out how to improve the social atmosphere of our schools. It is vital to spare these youngsters (and the millions who suffer in silence) from a continuation of the kinds of experiences that lead to such violent fantasies.

In short, the Columbine tragedy has alerted us to the existence of a serious problem in our schools—and this problem should be considered serious even if *no one* had been killed. Our sons and daughters are experiencing the kind of abuse that none of us would tolerate at our workplace. As the Secret Service report states, if anything like that kind of harassment occurred in the workplace, it would be illegal and subject to prosecution (Vossekuil et al., 2000).

BUILDING EMPATHY AND COMPASSION IN AUSTIN

What makes children and teens oriented toward finding weaknesses in others, then focusing on those weaknesses and proceeding to taunt, exclude, and bully their target? Is it part of being human? Is there a "natural" pecking order that cannot be modified and will inevitably assert itself? For this part of the story it is necessary to turn the clock back a few decades and travel from Littleton, Colorado, to Austin, Texas. The year was 1971. A highly explosive situation had developed in Austin—one that has played out in many cities across the United States. Austin's public schools had recently been desegregated (by court order) and, because the city had always been residentially segregated, white youngsters, African American youngsters, and Mexican American youngsters found themselves sharing the same classroom for the first time in their lives. Within a few weeks, longstanding, smoldering antipathy between these groups produced an atmosphere of turmoil and hostility that exploded into interethnic fistfights in corridors and schoolyards across the city.

The assistant superintendent of the Austin Public School System was a former student of mine. When the problem got out of hand, he called me in and asked me to consult. His aim was a modest one: He was not so ambitious as to believe that we could do much to reduce racial prejudice in the schools; he simply wondered if anything could be done to help students of different racial and ethnic groups avoid openly aggressing against one another while they were attending class or hanging out in the cafeteria or school grounds. My aim was a bit more ambitious. Because the schools were in crisis, I had pretty much of a *carte blanche* to implement any procedure that seemed promising—and I wanted to take full advantage of that situation to see if we could change attitudes and behavior.

Observing Classroom Dynamics

Our first step was to determine exactly what was going on in the classrooms that might be contributing to the problem. Accordingly, I entered the schools with a handful of graduate research assistants and we began observing classroom dynamics. After only a few days spent in systematic observation, my research assistants and I became convinced that the underlying intergroup hostility was probably being exacerbated by the pervasive competitive environment in which youngsters were expected to learn. Specifically, in every classroom we observed, the competition for grades and for the attention and respect of the teacher was intense and relentless.

Needless to say, this competitive environment was not unique to Austin. Competition was, and is, the dominant theme in almost every school in this country. The idea is to beat the other guy. And it begins early. In kindergarten, most kids play an apparently harmless little game called musical chairs. I am sure you remember how it works. The teacher sits down at the piano and plays a little song while the children march around the room. When the music stops, the children rush to the chairs to sit down. But the game is arranged so that there are not enough chairs—there is one less chair than there are children. So if a child is a bit slow or not terribly assertive, he or she gets left without a chair and is out of the game. What does a child learn from this game? I still remember playing that game when I was a child. I was shy and unaccustomed to the rough and tumble of the winner-take-all mentality. Consequently, the first time I played that game, I was among the first to be eliminated. A few of the other kids pointed their fingers at me, and some laughed derisively. I was terribly embarrassed. The next time we played the game, I was hell-bent on avoiding the indignity of being an early loser. So, as soon as the music stopped, I rushed toward an empty chair. If a little girl happened to be in my way, I shoved her aside; I was not going to lose again. The lesson is clear: The other kids are not on your team; they are competing against you for scarce resources. There will be winners and there will be losers. Which do you want to be?

The Process of Education

Let me take a step backward and present a broader view. What I am suggesting is that the classroom curriculum comprises only a small part of what a youngster actually learns in school. Students pay close attention to, and learn from, just about everything that happens in their school. For example, if the building is drafty, has broken windows, unswept floors, grimy walls, cracked linoleum, and leaky toilets, the students get the message that the adult community does not care a lot about their education.

What about the actual process of learning in school? It goes without saying that there are a great many ways to convey information to students. Perhaps we want the students to learn about World War II. The teacher can create two or three lectures about the causes and consequences of that war. Alternatively, the students can simply read the basic facts about World War II in a textbook. As a third option, the teacher can assign students to do their own research in the library, or have students interview people who served in the military or lived through the war period in the United States, Europe, and Asia. To demonstrate what they have learned, students might take a test, write a term paper, or give an oral presentation to the entire class. The teacher might also run the class as if it were a quiz show, where he or she asks questions and the students show their quickness and mastery of the subject by raising their hands as soon as they know the answer.

Each of these methods of conveying and retrieving information sends its own special message to students. Some of these messages may be unintended. Teachers who lecture send the message that they are an expert source of information offering the knowledge deemed important. Teachers who dispatch students to the library send the message that it is useful for students to become skillful researchers as well as learn about the topic at hand. Teachers who require students to interview a war veteran convey the implicit message that not all important information is contained in books or conveyed by people in the teaching profession. Teachers who run their class like a quiz show or contest indicate that quickness, assertiveness, and competitiveness are important aspects of the learning endeavor—and perhaps of life itself.

The point is that the learning students derive from the process of their educational experience is powerful indeed. As implied earlier, in classes where students are expected to raise their hands as soon as they know the answer and take tests graded on a curve, students are thereby encouraged to compete against each other. The implicit message is that the other students are competitors for scarce resources. It would not be surprising, then, if this process were to create tension among peers and discourage trust or friendship among youngsters who were not already friends beforehand.

In American schools, this kind of competitive process is the predominant method employed in most classrooms most of the time. High school students who have gone through 9 or 10 years of participation in such a competitive process are likely to view the world (both inside and outside of school) as one gigantic game of musical chairs, as a dog-eat-dog place where the prizes go to those who are quickest or strongest or most aggressive or most charming or most athletic. Such a process may implicitly encourage students to look for weaknesses or flaws in their peers—to find reasons for excluding or taunting those who falter or seem different or socially awkward—and to think of them as weird or as losers.

When my research assistants and I observed classrooms in Austin in 1971, it was the first time I had spent an entire day in elementary school since 1938. But it brought back a great many unhappy memories because, in terms of the classroom dynamics, very little had changed in those 33 years. Here is a description of a typical fifth-grade classroom that we observed in Austin:

The teacher stands in front of the class, asks a question, and waits for the children to indicate that they know the answer. Most frequently, six to ten youngsters raise their hands. But they do not simply raise their hands; they lift themselves a few inches off their chairs and stretch their arms as high as they can in an attempt to attract the teacher's attention. To say they are eager to be called on is an incredible understatement. Several other students sit quietly with their eyes averted, as if trying to make themselves invisible. These are the ones who do not know the answer. Understandably, they are trying to avoid eye contact with the teacher because they do not want to be called on.

When the teacher calls on one of the eager students, there are looks of disappointment, dismay, and unhappiness on the faces of the other students who were avidly raising their hands but were not called on. If the selected student comes up with the right answer, the teacher smiles, nods approvingly, and goes on to the next question. This is a great reward for the child who happens to be called on and answers correctly. At the same time that the fortunate student is coming up with the right answer and being smiled upon by the teacher, an audible groan can be heard coming from the children who were striving to be called on but were ignored. It is obvious they are disappointed because they missed an opportunity to show the teacher how smart and quick they are. Perhaps they will get an opportunity next time. In the meantime, the students who did not know the answer breathe a sigh of relief. They have escaped humiliation this time.

Upon interviewing several of the teachers, we learned that virtually all of them started the school year with a determination to treat every student equally and encourage all to do their best; nevertheless, the students quickly sorted themselves into different groups. The "winners" were the bright, eager, highly competitive students who fervently raised their hands, participated in discussions, and did well on tests. Understandably, teachers felt gratified that these students responded to their teaching, so they praised and encouraged these students, continued to call on them, and depended on them to keep the class going at a high level and at a reasonable pace.

Then there were the "losers." The teachers reported calling on these students occasionally at the beginning, but they almost invariably did not know the answer or were too shy to speak or could not speak English well. They seemed embarrassed to be in the spotlight; some of the other students made snide comments—sometimes under their breath, occasionally out loud. Because the schools in the poorer section of town were substandard, the African American and the Mexican American youngsters had received a poorer education prior to desegregation. Consequently, in Austin, it was frequently these students who were among the losers. This delineation tended, unfairly, to confirm the unflattering stereotypes that the white kids had about minority groups: Simply put, they considered kids from these groups to be stupid or lazy or both. The minority students also had preconceived notions about white kids—that they were pushy show-offs and teacher's pets. These stereotypes were also confirmed by the way most of the white students behaved in the competitive classroom.

After a while, the teachers typically became discouraged from trying to engage the students who were not doing well and felt it was kinder not to call on them and expose them to ridicule by the other students. In effect, these teachers made a silent pact with the "losers"; they would leave these students alone as long as they were not disruptive. Without really intending to do so, the teachers gave up on these students, and so did the rest of the class. Again, without really intending to do so, the teachers contributed to the difficulty the students were experiencing. After a while, these students tended to give up on themselves as well—perhaps believing that they *were* stupid.

Inventing and Testing the Jigsaw Intervention

It required only a few days of intensive observation and interviews for us to form a fairly clear idea of what was going on in these classrooms. We realized that we needed to do something drastic to shift the emphasis from a relentlessly competitive atmosphere to a more cooperative one. It was in this context that we invented the jigsaw technique.

Here is how the jigsaw classroom works: Students are placed in diverse, six-person learning groups. The day's lesson is divided into six paragraphs, so that each student has one segment of the written material. For example, if the students are to learn about the life of Eleanor Roosevelt, her biography is divided into six parts. Each student has possession of a unique and vital part of the information, which, like the pieces of a jigsaw puzzle, must be put together before anyone can learn the whole picture. The individual must learn his or her own section and teach it to the other members of the group, who do not have any other access to that material. Thus, if Debbie wants to do well on the ensuing exam about the life of Eleanor Roosevelt, she must pay close attention to Millie (who is reciting the information on Roosevelt's girlhood years), to Carol (who is describing Roosevelt's years in the White House), to Carlos (who is addressing Roosevelt's work at the United Nations), and so on.

Initially, at least one or two of the students in each group were already viewed as "losers" by their classmates. Carlos was one such student. Carlos was very shy and insecure in his new surroundings. English was his second language. He spoke it quite well but with an obvious Spanish accent. Try to imagine his experience: He attended an inadequately funded, substandard neighborhood school consisting entirely of Hispanic students like himself for his first 5 years. Then, in 1971, he is bussed across town to the middle-class area of the city and catapulted into a classroom with Anglo students who speak English fluently and seem to know much more than he does about all the subjects taught in the school. They seem eager to make him aware of his inadequacies by groaning when he is called upon to recite, giggling derisively, and mocking his accent.

When we restructured the classroom so that students were now working together in small groups, Carlos was initially terrified. For now, he could no longer slink down in his chair and hide in the back of the room. The jigsaw structure made it necessary for him to speak up when it was his turn to recite. In his first attempt at reporting, he blushed, stammered, and had difficulty articulating the material that he had learned. Skilled in the ways of the competitive classroom, the other students were quick to pounce on Carlos's weakness and began to ridicule him.

One of my research assistants was observing that group and heard some members of Carlos's group make comments such as, "Aw, you don't know it, you're dumb, you're stupid. You don't know what you're doing. You can't even speak English." Instead of admonishing them to "be nice" or "try to cooperate," she made one simple but powerful statement. It went something like this: "Talking like that to Carlos might be fun for you to do, but it's not going to help you learn anything about what Eleanor Roosevelt accomplished at the United Nations—and the exam will be given in about 15 minutes." My assistant was reminding the students that the situation had changed. The same behavior that might have been useful to them individually in the past, when they were competing against each other, was now going to cost them something very important: the chance to do well on the upcoming exam.

Needless to say, old, dysfunctional habits do not die easily—but they *do* die. Within a few days of working in the jigsaw fashion, Carlos's fellow group members realized that they needed to change their tactics. It was no longer in their own best interest to rattle Carlos; he was not the enemy, he was on their team. They needed him to perform well in order to do well themselves. Instead of taunting him and putting him down, they started to gently ask him questions. But how? What kind of questions? In effect, they had to put themselves in Carlos's shoes in order to find a way to ask questions that did not threaten him but would facilitate his attempts to recite in a clear and understandable manner. After a week or two, most of Carlos's group mates had developed into skillful interviewers, asking him relevant questions to elicit the vital information from him. They became more patient, figured out the most effective way to work with him, helped him out and encouraged him. The more they encouraged Carlos, the more he was able to relax; the more he was able to relax, the quicker and more articulate he became. Carlos's group mates began to see him in a new light. He became transformed in their minds from a "know-nothing loser who can't even speak English" to someone with whom they could work, someone they could appreciate, maybe even someone they could like.

Moreover, Carlos began to see *himself* in a new light: as a competent, contributing member of the class who could work with others from different ethnic groups. As his self-esteem increased, his performance improved even more; and as his performance continued to improve, his group mates continued to view him in an increasingly favorable light.

Within a few weeks, the success of the jigsaw technique was obvious to the classroom teachers. They spontaneously told us of their great satisfaction with the way the atmosphere of their classrooms had been transformed. Adjunct visitors (such as music teachers and the like) were little short of amazed at the dramatically changed atmosphere in the classrooms. Of course, as scientists, we were not content to rely on testimonials alone. Because we had randomly introduced the jigsaw intervention into some classrooms and not others, we were able to compare the progress of the "jigsaw students" with that of the students in traditional classrooms in a precise, scientific manner. After only 8 weeks there were clear differences, even though students spent only a small portion of their class time in jigsaw groups. When tested objectively, jigsaw students expressed significantly less prejudice and negative stereotyping, were more self-confident, and reported that they liked school better than students in traditional classrooms. Moreover, these self-report data were bolstered by hard behavioral data: For example, the children in jigsaw classes were absent less often than students in traditional classrooms. Systematic observation of the schoolyard and the cafeteria revealed far more intermingling of the races in schools using the jigsaw intervention than in schools using traditional methods only. Finally, on objective exams, the students in jigsaw classrooms performed significantly better than students learning the same material in traditional classrooms. Close inspection of the data revealed that the differences in objective exam performance were primarily due to improvements in the scores of students from minority groups; the Anglo students performed equally well in the jigsaw classrooms as in traditional classrooms (Lucker, Rosenfield, Sikes, & Aronson, 1977).

MECHANISMS UNDERLYING THE JIGSAW PROCESS

Why does cooperating with others have the beneficial effects of increasing the attractiveness of group mates and building empathy toward others? How might it be generalized so that members of the ingroup become more inclusive of, and less cruel to, outgroup members?

Peer Rewards and Increased Participation

Because students benefit from *each* student's performance in a cooperative task, they are prone to appreciate that performance by making encouraging statements to one another. This encouragement reinforces good performance, which in turn tends to raise the self-esteem of the person doing the reciting. The jigsaw method also requires people to participate more actively when they are required to recite and when they raise questions as active listeners. Active participation produces better learning than the passive condition of merely receiving information.

Empathic Role Taking

People working together in an interdependent fashion increase their ability to take one another's perspective. Suppose, for example, that Debbie and Carlos are in a jigsaw group. Carlos is reporting, and Debbie is having difficulty following him. She does not quite understand him because his style of presentation is different from that to which she is accustomed. Not only must she pay close attention, but she also must find a way to ask questions that Carlos will understand and that will elicit the additional information she needs. In order to accomplish this goal, she must get to know Carlos first, "put herself in his shoes," empathize. If Sally has still a different style, Debbie must shift gears and pay closer attention to her as well. After a while, Debbie gets into the habit of paying close attention to each of the people in her group, as she learns how to best treat each as an individual (Bridgeman, 1981).

I am reminded of a poignant scene from William Wharton's provocative novel *Birdy*. In this scene, one of the major protagonists, Alphonso, an army sergeant, develops an instant dislike for an overweight enlisted man, a clerk-typist named Ronsky. There are a great many things that Alphonso dislikes about Ronsky. At the top of his list is Ronsky's annoying habit of continually spitting. He spits all over his own desk, his typewriter, and anyone who happens to be in the vicinity. Alphonso cannot stand the guy and entertains fantasies of punching him out. Several weeks later, Alphonso learns that Ronsky had taken part in the Normandy invasion and had watched, in horror, as several of his buddies were cut down before they even had a chance to hit the beach. It seems that his constant spitting was a concrete manifestation of his attempt to get the bad taste out of his mouth. On learning this, Alphonso sees his former enemy in an entirely different light. He sighs with regret and says to himself: "Before you know it, if you're not careful, you can get to feeling for everybody and there's nobody left to hate."

Dissonance Reduction

One of the important mechanisms underlying our data is cognitive dissonance and its reduction. Several decades ago, Jecker and Landy (1969) demonstrated that doing a favor for a person increases our liking for the recipient of our largesse. The internal process hypothesized to mediate this response goes something like this: If I exert effort to help another, then anything about that person that I do not like produces dissonance. (e.g., "Why would I go out of my way to help someone I do not like?"). In order to reduce dissonance, I emphasize the recipient's positive qualities and deemphasize his or her negative qualities. Since the jigsaw method allows ample opportunity for favor-doing, all other things being equal, it should lead to greater liking among participants than traditional classroom methods. Moreover, being liked feels good, and good feelings tend to increase self-esteem, which, in turn, leads to better performance, greater liking for school, and so on.

Attribution of Success and Failure

Working together in the pursuit of common goals changes the "observer's" attributional patterns. There is some evidence to support the notion that cooperation increases the tendency for individuals to make the same kind of attribution for success and failure to their partners as they do to themselves. In one of our experiments (Stephan, Kennedy, & Aronson, 1977), we found that when people succeed at a task, they attribute their success dispositionally (i.e., to skill), but when they fail they tend to make a situational attribution (i.e., to bad luck). We went on to demonstrate that individuals engaged in an interdependent task make the same kinds of attributions to their partners' performances as they do to their own. That is, they give each partner the benefit of the doubt and treat him or her the way they treat themselves. This was not the case in competitive interactions.

Cooperation: Cornerstone of the Jigsaw Classroom and the Basketball Team

There is a rough similarity between the kind of cooperation that goes on in a jigsaw group and the kind of cooperation that is necessary for the smooth functioning of an athletic team. Take a basketball team, for example. If the team is to be successful, each player must play his or her role in a cooperative manner. If each player were hellbent on being the highest scorer on the team, then each would shoot whenever the opportunity arose. In contrast, on a cooperative team, the idea is to pass the ball crisply until one player manages to break clear for a relatively easy shot. If I pass the ball to Sam, and Sam whips a pass to Harry, and Harry passes to Tony who breaks free for an easy lay-up, I am elated even though I do not receive credit for either a field goal or an assist. This is true cooperation.

As a result of this cornerstone of cooperation in team sports, athletic teams frequently build a cohesiveness that extends to their relationship off the court. They become friends because they have learned to count on one another. There is one difference between the outcome of a typical jigsaw group and that of a typical high school basketball team, however—and it is a crucial difference. In high school, athletes tend to hang out with each other and frequently exclude nonathletes from their circle of close friends. In short, the internal cohesiveness of an athletic team often goes along with an exclusion of everyone else.

We circumvented this problem in the jigsaw classroom by the simple device of shuffling groups every 8 weeks. Once a group of students was functioning well together—once the barriers had been broken down and the students showed a great deal of liking and empathy for one another—we would reconfigure the groupings. At first, the students resisted this restructuring. Picture the scene: Debbie, Carlos, Tim, Patty, and Jacob have just gotten to know and appreciate one another and are doing incredibly good work as a team. Why would they want to leave this warm, efficient, and cozy group to join a group of relative strangers?

Now they are forced to become members of a new group—and that enforced change is one of the powerful aspects of this method. After spending a few weeks in the new group, the students invariably discover that the new people are just about as interesting, friendly, and wonderful as their former group mates. The new group is working well together and new friendships form. Then the students move on to their third group, and the same thing begins to happen. As they near the end of their time in the third group, it begins to dawn on most students that they did not happen to "luck out" and land in groups with four or five terrific people. Rather, they realize that just about *everyone* in their class is a worthy human being; all they need to do is pay attention to each person and try to understand him or her and good things will emerge. That is a powerful lesson— and one that few students forget.

LONG-TERM EFFECTS

The jigsaw intervention works *and* it is compatible with other teaching methods. We have found that, if the jigsaw method is used for as little as 1 hour per day, the positive effects are substantial. How permanent are these positive effects? If students participated in a jigsaw classroom in the fifth or sixth grade, would the positive impact remain even if they never experienced the jigsaw intervention again? Unfortunately, we do not have a definitive answer to this question. We do have some tangential evidence that the effects of the jigsaw method may become a permanent part of the individual's way of looking at the world. Earlier in this story, I mentioned empathic role taking as one of the mechanisms underlying the effectiveness of the jigsaw method in increasing compassion among group members. But the question is, does this compassion generalize to include people with whom one has never worked? Does the ability to empathize extend to strangers?

In a clever experiment, Bridgeman (1981) showed that the empathy required by the jigsaw method takes on the form of a more or less permanent ability that generalizes and is utilized outside the confines of the classroom. In her experiment, Bridgeman worked with fifth graders, half of whom had spent 2 months participating in jigsaw classes; the others had spent that time in traditional classrooms. Bridgeman showed them a series of stick-figure cartoons about a young boy their own age. In the first panel, the boy is looking sad as he waves goodbye to his father at the airport. In the next panel, a letter carrier delivers a package to the boy. In the final panel, the boy opens the package and finds a toy airplane inside and bursts into tears. Bridgeman asked the children why they thought the boy had burst into tears at the sight of the airplane. Nearly all of the children could answer correctly—because the toy airplane reminded him of how much he missed his father and that made him sad. Then Bridgeman asked the crucial question: "What did the letter carrier think when he saw the boy open the package and start to cry?"

Most children of this age make a consistent error; they assume that everyone knows what they know. Thus, the youngsters in the control group thought that the letter carrier would know the boy was sad because the gift reminded him of his father leaving. But the children who had participated in the jigsaw classroom responded differently. Because they were better able to take the perspective of the letter carrier—to put themselves in his shoes—they realized that he would be confused at seeing the boy cry over receiving a nice present because the letter carrier had not witnessed the farewell scene at the airport.

Offhand, the results of this experiment might not seem very important. After all, who cares whether kids have the ability to figure out what is in the letter carrier's mind? In point of fact, we should *all* care—a great deal. The extent to which children can develop the ability to see the world from the perspective of another human being has profound implications for interpersonal—even global—relations in general. When we have the empathy to feel another person's pain; when we can develop the ability to understand what another person is going through, it increases the probability that our hearts will open to that person—and open-heartedness makes it difficult to harm or taunt anyone. Moreover, Bridgeman's data suggest that empathy is a *skill*—not unlike the skill of riding a bike—that can be learned and used in a variety of situations. The implication of this finding is that the jigsaw classroom intervention might have long-lasting effects.

BACK TO LITTLETON

Following the Columbine massacre, there was a lot of negative publicity about how the atmosphere at Columbine High School might have contributed to the tragedy. Television, newspaper, and magazine stories about the school stressed how athletes dominated the social world there and how the unpopular students were taunted and excluded. The criticism, while not inaccurate, was unfair in the sense that Columbine was no different from just about every public high school in the country. In response to the criticism, some of the Columbine students attempted to justify their harassment of Harris and Klebold. Typical of these remarks was a comment made by a member of the Columbine football team who had been wounded in the attack:

> "Columbine is a good clean place except for those rejects. Most kids didn't want them there. They were into witchcraft. They were into voodoo. Sure we teased them. But what do you expect with kids who come to school with weird hairdos and horns on their hats? If you want to get rid of someone, usually you tease 'em." (in Gibbs & Roche, 1999)

It is my belief that if the jigsaw process had been widely used several years earlier in the elementary schools that supply the students for Columbine High School, the young man quoted above and his friends would almost certainly have developed some additional compassion and empathy as well as a greater tolerance for diversity. If so, it is likely that they would have been charmed and delighted rather than angered by the creativity of the kids "who come to school with weird hairdos and horns on their hats." What makes me think so? In Austin, as in dozens of communities throughout the country, the jigsaw process has been successful at overcoming one of the most hide-bound cliques imaginable: racial exclusion and intolerance. Accordingly, I am convinced that overcoming the relatively minor cliquishness that existed in Littleton would have been child's play by comparison.

Carrying this reasoning to its logical conclusion, I believe that, if the jigsaw method had been widely used in Littleton, the Columbine massacre might never have occurred, and those 15 people would still be alive. Admittedly, that is a bold statement—one not usually made by academicians. And, of course, it can never be proved. But I have a high degree of confidence because 31 years of research on the jigsaw method have made it undeniably clear: The jigsaw process builds empathy, and students in jigsaw classrooms are more open to one another, more compassionate, and more tolerant of diversity than students in traditional classrooms. Looking at the other side of the coin, in jigsaw classrooms, students who had previously grown accustomed to anticipating the school day with dread and anxiety wake up on school mornings with excitement and pleasant expectations. As one of the previously taunted kids put it in an unsolicited letter he wrote to me some *10 years* after his experience in a jigsaw classroom: "The kids I thought were cruel and hostile became my friends, and the teacher acted friendly and nice to me, and I actually began to love school, and I loved to learn things and I *still* love to learn." At the time he wrote that letter, the young man—one of seven children in a working-class Mexican American family—was a senior at a major university. The only member of his family ever to attend college, he was writing to tell me that he had just been accepted into Harvard Law School.

As I mentioned earlier, we scientists are trained to look askance at such testimonials; understandably, we prefer hard data from well-controlled experiments. In evaluating the jigsaw process, the hard data are clear and convincing and have been replicated scores of times. In this context, I hope you will forgive me if I confess that, on the deepest personal level, I find this testimonial to be particularly gratifying.

REFERENCES

Aronson, E. (2000). *Nobody left to hate: Teaching compassion after Columbine.* New York: Holt.

Aronson, E. (1978). *The jigsaw classroom.* Beverly Hills, CA: Sage.

Aronson, E. (1999). *The social animal.* New York: Worth.

Aronson, E. (1992). The jigsaw classroom: A cooperative strategy for reducing prejudice. In J. Lynch, C. Modgil, & S. Modgil (Eds.), *Cultural diversity and the schools* (pp. 186–214). London: Falmer Press.

Aronson, E., & Bridgeman, D. (1979). Jigsaw groups and the desegregated classroom: In pursuit of common goals. *Personality and Social Psychology Bulletin, 5,* 438–446.

Aronson, E., & Goode, E. (1980). Training teachers to implement jigsaw learning: A manual for teachers. in S. Sharan, P. Hare, C. Webb, & R. Hertz-Lazarowitz (Eds.), *Cooperation in education* (pp. 47–81). Provo, UT: Brigham Young University Press.

Aronson, E., & Patnoe, S. (1997). *Cooperation in the classroom: The jigsaw method.* New York: Longman.

Baumeister, R., Twenge, J., & Nuss, C. (2002). Effects of social exclusion on cognitive processes: Anticipated aloneness reduces intelligent thought. *Journal of Personality and Social Psychology, 83,* 817–827.

Bridgeman, D. (1981). Enhanced role-taking through cooperative interdependence: A field study. *Child Development, 52,* 1231–1238.

Gibbs, N. (1999, October 24). A week in the life of a high school, Webster Groves. *Time,* p. 6.

Gibbs, N. & Roche, T. (1999, December 20). The Columbine tapes. *Time,* p. 14.

Gilligan, J. (1992). *Violence: Our deadly epidemic and its causes.* New York: Grosset/Putnam.

Goldberg, W., & Connelly, M. (1999, October 20). *The New York Times,* p. 1.

Jacobs, J. (1999, December 20). *San Jose Mercury News,* p. 28.

Jecker, J., & Landy, D. (1969). Liking a person as a function of doing him a favor. *Human Relations, 22,* 371–378.

Lewin, T. (1999, May 2) Terror in Littleton: The teenage culture; Arizona high school provides glimpse into cliques. *The New York Times,* p. 4.

Lucker, W., Rosenfield, D., Sikes, J., & Aronson, E. (1977). Performance in the interdependent classroom: A field study. *American Educational Research Journal, 13,* 115–123.

Milgram, S. (1963). Behavioral study of obedience. *Journal of Abnormal and Social Psychology, 67,* 371–378

Stephan, C., Kennedy, J., & Aronson, E. (1977). Attribution of luck or skill as a function of cooperating or competing with a friend or acquaintance. *Sociometry, 40,* l07–111.

Tounsend, P. (1999, May 23). *Santa Cruz Sentinel,* p. 3.

Triplett, N. (1898). The dynamogenic factors in pace making and competition. *American Journal of Psychology, 9,* 507–533.

Twenge, J., Catanese, K., & Baumeister, R. (2002). Social exclusion causes self-defeating behavior. *Journal of Personality and Social Psychology, 83,* 606–615.

Vossekuil, B., Reddy, M., Fein, R., Borum, R., & Modzeleski, W. (2000). *U.S. Secret Service Safe School Initiative: An interim report on the prevention of targeted violence in schools.* Washington, DC: U.S. Secret Service, National Threat Assessment Center.

Williams, K., & Zadro, L. (2001). Ostracism: On being ignored, excluded, and rejected. M. R. Leary (Ed.), *Interpersonal rejection* (pp. 21–53). New York: Oxford University Press.

Index

Page numbers followed by *f* indicate figure; *n*, note; *t*, table.

489